THRIVING IN COLLEGE

with AVID® FOR HIGHER EDUCATION

A Customization of Thriving in Community College and Beyond, Third Edition by Joseph B. Cuseo, Aaron Thompson, and Julie A. McLaughlin.
AVID Contributions by Evelyn Hiatt

Collaborating with institutions of higher education to systemically address the goals of increased learning, persistence, completion and success in and beyond college

Kendall Hunt
publishing company

AVID Team

Project Leads: Jaime Sandoval and Julia Kendry
Instructional Strategists: Dr. Shannon McAndrews and Yvonne Ortiz
Subject Matter Experts: Dr. Michelle Duffy, Dr. Wayne Borin, Kristi Gerdes
Writers: Evelyn Hiatt

www.kendallhunt.com
Send all inquiries to:
4050 Westmark Drive
Dubuque, IA 52004-1840

Copyright © 2018 by Kendall Hunt Publishing Company

ISBN: 978-1-5249-3768-3

Published in the United States of America

BRIEF CONTENTS

CONTENTS

Chapter 8: Time Management Skills and Strategies

Chapter 9: Study and Test Wise in Higher Education Environments

Chapter 10: Academic Planning and Decision-Making

Chapter 11: Higher-Level Thinking

Chapter 12: Financial Literacy

Chapter 13: Career Planning and Decision-Making

FOREWORD

AVID strategies have a long history of effectiveness in advancing students' college *readiness*. These same strategies should prove equally effective in advancing students' college success. This book's focus on facilitating students' transition to college represents a natural extension of AVID's successful college-readiness system. It provides students with a critical bridge between secondary and postsecondary education, connecting these successive segments of the educational pipeline, enabling students to make a smoother, more seamless transition from high school to higher education.

The teaching and learning strategies identified in this book are well supported by postsecondary research on student learning and retention. One particular strand of this research shows that a distinguishing feature of colleges and universities that have made significant improvement in their graduation rates is they transformed themselves into student-centered campus cultures. One key characteristic of such a culture is the use of *student-centered pedagogy*. Prior to the turn of the 21st century, national reports on the quality of undergraduate education called for a paradigm shift—away from the traditional focus on teacher and the teaching process—to a new "learning paradigm" that focuses on the *learner* and the *learning* process. This new paradigm calls for a shift to a different starting point for improving the teaching–learning process that begins by centering on what the student (learner) is doing during the learning process, rather than what the teacher is doing (and covering) in class. In this paradigm, postsecondary pedagogy becomes more student-centered, with the instructor lecturing less and shifting more class time, control, and responsibility for learning to students. The student's role changes from being a passive recipient or receptacle for lecture-laden information to that of an active and engaged participant in the learning process. According to highly acclaimed educators, Paulo Freire and bell hooks (a.k.a., Linda Jean Hopkins), such engaging pedagogy liberates students from dependence on the teacher as absolute authority figure, empowering them with a personal voice and participatory role in the classroom. The strategies included in this book resonate resoundingly with this call for student-centered pedagogy; they place students at the center of the learning process, engaging them with the subject matter, with the instructor, and with other students.

The new learning paradigm also calls for a shift in the instructor's role from an information dispenser who simply disseminates discipline-specific knowledge (with a short shelf life) to an educational architect who designs classroom experiences that enable students to acquire transferable, durable lifelong-learning skills (e.g., problem solving, critical thinking, and communication). This book's extensive and intensive focus on student writing, inquiry, collaboration, organization, and reading (WICOR) responds resoundingly to the clarion call for cultivating learning skills that students can transfer across the curriculum and apply throughout life.

In addition to the use of learner-centered pedagogy, another key feature of a student-centered campus culture is focus on educating the student as a *"whole person"* (holistic development), including attention to social, emotional, and motivational factors that impact student success. The work of America's most prominent higher education scholars has demonstrated that a comprehensive, holistic approach to undergraduate education is essential for:

1. becoming an effective and authentic teacher (Palmer),
2. ensuring students' successful transition to college (Gardner),
3. promoting student engagement (Kuh),
4. increasing depth of student learning (Pascarella & Terenzini),
5. elevating student retention and college completion rates (Tinto),
6. advancing success rates of both underrepresented and first-generation students (Rendón).

It is safe to say that more research has been conducted on, and more evidence gathered for, the first-year experience (FYE) course than any other course in the history of American higher education. One would be hard pressed to find another curricular intervention that has undergone more rigorous evaluation and is better qualified to serve as an educational "best practice." However, not all FYE courses are created equal. Some of these courses focus exclusively on the development of academic skills (e.g., study skills courses) or acquiring major-specific information (e.g., discipline-based or pre-professional seminars).

This book takes a more comprehensive, holistic approach to promoting first-year student success that is consistent with the goals of a well-designed FYE course identified by Lee Upcraft and John Gardner in their seminal text, *The Freshman Year Experience*, namely: (1) developing academic and intellectual competencies, (2) establishing and maintaining interpersonal relationships, (3) developing a personal identity, (4) deciding on a career and lifestyle, and (5) maintaining health and wellness. This holistic type of FYE course has served as a national model for over 35 years and is the course in place at the University of South Carolina, home of the National Resource Center for the First-Year Experience & Students in Transition.

Unfortunately, research conducted by the College Board indicates that many postsecondary institutions do not take a holistic approach to promoting student success, often failing to pay sufficient attention to non-cognitive factors that affect student success. In particular, short shrift has been paid to developing students' sense of self-efficacy—the belief that through personal effort and use of effective strategies, students can control their education fate and achieve positive academic outcomes. Meta-analyses of multiple research studies indicate that academic self-efficacy is the most potent predictor of student retention and academic achievement (GPA) in college, particularly for underrepresented first-generation students. The scholar who originally researched and developed the concept of self-efficacy, Albert Bandura, discovered one very effective way for cultivating it is by supplying learners with early support that increases their prospects for initial success. This serves to increase their sense of self-competence and self-confidence, emboldening them to tackle subsequent challenges with more effort and persistence.

This book is intentionally designed to supply new college students with such competence- and confidence-building support. In so doing, it increases the likelihood they will experience initial success in college and develop the self-efficacy needed to meet the challenges that lie ahead of them.

Joseph B. Cuseo
Professor Emeritus, Psychology
Marymount California University

PREFACE

WELCOME TO OUR BOOK

PLAN AND PURPOSE OF THIS BOOK

This book is designed to help you make a smooth transition to college as well as equip you with strategies for success that you can use throughout college and beyond. Its aim is to promote the academic excellence and personal development of all students—whether you're a student who is (a) transitioning to college directly from high school or from a full-time or part-time job, (b) living on or off campus, or (c) attending college on a full-time or part-time basis. Whatever your previous educational record may have been, college is a new ball game played on a different field with different rules and expectations. If you haven't been a particularly successful student in the past, this book will help you become a successful student in the future. If you have been a successful student in high school, this book will make you an even stronger student in college.

One of the book's major goals is to help you put into practice a powerful principle of human learning and personal success: *mindfulness*. When you're mindful, you're aware of *what* you're doing and *if* you're doing it in the most effective way. Mindfulness or self-awareness is the critical first step toward self-improvement and success in any aspect of your life. If you develop the habit of remaining aware of whether you're "doing college" strategically (e.g., by using the key strategies identified in this book), you will have taken a huge step toward college success.

Rather than trying to figure out how to do college on your own through random trial-and-error, this book gives you a game plan for getting it right from the start and an inside track for getting off to a fast start. Its plan is built on a solid foundation of research that equips you with a comprehensive set of well-documented strategies for doing college successfully.

Specific action strategies make up the heart of this book. You will find that these practical strategies aren't presented simply as a laundry list of what-to-do tips dispensed by authority figures who think they know what's best for you. Instead, the recommendations are accompanied by evidence-based reasons for *why* they're effective and they're organized into broader *principles* that tie the strategies together into a meaningful plan. It's not only important for you to know *what* to do, but also *why* to do it. If you understand the reason behind a suggested strategy, you're more likely to take that strategy seriously and implement it effectively.

When specific strategies are organized into general principles, they become more powerful because you're able to see how the same principle may be generalized and applied across different subjects and situations.

> " Important achievements require a clear focus, all-out-effort, and a bottomless trunk full of strategies."
>
> —*Carol Dweck, Stanford professor, and author of* Mindset: The New Psychology of Success

From *Thriving in the Community College and Beyond: Strategies for Academic Success and Personal Development*, Third Edition by Joseph B. Cuseo, Aaron Thompson, and Julie A. McLaughlin. Copyright © 2016 by Kendall Hunt Publishing Company. Reprinted by permission.

Understanding the key principles that underlie effective strategies also empowers you to create additional strategies of your own that follow or flow from the same general principle. This promotes deeper, more powerful learning than simply collecting a bunch of tips about what you should or shouldn't do in college. We believe that you're ready and able to meet the challenge of deeper learning.

Since the strategies cited in this book are research-based, you'll find references cited regularly throughout all the chapters and a sizable reference section at the end of each chapter. Your professors will expect you to think critically and support your ideas with evidence. As authors, we should do the same and model that behavior for you.

You will find that the references cited represent a balanced blend of older, "classic" studies and more recent "cutting edge" research from a variety of fields. The time span of references cited serves to highlight the long-standing relevance of the ideas presented and their power to withstand the test of time. It also underscores the fact that the subject of success in college and beyond, like any other academic subject in the college curriculum, rests on a solid body of research and scholarship that spans multiple decades.

PREVIEW OF CONTENT

Chapter 1

Why Utilize AVID for Higher Education Strategies?

AVID for Higher Education(AHE) recognizes and values the importance of the first-year experience for college students, whether you have just completed high school or are returning after beginning a career or family. This book has been designed by experts in the field of higher education to intentionally target this transitional stage of the first year experience.

Chapter 2

College Knowledge

This chapter identifies top tips for academic success you can implement immediately, including what to do inside and outside the classroom. It also alerts you to in-class and out-of-class behavior that should be avoided in college.

Chapter 3

Engaging Your Mind, Engaging Your Campus

This chapter focuses on the "big picture": powerful principles you can implement to promote your own success and key campus resources you can use to help you succeed. It describes what these key principles and resources are, why they're effective, and how to capitalize on them.

Chapter 4

Effective Communication Strategies for You and Interacting with Others

This chapter identifies effective strategies for communicating with and relating to others, as well as ways to understand and regulate our emotions—such as stress, anxiety, anger, and depression. Implementing the recommended strategies should improve the quality of your performance in college and your career, as well as enhance your overall quality of life.

Chapter 5

Maximizing Wellness and Performance

This chapter examines strategies for maximizing wellness by maintaining a balanced diet, attaining quality sleep, promoting total fitness, and avoiding risky behaviors that jeopardize our health and impair our performance.

Chapter 6

Diversity and the College Experience

This chapter provides a framework to gain greater appreciation of human differences and develop skills for making the most of diversity in college and beyond. Through the lens of AVID for Higher Education, you will engage in a Socratic approach to the often emotionally charged topics that fall within the realm of Diversity, in order to intellectually and actively engage in the multi-perspective college learning experience.

Chapter 7

Goal Setting and Motivation in Higher Education Environments

This chapter lays out the key steps involved in the process of setting effective goals, identifies key self-motivational strategies for staying on track and sustaining progress toward goals, and describes how personal qualities such as self-efficacy, grit, and growth mindset are essential for achieving goals.

> In high school, a lot of the work was done while in school, but in college all of your work is done on your time. You really have to organize yourself in order to get everything done."
>
> —First-year student's response to a question about what was most surprising about college life

Chapter 8

Time Management Skills and Strategies

This chapter offers a comprehensive set of strategies for managing time, combating procrastination, and ensuring that your time-spending habits are aligned with your educational goals and priorities.

Chapter 9

Study and Test Wise in Higher Education Environments

This chapter supplies you with a systematic set of strategies for improving your performance on different types of tests that can be used before, during, and after exams, helping you to become more "test wise" and less "test anxious."

Chapter 10

Academic Planning and Decision-Making

This chapter will help you develop a plan for making educational decisions that will best enable you to reach your long-term goals. This chapter will equip you with effective strategies to pursue the educational path that is compatible with your personal interests, talents, and goals.

Chapter 11
Higher-Level Thinking
National surveys consistently show that the primary goal of college faculty is teaching students how to think critically. This chapter will help you understand what critical thinking is and empower you to think in this way. You will be provided with thinking strategies that move you beyond memorization to higher levels of thinking and learn how to demonstrate higher-level thinking on college exams and assignments.

Chapter 12
Financial Literacy
This chapter provides you with specific strategies for tracking cash flow, minimizing and avoiding debt, balancing time spent on schoolwork and working for pay, and making wise spending and saving decisions while you're in college.

Chapter 13
Career Planning and Decision-Making
This chapter will help you develop a plan for making career decisions that will best enable you to reach your long-term goals. This chapter will equip you with effective strategies for pursuing a career path that is aligned with your personal interests, goals, and talents.

Journal Reflection P.1

What chapters interest you? Why?

Which chapters do you believe are topics of "need" as you begin your first-year of college?

Process and Style of Presentation
As important as *what* information is contained in a book is *how* that information is presented. When writing this text, we made an intentional attempt to present information in a way that would: (a) stimulate your motivation to learn, (b) deepen your understanding of what you're learning, and (c) strengthen your retention (memory) for what you've learned.

We attempted to do this by incorporating the following principles of motivation, learning, and memory throughout the text.

- Each chapter begins with a **Preview** of the chapter's key goals and content, followed by a **Thought Starter**—a question designed to stimulate your thoughts and feelings about the upcoming material. This pre-reading exercise is designed to "warm up" or "tune up" your brain, preparing it to connect the ideas you're about to encounter in the chapter with the ideas you already have in your head. It's an instructional strategy that implements one of the most powerful principles of learning: we learn most effectively by relating what we're going to learn to what we've already learned and stored in our brain.

- Within each chapter, we periodically interrupt your reading with opportunities for *reflection*—**Think About It** questions that prompt you to pause and think about the material you've just read. These timely pauses for thought should keep you alert and mentally active throughout the reading process. They serve to intercept "attention drift" that normally takes place when the brain continually receives and processes information for an extended period, such as it does when reading (Willis, 2007). These reflections also deepen your understanding of the material because they ask you to *write* in response to your reading. Writing stimulates deeper learning and higher levels of thinking than simply underlining or highlighting sentences. We recommend keeping a record of your written responses to the textbook's reflection questions in a *learning journal*.

- **Exercises** at the *end* of each chapter ask you to reflect further on the knowledge you've acquired and transform that knowledge into informed action. We achieve *wisdom* when we move beyond simply acquiring knowledge to *applying* the knowledge—putting it into practice to help us become more wise, effective, and successful human beings (Staudinger, 2008).

  The strategic positioning of the *Thought Starter* questions at the beginning of each chapter, the *Think About It* reflections interspersed throughout the chapter, and the application *Exercises* at the end of the chapter will keep you actively involved at three key stages of the reading process: the beginning, middle, and end.

- **End-of-Chapter Reflections** ask you questions that allow you to reflect on what you learned in the chapter and how you can apply it to your success in college and life.

- Information is presented through **multiple modes of input**, which include: diagrams, pictures, cartoons, words of wisdom from famous and successful people, advice from current and former college students, and personal stories drawn from the authors' experiences. When you receive information through different formats, you process that information through multiple sensory modalities (input channels). This deepens learning by enabling your brain to lay down multiple memory tracks (traces) of the information it's taking in (Willis 2007).

What follows is a list of the book's seven key instructional features. *As you read these features, make a quick note in the side margin about how effective you think this feature will be in terms of motivating you to read and learn from the book.*

1. Research and Scholarly Support

The book's ideas and recommendations are grounded in research and scholarship drawn from a variety of academic fields. You will find references cited regularly throughout the chapters and a sizable reference section at the end of each chapter. The sheer quantity of references cited serves as testimony to the fact that the subject matter of this book is built on a solid body of research and scholarship, just like any other academic subject studied in the college curriculum. You'll also find that the references include a balanced blend of older, "classic" scholarship and more recent "cutting edge" research.

2. Boxed Summaries

At different points in the text, you will find boxes containing summaries of top tips for success. These summaries pull together key strategies relating to the same concept and organize them in the same place physically, which will help you organize and retain them mentally.

3. Quotes

The AVID symbol is intended to draw your attention to specific AHE student, faculty, and team members as well as influential people that relate to the concepts discussed at that point in the chapter. You'll find quotes from famous individuals who have lived in different historical periods and who have specialized in a variety of fields, including politics, philosophy, religion, science, business, music, art, and athletics. The wide-ranging time frames, cultures, and fields of study represented by the people quoted demonstrate that their words of wisdom are timeless and universal. It's our hope that the words of these highly successful and respected individuals will inspire you to put their words in practice.

You can also learn a lot from the firsthand experiences of current and former students. Throughout the book, you'll find comments and advice from students at different stages of the college experience, including college graduates (alumni). Studies show that students can learn a great deal from their peers—especially from more experienced peers who've "been there, done that." By hearing about their success stories and stumbling blocks, you can benefit from their college experiences to improve your college experience.

4. Author's Journey

In each chapter, you will find at least one author's experience related to the chapter topic. We share our own experiences as college students, our professional experiences working with students as instructors and advisors, and our personal experiences in other areas of our lives. Studies show that when people hear stories shared by others, their understanding and memory for key ideas contained in the stories is deepened and strengthened (McDrury and Alterio 2002). We share our stories for the purpose of personalizing the book and with the hope that you'll learn from our experiences—including learning from our mistakes!

Journal Reflection P.2

Have you received any tips or advice from friends or family about what to do, or what not to do in college?

_____

What kind of advice did you receive and who gave it to you?

_____

_____

_____

_____

_____

5. Note

Throughout the book, you will find AHE focused information or expert advice to provide additional information, a different perspective or a concept to consider in order to inform your decision making and next steps.

6. Journal Reflection

You will find at key locations in each chapter, guiding questions to spark your personal reflection and connections to the content, concept or topic. Ideally, consider capturing your personal journey and reflections in a separate journal or notebook. If you stay focused and engaged, you will be pleasantly surprised at your personal growth throughout the course.

7. Concept Maps (Graphic Organizers): Verbal-Visual Aids

Throughout the book, you will find ideas visually organized into diagrams, charts, and figures. When important concepts are represented in a visual-spatial format, we're more likely to retain them because two different memory traces are recorded in our brain: verbal (words) and visual (images).

8. Cartoons: Emotional-Visual Aids

You will find cartoons sprinkled throughout the text to lighten up the reading and provide you with a little entertainment. More importantly, the cartoons relate to an important concept and are also intended to strengthen your retention of that concept by reinforcing it with a visual image (drawing) and an emotional experience (humor). If the cartoon triggers at least a snicker, your body will release adrenaline—a hormone that facilitates memory formation. If it generates actual laughter, it will also stimulate your brain to release endorphins—natural, morphine-like chemicals that lower stress and elevate mood.

9. Learning More through the World Wide Web

At the end of each chapter are web-based resources containing additional information relating to the chapter's major ideas. One of the major goals of a college education is to prepare students to become independent, self-directed learners. We hope that the information presented in each chapter's topic will stimulate your interest and motivation to learn more about the topic. If it does, you can use the online resources cited at the end of the chapter to access additional information.

We firmly believe that the content of this book, and the manner in which the content is delivered, will empower you not only to survive college, but to *thrive* in college and beyond. The skills and strategies found on the following pages promote success throughout life. Self-awareness, effective planning and decision making, learning deeply and remembering longer, thinking critically and creatively, managing time and money effectively, communicating and relating effectively with others, and maintaining health and wellness are more than college success skills—they are *life* success skills.

Welcome to College

In the introduction to this book, you'll learn why college has the potential to be the most enriching experience of your life and one will benefit you throughout life. The first year of college is a particularly critical stage of your educational development. It's a transitional stage during which students encounter the greatest challenges, the most stress, the most academic difficulties, and the highest risk of dropping out. However, it's also the year when students experience the greatest amount of learning and personal growth. These findings highlight the power of the first-year experience, the value of first-year courses designed to promote college success, and the importance of books like this.

In the introduction, you'll find convincing evidence that new students who participate in first-year experience courses (college-success courses) are more likely to stick with college, complete their degree, and get the most out of their college experience.

It is our hope that the content of this book and the manner in which the content is presented will motivate and empower you to make the most of your college experience. Don't forget that the skills and strategies discussed are relevant to life beyond college. Effective planning and decision making, learning deeply and remembering longer, thinking critically and creatively, managing time and money responsibly, communicating and relating effectively with others, and maintaining health and wellness are more than just college skills: they are life skills.

Learning doesn't stop after college; it's a lifelong process. If you strive to apply the ideas in this book, you'll develop habits that will enable you to thrive in college and beyond.

> I've gotten a better sense of how to manage my life."
>
> I know that I have a lot to learn, but this class has given me the stepping stones to help me become the person that I want to be."
>
> —*Comments made by first-year students in a course that used this book*

REFERENCES

McDrury, J. and M. G.Alterio 2002. *Learning Through Storytelling: Using Reflection and Experience in Higher Education Contexts*. Palmerston North: Dunmore Press.

Staudinger, U. M. 2008. "A Psychology of Wisdom: History and Recent Developments." *Research in Human Development* 5: 107–20.

Willis, J. 2007. *Brain-friendly Strategies for the Inclusion Classroom*. Alexandria, VA: Association for Supervision and Curriculum Development.

ACKNOWLEDGEMENTS

Thriving in College and Beyond: AVID for Higher Education is adapted from the work of the following Higher Education experts:

—Dr. Joseph B. Cuseo, Emeritus, Marymount College

—Dr. Aaron Thompson, Executive Vice President and Chief Academic Office, The Kentucky Council on Postsecondary Education

—Julie A. McLaughlin, Cincinnati State Technical and Community College

AVID DESIGN AND DEVELOPMENT TEAM

PROJECT LEADS

Jaime Rae Sandoval

Julia Kendry

INSTRUCTIONAL STRATEGISTS

Dr. Shannon McAndrews

Yvonne Ortiz

WRITER

Evelyn Hiatt

SUBJECT MATTER EXPERTS

Dr. Michelle Duffy

Dr. Wayne Borin

Kristi Gerdes

Dr. R. Robin Withers

About the Authors

Joe Cuseo holds a doctoral degree in Educational Psychology and Assessment from the University of Iowa and is Professor Emeritus of Psychology. For more than 25 years, he directed the first-year seminar—a core college success course required of all new students. He's a 14-time recipient of the "faculty member of the year award" on his home campus—a student-driven award based on effective teaching and academic advising; a recipient of the "Outstanding First-Year Student Advocate Award" from the National Resource Center for The First-Year Experience and Students in Transition; and a recipient of the "Diamond Honoree Award" from the American College Personnel Association (ACPA) for contributions made to student development and the Student Affairs profession.

Currently, Joe serves as an educational advisor and consultant for AVID—a nonprofit organization whose mission is to promote the college access and success of underserved student populations. He has delivered hundreds of campus workshops and conference presentations across North America, as well as Europe, Asia, Australia, and the Middle East.

Aaron Thompson is the executive vice president and chief academic officer for the Kentucky Council on Postsecondary Education. He is also a professor of Sociology in the Department of Educational Leadership and Policy Studies at Eastern Kentucky University. Thompson has a Ph.D. in Sociology in areas of organizational behavior and race and gender relations. Dr. Thompson has over 27 years of leadership experience in higher education and business. In addition, he has spent numerous years serving on nonprofit boards in leadership roles. Thompson has researched, taught, and/or consulted in areas of diversity, leadership, ethics, multicultural families, race and ethnic relations, student success, first-year students, retention, cultural competence, and organizational design throughout his personal career. He has over 30 publications and numerous research and peer-reviewed presentations. Thompson has traveled throughout the Unite States and has given more than 700 workshops, seminars, and invited lectures in areas of race and gender diversity, living an unbiased life, overcoming obstacles to gain success, creating a school environment for academic success, cultural competence, workplace interaction, leadership, organizational goal setting, building relationships, the first-year seminar, and a variety of other topics. He has been or is a consultant to educational institutions (elementary, secondary, and postsecondary), corporations, nonprofit organizations, police departments, and other governmental agencies. His latest authored or co-authored books are: *Changing Student Culture from the Ground Up, The Sociological Outlook, Infusing Diversity and Cultural Competence into Teacher Education, Peer to Peer Leadership: Changing Student Culture from the Ground Up*. In addition to this text, he also co-authored *Thriving in College and Beyond: Research-Based Strategies for Academic Success, Diversity and the College Experience, Focus on Success,* and *Black Men and Divorce*.

Julie McLaughlin is department chair and professor of the First-Year Experience (FYE) courses, as well as co-chair of the FYE Advisory Committee, at Cincinnati State Technical and Community College. She has an M.A. in College Student Personnel from Eastern Michigan University. Julie is responsible for assisting in the creation of the three FYE courses that are offered at Cincinnati State, as well as the Psychology of Leadership course whose students serve as peer mentors in FYE courses. She is also responsible for overseeing the FYE curriculum and Instructor Development Program, with the assistance of full-time FYE faculty. McLaughlin is a five-time House-Bruckmann Faculty Excellence Award nominee. Julie previously served as an academic advisor and co-created the Athletic Advising Program at Cincinnati State which has been recognized as an exemplary practice by the National Academic Advising Association (NACADA), and she contributed to the NACADA monograph *Advising Student-Athletes: A Collaborative Approach to Success.* McLaughlin has presented at multiple national conferences for FYE and NACADA. She has also served as faculty for the Institute on First-Year Student Success in the Community College and the Institute on Developing and Sustaining First-Year Seminars presented by The National Resource Center for First-Year Experience and Students in Transition.

Evelyn Hiatt Bio Ta-Nahisi Coates has said "A life must be about something." When you are young, it can be difficult to see what that "something" is. As one chooses careers, builds relationships, makes life choices, a pattern emerges over time. I became an educator reluctantly, but in my forty-plus years in education, I've followed a clear path that has brought both personal satisfaction and, hopefully, some positive outcomes for students.

It began with my work at the Texas Legislature where I became interested in educational law and policies. My interest took me first to the Texas Education Agency where I became Senior Director for Advanced Academic Services and then to the Texas Coordinating Board for Higher Education, serving as Deputy Assistant Commissioner for College and Career Readiness. But the titles do not reflect the focus of my work. Early on, the vast inequities that existed in public education were obvious and, with whatever team I worked, our emphasis was on trying to balance the scales. It was not enough to open advanced opportunities for students of color, students from disadvantaged backgrounds, or second language learners. The students needed to understand the hard work that was needed to succeed in challenging educational options and to be provided with the skills necessary to meet those challenges. Whether in my official role at the TEA, where we initiated a program for AP Spanish to 7th Grade Native Spanish Speakers or as chair of the board of International Baccalaureate North America, I hoped to provide gateways that would encourage students to do their best both for themselves, their families, and their communities. AVID proved to be the natural extension of these roles. It offered me the chance to leave the office and be with both teachers and students who desperately wanted a chance—a chance AVID provided.

I have benefited greatly from my service. I've had the opportunity, not just to work with positive role models and compassionate educators such as Joe Cuseo and Aaron Thompson, but to call them friends. They however, are not the major benefit I've received. Ta-Nahisi Coates stated that he knows his struggle for equity will not be reached in his lifetime. Neither will educational excellence and equity be realized in my lifetime— but from the emails from students who attended the Texas Governor's School in the 1980's, to the public school teachers and principals who I taught at the University of Texas at Austin Extension, I know the struggle is in good hands and no matter how long it takes, ultimately will prevail.

CHAPTER 1

WHY UTILIZE AVID FOR HIGHER EDUCATION STRATEGIES?

WHY THRIVING IN COLLEGE AND BEYOND-AVID VERSION?

AVID for Higher Education (AHE) recognizes and values the importance of the first-year experience for college students, whether you have just completed high school or are returning after beginning a career or family. Professional learning, coaching, and resources have been designed and developed for faculty and students targeting this specific transitional stage in the educational arena.

What does that mean for you as students? Experts in the field of higher education intentionally developed and highlighted relevant and holistic strategies, practices, and information in order to foster your success as you embark on your first-year journey.

> When we began using annotations in this course, I felt everything we learned came together and they gave me an organized way to continue doing what I had begun doing in other courses to keep me engage in my reading. . . . My composition professor even complimented me, pointing out to the class that my textbook (in reference to the notes and highlighting I had done on an essay we read), "was how every college student's book should look."
>
> —Allison Scott

AHE EXPERIENCE

There are some challenges us vets do face when we get out and go to college. There is that natural gap in maturity [between] the regular college student versus the veteran student. While some students come in late on a regular basis, veteran students are often early to class. Also some students talk during a lecture, while a veteran student gives the instructor the utmost attention. But these are things that are drilled into our heads being raised in the military. Things like loyalty, respect, and integrity.

> — Veteran student

> The scariest thing for me to have done was to get out [of the military] and not have a plan. I firmly believe that you have to plan for success. Success doesn't just happen; you have to work for it."
>
> —First-year veteran student

Box 1.1

The Power of College: Economic and Personal Benefits of a College Education

Approximately 31% of Americans hold a four-year (bachelor's) degree (Lumina Foundation 2015). When they are compared with people from similar social and economic backgrounds who did not continue their education beyond high school, research reveals that a college education is well worth it—in terms of both personal development and career advancement.

Summarized below are positive outcomes associated with a college education and a college degree. Their wide-ranging impact on the whole person and society at large serve as testimony to the power of the college experience.

1. Economic and Career Benefits
- Job security and stability—college graduates have lower rates of unemployment and lower risk of being laid off work
- Higher income—the gap between the earnings of high school and college graduates is large and *growing*. Individuals holding a bachelor's degree

 It's an irrefutable fact that college gives you a significant and persistent advantage decade after decade."

—*Mary C. Daly, vice president of the Federal Reserve Bank of San Francisco (quoted in the Los Angeles Times, April 15, 2015)*

earn an average salary that's $17,500 higher than high school graduates. When these differences are calculated over a lifetime, the income of families headed by people with a bachelor's degree earn an income that's over a million dollars more than families headed by people with a high school diploma. (See **Figure 1.1**.)
- Better retirement and pension benefits
- Career versatility and mobility—greater ability to move out of one position into another (a college graduate has more job options)
- Career advancement—greater opportunity to move up to higher-level professional positions (in other words, a college graduate has more opportunities for job promotions)

FIGURE 1.1

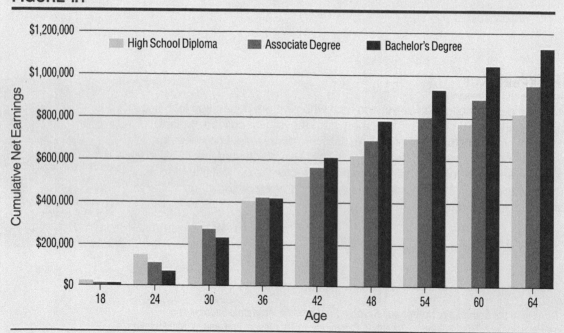

- Career satisfaction—college graduates are more likely to be in careers that interest them and in positions they find stimulating, challenging, and personally fulfilling
- Career autonomy—college graduates have more opportunities to work independently (without supervision) and make their own on-the-job decisions
- Career prestige—college graduates are more likely to hold higher status positions, (i.e., jobs considered to be desirable and highly regarded by society)

2. Advanced Intellectual Skills

College graduates possess:
- Greater knowledge
- More effective problem-solving skills—better ability to deal with complex and ambiguous (uncertain) problems
- Greater openness to new ideas
- More advanced levels of moral reasoning
- More effective consumer choices and decisions

> "Without exception, the observed changes [during college] involve greater breadth, expansion, and appreciation for the new and different . . . and the evidence for their presence is compelling."
>
> —*Ernest Pascarella and Pat Terenzini,* How College Affects Students

- Wiser long-term investments
- Clearer sense of self-identity—greater awareness and knowledge of personal talents, interests, values, and needs
- Greater likelihood of learning continually throughout life

3. Physical Health Benefits
- Better health insurance—college graduates are more likely to have insurance coverage and have more comprehensive coverage
- Better dietary habits
- Exercise more regularly
- Have lower rates of obesity
- Live longer and healthier lives

4. Social Benefits
- Greater social self-confidence
- Better ability to understand and communicate effectively with others

- Greater popularity
- More effective leadership skills
- Higher levels of marital satisfaction

5. Emotional Benefits
- Lower levels of anxiety
- Higher levels of self-esteem
- Greater sense of self-efficacy—college graduates believe they have more influence or control over the outcomes of their lives
- Higher levels of psychological well-being
- Higher levels of life satisfaction and happiness

6. Effective Citizenship
- Greater interest in national issues—both social and political
- Greater knowledge of current events
- Higher voting participation rates
- Higher rates of participation in civic affairs and community service

7. Higher Quality of Life for Their Children
- Less likely to smoke during pregnancy
- Provide better health care for their children
- Spend more time with their children
- More likely to involve their children in stimulating educational activities that advance their cognitive (mental) development
- More likely to save money for their children to go to college
- More likely to have children who graduate from college
- More likely that their children attain higher status, higher salary careers

> My three-month-old boy is very important to me, and it is important I graduate from college so my son, as well as I, live a better life".
>
> —*First-year student's response to the question: "What is most important to you?"*

Sources: Andres and Wyn (2010); Astin (1993); Bowen (1977, 1997); Baum, Ma, and Payea (2013); Carnevale, Strohl, and Melton (2011); Dee (2004); Feldman and Newcomb (1994); Hamilton (2011, 2014); Knox, Lindsay, and Kolb (1993); Lumina Foundation (2013, 2015); Pascarella and Terenzini (2005); Pew Research Center (2014); Seifert et al. (2008); SHEEO (2012); The Hamilton Project (2014); Tomsho (2009); U.S. Bureau of Labor Statistics (2015).

NOTE ✗

College is most likely one of the last times, as an adult, that you will be a member of a community with a wealth of resources, services, and faculty who are intentionally focused on your success!

❝

✗ *In (this class), I have learned many new things. . . . I use WICOR skills at my job. I got to know almost everyone in the class and something about their lives. When we see each other outside of class, we speak to each other and ask how each other's day is. I think the hardest part of not being in this class next semester is not seeing the (people) I have grown close to, twice a week. As a class, we have bonded and have kind of like our own little "family." I think what we learned besides WICOR, how to think deeper, and to question things is how to build friendships with other people who I would normally not talk to or do not have anything in common with.*

—AHE Student

FIRST YEAR OF COLLEGE

This book is designed to assist diverse college students with success skills, strategies, and insights of how to be academically successful with attention to your physical, emotional, and financial well-being.

The *first* year of college is undoubtedly the most important year of the college experience because it's a *transitional* stage. Students report the most change, the most learning, and the most development during their first year of college (Flowers et al. 2001; HERI 2014; Light 2001). Other research suggests that the academic habits students develop in their first year are likely to persist throughout their remaining years of college (Schilling 2001). When graduating seniors look back at their college experience, many of them say that their first year was the time of greatest change and the time when they made the most significant improvements in their approach to learning. Here's how one senior put it during a personal interview:

Interviewer: What have you learned about your approach to learning [in college]?

Student: I had to learn how to study. I went through high school with a 4.0 average. I didn't have to study. It was a breeze. I got to the university and there was no structure. No one took attendance to make sure I was in class. No one checked my homework. No one told me I had to do something. There were no quizzes on the readings. I did not work well with this lack of structure. It took my first year and a half to learn to deal with it. But I had to teach myself to manage my time. I had to teach myself how to study. I had to teach myself how to learn in a different environment (Chickering and Schlossberg 1998, p. 47).

In some ways, the first-year experience in college is similar to ocean surfing or downhill skiing: It can be filled with the most exciting thrills—greatest learning and development, but also the most dangerous spills—it's the year when students experience the most stress, the most academic difficulties, and the highest college withdrawal rates (American College Testing 2012; Bartlett 2002; Sax, Bryant, and Gilmartin 2004). The ultimate goal of downhill skiing and surfing is to experience the thrills, avoid the spills, and finish the run on your feet and feeling exhilarated. The same can be said for the first year of college; studies show that if students complete their first-year experience in good standing, their chances for successfully completing college increase dramatically (American College Testing 2009).

You'll find that the research cited and the advice provided in this book point to one major conclusion: Success in college depends on you—you make it happen by what you do and how well you capitalize on the resources available to you. Don't let college happen *to* you; make it happen *for* you—take charge of your college experience and take advantage of the college resources that are at your command.

After reviewing 40 years of research on how college affects students, two distinguished researchers reached the following conclusion:

> *The impact of college is largely determined by individual effort and involvement in the academic, interpersonal, and extracurricular*

[co-curricular] offerings on a campus. Students are not passive recipients of institutional efforts to "educate" or "change" them, but rather bear major responsibility for any gains they derive from their postsecondary [college] experience (Pascarella and Terenzini 2005, p. 602).

Compared to your previous experiences in school, college will provide you with a broader range of courses to choose from, more resources to capitalize on, and more decision-making opportunities. Your particular college experience will end up being different than any other college student because you have the freedom to actively shape and create it in a way that's uniquely your own.

AHE Experience

Many of these new students [displaced workers] feel that going back to school was the best thing that they have ever done. They feel better about themselves because of the daily challenges, making contacts and developing new relationships with classmates, and the thrill of learning helps them to believe in themselves and feel successful. I hear these comments: "This is a wonderful opportunity for me." "I realized what was important to me." "I've wanted to go back to school for a long time."

—Community college counselor

IMPORTANCE OF A FIRST-YEAR EXPERIENCE COURSE (ALSO KNOWN AS A FIRST-YEAR SEMINAR)

If you're reading this book, you are already beginning to take charge of your college experience because you're likely to be enrolled in a course that's designed to promote your college success. Research strongly indicates that new students who participate in first-year experience courses are more likely to continue in college until they complete their degree and perform at a higher level. These positive effects have been found for:

- All types of students (under-prepared and well-prepared, minority and majority, residential and commuter, male and female),
- Students at all types of colleges (two-year and four-year, public and private),
- Students attending colleges of all sizes (small, mid-sized, and large), and
- Students attending college in all locations (urban, suburban, and rural).

(Sources: Barefoot et al. 1998; Boudreau and Kromrey 1994; Cuseo 2011; Cuseo and Barefoot 1996; Fidler and Godwin 1994; Glass and Garrett 1995; Grunder and Hellmich 1996; Hunter and Linder 2005; Porter and Swing 2006; Shanley and Witten 1990; Sidle and McReynolds 1999; Starke, Harth, and Sirianni 2001; Thomson 1998; Tobolowsky 2005).

There has been more research on the first-year experience course and more evidence supporting its positive impact on student success than any other course in the college curriculum. Give this course your best effort and take full advantage of what it has to offer. If you do, you'll take an important first step toward excelling in college and in life beyond college.

I am very impressed by the displaced workers who are returning to school. While one would expect the workers to be down and depressed, most of them are viewing this as an opportunity to pursue an opportunity [and] a dream delayed."

—Community college counselor

DON'T BE UNWISE—AVIDIZE!

Everyone has told you college is not like high school. Whether you were a good student or just average, at least in high school, you knew the routine. If you were late on an assignment, you'd ask for extra credit. If you hadn't done all of the reading, but you'd been to class (or vice versa), sometimes you could bluff your way to at least a "c." You had a group of buddies, all locals, who you'd known forever. Alas, those days are gone.

College is high school on steroids! There's way more reading. And writing. You can't even understand what some of the questions are asking, let alone figure out a response. And there are all these new people from different towns, states, countries even. You feel as if you're all on your own. If you've been in the military, started a career or family, returning to school can be exciting and scary as you juggle multiple demands. It's easy to see how a person can become overwhelmed.

One of the most critical lessons that college offers is it forces you to take your learning into your own hands. While it is true that some professors do not take attendance, attending class, interacting with peer study groups, and becoming engaged on your campus is the strongest path to a successful and fulfilling college experience. How much you want to explore and grow is up to you. That can feel as daunting as the 150 pages of history you must read! How can you take things into your own hands if you don't have many ideas of what to do?

Not to worry. Help is on the way.

AVID for Higher Education (AHE) provides a set of strategies that are specifically designed to help you make it through the tough assignment, the confusing group work, and the tough questions. These strategies are not magic bullets. They require you to work hard, but you'll be working smarter. The more you practice them, the better you'll get and the easier assignments and relationships will be. Best of all, the strategies you're learning are not college-specific, the strategies are life skills that employers are looking for and will help you in your career and social life after you finish college.

Generally, the strategies are divided into five categories, focused on areas that research has proven to be important for success. These include tips on the following:

- writing more effective, succinct responses to questions,
- inquiring into issues and topics at a deeper and more insightful manner,
- collaborating with others from different backgrounds and with viewpoints in a collegial way,
- organizing your mind and surroundings so you can work more efficiently, and
- reading in such a way that you will gain greater understanding of the text and its relationship to other material you have heard and seen.

As you can see, its' a big canvas—one that pretty much covers all the facets of your experiences in college. We're going to provide you with brief overviews of each of these areas, but you'll only get the full benefit of them if you (a) use a journal or your laptop to complete the exercises included throughout this book, (b) use the online resources, which provide more information on the topics covered here, and if possible (c) discuss them and work on them with a study group or at least one of your classmates, which we recommend throughout the chapters. On this last point, connecting with your classmates and professor is possible both face-to-face and online. The point is adding these practices to your daily and weekly routines.

And remember, taking control of your learning also means knowing when you need to ask for assistance. A study group provides an ongoing and readily available set of classmates with whom you can share insights, suggestions, and learning. Your campus has trained tutors (many of them former AVID students) as well as advisors and counselors who can help you improve your curricular and co-curricular success in college. We'll give some tips about that as well.

And now, let's do a brief overview of the five important collegiate competencies that AHE refers to as WICOR (Writing, Inquiry, Collaboration, Organization, and Reading).

AHE DEEP DIVE INTO WRITING

Clear writing gives you voice. It enables you to write your thoughts in a coherent manner so not only you, but also your audience, has an understanding of your thoughts, feelings, and beliefs. If you have trouble writing, you probably understand Jimmy Santiago Baca (2014) when he says

> Ashamed of not understanding and fearful of asking questions, I dropped out of school in the ninth grade. . .
>
> There was nothing so humiliating as being unable to express myself, and my inarticulateness increased my sense of jeopardy. . . When at last I wrote my first words on the page, I felt an island rising beneath my feet like the back of a whale. As more and more words emerged, I could finally rest: I had a place to stand for the first time in my life. . . Through language I was free.

But in order to write well, you first must think clearly. You may remember when teachers asked you to do a rough draft and then to redo it, perhaps after someone else read it and made suggestions. Each step was a way of getting greater clarity in what you wanted to express. While mechanics are important—spelling, punctuation, and the like—our ability to organize what you write, your knowledge base, and your reasoning ability are critical aspects of making people understand your point of view. Within this book, we've included lots of short writing opportunities. Quickwrites, one minute papers, should be considered practice on how you might start to organize your thoughts for longer assignments. We also suggest you keep a journal in which you can keep your thoughts about your journey through college. Include your hopes and goals. This will help you to clarify what matters to you personally and how you feel about your progress. Many of the assignments included in this book are designed to give you a start on creating a journal on your college experiences.

Perhaps the most important thing to remember for your academic writing is the question. The question usually comes in the form of some type of prompt that tells you what the instructor wants you to do. For instance, you might be asked to analyze a text, or compare two events, or justify a character's actions. Each of these call for a different kind of response. In order to write clearly in these situations, you need to ask yourself some questions, such as "what am I being asked to do?" "Who is my audience?" or "Am I being asked to use various resources?" If you don't understand what you are being asked to do, seek assistance from another classmate or your instructor.

Do not consider your first draft your final paper. After you complete your assignment, it is helpful to have one of your peers review it to be sure you are addressing the question correctly. You don't want to ask someone, "so, what do you think?" but rather have certain components of the draft that you particularly want feedback on.

AHE Deep Dive into Inquiry

"Inquiring minds want to know." That may be the truest sentence ever written by the newspaper that uses it for its advertisement. Inquiring minds DO want to know and wanting to know is why you and your colleagues are in college. Whether your primary goal is to be a better person, get a better job, or read some better books, college is where you will find the opportunity to do all those things. All of these goals require that you be a good thinker and a good problem solver. And it all starts with questions. You will need to be able to form the right question to get the right answer. We want to introduce you to some ways of understanding the questions you are asked (even by yourself) and how you might approach coming up with appropriate answers.

Any compelling question is the start of a journey. Elie Wiesel noted, "In the word question, there is a beautiful word—*quest*. I love that word. We are all partners in a quest. The essential questions have no answers. You are my question, and I am yours—and then there is dialogue. The moment we have answers, there is no dialogue. Questions unite people." Like most quests, inquiry can be difficult, it can lead to dead ends. It can take longer than we anticipated and lead to unexpected conclusions. That's the fun of it. And that's why it's so important to understand what is being asked of us before we begin. So, let's take a step back before we start.

Think back to high school. The questions you were asked were often yes/no or fact-based questions. These were critical as before one can move on to more sophisticated thinking, they need to have a foundation of good, plain facts. On a car trip, we'd want to know mileage, traffic patterns, etc. All information that is easily gained from reputable sources. But what if the question was, "Would it be easier to make this journey by plane or by car?" That requires more thought and it asks us to compare two types of travel and suggest which would be easier and why. Taking it a step further, what if the question was, "How can self-driving cars impact Uber and other share-drive companies? This requires speculation based on facts. You need to evaluate data and synthesize it into a coherent response.

More complex questions get us to that deeper understanding of concepts and disciplines. AHE uses "Costa's Level of Questions" to analyze exactly what type of thinking and response is required.

* Level One questions focus on gathering and recalling information (Reading the lines)
* Level Two questions focus on making sense of gathered information (Reading between the lines)
* Level Three questions focus on applying and evaluating information (Thinking off the page)

Here's an example.

Level One: T/F: The earth's gravitational pull is different from the moon's.

Level Two: What are the implications of the different gravity on both the earth and moon?

Level Three: How did the political and social environment lead to the U.S. space programs journey to the moon in the 1960–1970s?

The first question is easily found. The second question calls on you to gather information and make some judgments based on a variety of sources. The third question requires information from a variety of disciplines, evaluation of that information, and an assessment of your part of why and how decisions were made about space travel. The questions call for increasingly complex information and increasingly sophisticated thinking. This is the heart of college learning—it is exciting, it is engaging, and it is hard work. All of the other skills AHE emphasizes are built around enabling you to have an easier time accessing complex information and on presenting sophisticated thoughts in a clear, coherent manner. Tips on:

* Writing helps you to communicate your ideas in a compelling and understandable way;
* Collaboration enables you to listen to and reflect on the ideas and work of others from diverse backgrounds;
* Organizational assists are designed for help you "clear the decks" and limit disruptions that can keep you from focusing on an assignment or issue; and
* Reading suggests how you can highlight the information that is most important for you to be considering.

Chapter 5 offers you a variety of ways of thinking about issues and concerns, both personal and academic. You will need the reading strategies we discuss to get the full benefit of that chapter. But for now, let's review some skills that will help you be successful in college and career. And in life.

AHE Deep Dive into Collaboration

According to AVID Center,

> Collaboration centers on the effective sharing of information amongst individuals. In an educational context, collaboration affords students the opportunity to work with peers in various group configurations as they engage subject matter across content areas. Collaboration is essential for student success as it entails experiencing the challenges and opportunities associated with a diversity of perspectives and working styles, which can deepen metacognitive thinking, accelerate learning, and broaden perspective. (AVID website)

Whew. In simpler terms, collaboration is about working together toward a shared outcome or goal. One of the benefits of your future education and career is that you will be working with others in collaborative settings This can be difficult—anytime personalities get together, they bring their egos along to make consensus more difficult. It is particularly difficult right now, as you begin your journey through college. You are surrounded by people who you don't know—how are you supposed to work together with them to achieve a common goal? The first step in this process is developing trust.

Many of your classes will start with "ice breakers," short informal exercises that let you tell a little about yourself and let you learn a little about others in your class. These usually involve some sort of question—What's your favorite movie? Which of your classes seems most interesting? They are introductory questions so you can get to know a little about other persons and grow comfortable with them. If they look familiar, it's because they are similar to the questions you might ask when meeting someone at a party or informal gathering. This would not be the time to ask about their greatest heartbreak or who they voted for in the last election. At this point you are only trying to get to learn a little about them and not delve into their deepest soul. One question will lead to another and, as you find out more, you will be able to determine whether or not this would be a good study partner and friend.

But many of our campus collaborations are assigned. It could be an "ad hoc" group that gets together to discuss a certain chapter or idea. Or it may be a formal study group, where you and several colleagues are assigned to study and work together in and out of class for the semester. In both cases, you didn't necessarily know the members of the group or they may be acquaintances that you didn't really enjoy that much. None of that matters. You will need to get along with and address the assignment given to the group.

At first, most people do not like group work—they prefer to work on their own because, they think, other people can't do the assignment as well as they can. Or they don't want to reveal to others that they are having trouble grasping certain concepts. In both cases, collaborative learning will be a welcome surprise. A collaborative learning environment supports both individual and group accountability. The success of each person is linked to the success of the group; individuals succeed to the extent that the group succeeds. Thus, students are motivated to help one another accomplish group goals (Johnson, Johnson, and Smith 1998). As important as what happens during the group work, what happens after—the debrief—is equally significant. The group should discuss what worked and what didn't in the development of their project. By talking out the highs and lows, each person learns more about how their role helped, or possibly slowed up, the process. This knowledge will make you a better student, and also a better friend for what you learn about collaboration is not simply an academic exercise. You will be in groups planning a party, deciding what restaurant to go to, organizing a weekend trip. You will use collaborative interpersonal skills in each of these endeavors.

In this book, you will find many activities that suggest working with a partner or with a group. If your class is not taught by an AHE instructor, this may be difficult to do, but you will find it worth the effort. Besides getting to know others better, the more you engage with others in learning, the more you will enjoy both college and the people with whom you meet. Various chapters in this book focus more deeply on collaborative learning and stress interpersonal skills. Additionally, we've included some of the easy activities you can use to get a group actively engaged in participating in the learning process.

AHE DEEP DIVE INTO ORGANIZING FOR SUCCESS

It doesn't seem like it should be so hard to get organized, but for some of us, it's a real chore. It was easier in high school, when everything was in one building and we had the same schedule from one week to the next. But now it's college and work and, well, LIFE!

We try to organize but somehow there's never enough time to do that. The papers/essays aren't where they should be, we forgot to purchase one of the texts needed for tomorrow's exam, and surely, we haven't lost the notes we took on Thursday. Where ARE they? We'll offer some assistance in each of these areas, but first things first.

Mindfulness

We're not talking meditation here, but mindfulness—being aware of yourself and your surroundings, focusing on how you feel, and how you perceive your world, right now. It's being actively aware of the present. In a sense, you are taking an objective view of yourself from the outside, making no judgment about the right or wrong of the situation. You are clearing your mind of all other thoughts, such as what you need to do for the test this afternoon or remembering to call your mom before lunch. It's all about you and how you experience the world. One student said anytime extraneous thoughts entered his mind, he would figuratively take a broom and sweep his brain clean. One strategy to consider is "Empty the Cup." It might be considered the beginning of mindfulness, as you and a classmate empty your thoughts to each other so you can proceed to your next task without thinking about all the things that weigh you down during a school day.

Why is this important to organization? Mindfulness is so important to doing good work that it is used intentionally by corporations—Apple, Google, and McKinsey—you might work for one day. They use it because they found that starting the day by clearing your mind and focusing on your environment made employees more relaxed and efficient. After they had focused on themselves, they were able to focus on the task at hand. But it's not something you do once and forget about the rest of the day. These corporations suggest doing mindful exercises several times a day: before work, at the end of an assignment, before going to bed. The UCLA Mindful Awareness Research Center (http://www.marc.ucla.edu) offers free exercises explained in both English and Spanish if you want to try some of the beginning activities.

Focused Note-Taking

Everyone takes notes, but everyone was neither taught how to take them nor, more importantly, how to use them. We're going through a quick review of one way you can take notes and use them to be more engaged in your courses. And the more engaged you are, the better your chances of doing well at both college and career.

To take focused notes, you divide your paper into three sections. While it's better to take notes in writing, we know you may be used to using your computer. Create a Cornell Note template or download one from numerous websites.

Notice that on the top of the page, there is room for you to write your subject, date, and most important, the Essential Question.[1] The essential question (EQ) informs you of what you need to be thinking about as your read or listen in class. If your instructor doesn't provide an EQ or statement of purpose, check your syllabus. However, sometimes you will have to proceed without this important guidepost.

On the right side of the page, take the notes from a lecture, discussion, or book. When you're finished with the class or text, review the notes and on the left side of the page, discuss them with your colleagues, and write any questions you have or key points you think are being made. This is best done with a partner so you can compare notes and see what you may have missed. Also, by sharing you may discover new insights and get the chance to explain your viewpoints to others. And take care with the questions you add to the left side of the page. Review those with your classmates and be sure you listen to their questions as well. You would be surprised how often a similar question may appear on an exam.

The bottom part of the page is devoted either to reflections you have about the work, or if your instructor asks, a summary of what you have reviewed. This section is important! One of the goals of college is to help you deepen and clarify your thinking. Reflecting on what you've read or discussing with others why it was meaningful are two ways you can achieve this goal. So, take the time to complete the Reflection section even if your instructor doesn't specifically ask it of you.

Getting the page in the correct form is not going to get you a good grade. It's what you put on that page that's critical, so here are some tips

---

[1] Instructor will not necessarily call the purpose of the lecture or reading an Essential Question. Sometimes they might say, "Today we're going to find out the effect of solute concentration on water potential as it relates to living plant tissues." That clearly tells you what the purpose of the lecture is and can easily be turned into an EQ. You need to listen carefully to those initial instructions.

for taking those notes. And we've included a sample from a student's actual notes so you can see how they look when well done.

1. Take 15–25 pages of quality focused notes per week. You may want to experiment by starting in one class and doing the notes faithfully, with both readings and lectures. Review them after class and write questions or highlights on the left side of the page. Use them as a study tool and see if your grades in that class suggest you might want to expand your experiment.

2. Use focused notes as an advanced study tool, which will be continually refined and studied independently. You may be going back and forth between earlier notes and later ones that relate to the topic or modify your thinking about its importance and meaning.

3. Create notes that track reading and research effectively. Some people find it helps to skip a line between major topics or to number the paragraphs that start a new topic.

4. Personalize your notes so key information stands out when you review your notes later. If you use highlighters, use different colors for main ideas of the reading or lecture, for key concepts, and for your questions.

5. Use notes during in-class and independently formed study groups. Take the time to review the notes with others and by yourself. Consider why a main theme is important and how it impacted the discipline you are studying. Write these questions about the notes on the left side of the page.

6. Refine the skill of writing higher-level summaries for focused notes that link all of the learning together.

It would be great if organizing your life would be as easy as organizing your notes, but alas, it's not. When you decide to get more organized, people will have many recommendations. Some suggest you organize everything in your life at once—clean out your car, your room, have a place for everything, and put everything in its place. Others say that being organized is a life style and it isn't going to happen all at once and suggest you focus on one thing at a time. We're only going to make some suggestions for your campus life:

- Organize your time. You'll find a whole chapter on time management and it's one you need to read carefully. However, we want to stress some points and suggest some ideas for you. First and probably most important, designate times when you will neither make calls nor write/receive texts. To do your best work, you need to focus. If you go through a kind of withdrawal when you can't respond to the text that comes in, inform everyone you're taking a short text break, say, 15 minutes so you can work. Build up your uninterrupted time to an hour, at which point you should be getting up and moving around anyway.

  When you get a long-term assignment, it's helpful to do some backward mapping about what is involved to complete the project. For example, if you put in your planner, "Paper due 10/16," it doesn't suggest all that's involved in getting that final paper into your instructor.

You need to decide on a topic, do research, determine what attachments or graphics you will want to include, write a rough draft, review and modify it, maybe have it read and critiqued by one of your classmates, type it up as a final, find a folder for it, and submit it. It seems overwhelming but if you did some backward mapping, and include it in your planner when you will do each of the tasks, you'll have begun to organize your time. For instance, if the paper is due by 10/16, you want to be sure you have it typed and final by 10/15. If a colleague was going to read it, you would need them to do that by 10/12 because you may need to retype it afterward, and so on. Also, remember that you probably will have more than one assignment in another class due sometime between now and 10/16. Doing this also will help you confront if and how much you procrastinate. The first time you say, "I can put off finally selecting my topic until next week." You're making your next deadline more difficult—and no more pleasant to do. In Chapter 7, you can find out more about battling procrastination—that enemy of organization.

And start tomorrow today. Spend just a few minutes before you go to bed making a list of what you need to do the next day. What do you plan to wear? Take it out and be sure it's clean and ready to wear. It will take you only a few moments but will contribute to making tomorrow a little easier. Read up on Chapter 2, which will be a great help in getting you to manage time rather than it managing you.

- Organize your work space. One of the biggest time wasters is looking for what you need to complete a task. If you have your own space or desk, ideally you will be able to organize it close to an outlet so your computer can be charged every time you use it. Keep the drawers clean, having only those things you need to work—pencils, pens, notepads, and glasses—inside them. If you keep written notes, put them in color-coded folders so you know exactly where they are. Use that same color for everything related to that course—if chemistry is a red folder, put additional notes, interviews, etc. in a chemistry folder that's titled in red on your computer.
- Organize your thoughts. It's great to have an exterior space that invites you to work and think seriously about your studies. But you also have to sweep your mind clean of extraneous thoughts and begin to focus on the subject at hand. Remember that we started with mindfulness and its importance in establishing you right in the present. As you begin major assignments or responsibilities—either at school or at home—practice mindfulness as a way of preparing for the tasks in front of you.

One easy way to organize your thoughts as you begin an assignment is the graphic organizer, K/W/H/L Chart. The charts headings stand for:

- *K*—what you already KNOW about the subject.
- *W*—what you WANT to learn.
- *H*—figuring out HOW you can learn more about the topic.
- *L*—what you LEARN as you read.

As you can see from the sample chart included, it can provide you with a good starting point for your studies. You'll find other strategies throughout this book that will help you. You'll be asked to "empty the cup," which serves many purposes, but one is to clear the mind of distractions. Sometimes you'll be asked to mark the text so you can better organize your studying. These strategies are suggestions that hopefully you will incorporate into your daily activities naturally without needing a reminder. But for now, do try to practice these strategies when you come to them in the following pages. Many chapters in this book go into more detail and offer suggestions and insights into both why organization is important and how you can conquer some of barriers that can get in the way of good habits.

AHE DEEP DIVE INTO READING

You think you know how to read—and you do. But do you know how to get the most out of your readings? We want to introduce you to some techniques you can use to read more deeply and with greater confidence. In college, professors expect students to be more analytical and thoughtful about what they read—they want you to interact with the text. They want you to think about what you read and draw your own conclusions about its meaning and importance. They expect students use what they read to prove or disprove what they say in class discussion. That can sound pretty formidable, but if you use these tips, you'll be among the top students in your class!

THE ACADEMIC READING PROCESS

At AVID for Higher Education, we use the Academic Reading Process that breaks down reading into several components. Some occur before reading, others after, but all focus on getting the most out of academic reading assignments. We'll run through the process now and then recommend how you can use it, not just in this course and with this book, but with all your academic work.

Planning for Reading: Knowing your syllabus says, "read pages 12–43," doesn't provide you with direction on why you were assigned the reading. To assist you in focusing, your instructor generally will provide you with a "reading prompt." A prompt can provide a background of the text or isolate the information that the instructor wants you to focus on as you read. It also (if you're at an AHE campus!) includes how you should interact with the text—circling main ideas or underlining important concepts (this will all be explained under). Finally, prompts also can include how you will show you have a good understanding of the text. Usually, the professor provides the prompt, but if you don't get a prompt, you might consider developing one of your own. You'll get some ideas on how you can do this as you read on. Also, note that each of the chapters in this book starts with a Purpose for Reading that serves as your prompt.

Building Vocabulary: Every year, new words that apply to technology, science, and everyday living are added to dictionaries around the world. Often, as you move from reading your history text to reading your science book, you will find that the same word often means something else in different disciplines or in our daily experiences. "Abstract" may be an adjective for "intangible" or "vague" when you hear it used in your English class when the author doesn't spell out exactly what he means. Your science professor might talk about an abstract as being a summary of a journal article. Think about the word, "model." It means a fashion model when you're reading Vogue, but a computer simulation in your chemistry book. Besides that, the more we read, the more we find ourselves confronting words or phrases that we *think* we know, but aren't quite sure.

Pre-Reading Strategies: You may wonder what you can do before you read to help you read. The possibilities are endless. One pre-read strategy is simply to review chapter headings and subheadings so you'll have a good idea of what the chapter is about before you've read a word of the text. You might look up the author to see if he's written other articles and is known for a viewpoint or opinion. By examining the pictures or scanning charts, you may see connections to other things you've learned. This will increase your interest in the reading as well as enable you to make predictions about that the reading is about.

Interacting with the Text: This is where the real fun starts. This is where you read and do what we refer to as "marking the texts." When we highlight text in our books, there's no distinction between things we are just interested in or concepts we need to remember because they are critical to understanding the discipline under review. When you mark the text, you are very conscious of using certain symbols to mean certain things. As examples, some ways of marking the text are as follows:

- **Circle the key terms**, which may be dates, names, new ideas, or propositions. If the author repeats a term several times, you can bet it's something important.
- **Underline main claims** that are made either for or against major ideas. A claim is something that is asserted as true. How well the author states his or her claims and backs it up will determine whether you believe what the author is asserting.
- **Bracket phrases** that support claims or provide evidence.
- **Make marginal notes** will be useful by including your questions, summarizing chunks of text, or relating it to other information you have. We'll talk more about making notes in the margins a little later.

These are only a few ways you can interact with the text but you should see that it's a much more specific and helpful way to review material that you've read. If you have rented your texts, you can still mark the text by using sticky notes attached to the pages of the book. We've provided a reference sheet on some of these techniques and you might want to keep a copy of it in your texts or on your computer.

Extending Beyond the Text: This gives you the opportunity to show what you know about your reading. Faculty may ask you to:

* summarize a chapter;
* compare two different readings; or
* determine how the text resonates with other text or current experiences/events occurring around the world.

Regardless of the assignment, your instructor is assuming you've not only read the material, but that you've thought about it and considered it in a variety of ways. All the techniques we've discussed, from vocabulary building to pre-reading, to interacting with the text, are designed to help you reach a deeper understanding of the material. This more complex and sophisticated understanding is, the more thoughtfully you'll be able to assignments and participating in class or study group discussions.

Throughout this book, we will be providing you with short exercises where you can see how these reading tips can help with your comprehension and enjoyment of the material. But you'll get more out of the exercises when you do them with other people. If your professor doesn't assign you to a study group, form one yourself. If that doesn't seem possible, scan a page or two from a chapter you've marked and exchange it with another student in the class. See how much you agreed with each other and discuss why you disagreed on some terms. Remember, you learn more when you share more.

BUT WHAT IF YOU NEED MORE?

Sometimes all the advice just confuses us and don't seem to be leading to the success we planned. You go to class. You read the book, but it just doesn't make sense. One of the most important aspects of taking responsibility for your own learning is knowing when you need someone to help you out. While your professors and teaching assistants are there to offer guidance, more intensive help is available through tutoring /mentoring facilities. On AHE campuses, AHE-trained tutors will be available to provide ongoing support in a variety of content areas and will critique assignments on occasion. They are trained to use the Socratic method—asking questions until you (yes you!) come up with the answers that solve your learning problems. But before you see a tutor, the burden is on you. You will be expected to have read the material and to attend class. These are the basics and the tutor uses these to further explain and assist you at understanding the finer points that you might be missing.

When you begin to feel that you are falling behind in your studies, make a tutorial appointment fast! The longer you go without understanding the content in your classes, the harder it will be to recoup. It is not a sign of weakness to go for assistance. It's a sign that you understand the importance of keeping up with your courses.

There are other supports available to you at most colleges and universities. While this resource provides more information on these options, remember that personal and academic counseling are part of the services campuses provide. Seeking out counseling for personal and financial problems is a positive action. It may offer you the peace of mind you need to do your best. The same goes for your physical health. Exercise helps clarify your thinking and helps your body in a variety of ways. And if you aren't feeling your best, the health clinic may be your best first line of defense. And don't ever think that asking for help is a sign of weakness. It only means that you want to be the best you can be. Take advantage of the opportunities you are offered.

Enjoy the journey!

REFERENCES

American College Testing. 2015. *College Student Retention and Graduation Rates from 2000 through 2015.* http://www.act.org/research/policymakers/pdf/retain_2015.pdf.

Andres, L., and J. Wyn. 2010. *The Making of a Generation: The Children of the 1970s in Adulthood.* Buffalo, NY: University of Toronto Press.

Astin, A. W. 1993. *What Matters in College?* San Francisco: Jossey-bass.

Baca, J. S. March 3, 2014. *Coming into Language.* https: //pen.org/coming-into-language.

Barefoot, B. O., C. L. Warnock, M. P. Dickinson, S. E. Richardson, and M. R. Roberts, eds. 1998. *Exploring the Evidence: Vol. 2. Reporting Outcomes of First-year Seminars.* Monograph No. 29. Columbia: National Resource Center for the First-year Experience and Students in Transition, University of South Carolina.

Bartlett, T. 2002. "Freshman Pay, Mentally and Physically, as they Adjust to College Life." *Chronicle of Higher Education* 48: 35–37.

Baum, S., J. Ma, and K. Payea. 2013. *Education Pays 2013: The Benefits of Higher Education for Individuals and Society.* Washington DC: The College Board. http://trends.collegeboard.org/sites/default/files/education-pays-2013-full-report-022714.pdf.

Boudreau, C., and J. Kromrey. 1994. "A Longitudinal Study of the Retention and Academic Performance of Participants in a Freshman Orientation Course." *Journal of College Student Development* 35: 444–49.

Bowen, H. R. 1977. *Investment in Learning: The Individual and Social Value of American Higher Education.* San Francisco: Jossey-bass.

Bowen, H. R. 1997. *Investment in Learning: The Individual and Social Value of American Higher Education.* 2nd ed. Baltimore: Johns Hopkins Press.

Carnevale, A. P., J. Strohl, and M. Melton. 2011. *What's in Worth? The Economic Value of College Majors.* Washington DC: Center on Education and the Workforce, Georgetown University. http:cew.georgetown.edu/whatsitworth/

Chickering, A. W., and N. K. Schlossberg. 1998. "Moving on: Seniors as People in Transition." In *The Senior Year Experience* edited by J. N. Gardner, G. Van der Veer, et al., 37–50. San Francisco: Jossey-bass.

Cuseo, J. B., and B. O. Barefoot. 1996. "A Natural Marriage: The Extended Orientation Seminar and the Community College." In *The Community College: Opportunity and Access for America's First-year Students* edited by J. Henkin, 59–68. Columbia: National Resource Center for the First-year Experience and Students in Transition, University of South Carolina.

Dee, T. 2004. "Are There Civic Returns to Education?" *Journal of Public Economics* 88: 1697–720.

Feldman, K. A., and T. M. Newcomb. 1994. *The Impact of College on Students.* New Brunswick: Transaction Publishers.

Fidler, P., and M. Godwin. 1994. "Retaining African-American Students through the Freshman Seminar." *Journal of Developmental Education* 17: 34–41.

Flowers, L., S. Osterlind, E. Pascarella, and C. Pierson. 2001. "How Much Do Students Learn in College? Cross-sectional Estimates Using the College Basic Academic Subjects Examination." *Journal of Higher Education* 72: 565–83.

Glass, J., and M. Garrett. 1995. "Student Participation in a College Orientation Course: Retention, and Grade Point Average." *Community College Journal of Research and Practice* 19: 117–32.

Grunder, P., and D. Hellmich. 1996. "Academic Persistence and Achievement of Remedial Students in a Community College's Success Program." *Community College Review* 24: 21–33.

Hamilton, W. December 29, 2011. "College Still Worth it, Study Says." *Los Angeles Times*, p. B2.

Hamilton, W. June 25, 2014. "College Still Good Bet, Study Says." *Los Angeles Times*, p. B4.

HERI (Higher Education Research Institute). 2014. *Your First College Year Survey 2014.* Los Angeles, CA: Cooperative Institutional Research Program, University of California-los Angeles.

Hunter, M. A., and C. W. Linder. 2005. "First-year Seminars." In *Challenging and Supporting the First-year Student: A Handbook for Improving the First Year of College*, edited by M. L. Upcraft, J. N. Gardner, B. O. Barefoot, et al., 275–91. San Francisco: Jossey-bass.

Johnson, D. W., R. T. Johnson, and K. A. Smith. 1998. *Active Learning: Cooperation in the College Classroom.* Edina, MN: Interaction Book Company.

Knox, W. E., P. Lindsay, and M. N. Kolb. 1993. *Does College Make a Difference? Long-term Changes in Activities and Attitudes.* Westport, CT: Greenwood.

Light, R. J. 2001. *Making the Most of College: Students Speak their Minds.* Cambridge, MA: Harvard University Press.

Lumina Foundation. 2013. *A Stronger Nation Through Higher Education.* Indianapolis IN: Author. http://www.pesc.org/library/docs/about_us/whitepapers/a-stronger-nation-2013lumina.pdf.

Lumina Foundation. 2015. *A Stronger Nation Through Higher Education*. Indianapolis IN: Author. http://www.luminafoundation.org/files/publications/A_stronger_nation_through_higher_education-2015.pdf.

Pascarella, E., and P. Terenzini. 2005. *How College Affects Students: A Third Decade of Research*. vol. 2. San Francisco: Jossey-bass.

Pew Research Center. February, 2014. *The Rising Cost of not Going to College*. http://www.pewsocialtrends.org/2014/02/11/the-rising-cost-of-not-going-to-college/.

Porter, S. R., and R. L. Swing. 2006. "Understanding How First-year Seminars Affect Persistence." *Research in Higher Education* 47(1): 89–109.

Sax, L. J., A. N. Bryant, and S. K. Gilmartin. 2004. "A Longitudinal Investigation of Emotional Health Among Male and Female First-year College Students." *Journal of the First-year Experience,* 16: 39–65.

Schilling, K. August, 2001. *Plenary Address*. Presented at The Summer Institute on First-year Assessment, Asheville, North Carolina.

Seifert, T. A., K. M. Goodman, N. Lindsay, J. D. Jorgensen, G. C. Wolniak, E. T. Pascarella, and C. Blaich. 2008. "The Effects of Liberal Arts Experiences on Liberal Arts Outcomes." *Research in Higher Education* 49: 107–25.

Shanley, M., and C. Witten. 1990. "University 101 Freshman Seminar Course: A Longitudinal Study of Persistence, Retention, and Graduation Rates." *NASPA Journal* 27: 344–52.

SHEEO (State Higher Education Executive Officers). 2012. *State Higher Education Finance, FY 2011*. http://www.sheeo.org/sites/default/files/publications/SHEF_FY11.pdf.

Sidle, M., and J. McReynolds. 1999. "The Freshman Year Experience: Student Retention and Student Success." *NASPA Journal* 36: 288–300.

Starke, M. C., M. Harth, and F. Sirianni. 2001. "Retention, Bonding, and Academic Achievement: Success of a First-year Seminar." *Journal of the First-year Experience and Students in Transition* 13(2): 7–35.

The Hamilton Project. 2014. *Major Decisions: What Graduates Earn over Their Lifetimes*. Washington, DC: Brookings Institution. http://www.hamiltonproject.org/papers/major_decisions_what_graduates_earn_over_their_lifetimes/

Thomson, R. 1998. "University of Vermont." In *Exploring the Evidence: Vol. 2. Reporting Outcomes of First-year Seminars*, edited by B. O. Barefoot, C. L. Warnock, M. P. Dickinson, S. E. Richardson, and M. R. Roberts, Monograph No. 29, 77–78. Columbia: National Resource Center for the First-year Experience and Students in Transition, University of South Carolina.

Tobolowsky, B. F. 2005. *The 2003 National Survey on First-year Seminars: Continuing Innovations in the College Curriculum,* Monograph No. 41. Columbia, SC: University of South Carolina, National Resource Center for the First-year Experience and Students in Transition.

Tomsho, R. April 22, 2009. "Study Tallies Education's Gap on GDP." *Wall Street Journal*. http://www.wsj.com/articles/SB124040633530943487

U.S. Bureau of Labor Statistics. 2015. *Employment Projections*. United States of Department of Labor. http://www.bls.gov/emp/ep_chart_001.htm.

Chapter 1 Reflection

After reading Chapter 1, how do you think this course will benefit you?

List and briefly describe three things you hope to learn or accomplish as a result of successfully completing this course.

COLLEGE KNOWLEDGE

EFFECTIVE COLLEGE BEHAVIOR IN CLASS AND ONLINE

This chapter identifies top tips for academic success you can implement immediately, including what to do inside and outside the classroom. It also alerts you to in-class and out-of-class behavior that should be avoided in college.

CHAPTER PREVIEW

Equip you with key academic strategies for getting off to a good start in college, and increase your awareness of behaviors that reflect academic incivility and lack of academic integrity.

LEARNING OBJECTIVE

You will understand and practice academic integrity as they begin their college career.

PERFORMANCE OBJECTIVE

What characteristics are valued in a collegiate setting?

PRE-REFLECTION

How can I interact with faculty and peers in an academic setting?

ESSENTIAL QUESTION

THOUGHT STARTER

 Journal Reflection 2.1

1. What three personal characteristics, qualities, or strategies do you think will be most important for college success?

_____

_____

_____

_____

Box 2.1

Birds of a Different Feather: High School vs. College

High School	College
Your classes are mostly arranged for you.	You arrange your own schedule in consultation with your advisor. Schedules tend to look lighter than they really are.
Your time is structured by others.	You manage your own time.
You go from one class directly to another, spending six hours per day—30 hours per week—in class.	You have free time between classes; class times vary throughout the day and evening; and you spend 12–16 hours each week in class if you are a full-time student.
The school year is 36 weeks long; some classes extend over both semesters, and some do not.	The academic year may be divided into separate semesters or quarters.
Teachers monitor class attendance.	Professors may not formally monitor class attendance; you're expected to have the self-discipline to show up and get down information that's presented in class.
Teachers often write information on the board for you to put in your notes.	Professors may lecture nonstop, expecting you to identify and write down important information in your notes. Professors don't record all their key points on the board. Notes that professors write on the board are used to supplement or complement the lecture, not to summarize for the lecture.
Teachers provide you with information you missed when you were absent.	Professors expect you to get information you missed from classmates.
You are given short reading assignments that are then discussed, and often reviewed, in class.	You're assigned substantial amounts of reading and writing that may not be directly addressed in class.
You seldom need to read anything more than once and sometimes listening in class is enough.	You need to review class notes and read material regularly.
Teachers present material to help you understand the textbook.	Professors may not follow the textbook, but you may be expected to relate class sessions to textbook readings.
You may have studied outside of class for zero to two hours per week.	You need to study for at least two to three hours outside of class for each hour spent in class.
Teachers remind you of assignments and due dates.	Professors expect you to consult the course syllabus for assignments and deadlines.

Source: Southern Methodist University (2006).

College teachers don't tell you what you're supposed to do. They just expect you to do it. High school teachers tell you about five times what you're supposed to do."
—*College sophomore (Appleby 2008)*

The transition from high school to college is often not easy, even for the smartest of students. As the chart above indicates, even things that seem the same, for example, reading assignments, examinations, and assessments, are different, more intense and require more time than they did just 3 months ago in high school.

If you have been out of school for a while, consider what has changed in your life since high school. You probably have more and different responsibilities now (e.g., a mortgage, children, etc.). Reflect on how you will manage these responsibilities with your college work (Chapter 4 on time management will give you some strategies). You will also notice the classroom environment has changed quite a bit over the years. You will rely on technology much more to assist with your education than you did years ago. If you need help with your technology skills, see if your school offers a basic technology course or has a technology help desk. You might also want to ask some of your more tech savvy classmates for some technology tips.

TOP TIPS FOR ACADEMIC SUCCESS

1. **Read the course syllabus carefully when you first receive it and refer to it throughout the term.** (See **Box 2.2** for details and strategies.)

BOX 2.2

Reading and Understanding a Syllabus

What's in a syllabus? A course syllabus is a document created by instructors that will probably be given to you on the first day of class. The syllabus has been called a contract between the student and the instructor. Please pay careful attention to all parts of the syllabus and make a copy to keep with you at all times. You are responsible for adhering to this contract. However, your instructor can change the syllabus as he/she deems necessary. A syllabus usually contains the following components (not necessarily in this order):

1. Course department, prefix, number, title, credit hours, semester and year, and course reference number.
2. Meeting times and location, instructor information (name, office location, office hours, contact information).
3. Catalog course description, including prerequisites and/or corequisites (courses students need to have taken before this one or at the same time); prerequisite skill sets (e.g., programming languages, familiarity with software).

4. Text(s) with dates, supplemental text(s), other required readings, and references readings (books, reserve readings, course readers, software, and supplies with information about where they can be obtained). You are expected to have these on the first day or soon after the first day.
5. Student learning outcomes and/or course objectives (this is what the instructor is telling you that he or she will work the lectures around, and you will have learning opportunities around them throughout the course). The tests, quizzes, papers, etc., are based on these objectives.
6. Skills and knowledge students will gain. These are the new items you will have learned after the course is completed. You may hear these referred to as competencies.
7. Course organization. This tells you step-by-step how this course will be taught.
8. Explanation of the topical organization of the course. This will give you an idea of the specific topics that will be covered in class.
9. Course requirements (what students will have to do in the course: assignments, exams, projects,

(continued)

BOX 2.2 *(continued)*

performances, attendance, participation, etc.). Usually the nature and format of assignments and the expected length of written work, as well as due dates for assignments and dates for exams, will be explained.

10. Evaluation and grading policy: what grades are based on, especially your final grade. Always keep up on what grade you have in class and discuss how to improve it with the instructor on a regular basis.

11. Course policies and expectations: may include policies on attendance, participation, tardiness, academic integrity, missing homework, missed exams, recording classroom activities, food in class, laptop use, cell phone use, etc.

12. Other expectations such as student behavior (e.g., respectful consideration of one another's perspectives, open-mindedness, creative risk-taking).

13. Course calendar/schedule (sometimes the instructor will put "tentative" before these words, letting you know it is subject to change). However, this is a class-to-class breakdown of topics and assignments (readings, homework, project due dates).

As a college student, you are responsible for knowing the contents of the course syllabus. It is not the instructor's responsibility to go over it with you. Be sure you read and understand your syllabi for all your courses. If you have any questions, be sure to ask your instructor right away.

HOW THE BRAIN RETAINS INFORMATION

In 1879, German researcher Hermann Ebbinghaus began examining the concept of forgetting. He created the curve of forgetting to describe how people retain or lose information. The curve is based on information retention rates following a 1-hour lecture. Basically, Ebbinghaus found that immediately following a lecture, a student remembers almost 100% of the information—it's jelling around in the short-term memory area of the brain. However, by Day 2, if a student has done nothing with that information, she or he will have lost 50%–80% of what was taught, and by Day 30, if nothing has been done with the information, a student will have lost approximately 97% of that lecture content. Ebbinghaus found that unless a student intentionally reviews the information periodically, the student will lose most of the information over time. He suggested that regular, intentional review of information will help with knowledge retention, and devised a formula to increase memory. Ebbinghaus' formula to increase memory is known as the 10-24-7 model.

The 10-24-7 model of instruction is based on research indicating when successful information retention occurs: within 10 minutes of hearing the lecture, when students review their notes; after 24 hours, when students revisit the notes again for about 10 more minutes; and on Day 7, when students review the notes for about 5 minutes. (It only takes 5 minutes to "reactivate the brain" with the same information.) From Day 8 to Day 30, students will only need to spend 2–4 minutes revisiting the notes to keep a high rate of retention. When Day 30 arrives and the students prepare for a test, the brain will only need a few minutes to reactivate the information. Exposure to the same information repeatedly means less and less time is needed to "activate" the information in students' long-term memory, making it easier to retrieve the information. By following the 10-24-7 model, students will keep 80%–100% of the information learned from the original lecture.

On the next pages are three different graphs illustrating how this model works.

THE CURVE OF FORGETTING

The curve of forgetting describes how people retain or lose information. The curve is based on information retention rates following a 1-hour lecture.

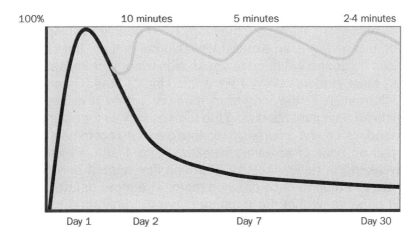

| 100% | 10 minutes | 5 minutes | 2-4 minutes |

| Day 1 | Day 2 | Day 7 | Day 30 |

On Day 1, at the beginning of the lecture, students know little or nothing about the topic, or 0%, (where the curve starts at the baseline). At the end of the lecture, they know 100% of what has been taught (where the curve rises to its highest point).

By Day 2, if students have done nothing with the information they learned in that lecture, did not think about it or read it again, they will have lost 50%–80% of what they learned. Brains are constantly recording information on a temporary basis: scraps of conversation heard while walking down the sidewalk, what the person at the front of the line is wearing. Because the information is not necessary, and it does not come up again, our brains dump it, along with what was learned in the lecture that actually was important!

By Day 7, most of what students learned has faded from memory, and by **Day 30** only about 2%–3% of the original lecture is retained! This timeline coincides with college midterm exams, and may explain the feeling students sometimes get while studying for exams—the feeling that they have never seen the information before. This means the information will need to be re-learned from scratch.

The shape of the curve can be changed! If information comes up again, it is a big signal to the brain to hold onto that specific chunk of information. When the same thing is repeated, the brain says, "Oh—there it is again, I'd better keep that." When exposed to the same information repetitively, it takes less and less time to "activate" the information in the long-term memory and it becomes easier to retrieve the information when needed.

Here's the Ebbinghaus 10-24-7 formula and the case for making time to review material:

1. Within 24 hours of receiving the information, spend 10 minutes reviewing it to raise the curve of forgetting to almost 100% again.
2. A week later (Day 7), it only takes 5 minutes to "reactivate" the same material, and again raise the curve.
3. By Day 30, the brain will only need 2–4 minutes to give the feedback, "Yup, I know that. Got it.

Often students feel they cannot possibly make time in their schedules for a review session every day; they may have trouble keeping up as it is. However, this review is an excellent investment of time. If a student does not review, he or she will need to spend significant time re-learning material later. Most students do not have this kind of time. Cramming rarely plants information in the long-term memory where it is needed to be accessible for assignments during the term as well as for exams.

Depending on the course load, the general recommendation is to spend half an hour or so every weekday, and 1 and a half to 2 hours every weekend in review activity. Perhaps the student only has time to review the information once or twice more. The more detailed graphs on the next page show that the memory curve will only drop to mid-range. That's okay; it's a lot better than the 2–3% that would have been retained if the information had not been reviewed at all.

Many students are amazed at the difference reviewing regularly makes in how much they understand and how well they understand and retain material. It is worth experimenting for a couple weeks just to see what a difference it makes!

Adapted from Counseling Services, Study Skills Program, University of Waterloo. Used by Permission. Based on Ebbinghaus's 1895 research.

Curve of Forgetting: Retention Over Time

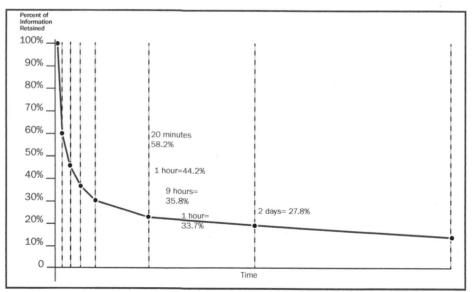

Rate of Forgetting with Study/Repetition

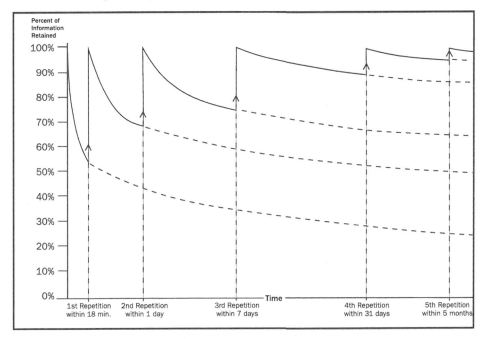

2. **Don't miss class.** Not surprisingly, the total amount of time you spend on learning is associated with how much you learn and how deeply you learn. This association leads to a straightforward recommendation: Attend all your classes in all your courses. It may be tempting to skip or cut classes because college professors are less likely to monitor your attendance or take roll than high school teachers. However, don't let this new freedom fool you into thinking that missing classes will not affect your course grades. Over the past 75 years, numerous studies have shown a direct relationship between class attendance and course grades—as one goes up or down, so does the other (Credé, Roch, Kieszczynka 2010; Launius 1997; Shimoff and Catania 2001; Tagliacollo, Volpato, and Pereira 2010). **Figure 2.1** depicts the results of a study conducted at the City Colleges of Chicago, which shows the relationship between students' class attendance during the first five weeks of the term and their final course grades.

> My biggest recommendation: GO TO CLASS. I learned this the hard way my first semester. You'll be surprised what you pick up just by being there. I wish someone would have informed me of this before I started school."
> —*Advice to new students from a college sophomore (Walsh 2005)*

NOTE

Look at going to class like going to work. If you miss work days, it lowers your pay; if you miss classes, it lowers your grades.

FIGURE 2.1: Percentage of Classes Attended and Final Course Grades

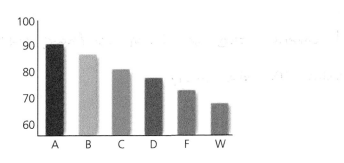

City Colleges of Chicago

> "I tend to sit at the very front of my classrooms. It helps me focus and take notes better. It also eliminates distractions."
>
> —First-year college student

NOTE

When you enter class, you have a choice about where you're going to sit. Choose wisely by selecting a location that will maximize your attentiveness to the instructor and your effectiveness as a note-taker.

3. **Adopt a seating location in class that maximizes attention and minimizes distraction.** Many years of research show that students who sit in the front and center of class tend to earn higher test scores and course grades (Benedict and Hoag 2004; Rennels and Chaudhair 1988; Tagliacollo, Volpato, and Pereira 2010). These results have been found even when students are assigned seats by their instructor, so it's not just a matter of more motivated and studious students sitting in the front of the room. Instead, the better academic performance achieved by students sitting front and center stems from learning advantages associated with this seating location.

    Sitting in the front of class can also reduce your level of anxiety about speaking in class because you will not have numerous class-mates sitting in front of you turning around to look at you when you speak.

    The *bottom line:* When you enter a classroom, get in the habit of heading for a seat in the front and center of class. In large classes, it's even more important to get to know your instructors—not only to improve your attention, note taking, and class participation—but also to improve your instructors' ability to remember who you are and how well you performed in class. This will work to your advantage when you ask your instructors for letters of recommendation later in your college career.

4. **Sit by people who will enable (not disable) your ability to listen and learn.** Intentionally sit near classmates who will not distract you or interfere with the quality of your note taking. Actively listening to and taking notes on lecture information is a demanding task that demands undivided attention.

Journal Reflection 2.2

When you enter a classroom, where do you usually sit?

I usually go for a middle row on the end.

Why do you sit there? Is it a conscious choice or more like an automatic habit?

I choose this so I can see/hear easily without being in the way.

Do you think that the seat you usually choose places you in the best possible position for listening and learning in the classroom? Why or why not?

Yes it puts me in a good position. I can hear/see fine where other students who may not hear/see very well should have access to front rows.

---

5. **Adopt a seating posture that screams attention.** Sitting upright and leaning forward increases attention because these signs of physical alertness reach the brain and stimulate mental alertness. Baseball players get into a ready position before a pitch is delivered to ready themselves to catch batted balls; similarly, learners who assume a ready position in the classroom put themselves in a better position to catch ideas batted around in class. Studies show that when humans are mentally alert and ready to learn, a greater amount of C-kinase (a brain chemical) is released at the connection point between brain cells, which increases the likelihood that neurological (learning) connections are formed between them (Howard 2014).

    Another advantage to being attentive in class is that it sends a clear message to your instructor that you're a courteous and conscientious student. This can influence your instructor's perception and evaluation of your academic performance; if at the end of the course you're on the border between a higher and lower grade, you're more likely to get the benefit of the doubt.

6. **Be a self-aware learner.** One characteristic of successful learners is that they self-monitor (check themselves) while learning to remain aware of:
    *   Whether they're using effective learning strategies (e.g., if they're giving their undivided attention to what they're learning)
    *   Whether they're truly comprehending what they are learning (e.g., if they're understanding it at a deep level or memorizing it at a surface level)
    *   How they're regulating or adjusting their learning strategies to meet the demands of different academic tasks and subjects (e.g., if they're reading technical material in a science textbook, they read at a slower rate and check their understanding more frequently than when reading a novel) (Pintrich and Schunk 2002).

    You can begin to establish good self-monitoring habits by getting in the routine of periodically pausing to reflect on the strategies you're using to learn and how you "do" college. For instance, you can ask yourself the following questions:
    *   Am I listening attentively to what my instructor is saying in class?
    *   Am I comprehending what I'm reading outside of class?

- Am I effectively using campus resources designed to support my success?
- Am I interacting with campus professionals who can contribute to my current success and future development?
- Am I interacting and collaborating with peers who can support (not sabotage) my learning and development?
- Am I effectively implementing college success strategies (such as those identified in this book)?

Journal Reflection 2.3

How would you rate your academic self-confidence at this point in your college experience? (Circle one.)

very confident   somewhat confident   (somewhat unconfident)   very unconfident

Why?

I have a hard time finding assignments online so I feel a little lost to the process.

THE IMPORTANCE OF TIME SPENT ON COURSEWORK OUTSIDE OF CLASS

In college, you will spend much less time sitting in class than you did in high school; however, you will be expected to spend much more time working on your courses outside of class. Less than 40% of beginning college students report having studied six or more hours per week during their final year in high school (Pryor et al. 2012) and only one-third expect to spend more than 20 hours per week preparing for class in college (National Survey of Student Engagement 2009).

Unfortunately, less than 10% of beginning college students say they will study at least two hours out of class for every hour spent in class—which is what most college faculty believe is necessary to do well in college (Kuh 2005). This has to change if college students are to earn good grades. **Just as successful athletes need to put in time and effort to improve their physical performance, successful students need to do the same to improve their academic performance.** Studies repeatedly show that the more time college students spend on academic work outside of class, the higher grades they earn in their college courses (National Survey of Student Engagement 2009). In one study of more than 25,000 college students it was found that the percentage of students receiving "A" grades was almost three times higher for students who spent 40 or more hours per week on academic work than it was for students who spent between 20 and 40 hours. For students who spent 20 or fewer hours per week on academic work, the percentage of them receiving a grade of "C" or below was almost twice as high as it was for students who spent 40 or more hours on academic work (Pace 1990, 1995).

If you need further motivation to achieve good grades, keep in mind that higher grades earned in college translates into career success after college. Research on college graduates indicates that the higher their grades were in college, the higher is: (a) their starting salary, (b) the status (prestige) of their first job, and (c) their career mobility (ability to change jobs or move into different positions). This relationship between higher college grades and greater career advantages exists for students at all types of colleges and universities—regardless of the reputation or prestige of the institution the students attended (Pascarella and Terenzini 1991, 2005). In other words, how well students do in college matters more to their career success than where they went to college.

> " I thought I would get a better education if the school had a really good reputation. Now, I think one's education depends on how much effort you put into it."
> —First-year college student

AUTHOR'S JOURNEY

When I went to college, I had to work to assist my family and to assist in paying for college. Although I was an 18-year-old, I came from a very poor family and it was part of my obligation to assist them financially, while it was more important to me to go to school and graduate so I could have a higher standard of living in comparison to my mother and father. Juggling my work life and school life quickly became a reality to which I had to adjust. Thus, I made sure I made the time to study and attend class as my first priority and worked with my employer to adjust my work hours around my classes. By placing my future above my immediate present, I was able to get my college degree and increase my earnings substantially beyond the earnings I had in college and way beyond my parents' earnings.

—Aaron Thompson

EFFECTIVE CLASSROOM BEHAVIOR: THE FUNDAMENTALS

In college, there will be expectations regarding appropriate behavior inside and outside the classroom. These expectations will vary, depending on the type of course you're taking—traditional face-to-face, online, technology-enhanced, or hybrid. With a few exceptions (e.g., you can wear pajamas while participating in an online course at home), the following expectations apply to all college courses.

Regardless of the type of course you take, you will be expected to know basic computer skills such as how to save, download, and send documents, etc. If you have minimal computer skills refer to the Learn Free Basic Computer Skills website (http://www.gcflearnfree.org/basic-computer-skills) for helpful information.

1. **Avoid inappropriate and "uncivil" classroom behavior.** The following behaviors indicate to the instructor and to your classmates that you're an unmotivated student. In addition, they create a classroom climate that disturbs or disrupts the learning process. Be sure not to engage in any of them.
   - Coming to class late and/or leaving early
   - Walking in and out of the classroom during class

- Talking with classmates while the instructor (or other classmates) is speaking
- Disregarding deadlines set by your instructor
- Using electronic devices for personal purposes
- Acting disinterested in class (e.g., looking at the window or putting your head on your desk)
- Doing homework during class time
- Sleeping in class
- Using electronic devices (see **Box 2.3**)

BOX 2.3

Guidelines for Civil and Responsible Use of Personal Technology in the College Classroom

Behavior that interferes with the right of others to learn or teach in the classroom is referred to as *classroom incivility*. Listed below are forms of classroom incivility that involve student use of personal technology. Be sure to avoid them.

Using Cell Phones

Keeping a cell phone on in class is a clear form of classroom incivility because it can interfere with the right of others to learn. In a study of college students who heard a cell phone ringing during class and were later tested on information presented in class, they scored approximately 25% lower for information that was presented at the time a cell phone rang. This drop in performance was found even if the material was covered by the professor just prior to the cell phone ringing and if it was projected on a slide while the phone rang. The study also showed that students' attention to information presented in class is significantly reduced when classmates frantically search through handbags or pockets to find and silence a ringing (or vibrating) phone (Shelton et al. 2009). These findings clearly suggest that cell phone use in class disrupts the learning process and the civil thing to do is:

> "
> The right to do something does not mean that doing it is right."
>
> —*William Safire, American author, journalist, and presidential speech writer*

- Turn your cell phone off before entering class, or keep it out of the classroom altogether. (You can use *studiousapp.com* to automatically silence your phone at times of the day when you're in class.) In rare cases where you may need to leave class to respond to an emergency, ask your instructor for permission in advance.
- Don't check your cell phone during the class period by turning it off and on.
- Don't look at your cell phone at any time during a test because your instructor may suspect that you're looking up answers to test questions.

Text Messaging

Although this form of electronic communication is silent, it still can distract or disturb your classmates. It's also discourteous or disrespectful to instructors when you put head down and turn your attention away from them while they're speaking in class. The bottom line: Be sensitive to your classmates and your instructor—don't text in class!

Surfing the Web

Although this can be done without creating distracting sounds, it still can create visual distractions. Unless you're taking class notes on it, keep your laptop closed to avoid distracting your classmates and raising your instructors' suspicion that you're a disinterested or disrespectful student.

Final Note: In addition to technological incivilities, other discourteous classroom behaviors include personal grooming, holding side conversations, and doing homework for other classes. Even if your attendance is perfect, "little things" you do in class that reflect inattention or disinterest can send a strong message to your instructors that you're an unmotivated and discourteous student.

Technology should be used sensitively and civilly not only inside the classroom, but outside the classroom as well. There are common rules of courtesy for Internet use (referred to as "netiquette") that should be used in social media. These rules are summarized in **Box 2.4**.

Box 2.4

Top 20 Rules to Follow for Appropriate Netiquette

1. The Internet is not private. What goes out on the airwaves stays on the airwaves! Do not post pictures to the Internet that you would not want your mom or younger cousin to see.
2. Avoid saying anything that could be interpreted as derogatory (e.g., no cursing).
3. Do not say harsh or mean things to someone over e-mail or text (this could be considered cyber bullying) and do not post nasty, mean, or insulting items about someone.
4. Do not respond to nasty e-mails sent to you.
5. Do not break up with a significant other via text or e-mail.
6. When you receive an e-mail that says to forward it to everyone you know, please don't.
7. Do not use ALL CAPITALS. IT IMPLIES YOU ARE SHOUTING!!!
8. When you send messages online, make sure you proofread and correct mistakes before sending.

9. Do not forward other people's e-mails without their permission.
10. Do not forward virus warnings. They are generally hoaxes.
11. Ask before you send huge attachments.
12. Keep your communications short and to the point.
13. Do not leave the subject field blank in e-mails.
14. Avoid posting personal messages to a listserv.
15. Avoid using texting language for e-mails or social media sites (use correct spellings and correct language mechanics).
16. Remember to treat others online as you would like to be treated.
17. Use the Internet in ways that do not take away from your learning, but add to it.
18. Allow an appropriate amount of time for a person to respond to a message (24–48 business hours).
19. Be sure to have an appropriate salutation (i.e., *good morning, hello*) and closing (i.e., *goodbye, see you tomorrow*, etc.) in your e-mails.
20. Avoid slang (i.e., *wha's up, yo*, etc.) and acronyms (*btw, lol*, etc.)

Also, be sure your communication with your instructor, both in and out of the classroom is appropriate, particularly when e-mailing your instructor. E-mailing and text messaging are very different forms of communication. Texting is very informal. E-mail, especially to an instructor, etc. is considered a professional form of communication. Be sure to treat it that way. First, be sure to send the e-mail from your school e-mail address. Other e-mails often go to spam or junk folders. Do not leave the subject line blank and be sure the subject pertains to your e-mail. Address your instructor appropriately. State your question or concern (be aware of your tone). Avoid all slang and close your e-mail appropriately. Appropriate response time for an e-mail is 24 business hours. Give your instructor enough time to respond to your e-mail and do not inundate their inbox with multiple e-mails about the same issue. See box below for an example of an appropriate e-mail to an instructor and one that could use some work.

HOW TO E-MAIL (OR NOT) YOUR INSTRUCTOR

An example of what not to do:

To: instructor@communitycollege.edu

From: pimpdaddy@bade-mail.com

Subject: WHATEVER!

Yo teach! Wha's up?

I know you did not give me an F on that test!!!! WTH!?!? I studied all night for that and I know I should not have failed. Tell me how you are gonna fix this cuz I gotta pass your class.

Peace!

An example of an appropriate e-mail:

To: instructor@communitycollege.edu

From: concernedstudent@communitycollege.edu

Subject: My test grade

Good morning instructor (name),

I am concerned about my grade on the last test. I got an F and I don't know what I did wrong. I studied all night for that test! Can I meet with you to discuss some strategies about how I might do better on the next test? I really want to pass this class.

Please let me know when you are available to meet. I appreciate your time.

Sincerely,

Concerned Student

It is important to pay attention to your behavior on social media (i.e., Facebook, Instagram, Twitter, etc.) as well. Once you post something on the Internet it is always out "in the cloud." Even when you delete a post, highly skilled people can find it. Coaches, potential employers, graduate schools, etc. are taking a closer look at social media profiles to aid in their decision making process. Just as you think before you speak, you should think before you post. Refrain from posting anything illegal, rude, disrespectful, or in poor taste. Also be sure to refrain from cyberbullying. People tend to be much more brave when they can hide behind a computer. Don't post anything online that you would not say in person. All of these things could affect your future in far more ways than you realize. In 2017, 10 students newly accepted to Harvard University were uninvited because of their tweets even though they were not yet enrolled.

> " Most colleges have policies on cyberbulling, social media expectations which when violated lead to probation, and sometimes expulsion.

2. **Avoid plagiarism.** Plagiarism is a violation of academic integrity that involves intentional or unintentional use of someone else's work

without acknowledging it, which gives the reader the impression that it's your own work. Listed below are common forms of plagiarism.

- Paying someone, or paying a service, for a paper and turning it in as your own work.
- Submitting an entire paper, or portion thereof, that was written by someone else.
- Copying sections of someone else's work and inserting it into your own work.
- Cutting paragraphs from separate sources and pasting them into the body of your own paper.
- Paraphrasing or rewording someone else's words or ideas without citing that person as a source. (Good strategies for paraphrasing without plagiarizing may be found at: http://www.upenn.edu/academicintegrity/ai_paraphrasing.html.)
- Placing someone else's exact words in the body of your paper and not placing quotation marks around them.
- Failing to cite the source of factual information in your paper that's not common knowledge.

Good examples of different forms of plagiarism may be found at: http://www.princeton.edu/pr/pub/integrity/pages/plagiarism/

Two other things to keep in mind:
- If you include information in your paper and just list its source in your reference (works cited) section—without citing the source in the *body* of your paper—this still qualifies as plagiarism.
- Be sure only to include sources in your reference section that you actually used and cited in the body of your paper. Although including sources in your reference section that aren't cited in your paper isn't technically a form of plagiarism, it may be viewed as being deceitful because you're "padding" your reference section, giving the reader the impression that you incorporated more sources into your paper than you actually did.

> When a student violates an academic integrity policy no one wins, even if the person gets away with it. It isn't right to cheat and it is an insult to everyone who put the effort in and did the work, and it cheapens the school for everyone. I learned my lesson and have no intention of ever cheating again."
>
> —*First-year student's reflection on an academic integrity violation.*

💡 Journal Reflection 2.4

Reflect back at the different forms of plagiarism just described. Were there any you were surprised to see, or didn't realize were plagiarism?

_____

_____

_____

_____

_____

_____

Post-reflection: What "notes to myself" do I want to remember from this chapter to project myself as a serious student while in college?

_____

_____

_____

_____

_____

_____

_____

Learning is the fundamental mission of all colleges and universities. One of the major goals of a college education is to help students become independent, self-directed learners. Learning doesn't stop after college graduation; it's a lifelong process that is essential for success in the 21st century. The ongoing information technology revolution, coupled with global interdependence, is creating a greater need for effective learning skills that can be used throughout life and in different cultural and occupational contexts. Today's employers value job applicants who have "learned how to learn" and will continue to be "lifelong learners" (SECFHE 2006).

> At first, I was resistant to learning WICOR. I already took notes, but I didn't touch it again until just before an exam. I realized I wasn't fully understanding the material when the professor asked me exam questions that extend beyond basic facts.
>
> —*Rising second-year student*

WHAT IS DEEP LEARNING?

When students learn deeply, they dive below the surface of shallow memorization; they go further by building mental bridges between what they're trying to learn and what they already know (Piaget 1978; Vygotsky 1978). Knowledge isn't acquired by simply pouring information into the brain as if it were an empty jar. It's a matter of attaching or connecting new ideas to ideas that are already stored in the brain. When this happens, facts are transformed into *concepts*—networks of connected or interrelated ideas. In fact, when something is learned deeply, the human brain actually makes a physical (neurological) connection between separate nerve cells (LeDoux 2002). (See **Figure 2.2.**)

Studies suggest that most college students don't engage in deep learning (Arum and Roksa 2011; Kuh 2005; Nathan 2005). They may show up for class most of the time, cram for their exams, and get their assignments done right before they're due. These learning strategies may enable students to survive college, but not thrive in college and achieve academic excellence.

FIGURE 2.2: Network of Brain Cells

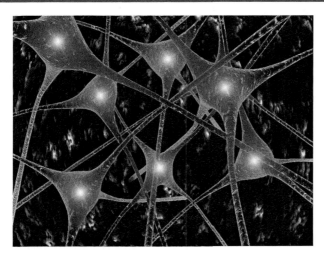

Deep learning involves making connections between what you're trying to learn and what you already know. When you learn something deeply, it's stored in the brain as a link in an interconnected network of brain cells.

©Jurgen Ziewe/Shutterstock.com

STAGES IN THE LEARNING AND MEMORY PROCESS

Learning deeply and retaining what you've learned is a process that involves three key stages:

1. **Sensory input (perception).** Taking information into the brain;
2. **Memory formation (storage).** Transforming that information into knowledge and storing it in the brain;
3. **Memory recall (retrieval).** Bringing that knowledge back to mind when you need it.

These three stages are summarized visually in **Figure 2.3**. These stages of the learning and memory process are similar to the way information is processed by a computer: (1) information is entered onto the screen (input), (2) that information is saved in a memory file (storage), and (3) the saved information is recalled and used when it's needed (retrieval). This three-stage process can serve as a framework for using the two major routes through which knowledge is acquired in college: from lectures and readings.

FIGURE 2.3: Key Stages in the Learning and Memory Process

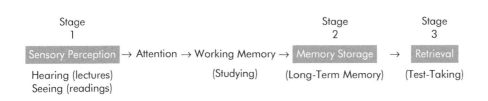

©Kendall Hunt Publishing Company.

EFFECTIVE LECTURE-LISTENING AND NOTE-TAKING STRATEGIES

The importance of developing effective listening skills in the college class-room was highlighted in a classic study of more than 400 students who were given a listening test at the start of their college experience. At the end of their first year in college, 49% of those students who scored low on the listening test were on academic probation—compared to only 4.4% of students who scored high on the listening test. On the other hand, 68.5% of students who scored high on the listening test were eligible for the honors program at the end of their first year—compared to only 4.17% of those students who had low listening test scores (Conaway 1982).

Journal Reflection 2.5

Do you think writing notes in class helps or hinders your ability to pay attention to and learn from your instructors' lectures?

Why?

Studies show that information delivered during lectures is the number one source of test questions (and answers) on college exams (Brown 1988; Kuhn 1988). When lecture information isn't recorded in students' notes and appears on a test, it has only a 5% chance of being recalled (Kiewra et al. 2000). Students who write notes during lectures achieve higher course grades than students who just listen to lectures (Kiewra 1985, 2005), and students with a more complete set of lecture notes are more likely to demonstrate higher levels of overall academic achievement (Johnstone and Su 1994; Kiewra and DuBois 1998).

Contrary to a popular belief that writing while listening interferes with the ability to listen, students report that taking notes actually increases their attention and concentration in class (Hartley 1998; Hartley and Marshall 1974). Studies also show that when students write down information that's presented to them, they're more likely to remember the most important aspects of that information when tested later (Bligh 2000). One study discovered that students with grade point averages (GPAs) of 2.53 or higher record more information in their notes and retain a larger percentage of the most important information than do students with GPAs of less than 2.53 (Einstein, Morris, and Smith 1985). These findings aren't surprising when you consider that hearing information, writing it and then seeing it after it's been written produces three different memory traces (tracks) in the brain, thus tripling your chances of remembering it.

Furthermore, when notes are taken, you're left with a written record of lecture information that can be studied later to improve your test performance. In contrast, if you take few or no notes, you're left with little or no information to study for upcoming exams. As previously noted, the majority of questions on professors' exams come from information contained in their lectures. So, come to class with the attitude that your instructors are dispensing answers to test questions as they speak and your job is to pick out and record these answers so you can pick up points on the next exam.

NOTE

Points your professors make in class that make it into your notes turn into points earned on your exams (and higher grades in your courses).

You can get the most out of lectures by employing effective strategies at three key times: before, during, and after *class.*

PRE-LECTURE STRATEGIES: WHAT TO DO *BEFORE* CLASS

1. **Check your syllabus to see where you are in the course and determine how the upcoming class fits into the total course picture.** By checking the course syllabus before individual class sessions you'll see how each part (class) relates to the whole (course). This strategy capitalizes on the brain's natural tendency to seek larger patterns and see the "big picture." The human brain is naturally inclined to connect parts into a whole (Caine and Caine 2011). It looks for meaningful patterns and connections rather than isolated bits and pieces of information (Jensen 2008). In **Figure 2.4**, notice how your brain naturally ties together and fills in the missing information to perceive a whole pattern that is meaningful.

2. **Get to class early so that you can review your notes from the previous class session and from any reading assignments relating to the day's lecture topic.** Research indicates that when students review information related to an upcoming lecture topic, they take more accurate and complete lecture notes (Jairam and Kiewra 2009; Kiewra 2005). Thus, a good way to improve your ability to learn from

FIGURE 2.4: Triangle Illusion

You perceive a white triangle in the middle of this figure. However, if you use three fingers to cover up the three corners of the white triangle that fall outside the other (background) triangle, the white triangle suddenly disappears. What your brain does is take these corners as starting points and fills in the rest of the information on its own to create a complete or whole pattern that has meaning to you. (Also, notice how you perceive the background triangle as a complete triangle, even though parts of its three sides sides are missing.)

lectures is to review your notes from the previous class session and read textbook information related to the lecture topic—*before* hearing the lecture. Reviewing previously learned information activates your prior knowledge, enabling you to connect lecture material to what you already know—a powerful way to promote deep learning (Bruner 1990; Piaget 1978; Vygotky 1978).

LISTENING AND NOTE-TAKING STRATEGIES: WHAT TO DO *DURING* CLASS

1. **Give lectures your undivided attention.** As previously noted, research shows that in all subject areas, the majority of test questions appearing on college exams come from the professor's lectures and students who take better class notes get better course grades (Brown 1988; Cuseo et al. 2013; Kiewra 2000). Studies also show that the more time students spend surfing the web or using Facebook during lectures, the lower their test scores. These results hold true for all students, regardless of how they scored on college admissions tests (Ravizza, Hambrick, and Fenn 2014).

   Remember that like all humans, not all professors are created equal. You'll have some that are more dynamic and easier to pay attention to than others. It's the less dynamic ones that will tempt you to lose attention and stop taking notes. Don't let the less engaging or less entertaining professors lower your course grades. Instead view them as a challenge; step up your focus of attention, continue taking notes to keep yourself engaged, and leave the course with the satisfaction of earning a good grade.

2. **Take your own notes in class.** Don't rely on someone else to take notes for you. Taking notes in your own words focuses your attention and ensures the notes you take make sense to you. Research indicates that students who record and review their own notes on information presented to them earn higher scores on memory tests for that information than do students who review notes taken by others (Jairam and Kiewra 2009; Kiewra 2005). Taking your own notes in your own words makes them *meaningful to you*. While it's a good idea to collaborate with classmates to compare notes for completeness and accuracy, or to pick up points you may have missed, you shouldn't rely on someone else to do your note-taking for you.

3. **Take notes in longhand rather than typing them on a laptop.** Studies show that when students use a keyboard to type notes, they're more likely to mindlessly punch in the exact words used by the instructor, rather than transforming the instructor's words into words that are meaningful to them. When tested on understanding and memory for key concepts presented in class, students who took notes in longhand outperformed those who typed notes on a keyboard (Mueller and Oppenheimer 2014). This may be due to the fact that the movements made during handwriting leave a motor (muscle) memory trace in the brain, which deepens learning and strengthens memory (Herbert 2014).

4. **Be alert to cues for the most important information contained in lectures.** Since the human attention span is limited, it's impossible to

attend to and make note of everything. Thus, we need to use our attention *selectively* to detect and select information that matters most. Here are some strategies for identifying and recording the most important information delivered by professors during lectures:

- Pay particular attention to information your instructors put *in print*—on the board, on a slide, or in a handout. If your instructor has taken the time and energy to write it out or type it out, this is usually a good clue that the information is important and you'll likely see it again—on an exam.
- Pay special attention to information presented during the *first and last few minutes of class*. Instructors are most likely to provide valuable reminders, reviews, and previews at the start and end of a class session.
- Look for *verbal and nonverbal cues* that signal the instructor is delivering important information. Don't just tune in when your professors are writing something down and tune out at other times. It's been found that students record almost 90% of material written on the board, but less than 50% of important ideas that professors state but don't write on the board (Johnstone and Su 1994; Locke 1977; Titsworth and Kiewra 2004). So, don't fall into the reflex-like routine of just taking notes when you see your instructor writing notes. Instead, listen actively to ideas you *hear* your instructor saying and take notes on these ideas as well. **Box 2.5** contains strategies for detecting clues to important information that professors are delivering orally in class.

Box 2.5

Detecting When Instructors Are Delivering Important Information during Lectures

Look for *verbal* cues, such as:

- Phrases signaling important information (e.g., "The point here is . . ." or "What's most significant about this is . . .").
- Information that's repeated or rephrased in a different way (e.g., "In other words, . . ", or "To put it another way . . .").
- Stated information that's followed by a question to check understanding (e.g., "Is that clear?" "Do you follow that?" "Does that make sense?" or "Are you with me?").

Watch for *vocal (tone of voice)* cues, such as:

- Information delivered in a louder tone or at a higher pitch than usual—which may indicate excitement or emphasis.

- Information delivered at a slower rate or with more pauses than usual—which may be your instructor's way of giving you more time to write down these important ideas.

Keep an eye out for nonverbal cues, such as:

- Information delivered by your instructor with more than the usual:
  a. Facial expressiveness (e.g., raised or furrowed eyebrows);
  b. Body movement (e.g., gesticulation and animation);
  c. Eye contact (e.g., looking directly and intently at the faces of students to see if they're following or understanding what's being said).
- Your instructor moving closer to the students (e.g., moving away from the podium or blackboard).
- Your instructor orienting his or her body directly toward the class (i.e., both shoulders directly or squarely facing the class).

5. **Keep taking notes even if you don't immediately understand what your instructor is saying.** If you are uncertain or confused about the material being presented, don't stop taking notes. Having notes on that material will at least leave you with a record to review later—when you have more time to think about it and make sense of it. If you still don't understand it after taking time to review it, seek clarification from your instructor, a classmate, or your textbook.

6. **Take organized notes.** If your instructor continues to make points relating to the same idea, take notes on that idea within the same paragraph. When the instructor shifts to a new idea, skip a few lines and shift to a new paragraph. Be alert to phrases that your instructor may use to signal a shift to a new or different idea (e.g., "Let's turn to . . ." or "In addition to . . ."). Use these phrases as cues for taking notes in paragraph form.

   By recording different ideas in different paragraphs, the organizational quality of your notes improves as will your comprehension and retention of them. Be sure to leave extra space between paragraphs (ideas) to give yourself room to add information that you may have initially missed, or to later translate the professor's words into your own words.

   Another popular strategy for taking organized notes is the *Cornell Note-Taking System*.

   There are several methods to take notes. It is important you find the note-taking method that works best for you. Examples include formal outlining, informal outlining, mapping, charting, and many others. Please refer to: http://www.redlands.edu/docs/Academics/1Five_Methods_of_Notetaking_2015.pdf for more information.

POST-LECTURE STRATEGIES: WHAT TO DO *AFTER* CLASS

1. **As soon as class ends, quickly check your notes for missing information or incomplete thoughts.** Information delivered during a lecture is likely to be fresh in your mind immediately after class. A quick check of your notes at this time will allow you to take advantage of your short-term memory. By reviewing and reflecting on your notes, you can help move that information into long-term memory before forgetting takes place. This quick review can be done alone or, better yet, with a motivated classmate. If you both have gaps in your notes, check them out with your instructor before he or she leaves the classroom. Even though it may be weeks before you'll be tested on the material, the quicker you pick up missed points and clear up sources of confusion, the better; it will help you understand upcoming material—especially upcoming material that builds on previously covered material. Catching confusion early in the game also enables you to avoid the mad last-minute rush of students seeking help from the instructor just before test time. You want to reserve the critical time just before exams to study notes you know are complete and

accurate, rather than rushing around trying to find missing information and seeking last-minute help on concepts presented weeks earlier.

Journal Reflection 2.6

Do you tend to stick around a few minutes after class sessions end to review your notes and clear up missing information or confusing points? Why?

_____

_____

_____

_____

What could you do immediately after class to be a more successful student?

_____

_____

_____

_____

_____

2. **Before the next class session meets, reflect on and review your notes to make sense of them.** Your professors will often lecture on information that you may have little prior knowledge about, so it's unrealistic to expect that you will understand everything that's being said the first time you hear it. Instead, set aside time to reflect on and review your notes as soon as possible after class has ended. During this review process, take notes on your notes by:

   * Translating technical information into your own words to make it more meaningful to you; and
   * Reorganizing your notes to get ideas related to the same point in the same place.

Studies show that students who organize their lecture notes into meaningful categories demonstrate superior recall of that information on memory tests—compared to students who simply review the notes they took in class (Howe 1970; Kiewra 2005).

NOTE

Effective note taking is a two-stage process: Stage 1 involves actively taking notes in class and stage 2 takes places after class— when you take time to reflect on your notes and process them more deeply.

AUTHOR'S JOURNEY

I spent my first year in college spending a lot of time trying to manipulate my schedule to create large blocks of free time. I took all of my classes in a row without a break to preserve some time at the end of the day for relaxation and hanging out with friends. Seldom did I even look at my notes until it was time to be tested on them. Thus, on the day before the test I was in a panic trying to cram the lecture notes into my head for the upcoming exam. Needless to say, I didn't perform well on many of my first tests. Eventually, a professor told me that if I spent some time each day rewriting my notes I would retain the material longer, increase my grades, and decrease my stress at test time. I employed this system and it worked wonderfully.

—Aaron Thompson

 Journal Reflection 2.7

Rate yourself in terms of how frequently you use these note-taking strategies according to the following scale:

4 = always, 3 = sometimes, 2 = rarely, 1 = never

1. I take notes aggressively in class.   4   3   2   1

2. I sit near the front of the class.   4   3   2   1

3. I sit upright and lean forward while in class.   4   3   2   1

4. I take notes on what my instructors say, not just what they write on the board.   4   3   2   1

5. I pay special attention to information presented at the start and end of class.   4   3   2   1

6. I take notes in paragraph form.   4   3   2   1

7. I review my notes immediately after class to check that they are complete and accurate.   4   3   2   1

What works for you? What might you try to improve your note-taking skills?

STRATEGIC READING

Expect to do more reading in college than you did in high school and be ready to be held accountable for the reading you're assigned. Information from assigned readings ranks right behind information from lectures as a source of test questions on college exams (Brown 1988; Cuseo et al. 2013). You're likely to find exam questions relating to reading assignments that your professors didn't talk about specifically in class (or even mention in class). College professors often expect you to relate or connect their lectures with material they've assigned you to read. Furthermore, professors often deliver class lectures with the assumption that students have done the assigned reading, so if you haven't done it, you're more likely to have difficulty following what your instructor is saying in class. Thus, you should do the assigned reading but also do it according to the schedule the instructor has established. By completing assigned reading in a timely manner, you will (a) be better positioned to understand class lectures, (b) acquire information that's likely to appear on exams but not covered in class, and (c) improve the quality of your participation in class.

The following research-based strategies can be used to improve your comprehension and retention of material you read.

Pre-Reading Strategies: What to Do *Before* Reading

1. **Before jumping into your assigned reading, first see how it fits into the overall organizational structure of the book and course.** You can do this efficiently by taking a quick look at the book's table of contents to see where the chapter you're about to read is placed in the overall sequence of chapters. Look especially at its relationship to the chapters that immediately precede and follow it. This strategy will give you a sense of how the particular part you're focusing on connects with the bigger picture. Research shows that if students have advanced knowledge about how material they're about to learn is organized—if they see how its parts relate to the whole before they start learning the specific parts—they're better able to comprehend and retain the material (Ausubel, Novak, and Hanesian 1978; Chen and Hirumi 2009). Thus, the first step toward improving reading comprehension and retention of a book chapter is to see how it relates to the book as a whole.

 Journal Reflection 2.8

When you open a textbook to read a chapter, how do you start the reading process? What's the first thing you do? Why?

2. **Preview the chapter by first reading its boldface headings and any chapter outline, objectives, summary, or end-of-chapter questions that may be included.** Before tackling the chapter's specific content, get in the habit of previewing what's in the chapter to get a general sense of its overall organization. If you dive into the specific details first, you may lose sight of how the smaller details relate to the larger picture. Since the brain's natural tendency is to perceive and comprehend whole patterns rather than isolated bits of information, start by seeing how the parts of the chapter relate to the whole. Just as looking at the whole picture of a completed jigsaw puzzle beforehand helps you connect its parts, so too does getting a picture of the whole chapter before reading its parts.

3. **Take a moment to think about what you may already know that relates to the main topic of the chapter.** This strategy will activate the areas of your brain where your prior knowledge about that topic is stored, thereby preparing it to make meaningful connections with the material you're about to read.

Strategies to Use *During* the Reading Process

1. **Read selectively to locate the most important information.** Effective reading begins with a plan for identifying what should be noted and remembered. Here are three key strategies you can use while reading to help you determine what information you should focus on and retain.

   - **Use boldface or dark-print headings and subheadings as cues for identifying important information.** These headings organize the chapter's major points; you can use them as "traffic" signs to direct you to the most important information in the chapter. Better yet, turn the headings into questions and read to find answers to them. This question-and-answer routine ensures that you read actively and with a purpose. (You can set up this strategy while previewing the chapter by placing a question mark after each heading contained in the chapter.) Creating and answering questions while reading also keeps you motivated because the questions stimulate curiosity and a desire to find answers to them (Walter, Knudsvig, and Smith 2003). Another advantage of posing and answering questions about what you're reading is that it's an effective way to prepare for exams—you're practicing exactly what you'll be expected to do on exams—answering questions.

   - **Pay close attention to information that's *italicized*, <u>underlined</u>, CAPITALIZED, or bulleted.** These features call attention to key terms that must be understood and built on before you can proceed to understand higher-level concepts covered later in the reading. Don't simply highlight these words because their special appearance suggests they're important. Read these terms carefully and be sure you understand them before you continue reading.

   - **Pay special attention to the first and last sentences in each paragraph.** These sentences provide an important introduction and conclusion to the key point contained in the paragraph. It's a good idea to reread the first and last sentences of each paragraph before you move on to the next paragraph, particularly when

NOTE

Your goal when reading is not just to cover the assigned pages, but to uncover the most important ideas contained on those pages.

reading material that's cumulative (builds on previously covered material), such as science and math.

2. **Take written notes on important information you find in your reading.** A good way to stop and think deeply about key ideas in your reading is to take notes on those ideas in your own words. Research shows that the common student practice of just highlighting the text (the author's words) is not a particularly effective strategy (Dunlosky et al. 2013). Highlighting is a passive learning process, whereas note-taking actively engages you in the reading process and enables you to transform the text into your own words. Don't slip into the habit of using your textbook simply as a coloring book in which the artistic process of highlighting information in spectacular, kaleidoscopic colors distracts you from the more important process of learning actively and thinking deeply about what you're reading. Highlighting is okay as long it's not the only thing you do while reading; take time to make notes on the material you've highlighted—in your own words—to ensure that you reflect on it and make it personally meaningful. Taking notes on information delivered during lectures will improve your performance on exams; taking notes on your reading assignments will do the same.

> ''
> I would advise you to read with a pen in your hand, and enter in a little book of short hints of what you find that is curious, or that might be useful; for this will be the best method of imprinting such particulars in your memory, where they will be ready."
>
> —Benjamin Franklin, 18th-century inventor, newspaper writer, and cosigner of the Declaration of Independence

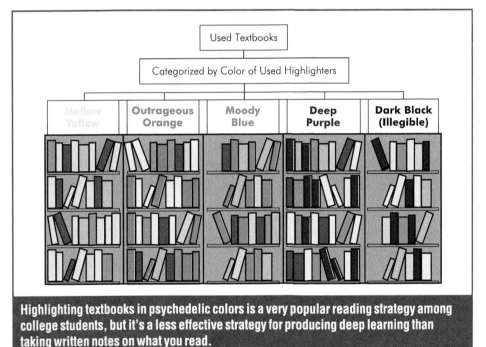

Highlighting textbooks in psychedelic colors is a very popular reading strategy among college students, but it's a less effective strategy for producing deep learning than taking written notes on what you read.

> ''
> I had the worst study habits and the lowest grades. Then I found out what I was doing wrong. I had been highlighting with a black magic marker."
>
> —Jeff Altman, American comedian

When you transform what someone else has written into your own words, you're implementing a powerful principle of deep learning: relating what you're trying to learn to what you already know (Demmert and Towner 2003). A good time for pausing and writing a brief summary of what you've read in your own words is when you encounter a boldface heading because it indicates you're about to encounter a new topic; this is the ideal time to deepen your knowledge of what you just finished reading and use that knowledge to help you understand what's coming next.

Journal Reflection 2.9

When reading a textbook, do you usually have the following tools on hand?

Highlighter: yes   no

Pen or pencil: yes   no

Notebook: yes   no

Class notes: yes   no

Dictionary: yes   no

Glossary: yes   no

If you don't usually have one or more of the above tools on hand while reading, which one(s) do you plan to have on hand in the future?

_____

_____

_____

_____

3. **Make use of visual aids that accompany the written text.** Don't fall into the trap of thinking that visual aids can or should be skipped because they're merely supplemental or ornamental. Visual aids, such as charts, graphs, diagrams, and concept maps are powerful learning and memory tools for a couple of reasons: (a) they enable you to "see" the information in addition to reading (hearing) it, and (b) they pull together separate ideas into a unified snapshot.

   Visual aids also improve learning and memory of written material by delivering information to the brain through a different sensory modality. In addition, periodically pausing to view visual aids adds variety and a change of pace to the reading process. Breaking up sustained periods of reading with a change of pace and different sensory input helps maintain your interest and attention (Malmberg and Murname 2002; Murname and Shiffrin 1991).

4. **Regulate or adjust your reading speed to the type of subject matter you're reading.** As you know, academic subjects vary in terms of their level of technicality and complexity. Reading material in a math or science textbook requires reading at a slower rate with more frequent pauses to check for understanding than reading a novel or a short story.

Post-Reading Strategies: What to Do *After* Reading

1. **End your reading sessions with a short review of the key information you've highlighted and taken notes on.** Rather than ending your reading session by trying to cover a few more pages, reserve the last five minutes to review the key ideas you already covered. Most

forgetting of information takes place immediately after we stop focusing on the information and turn our attention to another task (Averell and Heathcote 2011; Baddeley 1999). By taking a few minutes at the end of a reading session to review the most important information you've just read, you help your brain "lock" that information into long-term memory before getting involved with another task.

The graph in **Figure 2.5** represents the results of a classic experiment that tested how well information is recalled at various times after it was originally learned. As you can see on the far left of the graph, most forgetting occurs soon after information has been taken in (e.g., after 20 minutes, more than 60% of it was forgotten). The results of this classic study have been confirmed multiple times (Schacter 2001) and they underscore the importance of reviewing key information acquired through reading *immediately* after you've read it. By doing so, your memory for that information improves dramatically because you're intercepting the human "forgetting curve" at its steepest point of memory loss—just after information has been taken in.

FIGURE 2.5: The Forgetting Curve

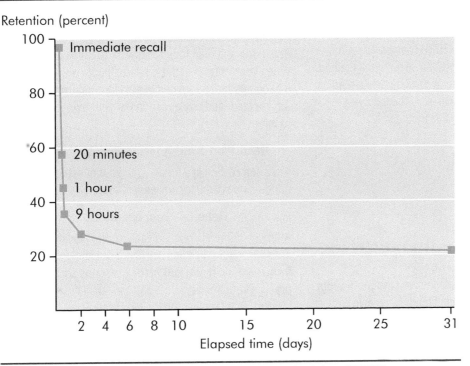

Source: Hermann Ebbinghaus, *Memory: A Contribution to Experimental Psychology*, 1885/1913

2. **After completing a reading assignment, if you're still confused about an important idea or concept contained in the reading, go to another source.** The problem may not be you—it may be the way the author has presented or explained it. You may be able to clear up your confusion by simply consulting another source or resource, such as those listed below.

   • **Look at how another book explains it.** Not all textbooks are created equal; some do a better job of explaining certain concepts than others. Check to see whether your library or campus book-store has other texts dealing with the same subject as your course. A different book may be able to explain a hard-to-understand concept much better than your assigned textbook.

- **Seek help from your instructor.** If you completed the reading assignment and made every effort to understand a particular concept but still can't grasp it, most instructors should be willing to assist you.
- **Seek help from learning assistance professionals or peer tutors in your Learning Center (Academic Support Center).** This is your key campus resource for help with reading assignments, particularly if your instructor is unavailable or unwilling to provide assistance.

BOX 2.6

SQ3R: A Method for Improving Reading Comprehension and Retention

A popular system for organizing and remembering key reading strategies, such as those discussed in this chapter, is the *SQ3R* system. SQ3R is an acronym for five steps that can be taken to increase textbook reading comprehension and retention, particularly when reading highly technical or complex material. The following sequences of steps comprise this method:

1. Survey
2. Question
3. Read
4. Recite
5. Review

S = Survey: Get a preview and overview of what you're about to read.

1. Use the chapter's title to activate your thoughts about the subject and get your mind ready to receive information related to it.
2. Read the introduction, chapter objectives, and chapter summary to become familiar with the author's purpose, goals, and key points.
3. Note the boldface headings and subheadings to get a sense of the chapter's organization before you begin reading. This supplies you with a mental structure or framework for making sense of the information you're about to read.
4. Take note of any graphics—such as charts, maps, and diagrams; they provide valuable visual support and reinforcement for the material you're reading.

5. Pay special attention to reading aids (e.g., italics and boldface font); use them to identify, understand, and remember key concepts.

Q = Question: Stay active and curious.

As you read, use boldface headings to formulate questions and read to find answers to those questions. When your mind is actively searching for answers, it becomes more engaged in the learning process. As you read, add any questions of your own that come to mind.

R = Read: Find answers to questions you've created.

Read one section at a time—with your questions in mind—and search for answers to these questions.

R = Recite: Rehearse your answers.

After you complete reading each section, recall the questions you asked and see if you can answer them from memory. If not, look at the questions again and practice your answers until you can recall them without looking. Don't move onto the next section until you're able to answer all questions in the section you've just completed.

R = Review: Look back and get a second view of the whole picture.

Once you've finished the chapter, review all the questions you've created for different parts or sections. See whether you can still answer them without looking. If not, go back and refresh your memory. Also, read the Chapter Summary. If any of the information in the summary seems unfamiliar, go back and find it and make sure you can relate it to what is in the summary.

Journal Reflection 2.10

Rate yourself in terms of how frequently you use the following reading strategies, using the following scale:

4 = always, 3 = sometimes, 2 = rarely, 1 = never

1. I read chapter outlines and summaries before I start reading the chapter content.   4   3   2   1

2. I preview a chapter's boldface headings and subheadings before I begin to read the chapter.   4   3   2   1

3. I adjust my reading speed to the type of subject I am reading.   4   3   2   1

4. I look up the meaning of unfamiliar words and unknown terms that I come across before I continue reading.   4   3   2   1

5. I take written notes on information I read.   4   3   2   1

6. I use the visual aids included in my textbooks.   4   3   2   1

7. I finish my reading sessions with a review of important information that I noted or highlighted.   4   3   2   1

What works for you? What might you do to improve reading strategies?

_____

_____

_____

_____

_____

_____

CHAPTER SUMMARY AND HIGHLIGHTS

This chapter highlighted the fact that successful students understand:

1. The differences between high school and college
2. The syllabus and class policies
3. What constitutes responsible classroom behavior
4. The dos and don'ts of technology

More specifically, this chapter suggested a number of "top tips" for getting off to a good start in college. These tips are summarized below:

Read the course syllabus. Review it carefully when you first receive it, save it, and refer to it throughout the term.

Don't miss class. Attend all your classes in all your courses. Studies repeatedly show that students who go to class earn higher grades. Look at going to class like going to work. If you miss work, you get lower pay; if you cut class, you get lower grades.

Intentionally choose a seat in class that maximizes attention and minimizes distraction. When you enter class, you have a choice about where you're going to sit. Choose wisely by selecting a location that will maximize your attentiveness to the instructor and your effectiveness as a note-taker. Many years of research show that students who sit in the front and center of class tend to earn higher exam scores and course grades.

Sit by people who will enable your ability to listen and learn. Intentionally sit near classmates who will not distract you or interfere with the quality of your note taking.

Be a self-aware learner. Successful students and success people are *mindful*—they watch what they're doing and remain aware of whether they're doing it effectively and to the best of their ability. You can be a self-aware learning by asking yourself questions such as:

- Am I listening attentively to what my instructor is saying in class?
- Am I comprehending what I'm reading outside of class?
- Am I effectively using campus resources designed to support my success?
- Am I interacting with campus professionals who can contribute to my current success and future development?
- Am I interacting and collaborating with peers who can support (not sabotage) my learning and development?
- Am I effectively implementing college success strategies (such as those identified in this book)?

Spend at least two hours on schoolwork out of class for every hour you spend in class. This is what most college faculty believe is necessary to succeed in college.

Avoid inappropriate classroom behavior, such as the following:

- Coming to class late and/or leaving early
- Walking in and out of the classroom during class
- Talking with classmates while the instructor is speaking
- Disregarding deadlines set by your instructor
- Using electronic devices for personal purposes
- Acting disinterested in class (e.g., looking at the window or putting your head on your desk)
- Doing homework during class time
- Using electronic devices in class (e.g., texting or surfing the web)

Avoid plagiarism. Plagiarism is a violation of academic integrity that involves intentional or unintentional use of someone else's work without acknowledging it, which gives the reader the impression that it's your own work. Common forms of plagiarism include:

- Paying someone, or paying a service, for a paper and turning it in as your own work.
- Submitting an entire paper, or portion thereof, that was written by someone else.
- Copying sections of someone else's work and inserting it into your own work.
- Cutting paragraphs from separate sources and pasting them into the body of your own paper.
- Paraphrasing or rewording someone else's words or ideas without citing that person as a source. (Good strategies for paraphrasing without plagiarizing may be found at: http://www.upenn.edu/academicintegrity/ai_paraphrasing.html.)
- Placing someone else's exact words in the body of your paper and not placing quotation marks around them.
- Failing to cite the source of factual information in your paper that's not common knowledge.

LEARNING MORE THROUGH THE WORLD WIDE WEB: INTERNET-BASED RESOURCES

For additional information on strategies for college success, see the following websites:

Using the College Syllabus
http://www.mycollegesuccessstory.com/academic-success-tools/course-syllabus.html

Classroom Etiquette & Civility
http://college.usatoday.com/2012/12/07/5-rules-for-college-classroom-etiquette/

Academic Integrity:
http://www.calea.org/calea-update-magazine/issue-100 who-s-watching-character-and-integrity-21st-century

REFERENCES

Appleby, D. C. June, 2008. *Diagnosing and Treating the Deadly 13th Grade Syndrome*. Paper presented at the Association of Psychological Science Convention, Chicago, IL.

Arum, R., and J. Roska. 2011. *Academically Adrift: Limited Learning on College Campuses*. Chicago: The University of Chicago Press.

Ausubel, D., J. Novak, and H. Hanesian. 1978. *Educational Psychology: A Cognitive View.* 2nd ed. New York: Holt, Rinehart & Winston.

Averell, L., and A. Heathcote. 2011. "The Form of the Forgetting Curve and the Fate of Memories." *Journal of Mathematical Psychology* 55(1): 25–35.

Baddeley, A. D. 1999. *Essentials of Human Memory.* Hove: Psychology.

Benedict, M. E., and J. Hoag. 2004. "Seating Location in Large Lectures: Are Seating Preferences or Location Related to Course Performance?" *Journal of Economics Education* 35: 215–31.

Bligh, D. A. 2000. *What's the Use of Lectures?* San Francisco: Jossey Bass.

Brown, R. D. 1988. "Self-quiz on Testing and Grading Issues." *Teaching at UNL (University of Nebraska Lincoln)* 10(2): 1–3.

Bruner, J. 1990. *Acts of Meaning.* Cambridge, MA: Harvard University Press.

Caine, R., and G. Caine. 2011. *Natural Learning for a Connected World: Education, Technology and the Human Brain.* New York, NY: Teachers College Press.

Chen, B., and A. Hirumi. 2009. "Effects of Advance Organizers on Learning for Differentiated Learners in a Fully Web-based Course." *International Journal of Instructional Technology & Distance Learning.* http://itdl.org/Journal/Jun_09/article01.htm

Conaway, M. S. 1982. "Listening: Learning Tool and Retention Agent." In *Improving Reading and Study Skills.* 51–63. San Francisco: Jossey-bass.

Credé, M., S. G. Roch, and U. M. Kieszczynka. 2010. "Class Attendance in College: A Meta-analytic Review of the Relationship of Class Attendance with Grades and Student Characteristics." *Review of Educational Research*, 80 (2): 272–95.

Cuseo, J. B., A. Thompson, M. Campagna, and V. S. Fecas. 2013. *Thriving in College & Beyond: Research-based Strategies for Academic Success and Personal Development.* 3rd ed. Dubuque, IA: Kendall Hunt.

Demmert, W. G., Jr., and J. C. Towner. 2003. *A Review of the Research Literature on the Influences of Culturally Based Education on the Academic Performance of Native American Students.* The Northwest Regional Educational Laboratory, Portland, Oregon. http://educationnorthwest.org/sites/default/files/cbe.pdf.

Dunlosky, J., K. A. Rawson, E. J. Marsh, M. J. Nathan, and D. T. Willingham. 2013. "Improving Students' Learning with Effective Learning Techniques: Promising Directions from Cognitive and Educational Psychology." *Psychological Science in the Public Interest* 14(1): 4–58.

Einstein, G. O., J. Morris, and S. Smith. 1985. "Note-taking, Individual Differences, and Memory for Lecture Information." *Journal of Educational Psychology* 77(5): 522–32.

Hartley, J. 1998. *Learning and Studying: A Research Perspective.* London: Routledge.

Hartley, J., and S. Marshall. 1974. "On Notes and Note Taking." *Universities Quarterly* 28: 225–35.

Herbert, W. 2014. "Ink on Paper: Some Notes on Note Taking." Association for Psychological Science (APS). http://www.psychologicalscience.org/index.php/news/were-only-human/ink-on-paper-some-notes-on-note-taking.html

Howard, P. J. 2014. *The Owner's Manual for the Brain: Everyday Applications of Mind-brain Research.* 4th ed. New York: HarperCollins.

Howe, M. J. 1970. "Note-taking Strategy, Review, and Long-term Retention of Verbal Information." *Journal of Educational Psychology* 63: 285.

Jairam, D., and K. A. Kiewra. 2009. "An Investigation of the SOAR Study Method." *Journal of Advanced Academics* August: 602–29.

Jensen, E. 2008. *Brain-based Learning.* Thousand Oaks, CA: Corwin Press.

Johnstone, A. H., and W. Y. Su. 1994. "Lectures: A Learning Experience?" *Education in Chemistry* 31(1): 65–76, 79.

Kiewra, K. A. 1985. "Students' Note-taking Behaviors and the Efficacy of Providing the Instructor's Notes for Review." *Contemporary Educational Psychology* 10: 378–86.

Kiewra, K. A. 2000. "Fish Giver or Fishing Teacher? The Lure of Strategy Instruction." *Teaching at UNL (University of Nebraska Lincoln)* 22(3): 1–3.

Kiewra, K. A. 2005. *Learn How to Study and SOAR to Success.* Upper Saddle River, NJ: Pearson Prentice Hall.

Kiewra, K. A., and N. F. DuBois. 1998. *Learning to Learn: Making the Transition from Student to Lifelong Learner.* Needham Heights, MA: Allyn and Bacon.

Kiewra, K. A., K. Hart, J. Scoular, M. Stephen, G. Sterup, and B. Tyler. 2000. "Fish Giver or Fishing Teacher? The lure of strategy instruction." *Teaching at UNL (University of Nebraska Lincoln)* 22(3).

Kuh, G. D. 2005. "Student Engagement in the First Year of College." In *Challenging and Supporting the First-year Student: A Handbook for Improving the First Year of College,* edited by M. L. Upcraft, J. N. Gardner, B. O. Barefoot, & Associates, 86–107. San Francisco: Jossey-bass.

Kuhn, L. 1988. "What Should We Tell Students About Answer Changing?" *Research Serving Teaching* 1(8).

Launius, M. H. 1997. "College Student Attendance: Attitudes and Academic Performance." *College Student Journal* 31 (1): 86–93.

LeDoux, J. 2002. *Synaptic Self: How Our Brains Become Who We Are.* New York: Penguin Books.

Locke, E. 1977. An Empirical Study of Lecture Note-taking Among College Students." *Journal of Educational Research* 77: 93–99.

Malmberg, K. J., and K. Murnane. 2002. "List Composition and the Word-frequency Effect for Recognition Memory." *Journal of Experimental Psychology: Learning, Memory, and Cognition* 28: 616–30.

Mueller, P. A., and D. M. Oppenheimer. 2014. "The Pen is Mightier Than the Keyboard: Advantages of Longhand over Laptop Note Taking." *Psychological Science* 25(6): 1159–68.

Murname, K., and R. M. Shiffrin. 1991. "Interference and the Representation of Events in Memory." *Journal of Experimental Psychology: Learning, Memory, & Cognition* 17: 855–74.

Nathan, R. 2005. *My Freshman Year: What a Professor Learned by Becoming a Student*. Ithaca, NY: Cornell University Press.

National Survey of Student Engagement. 2009. *NSSE Annual Results 2009. Assessment for Improvement: Tracking Student Engagement over Time.* Bloomington, IN: Author.

Pace, C. 1990. *The Undergraduates: A Report of Their Activities*. Los Angeles: University of California, Center for the Study of Evaluation.

Pace, C. May, 1995 *From Good Processes to good Products: Relating Good Practices in Undergraduate Education to Student Achievement.* Paper presented at the meeting of the Association for Institutional Research, Boston.

Pascarella, E., and P. Terenzini. 1991. *How College Affects Students: Findings and Insights from Twenty Years of Research.* San Francisco: Jossey-bass.

Pascarella, E., and P. Terenzini. 2005. *How College Affects Students: A Third Decade of Research* (Vol. 2). San Francisco: Jossey-bass.

Piaget, J. 1978. *Success and Understanding*. Cambridge, MA: Harvard University Press.

Pintrich, P. R., and D. H. Schunk. 2002. *Motivation in Education: Theory, Research, and Applications*. Upper Saddle River, NJ: Merrill-prentice Hall.

Pryor, J. H., L. De Angelo, B. Palucki-blake, S. Hurtado, and S. Tran. 2012. *The American Freshman: National Norms Fall 2011*. Los Angeles: Higher Education Research Institute, UCLA.

Ravizza, S. M., D. Z. Hambrick, and K. M. Fenn. 2014. "Non-academic Internet Use in the Classroom is Negatively Related to Classroom Learning Regardless of Intellectual Ability." *Computers & Education 78*: 109–14.

Rennels, M. R., and R. B. Chaudhair. 1988. "Eye-contact and Grade Distribution." *Perceptual and Motor Skills*, 67 (October): 627–32.

Schacter, D. L. 2001. *The Seven Sins of Memory: How the Mind Forgets and Remembers*. Boston: Houghton Mifflin.

SECFHE. 2006. *A National Dialogue: The Secretary of Education's Commission on the Future of Higher Education*. U.S. Department of Education Boards and Commissions: A Draft Panel Report. http://www.ed.gov/about/bdscomm/list/hiedfuture/reports/0809-draft.pdf

Shelton, J. T., E. M. Elliot, S. D. Eaves, and A. L. Exner. 2009. "The Distracting Effects of a Ringing Cell Phone: An Investigation of the Laboratory and the Classroom Setting." *Journal of Environmental Psychology* (March). http://news-info.wustl.edu/news/page/normal/14225.html.

Shimoff, E., and C. A. Catania. 2001. "Effects of recording attendance on grades in Introductory Psychology." *Teaching of Psychology* 23 (3): 192–5.

Tagliacollo, V. A., G. L. Volpato, and A. Pereira Jr. 2010. "Association of Student Position in Classroom and School Performance." *Educational Research* 1 (6): 198–201.

Titsworth, S., and K. A. Kiewra. 2004. "Organizational Lecture Cues and Student Note Taking." *Contemporary Educational Psychology 29*: 447–61.

Vygotsky, L. S. 1978. "Internalization of Higher Cognitive Functions." In *Mind in Society: The Development of Higher Psychological Processes*, edited and translated by M. Cole, V. John-steiner, S. Scribner, and E. Souberman. 52–57. Cambridge, MA: Harvard University Press.

Walsh, K. 2005. *Suggestions from More Experienced Classmates*. http://www.uni.edu/walsh/introtips.html.

Walter, T. W., G. M. Knudsvig, and D. E. P. Smith. 2003. *Critical Thinking: Building the Basics*. 2nd ed. Belmont, CA: Wadsworth.

Chapter 2 Exercises

2.1 Quote Reflections

Review the sidebar quotes contained in this chapter and select two that were especially meaningful or inspirational to you.

For each quote, provide a three- to five-sentence explanation why you chose it.

2.2 Reality Bite

Crime and Punishment: Plagiarism and Its Consequences

In an article that appeared in an Ohio newspaper, titled "Plagiarism persists in classrooms," an English professor is quoted as saying: "Technology has made it easier to plagiarize because students can download papers and exchange information and papers through their computers. But technology has also made it easier to catch students who plagiarize." This professor works at a college that subscribes to a website that matches the content of students' papers with content from books and online sources. Many professors now require students to submit their papers through this website. If students are caught plagiarizing, for a first offense, they typically receive an F for the assignment or the course. A second offense can result in dismissal or expulsion from college, which has already happened to a few students.

Reflection and Discussion Questions

1. What do you suspect are their primary motives or reasons why students plagiarize from the web?

2. What would you say is a fair or just penalty for those found guilty of a first plagiarism violation? What do you think would be fair penalty for a second violation?

3. How might web-based plagiarism be minimized or prevented from happening in the first place?

2.3 Syllabus Review

Review the syllabus (course outline) for all classes you're enrolled in this term, and complete the following information for each course.

Self-Assessment Questions

1. Is the overall workload what you expected? Are you surprised by the amount of work required in any particular course(s)?

2. At this point in the term, what do you see as your most challenging or demanding course or courses? Why?

3. Do you think you can handle the total workload required by the full set of courses you're enrolled in this term?

4. What adjustments or changes do you think you'll make to your previous learning and study habits to accommodate your academic workload this term?

2.4 Is it or is it Not Plagiarism?

The following four incidents were brought to a judicial review board to determine if plagiarism had occurred and, if so, what the penalty should be. After reading each case, answer the questions listed below it.

Case 1. A student turned in an essay that included substantial material copied from a published source. The student admitted that he didn't cite the sources properly, but argued that it was because he misunderstood the directions, not because he was attempting to steal someone else's ideas.

Is this Plagiarism?

How severe is it? (Rate it on a scale from 1 = low to 5 = high)

What should the consequence or penalty be?

How could the accusation of plagiarism be avoided?

Case 2. A student turned in a paper that was identical to a paper submitted by another student for a different course.

Is this plagiarism?

How severe is it? (Rate it on a scale from 1 = low to 5 = high)

What should the consequence or penalty be?

How could the accusation of plagiarism be avoided?

Case 3. A student submitted a paper he wrote in a previous course as an extra credit paper for a current course.

Is this plagiarism?

How severe is it? (Rate it on a scale from 1 = low to 5 = high)

What should the consequence or penalty be?

How could the accusation of plagiarism be avoided?

Case 4. A student submitted a paper in an art history that contained some ideas from art critics she read about and whose ideas she agreed with. The student didn't cite the critics as sources, but claimed it wasn't plagiarism because their ideas were merely their own subjective judgments or opinions, not facts or findings; furthermore, they were opinions she agreed with.

Is this plagiarism?

How severe is it? (Rate it on a scale from 1 = low to 5 = high)

What should the consequence or penalty be?

How could the accusation of plagiarism be avoided?

Chapter 2 Reflection

List five strategies discussed in this chapter that you intend to use to achieve college success, and explain HOW you plan to put them into practice.

CHAPTER 3

ENGAGING YOUR MIND, ENGAGING YOUR CAMPUS

USING POWERFUL PRINCIPLES OF STUDENT SUCCESS AND KEY CAMPUS RESOURCES

CHAPTER PREVIEW

This chapter focuses on the "big picture": powerful principles you can implement to promote your own success and key campus resources you can use to help you succeed. It describes what these key principles and resources are, why they're effective, and how to capitalize on them.

LEARNING OBJECTIVE

Alert you to the most powerful strategies and resources that you can use immediately to get off to a fast start in college and continually to achieve excellence throughout your college experience. To introduce novice college students to four principles and resources that will guide and support success in college and beyond.

PERFORMANCE OBJECTIVE

You will recognize and practice strategies and utilize resources that enable them to be successful at postsecondary institutions.

PRE-REFLECTION

What concerns do I have about starting college?

ESSENTIAL QUESTION

What strategies do students who thrive in college use in order to assure their academic success?

FIRST STEP OF COLLEGE SUCCESS: ACTIVE INVOLVEMENT (ENGAGEMENT)

Research indicates that active involvement may be the most powerful principle of human learning and college success (Astin 1993; Kuh et al. 2005). To succeed in college, you can't be a passive spectator; you need to be an active player.

Active involvement includes the following key components:

- The amount of *time* you devote to the college experience—inside and outside the classroom.
- The degree of *effort or energy* (mental and physical) you invest in the learning process.

THINK ABOUT IT

Pre-reading skills are very important skills to use to guide you to starting college on the right path. Take a moment and review the headings and sub-headings in this chapter. What do you predict is the gist of this chapter?

I always felt I had to work harder than normal, which made me feel insecure and frustrated. Taking this seminar class helped me understand how I learn best and what I can do to make learning more interesting and dig deeper into my reading.

—Second year AHE student

Tell me and I'll listen. Show me and I'll understand. Involve me and I'll learn.

—Teton Lakota Indian saying

NOTE

College provides a wealth of opportunities to interact with diverse ideas and people both inside and outside the classroom. Take advantage of these learning opportunities!

NOTE

Don't forget to add highlights from PPT's, discussions, or assignments to your Cornell Notes.

NOTE

Your role in the college classroom is not that of a passive spectator or an absorbent sponge who sits back and soaks up information through osmosis. Instead, it's like being an aggressive detective or investigative reporter on a search-and-record mission. Your job is to actively search for information by picking your instructor's brain, picking out the instructor's key points, and recording your "pickings" in your notebook.

Think of something you do with intensity, passion, and commitment. If you were to approach college in the same way, you would be faithfully implementing the principle of active involvement. Here's how you can apply both key components of active involvement—time and energy—to the major learning challenges you'll face in college.

Active Involvement in the Learning Process

College success will require that you work harder (put in more time than high school) and smarter (learn more strategically and effectively). Probably the most powerful principle of effective learning is active involvement (engagement); there's simply no such thing as "passive learning." You can ensure you're actively involved in the learning process by engaging in some form of *action* on what you're learning, such as the actions listed below.

- *Writing.* For example, when reading, take notes on what you're reading rather than passively highlighting sentences.
- *Speaking.* For example, rather than studying silently, explain what you're learning to a study group partner.
- *Organizing.* For example, create an outline, diagram, or concept map that pulls together the ideas you're learning.

Active Listening and Note Taking in Class

You will find that many college professors rely heavily on the lecture method—they profess their knowledge by speaking for long stretches of time and expect students to listen and take notes on the knowledge they dispense. This method of instruction places great demands on your ability to listen actively and take notes that are both accurate and complete. Research consistently shows that most test questions on college exams come from professors' lectures and students who take better class notes get better grades (Brown 1988; Cuseo et al. 2013; Kiewra 2000).

The best way to apply the principle of active involvement during a class lecture is to engage in the physical action of writing notes. Writing down what your instructor is saying in class "forces" you to pay closer attention to what is being said and reinforces your retention of what was said. By taking notes, you not only hear the information (auditory memory), you also see it on paper (visual memory) and feel it in the muscles of your hand as you write it (motor memory).

FOUR STEPS TO COLLEGE SUCCESS

Research points to four powerful principles of college success:

1. Active Involvement (Engagement)
2. Capitalizing on Campus Resources (Resourcefulness)
3. Interpersonal Interaction and Collaboration (Social Integration)
4. Reflection and Self-Awareness (Mindfulness)

(Sources: Astin 1993; Kuh et al. 2005; Light 2001; Pascarella and Terenzini 1991, 2005; Tinto 1993.)

FIGURE 3.1: The Diamond of College Success

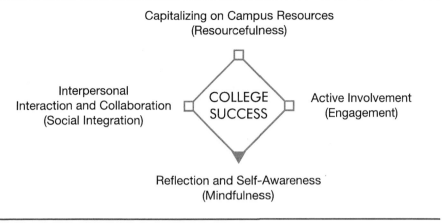

These four principles are presented in the beginning of this book because they represent the foundational basis for all success strategies discussed throughout the book.

THINK ABOUT IT

You've probably been taking notes for a long time, either in class or at your job. The problem is that few people have been taught *how* to take notes or *what* to do with them afterwards. We want to introduce you to Cornell Notes (CN). With CN, paper is divided into three sections. On the right side of the page, take the notes from a lecture, discussion, or book. When you're finished with the class or text, review the notes and on the left side of the page write any questions you have or key points you think are being made. The bottom part of the page is devoted either to reflections you have about the work, or if your instructor asks, a summary of what you have reviewed. Try to use CN to review this first section on Active Involvement. When you finish the Engagement section (and its boxes), reflect on which of the components of engagement you think will be hardest for you to do. Discuss it with a group of your classmates and see if they agree with you or have other concerns.

NOTE

Look back over your notes so far. . . . Is there a question you have that you might ask your professor in class or during office hours?

THINK ABOUT IT

If there is something that makes you uncomfortable in class, be sure to discuss with your professor during office hours or outside class (content, conflict with peer, etc.)

Box 3.1 contains a summary of top strategies for classroom listening and note taking that you can put into action right now.

BOX 3.1

Top Tips for Active Listening and Note Taking in the College Classroom

One task that you'll be expected to perform during the very first week of college is taking notes in class. Studies show that professors' lecture notes are the number one source of test questions (and test answers) on college exams. You can improve the quality of your note taking and your course grades by using the following strategies.

1. Get to every class. Whether or not your instructors take roll, you're responsible for all material covered

(continued)

BOX 3.1 *(continued)*

in class. Remember that a full load of college courses (12 units) only requires that you be in class about 13 hours per week. If you consider your class work to be a full-time job, any job that requires you to show up for only 13 hours a week is a pretty sweet deal; it's a deal that supplies you with much more educational freedom than you had in high school. To miss classes in college when you're required to spend so little time in class per week is an abuse of this educational freedom. It's also an abuse of the money that you, your family, and taxpaying American citizens are paying to support your college education.

2. Get to every class on time. During the first few minutes of a class session, instructors often share valuable information—such as important reminders, reviews, and previews.

3. Get organized. Bring the right equipment to class. Get a separate notebook for each class, write your name on it, date each class session, and store all class handouts in it.

4. Get in the right position.
   - The ideal place to sit in class is at the front and center of the room—where you're in the best position to hear and see what's going on.
   - The ideal social position to occupy in class is near motivated classmates who will not distract you, but motivate you to listen actively and take notes aggressively.

NOTE

These attention-focusing strategies are particularly important in large classes where you're likely to feel more anonymous, less accountable, and less engaged.

5. Get in the right frame of mind. Come to class with the attitude that you're there to pick your instructor's

brain, pick up answers to test questions, and pick up points to elevate your course grade.

6. Use Cornell Notes or other note taking strategy to record what is being said. Sometimes questions that students ask provide important information about what the lecturer thinks is important. Keep writing/typing. It is more important to have a lot of information rather than only look, listen, and record important points at all times in class. Pay special attention to whatever information instructors put in writing, whether it appears on the board, on a slide, or in a handout.

7. Talk with your professor. Look for opportunities to talk to your professors outside of class. Discuss exam, quiz or assignment, explore a topic in more depth or ask clarifying questions. Be sure to access office hours.

NOTE

Most college professors don't write all important information on the board for you; instead, they expect you to listen carefully and write it down yourself.

8. Finish strong. During the last few minutes of class, instructors often share valuable information, such as timely reminders, reviews, and previews.

9. Stick around. When class ends, don't bolt out of the room; instead, hang out for a few moments and quickly review your notes (by yourself or with a classmate). This quick end-of-class review will help your brain retain the information it just received. If you detect any gaps or confusing points in your notes, try to consult with your instructor immediately after class.

For more detailed ideas and strategies on listening and note taking, see Chapter 6, **p. 127.**

Finish class with a rush of attention, not a rush out the door!

Active Class Participation

Class participation increases your ability to stay alert and attentive in class, and it sends a clear message to your instructors that you are a motivated student who wants to learn. Class participation is also likely to account for a portion of your grade in many courses, so your attentiveness and involvement in class can have a direct, positive effect on your college grades. Look for opportunities to share feedback with peers one-on-one. Check in with professors to explore alternative ways to provide in writing (electronic or paper) feedback or ask clarifying questions.

Active Reading

Note-taking not only promotes active listening in class, it also promotes active reading out of class. Taking notes on what you're reading (or on information you've highlighted while reading) keeps you actively involved in the reading process because it requires more mental and physical energy than merely reading the material or passively highlighting sentences.

College professors also expect you to relate or connect what they talk about in class to the reading they've assigned. Thus, it's important to start developing good reading habits now. You can do so by using the top tips suggested in **Box 3.2**.

NOTE

Explore your campus... where are tutors available? Are there free tutor services?

THINK ABOUT IT

When you meet with your tutor, he or she may ask you if you have attended all classes. They are there because they want to help you, yet they also believe you need to attend class, and read required texts/readings.

NOTE

Model active participation by making one thoughtful comment per class or per week.

BOX 3.2

Top Tips for Strengthening Textbook Reading Comprehension and Retention

1. Get the textbooks required for your courses as soon as possible and get your reading assignments done on time. Information from reading assignments ranks right behind lecture notes as a source of test questions on college exams. Many professors deliver their lectures with the expectation that you've done the assigned reading and assume you can build on that knowledge to understand their lectures. If you haven't done the reading, you'll have more difficulty following what your instructor is saying in class. Thus, by not doing the assigned reading you pay a double penalty: you miss information from the reading that's not covered in class, which will likely appear on exams, and you miss understanding ideas presented in class that build on the reading.

   Take advantage of office hours to talk to your professor about the readings, assignments and expectations.

I recommend that you read the first chapters right away because college professors get started promptly with assigning certain readings. Classes in college move very fast because, unlike high school, you do not attend class five times a week but two or three times a week."

—*Advice to new college students from a first-year AHE student*

2. Read with the right equipment.
   - Bring a writing tool (pen, pencil, or keyboard) to record important information and a storage space (notebook or computer) in which you can save and later retrieve information acquired found in your reading for later use on tests and assignments.
   - Have a dictionary nearby to quickly find the meaning of unfamiliar words that may interfere with your ability to comprehend what you're reading. Looking up definitions of unfamiliar words helps you understand what you're reading and also builds your vocabulary. A strong vocabulary will

(continued)

Box 3.2 *(continued)*

improve your reading comprehension in all college courses, as well as your performance on standardized tests, such as those required for admission to graduate and professional schools.

- Check the back of your textbook for a glossary (list) of key terms included in the book. Each college subject and academic discipline has its own special language, and decoding it is often the key to understanding the concepts covered in the course. The glossary that appears at the end of your textbook is more than an ancillary add-on, it's a valuable tool that you can use to improve your comprehension of course concepts. Consider making a photocopy of the glossary at the back of your textbook so you can access it easily while you're reading—without having to repeatedly stop, hold your place, and go to the back of the text to find it.

3. Get in the right position. Sit upright and have light coming from behind you, over the side of your body opposite your writing hand. This will reduce the distracting and fatiguing effects of glare and shadows.

4. Get a sneak preview. Approach the chapter by first reading its boldface headings and any chapter outline, summary, or end-of-chapter questions that may be provided. This will supply you with a mental map of

the chapter's important ideas before you start your trip through it. Getting an overview of the chapter will help you keep track of its chapter's major ideas (the "big picture") and reduce your risk of getting lost in all the smaller details you encounter along the way.

5. Finish each of your reading sessions with a short review. Rather than using the last few minutes of a reading session to cover a few more pages, end it with a review of what you've highlighted or noted as important information. Since most forgetting takes place immediately after you stop processing (taking in) information and start doing something else, it's best to use your last minutes of reading time to "lock in" the most important information you've just read.

Note

When reading, your goal should be to discover or uncover the most important ideas, so the final step in the reading process should be to review (and lock in) the most important ideas you've discovered.

Note: For a more detailed discussion of reading comprehension and retention, see Chapter 2 (**pp. 52–53**).

3-2-1 Exercise

Name 3 things you learned about being actively engaged that you believe will assist you with being an attentive student.

Name 2 things that you plan on working on over the next semester/quarter.

Name 1 instructor who you will speak to out of class about their course over the next month.

SECOND STEP FOR COLLEGE SUCCESS: CAPITALIZING ON CAMPUS RESOURCES (RESOURCEFULNESS)

Successful people are *resourceful*; they seek out and take advantage of resources to help them reach their goals. Your campus is chock full of resources that have been intentionally designed to support your quest for educational and personal success. Studies show that students who utilize campus resources report higher levels of satisfaction with college and get more out of the college experience (Pascarella and Terenzini 1991, 2005).

Utilizing campus resources is a natural extension of the principle of active involvement. Successful students are *involved* students, both inside and outside the classroom. Out-of-class involvement includes involvement with campus resources. The first step toward making effective use of campus resources is becoming aware of the full range of resources available to you and what they can do for you. Listed below are key campus services that are likely to be available to you and what they can do for you.

Academic Support Services

This campus is designed to strengthen your academic performance. The individual and group tutoring provided here will help you master difficult course concepts and assignments, and the people working here are professionally trained to help you learn *how to learn.* Just as professors are experts in the subjects they teach, learning resource professionals are experts in the process of learning. They are professionals who can equip you with effective learning strategies that can be used in all courses, as well as specific strategies for dealing with the demands of certain courses and teaching styles. You're also likely to find trained peer tutors in this center who can often help you understand concepts better than more experienced professionals because they're closer to you in age and experience.

Studies show that college students who capitalize on academic support services outside the classroom achieve higher grades and are more likely to complete their college degree, particularly if they begin their involvement with these support services during their first year of college (Bailey 2009; Cuseo 2003). Students who seek and receive assistance from the Learning Center also show significant improvement in academic self-efficacy—that is, they develop a stronger sense of personal control over their academic performance and higher expectations for academic success (Smith, Walter, and Hoey 1992).

Despite the powerful advantages associated with student use of academic support services, these services are typically underused by college students—especially by students who need them the most (Cuseo 2003; Walter and Smith 1990). Unfortunately, some college students believe that seeking academic help is admitting they're not smart, self-sufficient, or able to succeed on their own. Don't buy into this myth. In high school, students may only go to an office on campus if they're required to (e.g., if they forgot to do something or did something wrong). In college, students go to campus offices to enhance their success by taking advantage of the services and support they provide.

Don't wait too long to get assistance! If, for example, you had difficulties with a subject in HS such as writing essays, or algebra, visit a tutor during your first week of college. Get ahead of your studies and connect to support services before you feel overwhelmed and/or confused.

Disability Services (a.k.a. Office for Students with Special Needs)

If you have a physical or learning disability that's interfering with your performance in college, or you think you may have such a disability, Disability Services is the campus resource to consult for assistance and support. Programs and services typically provided by this office include:

* Assessment for learning disabilities;
* Verification of eligibility for disability support services;

NOTE

Capitalizing on campus services is not only valuable, it's also "free"; the cost of these services has already been covered by your college tuition. By investing time and energy in campus resources, you maximize the return on your financial investment in college—you get a bigger bang for your buck.

NOTE

Using academic support services doesn't mean you're helpless, need remedial repair work, or require academic life support because you're on the verge of flunking out. Instead, it's a sign that you're a motivated and resourceful student who is striving for academic excellence.

" At colleges where I've taught, we found that the grade point average of students who used the Learning Center was higher than the college average, and honors students were more likely to use the center than other students."

—*Joe Cuseo, lead researcher for AHE Team*

Talk to your tutor about what academic concerns you are experiencing or anticipating have difficulties with during a course. Schedule time with a tutor early in the semester/quarter to keep your confidence up from the beginning.

"

When you're having trouble (be prepared—you will likely experience failing something), work through your fear, and ask for help early on. Help comes in a variety of forms. Help is getting a tutor when you feel confused by a reading or lecture. It means releasing notions that I can't share my burdens with a trusted professional. Getting help is letting go of assumptions that your professor will not understand or listen to how you feel or trepidation you are fulfilling a stereotype. See your professor during office hours. Develop a rapport. I am grateful some professors held my latest paper/grade hostage in an effort to bribe me to come see them outside of class.

—*AHE Professor (who was a first-generation college student)*

- Authorization of academic accommodations for students with disabilities; and
- Specialized counseling, advising, and tutoring.

College Media Center

This is your campus resource for finding information and completing research assignments (e.g., term papers and group projects). Librarians are professional educators who provide instruction outside the classroom; you can learn from them just as you can learn from faculty inside the classroom. They can help you develop research skills for accessing, retrieving, and evaluating information. These are lifelong learning skills that promote your educational success at all stages of the college experience as well as your professional and personal success beyond college.

Academic Advisement

Whether or not you have an assigned academic advisor, the Academic Advising Center is your campus resource for help with course selection, educational planning, and choosing or changing a major. Some campuses have faculty advisors who are housed in their respective departments. Be sure to find out who your advisor is and where he or she is located. Studies show that students who develop clear educational and career goals are more likely to persist in college and complete their college degree (Lotkowski, Robbins, and Noeth 2004). Research also indicates that most beginning college students need help clarifying their educational goals, deciding on a major, and identifying career options (Cuseo 2005; Tinto 2012). As a first-year college student, being undecided or uncertain about your educational and career goals is nothing to be embarrassed about. However, you should start thinking about your future now. Connect early and often with an academic advisor to help you clarify your educational goals and choose a field of study that best complements your interests, talents, and values.

Student Services

This is your campus resource for involvement in student life outside the classroom, including student clubs and organizations, recreational programs, leadership activities, and volunteer experiences. Research consistently shows that experiential learning outside the classroom contributes as much to your personal development and career success as class work (Kuh 1995; Kuh et al. 1994; Pascarella and Terenzini 2005). This is one reason why most campuses no longer refer to out-of-class experiences as "*extra*curricular" activities; instead they are referred to as "*co*-curricular" experiences—which conveys the message they're equally important as classroom-based learning. Studies show that students who become actively involved in campus life are more likely to:

- Enjoy their college experience;
- Graduate from college; and
- Develop leadership skills that enhance career performance beyond college (Astin 1993).

Devoting some out-of-class time to co-curricular experiences should not interfere with your academic performance. Keep in mind that in college you'll be spending much less time in the classroom than you did in high school. As mentioned previously, a full load of college courses (12 units) requires that you be in class for about 13 hours per week. This can leave you with sufficient time to become involved in learning experiences on or off campus. Research indicates that students' academic performance and progress to degree completion aren't impaired if they spend 20 or fewer hours on co-curricular and part-time work experiences (Advisory Committee on Student Financial Assistance 2008). In fact, they earn higher grades than students who don't get involved in any out-of-class activities (Pascarella 2001; Pascarella and Terenzini 2005).

Although co-curricular involvement is valuable, limit your involvement to no more than two or three major campus organizations at a time. Restricting the number of your out-of-class activities will not only enable you to keep up with your studies, it will be more impressive to future schools or employers because a long list of involvement in numerous activities may send the message that you're padding your resume with activities you participated in superficially (or never participated in at all).

At some institutions, Student Services covers a broad array of areas and departments, many of which are particularly important to first year students. These include:

- Veterans' Affairs: Colleges recognize that veterans either just starting or returning to college may have special issues concerning course requirements and finances. These campuses have special units that can assist veterans as they make their way through college. In addition, should veterans be in need of counseling services to adequately adjust to their life outside the military, many campuses have full-time counselors who can provide support in making the difficult transition to civilian life.

NOTE

Co-curricular experiences are also resume-building experiences, and campus professionals with whom you interact regularly while participating in co-curricular activities (e.g., director of student activities or dean of students) can be valuable resources for personal references and letters of recommendation.

Financial Aid

If you have questions concerning how to obtain assistance in paying for college, the staff in this office can guide you through the application process. The paperwork needed to apply for and secure financial aid can sometimes be confusing or overwhelming. Don't let the process of applying for financial aid intimidate you or prevent you from seeking financial aid because professional financial aid counselors can walk you through the process. They can also help you find:

- Part-time employment on campus through a work–study program;
- Low-interest student loans;
- Grants and scholarships.

If you have any doubt about whether you're using the most effective plan for financing your college education, make an appointment to see a professional in your Financial Aid Office right now.

- Federal and state laws governing loan and grant programs are always subject to change. Take responsibility to see if there have been changes in FAFSA or the Pell Grant program that could impact your status. In addition, it's a good thing to review possible grant options that may become available. Some of these will award funding to students in a specific field or from a specific county, so be sure to keep up-to-date on any small grants that can make a big difference.

- Office of Multi-Cultural Affairs/Diversity Office: As campuses become more diverse, they have become aware of the need to have professionals who can address the issues some of these students face. Often there are special clubs or meetings where first-generation college students, or students for whom English is a second language can meet to discuss unique problems they may be facing and to create their own solutions to various issues.

Counseling Center

NOTE

Personal counseling is not just for students experiencing emotional problems. It's for all students who want to enrich the quality of their life.

Beginning college is a huge transition and can cause confusion and uncertainty. If you begin to feel overwhelmed or uncertain about what to do visit the counseling center. Here's where you can get ideas and strategies for managing college stress, gaining greater self-awareness, and reaching your full potential. Personal counselors are professionals who do more than just help students maintain mental health; they also develop students' emotional intelligence, interpersonal skills, and personal growth.

THIRD STEP FOR COLLEGE SUCCESS: INTERPERSONAL INTERACTION AND COLLABORATION (SOCIAL INTEGRATION)

NOTE

Become familiar with your campus! Read the campus newspaper or visit the student union to learn about what resources, events, and activities are offered and taking place on campus.

Students who become socially integrated or connected with other members of the college community are more likely to complete their first year of college and go on to complete their college degree (Pascarella and Terenzini 2005; Tinto 1993). One of the most exciting and challenging times of your college career has already begun. You will be meeting people from other ethnic and racial groups, different generations, religions, countries, and customs. Some will be your fellow students, others will be faculty members or staff. All have had varied experiences—some will be military veterans, others parents or much younger than you. But for all the apparent differences, there are many similarities. Taking advantage of the diversity college offers is a rewarding experience you will relish throughout your postsecondary career. (For effective ways to make interpersonal connections with key members of your college community, see **Box 3.3.**)

BOX 3.3

Social Integration: Making Connections with Members of Your College Community

Listed below are top tips for making key social connections in college. Start developing these relationships right now so you can build a base of social support to

help you succeed during the critical first year of college.

- Connect with a student development professional you may have met during orientation.
- Join a college club, student organization, campus committee, intramural team, or volunteer service

group whose members share the same personal or career interests as you. If you can't find a club or organization you were hoping to join, consider starting it on your own. For example, if you're an English major, consider starting a Writing Club or a Book Club.
- Connect with a peer leader who has been trained to assist new students (e.g., orientation week leader, peer tutor, or peer mentor).
- Connect with classmates and team up with them to take notes, complete reading assignments, study for exams, or take classes together. Look especially to team up with a peer who may be in more than one class with you. (For more detailed information on forming collaborative learning teams, see Chapter 2, **pp. 44–45**.)
- Connect with peers who live near you or who commute to school from the same community in which you live. If your schedules are similar, consider carpooling together.
- Connect with faculty members—particularly in a field that you're considering as a major. Visit them during office hours, converse briefly with them after class, or communicate with them via e-mail.
- Connect with an academic advisor to discuss and develop your educational plans.
- Connect with academic support professionals in your college's Learning Center for personalized academic assistance or tutoring related to any course in which you'd like to improve your performance or achieve academic excellence.
- Connect with a college librarian to get early assistance or a head start on any research.
- Connect with a personal counselor or campus minister to discuss college adjustment or personal challenges you may be experiencing.

Four particular forms of interpersonal interaction have been found to promote student learning and motivation in college:

1. Student–faculty interaction,
2. Student–advisor interaction,
3. Student–mentor interaction, and
4. Student–student (peer) interaction.

Strategies for capitalizing on each of these key forms of interaction are provided below.

Interacting with Faculty Members

College success is strongly influenced by the frequency and quality of student–faculty interaction *outside the classroom*. Out-of-class contact with faculty is associated with the following positive outcomes for college students:

- Improved academic performance;
- Increased critical thinking skills;
- Greater satisfaction with the college experience;
- Increased likelihood of completing a college degree; and
- Stronger desire to pursue education beyond a four-year degree (Astin 1993; Pascarella and Terenzini 1991, 2005).

These positive outcomes are so powerful, strong, and widespread that we encourage you to immediately begin making connections with your professors outside of class time. Here are some of the easiest ways to do so.

1. **Seek contact with your instructors right after class.** If something covered in class captures your interest, approach your instructor to discuss it further. You could ask a quick question about something you weren't sure you understood, or have a short conversation about how the material covered in class really hit home for you or connected with something you learned in another course. Interacting briefly with instructors after class can help them get to know you as an individual and help you gain the confidence to approach them during office hours.

2. **Connect with course instructors during their office hours.** One of the most important pieces of information you'll find on a course syllabus is your instructor's office hours. College professors specifically reserve times in their weekly schedule to be available to students in their office. Try to visit the office of each of your instructors at least once, preferably early in the term, when quality time is easier to find.

3. **Connect with your instructors through e-mail.** Electronic communication is another effective tool for experiencing the benefits of student–faculty interaction outside the classroom, particularly if your professor's office hours conflict with your class schedule, work responsibilities, or family commitments. If you're a commuter student who doesn't live on campus, or if you're an adult student juggling family and work commitments along with your academic schedule, e-mail communication may be an especially effective and efficient way to interact with faculty. E-mail may also be a good way to initially communicate with instructors and build self-confidence to eventually seek out face-to-face interaction with them. However, if you miss class, don't use e-mail to ask such questions as:

   - Did I miss anything important in class today?
   - Could you send me your PowerPoint slides from the class I missed?

   Also, when using e-mail to communicate with your instructors, be sure to:

   - Include your full name in the message.
   - Mention the class or course in which you're enrolled.
   - Use complete sentences, correct grammar, and avoid informal "hip" expressions (e.g., "yo," "whatup").
   - Spell check and proofread your message before sending it.
   - Include your full contact information. (If you're communicating via Facebook, watch your screen name; for example, names like "Sexsea" or "Studly" wouldn't be appropriate.)
   - Give your instructor time to reply. (Don't expect an immediate response, particularly if you send your message in the evening or on a weekend.) (See Chapter 2, **p. 34,** for more netiquette guidelines.)

> " I wish that I would have taken advantage of professors' open-door policies when I had questions, because actually understanding what I was doing, instead of guessing, would have saved me a lot of stress and re-doing what I did wrong the first time."
>
> —*College sophomore (Walsh 2005)*

Interacting with Academic Advisors

If you need some help understanding college policies and procedures, or navigating the organizational maze of course options and course requirements, an academic advisor is the person to see. Advisors also serve as key referral agents who can direct you to, and connect you with, key campus support services that best meet your educational needs and career goals.

Your academic advisor should be someone whom you feel comfortable speaking with, someone who knows your name, and someone who's familiar with your personal interests and abilities. Give advisors the opportunity to get to know you personally, and seek their input on courses, majors, and any academic difficulties you may be experiencing.

If you've been assigned a specific advisor and cannot develop a good relationship with this person, ask the director of advising or academic dean if you could make a change. Consider asking your peers or peer leaders for their recommendations.

If your college does not assign you a personal advisor, but offers advising services in an Advising Center on a drop-by or drop-in basis, you may see a different advisor each time you visit the center. If you're not comfortable working with different advisors from one visit to the next, find one you like and make that person your advisor by scheduling appointments in advance. This will enable you to consistently connect with the same advisor and develop a close, ongoing relationship with that person.

NOTE

Advisors can be much more than course schedulers; they can be mentors. Unlike your course instructors—who may change from term to term—your academic advisor may be the one professional on campus with whom you have regular contact and a continuous relationship throughout your college experience.

 ## Journal Reflection 3.1

Do you have a personally assigned advisor?

_____

If yes, do you know who this person is and where he or she can be found?

_____

If you don't have a personally assigned advisor, where will you go if you have questions about your class schedule or educational plans?

_____

_____

_____

Interaction with Peers (Student–Student Interaction)

Peer support is important at any stage of the college experience, but it's especially valuable during the first term of college. It's at this stage when new students have a strong need for belongingness and social acceptance because they're in the midst of a major life transition. While new friends will be one of the 'take aways' from college it is especially important during the first year to be careful about how you spend your time. Spending the afternoon in the student union with friends may be a lot of fun, it will not get your essay written. As a new student, whether traditional or non-traditional, it may be useful to view your first-year experience through the lens of psychologist Abraham Maslow's hierarchy of human needs (see **Figure 3.2**).

FIGURE 3.2: Maslow's Theory of Self-Actualization

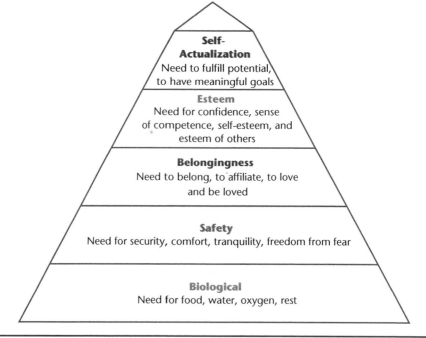

© Kendall Hunt Publishing Company

According to Maslow, humans only reach their full potential and achieve peak performance after their more basic emotional and social needs have been met (e.g., needs for personal safety, social acceptance, and self-esteem). Making early connections with your peers helps you meet these basic human needs, provides you with a base of social support that eases your integration into the college community, and prepares you to move up to higher levels of the need hierarchy (e.g., achieving academic excellence and reaching your educational goals).

Getting involved with campus organizations or activities is one way to connect with other students. In addition, try to interact with experienced students who have spent more time at college than you. Sophomores, juniors, and seniors can be valuable social resources for a new student. In particular, seek out contact with students who have been selected and trained as peer mentors or peer leaders.

Research clearly demonstrates that college students learn as much from peers as they do from instructors and textbooks (Astin 1993; Pascarella 2005). One study of more than 25,000 college students revealed that when peers interact with one another while learning, they achieve higher levels of academic performance and are more likely to persist to degree completion (Astin 1993).

Be observant—keep an eye out for peers who are successful. Start building your social support network by surrounding yourself with success-seeking and success-achieving students. Learn from them, emulate their productive habits and strategies, and use them as a social resource to promote your own success.

Collaborative Learning

Simply defined, collaborative learning is the process of two or more people working *interdependently* to advance each other's success—as opposed to working independently or competitively. Learning is strengthened when it takes place in a social context that involves interpersonal interaction. As scholars put it, human knowledge is "socially constructed" or built up through dialogue and an exchange of ideas; conversations with others become internalized as ideas in your mind and influence your way of thinking (Bruffee 1993). Thus, by having frequent, intelligent conversations with others, you broaden your knowledge base, deepen your learning, and elevate the quality of your thinking.

Research from kindergarten through college shows that students who learn collaboratively in teams experience significant gains in both academic performance and interpersonal skills (Cross, Barkley, and Major 2005; Cuseo 1996; Gilles and Adrian 2003; Johnson, Johnson, and Smith 1998). In one national study that involved in-depth interviews with more than 1,600 college students, it was discovered that almost all students who struggled academically had one particular study habit in common: they always studied alone (Light 2001).

To maximize the power of collaboration, use the following pair of guidelines to choose teammates who will enhance the quality and productivity of your learning team:

1. Observe your classmates with an eye toward identifying potentially good teammates. Look for motivated students who will actively contribute to your team's success (rather than those whom you suspect may just be hitchhikers looking for a free ride).
2. Don't team up exclusively with peers who are familiar with or similar to you in terms of their personal characteristics, backgrounds, and experiences. This familiarity can actually interfere with your team's performance by turning your learning team into a social group or gabfest that gets off track and onto topics that have nothing to do with studying (e.g., what you did last weekend or what you're planning to do next weekend). Instead, include teammates who differ from you with respect to such characteristics as: age, gender, race or ethnicity, and cultural or geographical background. Such variety brings different life experiences, styles of thinking strategies, and learning styles to your team, which enriches your team's diversity and learning capacity.

Keep in mind that collaborative learning can be much more than just forming study groups the night before an exam. You can team up with classmates more regularly to work on a variety of academic tasks, such as those listed below.

Note-Taking Teams. Immediately after class sessions end, take a couple of minutes to team up with other students to compare and share notes. Since listening and note-taking are demanding tasks, it's likely that a classmate will pick up an important point you missed and vice versa. By teaming up *immediately after class*, if you and your teammates find missing or confusing information, quickly consult with the instructor before leaving the room.

NOTE

Capitalize on the advantages of collaborating with peers of varied backgrounds and lifestyles. Studies show that we learn more from people who are different from us than from people similar to us (Pascarella 2001; Thompson and Cuseo 2014).

AUTHOR'S JOURNEY

During my first term in college, I was having difficulty taking complete notes in my biology course because the instructor spoke rapidly and with an unfamiliar accent. I noticed another student (Alex) sitting in the front row who was trying to take notes as best he could; however, he was experiencing the same difficulty as me. Following one particularly fast and complex lecture, we looked at each other and noticed we were both shaking our heads in frustration. We started talking about how frustrated we were and decided to join forces after every class to compare notes and identify points we missed or found confusing. First, we helped each other by comparing and sharing our notes in case one of us got something the other missed. If there were points we both missed or couldn't figure out, we went to the front of class together to consult with the instructor before he left the room. At the end of the course, Alex and I finished with the highest grades in the course.

—Joe Cuseo

Reading Teams. After completing reading assignments, team up with classmates to compare your highlighting and margin notes. See what you both identified as the most important material to be studied for upcoming exams.

Writing Teams. Students can provide each other with feedback to revise and improve their own writing. Studies show that when peers assess each other's writing, the quality of their individual writing gets better and they develop a more positive attitude about the writing process (Topping 1998). You can form peer writing teams to help at any or all of the following stages in the writing process:

1. Topic selection and refinement: to help one another come up with a list of possible topics and subtopics to write about;
2. Pre-writing: to clarify your writing purpose and audience;
3. First draft: to improve your general writing style and tone; and
4. Final draft: to proofread, detect, and correct clerical errors before submitting your written work.

NOTE

It's perfectly acceptable and ethical to team up with others to search for information and share resources. This isn't cheating or plagiarizing— as long as your final product is completed individually and what you turn into the instructor represents your own work.

Library Research Teams. Many first-year students are unfamiliar with the process of using a college or university library to conduct academic research. Some experience "library anxiety" and avoid even stepping foot into the library, particularly if it's a large and intimidating place (Malvasi, Rudowsky, and Valencia 2009). Forming library research teams is an effective way to develop a social support group that can make library research less intimidating by converting it from a solitary experience done alone to a collaborative venture done as a team. Working together with peers on any research task can reduce anxiety, create collective energy, and result in a final product that's superior to what could have been produced by a single person working independently.

Study Teams. When seniors at Harvard University were interviewed, nearly every one of them who had participated in study groups considered the experience to be crucial to their academic progress and success (Light 1990, 1992, 2001).

Additional research on study groups indicates that they are effective only if each member has done the required course work in advance of team meetings—for example, if all teammates attended class consistently and completed required readings (Light 2001). To fully capitalize and maximize the power of study teams, each team member should study individually *before* studying with the group and come to the group prepared with answers and ideas to share with teammates, as well as specific questions or points of confusion about which they hope to receive help from other members of the team. This ensures that all team members are individually accountable for their own learning and equally responsible for contributing to their teammates' learning.

Test Review Teams. After receiving your results on course examinations (and assignments) you can collaborate with peers to review your performance as a team. When you compare your answers to the answers of other students, you're better able to identify what you did well and where you lost points. By seeing the answers of teammates who received maximum credit on certain questions, you get a clearer picture of what went wrong and what you can do next time to get it right next time.

 Journal Reflection 3.2

Think about classmates in courses you're taking this term. Would you be willing to ask any of them if they'd like to form a learning team? Why?

NOTE

Don't forget that team learning goes beyond late-night study groups. Students could and should form learning teams in advance of exams to help each other with other academic tasks—such as note-taking, reading, writing, and library research.

NOTE

Adult collaborative groups function differently than K-12 groups. Address challenges and issues directly with your teammates and/or contact your professor for resolution.

FOURTH STEP FOR COLLEGE SUCCESS: REFLECTION AND SELF-AWARENESS (MINDFULNESS)

The final step in the learning process, whether it be learning in the classroom or learning from experience, is to step back from the process, thoughtfully review it, and connect it to what you already know. Reflection is the flip side of active involvement; both processes are necessary for learning to be complete. Active involvement ensures attention—it enables information to enter your brain—and reflection ensures consolidation—it converts that information into knowledge and remains in your brain on a long-term basis (Bligh 2000; Roediger, Dudai, and Fitzpatrick 2007).

Self-Awareness

In addition to reflecting on what you're learning, it's also important to reflect on yourself. This process is known as *introspection*—it involves turning inward to gain deeper self-awareness and understanding of who you are, what you're doing, and where you're going. Two forms of self-awareness are particularly important for success in college: (a) self-monitoring and (b) self-assessment. This is particularly important when you begin your college career. You may study—or party—a little too much and lose sleep. Your eating habits may change and you may find yourself under increased stress because of your coursework. These are all things that can impact your health, both physical and emotional. You'll need to pay attention to how you feel and modify your behavior accordingly. Think about things you can do to reduce stress and improve your physical health, things such as exercise or catching brief naps during the day. And don't forget the campus resources mentioned earlier in this chapter—they are there to help you. Remember, step back. Take a clear-eyed look at how you feel and consider your options.

Self-Monitoring

One characteristic of successful learners is that they self-monitor (check themselves) while learning to remain aware of:

- Whether they're using effective learning strategies (e.g., if they're giving their undivided attention to what they're learning);
- Whether they're truly comprehending what they are learning (e.g., if they're understanding it at a deep level or memorizing it at a surface level);
- How they're regulating or adjusting their learning strategies to meet the demands of different academic tasks and subjects (e.g., if they're reading technical material in a science textbook, they read at a slower rate and check their understanding more frequently than when reading a novel) (Pintrich and Schunk 2002).

You can begin to establish good self-monitoring habits by getting in the routine of periodically pausing to reflect on the strategies you're using to learn and how you "do" college. For instance, you can ask yourself the following questions:

- Am I listening attentively to what my instructor is saying in class?
- Am I comprehending what I'm reading outside of class?
- Am I effectively using campus resources designed to support my success?
- Am I interacting with campus professionals who can contribute to my current success and future development?
- Am I interacting and collaborating with peers who can support (not sabotage) my learning and development?
- Am I effectively implementing college success strategies (such as those identified in this book)?
- Am I spending more time on social activities and campus life than I should?
- Am I letting my social life interfere with reaching my academic goals?

> "We learn neither by thinking nor by doing; we learn by thinking about what we are doing."
> —George Stoddard, Professor Emeritus, University of Iowa

NOTE

Successful students and successful people are mindful—they watch what they're doing and remain aware of whether they're doing it effectively and to the best of their ability.

Self-Assessment

Simply defined, self-assessment is the process of reflecting on and evaluating your personal characteristics. The following are key target areas for self-assessment because they enable you to accurately identify and achieve your educational and personal goals:

* **Personal interests.** What you like to do or enjoy doing.
* **Personal values.** What's important to you and what you care about doing.
* **Personal abilities or aptitudes.** What you do well or have the potential to do well.
* **Learning habits.** What approaches, methods, or techniques you use to learn.
* **Learning styles.** How you like or prefer to learn.
* **Personality traits.** Your temperament, emotional characteristics, and social tendencies (e.g., whether you lean toward being outgoing or reserved).

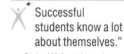

Successful students know a lot about themselves."

—*Claire Weinstein and Debra Meyer, professors of educational psychology at the University of Texas*

💡 Journal Reflection 3.3

Post-Chapter Reflection:

Based on this chapter, what strategies do you believe you can use during the next two weeks to enhance your academic success? Keep track of your progress in your journal.

CHAPTER SUMMARY AND HIGHLIGHTS

The key ideas contained in this chapter are summarized in the following self-assessment checklist of success promoting principles and practices.

A CHECKLIST OF SUCCESS PROMOTING PRINCIPLES AND PRACTICES

1. **Active Involvement (Engagement)**
   Inside the classroom, I will:
   ☑ *Get to class.* I'll treat it like a job and be there on all days I'm expected to.
   ☑ *Get involved in class.* I'll come prepared, listen actively, take notes, and participate. Outside the classroom, I will:

☑ *Read actively.* I'll take notes while I read to increase attention and retention.

☑ *Double up.* I'll spend twice as much time on academic work outside of class as I spend in class. If I'm a full-time student, I'll make it a full-time job and put in a 40-hour workweek (with occasional "overtime" as needed).

2. **Capitalizing on Campus Resources**

I will capitalize on academic and student support services available to me, such as the:

☑ Academic Support Services
☑ College Library
☑ Academic Advisement
☑ Student Development Services
☑ Financial Aid
☑ Counseling Center

3. **Interpersonal Interaction & Collaboration (Social Integration)**

I will interact and collaborate with the following members of my college community:

☑ Peers. I'll join student clubs and participate in campus organizations.

☑ Faculty members. I'll connect with my course instructors and other faculty members after class, in their offices, or via e-mail.

☑ Academic advisors. I'll see an advisor for more than course registration, and I'll find an advisor whom I can relate to and develop an ongoing relationship.

4. **Reflection & Self-Awareness (Mindfulness)**

I will engage in:

☑ Reflection. I'll step back from what I'm learning, review it, and connect it to what I already.

☑ Self-Monitoring. I'll maintain self-awareness of how I'm learning in college and if I'm using effective strategies.

☑ Self-Assessment. I'll reflect on and evaluate my personal interests, talents, learning styles, and learning habits.

In short, successful students are:

- **Involved.** They *get into* it by investing time and effort in the college experience;
- **Interactive.** They *team up* for it by interacting and collaborating with others;
- **Resourceful.** They *get help* with it by capitalizing on their surrounding resources; and
- **Reflective.** They *step back* from it to think about their performance and themselves.

Journal Reflection 3.4

Identify one way in which you will put each of the following four principles of college success into practice during the next few weeks.

1. Active Involvement (Engagement)

_____

_____

_____

_____

2. Utilizing Campus Resources (Resourcefulness)

_____

_____

_____

_____

3. Interpersonal Interaction and Collaboration (Social Integration)

_____

_____

_____

_____

4. Reflection and Self-awareness (Mindfulness)

_____

_____

_____

_____

LEARNING MORE THROUGH THE WORLD WIDE WEB: INTERNET-BASED RESOURCES

For additional information on strategies for college success, see the following websites:

http://www.cgcc.edu/success
http://www.dartmouth.edu/~acskills/success/
www.studygs.net
Ginsberg and Wlodkowskii Diversity and Motivation: Culturally Responsive Teaching in college.

REFERENCES

Advisory Committee on Student Financial Assistance. September, 2008. *Apply to Succeed: Ensuring Community College Students Benefit from Need-based Financial Aid*. Washington DC: Author. https://www2.ed.gov/about/bdscomm/list/acsfa/applytosucceed.pdf.

Astin, A. W. 1993. *What Matters in College?* San Francisco: Jossey-bass.

Bailey, G. 2009. *University of North Carolina, Greensboro Application for NADE Certification, Tutoring Program.* NADE Certification Council Archives. Searcy, AR: Harding University.

Bligh, D. A. 2000. *What's the Use of Lectures?* San Francisco: Jossey Bass.

Brown, R. D. 1988. "Self-quiz on Testing and Grading Issues." *Teaching at UNL (University of Nebraska–Lincoln)* 10 (2): 1–3.

Bruffee, K. A. 1993. *Collaborative Learning: Higher Education, Interdependence, and the Authority of Knowledge.* Baltimore: Johns Hopkins University Press.

Cross, K. P., E. F. Barkley, and C. H. Major. 2005. *Collaborative Learning Techniques: A Handbook for College Faculty.* San Francisco: Jossey-bass.

Cuseo, J. B. 1996. *Cooperative Learning: A Pedagogy for Addressing Contemporary Challenges and Critical Issues in Higher Education.* Stillwater, OK: New Forums Press.

Cuseo, J. B. 2003. Comprehensive Academic Support for Students During the First Year of College. In *Student Academic Services: An Integrated Approach,* edited by G. L. Kramer et al., 271–310. San Francisco: Jossey-bass.

Cuseo, J. B. 2005. "Decided," "Undecided," and "in Transition": Implications for academic advisement, career counseling, and student retention. In *Improving the First Year of College: Research and Practice,* edited by R. S. Feldman, 27–50. Mahwah, NJ: Lawrence Erlbaum.

Cuseo, J. B., A. Thompson, M. Campagna, and V. S. Fecas. 2013. *Thriving in College & Beyond: Research-based Strategies for Academic Success and Personal Development.* 3rd ed. Dubuque, IA: Kendall Hunt.

Gilles, R. M., and F. Adrian. 2003. *Cooperative Learning: The Social and Intellectual Outcomes of Learning in Groups.* London: Farmer Press.

Johnson, D., R. Johnson, and K. Smith. 1998. "Cooperative Learning Returns to College: What Evidence Is There that It Works?" *Change,* 30: 26–35.

Kiewra, K. A. 2000. "Fish Giver or Fishing Teacher? The Lure of Strategy Instruction." *Teaching at UNL (University of Nebraska–Lincoln)* 22 (3): 1–3.

Kuh, G. D. 1995. "The Other Curriculum: Out-of-class Experiences Associated with Student Learning and Personal Development." *Journal of Higher Education* 66 (2): 123–53.

Kuh, G. D. et al. 2005. Student Engagement in the First Year of College. In *Challenging and Supporting the First-year Student: A Handbook for Improving the First Year of College,* edited by M. L. Upcraft, J. N. Gardner, B. O. Barefoot, et al., 86–107. San Francisco: Jossey-bass.

Kuh, G. D., K. B. Douglas, J. P. Lund and J. Ramin-Gyurnek. 1994. *Student Learning Outside the Classroom: Transcending Artificial Boundaries.* ASHE-ERIC Higher Education Report No. 8. Washington, DC: George Washington University, School of Education and Human Development.

Light, R. L. 1990. *The Harvard Assessment Seminars.* Cambridge, MA: Harvard University Press.

Light, R. L. 1992. *The Harvard Assessment Seminars, Second Report.* Cambridge, MA: Harvard University Press.

Light, R. J. 2001. *Making the Most of College: Students Speak Their Minds.* Cambridge, MA: Harvard University Press.

Lotkowski, V. A., S. B. Robbins, and R. J. Noeth. 2004. *The Role of Academic and Non-academic Factors in Improving student retention.* ACT Policy Report. https://www.act.org/research/policymakers/pdf/college_retention.pdf.

Malvasi, M., C. Rudowsky, and J. M. Valencia. 2009. *Library Rx: Measuring and Treating Library Anxiety, a Research Study.* Chicago: Association of College and Research Libraries.

Pascarella, E. T. November/December, 2001. "Cognitive Growth in College: Surprising and Reassuring Findings from the National Study of Student Learning." *Change,* 21–27.

Pascarella, E. T. 2005. *How College Affects Students: Ten Directions for Future Research.* San Francisco: Jossey-bass.

Pascarella, E., and P. Terenzini. 1991. *How College Affects Students: Findings and Insights from Twenty Years of Research.* San Francisco: Jossey-bass.

Pascarella, E., and P. Terenzini. 2005. *How College Affects Students: A Third Decade of Research.* Vol. 2. San Francisco: Jossey-bass.

Pintrich, P. R., and D. H. Schunk. 2002. *Motivation in Education: Theory, Research, and Applications.* Upper Saddle River, NJ: Merrill-Prentice Hall.

Roediger, H. L., Y. Dudai, and S. M. Fitzpatrick. 2007. *Science of Memory: Concepts.* New York, NY: Oxford University Press.

Smith, J. B., T. L. Walter, and G. Hoey. 1992. "Support Programs and Student Self-efficacy: Do First-year Students Know When They Need Help?" *Journal of the Freshman Year Experience* 4 (2): 41–67.

Thompson, A., and J. Cuseo. 2014. *Diversity and the College Experience.* Dubuque, IA: Kendall Hunt.

Tinto, V. 1993. *Leaving College: Rethinking the Causes and Cures of Student Attrition.* 2nd ed. Chicago: University of Chicago Press.

Tinto, V. 2012. *Completing College: Rethinking Institutional Action.* Chicago: The University of Chicago Press.

Topping, K. 1998. "Peer Assessment between Students in Colleges and Universities." *Review of Educational Research* 68 (3): 249–76.

Walsh, K. 2005. *Suggestions from More Experienced Classmates.* http://www.uni.edu/walsh/introtips.html.

Walter, T. L., and J. Smith. April, 1990. *Self-assessment and Academic Support: Do Students Know They Need Help?* Paper presented at the annual Freshman Year Experience Conference, Austin, Texas.

Chapter 3 Exercises

3.1 Reality Bite-Case Study

Alone and Disconnected: Feeling like Calling It Quits

Josephine is a first-year student in her second week of college. She doesn't feel like she's fitting in with other students on her campus. She also feels a little guilty about the time she's taking time away from family and friends, and she fears that her ties with them will be weakened or broken if she continues spending so much time at school and on schoolwork. Josephine is feeling so torn between college, her family, and her old friends that she's beginning to have second thoughts about coming back next term.

Reflection and Discussion Questions

1. What would you say to Josephine that might persuade or motivate her to stay in college?

2. What could Josephine do to get more connected with her college community and feel less disconnected from her family and hometown friends?

3. What could Josephine do for herself right now to minimize the conflict she's experiencing between her commitment to college and her commitment to family and high school friends?

4. Can you relate to Josephine's situation? If yes, in what way? If no, why not?

3.2 Creating a Master List of Resources on Your Campus

Construct a master list of all support services that are available to you on your campus by consulting the following sources:

- Information published in your college catalog and student handbook
- Information posted on your college's website
- Information obtained by visiting with a professional in different offices or centers on your campus

1. Your final product will be a list that includes the following:

Campus Support Service	Type of Support Provided	Contact Person	Campus Location
_____	_____	_____	_____
_____	_____	_____	_____
_____	_____	_____	_____
_____	_____	_____	_____

etc.

Notes

- You can team up with other classmates to work collaboratively on this assignment. Members of your team could identify different campus resources to research and then share their findings with teammates.
- After completing this assignment, save your master list of support services for future use.

3.3 Utilizing Campus Resources

Look back at the campus resources you identified in the previous exercise, or those described on **pp. 66–70** of this chapter. Which of these resources do you plan to use this term?

Why did you identify these resources as your top priorities right now?

Ask your course instructor for recommendations about what campus resources you should consult during your first term on campus. Compare their recommendations with your selections.

Chapter 3 Reflection

WHAT do you believe is the most important principle of community college success?

WHY do you believe this is the most important one?

Explain HOW you will use this principle to assist you in being successful in college.

CHAPTER 4

EFFECTIVE COMMUNICATION STRATEGIES FOR YOU AND INTERACTING WITH OTHERS

RELATING TO OTHERS AND REGULATING EMOTIONS

CHAPTER PREVIEW

This chapter identifies effective strategies for communicating with and relating to others, as well as ways to understand and regulate our emotions—such as stress, anxiety, anger, and depression. Implementing the recommended strategies should improve the quality of your performance in college and your career, as well as enhance your overall quality of life.

PERFORMANCE OBJECTIVE

You will be able to implement strategies that will improve the quality of their academic and social performance.

THOUGHT STARTER

 Journal Reflection 4.1

When you think about someone being "intelligent," what personal characteristics come to mind?

_____

_____

_____

_____

_____

> " The most important single ingredient in the formula of success is knowing how to get along with people."
>
> —Theodore (Teddy) Roosevelt, 26th president of the United States and winner of the Nobel Peace Prize

If your answer to the preceding question focused on "intellectual" characteristics, your response reflected the traditional definition of intelligence. Human intelligence was once considered to be a general intellectual trait that could be measured by a single intelligence test score. Scholars have since discovered that the singular word "intelligence" needs to be replaced with the plural "intelligences" to reflect the fact that humans can and do display intelligence in many forms other than that measured by an IQ test. One of these other forms of human intelligence is referred to as *social intelligence* (a.k.a. "interpersonal intelligence"); it refers to the ability to communicate and relate effectively to others (Gardner 1993, 1999; Goleman 2006). It's been long known than interpersonal skills are essential for effective leadership (Avolio, Walumbwa, and Weber 2009), and more recent research indicates that social intelligence is a better predictor of personal and professional success than intellectual ability (Carneiro, Crawford, and Goodman 2006; Goleman 2006).

Another newly identified form of human intelligence is *emotional intelligence*—the ability to recognize our own emotions and the emotions of others, and behave in ways that have a positive impact on how others feel (Matthews, Zeidner, and Roberts 2007; Salovey and Mayer 1990). Research on emotional intelligence also reveals that it's a better predictor of personal and occupational success than performance on intellectual tests (Goleman 1995, 2000). Research also shows that emotional self-awareness—a key element of emotional intelligence—is a characteristic of effective leaders (Avolio and Luthans 2006; Goleman, Boyatzis, and McKee 2013).

THE IMPORTANCE OF SOCIAL RELATIONSHIPS AND SOCIAL INTELLIGENCE

Studies show that people with stronger social support networks are happier (Myers 1993, 2000) and live a longer life (Giles et al. 2005). The need to develop strong social support networks is particularly important in today's high-tech world of virtual reality and online (vs. in-person) communication, both of which make it easier to avoid face-to-face interaction with other people and increase the risk of social isolation and loneliness (Putman 2000).

 ### Journal Reflection 4.2

In your journal, draw the Circles of Support and indicate who you turn to when you are feeling low and in need of encouragement and cheering up. Are these the same people or different than those you identify for academic assistance?

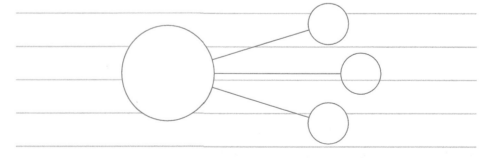

> " As a first-generation college student, it will be important to find ways to connect/share your life at school with those who love you. Some family wanted to be a part of this new adventure, but also fussed about me not visiting often. Overwhelmed, I was not clear how to navigate these two worlds. I remember the curiosity on my Abuelita's face, a woman with an eighth-grade education, when I explained the concepts from critical race theory and her enthusiasm as she sought to apply it to her factory union's complaints. The matriarch in my family and the woman who helped raise me—felt a part of my new life. Don't go at it alone.
>
> —*Professor (who was a first-generation college student)*

> " The Internet supposedly increases communication and brings humanity closer together. Instead, in my generation, I'm noticing quite the opposite. There seems to be less face-to-face communication. Everyone is hooked on social networking websites. We cowardly avoid interaction where there are no facial expressions or tones."
>
> —*First-year college student*

The quality of our social relationships rests heavily on two key skills:

- *interpersonal communication* skills—how well we communicate (verbally and nonverbally) when interacting with others, and
- *human relations* skills—how well we relate to and treat others (i.e., people skills).

Interpersonal Communication Skills

Listed below are strategies for strengthening interpersonal communication skills. Some of these strategies may seem very simple or obvious, but they are powerful. Perhaps it's because they're so simple that people simply overlook look them and forget to use them consistently. Don't be fooled by the seeming simplicity of the following suggestions and don't underestimate the positive impact they have on the quality of your interpersonal interactions and relationships.

It also is critical that one listens with empathy. Empathy relates to your ability to understand or relate to other people's positions and viewpoints (Bellet and Maloney 1991). It doesn't necessarily mean that you agree with that person, but that you do your best to understand where they are coming from and what they are trying to say. This can only be achieved by listening attentively and with an open mind.

1. **Take listening seriously.** When people hear the term "communication skills," the skills of speaking and writing usually come to mind. However, studies show that listening is the most frequently used communication skill; we spend more time listening than speaking, reading, and writing (Purdy and Borisoff 1996). Did you know that one study found that college students spend an average of 52.5% of their day listening? (Barker and Watson 2000). When people are asked to identify what they like most about their best friend, "a good listener" ranks among the top characteristics cited (Berndt 1992).

2. **Use active listening strategies.** We can listen to and understand spoken words at a rate four or more times faster than the average rate at which people speak (Barker and Watson 2000). This leaves plenty of time for our attention to drift and fall into the trap of *passive listening*—hearing the words with our ears, but not thinking about those words with our mind because our mind is somewhere else. To combat this tendency, we need to engage in *active listening*, which involves:

   - making the effort to focus full attention on the speaker's message (as opposed to just waiting for our turn to talk or thinking about what we're going to say next);
   - being an empathic listener who attends to the speaker's feelings and nonverbal messages;
   - being an engaged listener who checks for understanding, expresses interest, and encourages elaboration.

NOTE

In your journal, briefly describe an incident in which you did not listen as you should have when someone was confused and asking for advice. How did you respond?

"We have been given two ears and but a single mouth in order that we may hear more and talk less."

—Zeno of Citium, Ancient Greek philosopher and founder of Stoic philosophy

NOTE

When you listen actively and closely to others, it sends them the message that you respect them and their thoughts and feelings are worthy of receiving your undivided attention.

Active listening doesn't happen naturally; it's a skill developed through effort and practice that eventually becomes a regular habit. To develop the habit of active listening, engage in the following practices:

- While listening, monitor your understanding of what's being said. One way to check if you've followed the message is to occasionally summarize or paraphrase what you heard the speaker saying in your own words (e.g., "What I hear you saying is . . ."). This not only ensures you understand the message, it also sends the speaker the message that you're really listening to what's being said and taking it seriously.
- By sensing if a person is angry, hurt, or confused, you also get a notion of what your response might be. Not every conversation is about getting advice—sometimes it's about just having someone to talk to and sympathize.
- Check to be sure you're understanding what the person is *feeling* in addition to what the person is saying. Be sensitive to nonverbal messages, such as tone of voice and body language; they can often provide clues to the feelings behind the speaker's words. (For instance, speaking at a high rate and with high volume may indicate frustration or anger and speaking at a low rate and with low volume may indicate dejection or depression.)
- When you ask questions, allow the speaker time to formulate a thoughtful response. Be patient with some period of silence. If the silence continues, rephrase the question in a different way.
- Avoid the urge to interrupt the speaker when you think you have something important to say. Wait until the speaker has paused or completed her train of thought. Remember that the conversation, in this case, is not about you but about your friend or colleague.
- If the speaker pauses and you start to say something at the same time the speaker begins to speak again, don't overpower him by speaking louder; let him continue before you express your ideas.
- Be sure your nonverbal messages send the speaker the message that you're interested and non judgmental. (For positive, nonverbal communication signals to send while listening, see **Box 4.1**.)

BOX 4.1

Nonverbal Behaviors Associated with Active Listening in American Academic Settings

It's estimated that more than two-thirds of all human communication is nonverbal, and it's been found that nonverbal messages communicate stronger and truer messages than spoken language (Driver 2010; Navarro 2008). When there's inconsistency between an individual's verbal and nonverbal message (e.g., one shows interest, the other disinterest), we're more likely to perceive the nonverbal message as the true message (Ekman 2009).

Thus, "body language" may be the most powerful way a listener can communicate genuine interest in the speaker's message, as well as interest in and respect for the speaker. (Similarly, when we're speaking, awareness of our listeners' body language can provide us with important clues about whether we're holding or losing their interest.)

"The most important thing in communication is to hear what isn't being said."

—*Peter F. Drucker, Austrian author and founder of the study of "management"*

Good listeners listen with their whole body and they use body language to signal their attention and interest. The different body language signals we should send while listening may be summarized in the acronym SOFTEN:

S = Smile. Smiling sends signals of acceptance and interest. However, smiling should be periodic, not continuous. (A sustained smile can come across as an insincere or artificial pose.)

Sit Still. Fidgeting or squirming sends the message that you're bored or growing inpatient (and can't wait to move onto something else).

O = Open Posture. Avoid closed-posture positions, such as crossing your arms or folding your hands; they can send the message that you're not open to what the speaker is saying or passing judgment on what's being said.

F = Forward Lean. Leaning *forward* sends the message that you're looking forward to what the speaker is going to say next. In contrast, leaning back can send a signal that you're backing off from (losing interest in) what's being said, or that you're evaluating (psychoanalyzing).

Face the Speaker Directly. Line up your shoulders with the speaker's shoulders rather than turning one shoulder away—which sends the message that you want to get away or are giving the speaker the "cold shoulder."

T = Touch. An occasional light touch on the arm or hand can be a good way to communicate warmth—but not repeated touching, stroking, or rubbing—which could be interpreted as inappropriate intimacy (or sexual harassment).

E = Eye Contact. Lack of eye contact sends the message that you're looking around for something more interesting or stimulating than the speaker. However, eye contact shouldn't be continuous because that borders on staring or glaring. Instead, strike a happy medium by making *periodic* eye contact.

N = Nod Your Head. Nodding slowly and periodically while listening sends the signal that you're following what's being said and affirming the person saying it. However, avoid rapid and repeated head nodding; this sends the message that you want the speaker to hurry up and finish up so you can start talking!

Sources: Barker and Watson (2000); Nichols (2009); Purdy and Borisoff (1996)

An interesting exercise you can use to gain greater awareness of your nonverbal communication habits is to choose a couple of people whom you trust, and who know you well, and ask them to imitate your body language. This exercise can frequently be revealing (and sometimes very entertaining).

3. **Be open to listening to different conversational topics and viewpoints.** This is an issue of social etiquette and social ethics. It's also a learning issue because we learn the most from others whose interests and viewpoints don't duplicate our own. Thus, ignoring or blocking out information and ideas about topics that don't immediately interest you or support your particular perspective is not only a poor social skill, but also a poor learning strategy.

When others express ideas you don't agree with, you still owe them the courtesy of listening to what they have to say (and not immediately shaking your head, frowning, or interrupting them). After others finish expressing their point of view, you should then feel free to express your own. You certainly have the right to express your viewpoints, as long as you don't express them in such an opinionated way that it makes others feel their views weren't heard or welcomed.

4. **Communicate your ideas precisely and concisely.** When we speak, our goal should be to get to our point, make it, get "off stage," and give someone else a chance to talk. Nobody appreciates "stage hogs" who dominate the conversation and gobble up more than their fair share of conversation time.

   You can make your spoken messages less time-consuming and more to the point by avoiding tangents, unnecessary details, and empty fillers (e.g., "like," "kinda like," "I mean," "I'm all," and "you know").

5. **Take time to gather your thoughts before expressing them.** It's better to think silently *before* speaking aloud than to think aloud *while* talking. Giving forethought to what you're going to say will enable you to speak economically and open up more time for others to speak.

6. **Be comfortable with silent spells that may take place during conversations.** Silence can sometimes make us feel uncomfortable.

Silent spots in a conversation shouldn't always be viewed as a "communication breakdown." Instead, they may indicate that the people involved in the conversation are pausing to think deeply about what each other is saying and are comfortable enough with each other to allow these reflective pauses to take place.

 Journal Reflection 4.3

Revisit your journal entry (from above) concerning a peer or colleague that came to you for assistance or help. With new knowledge from this section, how would you adjust or change your response now?

_____

_____

_____

_____

_____

_____

> " We should be aware of the magic contained in a name. The name sets that individual apart; it makes him or her unique among all others. Remember that a person's name is to that person the sweetest and most important sound in any language."
>
> —*Dale Carnegie, author of the best-selling book, How to Win Friends and Influence People, and founder of The Dale Carnegie Course—a worldwide leadership training program for business professionals*

Human Relations Skills (a.k.a. "People Skills")

In addition to communicating well with others, another key component of social intelligence is *human relations* skills—how well we relate to and treat others. Listed below are specific strategies for strengthening human relations skills.

Learn and remember the names of people you meet. When you refer to a person by name, you affirm that person's individuality and unique identity. You've likely heard people say they just don't have a good memory for names, which implies that they will never be good at remembering names. However, the truth is that the ability to remember names is not some kind of natural talent or inherited ability that you either have or don't have. Instead, it's an acquired skill that's developed through intentional effort and effective use of memory improvement strategies, such as those described.

- Practice saying a person's name in the language and culture from where it originates. Encourage peers and colleagues to tell you the name they were born with and that they prefer, rather than an Americanized name.

- Pay close attention to the names of people you meet when you first meet them. The key first step to remembering someone's name is to actually hear it and get it into our brain. As obvious as this may seem, when we first meet someone, instead of listening actively and carefully for their name, we're often more focused on the first impression we're making on the person, or what we're going to say next. Consequently, when we *forget* someone's name, what really happened is that we didn't *get* the name (into our brain) in the first place because we were distracted by other thoughts.

- Strengthen your memory for the person's name by saying it soon after you first hear it. For instance, if your friend Gertrude has just introduced you to Geraldine, you might say: "Geraldine, how long have you known Gertrude?" When you recall a person's name shortly after you've heard it, you prevent memory loss at the time when it's most likely to occur—during the first minutes after information is taken into the brain. Using the person's name soon after you've heard it also serves to make that person feel welcomed and validated.

- Associate the person's name with other information you've learned or know about the person. For instance, you can associate the person's name with (a) your first topic of conversation, (b) some physical characteristic of the person, or (c) the place where you met. By making a mental connection between the person's name and another piece of information, you capitalize on the brain's natural tendency to store (retain) information as part of an interconnected network, rather than as isolated bits of information.

- Keep a name journal that includes the names of new people you meet, along with information about them (e.g., what they do and what their interests are). We write down things we don't want to forget to do, so why not do the same for the names of people we want to remember? Whenever you meet someone new, make note of that person's name by recording it in a name journal and accompany it with a short note of where you met and what you talked about.

Refer to people by name when you greet and interact with them. Once you've learned a person's name, use it when you interact with the person. By continuing to use people's names after you've learned them, you send the message you haven't forgotten who they are, and at the same time, you strengthen your memory of their names.

NOTE

Remembering names is not only a social skill that can bring you friends and improve your social life, it's also a powerful professional tool that can promote your career success in whatever field you choose to pursue.

❝ When I joined the bank, I started keeping a record of the people I met and put them on little cards, and I would indicate on the cards when I met them, and under what circumstances, and sometimes [make] a little notation which would help me remember a conversation."

—David Rockefeller, prominent American banker, philanthropist, and former CEO of the Chase Manhattan Bank

Remember information others share with you and refer to it when you interact with them. Ask people questions about their personal interests, plans, and experiences. Listen closely to their answers, especially to what seems most important to them, what they care about, or what interests them, and use this information in your future conversations with them. For one person that topic may be politics, for another it may be sports, for another it may be relationships.

When you see the person again, bring up something that was discussed in your last conversation. Get beyond the stock, generic questions that people routinely ask after they say "Hello" (e.g., "What's up? What's going on?"). Instead, ask about something specific you discussed with them last time you spoke (e.g., "How did you do on that math test last week?"). Our memories often reflect our priorities—we remember what's important to us. When you remember what others share with you, it shows them they're important to you.

Furthermore, when you show interest in others, you'll find that others start showing more interest in you. You're also likely to hear others say that you're a good listener and a great conversationalist.

Pay attention to the social and cultural cues on your campus. Some professors may be fine being called by their first name. Others may not. Always ask how peers and professors wish to be addressed. While references of respect like ma'am and sir may be acceptable in some cultural settings, be mindful that this is not gender inclusive. Try to use gender-neutral pronouns in your speech and refrain from guessing. Respect the name/identity that a person wants to be called/identified.

> "You can make more friends in 2 months by becoming interested in other people than you can in 2 years by trying to get other people interested in you."
>
> —*Dale Carnegie,* How to Win Friends and Influence People

STRATEGIES FOR MEETING PEOPLE AND FORMING FRIENDSHIPS

An important aspect of the college experience is meeting new people, learning from them, and forming lifelong friendships. Listed below are practical strategies for increasing the number and variety of people you meet and the quality of friendships you form.

> "I tend to have trouble meeting new people and I work a lot so I do not have much time. Through the class environment, having to work in groups, and participate in tutorials, I've met interesting people and some are close friends. We rely on each other when we are having a tough time and boost each other up. I don't have that support from family, so that has been really helpful for me.
>
> —*Third-year student*

1. **Place yourself in situations and locations where you will come in regular contact with others.** Physical proximity is the first step in the process of forming friendships—that is, people are more likely to become friends if they continue to find themselves in the same place at the same time (Latané et al. 1995). You can apply this principle by spending as much time on campus as possible and spending time in places where others are likely to be present (e.g., by eating your meals in the student cafeteria and studying in the college library). If you have the opportunity to live on campus, do so, because studies show that it helps students make social connections and increases their satisfaction with the college experience (Pascarella and Terenzini 2005; Tinto 2012). If you're a commuter student, make your college experience as similar as possible to that of a residential student. When your schedule permits, spend time on campus doing things other than attending class (e.g., study in the library and participate in campus events).

Journal Reflection 4.4

In an earlier journal entry, you were asked to identify a club or an activity that you might consider joining. Did you identify a club or an activity? Did you attend or join? Why or why not?

_____

_____

_____

_____

_____

2. **Put yourself in social situations where you're likely to meet people who share your interests, goals, and values.** People tend to form friendships with others who share similar interests, values, or goals (AhYun 2002). Friendships are more likely to form among people who have interests and values in common because they're more likely to spend time together doing things relating to their shared interests, and because they're more likely to validate each other's shared values (Festinger 1954; Suls, Martin, and Wheeler 2002).

    One straightforward way to find others with whom you have something in common is by participating in campus clubs and organizations that reflect your interests and values. (If you can't find one, start one of your own.) In addition, keep track of social events that are likely to attract others who share your interests, values, or goals by regularly checking your college newspaper, posted flyers on campus, and the Student Information Desk in your Student Activities Center. Be mindful of your time and commitments. Be careful not to overcommit or to engage in groups that might compromise your integrity or conflict with your core values.

> "Open your arms to change, but don't let go of your values."
> —*Dalai Lama, the current Dalai Lama, Tibetan Buddhist guru*

> "I'm genuine. I don't change depending on who I'm around."
> —*AHE Sophomore*

Dealing with Peer Pressure

Peer pressure can be very helpful in enjoying your college experience. Friends often encourage a person to try something new or join in an activity you might miss otherwise. But it takes good judgment on your part to know when you're being pressured to something that will deter you from succeeding in meeting your goals.

Good friends do not encourage someone to make bad choices. Always keep your required time and financial commitments—classes, exams, incidental expenses—in mind. If you need to study and a friend asks you to accompany him to a social event, explain why you have to decline. If they persist, suggest getting together at another time so they will know it isn't personal, it's just that something else is a priority at the moment. If they still persist, gently suggest they may not be listening carefully to your response!

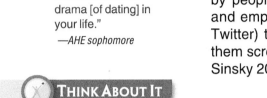

> " It's hard enough to have fun here with all the work you have to do. There's no reason to have the extra drama [of dating] in your life."
>
> —AHE sophomore

THINK ABOUT IT

Remember your social media life can negatively impact your daily life! Be cautious and smart!

3. **Meet others through social websites.** Facebook and other social websites represent an additional way to meet new people, join groups on campus, and check for announcements of parties or other social events. However, the people you respond to, the screen name you use and the messages you post on your page or 'wall' are public. Don't forget that cyberspace is public space, and it can be accessed by people beyond your social circle. For instance, some schools and employers review social networking sites (e.g., Facebook and Twitter) to check entries; they use the information they find to help them screen prospects and accept or reject applicants (Palank 2006; Sinsky 2011).

DATING AND ROMANTIC RELATIONSHIPS

Most people enjoy dating while they are in college. You may find that you have friends of both sexes, and you may "date" some of them casually, as in "Say if you're free on tomorrow night, let's go to the movie at the Ritz." Sometimes, a casual relationship can turn serious as you gain more insights into a person. Other times, you may date a person you're really interested in and hope to develop a serious romantic relationship.

Traditionally, romantic relationships begin through the process of dating. College students take different approaches to dating, ranging from not dating at all to dating with the intent of exploring or cementing long-term relationships.

Romantic Relationships

Dating relationships may eventually evolve into romantic relationships. Research on romantic relationships reveals they typically progress through the following stages (Bassham et al. 2013; Ruggiero 2011).

Stage 1. Passionate Love (Infatuation)

This is the very first stage of a romantic relationship, and it's characterized by the following features.

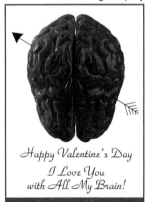

©MarkusManson/Shutterstock. com, compilation ©Kendall Hunt Publishing Company

Happy Valentine's Day I Love You with All My Brain!

Despite expressions like "I love you with all my heart," romantic love takes place in the human brain and is accompanied by major changes in the production of brain chemicals.

- *Erotic* love: relationship involves intense physical arousal and passion; attention is focused primarily on the partner's physical appearance and physical attraction between the partners is at a peak.
- *Impulsivity*: partners can quickly "fall into" love or be suddenly "swept off their feet" (e.g., "love at first sight").
- *Obsession*: partners can't stop thinking about each other (they're "madly in love").
- *Idealism*: The partners perceive each other and the relationship as being "perfect." They may say things like: "We're made for each other." "Nobody else has a relationship like ours." "We'll be together forever." Such idealistic thinking can make love "blind"—the partner's flaws and weaknesses are not seen (although they may be obvious to those outside of the relationship).
- *Attachment and Dependency*: The lovers feel insecure without each other and can't bear being separated (e.g., "I can't live without him"). As a result of such attachment and dependency, love at this stage

follows the principle: "I love you because I am loved" and "I love you because I need you."

- *Possessiveness and Jealousy*: Each lover feels that he or she has exclusive rights to the partner and may quickly become suspicious about the partner's fidelity, as well as jealous of anyone else who interacts with the partner in a friendly or affectionate manner.
- *Love Sickness*: If the relationship breaks up, intense depression or "love withdrawal" tends to follow the breakup, similar to withdrawal from a pleasure-producing drug. Studies show that the most common cause of despair or depression among college students is a romantic breakup (Foreman 2009).

Stage 2. Mature Love

The partners gradually "fall out" of first-stage (puppy) love and progress or "fall into" a more mature (advanced) stage of love that has the following characteristics.

- The partners become less selfish and self-centered and more selfless and other-centered. Love is no longer just a noun—an emotion or feeling within the person (e.g., "I'm in love"), but also an action verb—a way in which the partners act toward each other and treat one another (e.g., "we love each other"). More emphasis is placed on caring for the partner, rather than being cared for.
- The intense emotional "ups and downs" of early-stage love are now replaced by feelings of emotional serenity (mellowness) and evenness—a less extreme, but more consistently pleasant emotional-state characterized by slightly elevated levels of different brain chemicals (endorphins, rather than dopamine). Unlike infatuation or early-stage love, this pleasant emotional state does not decline with time; in fact, it may actually grow stronger as the relationship continues and matures (Bartels and Zeki 2000).
- Physical passion decreases. The "flames of the flesh" don't burn as intensely as in first-stage love, but a romantic afterglow continues. This afterglow is characterized by more emotional intimacy or psychological closeness between the partners and greater self-disclosure, mutual trust, and interpersonal honesty—all of which enhance both the physical and psychological quality of the relationship (Viorst 1998).
- Interest is now focused on the partner as a whole person, not just on the partner's physical qualities. The partners have a less idealistic, more realistic view of one another in which they recognize and accept each other's strengths and weaknesses. The partners genuinely like one another as persons (not just as lovers) and consider the other to be their "best" or "closest" friend.
- The partners have mutual trust and confidence in each other's commitment; they aren't plagued by feelings of suspicion, distrust, or petty jealousy. Each partner may have interests and close friends outside the relationship without the other becoming jealous (Hatfield and Rapson 1993, 2000).
- The partners have mutual concern for each other's growth and fulfillment. Rather than being envious or competitive, they take joy in each other's personal successes and accomplishments.

> I learned love and I learned you. I learned that, in order to love someone, you must be blind to the physical and the past. You must see their emotional and mental strengths and weaknesses, passions and dislikes, hobbies and pastimes."
>
> —*Letter written by first-year student*

- The relationship contains a balanced blend of independence and interdependence—is referred to as the "paradox (contradiction) of love"—because both partners maintain their independence and individuality yet feel more complete and fulfilled when they're together. The partners maintain their sense of personal identity and self-worth, but they're together, their respective identities become more complete.

NOTE

Relationships can become unhealthy and pose threats to our physical or psychological well-being. If you're in a relationship where you feel you're being repeatedly disrespected, excessively controlled, or are concerned for your safety, it's essential that you acknowledge and act upon these signals.

UNHEALTHY RELATIONSHIPS

Relationship abuse—whether emotional, psychological, physical, or sexual—is another threat to wellness and should *never* be tolerated. If you're in such a situation, or you have a friend who is, it's essential to address the issue immediately.

Sometimes the victims and offenders of relationship abuse don't recognize that they are, in fact, involved in an abusive relationship. Behaviors that characterize relationship violence include, but are not limited to, degrading language, dominating or dictating a partner's actions, as well as physical and/or sexual assault (Murray and Kardatzke 2007). Without such recognition, victims and perpetrators are likely to remain in their current relationship or continue to get involved in such relationships in the future (Miller 2011).

Unfortunately, the prevalence of relationship abuse is high among college-aged women and men. Studies show that 13%–42% of college students have been involved in relationships where they were the victims or perpetrators of physical abuse (Luthra and Gidycz 2006; Miller 2011). In another study, 88% of females and 81% of males reported being in relationships where they were either the victim or perpetrator of psychological (emotional) abuse (White and Koss 1991). It's important to note that relationship violence occurs among college students of all races, ethnicities, and socioeconomic groups (Malik, Sorenson, and Aneshensel 1997). Comparable levels of relationship violence have also been found among victims and perpetrators who are gay, bisexual, or straight (Freedner et al. 2002). Taken together, these data highlight the unfortunate fact that relationship abuse is all too common among college students and needs to be detected and addressed early in relationships—before it escalates to more violent levels.

Victims of relationship abuse are often reluctant to seek help because they fear embarrassment or retribution. If you find yourself in a violent relationship, it is important that you tell someone what's going on and get support. Don't let fear immobilize you. Talking to a trusted friend who has your health and safety in mind is a good place to start. Connecting with your college's counseling center is especially helpful because you can get professional assistance. Campus counseling centers are often staffed with professionals who have experience working with victims and perpetrators of relationship abuse, or they can refer you to professionals who do. See **Box 4.2** for a summary of the major types of relationship abuse and violence.

BOX 4.2

Sexual Abuse and Violence

Listed below are various forms of relationship abuse and violence. Note that these examples are not just physical or sexual in nature—emotional and psychological violence can be just as harmful to victims.

Sexual Harassment

Sexual harassment in college settings includes any unwanted or unwelcome sexual behavior initiated by another student or an employee of the college that interferes with one's education. Sexual harassment can take the following forms:

1. Verbal—such as, making sexual comments about someone's body or clothes; sexual jokes; or teasing— including spreading sexual rumors about a person's sexual activity or orientation; requesting sexual favors in exchange for a better grade, job, or promotion
2. Nonverbal—such as, staring or glaring at someone's body; making erotic or obscene gestures toward the person; sending obscene messages or unsolicited pornographic material
3. Physical—such as, contact by touching, grabbing, pinching, or brushing up against someone's body.

Recommendations for Dealing with Sexual Harassment:

- Make your objections clear and firm. Tell the harasser directly that you're offended by the unwanted behavior and that you know it constitutes sexual harassment.
- Keep a written record of any harassment. Record the date, place, and specific details about the harassing behavior.
- Become aware of the sexual harassment policy at your school. (Your school's policy is likely to be found in the *Student Handbook* or may be available from the Office of Human Resources.)
- If you're unsure about whether you're experiencing sexual harassment, or what to do about it, seek help from the Counseling Center or Office of Human Resources.
- Report it!

Note: Sexual harassment is one form of *peer harassment*, which is a broader category of harassment that includes taunting, bullying (in person or online), as well as harassment based on race or sexual orientation. All these behaviors violate the law, which guarantees all students the right to a learning environment that's conducive to learning. If you experience any of these forms of harassment, don't tolerate them silently, report them to school authorities.

NOTE

Title IX of the Education Amendment of 1972 is a federal civil rights law that prohibits discrimination on the basis of sex, which includes sexual harass-ment, rape, and sexual assault. A college or university may be held legally responsible when it knows about and ignores sexual harassment or assault in its programs or activities, whether the harassment is committed by a faculty member, staff member, or student. If you have been sexually harassed and believe that your campus has not responded effectively to your concern, you can contact or file a complaint with the Department of Education's Office of Civil Rights (http://www2. ed.gov/about/offices/list/ocr/docs/howto.html).

Abusive Relationships

An abusive relationship may be defined as a relation-ship in which one partner abuses the other—physically, verbally, or emotionally. Abusers are often dependent on their partners for their sense of self-worth; they commonly have low self-esteem and fear their partner will abandon them, so they attempt to prevent this abandonment by over controlling their partner. Frequently, abusers feel powerless or weak in other areas of their lives and overcompensate by attempting to gain power and personal strength by exerting power over their partner.

Potential Signs of Abuse:

- The abuser is possessive and tries to dominate or control all aspects of the partner's life (e.g., discour-ages the partner from having contact with friends or family members)

(continued)

BOX 4.2 *(continued)*

- The abuser frequently yells, shouts, intimidates, or makes physical threats toward the partner
- The abuser constantly puts down the partner and attempts to damage the partner's self-esteem
- The abuser displays intense and irrational jealousy (e.g., accusing the partner of infidelity without evidence)
- The abuser demands affection or sex when the partner is not interested or willing
- The abuser often appears charming to others in public settings, but is abusive toward the partner in private
- The abused partner behaves differently and is more inhibited when the abuser is around
- The abused partner fears the abuser.

Strategies for Avoiding or Escaping Abusive Relationships:

- Avoid relationship isolation; continue to maintain social ties with friends outside of the relationship.
- Don't make excuses for or rationalize the abuser's behavior (e.g., he was under stress or she was drinking)
- Get an objective, "third party" perspective by asking close friends for their views on your relationship. (Love can be "blind," so it's possible to be in denial about an abusive relationship and not "see" what's really going on.)
- Speak with a professional counselor on campus to help you see your relationships more objectively and for help with any relationship that you sense is becoming abusive.

Sexual Assault a.k.a. Sexual Violence

Sexual assault is an umbrella term used to describe a wide range of forced and/or unwanted sexual activity. This activity could include contact such as kissing, exhibitionism, groping, and rape. Victims might be coerced into sexual acts through verbal or nonverbal threats or through the use of substances, such as alcohol or drugs. Sexual assault doesn't always involve physical contact—acts such as voyeurism and exhibitionism can still count as unwanted sexual attention. Sexual assault refers to nonconsensual (unwanted or unwilling) sexual contact, which includes rape, attempted rape, and any

other type of sexual contact that a person forces on another without consent. *Rape* is a form of sexual assault or sexual violence that involves forced sexual penetration (intercourse), which takes place through physical force, by threat of bodily harm, or when the victim is incapable of giving consent due to alcohol or drug intoxication. Rape can be classified into two major categories:

1. Stranger Rape—when a total stranger forces sexual intercourse on the victim.
2. Acquaintance Rape or Date Rape—when the victim knows, or is dating, the person who forces unwanted sexual intercourse.

It's estimated that about 85% of reported rapes are committed by an acquaintance. Alcohol is frequently associated with acquaintance rapes because it lowers the rapist's inhibitions and reduces the victim's ability to judge whether it's a potentially dangerous situation. Since the partners are familiar with each other, the victim may feel that what happened was not sexual assault. However, here's the bottom line: Acquaintance rape *is* rape and it's still a crime because it involves nonconsensual sex.

Physical violence occurs in 11%–12% of same-gender couples. Incidents of violence happen at the same rate in same-gender couples and cross-gender couples. However, research suggests that the violence appears to be milder in same-gender couples. Research went on to conclude it is unclear how much of the violence should be classified as abuse and how much should be classified as "intimate terrorism." "Intimate terrorism" refers to physical and psychological violence that is used to dominate, control, intimidate, and degrade a partner (Johnson and Ferraro 2000; Rohrbaugh 2006).

Recommendations for Women to Reduce the Risk of Experiencing Sexual Assault:

- Don't drink to excess or associate with others who do.
- If you drink, or go to places where others drink, remain aware of the possibility of date rape

drugs being dropped into your drink. To guard against this risk, don't let others give you drinks, and hold onto your drink at all times (e.g., don't leave it, go to the restroom, and come back to drink it again).

- When you attend parties, go with friends so you can keep an eye out for one another.
- Clearly and assertively communicate what your sexual limits are. Use "I messages" to firmly resist unwanted sexual advances by rejecting the behavior rather than the person (e.g., "I'm not comfortable with your touching me like that").
- Carry mace or pepper spray and be prepared to use it if necessary.
- Take a self-defense class. Studies show that courses in resisting sexual assault reduce the risk of rape by almost 50% (Senn et al. 2015).

Recommendations for Men for Reducing the Risk of Committing Sexual Assault:

- Don't assume a woman wants to have sex just because she's:
  - (a) very friendly or flirtatious,
  - (b) dressed in a provocative way, or
  - (c) drinking alcohol.

- If a woman says "no," don't interpret that to mean she's really saying "yes."
- Don't think that just because you're "the man," you have to be the sexual initiator or aggressor.
- Interpret rejection of sexual advances by a woman to mean that woman just doesn't want to have sex. Don't take it as a personal insult or blow to your masculinity.

Sources: Karjane, and Cullen (2002, 2005); National Center for Victims of Crime (2012); Ottens and Hotelling (2001); Penfold (2006)

Journal Reflection 4.5

Have you ever known anyone who was involved in an abusive relationship?

In what way(s) was it abusive?

How did the abused partner handle it?

MANAGING INTERPERSONAL CONFLICT

Disagreement and conflict among people are inevitable aspects of social life. Research shows that even the most happily married couples don't experience perpetual marital bliss; they have occasional disagreements and discord (Gottman 1994, 1999).

Interpersonal conflict is something we can't expect to escape or eliminate; the best we can do is defuse it, contain it, and prevent it from reaching unmanageable levels. The interpersonal communication and human relations skills already discussed in this chapter can help minimize conflicts. In addition to these general social skills, the following set of specific strategies may be used to handle interpersonal conflicts constructively and compassionately.

1. **Approach the conflict with the attitude you're going to solve a problem, not win an argument.** Don't approach conflict with the attitude that you're going to get even or prove you're right. Winning the argument but not persuading the person to change the behavior that's causing the conflict is like winning a battle and losing the war. Instead, approach conflict resolution in a way that allows both parties to win—both of you can end up with a better relationship in the long run.

2. **Pick a private place and time to resolve the conflict.** Don't discuss the issue while others are present. Criticizing someone in the presence of others is akin to a public stoning; it's likely to cause resentment and intensify the conflict.

3. **Decompress emotionally before you express yourself verbally.** Sensitive issues shouldn't be discussed during a fit of anger (Daniels and Horowitz 1997). Your objective should be to solve the problem and resolve the conflict, not release your emotions. Taking the time to reflect, weigh your words, and respond in a mellow manner also communicates to the other person that you've given serious consideration to the matter and are not just storming in and firing away like a "loose cannon."

4. **Give the person a chance to respond.** Just because you're angry doesn't mean the person you're angry with must forfeit all rights to free speech and self-defense. By giving the other person a fair chance to be heard, you increase the likelihood that you'll receive a cooperative response. Don't jump the gun and pull the trigger before hearing the other side of the story and getting all the facts straight.

   After listening to the other person's response, check your understanding by summarizing it in your own words (e.g., "What I hear you saying is . . ."). This is an important step in the conflict-resolution process because conflicts often stem from a simple misunderstanding or failure to communicate. Sometimes just taking time to hear each other's side of the story can go a long way toward resolving the conflict.

5. **Acknowledge the person's perspectives and feelings.** After hearing the person's response, if you disagree with it, don't dismiss or discount the person's feelings. Avoid saying things like, "That's ridiculous!" or "That's no excuse!" Instead, acknowledge the persons' response by saying, "I can understand what you were thinking" or "I see how you might feel that way." Then follow by expressing how you believe your complaint is still justified.

NOTE

Things are better left unsaid until you find the right time and place to say them.

"Seek first to understand, then to be understood."

—*Stephen Covey, international best-selling author of* Seven Habits of Highly Effective People

6. **If things begin to get nasty, call for a time-out or cease-fire and postpone the discussion to allow both of you time to cool off.** When emotions and adrenaline run high, logic and reason tend to run low. This can result in one person saying something during a fit of anger that triggers an angry response from the other person; then the anger of both combatants continues to escalate until it turns into a blow-by-blow volley of verbal punches and counterpunches. An emotionally heated conversation may end up going something like this:

Person A: "You're way out of control."
Person B: "I'm not out of control; *you're* the one that's overreacting."
Person A: "*I'm* overreacting? You're the one who's acting like a jerk!"
Person B: "I may be *acting* like a jerk, but you're a real jerk!"

Blow-by-blow exchanges such as these are likely to turn up the emotional heat to a level so high that resolving the conflict takes a back seat to winning the fight. Both boxers need to back off, retreat to their respective corners, and try again later when neither is about to throw a knockout punch.

7. **Avoid absolute judgments or blanket statements.** Compare the following three pairs of statements:

(a) "You're no help at all." versus "You don't help me enough."
(b) "You never try to understand how I feel." versus "You don't try hard enough to understand how I feel."
(c) "I always have to clean up." versus "I'm doing more than my fair share of the cleaning."

The first statement in each of the preceding pairs represents an absolute statement that covers all times, situations, and circumstances. Such extreme, blanket criticisms send the message that the person is doing nothing right with respect to the issue in question. The second statement in each of the above pairs phrases the criticism in terms of degree or amount—the person is doing something right, but needs to do more of it—which is likely to be less threatening or humiliating (and probably closer to the truth).

8. **Conclude your discussion of the conflict on a warm, constructive note.** End it by ensuring that there are no hard feelings, and by letting the person know you're optimistic that the conflict can be resolved and your relationship strengthened.

9. **If the person makes a change in response to your request, express your appreciation.** Even if your complaint was legitimate and your request justified, the person's effort to accommodate your request shouldn't be taken for granted. (The last thing you want to say is something like: "That's more like it" or "It's about time!")

Expressing appreciation to the other person for making a change is not only a socially sensitive thing to do, it's also a self-serving thing to do. By recognizing and reinforcing the other person's changed behavior, you increase the likelihood that the positive change in behavior will continue and you'll continue to benefit from the change.

> To keep your marriage brimming with love . . . when you're wrong, admit it; when you're right, shut up."
> —Ogden Nash, American poet

NOTE ✗

After you have reached a solution, invite the person to go for coffee or for a walk, so both of you will have a positive memory of the exchange.

NOTE ✗

When dealing with interpersonal conflict, the goal should be reconciliation not retaliation.

❝

✗ *Don't find fault. Find a remedy."*

—*Henry Ford, founder of Ford Motor Company and one of the most widely admired people of the 20th century*

How Do I Make My Point?

You may have encountered people in the past who try to make a point but somehow don't quite do it. In many cases, these people are behaving in one of three ways. They may be:

1. Passive: weakly making a case for their point of view, possibly apologizing for feeling the way they do.
2. Aggressive: trying to assert their rights while diminishing yours. They may end trying to humiliate or bully you into accepting their viewpoints.
3. Passive aggressive people probably won't put up a fuss to express themselves, but they are passively aggressive—sulking or acting coldly. They may appear passive at first, because they seem to accede to your wishes. Their following behavior is hostile without being overtly aggressive.

There are much better ways to express your opinions without offending people. The following suggestions will help you to state your case in a calm and an assertive manner.

- **Focus on the *behavior* causing the conflict, not the person.** Avoid labeling the person as "selfish," "mean," or "inconsiderate." If you're upset because your roommate doesn't do his share of cleaning, stay away from aggressive labels such as "slob" or "slacker." This puts the person on the defensive and is likely to launch a counteroffensive assault on your personal flaws.

  Rather than focusing on the person's general character, focus on the specific action or behavior that's causing the problem (e.g., failing to do the dishes or leaving dirty laundry around the room). This lets the other person know exactly what behavior needs to be changed to resolve the conflict. It's much easier to change a specific behavior than it is to change a person's entire character or personality.

- **Use "I" messages that focus on how the other person's behavior affects you.** "I" messages are less aggressive because you're targeting the issue and how it's affecting you, not the other person (McKay, Davis, and Fanning 2009). By saying: "I feel angry when . . ." rather than "You make me angry when . . . ," you send the message that you're taking responsibility for the way you feel rather than guilt-tripping the person for making you feel that way. In contrast, "you" messages are more likely to launch the person on a counter offensive in an attempt to retaliate rather than cooperate (Bippus and Young 2005).

  Here are some specific tips for getting maximum mileage out of "I" messages.

  (a) Be *specific* about what *emotion* you're experiencing. Saying, "I feel neglected when you don't write or call" identifies what you're feeling more specifically than saying, "I wish you'd be more considerate." Describing what you feel in specific terms increases the persuasive power of your message and reduces the risk that the other person will misunderstand or discount it.

(b) Communicate what you want the other person to do in the form of a firm *request* rather than a demand or ultimatum. Saying, "I would like you to . . ." is less likely to put the person on the defensive than saying, "I insist . . ." or "I demand . . ."

(c) Be *specific* about what you want the person to *do* to resolve the conflict. Saying, "I would like for you to call me at least once a day" is more specific than saying, "I want you to keep in touch with me."

 Journal Reflection 4.6

You're working on a group project and your teammates aren't carrying their weight. You're getting frustrated and angry because you're doing almost all of the work yourself.

Construct an "I" message that communicates your concern to your teammates in an assertive, nonthreatening way.

_____

_____

_____

_____

_____

EMOTIONAL INTELLIGENCE

Excelling in college is a challenging task that will test your emotional strength and your ability to persist to task completion (graduation). Research indicates that college students who score higher on tests of emotional intelligence, such as the ability to identify their emotions and moods, are better able to focus their attention and stay absorbed ("in the zone") when completing challenging tasks and less likely to become frustrated or bored (Harris 2006; Wiederman 2007).

In one study involving nearly 4,000 first-year college students, it was found that students' level of optimism or hope for success during their first term on campus was a more accurate predictor of their first-year grades than was their SAT score or high school grade point average (Snyder et al. 1991). In contrast, negative emotions—such as anxiety and fear—can interfere with the brain's ability to (a) store and retrieve memories, and (b) engage in higher-level thinking (Caine and Caine 1994; Hertel and Brozovich 2010).

Discussed below are research-based strategies for minimizing negative emotions that sabotage success and maximizing positive emotions that promote success.

The "fight-or-flight" reaction occurs when we're under stress because it's a throwback to the time when ancient humans needed to fight with or flee from potential predators. Unlike that of other animals, our hair doesn't rise up and appear more intimidating to foes (but we still get "goosebumps" when we're nervous, and we still refer to scary events as "hair-raising" experiences).

Stress and Anxiety

One of the most common emotions we must monitor and manage is stress. Students report experiencing higher levels of stress in college than they did in high school (Bartlett 2002; Sax 2003).

But what exactly is stress? Stress has its roots in the "fight-or-flight" response—an automatic physical reaction wired into the body that enabled our human ancestors to engage in fight (attack) or flight (run away) when confronted by life-threatening predators. This suggests that stress isn't necessarily bad; in the right amount, it can actually be productive. For instance, a tightened guitar string generates better sound than a string that's too lax or loose, a tightened bow delivers a more powerful arrow shot, and a tightened muscle provides more strength or speed.

Keep in mind that stress can work for you as well as against you; it can either energize or sabotage your performance, depending on its level of intensity and the length of time it continues. Don't expect to stop or eliminate stress completely, nor should you want to; your goal should be to contain it and maintain it at a level where it's more productive than obstructive or destructive. Many years of research indicate that peak performance (mental and physical) is attained under conditions of *moderate* stress. (See **Figure 4.1.**) At an intermediate level, stress can enhance energy, attention, and motivation (Halvorson 2010; Sapolsky 2004).

FIGURE 4.1: Relationship between Arousal and Performance

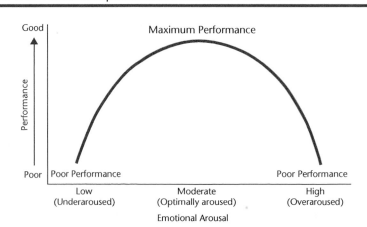

Moderate challenge that produces moderate stress typically promotes maximum (peak) performance.

Source: Williams, Landers, & Boutcher (1993).

Journal Reflection 4.7

Helping Trio: Complete a quickwrite that describes what you've found most stressful about being in college. In a group of three, share your quickwrite with others in your group and note down their suggestions that might help relieve the stress. Continue until everyone has provided both their quickwrite and their recommendations.

However, if stress becomes intense, excessive, and persistent, it now may be defined as *anxiety* (Mayo Clinic 2015a). Studies also show that students who experience high levels of academic stress and performance anxiety are more likely to use ineffective, "surface" approaches to learning that rely on memorization rather than effective, deep-learning strategies—such as reflection and seeking meaning (Biggs and Tang 2011; Ramsden 2003). Anxiety can interfere with mental performance on exams because anxious feelings and thoughts begin to preoccupy our mind, taking up valuable space in our limited attention span, leaving less room to process test information and engage in memory retrieval (Fernández-Castillo and Caurcel 2014).

Anxiety experienced over an extended period of time can also suppress the immune system, leaving us more vulnerable to flu, colds, and other infectious diseases. Studies show that the immune system of college students is suppressed (produces fewer antibodies) at very stressful times during the academic term—such as midterms and finals (Bosch et al. 2004; Deinzer et al. 2000).

Box 4.4 provides a summary of the signs or symptoms of anxiety. If these symptoms are experienced for more than a week, help should be sought to reduce them.

NOTE

Remember to visit your counseling center if you are feeling anxious or stressed.

 Journal Reflection 4.8

How would you rate your level of anxiety in the following situations?

1. Taking tests or exams   high moderate   low
2. Interacting in social situations   high moderate   low
3. Making decisions about the future   high moderate   low

Why did you rate them this way?

Box 4.3

Posttraumatic Stress Disorder: A Distinctive Form of Stress and Anxiety

Posttraumatic stress disorder (PTSD) is an anxiety disorder that arises after someone experiences a traumatic (dangerous or life-threatening) event, such as combat or sexual assault. It's natural to experience feelings of anxiety after such events, and the symptoms may last for weeks. However, if these feelings of anxiety do not gradually decline but remain or intensify over time and continue to interfere with the person's ability to carry out daily tasks, the person may be experiencing PTSD.

Symptoms of PTSD include the following:

- Constantly feeling tense or "on edge"
- Finding it difficult to concentrate
- Being easily startled
- Having difficulty sleeping

- Experiencing emotional numbness
- Having sudden outbursts of anger
- Blocking memories of the traumatic experience and events around the time of the experience
- Having flashbacks—reliving the trauma repeatedly and experiencing frightening thoughts and physical symptoms (e.g., a racing heart or sweating) that may occur spontaneously or be triggered by sights, sounds, or dreams that serve as reminders of the original traumatic experience
- Avoiding places, events, or objects that are reminders of the traumatic experience

If the preceding symptoms are occurring three or more months after a traumatic event, professional help should be sought. A good place to start would be the Counseling Center on campus or the PTSD Information Line at (802) 296-6300 (e-mail: ncptsd@va.gov).

Source: National Institute of Mental Health (2009).

> "My stress has caused me to lose a lot of weight; my appetite is cut in half. My sleep pattern is off; I have trouble falling/staying asleep. No matter how stressed I was in high school, this never happened [before]. What can I do to de-stress?"
>
> —*First-term college student*

Effective Methods for Managing Stress

If you perceive your level of stress reaching a point where it's beginning to interfere with the quality of your academic performance or your personal life, here are three key stress management methods that are well-supported by research in psychology and biology (Benson and Proctor 2011; Lehrer et al. 2007).

1. Deep (Diaphragmatic) Breathing

When people are experiencing excessive stress, their breathing pattern becomes fast, shallow, and irregular; they breathe through the mouth rather than the chest. Breathing associated with relaxation is just the opposite—slow, deep (from the diaphragm), and regular breathing that originates from the stomach.

In fact, studies show that when we slow down our breathing rate, other systems of our body slow down—for example, our heart rate and blood pressure drop (Benson and Proctor 2011).

2. Progressive Muscle Relaxation

Similar to stretching exercises to relax and loosen muscles before and after physical exercise, total body (head-to-toe) muscle relaxation can be achieved by progressively tensing and releasing the five sets of muscles listed below. Hold tension in each muscle area for about five seconds and then release slowly.

1. Wrinkle your forehead muscles and then release them.
2. Shrug your shoulders up as if to touch your ears and then drop them.
3. Make a tight fist with both hands and then open them.
4. Tighten your stomach muscles and then release them.
5. Tighten your toes by curling them under your feet and then raise them as high as you can.

> To relax, I like to stretch a lot."
> —*First-year college student*

When relaxing your muscles, take a deep breath and think or say: "Relax." By breathing deeply and thinking or hearing the word "relax" each time you release your muscles, the sound of the word "relax" becomes associated with your muscles being relaxed. When you find yourself in a stressful situation, take a deep breath and think or say the word "relax"; your stress level will drop because your muscles have been conditioned to relax in response to that word.

3. Mental Imagery

You can also reduce stress by *imagining* yourself in a calm, comfortable, and relaxing setting. Visualize images such as ocean waves, floating clouds, sitting in a warm sauna, or any sensory experience that tends to relax you. Try to use all of your senses—see it, hear it, smell it, touch it, and feel it. You can also create imaginary calming music in your head to accompany the visual image. The more senses you use, the more real the scene will seem and the more powerful its relaxing effects will be (Fezler 1989).

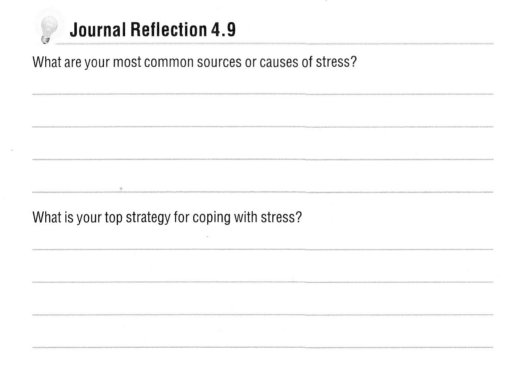

Journal Reflection 4.9

What are your most common sources or causes of stress?

_____

_____

_____

_____

What is your top strategy for coping with stress?

_____

_____

_____

_____

Would you say that you cope with stress well?

_____

_____

_____

_____

Simple Stress-Reduction Strategies and Habits

In addition to the formal stress-management techniques of diaphragmatic breathing, progressive muscle relaxation, and mental imagery, stress may be managed by simpler strategies and habits, such as those discussed below.

1. **Exercise.** Exercise reduces stress by increasing release of serotonin—a mellowing brain chemical that reduces feelings of tension (anxiety) and depression. Studies show that people who exercise regularly tend to report feeling happier (Myers 1993).

2. **Journaling.** Writing about our feelings in a personal journal helps us identify and express the emotions we're experiencing (a form of emotional intelligence), and provides us with a safe outlet for releasing stress (Seaward 2011). Writing about our emotions also reduces the risk that we'll deny or repress them—(push them out of conscious awareness).

3. **Substitute positive thoughts for negative thoughts.** Research indicates that the part of the human brain involved in thinking (the cortex) has many connections to the part of the brain responsible for emotions (the limbic system) (Goleman 1995; Zull 2002). Thus, our brain is wired in such a way that our thinking can directly influence our feelings. If thoughts influence emotions, then changing the way we think can change the emotions we experience, including our feelings of stress and anxiety.

    One of the keys to substituting positive for negative thoughts is to think about what you want to happen, not what you're afraid is going to happen (Halvorson 2010). If you're a pitcher in a baseball game and you start thinking you're going to walk a batter, stop thinking about whether you're going to throw balls and start thinking about throwing strikes. Similarly, if you're taking a test, stop thinking (and worrying) about losing points and start thinking (and focusing) on earning points. This will reduce your level of test anxiety.

4. **Take time for humor and laughter.** Research on the benefits of humor for reducing tension is clear and convincing. In one study, college students were suddenly told they had to give an impromptu (off the top of their head) speech. This unexpected assignment typically caused students' heart rate to elevate to an average of 110 beats per minute during delivery of the speech. However, students who watched

humorous episodes of sitcoms before delivering their impromptu speech had an average heart rate during the speech that was significantly lower (80–85 beats per minute)—indicating that experiencing humor reduces their level of anxiety (O'Brien, cited in Howard 2014).

Research also shows that humor strengthens our immune system after it's been suppressed or weakened. It does so by blocking the body's production of the stress hormone cortisol—a biochemical that suppresses our immune system when we're under stress (Berk, cited in Liebertz 2005b).

> The arrival of a good clown exercises a more beneficial influence upon the health of a town than the arrival of twenty asses laden with drugs."
> —*Thomas Sydenham, 17th-century physician*

DEPRESSION

Depression may be succinctly described as an emotional state characterized by a feeling of sadness accompanied by loss of interest, hope, and energy (Mayo Clinic 2015b). As the term implies, when we're depressed, our mood is lowered or pushed down. In contrast to anxiety, which typically involves worrying about something that's currently happening or is about to happen, depression more often relates to something that has already happened, particularly a *loss*, such as a lost relationship (e.g., broken romance or death of a family member) or a lost opportunity (e.g., losing a job or being rejected by a school) (Bowlby 1980; Price, Choi, and Vinokur 2002).

It's natural and normal to feel dejected after losses such as these. However, if the dejection reaches a point where we can't concentrate and complete our day-to-day tasks, and if this continues for an extended period of time, we may be experiencing what psychologists call *clinical depression* or *depressive disorder*—that is, depression so serious that we should receive immediate professional help. **Box 4.4** provides a summary of symptoms or signs of depression. If these symptoms continue to occur for two or more weeks, you should take action to relieve them.

NOTE

There's a difference between feeling despondent or down and being depressed. When psychologists use the word "depression," they're usually referring to clinical depression—a mood state so low that it's interfering with a person's ability to cope with day-to-day tasks, such as getting to school or going to work.

Strategies for Coping with Depression

Depression can vary widely in intensity. Moderate and severe forms of depression often require professional counseling or psychotherapy, and are often rooted in genetic or hereditary factors that cause imbalances in brain chemistry. The coping strategies described below can also be used for milder forms of depression that may be overcome through self-help and self-management. These strategies may be used in conjunction with professional help or medication to reduce the intensity and frequency of clinical depression.

1. **Focus on the present and the future, not the past.** Consciously combat the tendency to dwell on past losses or failures that can no longer be changed or controlled. Instead, focus on things you can control now.
2. **Make extra effort to engage in positive, emotionally uplifting behavior.** If our behavior is upbeat, our mind (mood) often follows suit. The expression, "Put on a happy face" can actually be an effective depression-reduction strategy because smiling produces changes in our facial muscles that trigger changes in brain chemistry—which, in turn, elevate our mood (Liebertz 2005a).

BOX 4.4

Recognizing the Symptoms of Depression

- Feeling low, down, dejected, sad, or blue
- Pessimistic feelings about the future (e.g., expecting failure or feeling helpless or hopeless)
- Decreased sense of humor
- Difficulty finding pleasure, joy, or fun in anything
- Lack of concentration
- Loss of motivation and interest in things previously found to be exciting or stimulating (e.g., loss of interest in school, sudden drop in rate of class attendance or completion of course assignments)
- Stooped posture (e.g., hung head or drawn face)
- Slower and softer speech rate
- Decreased animation and slower bodily movements
- Loss of energy
- Changes in sleeping patterns (e.g., sleeping more or less than usual)
- Changes in eating patterns (e.g., eating more or less than usual)
- Social withdrawal
- Neglect of physical appearance
- Consistently low self-esteem (e.g., thinking "I'm a loser")
- Strong feelings of worthlessness or guilt (e.g., thinking "I'm a failure")
- Suicidal thoughts (e.g., experiencing thoughts such as: "I can't take it anymore," "People would be better off without me," or "I don't deserve to live")

Note: Depression and suicidal thoughts occur at alarmingly high rates among college students. In one national study of more than 26,000 students at 70 campuses, it was found that 15% of the students surveyed reported they "seriously considered" suicide and more than 5%≈reported they actually attempted suicide. Unfortunately, however, only half the students who had suicidal thoughts sought counseling or treatment (Drum et al. 2009).

Recognizing the Symptoms of Anxiety

- Jitteriness or shaking—especially the hands
- Accelerated heart rate or heart palpitations (irregular heartbeat)
- Muscle tension. Tightness in the chest or upper shoulders or a tight feeling (lump) in the throat (the expressions "uptight" and "choking under pressure" derive from these symptoms of upper body tension)
- Body aches. Due to heightened muscle tension that can also lead to tension headaches, backaches, or chest pain (in extreme cases, it can feel like a heart attack)
- Sweating—especially sweaty (clammy) palms
- Cold, pale hands or feet. These symptoms are reflected in the expressions "white knuckles" and "cold feet," which have been used to describe someone who's highly anxious
- Dry mouth. Decreased production of saliva (hence, the expression "cotton mouth" and the tendency for nervous speakers to repeatedly sip water)
- Stomach discomfort or indigestion. Caused by increased secretion of stomach acid (as noted in the expression, "I feel like I have butterflies in my stomach")
- Gastrointestinal discomfort (e.g., stomach cramps, constipation, or diarrhea)
- Feeling faint or dizzy. Due to blood vessels constricting, which reduces oxygen flow to the brain
- Weakness and fatigue. A prolonged state of arousal and a sustained state of muscle tension can be physically exhausting
- Menstrual changes—missing or irregular menstrual periods
- Difficulty sleeping. Insomnia or interrupted (fitful) sleep
- Increased susceptibility to colds, flu, and other infections. Due to suppression of the body's immune system, resulting in lower production of antibodies

3. **Continue to engage in activities that are fun and enjoyable.** When we're down, we can fall into the downward spiral of not doing the things that bring us joy (because we're too down to do them); this brings us down further because we fail to do the very things that bring us up. When we're emotionally low, we should try even harder to

continue doing the things that bring us joy, such as socializing with friends and engaging in our usual recreational activities.

4. **Intentionally seek humor and opportunities to laugh.** In addition to reducing anxiety, laughter can lighten and brighten a dark mood. Furthermore, humor improves memory (Nielson, cited in Liebertz 2005a), which can combat the memory loss that typically accompanies depression.

5. **Continue getting things done.** When we're feeling down, staying busy and accomplishing things helps boost our mood because it provides us with a sense of achievement. Helping others less fortunate than ourselves can also be a particularly effective way to boost our mood because it gets us outside ourselves, increases our sense of self-esteem, and helps us realize that our issues may be minor compared to the problems faced by others.

6. **Make a conscious effort to focus on personal strengths and accomplishments.** Another way to drive away the blues is by keeping track of the positive developments in our life. We can do this by keeping a "positive events journal" in which we note the good things that happen to us and for us, such as the fortunate experiences in our life, the things we're grateful for, and our personal accomplishments or achievements. Positive journal entries leave us with a visible uplifting record that we can review anytime we're feeling down.

7. **If you're unable to overcome depression on your own, seek help from others.** In some cases, we may be able to help ourselves overcome emotional problems through personal effort and use of effective coping strategies—particularly if we experience depression or anxiety in milder forms and for shorter periods of time. However, overcoming more serious and long-lasting episodes of depression or anxiety isn't as simple as people make it out to be when they insensitively use expressions like: "Just deal with it," "Get over it," or "Snap out of it." More serious cases of depression and anxiety can be strongly associated with genetic factors, which are not completely within the person's control. In these cases, we shouldn't be reluctant to or embarrassed about seeking professional help.

> "The best way to cheer yourself up is to try to cheer somebody else up."
> —*Samuel Clemens, a.k.a. Mark Twain, writer, lecturer, and humorist*

 ## Journal Reflection 4.10

If you thought you were experiencing a serious episode of anxiety or depression, would you feel comfortable seeking help from a professional? If yes, why? If no, why not?

How do you think other students would react to your response?

_____

_____

_____

_____

_____

Using alcohol and/or other drugs to deal with stress, anxiety, or depression is not a healthy solution. Drugs and alcohol will be discussed further in the next chapter.

CHAPTER SUMMARY AND HIGHLIGHTS

Intellectual ability is only one form of human intelligence. Social and emotional intelligence are equally, if not more, important for living a successful, healthy, and happy life. The strategies discussed in this chapter should not be viewed merely as "soft skills," but as "hard core" skills essential for success in college and beyond.

Good communication skills (verbal and nonverbal) and good human relations skills ("people skills") are critical for the development of successful social relationships. We can improve our interpersonal interactions and relationships by working hard at remembering the names and interests of people we meet, being a good listener, and being open to different topics of conversation.

Interpersonal conflicts are an inevitable aspect of social life; we can't completely eliminate them, but we can minimize and manage them by using effective strategies to resolve conflicts assertively rather than aggressively, passively, or passive-aggressively.

Students report experiencing higher levels of stress in college than they did in high school. Strategies for reducing excess stress include formal stress-management techniques (e.g., deep, diaphragmatic breathing and progressive muscle relaxation), as well as simple stress-management strategies (e.g., exercising and journaling).

Along with anxiety, depression is the other major emotional problem that can afflict us.

Research on college students indicate that depression is associated with poorer academic performance in college and higher risk of withdrawing from college, even among highly motivated and academically well-prepared students. Mild depression may be overcome with a variety of self-help strategies. However, if symptoms of depression are severe and continue for two or more weeks, this suggests "clinical depression" or a "depressive disorder" is being experienced and professional help should be immediately sought.

LEARNING MORE THROUGH THE WORLD WIDE WEB: INTERNET-BASED RESOURCES

For additional information on social and emotional intelligence, see the following websites:

Social Intelligence and Interpersonal Relationships:
https://nationalvetcontent.edu.au/alfresco/d/d/workspace/
SpacesStore/5c14c044-6d26-4ab8-aef1-530948605d36/ims/shared/
resources/mag/web_conflict.htm
http://www.livestrong.com/article/132246-effective-interpersonal-communication-strategies/
http://www.yesintlcampus.com/index.asp?Cid=20&Tid=140&Sid=51680

Emotional Intelligence and Mental Health:
www.eqi.org/eitoc.htm
http://www.nimh.nih.gov/health/publications/depression-easy-to-read/
index.shtml
http://www.activeminds.org/issues-a-resources/mental-health-resources/
student-resources

REFERENCES

AhYun, K. 2002. "Similarity and Attraction." In *Interpersonal Communication Research*, edited by M. Allen, R. W. Preiss, B. M. Gayle, and N. A. Burrell, 145–67. Mahwah, NJ: Erlbaum.

Avolio, B. and F. Luthans. 2006. *The High Impact Leader*. New York: McGraw Hill.

Avolio, B. J., F. O. Walumbwa, and T. J. Weber. 2009. "Leadership: Current Theories, Research, and Future Directions." *Annual Review of Psychology* 60: 421–49.

Barker, L. and K. W. Watson. 2000. *Listen Up: How to Improve Relationships, Reduce Stress, and Be More Productive by Using the Power of Listening*. New York: St. Martin's Press.

Bartels, A. and S. Zeki. 2000. "The Neural Basis of Romantic Love." *European Journal of Neuroscience* 12: 172–93.

Bartlett, T. 2002. "Freshman Pay, Mentally and Physically, as They Adjust to College Life." *Chronicle of Higher Education* 48: 35–37.

Bassham, G., W. Irwin, H. Nardone, and J. M. Wallace. 2013. *Critical Thinking: A Student's Introduction*. 5th ed. New York: McGraw-Hill.

Bellet, P. S. and M. J. Maloney. 1991. "The importance of empathy as an interviewing skill in medicine." *JAMA* 266 (13): 1831–2. doi:10.1001/jama.1991.03470130111039.

Benson, H. and W. Proctor. 2011. *The Relaxation Revolution: The Science and Genetics of Mind Body Healing*. New York: Scribner.

Berndt, T. J. 1992. "Friendship and Friends' Influence in Adolescence." *Current Directions in Psychological Science* 1(5): 156–59.

Biggs, J. and C. Tang. 2011. *Teaching for Quality Learning at University*. New York: Open Education Press.

Bippus, A. M. and S. L. Young. 2005. "Owning Your Emotions: Reactions to Expressions of Self-versus Other-attributed Positive and Negative Emotions." *Journal of Applied Communication Research* 33(1): 26–45.

Bowlby, J. 1980. *Attachment and Loss: Loss, Sadness, and Depression. Vol. 3.* New York: Basic Books.

Caine, R. and G. Caine. 1994. *Making Connections: Teaching and the Human Brain*. Menlo Park, CA: Addison-Wesley.

Carneiro, P., C. Crawford, and A. Goodman. 2006. *Which Skills Matter?* Centre for the Economics of Education, London School of Economics, Discussion Paper 59. http://cee.lse.ac.uk/ceedps/ceedp59.pdf.

Daniels, D. and L. J. Horowitz. 1997. *Being and Caring: A Psychology for Living*. Prospect Heights, IL: Waveland Press.

Driver, J. 2010. *You Say More than You Think: A 7-day Plan for Using the New Body Language to Get What You Want*. New York: Crown Publishers.

Drum, D., C. Brownson, A. B. Denmark, S. E. Smith. 2009. "New Data on the Nature of Suicidal Crises in College Students: Shifting the Paradigm." *Professional Psychology: Research and Practice* 40(3): 213–22.

Ekman, P. 2009. *Telling Lies: Clues to Deceit in the Marketplace, Politics, and Marriage.* Revised ed. New York: W. W. Norton.

Fernández-Castillo, A., and M. J. Caurcel. 2014. "State Test-Anxiety, Selective Attention and Concentration in University Students." *International Journal of Psychology* 50(4): 265–71.

Festinger, L. 1954. "A Theory of Social Comparison Processes." *Human Relations* 7: 117–40.

Fezler, W. 1989. *Creative Imagery: How to Visualize in All Senses.* New York: Simon & Schuster.

Foreman, J. June 22, 2009. "Dear, I Love You with All My Brain." *Los Angeles Times.* http://www.latimes.com/features/health/la-he-love22-2009jun22,0,6897401.column.

Freedner, N., L. H. Freed, Y. W. Yang, and S. B. Austin. 2002. "Dating Violence among Gay, Lesbian, and Bisexual Adolescents: Results from a Community Survey." *Journal of Adolescent Health* 31: 469–74.

Gardner, H. 1993. *Frames of Mind: The Theory of Multiple Intelligences.* 2nd ed. New York: Basic Books.

Gardner, H. 1999. Intelligence Reframed: Multiple Intelligences for the 21st Century. New York: Basic Books.

Giles, L. C., F. V. Glonek, M. A. Luszcz, and G. R. Andrews. 2005. "Effect of Social Networks on 10-year Survival in Very Old Australians: The Australia Longitudinal Study of Aging." *Journal of Epidemiology and Community Health* 59: 574–79.

Goleman, D. 1995. *Emotional Intelligence: Why It Can Matter More than IQ.* New York: Random House.

Goleman, D. 2000. *Working with Emotional Intelligence.* New York: Bantam Dell.

Goleman, D. 2006. *Social Intelligence: The New Science of Human Relationships.* New York: Dell.

Goleman, D., Boyatzis, R., and McKee, A. 2013. *Primal Leadership: Realizing the Potential of Emotional Intelligence.* Boston, MA: Harvard Business School Press.

Gottman, J. 1994. *Why Marriages Succeed and Fail.* New York: Fireside.

Gottman, J. 1999. *The Seven Principles for Making Marriage Work.* New York: Three Rivers Press.

Halvorson, H. G. 2010. *Succeed: How We Can Reach Our Goals.* New York: Plume.

Harris, M. B. 2006. "Correlates and Characteristics of Boredom and Proneness to Boredom." *Journal of Applied Social Psychology* 30(3): 576–98.

Hatfield, E., and Rapson, R. L. 1993. *Love, Sex, and Intimacy: Their Psychology, Biology, and History.* New York: HarperCollins.

Hatfield, E., and Rapson, R. L. 2000. "Love." In *The Concise Corsini Encyclopedia of Psychology and Behavioral Science*, edited by W. E. Craighead and C. B. Nemeroff, 898–901. New York: John Wiley & Sons.

Hertel, P. T., and Brozovich, F. 2010. "Cognitive Habits and Memory Distortions in Anxiety and Depression." *Current Directions in Psychological Science* 19: 155–60.

Howard, P. J. 2014. *The Owner's Manual for the Brain: Everyday Applications of Mind-brain Research.* 4th ed. New York: HarperCollins.

Johnson, M. P., and Ferraro, K. J. 2000. "Research on domestic violence in the 1990s: Making distinctions." *Journal of Marriage and the Family* 62: 948–63.

Karjane, Fisher, and Cullen. 2002/2005. *Campus Sexual Assault: How America's Institutions of Higher Education Respond*, final report to the National Institute of Justice, October 2002, NCJ 196676.

Latané, B., J. H. Liu, A. Nowak, N. Bonevento, and L. Zheng, 1995. "Distance Matters: Physical Space and Social Impact." *Personality and Social Psychology Bulletin* 21: 795–805.

Lehrer, P., D. H. Barlow, R. L. Woolfolk, and W. E. Sime, eds. 2007. *Principles and Practice of Stress Management.* 3rd ed. New York: The Guilford Press.

Liebertz, C. 2005a. "A Healthy Laugh." *Scientific American Mind* 16(3): 90–91.

Liebertz, C. 2005b. "Want Clear Thinking? Relax." *Scientific American Mind* 16(3): 88–89.

Luthra, R., and C. A. Gidycz. 2006. "Dating Violence among College Men and Women: Evaluation of a Theoretical Model." *Journal of Interpersonal Violence.* 21: 717–31.

Malik, S., S. B. Sorenson, and C. S. Aneshensel. 1997. "Community and Dating Violence among Adolescents: Perpetration and Victimization." *Journal of Adolescent Health* 1997(5): 291–302.

Matthews, G., M. Zeidner, and R. D. Roberts. 2007. *The Science of Emotional Intelligence: Knowns and Unknowns.* New York: Oxford University Press.

Mayo Clinic. 2015a. *Anxiety: Definition.* http://www.mayoclinic.org/diseases-conditions/anxiety/basics/definition/con-20026282.

Mayo Clinic. 2015b. *Depression: Definition.* http://www.mayoclinic.org/diseases-conditions/depression/basics/definition/con-20032977.

McKay, M., M. Davis, and P. Fanning. 2009. *Messages: The Communication Skills Book.* 2nd ed. Oakland, CA: New Harbinbger.

Miller, L. M. 2011. "Physical Abuse in a College Setting: A Study of Perception and Participation in Abusive Dating Relationships." *Journal of Family Violence* 26(1): 71–80.

Murray, C. E. and K. N. Kardatzke. 2007. "Dating Violence among College Students: Key Issues for College Counselors." *Journal of College Counseling* 10 (1): 79.

Myers, D. G. 1993. *The Pursuit of Happiness: Who Is Happy and Why?* New York: Morrow.

Myers, D. G. 2000. *The American Paradox: Spiritual Hunger in an Age of Plenty.* New Haven, CT: Yale University Press.

National Center for Victims of Crime. 2012.

Navarro, J. 2008. *What Every BODY Is Saying.* New York: Harper Collins.

Nichols, M. P. 2009. *The Lost Art of Listening.* New York: Guilford Press.

Ottens, A. J., and K. Hotelling. 2001. *Sexual Violence on Campus: Politics, Programs, and Perspectives.* New York: Springer Publishing Company, Inc.

Palank, J. July 17, 2006. *Face It: "Book" no Secret to Employers.* http://www.washtimes.com/business/20060717-12942-1800r.htm.

Pascarella, E., and P. Terenzini. 2005. *How College Affects Students: A Third Decade of Research.* Vol. 2. San Francisco: Jossey-bass.

Penfold, R. B. 2006. *Dragonslippers: This Is What an Abusive Relationship Looks Like.* New York: Grove/Atlantic.

Price, R. H., J. N. Choi, and A. D. Vinokur. 2002. "Links in the Chain of Adversity Following Job Loss: How Financial Strain and Loss of Personal Control Lead to Depression, Impaired Functioning, and Poor Health." *Journal of Occupational Health Psychology* 7(4): 302–12.

Purdy, M., and D. Borisoff, eds. 1996. *Listening in Everyday Life: A Personal and Professional Approach.* Lanham, MD: University Press of America.

Putman, R. D. 2000. *Bowling Alone: The Collapse and Revival of American Community.* New York: Simon & Schuster.

Ramsden, P. 2003. *Learning to Teach in Higher Education.* 2nd ed. London: RoutledgeFalmer.

Rohrbaugh, J. B. 2006. "Domestic Violence in Same-Gender Relationships." *Family Court Review* 44(2): 287–99.

Ruggiero, V. R. 2011. *Beyond Feelings: A Guide to Critical Thinking.* New York: McGraw-Hill Education.

Salovey, P. and J. D. Mayer. 1990. "Emotional Intelligence." *Imagination, Cognition, and Personality* 9: 185–211.

Sapolsky, R. 2004. *Why Zebras Don't Get Ulcers.* New York: W. H. Freeman.

Sax, L. J. 2003. "Our Incoming Students: What Are They Like? *About Campus* July–August: 15–20.

Seaward, B. L. 2011. *Managing stress: Principles and Strategies for Health and Well-being.* Burlington, MA: Jones & Bartlett Learning.

Senn, C. Y., M. Eliasziw, P. C. Barata, W. E. Thurston, I. R. Newby-Clark, H. L. Radtke, and K. L. Hobden. 2015. "Efficacy of a Sexual Assault Resistance Program for University Women." *New England Journal of Medicine* 372: 2326–35.

Sinsky, R. 2011. "Reppler has a New Way to Rate Your Social Network Image." http://venturebeat.com/2011/09/27 /reppler/.

Snyder, C. R., C. Harris, J. R. Anderson, S. A. Holleran, L. M. Irving, S. T. Sigmon, L. Yoshinobu, J. Gibb, C. Langelle, and P. Harney. 1991. "The Will and the Ways: Development and Validation of an Individual-differences Measure of Hope." *Journal of Personality and Social Psychology* 60: 570–85.

Suls, J., R. Martin, and L. Wheeler. 2002. Social Comparison: Why, with Whom, and with What Effect? *Current Directions in Psychological Science* 11(5): 159–63.

Tinto, V. 2012. *Completing College: Rethinking Institutional Action.* Chicago: The University of Chicago Press.

Viorst, J. 1998. *Imperfect Control: Our Lifelong Struggles with Power and Surrender.* New York: Simon Schuster.

White, J. W. and M. P. Koss. 1991. "Courtship Violence: Incidence in a National Sample of Higher Education Students." *Violence and Victims* 6: 247–56.

Wiederman, M. W. 2007. "Gender Differences in Sexuality." *Family Journal Counseling and Therapy* 9(4): 468–71.

Zull, J. E. 2002. *The Art of Changing the Brain: Enriching Teaching by Exploring the Biology of Learning.* Sterling, VA: Stylus.

Chapter 4 Exercises

4.1 Quote Reflections

Review the sidebar quotes contained in this chapter and select two that were especially meaningful or inspirational to you.

For each quote, provide a three- to five-sentence explanation why you chose it.

4.2 Reality Bite

Caught Between a Rock and a Hard Place: Romantic Involvement versus Academic Commitment

Lauren has been dating her boyfriend (Nick) for about two months. She's convinced this is the real thing and that she's definitely in love. Lately, Nick has been asking her to skip class to spend more time with him. He tells Lauren: "If you really love me, you would do it for our relationship." Lauren feels that Nick truly loves her and wouldn't do anything to intentionally hurt her or interfere with her goals. So she accommodates Nick's request and begins skipping some classes to spend time with him. However, Lauren's grades soon start to slip; at the same time, Nick continues to demand more of her time.

Reflection and Discussion Questions

1. What concerns you most about Lauren's behavior?
2. What concerns you most about Nick's behavior?
3. Would you agree with Lauren's decision to start skipping classes?
4. If you were Lauren's friend, what advice would you give her?
5. If you were Nick's friend, what advice would you give him?
6. What might Lauren do to keep her grades up and still keep her relationship with Nick strong?

4.3 Reality Bite—Case Study

Mental Wellness

Leo was really looking forward to college, but he was not prepared to handle the stress and anxiety that came along with it. In high school, his teachers always reminded him when things were due and he hardly had any homework. Now his instructors expect him to read that silly syllabus and he has so much homework he does not know where to start! He is starting to fall behind and gets anxious and nervous any time he goes to class. His heart starts to race and his palms get really sweaty. The further he falls behind, the worse his stress and anxiety get. Soon he stops going to class altogether because he gets so worked up he literally makes himself sick.

Discussion Questions

1. How realistic do you think this case is? Why?
2. What could Leo have done to calm himself down so that he was able to go to his classes and be successful?
3. What do you think is going to happen to Leo?

4.4 Identifying Major Ways of Handling Interpersonal Conflict

Think of a social situation or relationship that's currently causing the most conflict in your life. Describe how this conflict could be approached in each of the following ways:

1. Passively:
2. Aggressively:
3. Passive–aggressively:
4. Assertively:

(See **pp. 104–105** for descriptions of each of these four approaches.)

Practice the *assertive* approach by role-playing it with a friend or classmate and consider applying it to the actual situation or relationship that's currently causing you the most conflict.

4.5 College Stress: Identifying Sources and Solutions

Read through the following 29 college stressors and rate them in terms of how much stress each one is currently causing you—on a scale of 1 to 5 (1 = lowest, 5 = highest).

Potential Stressors	Stress Rating				
Tests and exams	1	2	3	4	5
Assignments	1	2	3	4	5
Class workload	1	2	3	4	5
Pace of courses	1	2	3	4	5
Performing up to expectations	1	2	3	4	5
Handling personal freedom	1	2	3	4	5
Time pressure (e.g., not enough time)	1	2	3	4	5
Organizational pressure (e.g., losing things)	1	2	3	4	5
Living independently	1	2	3	4	5
The future	1	2	3	4	5
Decisions about a major or career	1	2	3	4	5
Moral and ethical decisions	1	2	3	4	5
Finding meaning in life	1	2	3	4	5
Emotional issues	1	2	3	4	5
Physical health	1	2	3	4	5
Social life	1	2	3	4	5
Intimate relationships	1	2	3	4	5
Sexuality	1	2	3	4	5
Family responsibilities	1	2	3	4	5
Family conflicts	1	2	3	4	5
Family pressure	1	2	3	4	5
Peer pressure	1	2	3	4	5
Loneliness or isolation	1	2	3	4	5
Roommate conflicts	1	2	3	4	5
Conflict with professors	1	2	3	4	5
Campus policies or procedures	1	2	3	4	5
Transportation	1	2	3	4	5
Technology	1	2	3	4	5
Safety	1	2	3	4	5

Review your ratings and record your three highest-rated stressors in the space below—along with: (a) a coping strategy you may use on your own to deal with that source of stress and (b) a campus resource you could use to obtain help with that source of stress.

Stressor #1: _____

Personal coping strategy:

Campus resource:

Stressor #2: _____

Personal coping strategy:

Campus resource:

Stressor #3: _____

Personal coping strategy:

Campus resource:

4.6 Do What You Are Reflection

Review your Do What You Are Report to answer the following questions.

1. What is your personality type?

2. What are the strengths of your personality type? How can you use these to assist in good communication with others?

3. What are the blind spots for your personality type? What can you do to improve in each of these areas to assist you in becoming a better communicator?

4. What are the strengths for your negotiation style? How can these help your negotiations with others?

5. What are the blind spots for your negotiation style? How could these impact your negotiations with others?

Chapter 4 Reflection

What is one healthy relationship you currently have that could positively affect your success in college? Explain.

What is one unhealthy relationship that could negatively affect your success in college? Explain. How can you make this relationship healthy, or what are other options you might have?

Think of a situation that is currently causing you stress. What is it? What are some ways you can address the situation so it will not cause you so much stress?

CHAPTER 5

MAXIMIZING WELLNESS AND PERFORMANCE

BODY, MIND, AND SPIRIT

This chapter examines strategies for maximizing wellness by maintaining a balanced diet, attaining quality sleep, promoting total fitness, and avoiding risky behaviors that jeopardize our health and impair our performance.

CHAPTER PREVIEW

Acquire wellness strategies that can be immediately practiced in the first year of college and beyond.

LEARNING OBJECTIVE

THOUGHT STARTER

 Journal Reflection 5.1

What would you say are the three most important things that college students could do to preserve their health and promote peak performance?

1. _____

2. _____

3. _____

WHAT IS WELLNESS?

Wellness may be defined as a high-quality state of health in which our risk of illness is minimized and the quality of our physical and mental performance is maximized. Research indicates that people who attend to multiple dimensions of self-development and live a well-rounded, well-balanced life are more likely to be healthy (physically and mentally) and successful (personally and professionally) (Covey 2004; Goleman 1995; Heath 1977).

> "Wellness is a multidimensional state of being describing the existence of positive health in an individual as exemplified by quality of life and a sense of well-being."
>
> —*Charles Corbin and Robert Pangrazi, President's Council on Physical Fitness and Sports*

> "Wellness is an integrated method of functioning, which is oriented toward maximizing the potential of the individual."
>
> —*H. Joseph Dunn, originator of the term, "wellness"*

> "May the sun bring you new energy by day; may the moon restore you by night. May the rain wash away your worries; may the breeze blow strength into your being."
>
> —*Apache Indian blessing*

The following eight dimensions of self-development are commonly cited as the key elements of the "wellness wheel"; they provide the foundation for a well-rounded life.

1. **Intellectual:** acquiring broad-based knowledge, learning how to learn, and learning how to think critically.
2. **Emotional:** understanding, managing, and expressing emotions and feelings.
3. **Social:** improving the quality and depth of interpersonal relationships.
4. **Ethical:** building moral character—making sound ethical judgments, developing a clear value system for guiding personal decisions, and demonstrating consistency between your convictions (beliefs) and your commitments (actions).
5. **Physical:** acquiring knowledge about the human body and applying that knowledge to prevent disease, promote wellness, and achieve peak performance.
6. **Spiritual:** devoting attention to the "big questions," such as the meaning or purpose of life, the inevitability of death, and the origins of human life and the natural world.
7. **Vocational:** exploring career options and pursuing a career path that capitalizes on your talents, interests, and values.
8. **Personal:** developing a strong sense of personal identity, a coherent self-concept, and the capacity to manage personal affairs and resources.

For specific skills and qualities associated with each of these dimensions of wellness, see **Exercise 5.3, pp. 155.**

As can be seen in **Figure 5.1**, numerous elements of the self join together to form the wellness wheel. These elements of wellness correspond closely to the components of holistic ("whole person") development, which is a primary goal of the college experience. One of the multiple

FIGURE 5.1: Components of the Wellness Wheel

advantages of a college education is that college graduates are more likely to live longer, healthier lives and experience higher levels of psychological well-being. Apparently, students learn something important about wellness in college that improves the overall quality of their lives.

PHYSICAL WELLNESS

The physical component of wellness is the primary focus of this chapter. It could be said that physical health is a precondition or prerequisite that enables all other elements of wellness to be experienced. It's hard to grow intellectually and professionally if you're not well physically, and it's hard to become wealthy and wise without first being healthy.

Physical wellness involves more than recovering from illness or disease after it occurs. Instead, it's engaging in health-promoting behaviors that proactively prevent illness from happening in the first place (Corbin, Pangrazi, and Franks 2000). Wellness puts into practice using two classic proverbs: "Prevention is the best medicine" and "An ounce of prevention is worth a pound of cure."

As depicted in **Figure 5.2**, there are three potential interception points for preventing illness, preserving health, and promoting peak performance; they range from reactive (after illness) to proactive (before illness). Wellness goes beyond maintaining physical health to attaining a higher quality of life that includes vitality (energy and vigor), longevity (longer life span), and life satisfaction (happiness).

> **NOTE**
>
> *Nurture balance by developing SMART health goals.*

> **"**
>
> Buono salute é la vera ricchezza ("Good health is true wealth.")"
> —*Italian proverb*

> **"**
>
> Health is a state of complete well-being, and not merely the absence of disease or infirmity."
> —*World Health Organization*

FIGURE 5.2: Potential Points for Preventing Illness, Preserving Health, and Promoting Peak Performance

Proactive		Reactive
1. Feeling great and attaining peak levels of performance	2. Not sick, but could be feeling better and performing at a higher level	3. Sick, unable to perform, and trying to regain health

©Kendall Hunt Publishing Company

During any major life transition, such as the transition to college, unhealthy habits add to the level of transitional stress (Khoshaba and Maddi 2005). In contrast, engaging in healthy habits is one way to manage and reduce stress at all stages of life—especially during stages of transition.

Elements of Physical Wellness

A healthy physical lifestyle includes three key components:

1. Nutrition
2. Rest
3. Healthy choices

NUTRITION

Similar to the way in which high-performance fuel improves the performance of an automobile, a high-quality (nutritious) diet improves the performance of the human body and mind, enabling each to operate at peak capacity. Unfortunately, we frequently pay more attention to the quality of fuel we put in our cars than to the quality of food we put into their bodies. We often eat without any intentional plan about what we should eat. We eat at places where we can get food fast conveniently without having to step out of our car (or off of our butts). America has become a "fast food nation"; we have grown accustomed to consuming food that can be accessed quickly, conveniently, cheaply, and in large (super-sized) portions (Schlosser 2005). National surveys reveal that less than 40% of American college students report that they maintain a healthy diet (Sax, Bryant, and Gilmartin 2004).

AUTHOR'S JOURNEY

When I first went away to college, I loved that I had the freedom to eat whatever I wanted, whenever I wanted. Food (and alcohol) were always readily available. During the first 18 years of my life, I never had any issues with my weight, so I didn't really think about what I was eating while in college. The late night pizza and ice cream runs caught up with me, and by the time I went home for the holiday break in December, I only had a few pairs of sweatpants that fit me. The fact that I was eating unhealthy foods and not exercising much had really caught up with me, and I gained over 20 pounds in four months. I have since learned how to eat healthier and exercise, but I have struggled with my weight ever since that first year of college.

—Julie McLaughlin

Journal Reflection 5.2

Have your eating habits changed since you've begun college? If yes, in what ways?

_____

_____

_____

_____

_____

_____

We should eat in a thoughtful, nutritionally conscious way, rather than solely out of convenience, habit, or pursuit of what's most pleasing to our taste buds. We should also "eat to win" by consuming the types of food that will best equip us to defeat disease and enables us to reach peak levels of physical and mental performance. The following nutrition management strategies may be used to enhance your body's ability to stay well and perform well.

Strategies for Healthy Eating

1. Have a Plan!

Living in dorms, hectic schedules, and adjusting to college life often negatively impact health. In your home, you may be able to purchase foods that are good for you as well as economical. However, when you are rushing to class or work, or with a group of classmates studying for a test, you may be tempted to stop at the first fast food you see or to eat junk food. Sometimes, that's going to happen, but you want such "binges" to be rare. To be sure that you can keep to a diet that feeds your mind and body positively, and you will need do develop a plan. For example, if you can keep the picture on **Figure 5.3** in mind and try to live by it, you will be eating a healthy diet. The MyPlate chart, developed by the American Dietetic Association, focuses on the nutrients needed for a healthy mind and body. If you go to www.ChooseMyPlate.gov or www.cnppusda.gov/ dietary guidelines, you can take control of your eating by developing your own nutritional plan.

FIGURE 5.3: MyPlate

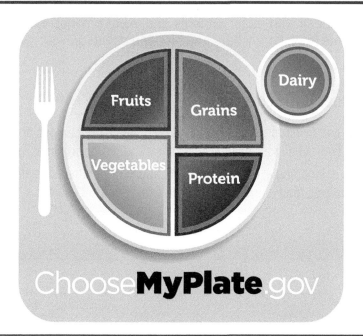

NOTE

Snap a photo of MyPlate to support you with healthy food choices.

Source: USDA

2. **Minimize your consumption of foods whose nutritional value is low (or zero) and that increase your risk of heart disease and cancer.**

    • Reduce intake of fried and fatty foods such as pizza, hamburgers, French fries, donuts, butter, and margarine. These foods not only contain lots of calories but also can increase the risk of heart disease because they contain saturated fats and trans fats—"bad" fats that tend to stick to blood vessel walls and increase the risk of blocking normal blood flow.

    • Reduce consumption of processed foods. Processed foods were originally natural foods, but synthetic ingredients have been added to them so that they can be preserved, packaged, jarred, canned, or bottled and sold later to the public in large or bulk quantities.

    • Reduce consumption of high-fat dairy products (e.g., cheese, butter, margarine, cream, and whole milk). High-fat dairy products are high in saturated fat and sodium, both of which increase the risk of heart disease.

    • Minimize consumption of animal meat, particularly red meat such as hamburger and steak. Meat often contains a large amount of saturated fat, which poses a major risk for heart disease. Americans tend to consume about twice as much protein as their bodies need (National Research Council 1989).

      If or when you consume meat, you can reduce its health risk by eating lean meat that has less fat and by removing any fatty skin from the meat (e.g., removing the skin from chicken or turkey).

3. **Reduce calorie intake and control weight.**

    • Decrease or eliminate junk-food snacks. Replace sugary and salty snacks with healthier munchies, such as fruits, nuts, seeds, and raw vegetables. Many of these healthier snacks are as sweet, crispy, or crunchy as junk food snacks. Natural fruits can provide sweetness with more nutrients and fewer calories than processed sweets (e.g., candy bars and blended coffee drinks).

 Journal Reflection 5.3

Identify five food restaurants or quick stops on or near your campus or near your home where you can choose healthy snacks, meals, and/or groceries.

Make a point of stopping at healthy choice locations rather than unhealthy ones. Consider keeping a food journal to guide you with your food choices.

- Decrease the tendency to pack most of your calories into one or two large meals per day. Most nutritionists recommend that people eat large meals less often and small meals more often. Six smaller meals or healthy snacks per day may be a more effective way to fuel the body than three full-sized meals (Khoshaba and Maddi 2004).
- Decrease the amount of juices you consume daily. They contain a large amount of calories. Eliminate sodas as they contain a large amount of sugar and empty calories.
- Reduce the total number of calories consumed during your evening meal. Remember that calories are measures of the amount of energy contained in food. One calorie may be described as one unit or degree of energy. If you consume a unit of energy and don't use it, you don't lose it; instead, you save it or store it—as fat. In other words, much like money, if you don't spend your income (caloric intake), you tend to save it in your body's bank of fat cells. Eating lots of calories in the evening and then lying down and sleeping soon thereafter means those evening calories don't get burned as physical energy, but are stored as body fat.
- Your first meal of the day should be the meal at which you consume most of your daily calories because you need energy for the next 16 or so hours that you'll be awake and moving. Unfortunately, Americans tend to do it backward by skipping or skimping at breakfast and piling on calories at dinner—a time of day when they don't need many calories because they'll soon be lying down and falling asleep.

4. **Make a conscious attempt to increase consumption of natural foods that have been available to humans throughout natural history.** The following foods aren't processed foods but natural foods that have been available to, and consumed by, humans for thousands of years. As a rule, the food that was good for our ancient ancestors and the survival of our species is good for us now. These are the foods that provide humans with the best protection against their two leading killers: heart disease and cancer.
   - Feast on fresh fruit. Fruit has multiple nutritional benefits, including high amounts of vitamins (especially A and C) and minerals.
   - Go for fresh (or frozen) vegetables. Fresh or frozen vegetables are superior to canned and processed vegetables. The natural oils in certain vegetables (e.g., olive, corn, avocado, and soy) are rich sources of unsaturated fat.
   - Go wild on grains. Whole-wheat bread and pasta, whole-grain cereals, oatmeal, and bran are examples of healthy grains.

     Natural grains contain complex carbohydrates, which the body uses to produce steady, ongoing energy. Complex carbohydrates are called "complex" because their molecular structure is harder for the body to digest and break down into blood sugar. Their more complex molecular structure slows the digestion process; as a result, they're absorbed into the bloodstream more slowly, which allows them to deliver energy to the body more gradually and evenly over an extended period (similar to a coated pill or time-released capsule).
   - Feed freely on fish. Fish are high in protein and low in saturated fat, and the natural oil in fish is high in unsaturated fat, which

flushes out and washes away cholesterol-forming fats from the bloodstream (Khoshaba and Maddi 2004).

- Consume lots of legumes. The word *legumes* derives from the Latin root *legumend,* meaning "to gather." This group includes plants and seeds, such as beans (black, red, and navy), lentils, Brussels sprouts, peas, and peanuts. Such foods are great sources of fiber, protein, iron, and B vitamins; plus, they are naturally cholesterol-free and low in saturated fat.

- Drink more water. Most people don't get the recommended amount of water (seven 8-ounce glasses per day). You need to hydrate your body. The body uses water much like a car uses motor oil and transmission fluid, to drive nutrients (fuel) to their proper destinations and to drive waste products out of the system. Water also improves your nervous system's ability to conduct electrochemical signals, which may benefit the brain's ability to process information more easily and more rapidly.

- If you're a woman, make a conscious effort to consume more calcium. Females should take in at least 1,200 mg of calcium per day (Gershoff and Whitney 1996) to reduce the risk of osteoporosis (thinning of bones and loss of bone mass or density), which increases risk for fractures and curvature of the upper spine.

5. **Maintain self-awareness of your eating habits.** In addition to planning our diet, effective nutrition management requires that we remain aware of our daily eating habits. We can monitor our eating habits by simply taking a little time to read the labels on food products before we put them into our shopping cart and into our body. Keeping a nutritional log or journal of what we eat in a typical week is an effective way to track the nutrients and caloric content of what we're consuming.

   When choosing our diet, we should also be mindful of our family history. Are there members of your immediate and extended family who have shown tendencies toward heart disease, diabetes, or cancer? If so, intentionally adopt a diet that reduces your risk for developing the types of illnesses that you may have genetic tendencies to develop. (For regularly updated information on dietary strategies for reducing the risk of common diseases, see the following website: https://fnic.nal.usda.gov/diet-and-disease).

EATING DISORDERS

NOTE

If you or someone you know might have an eating disorder do not be afraid to ask for help. Check in with the student union and/or counseling center for assistance.

While some students experience the "freshman 15"—a 15-pound weight gain during the first year of college (Brody 2003)—others experience eating disorders related to weight loss and losing control of their eating habits. These disorders are more common among females (National Institute of Mental Health 2014), largely because Western cultures place more emphasis and pressure on females to maintain lighter body weight and body size. Studies show that approximately one of every three college females reports worrying about her weight, body image, or eating habits (Leavy, Gnong, and Ross 2009).

Box 5.1 provides a short summary of the major eating disorders experienced by college students. These disorders are often accompanied by

BOX 5.1

Major Eating Disorders

Anorexia Nervosa

Individuals experiencing anorexia nervosa are dangerously thin, yet they see themselves as overweight and have an intense fear of gaining weight. Anorexics typically deny that they're severely underweight; and even if their weight drops to the point where they may look like walking skeletons, they may continue to be obsessed with losing weight, eating infrequently, and eating extremely small portions. Anorexics may also use other methods to lose weight, such as compulsive exercise, diet pills, laxatives, diuretics, or enemas.

Bulimia Nervosa

This eating disorder is characterized by repeated episodes of "binge eating"—consuming excessive amounts of food within a limited period of time. Bulimics tend to lose self-control during their binges and then try to compensate for overeating by engaging in behavior to purge their guilt and prevent weight gain. They may purge themselves by self-induced vomiting, consuming

> " I had a friend who took pride in her ability to lose 30 lbs. in one summer by not eating and working out excessively. I know girls that find pleasure in getting ill so that they throw up, can't eat, and lose weight."
>
> —*Comments written in a first-year student's journal*

excessive amounts of laxatives or diuretics, using enemas, or fasting. The binge–purge pattern typically takes place at least twice a week and continues for three or more months.

Unlike anorexics, bulimics are harder to detect because their binges and purges typically take place secretly and their body weight looks about normal for their age and height. However, similar to anorexics, bulimics fear gaining weight, aren't happy with their body, and have an intense desire to lose weight.

Binge-Eating Disorder

Like bulimia, binge-eating disorder involves repeated, out-of-control episodes of consuming large amounts of food. However, unlike bulimics, binge eaters don't purge after binging episodes.

Those suffering from binge-eating disorder demonstrate at least three of the following symptoms, two or more times per week, for several months:

1. Eating at an extremely rapid rate
2. Eating until becoming uncomfortably full
3. Eating large amounts of food when not physically hungry
4. Eating alone because of embarrassment about others seeing how much they eat
5. Feeling guilty, disgusted, or depressed after overeating.

Sources: American Psychiatric Association (2015); National Institute of Mental Health (2014).

emotional issues (e.g., depression and anxiety) that are serious enough to require professional treatment (National Institute of Mental Health 2014). The earlier these disorders are identified and treated, the better the prognosis or probability of complete and permanent recovery.

EXERCISE AND FITNESS

Wellness depends not only on fueling the body but using that fuel to move the body. We know that eating natural (unprocessed) foods is better for our health because those were the foods eaten by our ancient human ancestors, which has contributed to the survival of our species. Similarly exercise is another "natural" health-promoting activity that contributed to the health and survival of the human species (Booth and Vyas 2001).

> " If exercise could be packaged into a pill, it would be the single most widely prescribed and beneficial medicine in the nation."
>
> —*Robert N. Butler, former director of the National Institute of Aging*

The benefits of physical exercise for improving the longevity and quality of human life are simply extraordinary. If done regularly, exercise may well be the most effective "medicine" available to humans for preventing disease and preserving lifelong health. The major health-promoting benefits of exercise are described below.

Benefits of Exercise for the Body

1. **Exercise promotes cardiovascular health.** Simply stated, exercise makes the heart stronger. Since the heart is a muscle, like any other muscle in the body, its size and strength are increased by exercise. A bigger and stronger heart pumps more blood per beat, reducing the risk for heart disease and stroke (loss of oxygen to the brain) by increasing circulation of oxygen-carrying blood and increasing the body's ability to dissolve blood clots (Khoshaba and Maddi 2005).

   Exercise further reduces the risk of cardiovascular disease by: (a) decreasing the levels of triglycerides (clot-forming fats) in the blood, (b) increasing the levels of "good" cholesterol (high-density lipoproteins), and (c) preventing "bad" cholesterol (low-density lipoproteins) from sticking to and clogging up blood vessels.

2. **Exercise stimulates the immune system.** Exercise enables us to better fight off infectious diseases (e.g., colds and the flu) for the following reasons:

   - It reduces stress—which normally weakens the immune system.
   - It increases blood flow throughout the body, which increases circulation of antibodies that flush germs out of our system.
   - It increases body temperature, which helps kill germs in a way similar to how a low-grade fever kills germs when we're sick (Walsh et al. 2011).

3. **Exercise strengthens muscles and bones.** Exercise reduces muscle tension, which helps prevent muscle strain and pain (e.g., strengthening abdominal muscles reduces the risk of developing lower back pain). Exercise also maintains bone density and reduces the risk of osteoporosis (brittle bones that bend and break easily). It's noteworthy that our bone density before age 20 affects the bone density we will have for the remainder of life. Thus, by engaging in regular exercise early in life, we minimize risk of bone deterioration throughout life.

AUTHOR'S JOURNEY

I kept in shape when I was young by playing sports such as basketball and baseball. Whenever time in my schedule would allow, I'd play these sports for hours at a time. I enjoyed it so much that I didn't even realize I was exercising. My body fat was practically nonexistent, energy was ever flowing, and my athletic skills were ever-growing. Age has caught up with me and I can no longer play these sports. At this point in my life, I attempt to remain active through regularly scheduled workouts to keep my body fat in a reasonable double-digit category. This requires effective planning, time management, and willpower.

—Aaron Thompson

4. **Exercise promotes weight loss and weight management.** In a study of 188 countries, the highest proportion of overweight and obese people live in the United States, and the rate is increasing (Ng et al. 2014). The national increase in overweight Americans is due not only to our consuming more calories but also to our lower levels of physical activity (NIDDK 2010).

   Intentional exercise is our best antidote to all the inactivity that characterizes modern life. As a weight-control strategy, it's superior to dieting in one key respect: It raises the body's rate of metabolism—the rate at which consumed calories are burned as energy rather than stored as fat. In contrast, dieting lowers the body's rate of metabolism and the rate at which calories are burned (Agus et al. 2000; Leibel, Rosenbaum, and Hirsch 1995). After two to three weeks of low-calorie dieting without exercising, the body "thinks" it's starving, so it compensates by conserving more calories as fat so that it can be used for future energy (Bennett and Gurin 1983). In contrast, exercise speeds up basal metabolism—the body's rate of metabolism when it's resting. Thus, in addition to burning fat directly while exercising, exercise burns fat by continuing to keep the body's metabolic rate higher after we stop exercising and move on to do more sedentary things.

Benefits of Exercise for the Mind

In addition to its multiple benefits for the body, exercise benefits the mind. Here's a summary of the powerful effects that physical exercise has on our mental health and mental performance.

1. **Exercise increases mental energy and improves mental performance.** Have you noticed how red our face gets when we engage in strenuous physical activity? This rosy complexion occurs because physical activity pumps enormous amounts of blood into our head region and more oxygen into our brain. Exercise increases blood flow to all parts of the body, but since the brain uses more oxygen than any other organ of the body, it's the organ that benefits most from exercise. One well-designed study of more than 250 college students discovered that students who regularly engaged in vigorous physical activity had higher GPAs (Parker-Pope 2010).

   Furthermore, exercise is a stimulant whose stimulating effects are similar to those provided by popular energy drinks (e.g., Red Bull, Full Throttle, and Monster). However, exercise delivers these stimulating effects without the sugar, caffeine, and negative side effects of energy drinks—such as nervousness, irritability, increased blood pressure, and a sharp drop in energy ("crash") after the drink's stimulating effects wear off (Malinauskas et al. 2007).

2. **Exercise elevates mood.** Exercise stimulates release of: (a) endorphins—morphine-like chemicals found in the brain that produce a natural high and (b) serotonin—a mellowing brain chemical that reduces feelings of tension, anxiety, and depression. Studies show that people who exercise regularly report feeling happier (Myers 1993).

3. **Exercise improves self-esteem.** Exercise can enhance our sense of self-worth by providing us with a feeling of accomplishment and improving our physical self-image (e.g., better weight control, muscle tone, and skin tone).

4. **Exercise deepens and enriches the quality of sleep.** Sleep research indicates that if we engage in exercise at least three hours

> "I'm less active now than before college because I'm having trouble learning how to manage my time."
> —AHE First-year student

NOTE

Five-, seven-, or ten-minute workouts can be key pieces in a balanced exercise plan. Take the stairs instead of the elevator or escalator . . . every step counts!

> "To keep the body in good health is a duty, otherwise we shall not be able to keep our mind strong and clear."
> —Buddha, founder of Buddhism

> "It is exercise alone that supports the spirits, and keeps the mind in vigor."
> —Marcus Cicero, ancient Roman orator and philosopher

before bedtime, it helps us fall asleep, stay asleep, and sleep more deeply (Singh, Clements, and Fiatarone 1997; Youngstedt 2005). This is why exercise is a common component of treatment programs for people suffering from insomnia (Dement and Vaughan 2000).

Guidelines and Strategies for Maximizing the Effectiveness of Exercise

Although specific types of exercises benefit the body and mind in different ways, there are general guidelines that can be followed to maximize the positive impact of any exercise routine or personal fitness program. These guidelines are discussed below.

1. **Warm up before exercising and cool down after exercising.** Begin and end your workout with a five- to ten-minute warm-up and cooldown. Your body will thank you!
2. **Engage in cross-training to attain total body fitness.** A balanced, comprehensive fitness program includes cross-training—a combination of different exercises to achieve total body fitness. We should strive to combine exercises that enable us to achieve all of the following physical benefits:
   * Endurance and weight control (e.g., running, cycling, or swimming);
   * Muscle strength and tone (e.g., weight training, push-ups, or sit-ups); and
   * Flexibility (e.g., yoga, Pilates, or tai chi).
3. **Include *interval training* as part of your exercise plan.** Interval training involves interspersing high-intensity exercise workouts with low-intensity exercise or short rest periods (Roxburgh et al. 2014), such as interspersing walking with short bursts of running. Research indicates that alternating between higher- and lower-intensity exercises effectively strengthen the heart muscle and increases its oxygen-carrying capacity; it also burns calories faster and enables you to exercise longer and at more intense levels (Mayo Clinic 2015; Mazurek et al. 2014).
4. **Exercise regularly, allowing strength and stamina to increase gradually.** The key to attaining fitness and avoiding injury is body training, not body straining. One strategy for ensuring you're not straining your body is to see if you can talk while you're exercising. If you can't continue speaking without stopping to catch your breath, this may indicate you're overdoing it.
5. **Take advantage of exercise and fitness resources on your campus.** Your college tuition pays use of the campus gym or recreation

AUTHOR'S JOURNEY

I had a habit of exercising too intensely—to the point where my body felt sore for days after I worked out. I eventually discovered a way to avoid overdoing it. When listening to music through headphones while exercising, I'd see if I could sing along with the music without having to stop and catch my breath. If I could, I knew I wasn't overextending myself. This strategy has helped me manage my exercise intensity level and reduce my day-after exercise soreness. (Plus, I've gained more confidence as a vocalist because my singing sounds a lot better when my ears are covered with headphones.)

—Joe Cuseo

center, so take advantage of it. If exercise groups or clubs meet on campus, join them; they can provide you with a motivational support group that converts exercise from a solitary routine into a social experience. (It's also a good way to meet people.)

6. **Take advantage of natural opportunities for physical activity that present themselves during the day.** Exercise can take place in places beyond a gym or fitness center and outside scheduled workout times. Opportunities for exercise are available to us as we go about our daily activities. If you can walk or ride your bike to class, do that instead of driving a car or riding a bus. If you can climb some stairs instead of taking an elevator, take the route that requires more bodily activity.

 ### Journal Reflection 5.4

Develop a balanced routine that includes food, exercise, and sleep schedules, post it in a spot that you see every day or as your screen saver to motivate and remind you of your SMART goals.

How are you doing with your plan?

Not great. I have 3 planners and not enough time in the day to get everything done.

How are you feeling about yourself and your health?

I'm very discouraged and feeling like maybe college isn't for me.

REST AND SLEEP

We often underestimate the power of sleep and think we can cut down on the time we spend sleeping without compromising the quality of our lives. However, as discussed below, the amount of sleep we get plays a pivotal role for preserving our health and enhancing our performance.

The Value and Purpose of Sleep

Resting and reenergizing the body are the most obvious purposes of sleep. Listed below are other benefits of sleep that are less well known but equally important (Dement and Vaughan 2000; Horne 1988).

> Sleep deprivation is a major epidemic in our society. Americans spend so much time and energy chasing the American dream that they don't have much time left for actual dreaming."
>
> —*William Dement, pioneering sleep researcher and founder of the American Sleep Disorders Association*

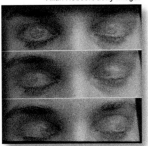

Studies show that dreaming during the REM stage of sleep helps us cope with stress and retain memories.

1. **Sleep restores and preserves the power of the immune system.** Studies show that when humans and other animals lose sleep, it lowers their production of disease-fighting antibodies, making them more susceptible to illness, such as common colds and the flu (Bryant, Trinder, and Curtis 2004).
2. **Sleep helps us cope with daily stress.**
3. **Sleep helps the brain form and retain memories.**

The Importance of Sleep for College Students

College students tend to have poorer sleep habits and experience more sleep problems than the general population. Heavier academic workloads, more opportunities for late-night socializing, and more frequent late-night (or all-night) study sessions often lead to more irregular sleep schedules and more sleep deprivation among college students. It's estimated that 60% of college students get an insufficient amount of sleep—a rate twice that of the general population (Kingkade 2014).

How much sleep do we need and should we get? The answer lies in our genes and varies from person to person. On average, adults need seven to eight hours of sleep per day and teenagers need slightly more—about nine hours (Ohayon et al. 2004). Research shows that college students get an average of less than seven hours of sleep each night (Hicks, cited in Zimbardo, Johnson, and McCann 2012), which means they're not getting the amount of sleep needed for optimal academic performance.

> "First of all, you should probably know that your body will not function without sleep. I learned that the hard way."
>
> —*words written by AHE First-year student in a letter of advice to incoming students*

When our body is deprived of the amount of sleep it's genetically designed to receive, it accumulates "sleep debt," which, like financial debt, must be paid back (Dement and Vaughan 2000). If our sleep debt isn't repaid, it catches up to us and we pay for it by experiencing lower energy, lower mood, poorer health, and poorer performance (Van Dongen et al. 2003). For example, studies show that the negative effects of sleep loss on driving an automobile are similar to the effects of drinking alcohol (Arnedt et al. 2001; Fletcher et al. 2003). Studies of sleep-deprived college students indicate that their academic performance is poorer than students who get sufficient sleep (Spinweber, cited in Zimbardo, Johnson, and McCann 2012).

Strategies for Improving Sleep Quality

Since sleep has such powerful benefits for both the body and mind, if you can improve the quality of your sleep, you can improve your physical and mental well-being. Listed below are specific strategies for improving sleep quality, which, in turn, should improve your health and performance.

1. **Become more aware of your sleep habits by keeping a sleep log or sleep journal.** Make note of what you did before going to bed on nights when you slept well or poorly. Tracking your sleep experiences in a journal may enable you to detect a pattern or relationship between certain things you do (or don't do) during the day on those nights when you sleep well. If you discover a pattern, you may have found yourself a routine to follow that gets you a good night's sleep on a consistent basis.
2. **Try to get into a regular sleep schedule by going to sleep and getting up at about the same time each day.** The human body

functions best when it's on a biological rhythm of set cycles. If you can get your body on a regular sleep cycle, you can get into a biological rhythm that makes it easier for you to fall asleep, stay asleep, and wake up naturally from sleep—according to your body's own "internal alarm clock."

Establishing a stable sleep schedule is particularly important around midterms and finals. Unfortunately, however, these are the times during the term when just the opposite happens. Normal sleep cycles are disrupted by cramming in last-minute studying, staying up later, getting up earlier, or pulling all-nighters and not sleeping at all. Sleep research shows that if students want to be at their physical and mental best for upcoming exams, they should get themselves on a regular sleep schedule of going to bed about the same time and getting up about the same time for at least one week before exams are to be taken (Dement and Vaughan 2000).

3. **Attempt to get into a relaxing pre-bedtime ritual each night.** Taking a hot bath or shower, consuming a hot (noncaffeinated) beverage, or listening to relaxing music are bedtime rituals that can get you into a worry-free state before sleep and help you fall asleep sooner. In addition, making a list of things you intend to do the next day before going to bed may help you relax and fall asleep because you know you're organized and ready to handle the following day's tasks.

A light review of class notes or reading highlights just before bedtime can be a good nighttime ritual because sleep helps you retain what you experienced just before falling asleep. Many years of research indicate that the best thing you can do after attempting to learn information is to "sleep on it," probably because your brain can focus on processing and storing that information without interference from external stimulation or outside distractions (Jenkins and Dallenbach 1924; Kuriyama et al. 2008).

Journal Reflection 5.5

What do you do on most nights immediately before going to bed? Do you think this helps or hinders the quality of your sleep?

_____

_____

_____

_____

_____

4. **Avoid intense mental activity just before going to bed.** Light mental work may serve as a relaxing presleep ritual, but cramming intensely

for a difficult exam or doing intensive writing before bedtime will put you in a state of mental arousal, which can interfere with your ability to wind down and fall asleep.

5. **Avoid intense physical exercise before bedtime.** Physical exercise elevates muscle tension and increases oxygen flow to the brain, both of which will hinder your ability to fall asleep. If you like to exercise in the evening, it should be done at least three hours before bedtime (Epstein and Mardon 2007).

6. **Avoid consuming sleep-interfering foods, beverages, or drugs in the late afternoon or evening.** In particular, avoid the following substances near bedtime:

   • **Caffeine.** It's a stimulant drug; for most people, it will stimulate their nervous system and keep them awake.

   • **Nicotine.** Another stimulant drug that's also likely to reduce the depth and quality of your sleep. (Note: Smoking hookah through a water pipe delivers the same amount of nicotine as a cigarette.)

   • **Alcohol.** It's a depressant (sedative) that makes you feel sleepy in larger doses; however, in smaller doses, it can have a stimulating effect. Furthermore, alcohol in any amount disrupts the quality of sleep by reducing the amount of time we spend in dream-stage sleep. (Marijuana does the same.)

   • **High-fat foods.** Eating just before bedtime (or during the night) increases digestive activity in the stomach. This "internal noise" is likely to interfere with the soundness of our sleep. Peanuts, beans, fruits, raw vegetables, and high-fat snacks should especially be avoided because these are harder-to-digest foods.

7. **Make sure the temperature in the room where you're sleeping is not warmer than 70 degrees (Fahrenheit).** Warm temperatures often make us feel sleepy, but they usually don't help us stay asleep or sleep deeply. This is why people have trouble sleeping on hot summer evenings. High-quality, uninterrupted sleep is more likely to take place at room temperatures around 65 degrees (Lack et al. 2008).

NOTE

Substances that make us feel sleepy or cause us to fall asleep (e.g., alcohol and marijuana) typically reduce the quality of our sleep by interfering with dream sleep.

SUBSTANCE ABUSE AND RISKY BEHAVIOR

In addition to putting healthy nutrients into our body, as well as exercising and resting it, there are two other important elements of physical wellness: (a) keeping risky substances out of our body and (b) avoiding risky behaviors that threaten our body's well-being.

Alcohol Use among College Students

Research indicates that first-year college students drink more than they did in high school (Johnston et al. 2005) and that alcohol abuse is higher among first-year college students than students at more advanced stages of their college experience (Bergen-Cico 2000). The most common reason why first-year students drink is to "fit in" or to feel socially accepted (Meilman and Presley 2005). If you choose to drink, make sure that it's *your* choice, not a choice imposed on you through social pressure or conformity. Since it's a substance commonly accessible at college parties and social gatherings, you'll be confronted with two choices:

1. To drink or not to drink
2. To drink responsibly or irresponsibly

If you decide to drink, here are some quick tips for drinking safely and responsibly:

- **Eat well before drinking and snack while drinking.** This will help lower the peak level of alcohol in your bloodstream.
- **Drink slowly.** Sip, don't gulp, and avoid "shot-gunning" or "chug-a-lugging" drinks.
- **Space out drinking over time.** (This gives the body time to metabolize the alcohol you've consumed and keeps your blood-alcohol level manageable.)
- **Alternate water and alcoholic drinks.**
- **Maintain awareness of how much you're drinking while you're drinking by monitoring your physical and mental state.** Slow down or stop drinking after you've reached a state of moderate relaxation or a mild loss of inhibition. When folks drink to the point of slurring their speech, nodding out, or vomiting in the restroom, they're not exactly the life of the party.

In addition, remember that alcohol is costly—both in terms of money and calories. Thus, reducing the amount we drink is not only a better way to manage our health; it's also a better way to manage our money and weight.

Alcohol Abuse among College Students

College students' expectations are that they should drink (or drink to excess) accounts, at least in part, for the fact that the number one drug problem on college campuses is *binge drinking*—periodic drinking episodes during which a large amount of alcohol (four to five drinks) is consumed in a short period of time, resulting in an acute state of intoxication, a.k.a., a "drunken state" (Marczinski, Estee, and Grant 2009). Consumed in moderate amounts, alcohol is a relaxing beverage; in larger doses, it's a mind-altering drug. Like any other mind-altering substance, it has the potential to be addictive; approximately 7%–8% of people who drink experience alcohol dependency (alcoholism) (Julien, Advokat, and Comaty 2011). If there's a history of alcohol dependency in your family, be particularly cautious about your drinking habits.

Although binge drinking isn't necessarily a form of alcohol dependency, it's still a form of alcohol abuse because it has direct, negative effects on the health and well-being of the drinker (as well as others who have contact with the drinker). Research indicates that repeatedly getting drunk reduces the size and effectiveness of the part of the brain involved with memory formation (Brown et al. 2000). These findings have led researchers to a simple conclusion: Each time we get drunk, the dumber we get (Weschsler and Wuethrich 2002).

Binge drinking also reduces our inhibitions about engaging in risk-taking behavior, which, in turn, increases our risk of personal accidents, injuries, and illnesses. It's noteworthy that the legal age for consuming alcohol was once lowered to 18 years; it was raised back to 21 because the number of drunk-driving accidents and deaths among teenage drinkers increased dramatically when the legal age was lowered (NHTSA/FARS and U.S. Census Bureau 2012). Traffic accidents still account for more deaths of Americans between the ages of 15 and 24 than any other single cause (Centers for Disease Control and Prevention 2010).

Who's In Charge?

Drugs and Alcohol

It's "Thirsty Thursday" and your friend convinces you to go to a party with him. You tell him that you have class at 9:00 and you cannot miss it. He assures you that you will be home before midnight. You go to the party and you are having a great time. Everyone is drinking so you decide you should join in (even though you are underage). You drink more than your fair share and stumble in at 3 a.m. Your friend makes sure you get to bed OK and even sets your alarm for 8:30 so that you can make it to your 9:00 class. You are sick all night because you drank too much and you pass out on the bathroom floor. You finally get up around 11:00 and realize you missed class. You hear from a classmate that the teacher gave a pop quiz. You are irate with your friend because it is all his fault that you missed class and the quiz! Could you have handled this situation differently? If so, how? Who really is to blame for you missing class and the quiz?

_____

_____

_____

_____

_____

_____

_____

Arguably, no other drug reduces a person's inhibitions as dramatically as alcohol. When people consume a substantial amount of alcohol, they often become substantially less cautious about doing things they normally wouldn't do. This chemically induced sense of confidence—sometimes referred to as "liquid courage"—can override the process of logical thinking and decision making, increasing the drinker's willingness to engage in irrational, risk-taking behavior (e.g., engaging in dangerous stunts). Binge drinkers are also more willing to engage in reckless driving—increasing their risk of injury or death—and reckless (unprotected) sex—increasing their risk of accidental pregnancy or contracting sexual transmitted infections (STIs). It could be said that binge drinking leads drinkers to think they're invincible, immortal, and infertile.

This lack of inhibition happens because alcohol is a depressant drug, which depresses (slows down) signals normally sent from the upper, front part of the brain (the "human brain") that's responsible for rational thinking. This is the part of the brain that normally controls or inhibits the lower, middle part of the brain (the "animal brain")—which is responsible for basic animal drives, such as sex and aggression (see **Figure 5.4**). When the upper (rational) brain's messages are slowed by alcohol, the animal brain is freed from the signals that normally restrain or inhibit it, allowing its basic drives to be released or expressed. This is the underlying biological reason why excessive alcohol use increases the risk of aggressive behavior, such as: reckless driving, damaging property, fighting, sexual harassment, sexual abuse, and relationship violence (Abbey 2002; Bushman and Cooper 1990).

FIGURE 5.4: How Alcohol Works in the Brain to Reduce Personal Inhibitions

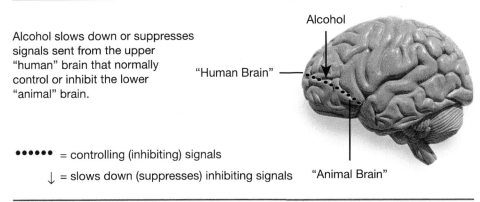

Alcohol slows down or suppresses signals sent from the upper "human" brain that normally control or inhibit the lower "animal" brain.

●●●●●● = controlling (inhibiting) signals

↓ = slows down (suppresses) inhibiting signals

©Kendall Hunt Publishing Company.

The point we're making here is not to scare you away from even thinking about drinking, nor is it to "guilt" you if you already drink. The point being made is: If you don't drink and don't care to drink, don't be pressured into drinking; and if you do drink, don't do it in excess or in binges.

Perscription and Illegal Drug Abuse

Alcohol can be legally used by anyone 21 years of age and older; other substances cannot be legally used by anyone at any age. While the college years are often a time for exploring and experimenting with different ideas, feelings, and experiences, experimenting with illegal drugs can be risky. Even if we know how an illegal drug affects people in general, we don't know how it will affect us individually because each person has a unique genetic makeup. Furthermore, unlike legal drugs, which have to pass through rigorous testing by the Federal Drug Administration before being approved for public consumption, we don't have similar safeguards for the production and packaging of illegal drugs. For instance, we don't know if or what the drug may have been "cut" (mixed) with during the production process. Thus, we're not just taking a criminal risk by using an illegal substance, we're also taking a health risk by consuming an *unregulated* substance. Our bottom-line recommendation is: When in doubt,

THINK ABOUT IT

Prescription drug abuse deaths are increasing at an alarming rate. Do not be fooled, just because you have a prescription does not mean you will not become addicted.

keep it out. Don't put anything into your body that's unregulated and whose impact may be unpredictable.

Listed below are the major types of illegal drugs, accompanied by a short description of their effects. Following the list, **Box 5.2** contains a summary of the major motives or reasons why people use drugs.

- **Cocaine (coke, crack).** A stimulant that's typically snorted or smoked and produces a strong "rush" (an intense feeling of euphoria)
- **Amphetamines (speed, meth).** A strong stimulant that increases energy and general arousal; it's usually taken in pill form but may also be smoked or injected
- **Ecstasy (X).** A stimulant typically taken in pill form that speeds up the nervous system and reduces social inhibitions
- **Hallucinogens (psychedelics).** Drugs that alter or distort perception—such as, LSD ("acid") and hallucinogenic mushrooms ("shrooms")
- **Narcotics (e.g., heroin and prescription pain pills).** Sedative drugs that slow down the nervous system and produce feelings of relaxation. (Heroin is a particularly powerful narcotic that's typically injected or smoked and produces an intense "rush" of euphoria.)
- **Marijuana (weed, pot).** Still an illegal drug in most states, it's primarily a depressant or sedative drug that slows down the nervous system and induces feelings of relaxation. It is important to note that while marijuana may be legal in some states, federal law (marijuana is illegal) overrides state law when an institutions receive federal funds. Thus, marijuana is illegal on almost all college campuses regardless of the state law.
- **Date rape drugs.** Depressant (sedative) drugs that induce sleepiness, memory loss, and possible loss of consciousness; they're typically colorless, tasteless, and odorless, so they can be easily mixed into a drink without the person noticing it, rendering that person vulnerable to rape or other forms of sexual assault. The most common date rape drugs are Rohypnol ("roofies") and GHB ("liquid E").
- **Synthetic drugs.** There has been a recent rise in the use of synthetic drugs (bath salts, K2, Spice). Legalities vary from state to state, but there is no regulation on these chemical compounds. Because of this, these substance can be just as dangerous (if not more so) than traditional illegal drugs.

Journal Reflection 5.6

What drugs (if any) have you seen being used on your campus?

_____

_____

_____

_____

How would the type and frequency of drug use on your campus compare to what you saw in high school?

Much less. My highschool was bad about substance abuse. I haven't seen any on campus at all.

BOX 5.2

Motives (Reasons) for Drug Use

People use drugs for a variety of reasons, the most common of which are listed below. If we remain aware of these motives, we reduce the risk that we'll do drugs for unconscious or subconscious reasons.

1. **Social Pressure.** To "fit in" or be socially accepted (e.g., drinking alcohol because everyone seems to be doing it)
2. **Recreational (Party) Use.** For fun, stimulation, or pleasure (e.g., smoking marijuana at parties to relax, loosen inhibitions, and have a "good time")
3. **Experimental Use.** Doing drugs out of curiosity—to test out its effects (e.g., experimenting with LSD to see what it's like to have a psychedelic or hallucinogenic experience)

4. **Therapeutic Use.** Using prescription or over-the-counter drugs for medical purposes (e.g., taking Prozac for depression or Adderall to treat attention deficit disorder)
5. **Performance Enhancement.** To improve physical, mental, or social performance (e.g., taking steroids to improve athletic performance, stimulants to stay awake all night and cram for an exam, or alcohol to reduce social inhibitions and become more outgoing)
6. **Escapism.** To escape a personal problem or an unpleasant emotional state (e.g., taking ecstasy to escape depression or boredom)
7. **Addiction.** Physical or psychological dependence resulting from habitual use of a drug (e.g., continuing to use nicotine or cocaine because stopping triggers withdrawal symptoms such as anxiety and depression)

💡 Journal Reflection 5.7

What motives for drug use listed in **Box 5.2** would you say are the most common reasons for drug use on your campus?

Any drug has the potential to be addictive (habit forming), especially if it's injected intravenously (directly into a vein) or smoked (inhaled through the lungs). These routes of delivery are particularly dangerous because they allow the drug to reach the brain faster and heighten its peak effect (the intensity of its highest point of impact). This rapid and high-peak effect is immediately followed by a rapid and sharp drop ("crash") (see **Figure 5.5**). This peak-to-valley, roller-coaster experience creates a greater risk for craving the drug again, thereby increasing the user's risk of dependency (addiction).

FIGURE 5.5: Drugs Smoked Produce a Higher and More Rapid Peak Effect

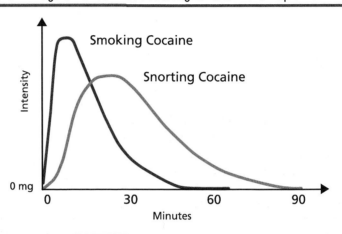

©Kendall Hunt Publishing Company

Here's a list of the most common signs that a person's drug use (including alcohol) is moving in the direction of *dependency* (*addiction*):

- Steadily increasing the amount (dose) of the drug and/or using it more often
- Difficulty cutting back (e.g., unable to use the drug less frequently or in smaller amounts)
- Difficulty controlling or limiting the amount taken after starting
- Keeping a steady supply of the drug on hand
- Spending more money on the drug than the person can afford
- Using the drug alone
- Hiding or hoarding the drug
- Lying about drug use to family and friends
- Reacting angrily or defensively when questioned about use of the drug
- Being "in denial" about abusing the drug (e.g., "I don't have a problem")
- Rationalizing drug abuse (e.g., "I'm just partying. It's a normal part of the college experience.")
- When continuing to use the drug matters more to the user than the personal and interpersonal problems caused by its use.
- Stealing from family, friends, anyone, in order to fund their habit

SEXUALLY TRANSMITTED INFECTIONS (STIs)

STIs represent a group of contagious infections spread through sexual contact that can threaten our health and well-being. Latex condoms provide the best protection against STIs (Holmes, Levine, and Weaver 2004). In addition, having sex with fewer partners reduces the risk of contracting an STI. Obviously, not engaging in sexual intercourse is the most foolproof way to eliminate the risk of an STI (and unwanted pregnancy). When it comes to sexual intercourse, we have three basic options: Do it recklessly, do it safely, or don't do it. If you choose the last option (abstinence), it doesn't mean you're a cold or unaffectionate prude. All it means is that you're choosing not to have sexual intercourse at this particular time in your life.

More than 25 types of STIs have been identified and virtually all of them are effectively treated if detected early. Listed below is a summary of the major forms of STIs. If ignored, some STIs can progress to the point where they result in serious infection and possible infertility (Cates et al. 2004). Experiencing pain during or after urination, or unusual discharge from the penis or vaginal areas, is common early symptoms of STI. But the symptoms can sometimes be subtle and undetectable. If you have any doubt, play it safe and check it out immediately by visiting the Health Center on your campus. Any advice or treatment you receive there will remain confidential. If you discover that you have an STI, immediately inform anyone you've had sex with, so he or she can receive early treatment before the disease progresses. This isn't just a polite thing to do; it's the right (ethical) thing to do.

STIs Caused by Bacteria

Gonorrhea. This is a common STI with few symptoms but serious consequences if it is left untreated. In 2007, there were 355,991 cases reported; however, the Centers for Disease Control and Prevention (CDC) estimates there are nearly twice as many infections annually than the number reported (Weinstock, Berman, and Cates 2004). Men typically experience creamy, yellow-colored, pus-like discharge from the penis, and burning when urinating. Women experience few early symptoms, but the disease can lead to later pelvic infections and possible infertility. The best way to detect gonorrhea, or any other STI that produces early symptoms that are not visible, is to have a laboratory test done by a doctor or health care provider. Gonorrhea can be treated and completely cured with antibiotics.

Chlamydia. This is the number one bacterial STI; it's estimated to infect more than 10% of college students. In 2007, there were 1,108,374 chlamydia diagnoses reported, the largest number of cases ever reported to the CDC for any condition. Symptoms include a clear, mucous-like discharge and a burning sensation when urinating. Men may experience pain in the testes, and women may experience pain in the abdomen. However, women typically experience few or no early symptoms.

Genital Herpes. Typically produces painful blisters on the genitals or in the anus, which may itch and burn, especially during and following urination. Symptoms may disappear and come back, but are never cured. Later attacks tend to be less severe than the first attack. The frequency and intensity of outbreaks can be reduced with prescription medication (e.g., acyclovir capsules).

Syphilis. Men first experience ulcers (open sores) on the penis. Women may first develop ulcers in the vagina, but they can be overlooked, allowing the disease to progress. Syphilis is totally curable with antibiotics.

STIs Caused by Viruses

Human Papilloma Virus (HPV). Overall, this is the most common STI among young, sexually active people. HPV is a virus that may cause warts in the genital area, but it typically does not produce noticeable symptoms in its early stages. Sometimes, the disease may also cause lesions (abnormal tissue changes) that are not visible, but when they appear, they look like small hard, cauliflower-like spots. Men can experience warts on the penis. HPV is treatable with laser or chemical treatment, which basically burn off the lesions. If untreated, HPV can lead to cancer of the cervix in women. If you are or have been sexually active, check with the health center on your campus to find out about the HPV vaccine that is available for both men and women. The Center for Disease Control recommends getting the vaccine between the ages of 11 and 13, before most people are active sexually. However, whenever the vaccine is administered, it will prevent your exposure to the two forms of HPV viruses that are most responsible for cervical cancer.

Human Immunodeficiency Virus (HIV). Early symptoms include fever, night sweats, swollen lymph nodes, diarrhea, chronic fatigue, and weight loss. About one-half of people with HIV experience these flu-like symptoms, but one-half show no symptoms at all. Thus, the disease may go undetected until the person is given a blood test for some other reason. Most cases of HIV are transmitted through sexual contact; however, the disease may also be contracted through the sharing of intravenous needles. The most serious form of HIV is acquired immune deficiency syndrome (AIDS), which is a life-threatening condition, because the person's immune system becomes severely impaired and leaves the infected person vulnerable to cancer and diseases of the nervous system. HIV infection is just one of the reasons you should never have unprotected sex, especially with new partners whose former experiences may be unknown to you.

Hepatitis B or Hepatitis C. About one-half of the people with hepatitis experience flu-like symptoms, and one-half show no symptoms at all. Thus, the disease may go undetected until the person is given a blood test for some other reason.

Who's In Charge?

STIs

You have been seeing a new guy for almost a month and decide you are ready have sex. He tells you not to worry because he has been tested for STIs and the test came back clean. Since you are both really into each other and have decided to be exclusive and you are on the pill, you decide there is no need to use a condom. Sex is so much better without them! A few weeks later you notice an odd-smelling discharge and go to the doctor only to find out you have an STI. What could you have done to prevent getting the STI? Many people blame the partner, but in this case, could the situation have been prevented? How?

_____

_____

_____

_____

_____

Pubic Lice (a.k.a. "Crabs"). Caused by tiny lice that are called "crabs" (because they look like sea crabs), which breed in pubic hair around the genitals. These creatures are not dangerous but can cause intense itching.

UNPLANNED PREGNANCY AND COLLEGE STUDENTS

Although many might think this topic is not necessary to talk about for students in colleges, it is! The rate of unplanned pregnancies is actually increasing (and not decreasing) among 20- to 24-year olds (Guttmacher Institute 2009). Possibly the most important thing to know regarding college students and unplanned pregnancy is that 61% of women who have children after enrolling in a college do not finish their education. This number is 65% higher than for women who do not have children while in college (Bradburn 2002).

Many students believe that preventing pregnancy while in school is important. Three-quarters of students report that preventing unplanned pregnancy is important to them, and eight in ten say that having a child while in school would make it harder to accomplish their goals. Research supports this belief. Students who are parents, particularly those who are single parents, often do not do as well in college as their peers without children (Prentice, Storin, Robinson 2012). Thus, having unprotected sex can lead to multiple unplanned outcome

Birth Control Facts

True or False: It is necessary to "take a break" from the pill every couple years.

True or False: An IUD can only be used by women who have already given birth.

True or False: It is okay to use petroleum jelly or Vaseline as a lubricant when using latex condoms.

True or False: A woman with a regular, 28-day cycle is most likely to get pregnant about two weeks after the first day of her period.

Among couples who have sex regularly, what percentage will get pregnant within one year if they use no birth control at all? 15%, 33%, 60%, 85%, or 97%?

If you would like more information refer to Bedsider.org to watch the "Fact or Fiction" videos about other myths.

Fog Zone (http://thenationalcampaign.org/sites/default/files/resource-supporting-download/myths.pdf) and Magical Thinking (http://thenationalcampaign.org/sites/default/files/resource-primary-download/magicalthinking.pdf) publications.

Answers: false, false, false, true, 85%.

NOTE

Avoid whenever possible walking on campus late at night alone. Take advantage of campus security services.

CAMPUS SAFETY

College campuses are generally safe and no more prone to crime than other locations or organizations. However, crimes do occur on campuses and one element of wellness is reducing your risk of being victimized by crimes, particularly crimes that threaten your physical well-being. Listed below are some top tips on doing so.

- After dark, don't walk alone; use a buddy system.
- At night or when walking alone, don't get so absorbed in texting or listening to iTunes that you tune out or block out what's going on around you.
- If you're carrying valuable electronics, keep them concealed.
- Check if your campus has an escort service at night; if it does, take advantage of it.
- Call ahead for campus shuttles and escort services to reduce the amount of time you're waiting for a ride.
- Have your keys out and ready before entering your building or your car, and double-check to be sure the door locks behind you.
- Know the phone number and location of the office for campus safety.
- Be aware of the location of emergency phones in academic buildings.
- Put emergency numbers in your cell phone.

(Sources: Lucier, 2015; "Staying Safe on Campus," 2012.)

Mobile apps are also available to promote your safety. For instance, "Circle of 6" (www.circleof6app.com/) is a free mobile map that allows you to choose a network of six friends whom you can contact with emergency text messages, such as: "Call me immediately," "Come and get me," or "I need help getting home safely." When you text a message, your GPS location is included. This app was a co-winner of the national "Apps Against Abuse Challenge" sponsored by the White House (Rivera 2015).

"ArcAngel" (www.patrocinium.com/arcangel) is another mobile safety app that notifies you within seconds of an emergency or if you're near danger (e.g., a crime scene, fire, or flood); it also provides ongoing status reports throughout the emergency and recommends evacuation routes as needed. If you need help, you can click a button that informs local authorities, campus security teams, and family members of your exact location.

Take advantage of these new safety technologies to lower your risk of being victimized by crime and avoiding dangerous situations.

CHAPTER SUMMARY AND HIGHLIGHTS

Wellness is a state of high-quality health and personal well-being that promotes peak physical and mental performance. It requires a healthy lifestyle that includes the following key elements: (a) supplying our body with effective fuel (nutrition) for optimal energy, (b) using energy to engage in heath-preserving exercise, and (c) giving our body adequate rest (sleep) so that it can recover and replenish the energy it has expended.

Research findings and recommendations from health care professionals indicate that physical wellness is most effectively promoted by adopting the following strategies:

- **Watch what we eat.** In particular, we should increase consumption of natural fruits, vegetables, legumes, whole grains, fish, and water and decrease consumption of processed foods, fatty foods, fried foods, fast foods, and foods purchased from vending machines. Although the expression, "you are what you eat" may be a bit of an exaggeration, it contains a kernel of truth because the food we consume does affect our health, our emotions, and our performance.
- **Become more physically active.** To counteract the sedentary lifestyle created by life in modern society and attain total fitness, we should engage in a balanced blend of exercises that build stamina, strength, and flexibility.
- **Don't cheat on sleep.** Humans typically do not get the amount of sleep they need to perform at peak levels. College students, in particular, need to get more sleep than they usually do and develop more regular (consistent) sleep habits.
- **Drink alcohol responsibly or not at all.** Avoid excessive consumption of alcohol or other mind-altering substances that can threaten our

physical health, impair our mental judgment, and reduce our inhibitions about engaging in dangerous, risk-taking behavior.

- **Avoid use of illegal substances or prescription drugs that are unregulated**—particularly substances whose effects may be unpredictable and that pose a high risk for dependency (addiction).
- **Minimize the risk of contracting sexually transmitted infections.** There are three basic strategies for doing so: using latex condoms during sex, limiting the number of sexual partners, or choosing not to be sexually active.
- **Minimize the risk of unwanted pregnancy.** The rate of unwanted pregnancies is increasing among college-aged students; the risk can be reduced by engaging in protected sex or postponing sex.

The wellness-promoting strategies discussed in this chapter are effective ways to preserve health and promote peak performance, both in college and beyond.

LEARNING MORE THROUGH THE WORLD WIDE WEB: INTERNET-BASED RESOURCES

For additional information on health and wellness, see the following websites.

Nutrition:
www.eatright.org
http://www.educationdive.com/news/10-mobile-apps-making-campuses-safer/241575/

Physical Activities & Fitness:
http://archive.ncppa.org/resources/coalitions/

Sleep:
www.sleepfoundation.org
www.drugabuse.com/library/oxycodone-abuse

Drugs & Abuse (including alcohol):
http://www.drugabuse.gov/drugs-abuse
http://www.wise-drinking.com/ (an app on responsible drinking)
https://www.cdc.gov/hpv/parents/questions-answers.html

Mental Health:
http://www.activeminds.org/issues-a-resources/mental-health-resources/student-resources

Sexual Harassment, Assault, & Abuse
http://uhs.princeton.edu/medical-services/sexual-health-and-wellness

Safer Sex
www.Bedsider.org/studentsexlife
https://aidsinfo.nih.gov/understanding-hiv-aids/fact.../the-basics-of-hiv-prevention

REFERENCES

Abbey, A. 2002. "Alcohol-Related Sexual Assault: A Common Problem Among College Students." *Journal of Studies on Alcohol* 14: 118–28.

Agus M. S., J. F. Swain, C. L. Larson, E. A. Eckert, and D. S. Ludwig. 2000. "Dietary Composition and Physiologic Adaptations to Energy Restriction." *American Journal of Clinical Nutrition* 74(4): 901–07.

American Psychiatric Association. 2015. *Diagnostic and Statistical Manual of Mental disorders, DSM-IV-TR*. 5th ed. Washington, DC: Author.

Arnedt, J. T., G. J. S. Wilde, P. W. Munt, and A. W. MacLean. 2001. "How Do Prolonged Wakefulness and Alcohol Compare in the Decrements they Produce on a Simulated Driving Task?" *Accident Analysis and Prevention* 33: 337–44.

Bennett, W., and J. Gurin. 1983. *The Dieter's Dilemma*. New York: Basic Books.

Bergen-Cico, D. 2000. "Patterns of Substance Abuse and Attrition Among First-year Students." *Journal of the First-year Experience and Students in Transition* 12(1): 61–75.

Booth, F. W., and D. R. Vyas. 2001. "Genes, Environment, and Exercise." *Advances in Experimental Medicine and Biology* 502: 13–20.

Bradburn, E. M. 2002. *Short-term Enrollment in Postsecondary Education: Student Background and Institutional Differences in Reasons for Early Departure, 1996–1998*. Washington, DC: National Center for Education Statistics, U.S. Department of Education.

Brown, S. A., S. F. Tapert, E. Granholm, and D. C. Delis. 2000. "Neurocognitive Functioning of Adolescents: Effects of Protracted Alcohol Use." *Alcoholism: Clinical & Experimental Research* 24(2): 164–71.

Bushman, B. J., and H. M. Cooper. 1990. "Effects of Alcohol on Human Aggression: An Integrative Research Review." *Psychological Bulletin* 107(3): 341–54.

Cates, J. R., N. L. Herndon, S. L. Schulz, and J. E. Darroch. 2004. *Our Voices, Our Lives, Our Futures: Youth and Sexually Transmitted Diseases*. Chapel Hill, NC: University of North Carolina at Chapel Hill School of Journalism and Mass Communication.

Centers for Disease Control and Prevention. 2010. *Teen Drivers Fact Sheet*. http://www.cdc.gov/motorvehiclesafety/teen_drivers/teendrivers_factsheet.html.

Colcombe, S. J., K. Erickson, P. E. Scalf, J. S. Kim, R. Prakash, and E. McAuley. 2006. "Aerobic Exercise Training Increases Brain Volume in Aging Humans." *Journal of Gerontology: Medical Sciences* 61A(11): 1166–70.

Corbin, C. B., R. P. Pangrazi, and B. D. Franks. 2000. "Definitions: Health, Fitness, and Physical Activity." *President's Council on Physical Fitness and Sports Research Digest* 3(9): 1–8.

Covey, S. R. 2004. *Seven Habits of Highly Effective People*. 3rd ed. New York: Fireside.

Dement, W. C., and C. Vaughan. 2000. *The Promise of Sleep: A Pioneer in Sleep Medicine Explores the Vital Connection between Health, Happiness, and a Good Night's Sleep*. New York: Dell.

Epstein, L., and S. Mardon. 2007. *The Harvard Medical School Guide to a Good Night's Sleep*. New York: The McGraw-Hill Companies.

Fletcher, A., N. Lamond, C. J. van den Heuvel, and D. Dawson. 2003. "Prediction of Performance During Sleep Deprivation and Alcohol Intoxication using a Quantitative Model of Work-related Fatigue." *Sleep Research Online* 5: 67–75.

Goleman, D. 1995. *Emotional Intelligence: Why It Can Matter more than IQ*. New York: Random House.

Guttmacher Institute. 2009. *A Real-time Look at the Impact of the Recession on Women's Family Planning and Pregnancy Decisions*. New York: Guttmacher Institute.

Heath, H. 1977. *Maturity and Competence: A Transcultural View*. New York: Halsted Press.

Holmes, K. K., R. Levine, and M. Weaver. 2004. "Effectiveness of Condoms in Preventing Sexually Transmitted Infections." *Bulletin of the World Health Organization* 82: 254–464.

Jenkins, J. G., and K. M. Dallenbach. 1924. Oblivescence during Sleep and Waking. *American Journal of Psychology* 35: 605–12.

Johnston, L. D., P. M. O'Malley, J. G. Bachman, and J. E. Schulenberg. 2005. *Monitoring the Future National Survey Results on Drug Use, 1975–2004: Vol 2. College Students and Adults Ages 19–45*. National Institute on Drug Abuse: Bethesda, MD: 2005. NIH Publication No. 05-5728.

Julien, R. M., C. D. Advokat, and J. E. Comaty. 2011. *A Primer of Drug Action*. New York: Worth.

Khoshaba, D., and S. R. Maddi. 2005. *HardiTraining: Managing Stressful Change*. 4th ed. Newport Beach, CA: Hardiness Institute.

Kingkade, T. August 27, 2014. "Sleepy College Students Are Worried about Their Stress Levels." *The Huffington Post*. http://www.huffingtonpost.com/2014/08/27/college-students-sleep-stress_n_5723438.html

Kramer, A. F., and K. I. Erickson. 2007. "Capitalizing on Cortical Plasticity: Influence of Physical Activity on Cognition and Brain Function." *Trends in Cognitive Sciences* 11(8): 342–48.

Kuriyama, K., K. Mishima, H. Suzuki, S. Aritake, and M. Uchiyama. 2008. "Sleep Accelerates Improvement in Working Memory Performance." *The Journal of Neuroscience* 28(4): 10145–50.

Lack, L. C., M. Gradisar, E. J. W. Van Someren, H. R. Wright, and K. Lushington. 2008. The Relationship between Insomnia and Body Temperatures. *Sleep Medicine Reviews* 12(4): 307–17.

Leavy, P., A. Gnong, and L. S. Ross. 2009. "Femininity, Masculinity, and Body Image Issues among College-age Women: An In-depth and Written Interview Study of the Mind-body Dichotomy." *The Qualitative Report* 14(2): 261–92.

Leibel, R. L., M. Rosenbaum, and J. Hirsch. 1995. "Changes in Energy Expenditure Resulting from Altered Body Weight." *New England Journal of Medicine* 332: 621–28.

Lucler, K. L. 2015. "15 Ways to Stay Safe while in College." http://collegelife.about.com/od/healthwellness/qt/SafetyTips.htm

Malinauskas, B. M., V. G. Aeby, R. F. Overton, T. Carpenter-Aeby, and K. Barber-Heidal. 2007. "A Survey of Energy Drink Consumption Patterns among College Students." *Nutrition Journal* 6(1): 35.

Marczinski, C., G. Estee, and V. Grant. 2009. *Binge Drinking in Adolescent and College Students*. New York: Nova Science Publishers.

Mayo Clinic. 2015. "Rev Up Your Workout with Interval Training: Interval Training Can Help You Get the most Out of Your Workout." http://www.mayoclinic.org/healthy-living/fitness/in-depth/interval-training/art-20044588?pg=1

Mazurek K., K. Karwczyk, P. Zemijeeski, H. Norkoski, and M. Czajkowska. 2014. "Effects of Aerobic Interval Training versus Continuous Moderate Exercise Programme on Aerobic and Anaerobic Capacity, Somatic Features and Blood Lipid Profile in Collegiate Females." *Annals of Agricultural and Environmental Medicine* 21(4): 844–49.

Meilman, P. W., and C. A. Presley. 2005. "The First-year Experience and Alcohol Use." In *Challenging and Supporting the First-year Student: A Handbook for Improving the First Year of College*, edited by M. L. Upcraft, J. N. Gardner, B. O. Barefoot, et al. 445–68. San Francisco: Jossey-bass.

Myers, D. G. 1993. *The Pursuit of Happiness: Who Is Happy and Why?* New York: Morrow.

National Institute of Mental Health. 2014. *What Are Eating Disorders?* Washington, DC: U.S. Department of Health and Human Services. http://www.nimh.nih.gov/health/publications/eating-disorders-new-trifold/index.shtml.

Ng, M., T. Fleming, M. Robinson, B. Thomson, N. Graetz, C. Margono, E. C. Mullany, et al. 2014.

"Global, Regional, and National Prevalence of Overweight and Obesity in Children and Adults during 1980–2013: A Systematic Analysis for the Global Burden of Disease Study 2013. *The Lancet* 384 (9945): 766–81.

NHTSA/FARS and U.S. Census Bureau. 2012. *Underage Drunk Driving Fatalities*. www.centurycouncil.org/drunk-driving/underage-drunk-driving-fatalities.

NIDDK (National Institute of Diabetes and Digestive Kidney Diseases). 2010. *Overweight and Obesity Statistics*. Washington, DC: U.S. Department of Health and Human Services.

Ohayon, M. M., M. A. Carskadon, C. Guilleminault, and M. V. Vitiello. 2004. "Meta-Analysis of Quantitative Sleep Parameters from Childhood to Old Age in Healthy Individuals: Developing Normative Sleep Values Across the Human Lifespan." *Sleep* 27: 1255–73.

Parker-Pope, T. 2010. "Vigorous exercise linked with better grades." http://query.nytimes.com/gst/fullpage.html?res=9A03EEDE103EF93BA35755C0A9669D8B63.

Prentice. M., C. Storin, and G. Robinson. 2012. *Make It Personal: How Pregnancy Planning and Prevention Help Students Complete College*. Washington, DC: American Association of Community Colleges.

Rivera, C. July 1, 2015. "College Safety Gets a Tech Boost." *Los Angeles Times*, B2.

Roxburgh, B. H., P. B. Nolan, R. M. Weatherwax, L. C. Dalleck, 2014. "*Is Moderate Intensity Exercise Training Combined with High Intensity Interval Training more Effective at Improving Cardiorespiratory Fitness than Moderate Intensity Exercise Training Alone?*" *Journal of Sports Science and Medicine* 13(3):702–07.

Sax, L. J., A. N. Bryant, and S. K. Gilmartin, 2004. "A Longitudinal Investigation of Emotional Health among Male and Female First-year College Students." *Journal of the First-year Experience and Students in Transition* 16(2): 29–65.

Schlosser, E. 2005. *Fast Food Nation: The Dark Side of the All-American Meal*. New York: Harper Perennial.

Singh, N. A., K. M. Clements, and M. A. Fiatarone. 1997. "A Randomized Controlled Trial of the Effect of Exercise on Sleep." *Sleep* 20: 95–101.

Staying Safe on Campus. July 20, 2012. http://www.nytimes.com/2012/07/20/education/edlife/students-fear-venturing-out-alone-at-night-on-campus.html?pagewanted=all.

Van Dongen, H. P., G. Maislin, J. M. Mullington, and D. F. Dinges. 2003. "The Cumulative Cost of Additional Wakefulness: Dose Response Effects on Neurobehavioral Functions and Sleep Physiology from Chronic Sleep Restriction and Total Sleep Deprivation." *Sleep* 26: 117–26.

Walsh, N. P., M. Gleeson, R. J. Shephard, J. A. Woods, N. C. Bishop, M. Fleshner, C. Green, B. K. Pedersen, L. Hoffman-Goetz, C. J. Rogers, H. Northoff, A. Abbasi, and P. Simon. 2011. "Position Statement. Part One: Immune Function and Exercise." *Exercise Immunology Review* 17: 6–63.

Weinstock, H., S. Berman, and W. Cates, Jr. 2004. "Sexually Transmitted Diseases among American youth: Incidence and Prevalence Estimates, 2000." *Perspectives on Sexual and Reproductive Health* 36(10): 6–10.

Weschsler, H., and B. Wuethrich. 2002. *Dying to Drink: Confronting Binge Drinking on College Campuses.* Emmaus, PA: Rodale.

Youngstedt, S. D. 2005. "Effects of exercise on sleep." *Clinical Sports Medicine* 24(2): 355–65.

Zimbardo, P. G., R. L. Johnson, and V. McCann. 2012. *Psychology: Core Concepts.* 7th ed. Boston: Pearson.

Chapter 5 Exercises

5.1 Quote Reflections

Review the sidebar quotes contained in this chapter and select two that were especially meaningful or inspirational to you.

For each quote, provide a three- to five-sentence explanation why you chose it.

5.2 Reality Bite

Concerns about Eating: Too Much or Too Little?

The following e-mail message was sent by an underweight, 25-year-old woman (Nancy) who was seeking advice:

I have a big worry: I eat normally during the day but I eat two scoops of ice cream at the end of the day followed by a large package of cookies. I am not exaggerating the situation. Last week, I could only stuff myself with two scoops of ice cream after dinner, but these days it's getting worse—now that I can add bread and buttery cookies (a whole packet, not those mini ones, mind you). What should I do? I know that I should gain weight but I should be getting the extra pounds by more normal means like meat or milk—and I am really worried that once this binge and indulgence becomes a habit, it's difficult to get rid of.

Discussion Questions

Nancy goes on to ask the following questions about her condition. As you read each question, respond to it with the advice you think would be best.

1. Is it okay that I eat that much at the end of each day rather than distributing it equally throughout the day? (Though the former way seems better, I can tell myself, "Hey, girl, after all, you are eating less than your sister!")

2. I am eating junk food—ice cream, loads of biscuits, bread, those Garden chocolate roll cakes, chocolate fingers, chocolate McVita's, buttery cookies...It seems that this is not as healthy as gaining weight by eating meat, milk, or carbohydrates. Is this true?

3. Is it unhealthy to eat just before bed?

4. Could it become difficult to stop?

5. Am I controlled by food?

6. Now that I am eating more than my sister, I am really scared indeed, not only because I am eating far more than her but also because I am having fat deposited in undesirable parts of my body and getting a totally worse figure than she has—that fat which I had tried so hard for three years to get rid of. Any advice?

5.3 Holistic Development Needs and Priorities: A Self-Assessment

Development of the whole self is an essential goal of the liberal arts and general education. As you read through the specific skills and qualities associated with the following dimensions of holistic ("whole person") development, rate each one in terms of its *importance to you* on a scale of 1 to 5, with 5 being highest and 1 lowest.

Skills and Qualities Associated with the Dimensions of Holistic (Whole-Person) Development

1. ***Intellectual* Development:** acquiring a broad base of knowledge, learning how to learn deeply and think critically.

    Specific Objectives & Attributes:

    _____ Becoming aware of your intellectual abilities, interests, and learning styles

    _____ Improving your focus of attention and concentration

    _____ Moving beyond memorization to learning at a deeper level

    _____ mproving your ability to retain knowledge on a long-term basis

    _____ Acquiring effective research skills for finding information from a variety of sources and systems

    _____ Learning how to view issues from multiple angles or perspectives (psychological, social, political, economic, etc.)

    _____ Responding constructively to differing viewpoints or opposing arguments

    _____ Critically evaluating ideas in terms of their truth and value

    _____ Detecting and rejecting persuasion tactics that appeal to emotion rather than reason

    _____ hinking creatively and innovatively

    > Intellectual growth should commence at birth and cease only at death."
    >
    > —Albert Einstein, Nobel Prize–winning physicist

2. **Emotional Development:** understanding, managing, and expressing emotions.

    Specific Objectives and Attributes:

    _____ Dealing with personal emotions in an honest, nondefensive manner

    _____ Maintaining a healthy balance between emotional control and emotional expression

    _____ Responding with empathy and sensitivity to emotions experienced by others

    _____ Using effective stress management strategies to control anxiety and reduce tension

    _____ Dealing effectively with depression

    _____ Dealing effectively with anger

    _____ Responding constructively to frustrations and setbacks

    _____ Dealing effectively with fear of failure and lack of self-confidence

    _____ Maintaining optimism and enthusiasm

    _____ Accepting feedback from others in a constructive, nondefensive manner

    > It's not stress that kills us, it is our reaction to it."
    >
    > —Hans Selye, Canadian endocrinologist and author of Stress Without Distress

3. **Social Development:** Improving the quality and depth of interpersonal relationships.

Specific Objectives and Attributes:

_____ Increasing social self-confidence

_____ Improving listening and conversational skills

_____ Overcoming shyness

_____ Relating to others in an open, nondefensive and nonjudgmental manner

_____ Forming meaningful friendships

_____ Learning how to resolve interpersonal conflicts effectively

_____ Developing greater empathy for others

_____ Relating effectively to others from different cultural backgrounds and lifestyles

_____ Collaborating effectively with others when working in groups or teams

_____ Strengthening leadership skills

> Chi rispetta sara rippetato."
> ("Respect others and you will be respected.")
> —*Italian proverb*

4. **Ethical (Character) Development:** Developing a clear value system for guiding personal decisions, making sound ethical judgments, and demonstrating consistency between convictions (beliefs) and commitments (actions).

Specific Objectives and Attributes:

_____ Gaining deeper awareness of your personal values and ethical priorities

_____ Making personal choices and life decisions based on a meaningful value system

_____ Developing the capacity to think and act with personal integrity and authenticity

_____ Resisting social pressure to act in ways that are inconsistent with your values

_____ Treating others in a fair and just manner

_____ Exercising personal freedom responsibly without infringing on the rights of others

_____ Increasing awareness of and commitment to human rights and social justice

_____ Developing the courage to challenge or confront others who violate human rights and social justice

_____ Using electronic technology in a civil and ethical manner

_____ Becoming a more engaged and responsible citizen

> If you don't stand for something you will fall for anything."
> —*Malcolm X, African American Muslim minister, public speaker, and human rights activist*

5. **Physical Development:** Acquiring knowledge about the human body and how to apply that knowledge to prevent disease, preserve wellness, and promote peak performance.

Specific Objectives and Attributes:

_____ Becoming more aware of your physical condition and state of health

_____ Applying knowledge about exercise and fitness to improve your physical and mental health

_____ Developing sleep habits that maximize physical and mental well-being

_____ Maintaining a healthy balance between work, recreation, and relaxation

_____ Applying knowledge about nutrition to reduce risk of illness and promote peak performance levels

> A man too busy to take care of his health is like a mechanic too busy to take care of his tools."
> —*Spanish proverb*

_____ Becoming knowledgeable about nutritional imbalances and eating disorders

_____ Developing a positive physical self-image

_____ Increasing knowledge about the effects of drugs and how they affect the body and mind

_____ Becoming more knowledgeable about human sexuality and sexual diversity

_____ Understanding how biological differences between the sexes affect how males and females communicate and relate to each other

6. **Spiritual Development:** Devoting attention to the "big questions" about the meaning or purpose of life, the inevitability of death, and the origins of human life and the natural world.

Specific Objectives and Attributes:

_____ Developing or refining your philosophy of life

_____ Exploring the unknown or what cannot be completely understood scientifically

_____ Appreciating the mysteries associated with the origin of the universe

_____ Searching for the connection between the self and the larger world or cosmos

_____ Searching for the mystical or supernatural—that which transcends the boundaries of the natural world

_____ Examining questions relating to death and life after death

_____ Exploring questions about the possible existence of a supreme being or higher power

_____ Gaining knowledge about different approaches to spirituality and their underlying beliefs or assumptions

_____ Understanding the difference and relationship between faith and reason

_____ Becoming more aware and accepting of diverse religious beliefs and practices

> "We are not human beings having a spiritual experience. We are spiritual beings having a human experience."
>
> —Pierre Teilhard de Chardin, French philosopher, geologist, paleontologist, and Jesuit priest

7. **Vocational Development:** Exploring career options and pursuing a career path that is compatible with your interests, talents, and values.

Specific Objectives and Attributes:

_____ Understanding the relationship between majors and careers

_____ Using effective strategies for exploring and identifying potential careers

_____ Identifying career options that capitalize on your personal interests, talents, needs, and values

_____ Acquiring work experience related to your vocational interests

_____ Creating an effective resume or portfolio

_____ Developing effective strategies for selecting personal references and acquiring letters of recommendation

_____ Implementing effective job search strategies

_____ Learning how to write persuasive letters of inquiry and letters of application for employment positions

_____ Acquiring networking skills for connecting with potential employers

_____ Developing strategies for performing successfully in job interviews

> "Your work is to discover your work and then with all your heart to give yourself to it."
>
> —Hindu Siddhartha Prince Gautama Siddharta, a.k.a. Buddha, founder of the philosophy and religion of Buddhism

8. **Personal Development:** Developing a strong sense of personal identity, a coherent self-concept, and the ability to manage personal affairs and resources.

Specific Objectives and Attributes:

_____ Discovering your identity and clarifying your self-concept (Answering the question: Who am I?)

_____ Finding a sense of purpose and direction in life (Answering the question: Who will I become?)

_____ Developing greater self-respect and self-esteem

_____ Increasing self-confidence

_____ Developing self-efficacy—belief that the outcomes of your life are within your control and can be influenced by personal initiative and effort

_____ Strengthening skills for managing personal resources (e.g., time and money)

_____ Becoming more independent, self-directed, and self-reliant

_____ Setting realistic goals and priorities

_____ Developing the self-motivation and self-discipline needed to reach long-term goals

_____ Developing the resiliency to overcome obstacles and convert setbacks into comebacks

> Remember, no one can make you feel inferior without your consent."
>
> —*Eleanor Roosevelt, former United Nations diplomat and humanitarian*

Based on your total score in each area, what aspect(s) of self-development appear to be most and least important to you? How would you explain (or what do you think accounts for) this discrepancy?

Add up your total score for each of the eight areas of holistic development.

a. Do your totals in each of the eight areas suggest that all aspects of self-development are about equally important to you and that you're striving to become a well-rounded person?

b. If yes, why? If no, why not?

5.4 Wellness Self-Assessment for Self-Improvement

For each aspect of wellness listed below, rate yourself in terms of how close you are to doing what you should be doing (1 = furthest from the ideal, 5 = closest to the ideal).

	Nowhere Close to What I Should Be Doing		Not Bad but Should Be Better		Right Where I Should Be
Nutrition	1	2	3	4	5
Exercise	1	2	3	4	5
Sleep	1	2	3	4	5
Alcohol and Drugs	1	2	3	4	5

For each area in which there's a gap between where you are now and where you should be, identify the best action you could take to reduce or eliminate the gap.

5.5 Nutritional Self-Assessment and Self-Improvement

1. Go to: *www.ChooseMyPlate.gov*.

2. For each of the five food groups listed below, record in the first column the amount you *should* be consuming daily; in the second column, estimate the amount you *do* consume daily.

Basic Food Type	Amount Recommended	Amount Consumed
Fruits		
Vegetables		
Grains		
Protein Foods		
Dairy		

3. For any food group that you're consuming less than the recommended amounts, use the website to find foods that would enable you to meet the recommended daily amount. Write down those food items, and answer the following questions about each of them:

   a. How likely is it that you'll actually add these food items to your regular diet?

   Very Likely   Possibly   Very Unlikely

   b. For those food items you identified as "very unlikely," why would you be unlikely to add these items to your regular diet?

Chapter 5 Reflection

What is the one area of your health that could most affect your success in college. Explain?

What are three action steps you can take to improve in this area?

1.

2.

3.

Write three health goals you have set for yourself. (Remember to use the goal-setting strategies you learned about in Chapter 3.)

CHAPTER 6

DIVERSITY AND THE COLLEGE EXPERIENCE

LEARNING ABOUT AND FROM HUMAN DIFFERENCES

This chapter clarifies what "diversity" means through the AVID lens and demonstrates how experiencing diversity can deepen:

- Learning,
- Promote critical and creative thinking, and
- Contribute to your personal and professional development.

Simply stated, we learn more from people who differ from us than we do from people similar to us. There is more diversity among college students today than at any other time in history. This chapter will help you capitalize on this learning opportunity.

CHAPTER PREVIEW

This chapter provides a framework to gain greater appreciation of human differences and develop skills for making the most of diversity in college and beyond.

LEARNING OBJECTIVE

You will engage in a Socratic approach to the often emotionally charged topics that fall within the realm of Diversity, in order to intellectually and actively engage in the multiperspective college learning process.

PERFORMANCE OBJECTIVE

 Journal Reflection 6.1

THOUGHT STARTER

Complete the following sentence:

When I hear the word *diversity*, the first thing that comes to my mind is . . .

Collection of differences

WHAT IS DIVERSITY?

Literally translated, the word *diversity* derives from the Latin root *diversus*, meaning "various" or "variety." Thus, human diversity refers to the variety that exists in humanity (the human species). The relationship between humanity and diversity may be compared to the relationship between sunlight and the variety of colors that make up the visual spectrum. Similar to how sunlight passing through a prism disperses into the variety of colors that comprise the visual spectrum, the human species on planet earth is dispersed into a variety of different groups that comprise the human spectrum (humanity).

Human diversity is manifested in a multiplicity of ways, including differences in physical features, national origins, cultural backgrounds, and sexual orientations. Some dimensions of diversity are easily detectable, others are very subtle, and some are invisible.

In this chapter, we will rely on the AVID Culturally Relevant Teaching Philosophy in order to establish a Socratic Framework in which to engage in intellectual conversations. Federal, State, College, and University frameworks and definitions may vary across the nation and internationally, it is AVID's intent to address a common definition throughout our resources and aligned with our AVID Professional Learning for educators to establish a common understanding prior to diving into what might be emotionally charged conversations. At AVID, we call these "courageous, intentional conversations," meaning we have conversations about our experiences in a structured format with clear guidelines and parameters. In this book, which is designed for college students, our intention is to guide them through the sometimes challenging experiences, conversations, and assignments that they will be asked to engage in both inside and outside the college classroom.

Diversity includes discussion of equal rights and social justice for minority groups, but it's a broader concept that involves much more than political issues. In a national survey of American voters, the vast majority of respondents agreed that diversity is more than just "political correctness" (National Survey of Women Voters 1998). Diversity is also an *educational* issue—an integral element of a college education that contributes to the learning, personal development, and career preparation of *all* students. It enhances the quality of the college experience by bringing multiple perspectives and alternative approaches to *what* is being learned (the content) and *how* it's being learned (the process).

NOTE

Explore a wealth of free resources on Teaching Tolerance website.

https://www.tolerance.org/

THINK ABOUT IT

Explore the following book-Culturally Proficient Leadership: The Personal Journey Begins Within (Terrell and Lindsey 2009) Corwin Press

"We are all brothers and sisters. Each face in the rainbow of color that populates our world is precious and special. Each adds to the rich treasure of humanity."

—Morris Dees, civil rights leader and cofounder of the Southern Poverty Law Center

Journal Reflection 6.2

Diversity understanding begins with you and your journey. Reflect on your own experience, when did you first encounter or become aware of racial, cultural, ethnic, or gender differences? How did this first encounter impact or shape your own beliefs and values?

I have always been exposed to racial and cultural diversity.

WHAT IS RACIAL DIVERSITY?

A *racial group (race)* is a group of people who share distinctive physical traits, such as skin color or facial characteristics. The variation in skin color we now see among humans is largely due to biological adaptations that have evolved over thousands of years among groups of humans who migrated to different climatic regions of the world. Currently, the most widely accepted explanation of the geographic origin of modern humans is the "Out of Africa" theory. Genetic studies and fossil evidence indicate that all Homo sapiens inhabited Africa 150,000–250,000 years ago; over time, some migrated from Africa to other parts of the world (Mendez et al. 2013; Meredith 2011; Reid and Hetherington 2010). Darker skin tones developed among humans who inhabited and reproduced in hotter geographical regions nearer the equator (e.g., Africans). Their darker skin color helped them adapt and survive by providing them with better protection from the potentially damaging effects of intense sunlight (Bridgeman 2003). In contrast, lighter skin tones developed over time among humans inhabiting colder climates that were farther from the equator (e.g., Scandinavia). Their lighter skin color enabled them to absorb greater amounts of vitamin D supplied by sunlight, which was in shorter supply in those regions of the world (Jablonksi and Chaplin 2002).

Currently, the U.S. Census Bureau has identified five races (U.S. Census Bureau 2012):

White: a person whose lineage may be traced to the original people inhabiting Europe, the Middle East, or North Africa.

Black or African American: a person whose lineage may be traced to the original people inhabiting Africa.

American Indian or Alaska Native: a person whose lineage may be traced to the original people inhabiting North and South America (including Central America), and who continue to maintain their tribal affiliation or attachment.

Asian: a person whose lineage may be traced to the original people inhabiting the Far East, Southeast Asia, or the Indian subcontinent, including: Cambodia, China, India, Japan, Korea, Malaysia, Pakistan, the Philippine Islands, Thailand, and Vietnam.

Native Hawaiian or Other Pacific Islander: a person whose lineage may be traced to the original people inhabiting Hawaii, Guam, Samoa, or other Pacific islands.

It's important to keep in mind that racial categories are not based on scientific evidence; they merely represent group classifications constructed by society (Anderson and Fienberg 2000). No identifiable set of genes distinguishes one race from another; in fact, there continues to be disagreement

> Ethnic and cultural diversity is an integral, natural, and normal component of educational experiences for all students."
> —*National Council for Social Studies*

NOTE

Diversity is a human issue that embraces and benefits all people; it's not a code word for "some" people. Although one major goal of diversity is to promote appreciation and equitable treatment of particular groups of people who've experienced discrimination, it's also a learning experience that strengthens the quality of a college education, career preparation, and leadership potential.

THINK ABOUT IT

Be aware that the Federal U.S. Census Bureau is one form of racial category often utilized on college and university campuses. Other organizations have different categories that may broaden and include ethnic and cultural identity groups.

among scholars about what groups of people constitute a human race or whether distinctive races actually exist (Wheelright 2005). In other words, you can't do a blood test or some type of internal genetic test to determine a person's race. Humans have simply decided to categorize themselves into races on the basis of certain external differences in their physical appearance, particularly the color of their outer layer of skin. The U.S. Census Bureau could have decided to divide people into "racial" categories based on other physical characteristics, such as eye color (blue, brown, and green), hair color (brown, black, blonde, or red), or body length (tall, short, or mid-sized).

AUTHOR'S JOURNEY

My father stood approximately six feet tall and had straight, light brown hair. His skin color was that of a Western European with a very slight suntan. My mother was from Alabama; she was dark in skin color with high cheekbones and had long curly black hair. In fact, if you didn't know that my father was of African American descent, you would not have thought he was black.

All of my life I've thought of myself as African American and all people who know me have thought of me as African American. I've lived half of a century with that as my racial identity. Several years ago, I carefully reviewed records of births and deaths in my family history and discovered that I had less than 50% African lineage. Biologically, I am no longer black; socially and emotionally, I still am. Clearly, my "race" has been socially constructed, not biologically determined.

—Aaron Thompson

NOTE

Search YouTube for the video on "Race, Ethnicity, Nationality, and Jellybeans."

While humans may display diversity in the color or tone of their external layer of skin, the reality is that all members of the human species are remarkably similar at an internal biological level. More than 98% of the genes of all humans are exactly the same, regardless of what their particular race may be (Bronfenbrenner 2005). This large amount of genetic overlap accounts for our distinctively "human" appearance, which clearly distinguishes us from all other living species. All humans have internal organs that are similar in structure and function, and despite variations in the color of our outer layer of skin, when it's cut, all humans bleed in the same color.

AUTHOR'S JOURNEY

I was sitting in a coffee shop in the Chicago O'Hare airport while proofreading my first draft of this chapter. I looked up from my work for a second and saw what appeared to be a white girl about 18 years of age. As I lowered my head to return to work, I did a double-take and looked at her again because something about her seemed different or unusual. When I looked more closely at her the second time, I noticed that although she had white skin, the features of her face and hair appeared to be those of an African American. After a couple of seconds of puzzlement, I figured it out: she was an *albino* African American. That satisfied my curiosity for the moment, but then I began to wonder: Would it still be accurate to say she was "black" even though her skin was not black? Would her hair and facial features be sufficient for her to be considered or classified as black? If yes, then what would be the "race" of someone who had black skin tone, but did not have the typical hair and facial features characteristic of black people? Is skin color the defining feature of being African American or are other features equally important?

I was unable to answer these questions, but found it amusing that all of these thoughts were crossing my mind while I was working on a chapter dealing with diversity. On the plane ride home, I thought again about that albino African American girl and realized that she was a perfect example of how classifying people into "races" isn't based on objective, scientific evidence, but on subjective, socially constructed categories.

—Joe Cuseo

Categorizing people into distinct racial or ethnic groups is becoming even more difficult because members of different ethnic and racial groups are increasingly forming cross-ethnic and interracial families. By 2050, the number of Americans who identify themselves as being of two or more races is projected to more than triple, growing from 5.2 million to 16.2 million (U.S. Census Bureau 2008).

Journal Reflection 6.3

What race(s) do you consider yourself to be? Why?

White, with native heritage.

Would you say you identify strongly with your racial identity, or are you rarely conscious of it? Why?

Just conscious. Race has nothing to do with my identity. My personality and core beliefs do.

WHAT IS CULTURAL DIVERSITY?

"Culture" may be defined as a distinctive pattern of beliefs and values learned by a group of people who share the same social heritage and traditions. In short, culture is the whole way in which a group of people has learned to live (Peoples and Bailey 2011); it includes their style of speaking (language), fashion, food, art and music, as well as their beliefs and values. **Box 6.1** contains a summary of key components of culture that a group may share.

NOTE

The reality of our own culture is not the reality of other cultures. Our perceptions of the outside world are shaped (and sometimes distorted) by our prior cultural experiences.

Box 6.1

Key Components of Culture

Language

How members of the culture communicate through written or spoken words; their particular dialect; and their distinctive style of nonverbal communication (body language).

Space

How cultural members arrange themselves with respect to social–spatial distance (e.g., how closely they stand next to each other when having a conversation).

Time

How the culture conceives of, divides, and uses time (e.g., the speed or pace at which they conduct business).

Aesthetics

How cultural members appreciate and express artistic beauty and creativity (e.g., their style of visual art, culinary art, music, theater, literature, and dance).

Family

The culture's attitudes and habits with respect to interacting with family members (e.g., customary styles of parenting their children and caring for their elderly).

Economics

How the culture meets its members' material needs, and its customary ways of acquiring and distributing wealth (e.g., general level of wealth and gap between the very rich and very poor).

Gender Roles

The culture's expectations for "appropriate" male and female behavior (e.g., whether or not women are able to hold the same leadership positions as men).

Politics

How decision-making power is exercised in the culture (e.g., democratically or autocratically).

Science and Technology

The culture's attitude toward and use of science or technology (e.g., the degree to which the culture is technologically "advanced").

Philosophy

The culture's ideas or views on wisdom, goodness, truth, and social values (e.g., whether they place greater value on individual competition or collective collaboration).

Spirituality and Religion

Cultural beliefs about a supreme being and an afterlife (e.g., its predominant faith-based views and belief systems about the supernatural).

 *is this really relevant?*

💡 Journal Reflection 6.4

Select one or two components from the list in Box 6.1. Explain how the component(s) expresses itself or is "lived out" in your life.

_____

_____

_____

_____

AUTHOR'S JOURNEY

I was watching a basketball game between the Los Angeles Lakers and Los Angeles Clippers when a short scuffle broke out between the Lakers' Paul Gasol—who is Spanish—and the Clippers' Chris Paul—who is African American. After the scuffle ended, Gasol tried to show Paul there were no hard feelings by patting him on the head. Instead of interpreting Gasol's head pat as a peace-making gesture, Paul took it as a putdown and returned the favor by slapping (rather than patting) Paul in the head.

This whole misunderstanding stemmed from a basic difference in nonverbal communication between the two cultures. Patting someone on the head in European cultures is a friendly gesture; European soccer players often do it to an opposing player to express no ill will after a foul or collision. However, this same nonverbal message meant something very different to Chris Paul—an African American raised in urban America.

—*Joe Cuseo*

WHAT IS AN ETHNIC GROUP?

A group of people who share the same culture is referred to as an *ethnic group*. Thus, "culture" refers to *what* an ethnic group shares in common (e.g., language and traditions) and "ethnic group" refers to the *people* who share the same culture that's been *learned* through common social experiences. Members of the same racial group—whose shared physical characteristics have been *inherited*—may be members of different ethnic groups. For instance, white Americans belong to the same racial group, but differ in terms of their ethnic group (e.g., French, German, Irish) and Asian Americans belong to the same racial group, but are members of different ethnic groups (e.g., Japanese, Chinese, Korean).

Currently, the major cultural (ethnic) groups in the United States include:

- Native Americans (American Indians)
  - Cherokee, Navaho, Hopi, Alaskan natives, Blackfoot, and so on.
- European Americans (Whites)
  - Descendents from Western Europe (e.g., United Kingdom, Ireland, Netherlands), Eastern Europe (e.g., Hungary, Romania, Bulgaria), Southern Europe (e.g., Italy, Greece, Portugal), and Northern Europe or Scandinavia (e.g., Denmark, Sweden, Norway)
- African Americans (Blacks)
  - Americans whose cultural roots lie in the continent of Africa (e.g., Ethiopia, Kenya, Nigeria) and the Caribbean Islands (e.g., Bahamas, Cuba, Jamaica)
- Hispanic Americans (Latinos)
  - Americans with cultural roots in Mexico, Puerto Rico, Central America (e.g., El Salvador, Guatemala, Nicaragua), and South America (e.g., Brazil, Columbia, Venezuela)
- Asian Americans
  - Americans whose cultural roots lie in East Asia (e.g., Japan, China, Korea), Southeast Asia (e.g., Vietnam, Thailand, Cambodia), and South Asia (e.g., India, Pakistan, Bangladesh)
- Middle Eastern Americans
  - Americans with cultural roots in Iraq, Iran, Israel, and so on.

THINK ABOUT IT

This personal journey highlights the importance of being culturally aware and sensitive in our personal and professional interactions.

NOTE

Be aware that Federal, State, College, and Universities may utilize different categories that may broaden and include additional ethnic and cultural identity groups.

Journal Reflection 6.5

What ethnic group(s) are you a member of, or do you identify with? What would you say are the key cultural values shared by your ethnic group(s)? Why?

_____

_____

_____

Which ethnic group(s) do you know the least about?

_____

_____

Which ethnic group(s) would you like to learn more about and why?

_____

_____

_____

_____

NOTE

Visit the Federal Government Census website for the latest statistics https://www.census.gov

European Americans are still the majority ethnic group in the United States; they account for more than 50% of the American population. Native Americans, African Americans, Hispanic Americans, and Asian Americans are considered to be _minority_ ethnic groups because each of these groups represents less than 50% of the American population.

As with racial grouping, classifying humans into different ethnic groups can be very arbitrary and subject to debate. Currently, the U.S. Census Bureau classifies Hispanics as an ethnic group rather than a race. However, among Americans who checked "some other race" in the 2000 Census, 97% were Hispanic. This finding suggests that Hispanic Americans consider themselves to be a racial group, probably because that's how they're perceived and treated by non-Hispanics (Cianciatto 2005). It's noteworthy that the American media used the term "racial profiling" (rather than ethnic profiling) to describe Arizona's controversial 2010 law that allowed police to target Hispanics who "look" like illegal aliens from Mexico, Central America, and South America. Once again, this illustrates how race and ethnicity are subjective, socially constructed concepts that reflect how people perceive and treat different social groups, which, in turn, affects how members of these groups perceive themselves.

THE RELATIONSHIP BETWEEN DIVERSITY AND HUMANITY

As previously noted, diversity represents variations on the same theme: being human. Thus, humanity and diversity are interdependent, complementary concepts. To understand human diversity is to understand both our differences and *similarities* (Public Service Enterprise Group 2009). Diversity appreciation includes appreciating both the unique perspectives of different cultural groups as well as universal aspects of the human experience that are common to all groups—whatever their particular cultural background happens to be. Members of all racial and ethnic groups live in communities, develop personal relationships, have emotional needs, and undergo life experiences that affect their self-esteem and personal identity. Humans of all races and ethnicities experience similar emotions and reveal those emotions with similar facial expressions (see **Figure 6.1**).

THINK ABOUT IT

Be mindful of Social Construction of Race.

FIGURE 6.1: Humans all over the world display the same facial expressions when experiencing and expressing different emotions. See if you can detect the emotions being expressed in the following faces. (To find the answers, turn your book upside down.)

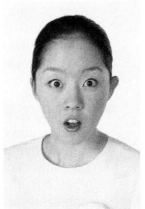

Answers: The emotions shown. Top, left to right: anger, fear, and sadness. Bottom, left to right: disgust, happiness, and surprise.

All images ©JupiterImages Corporation.

"We have become not a melting pot but a beautiful mosaic."

—*Jimmy Carter, 39th president of the United States and winner of the Nobel Peace Prize*

Other characteristics that anthropologists have found to be shared by all humans in every corner of the world include: storytelling, poetry, adornment of the body, dance, music, decoration with artifacts, families, socialization of children by elders, a sense of right and wrong, supernatural beliefs, and mourning of the dead (Pinker 2000). Although different cultural groups may express these shared experiences in different ways, they are universal experiences common to all human cultures.

Journal Reflection 6.6

Identify human experiences that are universal in addtion to those already mentioned.

NOTE

When we appreciate diversity in the context of humanity, we capitalize on the variety and versatility of human differences while preserving the collective strength and synergy of human unity.

©steven r. hendricks/Shutterstock.com

Cultural differences can exist within the same society (multicultural society), within a single nation (domestic diversity), or across different nations (international diversity).

You may have heard the question: "We're all human, aren't we?" The answer to this important question is "yes and no." Yes, we are all the same, but not in the same way. A good metaphor for understanding this apparent contradiction is to visualize humanity as a quilt in which we're all united by the common thread of humanity—the universal bond of being human. (Much like the quilt below.) The different patches comprising the quilt represent diversity—the distinctive or unique cultures that comprise our shared humanity. The quilt metaphor acknowledges the identity and beauty of all cultures. It differs from the old American "melting pot" metaphor, which viewed cultural differences as something to be melted down and eliminated. It also differs from the old "salad bowl" metaphor that depicted America as a hodgepodge or mishmash of cultures thrown together without any common connection. In contrast, the quilt metaphor suggests that the unique cultures of different human groups should be preserved, recognized, and valued; at the same time, these cultural differences join together to form a seamless, unified whole. This blending of diversity and unity is captured in the Latin expression *E pluribus unum* ("Out of many, one")—the motto of the United States—which you'll find printed on all its currency.

AUTHOR'S JOURNEY

When I was 12 years old and living in New York City, I returned from school one Friday and my mother asked me if anything interesting happened at school that day. I told her that the teacher went around the room asking students what they had for dinner the night before. At that moment, my mother became a bit concerned and nervously asked me: "What did you tell the teacher?" I said: "I told her and the rest of the class that I had pasta last night because my family always eats pasta on Thursdays and Sundays." My mother exploded and fired back the following question at me in a very agitated tone, "Why didn't you tell her we had steak or roast beef?" For a moment, I was stunned and couldn't figure out what I'd done wrong or why I should have lied about eating pasta. Then it dawned on me: My mom was embarrassed about being Italian American. She wanted me to hide our family's ethnic background and make it sound like we were very "American."

As I grew older, I understood why my mother felt the way she did. She grew up in America's "melting pot" generation—a time when different American ethnic groups were expected to melt down and melt away their ethnicity. They were not to celebrate their diversity; they were to eliminate it.

—Joe Cuseo

WHAT IS INDIVIDUALITY?

It's important to keep in mind that there are individual differences among members of any racial or ethnic group that are greater than the average difference between groups. Said in another way, there's more variability (individuality) within groups than between groups. For example, among members of the same racial group, individual differences in their physical attributes (e.g., height and weight) and psychological characteristics (e.g., temperament and personality) are greater than any average difference that may exist between their racial group and other racial groups (Caplan and Caplan 2008).

As you proceed through your college experience, keep the following key distinctions in mind:

* **Humanity.** All humans are members of the *same group*—the human species.
* **Diversity.** All humans are members of *different groups*—such as, different racial and ethnic groups.
* **Individuality.** Each human is a *unique individual* who differs from all other members of any group to which he or she may belong.

MAJOR FORMS OR TYPES OF DIVERSITY IN TODAY'S WORLD

Ethnic and Racial Diversity

America is rapidly becoming a more racially and ethnically diverse nation. Minorities now account for 36.6% of the total population—an all-time high; in 2011, for the first time in U.S. history, racial and ethnic minorities made up more than half (50.4%) of all children born in America (Nhan 2012). By the middle of the twenty-first century, minority groups are expected to comprise 54% of the American population and more than 60% of the nation's children will be members of minority groups (U.S. Census Bureau 2008).

NOTE

While it's valuable to learn about differences between different human groups, there are substantial individual differences among people within the same racial or ethnic group that should neither be ignored nor overlooked. Don't assume that individuals with the same racial or ethnic characteristics share the same personal characteristics.

More specifically, by 2050 the American population is projected to be more than 30% Hispanic (up from 15% in 2008), 15% Black (up from 13% in 2008), 9.6% Asian (up from 5.3% in 2008), and 2% Native Americans (up from 1.6% in 2008). The Native Hawaiian and Pacific Islander population is expected to more than double between 2008 and 2050. During this same timeframe, the percentage of white Americans will decline from 66% (2008) to 46% (2050). As a result of these demographic trends, today's ethnic and racial minorities will become the "new majority" of Americans by the middle of the twenty-first century (see **Figure 6.2**).

FIGURE 6.2: The "New Majority"

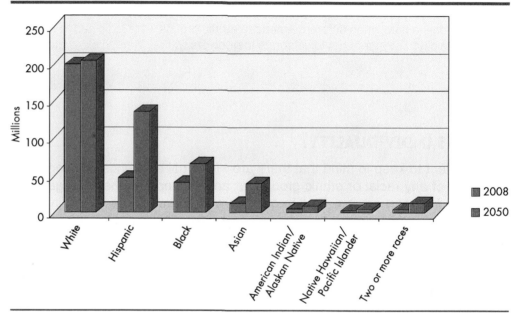

©Kendall Hunt Publishing Company

The growing racial and ethnic diversity of America's population is reflected in the growing diversity of students enrolled in its colleges and universities. In 1960, whites made up almost 95% of the total college population; in 2010, that percentage had decreased to 61.5%. Between 1976 and 2010, the percentage of ethnic minority students in higher education increased from 17% to 40% (National Center for Education Statistics 2011). This rise in ethnic and racial diversity on American campuses is particularly noteworthy when viewed in light of the historical treatment of minority groups in the United States. In the early nineteenth century, education was not a right, but a privilege available only to those who could afford to attend private schools. It was experienced largely by Protestants of European descent (Luhman 2007).

 Journal Reflection 6.7

1. What diverse groups do you see represented on your campus?

2. Are there groups on campus you didn't expect to see or to see in such large numbers?

NOTE ✗

Explore and learn more about Brown v. Board of Education in relationship to today's educational system.

3. Are there groups on campus you expected to see but don't see or, see in smaller numbers than you expected?

> Of all the civil rights for which the world has struggled and fought for 5,000 years, the right to learn is undoubtedly the most fundamental."
>
> —W. E. B. Du Bois, African American sociologist, historian, and civil rights activist

The rise in ethnic and racial diversity on American campuses is particularly noteworthy when viewed in light of the historical treatment of minority groups in the United States. Members of certain minority groups were left out of the educational process altogether, or were forced to be educated in racially segregated settings. For example, Americans of color were once taught in separate, segregated schools that were typically inferior in terms of educational facilities. It was not until the groundbreaking Supreme Court ruling in *Brown v. Board of Education* (1954) that the face of education for people of color changed with the ruling that "separate educational facilities are inherently unequal." The decision made it illegal for Kansas and 20 other states to deliver education in segregated classrooms.

BOX 6.2

Diversity in America's Community Colleges

58% of community college students are women

53% are 22 years of age or older

Among full-time students, 50% are employed part-time and 27% are employed full-time

Among part-time students, 50% are employed full-time and 33% are employed part-time

39% are the first in their family to attend college

36% are members of a minority ethnic or racial group

17% are single parents

American Association of Community Colleges (2009)

AUTHOR'S JOURNEY

My mother was a direct descendent of slaves and moved with her parents from the Deep South at the age of 17. My father lived in an all-Black coal mining camp, into which my mother and her family moved in 1938. My father remained illiterate because he was not allowed to attend public schools in eastern Kentucky. In the early 1960s my brother, my sister, and I were integrated into the White public schools. Physical violence and constant verbal harassment caused many other Blacks to forgo their education and opt for jobs in the coal mines at an early age. But my father remained constant in his advice to me: "It doesn't matter if they call you n_____; but don't you ever let them beat you by walking out on your education." He would say to me, "Son, you will have opportunities that I never had. Just remember, when you do get that education, you'll never have to go in those coal mines and have them break your back. You can choose what you want to do, and then you can be free man."

My parents, who could never provide me with monetary wealth, truly made me proud of them by giving me the gift of insight and an aspiration for achievement.

—Aaron Thompson

Socioeconomic Diversity

Human diversity also exists among groups of people in terms of their socioeconomic status (SES), which is determined by their level of education, level of income, and the occupational prestige of the jobs they hold. Groups are stratified (divided) into lower, middle, or upper classes, and groups occupying lower social strata have less economic resources and social privileges (Feagin and Feagin 2007).

Young adults from high-income families are more than seven times likely to have earned a college degree and hold a prestigious job than those from low-income families (Olson 2007). Sharp discrepancies also exist in income level among different racial, ethnic, and gender groups. In 2012, the median income for non-Hispanic white households was $57,009, compared to $39,005 for Hispanics and $33,321 for African Americans (DeNavas-Walt, Proctor, and Smith 2013). From 2005 to 2009, household wealth fell by 66% for Hispanics, 53% for Blacks, and 16% for Whites, largely due to the housing and mortgage collapse—which had a more damaging effect on lower-income families (Kochlar, Fry, and Taylor 2011).

Despite its overall wealth, the United States is one of the most impoverished of all developed countries in the world (Shah 2008). The poverty rate in the United States is almost twice the rate of other economically developed countries around the world (Gould and Wething 2013). In 2012, more than 16% of the American population, and almost 20% of American children, lived below the poverty line ($23,050 yearly income for a family of four) (U.S. Census Bureau 2013).

 ### Journal Reflection 6.8

Are you the first in your family to attend college?

Whether yes or no, how does that make you feel?

International Diversity

If it were possible to reduce the world's population to a village of precisely 100 people, with all existing human ratios remaining about the same, the demographics of this world village would look something like this:

61 would be Asians; 13 would be Africans; 12 would be Europeans; 9 would be Latin Americans; and 5 would be North Americans (citizens of the United States and Canada)
50 would be male, 50 would be female
75 would be non-white; 25 white
67 would be non-Christian; 33 would be Christian
80 would live in substandard housing
16 would be unable to read or write
50 would be malnourished and 1 would be dying of starvation
33 would be without access to a safe water supply
39 would lack access to modern sanitation
24 would have no electricity (and of the 76 who have electricity, most would only use it for light at night)
8 people would have access to the Internet
1 would have a college education
1 would have HIV
2 would be near birth; 1 near death
5 would control 32% of the entire world's wealth; all 5 would be U.S. citizens
48 would live on less than $2 a day
20 would live on less than $1 a day (Family Care Foundation 1997–2012).

In this world village, English would not be the most common language spoken—it would be third, following Chinese and Spanish (Lewis, Paul, and Fennig 2014).

The need for American college students to develop an appreciation of international diversity is highlighted by a study conducted by an anthropologist who went "undercover" to pose as a student in a university residence hall. She found that the biggest complaint international students had about American students was their lack of knowledge of other countries and the misconceptions they held about people from different nations (Nathan 2005). When you take the time to learn about other countries and the cultures of people who inhabit them, you move beyond being just a citizen of your own nation, you become *cosmopolitan*—a citizen of the world.

Generational Diversity

Humans are also diverse with respect to the historical time period in which they grew up. The term "generation" refers to a cohort (group) of individuals born during the same period in history whose attitudes, values, and habits have been shaped by events that took place in the world during their formative years of development. People growing up in different generations are likely to develop different attitudes and beliefs because of the different historical events they experienced during their upbringing.

Box 6.3 contains a brief summary of different generations, the key historical events they experienced, and the personal characteristics commonly associated with each generational group (Lancaster and Stillman 2002).

BOX 6.3

Generational Diversity: A Snapshot Summary

- **The Traditional Generation (a.k.a. "Silent Generation")** (born 1922–1945). This generation was influenced by events such as the Great Depression and World Wars I and II. Characteristics associated with people growing up at this time include loyalty, patriotism, respect for authority, and conservatism.
- **The Baby Boomer Generation** (born 1946–1964). This generation was influenced by events such as the Vietnam War, Watergate, and the civil rights movement. Characteristics associated with people growing up at this time include idealism, emphasis on self-fulfillment, and concern for social justice and equal rights.
- **Generation X** (born 1965–1980). This generation was influenced by Sesame Street, the creation of MTV, AIDS, and soaring divorce rates. They were the first "latchkey children"—youngsters who used their own key to let themselves into their home after school—because their mother (or single mother) was working outside the home. Characteristics associated with people growing up at this time include self-reliance, resourcefulness, and ability to adapt to change.
- **Generation Y (a.k.a. "Millennials")** (born 1981–2002). This generation was influenced by the

September 11, 2001, terrorist attack on the United States, the shooting of students at Columbine High School, and the collapse of the Enron Corporation. Characteristics associated with people growing up at this time include a preference for working and playing in groups, familiarity with technology, and willingness to engage in volunteer service in their community (the "civic generation"). This is also the most ethnically diverse generation, which may explain why they're more open to diversity than previous generations and are more likely to view diversity positively.

- **Generation Z (a.k.a. "The iGeneration")** (born 1994–present). This generation includes the latter half of Generation Y. They grew up during the wars in Afghanistan and Iraq, terrorism, the global recession, and climate change. Consequently, they have less trust in political systems and industrial corporations than previous generations. During their formative years, the world wide web was in place, so they're quite comfortable with technology and rely heavily on the Internet, Wikipedia, Google, Twitter, MySpace, Facebook, Instant Messaging, image boards, and YouTube. They expect immediate gratification through technology and accept the lack of privacy associated with social networking. For these reasons, they're also referred to as the "digital generation."

 Journal Reflection 6.9

Look back at the characteristics associated with your generation. Which of these characteristics accurately reflect your personal characteristics and those of your closest friends? Which do not?

If you were or are working in a cross-generational group, what might you consider when approaching the group work? Why?

_____

_____

_____

_____

Sexual Diversity: LGBT, LGBTQ, LGBTQA, TBL

These acronyms refer to lesbian, gay, bisexual, transgender, queer or questioning, and asexual or ally but all of the different identities within "LGBT" are often grouped together. These groups are very present on college campuses and there are specific needs and concerns related to each individual identity.

Humans experience and express sexuality in diverse ways. "Sexual diversity" refers to differences in human *sexual orientation*—the gender (male or female) an individual is physically attracted to, and *sexual identity*—the gender an individual identifies with or considers himself or herself or to be. The spectrum of sexual diversity includes:

Heterosexuals—males who are sexually attracted to females, and females who are sexually attracted to males

Gays—males who are sexually attracted to males

Lesbians—females who are sexually attracted to females

Bisexuals—individuals who are sexually attracted to males and females

Transgender—individuals who do not identify with the gender they were assigned at birth, or don't feel they belong to a single gender (e.g., transsexuals, transvestites, and bigender).

Other terms are often grouped and discussed in these diverse communities. They are:

Asexual: A person who generally does not feel sexual attraction or desire to any group of people. Asexuality is not the same as celibacy.

Ally: Typically any non-LGBT person who supports and stands up for the rights of LGBT people, although LGBT people can be allies, such as a lesbian who is an ally to a transgender person.

Biphobia: Aversion toward bisexuality and bisexual people as a social group or as individuals. People of any sexual orientation can experience such feelings of aversion. Biphobia is a source of discrimination against bisexuals, and may be based on negative bisexual stereotypes or irrational fear.

Cisgender: Types of gender identity where an individual's experience of their own gender matches the sex they were assigned at birth.

> **THINK ABOUT IT**
>
> Explore the following organizations for more resources, information, and support.
> PFLAG
> GLAAD
> GLSEN
> The Trevor Project

Coming Out: The process of acknowledging one's sexual orientation and/or gender identity to other people. For most LGBT people, this is a lifelong process.

Gender expression: A term that refers to the ways in which we each manifest masculinity or femininity. It is usually an extension of our "gender identity," our innate sense of being male, female, or others. Each of us expresses a particular gender every day—by the way we style our hair, select our clothing, or even the way we stand. Our appearance, speech, behavior, movement, and other factors signal that we feel—and wish to be understood as—masculine or feminine, or as a man or a woman.

Gender identity: The sense of "being" male, female, genderqueer, agender, etc. For some people, gender identity is in accord with physical anatomy. For transgender people, gender identity may differ from physical anatomy or expected social roles. It is important to note that gender identity, biological sex, and sexual orientation are separate and that you cannot assume how someone identifies in one category based on how they identify in another category.

Genderqueer: A term that refers to individuals or groups who "queer" or problematize the hegemonic notions of sex, gender, and desire in a given society. Genderqueer people possess identities that fall outside of the widely accepted sexual binary (i.e., "men" and "women"). Genderqueer may also refer to people who identify as both transgendered AND queer—that is, individuals who challenge both gender and sexuality regimes and see gender identity and sexual orientation as overlapping and interconnected.

Heterosexual: A person who is only attracted to members of the opposite sex. In addition, called "straight."

Homophobia: A range of negative attitudes and feelings toward homosexuality or people who are identified or perceived as being lesbian, gay, bisexual, or transgender (LGBT). It can be expressed as antipathy, contempt, prejudice, aversion, or hatred; may be based on irrational fear; and is sometimes related to religious beliefs.

Homosexual: A clinical term for people who are attracted to members of the same sex. Some people find this term offensive.

Intersex: A person whose sexual anatomy or chromosomes do not fit with the traditional markers of "female" and "male." For example: people born with both "female" and "male" anatomy (penis, testicles, vagina, uterus); people born with XXY chromosomes.

In the closet: Describes a person who keeps their sexual orientation or gender identity a secret from some or all people.

Queer: (1) An umbrella term sometimes used by LGBTQA people to refer to the entire LGBT community. (2) An alternative that some people use to "queer" the idea of the labels and categories such as lesbian, gay, bisexual, and so on. Similar to the concept of genderqueer. It is important to note that the word queer is an in-group term, and a word that can be considered offensive to some people, depending on their generation, geographic location, and relationship with the word.

Questioning: For some, the process of exploring and discovering one's own sexual orientation, gender identity, or gender expression.

Pansexual: A person who experiences sexual, romantic, physical, and/or spiritual attraction for members of all gender identities/expressions, not just people who fit into the standard gender binary (i.e., men and women).

Sexual orientation: The type of sexual, romantic, and/or physical attraction someone feels toward others. Often labeled based on the gender identity/expression of the person and who they are attracted to. Common labels: lesbian, gay, bisexual, pansexual, and so on.

Transphobia: The fear or hatred of transgender people or gender nonconforming behavior. Like biphobia, transphobia can also exist among lesbian, gay, and bisexual people as well as among heterosexual people.

Transsexual: A person whose gender identity is different from their biological sex, who may undergo medical treatments to change their biological sex, oftentimes to align it with their gender identity, or they may live their lives as another sex.

For more information:
- http://itspronouncedmetrosexual.com/2013/01/a-comprehensive-list-of-lgbtq-term-definitions/
- http://gillfoundation.org/grants/gender-expression-toolkit/gender-expression/

College campuses across the country are increasing their support for GLBT (gay, lesbian, bisexual, transgendered) students, creating centers and services to facilitate their acceptance and adjustment. These centers and services play an important role in combating homophobia and related forms of sexual prejudice on campus, while promoting awareness and tolerance of all forms of sexual diversity. By accepting individuals who span the spectrum of sexual diversity, we acknowledge and appreciate the reality that heterosexuality isn't the one-and-only form of human sexual expression (Dessel 2012). This growing acknowledgment is reflected in the Supreme Court's historic decision to legalize same-sex marriage nationwide (Dolan and Romney 2015).

Journal Reflection 6.10

Growing up, what was your families perspective(s) on Sexual Diveristy?

As an adult, has your perspective(s) changed or altered since childhood?

If so, how and why?

OVERCOMING BARRIERS TO DIVERSITY

Before we can capitalize on the benefits of diversity, we need to overcome obstacles that have long impeded our ability to appreciate and seek out diversity. These major impediments are discussed below.

FIGURE 6.3:
Optical Illusion

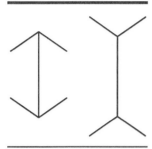

©Kendall Hunt Publishing Company

Ethnocentrism

A major advantage of culture is that it builds group solidarity, binding its members into a supportive, tight-knit community. Unfortunately, culture not only binds us, it can also blind us from taking different cultural perspectives. Since culture shapes thought and perception, people from the same ethnic (cultural) group run the risk of becoming *ethnocentric*—centered on their own culture to such a degree they view the world solely through their own cultural lens (frame of reference) and fail to consider or appreciate other cultural perspectives (Colombo, Cullen, and Lisle 2013). Optical illusions are a good example of how our particular cultural perspective can influence (and distort) our perceptions. Compare the lengths of the two lines in **Figure 6.3**.

If you perceive the line on the right to be longer than the one on the left, your perception has been shaped by Western culture. People from Western cultures, such as Americans, perceive the line on the right to be longer. However, both lines are actually equal in length. (If you don't believe it, take out a ruler and measure them.) Interestingly, this perceptual error isn't made by people from non-Western cultures—whose living spaces and architectural structures are predominantly circular (e.g., huts or igloos)—in contrast to rectangular-shaped buildings with angled corners that typify Western cultures (Segall, Campbell, and Herskovits 1966).

The optical illusion depicted in Figure 6.3 is just one of a number of illusions experienced by people in certain cultures, but not others (Shiraev and Levy 2013). Cross-cultural differences in susceptibility to optical illusions illustrate how strongly our cultural experiences can influence and sometimes misinform our perception of reality. People think they are seeing things objectively (as they actually are) but they're really seeing things subjectively—as viewed from their particular cultural perspective.

If our cultural experience can influence our perception of the physical world, it can certainly shape our perception of social events and political issues. Research in psychology indicates that the more exposure humans have to somebody or something, the more familiar it becomes and the more likely it will be perceived positively and judged favorably. The effect of familiarity is so prevalent and powerful that social psychologists have come to call it the "familiarity principle"—that is, what is familiar is perceived as better or more acceptable

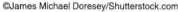
©James Michael Doresey/Shutterstock.com

People whose cultural experiences involve living and working in circular structures would not be fooled by the optical illusion in Figure 6.3.

(Zajonc 1968, 1970, 2001). Thus, we need to be mindful that the familiarity of our cultural experiences can bias us toward seeing our culture as normal or better. By remaining open to the viewpoints of people who perceive the world from different cultural vantage points, we minimize our cultural blind spots, expand our range of perception, and position ourselves to perceive the world with greater clarity and cultural sensitivity.

Stereotyping

"Stereotype" derives from two different roots: *stereo*—to look at in a fixed way—and *type*—to categorize or group together, as in the word "typical." Thus, to stereotype is to view individuals of the same type (group) in the same (fixed) way.

Stereotyping overlooks or disregards individuality; all people sharing the same group characteristic (e.g., race or gender) are viewed as having the same personal characteristics—as in the expression: "You know how they are; they're all alike." Stereotypes can also involve *bias*—literally meaning "slant"—a slant that can tilt toward the positive or the negative. Positive bias results in favorable stereotypes (e.g., "Asians are great in science and math"); negative bias leads to unfavorable stereotypes (e.g., "Asians are nerds who do nothing but study"). Here are some other examples of negative stereotypes:

* Muslims are religious terrorists.
* Whites can't jump (or dance).
* Blacks are lazy.
* Irish are alcoholics.
* Gay men are feminine; lesbian women are masculine.
* Jews are cheap.
* Women are weak.

While few people would agree with these crass stereotypes, overgeneralizations are often made about members of certain groups. Such negative overgeneralizations malign the group's reputation, rob group members of their individuality, and can weaken their self-esteem and self-confidence (as illustrated by the following experience).

AUTHOR'S JOURNEY

When I was six years old, I was told by a six-year-old girl from a different racial group that all people of my race could not swim. Since I couldn't swim at that time and she could, I assumed she was correct. I asked a boy, who was a member of the same racial group as the girl, whether her statement was true. He responded emphatically: "Yes, it's true!" Since I was from an area where few other African Americans were around to counteract this belief about my racial group, I continued to buy into this stereotype until I finally took swimming lessons as an adult. After many lessons, I am now a lousy swimmer because I didn't even attempt to swim until I was an adult. Moral of this story: Group stereotypes can limit the confidence and potential of individual members of the stereotyped group.

—*Aaron Thompson*

Whether you are male or female, don't let gender stereotypes limit your career options.

 Journal Reflection 6.11

1. Have you ever been stereotyped based on your appearance or group membership? If so, what was the stereotype and how did it make you feel?

2. Have you ever unintentionally perceived or treated a person in terms of a group
stereotype rather than as an individual? What assumptions did you make about
that person? Was that person aware of, or affected by, your stereotyping?

_____

_____

_____

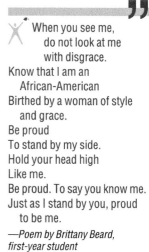

Prejudice

If all members of a stereotyped group are judged and evaluated in a negative way, the result is _prejudice_. The word "prejudice" literally means to "pre-judge." Typically, the prejudgment is negative and involves _stigmatizing_—ascribing inferior or unfavorable traits to people who belong to the same group. Thus, prejudice may be defined as a negative stereotype held about a group of people that's formed before the facts are known.

People who hold a group prejudice typically avoid contact with members of that group. This enables the prejudice to continue unchallenged because there's little opportunity for the prejudiced person to have a positive experience with members of the stigmatized group that could contradict or disprove the prejudice. Thus, a vicious cycle is established in which the prejudiced person continues to avoid contact with individuals from the stigmatized group; this, in turn, continues to maintain and reinforce the prejudice

 ### Journal Reflection 6.12

Prejudice and discrimination can be subtle and only begin to surface when the social or emotional distance among members of different groups grows closer. Rate your level of comfort (high, moderate, or low) with the following situations.

Someone from another racial group:

1. Going to your school	high	moderate	low
2. Working in your place of employment	high	moderate	low
3. Living on your street as a neighbor	high	moderate	low
4. Living with you as a roommate	high	moderate	low
5. Socializing with you as a personal friend	high	moderate	low
6. Being your most intimate friend or romantic partner	high	moderate	low
7. Being your partner in marriage	high	moderate	low

Identify and describe what influences impacted your high, moderate, and low responses.

_____

_____

_____

Once prejudice has been formed, it often remains intact and resistant to change through the psychological process of *selective perception*—the tendency for biased (prejudiced) people to see what they *expect* to see and fail to see what contradicts their bias (Hugenberg and Bodenhausen 2003). Have you ever noticed how fans rooting for their favorite sports team tend to focus on and "see" the calls of referees that go against their own team, but don't seem to react (or even notice) the calls that go against the opposing team? This is a classic example of selective perception. In effect, selective perception transforms the old adage, "seeing is believing," into "believing is seeing." This can lead prejudiced people to focus their attention on information that's consistent with their prejudgment, causing them to "see" what supports or reinforces it and fail to see information that contradicts it.

Making matters worse, selective perception is often accompanied by *selective memory*—the tendency to remember information that's consistent with one's prejudicial belief and to forget information that's inconsistent with it or contradicts it (Judd, Ryan, and Parke 1991). The mental processes of selective perception and selective memory often work together and often work *unconsciously*. As a result, prejudiced people may not even be aware they're using these biased mental processes or realize how these processes are keeping their prejudice permanently intact (Baron, Brauscombe, and Byrne 2008).

Journal Reflection 6.13

Have you experienced selective perception or selective memory—people seeing or recalling what they believe is true (due to bias), rather than what's actually true? What happened and why do you think it happened? What was your response?

_____

_____

_____

_____

_____

Discrimination

Literally translated, the term *discrimination* means "division" or "separation." Whereas prejudice involves a belief, attitude or opinion, discrimination involves an *act* or *behavior*. Technically, discrimination can be either positive or negative. A discriminating eater may only eat healthy foods, which is a positive quality. However, discrimination is most often associated with a harmful act that results in a prejudiced person treating another individual, or group of individuals, in an unfair manner. Thus, it could be said that discrimination is prejudice put into action. For instance, to fire or not hire people on the basis of their race, gender, or sexual orientation is an act of discrimination.

Box 6.4 below contains a summary of the major forms of discrimination, prejudice, and stereotypes that have plagued humanity. As you read through the following list, place a check mark next to any item that you, a friend, or family member has experienced.

BOX 6.4

Stereotypes, Prejudices, and Forms of Discrimination: A Snapshot Summary

- Ethnocentrism: viewing one's own culture or ethnic group as "central" or "normal," while viewing different cultures as "deficient" or "inferior."

    Example: Viewing another culture as "abnormal" or "uncivilized" because its members eat animals our culture views as unacceptable to eat, although we eat animals their culture views as unacceptable to eat.
- Stereotyping: viewing all (or virtually all) members of the same group in the same way—as having the same personal qualities or characteristics.

    Example: "If you're Italian, you must be in the Mafia, or have a family member who is."
- Prejudice: negative prejudgment about another group of people.

    Example: Women can't be effective leaders because they're too emotional.
- Discrimination: unequal and unfair treatment of a person or group of people—prejudice put into action.

    Example: Paying women less than men for performing the same job, even though they have the same level of education and job qualifications.
- Segregation: intentional decision made by a group to separate itself (socially or physically) from another group.

    Example: "White flight"—white people moving out of neighborhoods when people of color move in.
- Racism: belief that one's racial group is superior to another group and expressing that belief in attitude (prejudice) or action (discrimination).

    Example: Confiscating land from American Indians based on the unfounded belief that they are "uncivilized" or "savages."
- Institutional Racism: racial discrimination rooted in organizational policies and practices that disadvantage certain racial groups.

    Example: Race-based discrimination in mortgage lending, housing, and bank loans.
- Racial Profiling: investigating or arresting someone solely on the basis of the person's race, ethnicity, or national origin—without witnessing actual criminal behavior or possessing incriminating evidence.

    Example: Police making a traffic stop or conducting a personal search based solely on an individual's racial features.
- Slavery: forced labor in which people are considered to be property, held against their will, and deprived of the right to receive wages.

    Example: Enslavement of Blacks, which was legal in the United States until 1865.
- "Jim Crow" Laws: formal and informal laws created by Whites to segregate Blacks after the abolition of slavery.

(continued)

Box 6.4 *(continued)*

Example: laws in certain parts of the United States that once required Blacks to use separate bathrooms and be educated in separate schools.

- Apartheid: an institutionalized system of "legal racism" supported by a nation's government. (Apartheid derives from a word in the Afrikaan language, meaning "apartness.")

    Example: South Africa's national system of racial segregation and discrimination that was in place from 1948 to 1994.

- Hate Crimes: criminal action motivated solely by prejudice toward the crime victim.

    Example: Acts of vandalism or assault aimed at members of a particular ethnic group or persons of a particular sexual orientation.

- Hate Groups: organizations whose primary purpose is to stimulate prejudice, discrimination, or aggression toward certain groups of people based on their ethnicity, race, religion, and so on.

    Example: The Ku Klux Klan—an American terrorist group that perpetrates hatred toward all non-white races.

- Genocide: mass murdering of a particular ethnic or racial group.

    Example: The Holocaust, in which millions of Jews were systematically murdered during World War II. Other examples include the murdering of Cambodians under the Khmer Rouge regime, the murdering of Bosnian Muslims in the former country of Yugoslavia, and the slaughter of the Tutsi minority by the Hutu majority in Rwanda.

- Classism: prejudice or discrimination based on social class, particularly toward people of lower socioeconomic status.

    Example: Acknowledging the contributions made by politicians and wealthy industrialists to America, while ignoring the contributions of poor immigrants, farmers, slaves, and pioneer women.

- Religious Intolerance: denying the fundamental human right of people to hold religious beliefs, or to hold religious beliefs that differ from one's own.

    Example: An atheist who forces nonreligious (secular) beliefs on others, or a member of a religious group who believes that people who hold different religious beliefs are infidels or "sinners" whose souls will not be saved.

- Anti-Semitism: prejudice or discrimination toward Jews or people who practice the religion of Judaism.

    Example: Disliking Jews because they're the ones who "killed Christ."

- Xenophobia: fear or hatred of foreigners, outsiders, or strangers.

    Example: Believing that immigrants should be banned from entering the country because they'll undermine our economy and increase our crime rate.

- Regional Bias: prejudice or discrimination based on the geographical region in which an individual is born and raised.

    Example: A northerner thinking that all southerners are racists.

- Jingoism: excessive interest and belief in the superiority of one's own nation—without acknowledging its mistakes or weaknesses—often accompanied by an aggressive foreign policy that neglects the needs of other nations or the common needs of all nations.

    Example: "Blind patriotism"—failure to see the shortcomings of one's own nation and viewing any questioning or criticism of one's own nation as being disloyal or "unpatriotic." (As in the slogan, "America: right or wrong" or "America: love it or leave it!")

- Terrorism: intentional acts of violence committed against civilians that are motivated by political or religious prejudice.

    Example: The September 11, 2001, attacks on the United States.

- Sexism: prejudice or discrimination based on sex or gender.

    Example: Believing that women should not pursue careers in fields traditionally filled only by men (e.g., engineering or politics) because they lack the innate qualities or natural skills to do so.

- Heterosexism: belief that heterosexuality is the only acceptable sexual orientation.

    Example: Believing that gays should not have the same legal rights and opportunities as heterosexuals.

- Homophobia: extreme fear or hatred of homosexuals.

    Example: Creating or contributing to anti-gay websites or "gay bashing" (acts of violence toward gays).

- Ageism: prejudice or discrimination toward certain age groups, particularly toward the elderly.

    Example: Believing that all "old" people have dementia and shouldn't be allowed to drive or make important decisions.

- Ableism: prejudice or discrimination toward people who are disabled or handicapped (physically, mentally, or emotionally).

    Example: Intentionally avoiding social contact with people in wheelchairs.

Journal Reflection 6.14

After reading, "A Snapshot Summary", what reactions (positive and negative) did you identify, why do you think you reacted the way you did?

In small groups, give an example or share your reflection.

_____

_____

_____

_____

_____

_____

> "I grew up in a very racist family. Even just a year ago, I could honestly say 'I hate Asians' with a straight face and mean it. My senior AP language teacher tried hard to teach me not to be judgmental. He got me to be open to others, so much so that my current boyfriend is half Chinese."
>
> —*AHE first-year student*

STRATEGIES FOR OVERCOMING STEREOTYPES AND PREJUDICES

We may hold prejudices, stereotypes, or subtle biases that bubble beneath the surface of our conscious awareness. The following practices and strategies can help us become more aware of our unconscious biases and relate more effectively to individuals from diverse groups.

Consciously avoid preoccupation with physical appearances. Remember the old proverb: "It's what inside that counts." Judge others by the quality of their inner qualities, not by the familiarity of their outer features. Get beneath the superficial surface of appearances and relate to people not in terms of how they look but who they are and how they act.

Form impressions of others on a person-to-person basis, not on the basis of their group membership. This may seem like an obvious and easy thing to do, but research shows that humans have a natural tendency to perceive individuals from unfamiliar groups as being more alike (or all alike) than members of their own group (Taylor, Peplau, and Sears 2006). Thus, we need to remain mindful of this tendency and make a conscious effort to perceive and treat individuals of diverse groups as unique human beings, not according to some general (stereotypical) rule of thumb.

NOTE

It's valuable to learn about different cultures and the common characteristics shared by members of the same culture; however, this shouldn't be done while ignoring individual differences. Don't assume that all individuals who share the same cultural background share the same personal characteristics.

Journal Reflection 6.15

Your comfort level while interacting with people from diverse groups is likely to depend on how much prior experience you've had with members of those groups. Rate the amount or variety of diversity you have experienced in the following settings:

1. The high school you attended   high   moderate   low

2. The college or university you now attend   high   moderate   low

3. The neighborhood in which you grew up   high   moderate   low

4. Places where you have been employed   high   moderate   low

Which setting had the *most* and the *least* diversity?

_____

_____

_____

_____

What do you think accounted for this difference?

_____

_____

_____

_____

_____

Place yourself in situations and locations on campus where you will come in regular contact with individuals from diverse groups. Distancing ourselves from diversity ensures we'll never experience diversity and benefit from it. Research in social psychology shows that relationships are more likely to form among people who come in regular contact with one another (Latané et al. 1995), and research on diversity reveals that when there's regular contact between members of different racial or ethnic groups, stereotyping is sharply reduced and intercultural friendships are more likely to develop (Pettigrew 1997, 1998). You can create these conditions by making an intentional attempt to sit near diverse students in the classroom, library, or student café, and by joining them for class discussion groups or group projects.

Take advantage of social media to "chat" virtually with students from diverse groups on your own campus, or students on other campuses. Electronic communication can be a convenient and comfortable way to initially interact with members of diverse groups with whom you have had little prior experience. After interacting *online*, you're more likely to feel more comfortable about interacting *in person*.

Engage in co-curricular experiences involving diversity. Review your student handbook to find co-curricular programs, student activities, student clubs, or campus organizations that emphasize diversity awareness and appreciation. Studies indicate that participation in co-curricular experiences relating to diversity promotes critical thinking (Pascarella and Terenzini 2005) and reduces unconscious prejudice (Blair 2002).

Consider spending time at the multicultural center on your campus, or joining a campus club or organization that's devoted to diversity awareness (e.g., multicultural or international student club). Putting yourself in these situations will enable you to make regular contact with members of cultural groups other than your own; it also sends a clear message to members of these groups that you value their culture because you've taken the initiative to connect with them on "their turf."

If your campus sponsors multicultural or cross-cultural retreats, strongly consider participating in them. A retreat setting can provide a comfortable environment in which you can interact personally with diverse students without being distracted by your customary social circle and daily routine.

If possible, participate in a study abroad or travel study program that gives you the opportunity to live in another country and interact directly with its native citizens. In addition to coursework, you can gain international knowledge and a global perspective by participating in programs that enable you to actually *experience* a different country. You can do this for a full term or for a shorter time period (e.g., January, May, or summer term). To prepare for international experiences, take a course in the language, culture, or history of the nation to which you will be traveling.

Research on students who participate in study abroad programs indicates that these experiences promote greater appreciation of cross-cultural differences, greater interest in world affairs, and greater commitment to peace and international cooperation (Bok 2006; Kaufmann et al. 1992). Additional research shows that study abroad benefits students' personal development, including improved self-confidence, sense of independence, and ability to function in complex environments (Carlson et al. 1990; IES Abroad News 2002).

Incorporate diversity courses into your planned schedule of classes. Review your college catalog (bulletin) and identify courses that are designed to promote understanding or appreciation of diversity. These courses may focus on diverse cultures found within the United States (sometimes referred to as multicultural courses) or diverse cultures associated with different countries (sometimes referred to as international or cross-cultural courses).

In a national study of college students who experienced multicultural courses, it was discovered that students of all racial and ethnic groups made significant gains in learning and intellectual development (Smith 1997; Smith et al. 1997).

Taking courses focusing on international diversity can help you develop the global perspective needed for success in today's international economy and enhance the quality of your college transcript (Brooks 2009; Cuseo et al. 2013; National Association of Colleges and Employers 2003).

Be on the lookout for diversity implications associated with topics you're reading about or discussing in class. Consider the multicultural and cross-cultural ramifications of material you're studying and use examples of diversity to support or illustrate your points. If you're allowed to choose a topic for a research project, select one that relates to diversity or has implications for diversity.

Seek out the views and opinions of classmates from diverse backgrounds. Discussions among students of different races and cultures can reduce prejudice and promote intercultural appreciation, but only if each member's cultural identity and perspective is sought out and valued by members of the discussion group (Baron, Brauscombe, and Byrne 2008). During class discussions, you can demonstrate leadership by seeking out views and opinions of classmates from diverse backgrounds and ensuring that the ideas of people from minority groups are included and respected. In addition, after class discussions, you can ask students from different backgrounds if there was any point made or position taken in class that they would have strongly questioned or challenged.

If there is little or no diversity among students in class, encourage your classmates to look at the topic from diverse perspectives. For instance, you might ask: "If there were international students here, what might they be adding to our discussion?" or, "If members of certain minority groups were here, would they be offering a different viewpoint?"

If you are given the opportunity to form your own discussion groups and group project teams, join or create groups composed of students from diverse backgrounds. You can gain greater exposure to diverse perspectives by intentionally joining or forming learning groups with students who differ in terms of gender, age, race, or ethnicity. Including diversity in your discussion groups not only creates social variety, it also enhances the quality of your group's work by allowing members to gain access to and learn from multiple perspectives. For instance, in learning groups that are diverse with respect to age, older students will bring a broad range of life experiences that younger students can draw upon and learn from, while younger students can provide a more contemporary and idealistic perspective to the group's discussions. Gender diversity is also likely to infuse group discussions with different learning styles and approaches to understanding issues. Studies show that males are more likely to be "separate knowers"—they tend to "detach" themselves from the concept or issue being discussed so they can analyze it. In contrast, females are more likely to be "connected knowers"—they tend to relate personally to concepts and connect them with their own experiences and the experiences of others. For example, when interpreting a poem, males are more likely to ask: "What techniques can I use to analyze it?" In contrast, females would be more likely to ask: "What is the poet trying to say to me?" (Belenky et al. 1986). It's also been found that females are more likely to work collaboratively during group discussions and collect the ideas of other members; in contrast, males are more likely to adopt a competitive approach and debate the ideas of others (Magolda 1992). Both of these styles of learning are valuable and you can capitalize on these different styles by forming gender-diverse discussion groups.

Form collaborative learning teams with students from diverse backgrounds. A learning *team* is more than a discussion group that tosses around ideas; it moves beyond discussion to *collaboration*—its members "co-labor" (work together) to reach the same goal. Research from kindergarten through college indicates that when students collaborate in teams, their academic performance and interpersonal skills are strengthened (Cuseo 1996). In addition, when individuals from different racial groups work collaboratively toward the same goal, racial prejudice is reduced and interracial friendships are more likely to be formed (Allport 1954; Amir 1976; Brown et al. 2003; Dovidio, Eller, and Hewstone 2011). These positive developments may be explained, in part, by the fact that when members of diverse groups come together on the same team, nobody is a member of an "out" group ("them"); instead, everybody belongs to the same "in" group ("us") (Pratto et al. 2000; Sidanius et al. 2000).

In an analysis of multiple studies involving more than 90,000 people from 25 different countries, it was found that when interaction between members of diverse groups took place under the conditions described in **Box 6.5**, prejudice was significantly reduced (Pettigrew and Tropp 2000) and the greatest gains in learning took place (Johnson, Johnson, and Smith 1998; Slavin 1995).

Box 6.5

Tips for Teamwork: Creating Diverse and Effective Learning Teams

1. Intentionally form learning teams with students who have different cultural backgrounds and life experiences. Teaming up only with friends or classmates whose backgrounds and experiences are similar to yours can actually impair your team's performance because teammates can get off track and onto topics that have nothing to do with the learning task (e.g., what they did last weekend or what they're planning to do next weekend).

2. Before jumping into group work, take some time to interact informally with your teammates. When team members have some social "warm up" time (e.g., time to learn each other's names and learn something about each other), they feel more comfortable expressing their ideas and are more likely to develop a stronger sense of team identity. This feeling of group solidarity can create a foundation of trust among group members, enabling them to work together as a team, particularly if they come from diverse (and unfamiliar) cultural backgrounds.

    The context in which a group interacts can influence the openness and harmony of their interaction. Group members are more likely to interact openly and collaboratively when they work in a friendly, informal environment that's conducive to relationship building. A living room or a lounge area provides a warmer and friendlier team-learning atmosphere than a sterile classroom.

3. Have teammates work together to complete a single work product. One jointly created product serves to highlight the team's collaborative effort and collective achievement (e.g., a completed sheet of answers to questions, or a comprehensive list of ideas). Creating a common final product helps keep individuals thinking in terms of "we" (not "me") and keeps the team moving in the same direction toward the same goal.

4. Group members should work interdependently—they should depend on each other to reach their common goal and each member should have equal opportunity to contribute to the team's final product. Each teammate should take responsibility for making an indispensable contribution to the team's end product, such as contributing: (a) a different piece of *information* (e.g., a specific chapter from the textbook or a particular section of class notes), (b) a particular form of *thinking* to the learning task (e.g., analysis, synthesis, or application), or (c) a different *perspective* (e.g., national, international, or global). Said in another way, each group member should assume personal responsibility for a piece that's needed to complete the whole puzzle.

(continued)

Box 6.5 *(continued)*

Similar to a sports team, each member of a learning team should have a specific role to play. For instance, each teammate could perform one of the following roles:

- manager—whose role is to assure that the team stays on track and keeps moving toward its goal;
- moderator—whose role is to ensure that all teammates have equal opportunity to contribute;
- summarizer—whose role is to monitor the team's progress, identifying what has been accomplished and what still needs to be done;
- recorder—whose role is to keep a written record of the team's ideas.

5. After concluding work in diverse learning teams, take time to reflect on the experience. The final step in any learning process, whether it be learning from a lecture or learning from a group discussion, is to step back from the process and thoughtfully review it. Deep learning requires not only effortful action but also thoughtful reflection (Bligh 2000; Roediger, Dudai, and Fitzpatrick 2007). You can reflect on your experiences with diverse learning groups by asking yourself questions that prompt you to process the ideas shared by members of your group and the impact those ideas had on you. For instance, ask yourself (and your teammates) the following questions:

What major similarities in viewpoints did all group members share? (What were the common themes?)
- What major differences of opinion were expressed by diverse members of our group? (What were the variations on the themes?)
- Were there particular topics or issues raised during the discussion that provoked intense reactions or emotional responses from certain members of our group?
- Did the group discussion lead any individuals to change their mind about an idea or position they originally held?

When contact among people from diverse groups takes place under the five conditions described in this box, group work is transformed into *teamwork* and promotes higher levels of thinking and deeper appreciation of diversity. A win-win scenario is created: Learning and thinking are strengthened while bias and prejudice are weakened (Allport 1979; Amir 1969; Aronson, Wilson, and Akert 2013; Cook 1984; Sherif et al. 1961).

 Journal Reflection 6.16

Have you had an experience with a member of an unfamiliar racial or cultural group that caused you to change your attitude or viewpoint toward that group? Explain in a positive manner.

_____

_____

_____

_____

_____

Take a stand against prejudice or discrimination by constructively disagreeing with students who make stereotypical statements and prejudicial remarks. By saying nothing, you may avoid conflict, but your silence may be perceived by others to mean that you agree with the person who made the prejudicial remark. Studies show that when members of the same group observe another member of their own group making prejudicial comments, prejudice tends to increase among all group members—probably due to peer pressure of group conformity (Stangor, Sechrist, and Jost 2001). In contrast, if a person's prejudicial remark is challenged by a member of one's own group, particularly a fellow member who is liked and respected, that person's prejudice decreases along with similar prejudices held by other members of the group (Baron, Brauscombe, and Byrne 2008). Thus, by taking a leadership role and challenging peers who make prejudicial remarks, you're likely to reduce that person's prejudice as well as the prejudice of others who hear the remark. In addition, you help create a campus climate in which students experience greater satisfaction with their college experience and are more likely to complete their college degree. Studies show that a campus climate which is hostile toward students from minority groups lowers students' level of college satisfaction and college completion rates of both minority and majority students (Cabrera et al. 1999; Eimers and Pike 1997; Nora and Cabrera 1996).

NOTE

By actively opposing prejudice on campus, you demonstrate diversity leadership and moral character. You become a role model whose actions send a clear message that valuing diversity is not only the smart thing to do, it's the right thing to do.

Journal Reflection 6.17

If you heard another student telling an insulting racial or gender joke, do you think you would do anything about it? What might you do? Why?

_____

_____

_____

_____

_____

THE BENEFITS OF EXPERIENCING DIVERSITY

Thus far, this chapter has focused on *what* diversity is; we now turn to *why* diversity is worth experiencing. National surveys show that by the end of their first year in college, almost two-thirds of students report "stronger" or "much stronger" knowledge of people from different races and cultures than they had when they first began college, and the majority of them became more open to diverse cultures, viewpoints and values (HERI 2013, 2014). Students who develop more openness to and knowledge of diversity are likely to experience the following benefits.

> "
> Do the hard work to grow comfortable in your own skin, hair, size, and identity. If you leave college the same as when you came in, you didn't seize the opportunity—you paid for an expensive piece of paper. Surround yourself with diverse people and ideas. Embrace all of who you are and your interests. Be patient with yourself. Enjoy the journey because there is truly no other time in your life that will be quite like it.
>
> *—College graduate*

NOTE

The more you learn from people who are different than yourself, the more you learn about yourself.

Diversity Increases Self-Awareness and Self-Knowledge

Interacting with people from diverse backgrounds increases self-knowledge and self-awareness by enabling you to compare your life experiences with others whose experiences may differ sharply from your own. When you step outside yourself to contrast your experiences with others from different backgrounds, you move beyond ethnocentrism and gain a *comparative perspective*—a reference point that positions you to see how your particular cultural background has shaped the person you are today.

A comparative perspective also enables us to learn how our cultural background has advantaged or disadvantaged us. For instance, learning about cross-cultural differences in education makes us aware of the limited opportunities people in other countries have to attend college and how advantaged we are in America—where a college education is available to everyone, regardless of their race, gender, age, or prior academic history.

Diversity Deepens Learning

Research consistently shows that we learn more from people who differ from us than we do from people similar to us (Pascarella 2001; Pascarella and Terenzini 2005). Learning about different cultures and interacting with people from diverse cultural groups provides our brain with more varied routes or pathways through which to connect (learn) new ideas. Experiencing diversity "stretches" the brain beyond its normal "comfort zone," requiring it to work harder to assimilate something unfamiliar. When we encounter the unfamiliar, the brain has to engage in extra effort to understand it by comparing and contrasting it to something we already know (Acredolo and O'Connor 1991; Nagda, Gurin, and Johnson 2005). This added expenditure of mental energy results in the brain forming neurological connections that are deeper and more durable (Willis 2006). Simply stated, humans learn more from diversity than they do from similarity or familiarity. In contrast, when we restrict the diversity of people with whom we interact (out of habit or prejudice), we limit the breadth and depth of our learning.

Diversity Promotes Critical Thinking

Studies show that students who experience high levels of exposure to various forms of diversity while in college—such as participating in multicultural courses and campus events and interacting with peers of different ethnic backgrounds—report the greatest gains in:

- thinking *complexity*—ability to think about all parts and sides of an issue (Association of American Colleges and Universities 2004; Gurin 1999),
- *reflective* thinking—ability to think deeply about personal and global issues (Kitchener, Wood, and Jensen 2000), and
- *critical* thinking—ability to evaluate the validity of their own reasoning and the reasoning of others (Gorski 2009; Pascarella et al. 2001).

These findings are likely explained by the fact that when we're exposed to perspectives that differ from our own, we experience "cognitive dissonance"—a state of cognitive (mental) disequilibrium or imbalance that "forces" our mind to consider multiple perspectives simultaneously;

this makes our thinking less simplistic, more complex, and more comprehensive (Brookfield 1987; Gorski 2009).

Diversity Stimulates Creative Thinking

Cross-cultural knowledge and experiences enhance personal creativity (Leung et al. 2008; Maddux and Galinsky 2009). When we have diverse perspectives at our disposal, we have more opportunities to shift perspectives and discover "multiple partial solutions" to problems (Kelly 1994). Furthermore, ideas acquired from diverse people and cultures can "cross-fertilize," giving birth to new ideas for tackling old problems (Harris 2010). Research shows that when ideas are generated freely and exchanged openly in groups comprised of people from diverse backgrounds, powerful "cross-stimulation" effects can occur, whereby ideas from one group member trigger new ideas among other group members (Brown, Dane, and Durham 1998). Research also indicates that seeking out diverse alternatives, perspectives, and viewpoints enhances our ability to reach personal goals (Stoltz 2014).

In contrast, when different cultural perspectives are neither sought nor valued, the variety of lenses available to us for viewing problems is reduced, which, in turn, reduces our capacity to think creatively. Ideas are less likely to diverge (go in different directions); instead, they're more likely to converge and merge into the same cultural channel—the one shared by the homogeneous group of people doing the thinking.

Diversity Enhances Career Preparation and Career Success

Whatever line of work you decide to pursue, you're likely to find yourself working with employers, coworkers, customers, and clients from diverse cultural backgrounds. America's workforce is now more diverse than at any other time in history and will grow ever more diverse throughout the twenty-first century; by 2050, the proportion of American workers from minority ethnic and racial groups will jump to 55% (U.S. Census Bureau 2008).

National surveys reveal that policymakers, business leaders, and employers seek college graduates who are more than just "aware" of or "tolerant" of diversity. They want graduates who have actual *experience* with diversity (Education Commission of the States 1995) and are able to collaborate with diverse coworkers, clients, and customers (Association of American Colleges and Universities 2002; Hart Research Associates 2013). Over 90% of employers agree that all students should have experiences in college that teach them how to solve problems with people whose views differ from their own (Hart Research Associates 2013).

The current "global economy" also requires skills relating to international diversity. Today's work world is characterized by economic interdependence among nations, international trading (imports/exports), multinational corporations, international travel, and almost instantaneous worldwide communication—due to rapid advances in the world wide web (Dryden and Vos 1999; Friedman 2005). Even smaller companies and corporations have become increasingly international in nature (Brooks 2009). As a result, employers in all sectors of the economy now seek job candidates

NOTE

By drawing on ideas generated by people from diverse backgrounds and bouncing your ideas off them, divergent or expansive thinking is stimulated; this leads to synergy (multiplication of ideas) and serendipity (unexpected discoveries).

NOTE

The wealth of diversity on college campuses today represents an unprecedented educational opportunity. You may never again be a member of a community with so many people from such a wide variety of backgrounds. Seize this opportunity to strengthen your education and career preparation.

who possess the following skills and attributes: sensitivity to human differences, ability to understand and relate to people from different cultural backgrounds, international knowledge, and ability to communicate in a second language (Fixman 1990; Hart Research Associates 2013; National Association of Colleges and Employers 2007; Office of Research 1994).

As a result of these domestic and international trends, *intercultural competence* has become an essential skill for success in the twenty-first century (Thompson and Cuseo 2014). Intercultural competence may be defined as the ability to appreciate and learn from human differences and to interact effectively with people from diverse cultural backgrounds. It includes "knowledge of cultures and cultural practices (one's own and others), complex cognitive skills for decision making in intercultural contexts, social skills to function effectively in diverse groups, and personal attributes that include flexibility and openness to new ideas" (Wabash National Study of Liberal Arts Education 2007).

Journal Reflection 6.18

What intercultural skills do you think you already possess?

_____

_____

_____

_____

_____

What intercultural skills do you think you need to develop?

_____

_____

_____

_____

_____

_____

CHAPTER SUMMARY AND HIGHLIGHTS

Diversity refers to the variety of groups that comprise humanity (the human species). Humans differ from one another in multiple ways, including physical features, religious beliefs, mental and physical abilities, national origins, social backgrounds, gender, and sexual orientation. Diversity involves the important political issue of securing equal rights and social justice for all people; however, it's also an important *educational* issue—an integral element of the college experience that enriches learning, personal development, and career preparation.

When a group of people share the same traditions and customs, it creates a culture that serves to bind people into a supportive, tight-knit community. However, culture can also lead its members to view the world solely through their own cultural lens (known as ethnocentrism), which can blind them to other cultural perspectives. Ethnocentrism can contribute to stereotyping—viewing individual members of another cultural group in the same (fixed) way, in which they're seen as having similar personal characteristics.

Stereotyping can result in prejudice—a biased prejudgment about another person or group of people that's formed before the facts are known. Stereotyping and prejudice often go hand in hand because if the stereotype is negative, members of the stereotyped group are then judged negatively. Discrimination takes prejudice one step further by converting the negative prejudgment into behavior that results in unfair treatment of others. Thus, discrimination is prejudice put into action.

Once stereotyping and prejudice are overcome, we are positioned to experience diversity and reap its multiple benefits—which include sharper self-awareness, deeper learning, higher-level thinking, and better career preparation.

The increasing diversity of students on campus, combined with the wealth of diversity-related educational experiences found in the college curriculum and co-curriculum, presents you with an unprecedented opportunity to infuse diversity into your college experience. Seize this opportunity and capitalize on the power of diversity to increase the quality of your college education and your prospects for success in the twenty-first century.

LEARNING MORE THROUGH THE WORLD WIDE WEB: INTERNET-BASED RESOURCES

For additional information on diversity, see the following websites:

Stereotyping: ReducingStereotypeThreat.org at www.reducingstereotypethreat.org

Prejudice & Discrimination: Southern Poverty Law Center at www.splcenter.org/

Human Rights:
Amnesty International at www.amnesty.org/en/discrimination
Center for Economic & Social Justice at www.cesj.org

Sexism in the Media:
"Killing Us Softly" at www.youtube.com/watch?v=PTImho_RovY
LGBT Acceptance & Support: "It Gets Better Project," at www.itgetsbetter.org
Teaching Tolerance webpage
Terrel and Lindsey book
Brown v. Board of Ed.
Sexual Diversity organizations

REFERENCES

Acredolo, C., and J. O'Connor. 1991. "On the Difficulty of Detecting Cognitive Uncertainty." *Human Development* 34: 204–23.

Allport, G. W. 1954. *The Nature of Prejudice.* Cambridge, MA: Addison-Wesley.

Allport, G. W. 1979. *The Nature of Prejudice.* 3rd ed. Reading, MA: Addison-Wesley.

American Association of Community Colleges. 2009. 2009 Fact Sheet. http://www.aacc.nche.edu/About/Documents/factsheet2009.pdf.

Amir, Y. 1969. "Contact Hypothesis in Ethnic Relations." *Psychological Bulletin* 71: 319–42.

Amir, Y. 1976. "The Role of Intergroup Contact in Change of Prejudice and Ethnic Relations." In *Towards the Elimination of Racism*, edited by P. A. Katz, 245–308. New York: Pergamon Press.

Anderson, M., and S. Fienberg. 2000. "*Race and Ethnicity and the Controversy Over the US Census.*" *Current Sociology* 48 (3): 87–110.

Aronson, E., T. D. Wilson, and R. M. Akert. 2013. *Social Psychology.* 8th ed. Upper Saddle River, NJ: Pearson/Prentice Hall.

Association of American Colleges & Universities (AAC&U). 2002. *Greater Expectations: A New Vision for Learning as a Nation Goes to College.* Washington, DC: Author.

Association of American Colleges & Universities (AAC&U). 2004. *Our Students' Best Work.* Washington, DC: Author.

Baron, R. A., R. N. Branscombe, and D. R. Byrnne. 2008. *Social Psychology.* 12th ed. Boston, MA: Allyn and Bacon.

Belenky, M. F., B. Clinchy, N. R. Goldberger, and J. M. Tarule. 1986. *Women's Ways of Knowing: The Development of Self, Voice, and Mind.* New York: Basic Books.

Blair, I. V. 2002. "The Malleability of Automatic Stereotypes and Prejudice." *Personality and Social Psychology Review* 6 (3): 242–61.

Bligh, D. A. 2000. *What's the Use of Lectures?* San Francisco: Jossey Bass.

Bok, D. 2006. *Our Underachieving Colleges: A Candid Look at How Much Students Learn and Why They Should Be Learning More.* Princeton, New Jersey: Princeton University Press.

Bridgeman, B. 2003. *Psychology and Evolution: The Origins of Mind.* Thousand Oaks, CA: Sage Publications.

Bronfenbrenner, U., ed. 2005. *Making Human Beings Human: Bioecological Perspectives on Human Development.* Thousand Oaks, CA: Sage.

Brookfield, S. D. 1987. *Developing Critical Thinkers.* San Francisco: Jossey-bass.

Brooks, I. 2009. Organisational Behaviour. 4th ed. Englewood Cliffs, NJ: Prentice Hall.

Brown, T. D., F. C. Dane, and M. D. Durham. 1998. "Perception of Race and Ethnicity." *Journal of Social Behavior and Personality* 13 (2): 295–306.

Brown, K. T., T. N. Brown, J. S. Jackson, R. M. Sellers, and W. J. Manuel. 2003. "Teammates On and Off the Field? Contact with Black Teammates and the Racial Attitudes of White Student Athletes.*" Journal of Applied Social Psychology* 33: 1379–403.

Cabrera, A., A. Nora, P. Terenzini, E. Pascarella, and L. S. Hagedorn. 1999. "Campus Racial Climate and the Adjustment of Students to College: A Comparison Between White Students and African American Students." *The Journal of Higher Education* 70 (2): 134–60.

Caplan, P. J., and J. B. Caplan. 2008. *Thinking Critically About Research on Sex and Gender.* 3rd ed. New York: HarperCollins College Publishers.

Carlson, J. N., Keller, R. W., Glick, S. D. 1990. "Individual Differences in the Behavioral Effects of Stressors Attributable to Lateralized Differences in Mesocortical Dopamine Systems." *Society for Neuroscience Abstracts* 16.233.

Ciancotto, J. 2005. *Hispanic and Latino Same-sex Couple Households in the United States: A Report from the 2000 Census.* New York: The National Gay and Lesbian Task Force Policy Institute and the National Latino/a Coalition for Justice.

Colombo, G., R. Cullen, and B. Lisle. 2013. *Rereading America: Cultural Contexts for Critical Thinking and Writing.* 9th ed. Boston: Bedford Books of St. Martin's Press.

Cook, S. W. 1984. "Cooperative Interaction in Multiethnic Contexts." In *Groups in Contact: The Psychology of Desegregation,* edited by N. Miller and M. B. Brewer, 291–302. New York: Academic Press.

Cuseo, J. B. 1996. *Cooperative Learning: A Pedagogy for Addressing Contemporary Challenges and Critical Issues in Higher Education.* Stillwater, OK: New Forums Press.

Cuseo, J. B., A. Thompson, J. McLaughlin. 2013. *Thriving in Community College & Beyond: Strategies for Academic Success and Personal Development.* Dubuque, IA: Kendall Hunt Publishing Company.

DeNavas-Walt, C., B. D. Proctor, and J. C. Smith. 2013. *Income, Poverty, and Health Insurance Coverage in the United States, 2012.* U.S. Census Bureau, Current Population Reports, P60-245, Washington, DC: U.S. Government Printing Office.

Dessel, A. 2012. "Effects of Intergroup Dialogue: Public School Teachers and Sexual Orientation Prejudice." *Small Group Research* 41 (5): 556–92.

Dolan, M., and L. Romney. June 27, 2015. "Law in California Is Now a Right for All." *Los Angeles Times*: A1 and A8.

Dovidio, J. F., A. Eller, and M. Hewstone. 2011. "Improving Intergroup Relations Through Direct, Extended and Other Forms of Indirect Contact." *Group Processes & Intergroup Relations* 14: 147–60.

Dryden, G., and J. Vos. 1999. *The Learning Revolution: To Change the Way the World Learns.* Torrance, CA and Auckland, New Zealand: The Learning Web.

Education Commission of the States. 1995. *Making Quality Count in Undergraduate Education.* Denver, CO: ECS Distribution Center.

Eimers, M. T., and G. R. Pike. 1997. "Minority and Nonminority Adjustment to College: Differences or Similarities." *Research in Higher Education* 38 (1): 77–97.

Erickson, B. L., C. B. Peters, and D. W. Strommer. 2006. *Teaching First-year College Students.* San Francisco: Jossey-bass.

Family Care Foundation. 1997–2012. *If the World Were a Village of 100 People.* http://www.familycare.org/special-interest/if-the-world-were-a-village-of-100-people/.

Feagin, J. R., and C. B. Feagin. 2007. Racial and Ethnic Relations. 8th ed. Englewood Cliffs, NJ: Prentice Hall.

Fixman, C. S. 1990. "The Foreign Language Needs of U.S. Based Corporations." *Annals of the American Academy of Political and Social Science* 511: 25–46.

Friedman, T. L. 2005. *The World Is Flat: A Brief History of the Twenty-First Century: Revitalizing the Civic Mission of Schools.* Alexandria, VA.

Gorski, P. C. 2009. *Key Characteristics of a Multicultural Curriculum.* Critical Multicultural Pavilion: Multicultural Curriculum Reform (An EdChange Project). www.edchange.org/multicultural/curriculum/characteristics.html.

Gould, E., and H. Wething. 2013. "Health Care, the Market and Consumer Choice." *Inquiry* 50 (1): 85–6.

Gurin, P. 1999. "New Research on the Benefits of Diversity in College and Beyond: An Empirical Analysis." *Diversity Digest* 3 (3), 5–15. http://www.diversityweb.org/Digest/Sp99/benefits.html.

Harris, A. 2010. "Leading System Transformation." *School Leadership and Management* 30 (3): 197–207.

Hart Research Associates. 2013. *It Takes more than a Major: Employer Priorities for College Learning and Student Success.* Washington, DC: Author.

HERI (Higher Education Research Institute). 2013. *Your First College Year Survey 2012.* Los Angeles, CA: Cooperative Institutional Research Program, University of California-los Angeles.

HERI (Higher Education Research Institute). 2014. *Your First College Year Survey 2014.* Los Angeles, CA: Cooperative Institutional Research Program, University of California-los Angeles.

Hugenberg, K., and G. V. Bodenhausen. 2003. "Facing Prejudice: Implicit Prejudice and the Perception of Facial Threat." *Psychological Science* 14: 640–43.

IES Abroad News. 2002. Study Abroad: A Lifetime of Benefits. www.iesabroad.org/study-abroad/news/study-abroad-lifetime-benefits.

Jablonski, N. G., and G. Chaplin. 2002. "Skin Deep." *Scientific American* (October): 75–81.

Johnson, D., R. Johnson, and K. Smith. 1998. "Cooperative Learning Returns to College: What Evidence Is There that It Works?" *Change* 30: 26–35.

Judd, C. M., C. S. Ryan, and B. Parke. 1991. "Accuracy in the Judgment of In-Group and Out-Group Variability." *Journal of Personality and Social Psychology* 61: 366–79.

Kaufmann, N. L., J. M. Martin, and H. D. Weaver. 1992. *Students Abroad: Strangers at Home: Education for a Global Society.* Yarmouth, ME: Intercultural Press.

Kelly, K. 1994. *Out of Control: The New Biology of Machines, Social Systems, and the Economic World.* Reading, MA: Addison-Wesley.

Kitchener, K., P. Wood, and L. Jensen. August, 2000. *Curricular, Co-curricular, and Institutional Influence on Real-World Problem-Solving.* Paper Presented at the Annual Meeting of the American Psychological *Association*, Boston.

Kochlar, R., R. Fry, and P. Taylor. 2011. "Wealth Gaps Rise to Record Highs Between Whites, Blacks, Hispanics, Twenty-to-One." *Pew Research Social and Demographics Trends* (July). http://www.pewsocialtrends.org/2011/07/26/wealth-gaps-rise-to-record-highs-between-whites-blacks-hispanics/.

Lancaster, L., and D. Stilman. 2002. *When Generations Collide: Who They Are. Why They Clash.* New York: HarperCollins.

Latané, B., J. H. Liu, A. Nowak, N. Bonevento, and L. Zheng. 1995. "Distance Matters: Physical Space and Social Impact." *Personality and Social Psychology Bulletin* 21: 795–805.

Leung, A. K., W. W. Maddux, A. D. Galinsky, and C.-Y. Chiu. 2008. "Multicultural Experience Enhances Creativity: The When and How." *American Psychologist* 63 (3): 169–81.

Lewis, M., G. W. Paul, and C. D. Fenning, eds. 2014. *Ethnologue: Languages of the World*. 17th ed. Dallas, Texas: SIL International. Online Version: http://www.ethnologue.com.

Luhman, R. 2007. *The Sociological Outlook*. Lanham, MD: Rowman & Littlefield.

Maddux, W. W., and A. D. Galinsky. 2009. "Cultural Borders and Mental Barriers: the Relationship Between Living Abroad and Creativity." *Journal of Personality and Social Psychology* 96 (5): 1047–61.

Magolda, M. B. B. 1992. *Knowing and Reasoning in College*. San Francisco: Jossey-bass.

Mendez, F., T. Krahn, B. Schrack, A. M. Krahn, K. Veeramah, A. Woerner, F. L. Fomine, M. Bradman, N., M. Thomas, T. Karafet, and M. Hammer. 2013. "An African American Paternal Lineage Adds an Extremely Ancient Root to the Human Y Chromosome Phylogenetic Tree." *The American Journal of Human Genetics* 92: 454–59.

Meredith, M. 2011. *Born in Africa: The Quest for the Origins of Human Life*. New York: Public Affairs.

Nagda, B. R., P. Gurin, and S. M. Johnson. 2005. "Living, Doing and Thinking Diversity: How Does Pre-college Diversity Experience Affect First-year Students' Engagement with College Diversity?" In *Improving the First Year of College: Research and Practice*, edited by R. S. Feldman, 73–110. Mahwah, NJ: Lawrence Erlbaum.

Nathan, R. 2005. *My Freshman Year: What a Professor Learned by Becoming a Student*. London: Penguin.

National Center for Education Statistics. 2011. *Digest of Education Statistics, Table 237. Total Fall Enrollment in Degree-granting Institutions, by Level of Student, Sex, Attendance Status, and Race/Ethnicity: Selected Years, 1976 Through 2010*. Alexandria, VA: U.S. Department of Education. http://neces.ed/gov/programs/digest/d11/tables/dt11_237.asp

National Association of Colleges and Employers (NACE). 2003. Job Outlook 2003 Survey. Bethlehem, PA: Author.

National Association of Colleges and Employers (NACE). 2007. Job Outlook 2007 Survey. Bethlehem, PA: Author

National Survey of Women Voters. 1998. *Autumn Overview Report Conducted by DYG Inc.* http://www.diversityweb.org/research_and_trends/research_evaluation_impact_/campus_community_connections/national_poll.cfm

Nhan, D. 2012. "Census: Minorities Constitute 37 Percent of U.S. Population." *National Journal: The Next America-demographics 2012*. http://www.nationaljournal.com/thenextamerica/demographics/census-minorities-constitute-37-percent-of-u-s-population-20120517

Nora, A., and A. Cabrera, 1996. "The Role of Perceptions of Prejudice and Discrimination on the Adjustment of Minority College Students." *The Journal of Higher Education* 67 (2): 119–48.

Office of Research. 1994. *What Employers Expect of College Graduates: International Knowledge and Second Language Skills*. Washington, DC: Office of Educational Research and Improvement, U.S. Department of Education.

Olson, L. 2007. "What Does "Ready" Mean?" *Education Week* 40: 7–12.

Pascarella, E. T. November/December, 2001. "Cognitive Growth in College: Surprising and Reassuring Findings from the National Study of Student Learning." *Change* 21–7.

Pascarella, E. T., and P. T. Terenzini. 2005. *How College Affects Students, Volume 2, A Third Decade of Research*. San Francisco, CA: Jossey-bass.

Pascarella, E., B. Palmer, M. Moye, and C. Pierson. 2001. "Do Diversity Experiences Influence the Development of Critical Thinking?" *Journal of College Student Development* 42 (3): 257–91.

Peoples, J., and G. Bailey. 2011. *Humanity: An Introduction to Cultural Anthropology*. Belmont, CA: Wadsworth, Cengage Learning.

Pettigrew, T. F. 1997. "Generalized Intergroup Contact Effects on Prejudice." *Personality and Social Psychology Bulletin* 23: 173–85.

Pettigrew, T. F. 1998. "Intergroup Contact Theory." *Annual Review of Psychology* 49: 65–85.

Pettigrew, T. F., and L. R. Tropp. 2000. "Does Intergroup Contact Reduce Prejudice? Recent Meta-analytic Findings." In *Reducing Prejudice and Discrimination*, edited by S. Oskamp, 93–114. Mahwah, NJ: Lawrence Erlbaum Associates.

Pinker, S. 2000. *The Language Instinct: The New Science of Language and Mind*. New York: Perennial.

Pratto, F., J. H. Liu, S. Levin, J. Sidanius, M. Shih, H. Bachrach, and P. Hegarty. 2000. "Social Dominance Orientation and the Legitimization of Inequality Across Cultures." *Journal of Cross-Cultural Psychology* 31: 369–409.

Public Service Enterprise Group (PSEG). 2009. *Diversity*. www.pseg.com/info/environment/sustainability/2009/.../diversity.jsp

Reid, G. B. R., and R. Hetherington. 2010. *The Climate Connection: Climate Change and Modern Evolution*. Cambridge, UK: Cambridge University Press.

Roediger, H. L., Y. Dudai, and S. M. Fitzpatrick. 2007. *Science of Memory: Concepts*. New York, NY: Oxford University Press.

Segall, M. H., D. T. Campbell, and M. J. Herskovits. 1966. *The Influence of Culture on Visual Perception*. Indianapolis: Bobbs-Merrill.

Shah, A. 2009. *Global Issues: Poverty Facts and Stats.* http://www.globalissues.org/article/26/poverty-facts-and-stats.

Sherif, M., D. J. Harvey, B. J. White, W. R. Hood, and C. W. Sherif. 1961. *The Robbers' Cave Experiment.* Norman, OK: Institute of Group Relations.

Shiraev, E. D., and D. Levy. 2013. *Cross-cultural Psychology: Critical Thinking and Contemporary Applications.* 5th ed. Upper Saddle River, NJ: Pearson Education.

Sidanius, J., S. Levin, H. Liu, and F. Pratto. 2000. "Social Dominance Orientation, Anti-egalitarianism, and the Political Psychology of Gender: An Extension and Cross-cultural Replication." *European Journal of Social Psychology* 30: 41–67.

Slavin, R. E. 1995. *Cooperative Learning.* 2nd ed. Boston: Allyn & Bacon.

Smith, D. G., L. Guy, G. L. Gerbrick, M. A. Figueroa, G. H. Watkins, T. Levitan, L. C. Moore, P. A. Merchant, H. D. Beliak, and B. Figueroa. 1997. *Diversity Works: The Emerging Picture of How Students Benefit.* Washington, DC: Association of American Colleges and Universities.

Stangor, C., G. B. Sechrist, and J. T. Jost. 2001. "Changing Racial Beliefs by Providing Consensus Information." *Personality and Social Psychology Bulletin* 27: 484–94.

Stoltz, P. G. 2014. *Grit: The New Science of What It Takes to Persevere, Flourish, Succeed.* San Luis Obispo: Climb Strong Press.

Taylor, S. E., L. A. Peplau, and D. O. Sears. 2006. *Social Psychology.* 12th ed. Upper Saddle River, NJ: Pearson/Prentice-Hall.

Thompson, A., and J. Cuseo. 2014. *Diversity and the College Experience.* Dubuque, IA: Kendall Hunt.

U. S. Census Bureau. 2008. *Bureau of Labor Statistics.* Washington, DC: Author.

U. S. Census Bureau. 2013. *Poverty.* Washington, DC: Author. https://www.census.gov/hhes/www/poverty/data/threshld/.

Wabash National Study of Liberal Arts Education. 2007. *Liberal Arts Outcomes.* http:www.liberalarts.wabash.edu/ study-overview/.

Wheelright, J. March, 2005. "Human, Study Thyself." *Discover:* 39–45.

Willis, J. 2006. *Research-Based Strategies to Ignite Student Learning: Insights from a Neurologist and Classroom Teacher.* Alexandria, VA: ASCD.

Zajonc, R. B. 1968. "Attitudinal Effects of Mere Exposure." *Journal of Personality and Social Psychology 9* (monograph supplement no. 2, part 2): 1–27.

Zajonc, R. B. 1970. "Brainwash: Familiarity Breeds Comfort." *Psychology Today* (February): 32–5, 60–2.

Zajonc, R. B. 2001. "Mere Exposure: A Gateway to the Subliminal." *Current Directions in Psychological Science* 10: 224–28.

Chapter 6 Exercises

6.1 Quote Reflections

Review the sidebar quotes contained in this chapter and select two that were especially meaningful or inspirational to you.

For each quote, provide a three- to five-sentence explanation why you chose it.

6.2 Reality Bite

Hate Crime: A Racially Motivated Murder

Jasper County, Texas, has a population of approximately 31,000 people. In this county, 80% of the people are White, 18% are Black, and 2% are of other races. The county's poverty rate is considerably higher than the national average, and its average household income is significantly lower. In 1998, the mayor, the president of the Chamber of Commerce, and two councilmen were Black. From the outside, Jasper appeared to be a town with racial harmony, and its Black and White leaders were quick to state that there was no racial tension in Jasper.

However, one day, James Byrd Jr.—a 49-year-old African American man—was walking home along a road one evening and was offered a ride by three White males. Rather than taking Byrd home, Lawrence Brewer (age 31), John King (age 23), and Shawn Berry (age 23), three men linked to White-supremacist groups, took Byrd to an isolated area and began beating him. They then dropped his pants to his ankles, painted his face black, chained Byrd to their truck, and dragged him for approximately three miles. The truck was driven in a zigzag fashion to inflict maximum pain on the victim. Byrd was decapitated after his body collided with a culvert in a ditch alongside the road. His skin, arms, genitalia, and other body parts were strewn along the road, while his torso was found dumped in front of a Black cemetery. Medical examiners testified that Byrd was alive for much of the dragging incident.

When they were brought to trial, the bodies of Brewer and King were covered with racist tattoos; they were eventually sentenced to death. As a result of the murder, Byrd's family created the James Byrd Foundation for Racial Healing. A wrought iron fence that separated Black and White graves for more than 150 years in Jasper Cemetery was removed in a special unity service. Members of the racist Ku Klux Klan have since visited the gravesite of Byrd several times, leaving racist stickers and other marks that angered the Jasper community and Byrd's family.

Source: Louisiana Weekly (February 3, 2003).

Reflection Questions

1. What factors do you think were responsible for this incident?

2. Could this incident have been prevented? If yes, how? If no, why not?

3. How likely do you think an incident like this could take place in your hometown or near your college campus?

4. If this event happened to take place place in your hometown, how do you think members of your community would react?

5. Events like this is still occurring today, what resources or organizations on your campus provide guidance, information, and support for you to address discrimination? If not, who on campus would be able to assist you?

6.3 Gaining Awareness of Your Group Identities

We are members of multiple groups at the same time and our membership in these overlapping groups can influence our personal development and identity. In the following figure, consider the shaded center circle to be yourself and the six unshaded circles to be six different groups you belong to and that you think have influenced your development.

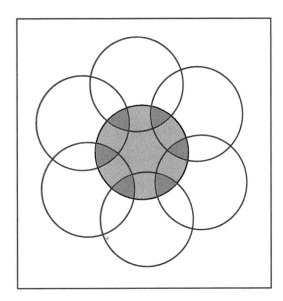

Fill in the unshaded circles with the names of groups to which you think you belong that have had the most influence on your personal development and identity. Don't feel you have to fill in all six circles. What's more important is to identify those groups that you think have had a significant influence on your personal development or identity.

Reflection Questions

1. Which one of your groups has had the greatest influence on your personal development or identity? Why?

2. Have you ever felt limited or disadvantaged by being a member of any your group(s) to which you belonged? Why?

3. Have you ever felt advantaged or privileged by your membership in any group(s)? Why?

6.4 Intercultural Interview

1. Identify a person on your campus who is a member of an ethnic or racial group that you've had little previous contact. Ask that person for an interview, and during the interview, include the following questions:

    •   What does "diversity" mean to you?

    •   What prior experiences have affected your current viewpoints or attitudes about diversity?

    •   What would you say have been the major influences and turning points in your life?

    •   Who would you cite as your positive role models, heroes, or sources of inspiration?

- What societal contributions made by your ethnic or racial group would you like others to be aware of and acknowledge?

- What do you hope will never again be said about your ethnic or racial group?

2. If you were the interviewee instead of the interviewer, how would you have answered the above questions?

3. What do you think accounts for the differences (and similarities) between your answers to the above questions and those provided by the person you interviewed?

6.5 Hidden Bias Test

Go to www.tolerance.org/activity/test-yourself-hidden-bias and take one or more of the hidden bias tests on this website. These tests assess subtle bias with respect to gender, age, ethnic minority groups, religious denominations, sexual orientations, disabilities, and body weight.

1. After completing the test, answer the following questions:

2. Did the results reveal any biases you weren't unaware of?

3. Did you think the assessment results were accurate or valid?

4. What do you think best accounts for or explains your results?

If your closest family member and best friend took the test, how do you think their results would compare with yours?

Chapter 6 Reflection

After reading this chapter, has your definition of diversity changed? Explain.

List and describe five ways appreciating diversity will assist you in being successful in college and/or life.

1.

2.

3.

4.

5.

Are there any areas of diversity you feel you need to be more comfortable with? What are the areas and HOW will you become more comfortable with them?

GOAL SETTING AND MOTIVATION IN HIGHER EDUCATION ENVIRONMENTS

MOVING FROM INTENTION TO ACTION

This chapter lays out the key steps involved in the process of setting effective goals, identifies key self-motivational strategies for staying on track and sustaining progress toward goals, and describes how personal qualities such as self-efficacy, grit, and growth mindset are essential for achieving goals.	**CHAPTER PREVIEW**
Help you set meaningful goals and maintain motivation to achieve your goals. To enable students to articulate their goals and develop a plan to achieve them.	**LEARNING OBJECTIVE**
You will recognize and practice strategies while accessing resources that enable them to be successful in postsecondary institutions.	**PERFORMANCE OBJECTIVE**
Do a quickwrite explaining what your current academic goal is, why and how you decided upon that goal. Be sure and make it a SMART goal.	**PRE-REFLECTION**
What steps do I need to take to meet my academic goals in college?	**ESSENTIAL QUESTION**

THE RELATIONSHIP BETWEEN GOAL SETTING AND SUCCESS

Achieving success begins with setting goals. Research shows that people who set goals and develop plans to reach them are more likely to reach them (Halvorson 2010), and successful people set goals on a regular basis (Locke and Latham 1990). By definition, success involves a sequence of actions that leads to a desired outcome; the process starts with identifying an end (goal) and then finding a means (sequence of steps) to reach that goal.

Motivation begins with dreams and great intentions that get turned into realistic goals. Depending on the length of time it takes to reach them

> "The tragedy of life doesn't lie in not reaching your goal. The tragedy of life lies in having no goal to reach."
>
> —*Benjamin Mays, minister, scholar, activist, president of Morehouse College*

> This first semester has taught me to believe in myself and my own intelligence.
>
> —*Allison Scott*

and the order in which they are to be achieved, goals may be classified into three general categories: long-range, mid-range, and short-range. Short-range goals need to be completed before a mid-range goal can be reached, and mid-range goals must be reached before a long-range goal can be achieved. For example, if your long-range goal is a successful career that requires a college degree, your mid-range goal is completing all the coursework required for a degree that will allow you entry into that career. To reach your mid-range goal of a college degree, you need to start by successfully completing the courses you're taking this term (your short-range goal).

This goal-setting process is called *means-end analysis*; it involves working backward from your long-range goal (the end) and identifying what mid-range and short-range subgoals (the means) must be reached in order to achieve your long-range goal (Brooks 2009; Newell and Simon 1959). Engaging in this process doesn't mean you're locking yourself into a premature plan that will restrict your flexibility or options. It's just a process that (a) gets you to think about where you want to go, (b) provides some sense of direction about how to get there, and (c) starts moving you in the right direction.

In Chapter 1, we introduced you to Marking the Text and in Chapter 2, we provided an overview of Cornell Notes. Now we're going to present "Writing in the Margins." There are lots of ways to use this skill to improve your study skills and memory of important reading You can summarize the ideas of the texts, add questions you might have, and you can connect the ideas you've read with other readings or lectures you've heard. It's just one more way of translating what you're reading into your own thoughts and words. When you finish the chapter, you might want to get together with another student to compare your ideas and answer each others questions.

CHARACTERISTICS OF A WELL-DESIGNED GOAL

Try hard and do their very best (Halvorson 2010; Latham and Locke 2007). The acronym "SMART" is a well-known mnemonic device (memory strategy) for recalling all the key components of a well-designed goal (Doran 1981; Meyer 2003). **Box 7.1** describes the different components of a SMART goal.

BOX 7.1

The *SMART* Method of Goal Setting

A *SMART* goal is one that's:

Specific—it states precisely what the goal is, targets exactly what needs to be done to achieve it, and provides a clear picture of what successfully reaching the goal looks like.

Example: By spending 25 hours per week on my coursework outside of class and by using the effective learning strategies (such as those recommended in this book), I'll achieve at least a 3.0 grade point average this term. (Note that this is a much more specific goal than saying, "I'm really going to work hard this term.")

*M*eaningful (and *M*easurable)—the goal really matters to you (not someone else) and the progress you're making toward the goal can be clearly measured (tracked).

" Dreams can be fulfilled only when they've been defined."

—Ernest Boyer, former United States Commissioner of Education

Example: Achieving at least a 3.0 grade point average this term is important to me because it will enable me to get into the field I'd like to major in. I'll measure my progress toward this goal by calculating the grade I'm earning in each of my courses this semester at regular intervals throughout the term.

*A*ctionable (i.e., *A*ction-Oriented)—the actions or behaviors that will be taken to reach your goal are clearly specified.

Example: I will achieve at least a 3.0 grade point average this term by (a) attending all classes, (b) taking detailed notes in all my classes, (c) completing all reading assignments before their due dates, and (d) avoiding cramming by studying in advance for all my major exams.

*R*ealistic—there is a good chance of reaching the goal, given the time, effort, and skills needed to get there.

Example: Achieving a 3.0 grade point average this term is a realistic goal because my course load is manageable, I will be working no more than 15 hours per week at my part-time job, and I'll be able to get help from campus support services for any academic skills or strategies that need to be strengthened.

*T*ime-framed—the goal has a deadline plus a timeline or timetable that includes short-range (daily), mid-range (weekly), and long-range (monthly steps).

Example: To achieve at least a 3.0 grade point average this term, first I'll acquire all the information I need to learn by taking complete notes in my classes and complete all reading assignments (short-range step). Second, I'll learn the information I've acquired from my notes and readings, break it into parts and study the parts in separate sessions in advance of major exams (mid-range step). Third, on the day before exams, I'll review all the information I previously studied in parts so I avoid cramming and get a good night's sleep (long-range step).

Note: The SMART process can be used to set goals in any area of your life or dimension of personal development, such as:

- self-management (e.g., time management and money management goals),
- physical development (e.g., health and fitness goals),
- social development (e.g., relationship goals),
- emotional development (e.g., stress management or anger management goals),
- intellectual development (e.g., learning and critical thinking goals),
- career development (e.g., career exploration and preparation goals),
- any other element of holistic (whole-person) development discussed in Chapters 11.

In addition to the effective goal-setting properties associated with the SMART method, research reveals that the following goal-setting features characterize people who set and reach important goals. To be effective, be sure to:

1. Set *improvement (get-better) goals* that emphasize progress and growth, rather than perfection (be-good) goals.
2. Focus on outcomes you have *influence or control over*, not on outcomes that are beyond your control. For example, a controllable goal for an aspiring actress would be to improve her acting skills and opportunities, rather than to become a famous movie star—which will depend on factors that are beyond her control. There are several goals you have related to your future—academic, personal, career. These disparate goals influence each other. For example, you may have a goal to complete college with a 3.0 (academic) so you can be admitted to a good graduate school that relates to your future career plans (career) and the career you are interested in enables you to travel internationally (personal). At various times, one goal takes priority over others. This is natural.

NOTE

Review the goal you wrote in the pre-reflection exercise at the beginning of this chapter. Check to ensure it is in the SMART format.

NOTE

It is a good idea to have a plan B, which may include an alternative method of achieving your goal if you are confronted by seemingly insurmountable obstacles.

"
Develop an inner circle of close associations in which the mutual attraction is not sharing problems or needs. The mutual attraction should be values and goals."

—Denis Waitley, former mental trainer for U.S. Olympic athletes and author of Seeds of Greatness

NOTE

Think about your class mates: Who would be helpful in accomplishing your goal? Who would support me when I am feeling like the barriers are insurmountable?

And as important, Who would suggests activities that would keep me from meeting my goal?

NOTE

Be sure to ask yourself: Who can help me stick to my plan and complete the steps needed to reach my goal? You can harness the power of social support by surrounding yourself with peers who are committed to successfully achieve their educational goals and by avoiding "toxic" people who are likely to poison your plans or dampen your dreams.

3. Set goals that are *challenging and effortful*. Goals worth achieving require that we stretch ourselves and break a sweat; they require endurance, persistence, and resiliency. Studies of successful people in all occupations indicate that when they set goals that are attainable but also *challenging*, they pursue those goals more strategically, with more intensity, and with greater commitment (Latham and Locke 2007; Locke and Latham 2002). There's another advantage of setting challenging goals: Achieving them supplies us with a stronger sense of accomplishment, satisfaction, and self-esteem.

4. Anticipate *obstacles* they may encounter along the path to their goal and have a plan in place for dealing with them. You need to be optimistic about succeeding, but that doesn't mean you should be a blind optimist; they realize the road will be tough and they have a realistic plan in place for dealing with the rough spots (Oettingen 2000; Oettingen and Stephens 2009). Thus a well-designed goal should not only include specific information about how the goal will be achieved, but also specific plans to handle anticipated impediments along the way—for example, identifying what resources and social support networks may be used to keep you on track and moving forward.

Capitalize on resources that can help you stay on track and moving toward your goal. Research indicates that success in college involves a combination of what students do for themselves (personal responsibility) and how they to capitalize on resources available to them (Pascarella and Terenzini 1991, 2005). Successful people are resourceful; they seek out and take advantage of resources to help them reach their goals. Use your campus (and community) to help you achieve your long-range goals (e.g., academic advising and career counseling).

Much has been said about the dangers of "peer pressure," but much less attention has been paid to the benefits of "peer power." The power of social support groups for helping people achieve personal goals is well documented by research in different fields (Brissette, Cohen, and Seeman 2000; Ewell 1997). There's also a long historical trail of research pointing to the power of peers for promoting the development and success of college students (Astin 1993; Feldman and Newcomb 1994; Pascarella and Terenzini 2005).

Studies show that making a commitment to a goal in the presence of others increases our commitment to that goal because our successful pursuit of it is viewed not only through our own eyes, but through the eyes of others as well (Hollenbeck, Williams, and Klein 1989; Locke 2000).

 ## Journal Reflection 7.1

What *obstacles* or *impediments* do you anticipate may interfere with your goal of succeeding in college and completing your college degree?

What *campus resources* do you think would be most helpful for dealing with your anticipated obstacles?

THINK ABOUT IT

Take this opportunity to work with a motivated peer and do a quick review of previous chapters. Share SMART goals with another colleague/peer and each of you share your progress, barriers that have gotten in the way and successes. Together review what campus resources are available and determine which would be helpful for continued academic success.

STRATEGIES FOR MAINTAINING MOTIVATION AND PROGRESS TOWARD YOUR GOALS

The word *motivation* derives from the Latin *movere*, meaning "to move." Success comes to those who overcome inertia—they start moving toward their goal; then they maintain momentum until their goal is reached. Goal-setting only creates the potential for success; it takes motivation to turn this potential into reality by converting intention into action. Studies show that goal-setting is just the first step in the process; it must be accompanied by a strong commitment to achieve the goal that has been set (Locke 2000; Locke and Latham 1990).

Reaching challenging goals requires that you maintain motivation and sustain effort over an extended period of time. Listed below are strategies for doing so.

Put your goals in writing and make them visible. Written goals can serve almost like a written contract that holds you accountable for following through on your commitments.

By placing written goals where you can't help but see them on a daily basis (e.g., your laptop, refrigerator, and bathroom mirror), you're less likely to "lose sight" of them and more likely to continue pursuing them. What's kept in sight is kept in mind.

Keep your eye on the prize. Visualize reaching your long-range goals; picture it by creating vivid mental images of your future success. For example, if your goal is to achieve a college degree, visualize a crowd of cheering family, friends, and faculty at your graduation. (You could even add musical accompaniment to your visualization

As a 37-year-old single mother, returning to college was exciting and frightening. I worried about how my kids would manage in my absence. I felt intimidated about my ability to be in school. I was doing Algebra again. What?! But I knew that this would help provide my kids an example of what's possible for their lives. I found peers like me to study with and sometimes, vent about our challenges. We supported each other by babysitting each other's kids and making sure we shared notes when we had to miss a class. We shared information when we found out about campus changes or resources that could help.

—*College graduate*

by playing a motivational song in your head—e.g., "We are the Champions" by Queen.) Imagine cherishing this proud memory for the rest of your life and being in a career your college degree enabled you to enter.

In addition to visualizing the positive consequences of achieving your goal, you can also motivate yourself by visualizing the negative consequences of not achieving it—as illustrated by the following experience.

Visualize completing the steps leading to your goal. You need to visualize not just the success itself (the end goal), but also the steps you'll take along the way. "Just picturing yourself crossing the finish line doesn't actually help you get there—but visualizing how you run the race (the strategies you will use, the choices you will make, the obstacles you will face) not only will give you greater confidence, but also leave you better prepared for the task ahead" (Halvorson 2010, p. 208).

Thus, reaching a long-term goal requires focusing on the prize—your dream and *why* it's important to you; this "big picture" view provides the inspiration. At the same time, however, you have to focus on the little things—*what* it will take to get there—the nitty-gritty of due dates, to-do lists, and day-to-day tasks. This is the perspiration that transforms inspiration into action, enabling you to plug away and stay on track until your goal is achieved.

It could be said that successfully achieving a long-term goal requires two lenses, each of which provides you with a different focus point: (a) a wide-angle lens that gives you a big picture view of a future that's far ahead of you (your ultimate goal), and (b) a narrow-angle lens that allows you to focus intently on the here and now—on the steps that lie immediately ahead of you. Alternating between these two perspectives allows you to view your small, short-term chores and challenges (e.g., completing an assignment that's due next week) in light of the larger, long-range picture (e.g., college graduation and a successful future).

Keep a record of your progress. Keeping a regular record of your personal progress increases motivation by providing you with frequent *feedback* about whether you're on track and positive *reinforcement* for staying on track (Bandura and Cervone 1983; Schunk 1995).

Mark down your accomplishments in red on a calendar, or use your journal of the short- and mid-range goals you've reached. These markings serve as benchmarks, supplying you with concrete evidence and a visible reminder of your progress. You can also mark your progress on a chart or graph, or list your achievements in a resume or portfolio. Place these displays of progress where you can see them on a daily basis and use them as a source of motivation to keep striving toward your ultimate goal (Halvorson 2010).

This practice of ongoing (daily) assessment of our personal progress toward goal completion is a simple, yet powerful form of self-reflection that's associated with success. Research on successful people reveals that they reflect regularly on their daily progress to ensure they're on track and progressing steadily toward their goals (Covey 1990).

Reward yourself for reaching milestones on the path toward your goal. Reaching a long-range goal is clearly rewarding because it marks the end of the trip and arrival at your desired destination. However, reaching short- and mid-range goals are not as self-rewarding because they're merely the means to the end. Thus, you need to make intentional attempts to reward yourself for climbing these smaller, yet essential stepping stones on the path to the mountain peak.

The behaviors needed to persist and persevere through all the intermediate steps needed to reach a long-range goal is more likely to take place if these behaviors are followed by reward (positive reinforcement). The process of setting small goals, moving steadily toward them, and rewarding yourself for reaching them is a simple, yet powerful self-motivational strategy. It helps you maintain momentum over an extended period of time, which is exactly what's required to reach a long-range goal. When you achieve short- and mid-range goals, check them off as milestones and reward yourself for reaching them (e.g., celebrate successful completion of midterms or finals by treating yourself to something you really enjoy).

NOTE

Reward yourself for short- and long-term goal success! Share your success at short-term and long-term goals with faculty, peers, and family!

 Journal Reflection 7.2

For you, what would be effective rewards for making progress toward your goals and serve as motivators to keep you going?

CHARACTERISTICS OF SUCCESSFUL PEOPLE

Achieving success involves effective use of goal-setting and motivational strategies, but it takes something more. Ultimately, success emerges from the inside out; it flows from personal qualities and attributes found within a person. Studies of successful people who achieve their goals reveal they possess the following personal characteristics. Keep these characteristics in mind as you set and pursue your goals.

THINK ABOUT IT

How are you progressing with your academic vocabulary?

Internal Locus of Control

Successful people have what psychologists call an "internal locus of control"; they believe that the locus (location or source) of control for events in their life is *internal*—"inside" them and within their control—rather than *external*—outside them and beyond their control. They believe that success is influenced more by attitude, effort, commitment, and preparation than by inherited ability, inborn intelligence, luck, chance, or fate (Carlson et al. 2009; Jernigan 2004; Rotter 1966).

Research shows that individuals with a strong internal locus of control display the following positive qualities:

1. Greater independence and self-direction (Van Overwalle, Mervielde, and De Schuyer 1995),
2. More accurate self-assessment of strengths and weaknesses (Hashaw, Hammond, and Rogers 1990), and
3. Higher levels of learning and achievement (Wilhite 1990).

Self-Efficacy

An internal locus of control contributes to the development of another positive trait that psychologists refer to as *self-efficacy*—the belief that you have power to produce a positive effect on the *outcomes* of your life (Bandura 1994). People with low self-efficacy tend to feel helpless, powerless, and passive; they think (and allow) things to happen to them rather than taking charge and making things happen for them. College students with a strong sense of self-efficacy believe they're in control of their educational success and can shape their future, regardless of their past experience or current circumstances.

Students with a strong sense of *academic self-efficacy* have been found to:

1. Put considerable effort into their studies;
2. Use active learning strategies;
3. Capitalize on campus resources; and
4. Persist in the face of obstacles (Multon, Brown, and Lent 1991; Zimmeman 1995, 2000).

Students with a strong sense of self-efficacy also possess a strong sense of personal responsibility. As the breakdown of the word "responsible" implies, they are "response" "able"—they believe they're able to respond to personal challenges, including academic challenges.

 Journal Reflection 7.3

In what area or areas of your life do you feel that you've been able to exert the most control and achieve the most positive results?

_____

_____

_____

_____

Do you think this could impact your attaining your SMART academic goal? Why or Why not?

_____

_____

_____

_____

_____

What strategies have you used in the area of your life where you've been able to exert the most personal control and achieve the most positive outcomes?

_____

_____

_____

_____

_____

Could you apply any of these same strategies to those areas in which you need to gain more control? How?

_____

_____

_____

_____

_____

_____

GRIT

When you expend significant effort, energy, and sacrifice over a sustained period of time to achieve a goal, you're demonstrating grit (Stoltz 2014). People with grit have been found to possess the following qualities (Duckworth et al. 2007).

Persistence. They hang in there and persevere effort until they reach their goals. When the going gets tough, they don't give up—they step it up. They have the fortitude to persist in the face of frustration and adversity.

Tenacity. They pursue their goals with relentless determination. If they encounter something along the way that's hard to do, they work harder to do it.

Resilience. They bounce back from setbacks and keep striving to reach their goals. They adopt the mindset that they'll bounce back from setbacks and turn them into comebacks.

It's noteworthy that the word *problem* derives from the Greek root *proballein*, meaning "to throw forward." This suggests that a problem is an

> Grit is perseverance and passion for long-term goals. Sticking with your future day in, day out, not just for the week, not just for the month, but for years and working really hard to make that future a reality."
>
> —Angela Duckworth, psychologist, University of Pennsylvania

> "What happens is not as important as how you react to what happens."
>
> —Thaddeus Golas, Lazy Man's Guide to Enlightenment

> "When written in Chinese, the word 'crisis' is composed of two characters. One represents danger, and the other represents opportunity."
>
> —John F. Kennedy, 35th president of the United States

 NOTE

Don't let early setbacks bring you down emotionally or motivationally. Reflect on them, learn from them, and make sure they don't happen again.

opportunity to move ahead. You can take this approach to problems by re-wording or rephrasing the problem you're experiencing in terms of a positive goal statement. (For example, "I'm flunking math" can be reframed as: "My goal is to get a grade of C or better on the next test to pull my overall course grade into passing territory.")

Similarly, the root of the word *failure* is *fallere*—meaning to "trip or fall." Thus, failing at something doesn't mean we've been defeated, it just means we've stumbled and taken a temporary spill. Success can still be achieved after a fall if we don't give up, but get up and get back to taking the next step needed to reach our goal. By viewing poor academic performances and other setbacks (particularly those occurring early in your college experience) not as failures but as learning opportunities, you put yourself in a position to bounce back and transform your setbacks into comebacks. Here are some notable people who did so:

- Louis Pasteur, famous bacteriologist, failed his admission test to the University of Paris;
- Albert Einstein, Nobel Prize–winning physicist, failed math in elementary school;
- Thomas Edison, prolific inventor, once expelled from school as "uneducable";
- Michael Jordan, Hall of fame basketball player, cut from his high school team as a sophomore.

Journal Reflection 7.4

What would you say is the biggest setback or obstacle you've overcome in your life thus far?

_____

_____

_____

_____

How did you overcome it? What enabled you to get past it? What did you do to prevent it from stopping you?

_____

_____

_____

_____

_____

_____

Self-Discipline. People with grit have the *self-control*—they keep their actions aligned with their goal, staying on course and moving in the right direction—despite distractions and temptations (Halvorson 2010). They're able to sacrifice immediate, short-sighted needs and desires to do what has to be done to get where they want to be in the long run.

Setting long-range goals is important but having the self-discipline to reach them is another matter. Each day, whether we're aware of it or not, we're tempted to make choices and decisions that interfere with our ability to reach our goals. We need to remain mindful about whether these choices are moving us in the direction of our goals or taking us off course.

AUTHOR'S JOURNEY

When I entered college in the mid-1970s, I was a first-generation student from an extremely impoverished background. Not only did I have to work to support my education, I also needed to assist my family financially. I stocked grocery store shelves at night during the week and waited tables at a local country club on the weekends. Managing my time, school, work, and life required a lot of self-discipline. However, I always understood that my goal was to graduate from college and all of my other commitments supported that goal. One of my greatest achievements in life was to keep my mind and body focused on the ultimate prize of getting a college education. That achievement has paid off for me many times over the course of my life.

—Aaron Thompson

Journal Reflection 7.5

Think about something in your life that you sacrificed for and persisted at for the longest period of time before getting there. What is it? Do you see ways in which you could apply the same approach to achieving your goals in college? Explain.

GROWTH MINDSET

A *mindset* is a powerful belief. People with a *growth mindset* believe that intelligence and other positive qualities can be grown or developed. People with a *fixed mindset* believe just the opposite: they think that intelligence and personal characteristics are deep-seated traits that are set and unlikely to change (Dweck 2006).

Listed below are opposing pairs of traits—one representing a fixed mindset (FM) and the other representing a growth mindset (GM). **As you read through them, honestly assess whether you lean more toward a fixed or growth mindset by circling either FM or GM for each pair of traits.**

I try to get better at what I do. (GM)
I try to show others (including myself) how good I am. (FM)

I try to validate myself by proving how smart or talented I am. (FM)
I validate myself by stretching myself to become smarter and more talented. (GM)

I believe that if I cannot learn to do something easily, I'm not smart. (FM)
I believe that I can learn to do something well even if it doesn't come easily at first. (GM)

I evaluate my performance by comparing it to the performance of others. (FM)
I evaluate my performance by comparing it to my past performances. (GM)

I believe I have a certain amount of intelligence and not much can be done to change it. (FM)
I believe that the amount of intelligence I start with isn't the amount I'll end up with. (GM)

I think that intelligence and personal qualities are inherited and hard to change. (FM)
I think that intelligence and personal qualities are learned and changeable. (GM)

I think success is a matter of having ability. (FM)
I think success is a matter of getting ability. (GM)

I focus on demonstrating my skills to others. (FM)
I focus on developing my skills. (GM)

I focus on proving myself (as being good or smart). (FM)
I focus on improving myself (by getting better). (GM)

I feel smart when I complete tasks quickly and without mistakes. (FM)
I feel smart when I work on something for awhile before figuring it out. (GM)

I avoid seeking constructive criticism from others because it will expose my weaknesses. (FM)
I seek out constructive criticism from others to improve myself. (GM)

I feel threatened by the success of others. (FM)
I feel I can be inspired by and learn from the success of others. (GM)

I tend to peak early and don't continually progress to higher levels of achievement. (FM)

> " No matter what your ability is, effort is what ignites that ability and turns it into accomplishment."
>
> —Carol Dweck, Stanford psychologist and author of Mindset

I tend to keep progressing toward increasingly higher levels of achievement. (GM)

I think success should be effortless. (FM)
I think success should be effortful. (GM)

I view challenges as threatening because they may prove I'm not smart. (FM)
I view challenges as opportunities to develop new skills. (GM)

I believe effort creates talent. (GM)
I believe effort is for those who can't make it on talent. (FM)

I focus on self-improvement—about becoming the best I can be. (GM)
I focus on self-validation—about proving I'm already good. (FM)

I look at grades as labels that judge or measure my intelligence. (FM)
I look at grades as a source of feedback for improving my performance. (GM)

Journal Reflection 7.6

Look back at the above pairs of statements and compare the total number of fixed mindset (FM) and growth mindset (GM) statements you circled.

Do your totals suggest that, in general, you lean more toward a growth or fixed mindset?

_____

_____

_____

_____

Review your long-term SMART goal from Journal 7.1 What approaches will you take to ensure your still reach your long-term goals?

_____

_____

_____

_____

_____

Numerous studies show that a growth mindset is strongly associated with goal achievement and personal success (Dweck 2006). In one study, the mindset of pre-med students taking a difficult chemistry course was measured at the start of the semester and their performance was tracked throughout the term. Students with a growth mindset consistently earned higher grades in the course. Even when students with a growth mindset did poorly on a particular test, they improved on the next one. In contrast, the performance of students with a fixed mindset showed no pattern of improvement from one exam to the next (Dweck 2006).

In another study, students with a growth mindset (who believed their goal in college courses was to improve their grade as the course progressed) were compared to students with a fixed mindset (who believed their goal was to prove how smart they were). Students with a growth mindset achieved higher overall course grades and did so because they improved with each exam. They didn't have higher grades on the first exam, but began earning higher grades on later exams. The opposite pattern was true for fixed mindset students—their performance actually remained the same or declined over time—particularly if their first exam score was low (Halvorson 2010).

It's been found that students can have different mindsets for different subjects and situations. Some students may have a fixed mindset for learning math, but a growth mindset for learning other subjects. However, the most important thing to remember about mindsets is that, although they're powerful, they're just beliefs held in our mind. Thus, mindsets can be changed from fixed to growth for any subject or situation. By so doing, we increase the likelihood of achieving our goals and reaching our full potential (Dweck 2006).

CHAPTER SUMMARY AND HIGHLIGHTS

A key to success is challenging ourselves to set ambitious, yet realistic goals. Studies consistently show that goal-setting is a more effective self-motivational strategy than simply telling ourselves to "try hard" or "do our best." Achieving success begins with setting goals and successful people set goals on a regular basis.

The acronym "SMART" is a popular mnemonic device (memory strategy) for recalling all the key components of a well-designed goal. A ***SMART*** goal is one that is:

Specific—it states precisely what the goal is and what you will do to achieve it.

Meaningful (and Measurable)—it's a goal that really matters to you and your progress toward reaching it can be steadily measured or tracked.

Actionable (or Action-Oriented) —it identifies concrete actions and specific behaviors you'll engage in to reach the goal.

Realistic—the goal is attainable and you're aware of the amount of time, effort, and skill it will take to attain it, as well as obstacles you'll need to overcome along the way.

Time-framed—the goal has a deadline and a timeline that includes a sequence of short-range, mid-range, and long-range steps.

In addition to the effective goal-setting properties associated with the SMART method, research reveals that the following goal-setting features characterize people who set and reach important goals.

1. Effective goal-setters set *improvement (get-better) goals* that emphasize progress and growth, rather than perfection (be-good) goals.
2. Effective goal-setters focus on what outcomes can *influence or control*, not on outcomes that are beyond their control.
3. Effective goal-setters set goals that are *challenging and effortful*.
4. Effective goal-setters anticipate *obstacles* they may encounter along the path to their goal and have a plan in place for dealing with them.

Setting goals ignites motivation, but maintaining motivation after it's been ignited requires use of effective self-motivational strategies. You can maintain your motivation by using such strategies as:

*   Visualizing reaching your long-range goals;
*   Putting your goals in writing;
*   Creating a visual map of your goals;
*   Keeping a record of your progress toward your goals;
*   Rewarding yourself for milestones you reach along the path to your goals;
*   Converting setbacks into comebacks by learning from mistakes and maintaining positive expectations.

Studies of successful people who achieve their goals reveal they possess the following personal characteristics.

Internal Locus of Control. They believe that the locus (location or source) of control for events in their life is *internal*—"inside" them and within their control—rather than *external*—outside them and beyond their control.

Self-Efficacy. They believe they have power to produce a positive effect on the *outcomes* of their lives. They believe success is something that's earned and the harder they work at it, the more likely they'll get it.

Grit. They expend significant effort, energy, and sacrifice over an extended period of time to achieve their goals. People with grit have been found to possess the following qualities:

*   *Persistence*—when the going gets tough, they don't give up, they step it up; they have the fortitude to persist in the face of frustration and adversity.
*   *Tenacity*—they pursue their goals with relentless determination; if they encounter something along the way that's hard to do, they work harder to do it.
*   *Resilience*—they bounce back from setbacks and turn them into comebacks.
*   *Self-Discipline*—they have *self-control*—they resist the impulse to pursue instant gratification and do what they feel like doing instead of what should be done to reach their goal; they're able to sacrifice

NOTE

Achieving success isn't a short sprint; it's a long-distance run that takes patience and perseverance. Goal-setting is the key that gets us off the starting blocks and motivation is the fuel that keeps us going until we cross the finish line.

immediate, short-sighted needs and desires to do what has to be done to get where they want to be in the long run.

Growth Mindset. They believe that intelligence and other positive qualities can be grown or developed. In contrast, people with a "fixed mindset" believe that intelligence and personal characteristics are deep-seated traits that are set and unlikely to change.

LEARNING MORE THROUGH THE WORLD WIDE WEB: INTERNET-BASED RESOURCES

For additional information on goal-setting and motivation, see the following websites.

Goal Setting:
https://www.mindtools.com/page6.html

Self-Motivational Strategies:
www.selfmotivationstrategies.com

Self-Efficacy:
www.psychologytoday.com/blog/flourish/201002/
if-you-think-you-can-t-think-again-the-sway-self-efficacy

Grit & Resilience:
https://undergrad.stanford.edu/resilience

Growth Mindset:
www.ted.com/talks/carol_dweck_the_power_of_believing_that_you_can_
improve?language=en

REFERENCES

Astin, A. W. 1993. *What Matters in College?* San Francisco: Jossey-bass.

Bandura, A. 1994. Self-efficacy. In *Encyclopedia of Human Behavior*, edited by V. S. Ramachaudran. Vol. 4, 71–81. New York: Academic Press.

Bandura, A., and D. Cervone. 1983. "Self-Evaluative and Self-Efficacy Mechanisms Governing the Motivational Effects of Goal Systems." *Journal of Personality and Social Psychology* 45 (5): 1017–28.

Brissette, I., S. Cohen, and T. E. Seeman. 2000. "Measuring Social Integration and Social Networks." In *Social Support Measurement and Intervention*, edited by S. Cohen, L. G. Underwood, and B. H. Gottlieb, 53–85. New York: Oxford University Press.

Brooks, K. 2009. *You Majored in What? Mapping Your Path from Chaos to Career.* New York: Penguin.

Carlson, N. R., H. Miller, C. D. Heth, J. W. Donahoe, and G. N. Martin. 2009. *Psychology: The Science of Behaviour.* 7th ed. Toronto, ON: Pearson Education Canada.

Covey, S. R. 1990. Seven Habits of Highly Effective People. 2nd ed. New York: Fireside.

Doran, G. T. 1981. "There's a S.M.A.R.T. Way to Write Management's Goals and Objectives." *Management Review* 70 (11): 35–6.

Duckworth, A. L., C. Peterson, M. D. Matthews, and D. R. Kelly. 2007. "Grit: Perseverance and Passion for Long-term Goals." *Journal of Personality and Social Psychology* 92 (6): 1087–101.

Dweck, C. S. 2006. *Mindset: The New Psychology of Success.* New York: Random House.

Ewell, P. T. 1997. "Organizing for Learning." *AAHE Bulletin* 50 (4), 3–6.

Feldman, K. A., and T. M. Newcomb. 1994. *The Impact of College on Students.* New Brunswick, NJ: Transaction Publishers (original work published 1969).

Halvorson, H. G. 2010. *Succeed: How We can Reach our Goals*. New York: Plume.

Hashaw, R. M., C. J. Hammond, and P. H. Rogers. 1990. "Academic Locus of Control and the Collegiate Experience." *Research & Teaching in Developmental Education* 7 (1): 45–54.

Hollenbeck, J. R., C. R. Williams, and H. J. Klein. 1989. "An Empirical Examination of the Antecedents of Commitment to Difficult Goals." *Journal of Applied Psychology* 74 (1): 18–23.

Jernigan, C. G. 2004. "What Do Students Expect to Learn? The Role of Learner Expectancies, Beliefs, and Attributions for Success and Failure in Student Motivation." *Current Issues in Education* [On-line], 7 (4). Retrieved January 16, 2012, from cie.asu.edu/ojs/index.php/cieatasu/article/download/824/250

Latham, G. and E. Locke. 2007. "New Developments in and Directions for Goal-setting Research." *European Psychologists* 12: 290–300.

Locke, E. A. 2000. Motivation, Cognition, and Action: "An Analysis of Studies of Task Goals and Knowledge." *Applied Psychology: An International Review* 49: 408–29.

Locke, E. A., and G. P. Latham. 1990. *A Theory of Goal Setting and Task Performance*. Englewood Cliffs, NJ: Prentice Hall.

Locke, E. A., and G. P. Latham. 2002. "Building a Practically Useful Theory of Goal Setting and Task Motivation." *American Psychologist*, 57, 705–17.

Meyer, P. J. 2003. "What Would You Do if You Knew You Couldn't Fail? Creating S.M.A.R.T. Goals." *In Attitude Is Everything: If You Want to Succeed Above and Beyond.* Meyer Resource Group, Incorporated.

Multon, S. D., K. D., Brown, and R. W. Lent. 1991. "Relation of Self-efficacy Beliefs to Academic Outcomes: A Meta-Analytic Investigation." *Journal of Counseling Psychology* 38 (1): 30–8.

Newell, A., and H. A. Simon. 1959. *The Simulation of Human Thought.* Santa Monica, CA: Rand Corporation.

Oettingen, G. 2000. "Expectancy Effects on Behavior Depend on Self-Regulatory Thought." *Social Cognition* 14: 101–29.

Oettingen, G., and E. Stephens. 2009. "Mental Contrasting Future and Reality: A Motivationally Intelligent Self-Regulatory Strategy." In *The Psychology of Goals*, edited by G. Moskowitz and H. Grant. New York: Guilford.

Pascarella, E., and P. Terenzini. 1991. *How College Affects Students: Findings and Insights from Twenty Years of Research.* San Francisco: Jossey-bass.

Pascarella, E., and P. Terenzini. 2005. *How College Affects Students: A Third Decade of Research.* Vol. 2. San Francisco: Jossey-bass.

Rotter, J. 1966. "Generalized Expectancies for Internal versus External Controls of Reinforcement." *Psychological Monographs: General and Applied* 80 (609): 1–28.

Schunk, D. H. 1995. "Self-Efficacy and Education and Instruction." In *Self-Efficacy, Adaptation, and Adjustment: Theory, Research, and Application*, edited by J. E. Maddux, 281–303. New York: Plenum Press.

Snyder, C. R. 1995. Conceptualizing, Measuring, and Nurturing Hope." *Journal of Counseling and Development* 73 (January/February): 355–60.

Stoltz, P. G. 2014. *Grit: The New Science of What It Takes to Persevere, Flourish, Succeed.* San Luis Obispo: Climb Strong Press.

Van Overwalle, F. I., I. Mervielde, and J. De Schuyer. 1995. "Structural Modeling of the Relationships Between Attributional Dimensions, Emotions, and Performance of College Freshmen." *Cognition and Emotion* 9 (1): 59–85.

Wilhite, S. 1990. "Self-efficacy, Locus of Control, Self-Assessment of Memory Ability, and Student Activities as Predictors of College Course Achievement." *Journal of Educational Psychology* 82 (4): 696–700.

Chapter 7 Exercises

7.1 Quote Reflections

Review the sidebar quotes contained in this chapter and select two that were especially meaningful or inspirational to you.

For each quote, write a three- to five-sentence explanation why you chose it.

7.2 Reality Bite

Goals and Motivation

Lorraine has decided to go to her local community college to become an RN. She knows that nurses make good money and it is easy to get a job in the profession right now. All she really cares about is having a good job and making money. She did not realize the classes would be difficult and she has a hard time getting through them since she really is not that interested in them. She started her clinicals and HATED what she was being asked to do. She was not prepared for all the bodily fluids she would see in one day. Lorraine decides nursing is not for her and is angry that no one told her she would hate it this much! She has to find a different major now that will still make a lot of money, but she is angry that she wasted more than a year of her life as well as the money she has spent on her education.

1. Why do you think Lorraine is really unhappy with the events that have unfolded during the past year?

2. What could Lorraine have done differently to avoid this situation?

3. What goals would you suggest Lorraine set for herself?

Lorraine is clearly motivated by money; is that what is going to make her happy? Why or why not?

7.3 Clarifying Your Goals

Take a moment to answer the following questions as honestly as possible:

- What are my highest priorities?
- What competing needs and priorities do I need to keep in check?
- How will I maintain balance across different aspects of my life?
- What am I willing and able to give up in order to achieve my educational and personal goals?
- How can I maintain motivation on a day-to-day basis?
- Who can I collaborate with to reach my goals and what will that collaboration involve?

7.4 Review your short- and long-term SMART goals

Think of an aspect of your life where there's a significant gap between what you'd like it to be (the ideal) and where you are (the reality).

Use the following form to identify a goal you could pursue to reduce this gap.

Goal: _____

What specific *actions* will be taken?

When will these actions be taken?

What *obstacles or roadblocks* do you anticipate?

What *resources* could you use to overcome your anticipated obstacles or roadblocks?

How will you *measure your progress*?

How will you know when you *reached or achieved* your goal?

7.5 Converting Setbacks into Comebacks: Transforming Pessimism into Optimism through Positive Self-Talk

In Hamlet, Shakespeare wrote: "There is nothing good or bad, but thinking makes it so." His point was that experiences have the potential to be positive or negative, depending on how people interpret them and react to them.

Listed below is a series of statements representing negative, motivation-destroying interpretations and reactions to a situation or experience:

a. "I'm just not good at this."

b. "There's nothing I can do about it."

c. "Nothing is going to change."

d. "This always happens to me."

e. "Everybody is going to think I'm a loser."

For each of the preceding statements, replace the negative statement with a statement that represents a more positive, self-motivating interpretation or reaction.

7.6 Self-Assessment of Hope

Studies of people who have changed their lives in productive ways indicate they exhibit "high hope" by engaging in certain behaviors that enable them to find the will and the way to reach their personal goals (Snyder 1995). A sample of hopeful behaviors is listed below. Assess yourself on these behaviors, using the following scale:

1 = Never
2 = Rarely
3 = Frequently
4 = Almost Always

Behavior Exhibited by People Possessing High Levels of Hope

_____ When I think of goals, I think of challenges, rather than setbacks and failures.

_____ I seek out stories about how other people have succeeded to inspire me and give me new ideas on how to be successful.

_____ I find role models I can emulate and who can advise, guide, or mentor me.

_____ I tell my friends about my goals and seek their support to help me reach my goals.

_____ I use positive self-talk to help me succeed.

_____ I think that mistakes I make along the way to my goals are usually the result of using a wrong strategy or making a poor decision, rather than lack of talent or ability on my part.

_____ When I struggle, I remember past successes and things I did that worked.

_____ I reward myself when reaching smaller, short-term goals I accomplish along the way to larger, long-term goals.

Adapted from: Snyder, C. R. (1995). Conceptualizing, measuring, and nurturing hope. *Journal of Counseling and Development, 73* (January/February), 355–360.

Self-Assessment Reflections

For any item you rated "1" or "2," explain:

a. *Why* you "rarely" or "never" engage in the practice;

b. *If* you intend to engage in the practice more frequently in the future;

c. *How likely* is it that you'll engage in the practice more frequently in the future;

d. *When do* you plan to begin engaging in the practice.

Chapter 7 Reflection

What do I believe are my strongest attributes that will help me attain my SMART goals?

What may hold me back?

How might I use my strengths to overcome those things that might stand in the way to accomplishing my goals?

TIME MANAGEMENT SKILLS AND STRATEGIES

PRIORITIZING TASKS, PREVENTING PROCRASTINATION, AND PROMOTING PRODUCTIVITY

This chapter offers a comprehensive set of strategies for managing time, combating procrastination, and ensuring that your time-spending habits are aligned with your educational goals and priorities.	**CHAPTER PREVIEW**
To equip you with a set of strategies for setting priorities, planning your time and completing tasks in a timely and productive manner.	**LEARNING OBJECTIVE**
You will recognize the importance of time management and be able to establish a schedule that enables you to meet your goals efficiently and on time.	**PERFORMANCE OBJECTIVE**
Do I spend my time in a way that enables me to be successful in college?	**PRE-REFLECTION**
How can I create a schedule that enables me to balance my college and life responsibilities?	**ESSENTIAL QUESTION**

 **THINK ABOUT IT**

Purpose for Reading this Chapter: Time management is a critical component of success at college. Read Chapter 4 and summarize the main ideas in the margins of the text. When you have completed your reading, write a short reflective piece explaining what one behavior you believe needs to be modified if you are to be successful at managing your time and achieving the SMART goal you have set for yourself.

From *Thriving in the Community College and Beyond: Strategies for Academic Success and Personal Development*, Third Edition by Joseph B. Cuseo, Aaron Thompson, and Julie A. McLaughlin. Copyright © 2016 by Kendall Hunt Publishing Company. Reprinted by permission.

" The major difference [between high school and college] is time. You have so much free time on your hands that you don't know what to do for most of the time."

—*First-year college student (Erickson & Strommer, Teaching College Freshmen)*

" I cannot stress enough that you need to intelligently budget your time."

—*Advice to new college students from a student finishing his first year in college*

THE IMPORTANCE OF TIME MANAGEMENT

For many first-year students, the beginning of college means the beginning of more independent living and self-management. Even if you've lived on your own for some time, managing time is an important skill to possess because you're likely juggling multiple responsibilities, including school, family, and work. Studies show that most first-year community college students are attending classes while working either part-time or full-time (American Association of Community Colleges 2009). To have any realistic chance of achieving our goals, we need an intentional and strategic plan for spending our time in a way that aligns with our goals and enables us to make steady progress toward them. Thus, setting goals, reaching goals, and managing time are interrelated skills.

Most college students struggle to at least some extent with time management, particularly first-year students who are transitioning from the lockstep schedules of high school and careers to the more unstructured time associated with college course schedules. National surveys indicate that almost 50% of first-year college students report difficulty managing their time effectively (HERI 2014). In college, the academic calendar and class scheduling patterns in college differ radically from high school. There's less "seat time" in class each week and college students are expected to do much more academic work on their courses outside of class time, which leaves them with a lot more "free time" to manage.

Simply stated, college students who have difficulty managing their time have difficulty managing college. One study compared college sophomores who had an outstanding first year (both academically and personally) with sophomores who struggled in their first year. Interviews with both groups revealed there was one key difference between them: sophomores who experienced a successful first year repeatedly brought up the topic of time during the interviews. The successful students said they had to think carefully about how they spent their time and that they needed to budget their time. In contrast, sophomores who experienced difficulty in their first year of college hardly talked about the topic of time during their interviews, even when they were specifically asked about it (Light 2001).

Studies also indicate that people of all ages report time management to be a critical element of their life. Working adults report that setting priorities and balancing multiple responsibilities (e.g., work and family) can be a stressful juggling act (Harriott and Ferrari 1996). For them, time management and stress management are interrelated. These findings suggest that time management is more than just a college success skill; it's also as a life management and life success skill.

In the preface, we said that one of the purposes of this book was to make you more aware of your actions and their implications. Time management is a cornerstone of mindfulness. The more aware you are of how you spend your time, the more aware you will be of what it takes for you to complete assignments as well as what expectations you need to set for yourself. Keeping track of your time keeps you, and not external forces, in control of your actions.

AUTHOR'S JOURNEY

I started the process of earning my doctorate a little later in life than other students. I was a married father with a preschool daughter (Sara). Since my wife left for work early in the morning, it was always my duty to get up and get Sara's day going in the right direction. In addition, I had to do the same for myself. Three days of my week were spent on campus in class or in the library. (We didn't have quick access to research on home computers then as you do now.) The other two days of the workweek and the weekend were spent on household chores, family time, and studying.

I knew that if I was to have any chance of finishing my Ph.D. in a reasonable amount of time, I had to adopt an effective schedule for managing my time. Each day of the week, I held to a strict routine. I got up in the morning, ate breakfast while reading the paper, got Sara ready for school, and got her to school. Once I returned home, I put a load of laundry in the washer, studied, wrote, and spent time concentrating on what I needed to do to be successful from 8:30 a.m. to 12:00 p.m. every day. At lunch, I had a pastrami and cheese sandwich and a soft drink while rewarding myself by watching *Perry Mason* reruns until 1:00 p.m. I then continued to study until it was time to pick up Sara from school. Each night I spent time with my wife and daughter and then prepared for the next day. I lived a life that had a preset schedule. By following that schedule, I was able to successfully complete my doctorate in a reasonable amount of time while giving my family the time they needed. (By the way, I still watch *Perry Mason* reruns.)

—Aaron Thompson

STRATEGIES FOR MANAGING TIME AND TASKS

Effectively managing our time and our tasks involves three key processes:

1. **Analysis**—breaking down time to see how much of it we have and what we're spending it on;
2. **Itemizing**—identifying and listing the tasks that we need to complete and when we need to complete them; and
3. **Prioritizing**—ranking our tasks in terms of their importance and attacking them in order of their importance.

The following strategies can be used to implement these three processes and should help you open up more time in your schedule, enabling you to discover new ways to use your time more productively.

Download the chart on the next page (week at a glance grid, p. 251). Complete this chart for a typical week. Put all your required activities (course classes, labs, work) in black or blue ink and complete the rest of the chart in red or green showing how you spend all the rest of your waking time (exercise, outside reading, course work, meeting and chatting with friends and family, and texting). Every block should be completed even if it just says "unplanned time." Thinking about the sentence, "Simply stated, college students who have difficulty managing their time have difficulty managing college." Based on what you have placed on your chart, do you think you could use some help managing your time?

Keep this chart handy—we'll use it again.

Journal Reflection 8.1

1. What is your greatest time waster?

_____

_____

_____

_____

2. Is there anything you can do right now to stop or eliminate it?

_____

_____

_____

_____

_____

> Taking an inventory of how I spent my days for an entire week helped me see where I was wasting a lot of time and how I could find time to study more without pulling all nighters. Life still happens, but now I have a better plan to be able to get back on track and I'm not so stressed during exams now.
>
> —AHE second-year student

Become more aware of how your time is spent by breaking it into smaller units. How often have you heard someone say, "Where did all the time go?" or "I just can't seem to find the time!" One way to find out where all our time goes and find more time to get things done is by doing a *time analysis*—a detailed examination of how much total time we have and where we're spending it—including patches of wasted time when we get little done and nothing accomplished.

Identify *what* specific tasks you need to accomplish and when you need to accomplish them. One characteristic of successful people is that they are list makers; they make lists for things they want to accomplish each day (Covey 2004). When noting what needs to be done, refer to each course's syllabus. Be sure to include when exams are being given and when assignments are due. Be sure to add the dates to your agenda (paper or electronic).

NOTE

When we write out things we need to do, we're less likely to block them out and forget to do them.

Journal Reflection 8.2

Do you make a to-do list of things you need to get done each day? (Circle one.)

never   seldom   often   almost   always

If you circled "never" or "seldom," why don't you?

_____

_____

Take advantage of time planning and task management tools, such as the following:

- *Smartphone.* These devices can be used for more than checking social networking sites and sending or receiving text messages. They can be used as a calendar tool to record due dates and set up alert functions to remind you of deadlines. Many smartphones also allow you to set up task or to-do lists and set priorities for each item entered. A variety of apps are now available for planning tasks and tracking time spent on tasks (e.g., see: http://www.rememberthemilk.com; other apps available include cozi, an organization app, and pomodoro, an app intended to boost productivity). Take advantage of cutting edge tools, but at the same time, keep in mind that planners don't plan time, people do. Effectively planning time and tasks flows from a clear vision of your goals and priorities.
- *Small, portable planner.* You can use this device to list all your major assignments and exams for the term, along with their due dates. Check and add to your list throughout the day.
- *Large, stable calendar.* In the calendar's date boxes, record your major assignments for the term. The calendar should be posted in a place you can see every day (e.g., bedroom or refrigerator). If you repeatedly see the things you have to do, you're less likely to overlook them, forget about them, or subconsciously push them out of your mind because you'd really prefer not to do them.

AUTHOR'S JOURNEY

My mom ensured I got up for school on time. Once I got to school the bell would ring to let me know to move on to the next class. When I returned home, I had to do my homework and chores. My daily and weekly schedules were dictated by someone else.

When I entered college, I quickly realized that I needed to develop my own system for being organized, focused, and productive without the assistance of my mother or school authorities. Since I came from a modest background, I had to work my way through college. Juggling schedules became an art and science for me. I knew the things that I could not miss, such as work and school, and the things I could miss—TV and girls. (OK, TV, but not girls.)

After college, I spent 10 years in business—a world where I was measured by being on time and delivering a productive "bottom line." It was during this time that I discovered a scheduling book. When I became a professor, I had other mechanisms to make sure I did what I needed to do when I needed to do it. This was largely based on when my classes were offered. Other time was dedicated to working out and spending time with my family. Now, as an administrator, I have an assistant who keeps my schedule for me. She tells me where I am going, how long I should be there, and what I need to accomplish while I am there. Unless you take your parents with you or have the luxury of a personal assistant, it's important to schedule your time. Use a planner!

—*Aaron Thompson*

Prioritize: rank tasks in order of their importance. After you itemize your work tasks by identifying and listing them, the next step is to *prioritize* them—determine the order or sequence in which they get done. Prioritizing basically involves ranking tasks in terms of their importance, with the highest priority tasks placed at the top of the list to ensure they're tackled first.

How do you decide on what tasks are to be ranked highest and tackled first? Here are two key criteria (standards of judgment) for determining your highest priority tasks:

- **Urgency.** Tasks that are closest to their deadline or due date should receive highest priority. Finishing an assignment that's due tomorrow should receive higher priority than starting an assignment that's due next month.
- **Gravity.** Tasks that carry the greatest weight (count the most) should receive highest priority. If an assignment worth 100 points and an assignment worth 10 points are due at the same time, the 100-point task should receive higher priority. We want to be sure to invest our work time on tasks that matter most. Similar to investing money, we should invest our time on tasks that yield the greatest pay-off.

An effective strategy for prioritizing tasks is to divide them into "A," "B," and "C" lists (Lakein 1973; Morgenstern 2004). The "A" list is reserved for *essential* (nonnegotiable) tasks—those that that *must* be done now. The "B" list is for *important* tasks—those that *should* be done soon. The "C" list is for *optional* tasks—those that *could* or *might* be done if there's time remaining after the more important tasks on lists A and B have been completed. Organizing tasks and time in this fashion helps you decide how to divide your labor in a way that ensures you "put first things first."

NOTE

Put first things first: Plan your work by identifying your most important and most urgent tasks, and work your plan by attacking these tasks first.

"

"When I have lots of homework to do, I suddenly go through this urge to clean up and organize the house. I'm thinking, 'I'm not wasting my time. I'm cleaning up the house and that's something I have to do.' But all I'm really doing is avoiding school work."

—*College sophomore*

AUTHOR'S JOURNEY

My mom is a schoolteacher, and when my sister and I were growing up she had a strict policy: when we came home from school we could have a snack, but after that we were not allowed to do anything else until our homework was finished. I remember that on days when it was really nice outside, I would beg and plead (and sometimes even argue) with my mom about going outside to play. She always won, and often I had wasted so much time arguing that I completely missed out on the opportunity to play at all. At the time I thought my mom was really mean. As I grew older (in high school and college), though, it became easy to put my homework first. My mom had taught me the importance of prioritizing and completing important things (like homework) before things that were not as important.

—*Julie McLaughlin*

CREATING A TIME-MANAGEMENT PLAN

Don't buy into the myth that taking time to plan takes time away from getting started and getting things done. Time management experts estimate that the amount of time planning your total work actually reduces your total work time by a factor of three: for every one unit of time you spend planning, you save three units of time working (Goldsmith 2010; Lakein 1973). For example, 5 minutes of planning time will typically save you 15 minutes of total work time, and 10 minutes of planning time will save you 30 minutes of work time.

Planning your time saves you time because it ensures you start off in the right direction. If you have a plan of attack, you're less vulnerable to "false starts"—starting your work and then discovering you're not on the right track or not doing things in the right sequence, which forces you to retreat and start all over again.

Once you have accepted the idea that taking time to plan your time will save you time in the long run, you're ready to create a plan for effectively managing time. Listed below are specific strategies for doing so.

 ## Journal Reflection 8.3

Look at the grid you completed on how you spend your time. Use the A, B, and C approach discussed above to note essential (A), important (B), and (C) optional tasks. Share this with a class mate and discuss whether you think you have a schedule that enables you to reach one of the subgoals of your SMART goal.

_____

_____

_____

_____

Take *portable work* with you during the day that you can work at any place at any time. This will enable you to take advantage of "dead time" such as time spent sitting and waiting for appointments or transportation. Portable work allows you to resurrect dead time and transform it into productive work time. Not only is this a good time management strategy, it's a good stress management strategy because you replace the frustration and boredom associated with having no control over "wait time" with a sense of accomplishment.

Make good use of your *free time between classes* by working on assignments and studying in advance for upcoming exams. See **Box 8.1** for a summary of how you can use your out-of-class time to improve your academic performance and course grades.

 ### THINK ABOUT IT

A really helpful thing you can do to get started at a big task is to be organized. Think through the assignment—do you need note cards, or printouts from your computer? Will you need drawing paper to sketch out certain pictures. Do you need to scan pages from a book? Whatever you will need to complete your assignment should be planned for in advance so you don't need to get up and get a pen or search through notebooks or files to find a set of notes. If you're not very good at organizing for assignments, put it on your calendar as a separate item—arc out the first half hour as "Organize materials" for whatever the assignment is. The less time you spend hunting for things later, the more time you'll have to focus on the project at hand.

NOTE

Developing awareness of how our time is spent is more than a brainless, clerical activity. When it's done well, it becomes an exercise in self-awareness and values clarification— how we spend our time is a true test of who we are and what we really value.

"

X I used to be able to remember the major things I needed to do in the day. As my work, personal, and school responsibilities increased, I realized I spent most of my time reacting to what would come up instead of having a plan. Backwards mapping with projects, planning my kids' medical appointments, major deadlines and busy periods at work, helped me plan more effectively and gave me less stress.
—AHE Third-year student

NOTE

College professors are more likely than high school teachers to expect you to rely on your course syllabus to keep track of what you have to do and when you have to do it. Your instructors may not remind you about upcoming papers, tests, quizzes, assignments, etc.

BOX 8.1

Making Productive Use of "Free Time" Outside the Classroom

Compared to high school, "homework" in college often doesn't involve turning in assignments on a daily or weekly basis. Academic work assigned to be done outside the college classroom may not even be collected and graded. Instead, it's often done for your own benefit to help you prepare for upcoming exams and complete written reports (e.g., assigned reading and assigned problems in math and science). Rather than formally assigning and collecting this work as homework, your professors expect that you will do this work on your own and without supervision.

> In high school we were given a homework assignment every day. Now we have a large task assigned to be done at a certain time. No one tells [us] when to start or what to do each day."
>
> —*First-year college student*

Listed in this box are strategies for working independently and in advance of college exams and assignments. By building time for each of these activities into your regular schedule, you'll make more productive use of out-of-class time, decrease your level of stress, and strengthen your academic performance.

Doing Out-of-Class Work in Advance of Exams

- Complete reading assignments relating to lecture topics *before* the topic is discussed in class.
- Review class notes from your last class before the next class to build a mental bridge from one class to the next. Reviewing your notes give you the opportunity to check if there's information you don't understand or did not cover adequately at the time.

    By reviewing your class notes on a regular basis, you will improve your ability to understand each upcoming lecture and reduce the total time you'll need to spend studying your notes the night before an exam.

- Review your reading notes and highlights to improve retention of important material. If you find parts of the text that you marked or notes in the margin that are still confusing, discuss them with your course instructor during office hours or with a fellow classmate outside of class.
- Integrate class material with reading material. Connect related information from your lecture notes and reading notes and get them in the same place (e.g., on the same index card).
- Use a "part-to-whole" study method whereby you study material from your class notes and assigned reading in small pieces (parts) during short, separate study sessions in advance of the exam; then make your last study session before the exam a longer review session during which you re-study all the small parts (the whole) at the same time. As will be fully explained in Chapter 6, material studied in advance of an exam remains in your brain and is still there when you later review it. Even if it doesn't immediately come back to mind when you first start reviewing it, you'll relearn it much faster than you did the first time.

Doing Out-of-Class Work in Advance of Term Papers and Research Reports

Work on large, long-range assignments due at the end of the term by breaking them into smaller, short-term tasks completed at separate times during the term. For instance, a large term paper may be broken up into the following smaller tasks and completed in separate installments.

1. Search for and decide on a topic.
2. Locate sources of information on the topic.
3. Organize information obtained from your sources into categories.
4. Develop an outline of your paper's major points and the order or sequence in which you plan to present them.
5. Construct a first draft of your paper (and, if necessary, a second or third draft).
6. Write a final draft of your paper.
7. Proofread your final draft for spelling and grammatical errors before turning it in.
8. Make use of the writing center or peer writing tutors in the development of subsequent drafts.

A good time management plan transforms intention into action.
Once you've planned the work, the next step is to work the plan. A time
management plan turns into an action plan when you: (a) preview what
you intend to do, (b) review whether you actually did what you intended
to do, and (c) close the gap between your intentions and actions. The
action plan begins with your *daily to-do list*, bringing that list with you
as the day begins, and checking off items on the list as they're completed during the day. At the end of the day, the list is reviewed to
determine what got done and what still needs to be done. The uncom-
pleted tasks then become high priorities on the following day's
to-do list.

Not being able to complete many of your intended daily tasks may
mean that you need to modify your time management plan by adding
more work time or subtracting some non-work activities that are drawing
time and attention away from your work (e.g., responding to phone calls
and text messages during your planned work times). If you're consistently
falling short of achieving your daily goals, honestly ask yourself if you're
spending too much time on less important things (e.g., TV, video games,
Facebook).

**A good time management plan includes reserving time for the
unexpected.** Always hope for the best, but prepare for the worst. Your
plan should include a buffer zone or safety net that contains extra
time in case you encounter unforeseen developments or unexpected
emergencies.

A good time management plan contains time for work and play. Your
plan shouldn't consist solely of a daunting list of work tasks you have to
do; it should also include fun things you like to do. Plan time to relax, re-
fuel, and recharge. Consider following the daily "8-8-8 rule"—8 hours for
sleep, 8 hours for school, and 8 hours for other activities.

If you schedule things you like to do, you're more likely do to the things
you have to do. You're much more likely to faithfully execute your plan if
play time is scheduled along with work time, allowing play activities to
serve as a reward for completing your work tasks.

A good time management plan has some flexibility. A time management plan shouldn't enslave you to a rigid work schedule. The plan
should be flexible enough to allow you to occasionally bend it without
breaking it. However, you should plan to make up the work time you
lost. In other words, you can borrow or trade work time for play time,
but don't "steal" it; plan to pay back the work time you borrowed by substituting it for play time that was planned for another time. If you decide
not to do work you planned, the next best thing to do is re-plan when
you'll do it.

THINK ABOUT IT

Short exercise breaks not
only work for your body,
they also work for your
brain. Your brain
appreciates the down
time and will come back
to your study time, ready
to go!

NOTE

*Try doubling up! When
including exercise in your
time management plan (you
did include it, didn't you?),
remember that you should
take brief breaks—10 to
15 minutes every hour to get
up and move.*

NOTE

*An effective time manage-
ment plan helps you stress
less, learn more, and earn
higher grades while
reserving time for other
things that are important to
you, enabling you to attain
and maintain balance in
your life.*

NOTE

*When you create a personal
time management plan,
remember it's your
plan—you own it and you
run it. It shouldn't run you.*

TIME AND ENERGY MANAGEMENT

Time management, one of the most important skills for college students, should to be developed early in their college careers. Informal surveys of incoming freshman report that students have a lot of unstructured time they do not know how to fill. New college attendees find themselves surrounded by multiple social opportunities and other distractions. For some first-year students, leaving home and being without parental control for the first time is both exhilarating and challenging. New students need to strike a healthy balance between maintaining or loosening ties with family or former friends and developing new relationships, while adapting to the many demands of their new learning environment. Moreover, they need to make friends and develop habits that support, rather than sabotage, their college success. Commuter and non-traditional students face similar challenges in identifying and navigating new priorities and demands on their time.

Students are faced with many activities and prioritizing can be daunting: work, social life, family responsibilities, and school. College classes generally meet only a few times a week and students often are unaware that instructors expect them to spend significant out-of-class time on assignments and activities. Their newly-found freedom leads to difficulty in making decisions about how to prioritize social life, manage a work schedule, and go to school, without the benefit of the familiar structure they experienced in high school.

Exacerbating the problem, homework may not be collected or graded, and the student may not see any relationship between reading assignments and classroom activities. Developing skills for time management will help them analyze how they spend their time; create a weekly schedule that they can use throughout the semester; work with others to make better use of their time. Finding efficiency in activities that must be completed, and sufficiently planning for assignments so they can be completed without procrastination, will reduce stress, depression, and sleepless nights.

Goals

*   To assess how students think they are spending their time on a weekly basis, plus how they are actually using it
*   To understand what activities are essential for success in college
*   To complete a realistic weekly schedule, assigning specific times to their tasks, activities and assignments
*   To analyze ways to make their time more structured and efficient
*   To categorize and prioritize their activities, allowing time for activities that improve their overall health
*   To identify support structures to help them achieve goals

Materials

*   Colors (markers, colored pencils, and crayons)
*   A calendar (paper or electronic)
*   Copies of Student Handouts:

    8.1 Time Audit Worksheet
    8.2 Guiding Questions for Time Audit Worksheet
    8.3 Weekly Schedule

Instructions

1. Students take 2–3 minutes to quickwrite (see Section 8.2 *Writing and Speaking to Learn*) a response to the following:
   a. How do you spend your time?
   b. What are the five most important things that you currently want to spend time on in your life? Remind them to consider all activities including sleeping, "Facebooking" and texting.

2. Students prioritize their lists. Instruct them to put an "A" next to activities that are of highest priority, "B" next to those that are not quite so high a priority, and "C" next to those that should be done only after everything else is completed.

3. Create groups four to five students. Each group is to make a list of activities including the hours per week (on average) they spend on each activity.

4. Have each group report to the class. As they report, write their responses on the board or chart paper. This can also be done with the entire class, working collaboratively.

5. Add up the total hours and find the difference between that total and the actual number of hours in the week (168).

6. Have the groups or the class decide what the most important activities are in relation to success in academics. What activities can be eliminated or reduced? How can they restructure their time to make themselves more productive?

7. Finish the activity by asking each student to put in writing the changes she or he will commit to making in their schedule.

8. Hand out the *Time Audit Worksheet* and ask students to fill out their activities for a typical week.

9. Pair students and have them share their schedules.

10. Students will answer the *Guiding Questions* with their partner.

11. Lead a class discussion on ways to manage time better so that they can focus on necessary class-related activities.

12. Ask each class member to fill out a *Weekly Schedule*.

13. Remind students to include the activities important to their college success in their schedule. If they are not scheduled, ask how they can make time for those activities. What can be reprioritized?

Extended Activities

1. After several weeks, ask students to compare their Weekly Schedule with their Time Audit Worksheet. Have them share with the class if they have modified their schedules based on the demands they face.

2. Ask students to write a brief reflection on their use of this strategy. What, if any, changes need to occur?

Time Audit Worksheet

Fill in the grid below with your *regular* weekly schedule: the hours you typically spend studying, relaxing, watching TV, texting, sleeping, on Facebook, eating, etc. Be honest. It is important that you put in the correct amount of time spent on each activity.

	Monday	Tuesday	Wednesday	Thursday	Friday	Saturday	Sunday
6:00 am							
7:00 am							
8:00 am							
9:00 am							
10:00 am							
11:00 am							
12:00 pm							
1:00 pm							
2:00 pm							
3:00 pm							
4:00 pm							
5:00 pm							
6:00 pm							
7:00 pm							
8:00 pm							
9:00 pm							
10:00 pm							
11:00 pm							
12:00 am							

Guiding Questions for Time Audit Worksheet

What things do you currently spend the most time on during a typical week?

What things do you spend the least time on during a typical week?

How many hours do you spend in class every day? _____

How many hours do you spend studying every day? _____

Do you feel like this school-centered time is sufficient? Explain:

Are you satisfied with how you spend your time every day? ☐ Yes ☐ No

If you are not satisfied with how you spend your time, what can you do that would make you more satisfied?

How could you reorder your time to make it more efficient?

Weekly Schedule

Schedule for the week of _____

Instructions: Fill in the grid with your weekly schedule.

This week's primary goal: _____

	Monday	Tuesday	Wednesday	Thursday	Friday	Saturday	Sunday
6:00 am							
7:00 am							
8:00 am							
9:00 am							
10:00 am							
11:00 am							
12:00 pm							
1:00 pm							
2:00 pm							
3:00 pm							
4:00 pm							
5:00 pm							
6:00 pm							
7:00 pm							
8:00 pm							
9:00 pm							
10:00 pm							
11:00 pm							
12:00 am							

DEALING WITH PROCRASTINATION

A major enemy of effective time management is procrastination. If your philosophy is: "This can wait until tomorrow," you're promoting a perpetual pattern of postponing what needs to be done until the last possible moment, forcing you to rush frantically to finish work on time and turn in work that's inferior or incomplete (or not turn anything in at all).

©Kendall Hunt Publishing Company.

List of Things To Do Today	List of Things Due Today
1. Write Paper	1. Turn in Paper
2. Study for Math Test	2. Take Math Test
3. Prepare Speech	3. Deliver Speech

Next time I'll start sooner!

A procrastinator's idea of planning ahead and working in advance often boils down to this scenario.

Research shows that 80% to 95% of college students procrastinate (Steel 2007) and almost 50% report that they procrastinate consistently (Onwuegbuzie 2000). Procrastination is such a serious issue for college students that some campuses have opened "procrastination centers" to help them (Burka and Yuen 2008).

AUTHOR'S JOURNEY

During my early years in college, I was quite a procrastinator. During my sophomore year, I waited to do a major history paper until the night before it was due. Back then, I had a word processor that was little more than a typewriter; it allowed you to save your work to a floppy disk before printing. I finished writing my paper around 3:00 a.m. and hit "print," but halfway through the printing I ran out of paper. I woke up my roommate to ask if she had paper, but she didn't. So, at 3:00 a.m. I was forced to get out of my pajamas, get into my street clothes, get into my car, and drive around town to find someplace open at three in the morning that sold typing paper. By the time I found a place, got back home, printed the paper, and washed up, it was time to go to class. I could barely stay awake in any of my classes that day, and when I got my history paper back, the grade wasn't exactly that I was hoping for. I never forgot that incident. My procrastination on that paper caused me to lose sleep the night before it was due, lose attention in all my other classes on the day it was due, and lose points on the paper that I managed to do. Thereafter, I was determined not to let procrastination get the best of me.

—Julie McLaughlin

MYTHS THAT PROMOTE PROCRASTINATION

To have any hope of putting a stop to procrastination, procrastinators need to let go of two popular myths or misconceptions about time and performance.

Myth 1. "I work better under pressure" (e.g., on the day or night before something is due). Procrastinators often confuse desperation with motivation. Their belief that they work better under pressure is usually a rationalization to justify the fact that they *only* work under pressure—when they have to work because they've run out of time and are under the gun of a looming deadline.

Myth 2. "Studying in advance is a waste of time because you will forget it all by test time." This myth is used by procrastinators to justify putting off all studying until the night before an exam. Research indicates that procrastinators suffer from higher rates of stress-related physical disorders, such as insomnia, stomach problems, colds, and flu (McCance and Pychyl 2003). Working under time pressure also increases performance pressure by leaving the procrastinators with (a) no margin of error to correct mistakes, (b) no time to seek help on their work, and (c) no chance to handle random catastrophes or setbacks that may arise at the last minute.

Psychological Causes of Procrastination

Sometimes, procrastination has deeper psychological roots. People may procrastinate for reasons that relate more to emotional issues than poor time management habits. Studies show that some people procrastinate as a psychological strategy to protect their self-esteem. Referred to as *self-handicapping* (Rhodewalt and Vohs 2005), this strategy is used by some procrastinators, often unconsciously, to give themselves a "handicap," or disadvantage. By starting their work at the last possible moment, if their performance turns out to be less than spectacular, they can always conclude (rationalize) that it was because they were performing under a handicap—lack of time rather than lack of ability (Chu and Cho 2005).

 Journal Reflection 8.4

Do you tend to put off work for so long that getting it done turns into an emergency or panic situation?

If your answer is yes, why do you think you put yourself in this position?

If your answer is no, what motivates or enables you to avoid this scenario?

_____

_____

_____

_____

_____

In addition to self-handicapping, other psychological factors have been found to contribute to procrastination, including the following:

- **Fear of failure.** The procrastinator feels better about not turning in work than turning it in and getting negative feedback (Burka and Yuen 2008; Solomon and Rothblum 1984);

- **Perfectionism.** The procrastinator has unrealistically high personal standards or expectations, which leads to the belief that it's better to postpone work or not do it than to risk doing it less than perfectly (Kachgal, Hansel, and Nuter 2001);

- **Fear of success.** The procrastinator fears that doing well will show others that he has the ability to achieve success, leading others to expect him to maintain those high standards in the future (Beck, Koons, and Milgram 2000; Ellis and Knaus 2002);

- **Indecisiveness.** The procrastinator has difficulty making decisions, including decisions about what to do first, when to do it, or whether to do it (Anderson 2003; Steel 2007), so they delay doing it or don't do it at all; and

- **Thrill seeking.** The procrastinator is hooked on the adrenaline rush triggered by rushing around to get things done just before a deadline (Szalavitz 2003).

THINK ABOUT IT

Some tips for preventing and overcoming procrastination

- Practice, practice, practice. Time management is like anything else—the more you practice, the better you get at it. Managing your time can be difficult, especially with friends urging you to join them at the union or off campus. Practicing the strategies in this chapter may be hard at first, but the more often you achieve your goals, the easier you will find it—and the more you will want to continue getting better at managing your time. Research suggests that if you turn an intention into a pledge ("I commit to finishing this reading by tomorrow") you will be more likely to accomplish it (Gollwitzer 1999, Gollwitzr and Sheeran 2006).
- Be mindful of what works for you. Some people get "start-up stress" when they are about to begin a task and therefore become anxious (Burke and Yuen 2008). If that's the case, sequence your work so you're starting with what interests you the most and ride this enthusiasm through to less exciting parts of the assignment. In other cases, people find it easier to do the difficult, more complex components first so they can get them out of the way and have an easier time at the conclusion. This awareness of what works for you is important to getting started and maintaining motivation until you conclude your assignment.

  If an assignment seems to big, chunk it. Remember how you created subgoals for your SMART goal? Do the same process here. If your big assignment is a term paper, your intermediate steps are to determine your topic, find resources for research, organize your notes, etc. As you check off items, you will feel a sense of accomplishment as you realize how much you have completed of the major assignment.
- You haven't won until you're done. Sometimes things seem to be going well and you begin to think that your task won't take as long as you thought. It's not complete—until it's complete. If you wear a device that tracks your exercise, a fitbit or garmin for example, getting close to your goal is not good enough. You need to complete your steps or minutes in order to get the star. The same goes for your academic work. When you're close to completion, charge for the finish line. And if you finish early, give yourself a treat.
- Organization matters. Disorganization is a major factor of procrastination "I can't find a pen, so I guess I'll watch TV for a while" (Steel 2007). We've already talked about thinking through your assignments and getting all the materials handy. But think of other ways you can organize. Try color coding your folders by class, or by weeks—whatever works to keep you orderly when it comes to your courses and work.
- Location, location, location. Try to have one place you can establish as your work space. It's easy if you have your own desk at home or in your dorm where you can organize your books, folders, and computer. But if necessary, find a place on campus that is quiet where you can organize your materials and be free from distractions.
- Participate in a study group. On some campuses, study groups for specific classes will be created, but if not, form you own. This is not necessarily a group of your "besties." A study group is composed of your colleagues serves as an "academic support group" that untangles questions and issues you or they might have in a course. You learn from each other, sharing resources, organizational tips, and offering diverse opinions.
- A friend in need. One of the best things about college is that you will make lifelong friendships along the way. And good friends will want to help you accomplish your goals. Of course you want to be part of the crowd, but you know what you need to do to complete your tasks. Let your friends know your daily schedule, text them to tell you when you shouldn't be disturbed. Suggest where you can meet to celebrate when you finish your work. Good friends will understand that you can't be available all the time. Better friends will encourage you to stay the course and complete your work.

AUTHOR'S JOURNEY

The two biggest projects I've had to complete in my life were writing my doctoral thesis and writing this book. The strategy that enabled me to complete both of these large tasks was to set short-term deadlines for myself (e.g., complete five to ten pages each week). I psyched myself into thinking that these little, self-imposed due dates were really drop-dead deadlines that I had to meet. This strategy allowed me to divide one monstrous chore into a series of smaller, more manageable mini-tasks. It was like taking a huge, indigestible meal and breaking it into small, bite-sized pieces that could be easily ingested and gradually digested over time.

—*Joe Cuseo*

> I long to accomplish some great and noble task, but it is my chief duty to accomplish small tasks as if they were great and noble."
>
> —*Helen Keller, seeing- and hearing-impaired author and activist for the rights of women and the handicapped*

CHAPTER SUMMARY AND HIGHLIGHTS

Effective goal-setting gets you going, but effective time management gets things done. To manage time effectively, we need to

- *Analyze* it. Break down time and become aware of how we spend it;
- *Itemize* it. Identify the tasks we need to accomplish and their due dates; and
- *Prioritize* it. Tackle our tasks in order of their importance.

Developing a comprehensive time management plan for academic work involves long-, mid-, and short-range steps that involve:

- Planning the total term (long-range step);
- Planning your week (mid-range step); and
- Planning your day (short-range step).

A good time management plan includes the following features:

- It transforms intention to action.
- It includes time to take care of unexpected developments.
- It contains time for work and play.
- It gives you the flexibility to accommodate unforeseen opportunities.

The enemy of effective time management is procrastination. Overcoming it involves letting go of two major myths:

- Better work is produced "under pressure"—on the day or night before it's due.
- Studying in advance is a waste of time—because you'll forget it all by test time.

Effective strategies for beating the procrastination habit include the following:

- Organize your work materials to make it easy and convenient for you to start working.
- Organize your work place or space so that you work in a location that minimizes distractions and temptations not to work.

- Intentionally arrange your work schedule so that you are working on more enjoyable or stimulating tasks at times when you're less vulnerable to procrastination.
- If you're close to finishing a task, finish it, because it's often harder to restart a task than to complete one that's already been started.
- Divide large tasks into smaller, more manageable units and tackle them in separate work sessions.

Mastering the skill of managing time is critical for success in college and beyond. Time is one of our most powerful personal resources; the better we manage it, the more likely we are to achieve our goals and gain control of our life.

Learning More through the World Wide Web: Internet-Based Resources

For additional information on managing time, and preventing procrastination, see the following websites:

Time-Management Strategies for All Students:
www.studygs.net/timman.htm

www.pennstatelearning.psu.edu/resources/study-tips/time-mgt

Time-Management Strategies for Adult Students:
www.essortment.com/lifestyle/timemanagement_sjmu.htm

Beating Procrastination:
www.mindtools.com/pages/article/newHTE_96.htm

http://success.oregonstate.edu/learning-corner/time-management/managing-procrastination

References

American Association of Community Colleges 2009 Fact Sheet. 2009. http://www.aacc.nche.edu/About/Documents/factsheet2009.pdf.

Anderson, C. J. 2003. "The Psychology of Doing Nothing: Forms of Decision Avoidance Result from Reason and Emotion." *Psychological Bulletin* 129: 139–67.

Beck, B. L., S. R. Koons, and D. L. Milgram. 2000. "Correlates and Consequences of Behavioural Procrastination: The Effects of Academic Procrastination, Self-consciousness, Self-esteem and Self-handicapping [Special issue]. *Journal of Social Behaviour & Personality* 15(5): 3–13.

Burka, J. B., and L. M. Yuen. 2008. *Procrastination: Why You Do It, What to Do About It Now*. Cambridge, MA: De Capo Press.

Chu, A. H. C., and J. N. Cho. 2005. "Rethinking Procrastination: Positive Effects of "Active"

Procrastination Behavior on Attitudes and Performance." *The Journal of Social Psychology* 145(3): 245–64.

Covey, S. R. 2004. *Seven Habits of Highly Effective People*. 3rd ed. New York: Fireside.

Ellis, A., and W. J. Knausm. 2002. *Overcoming Procrastination*. Rev. ed. New York: New American Library.

Goldsmith, E. B. 2010. *Resource Management for Individuals and Families*. 4th ed. Upper Saddle River, NJ: Prentice Hall.

Harriot, J. and J. R. Ferrari. 1996. "Prevalence of Procrastination among Samples of Adults." *Psychological Reports* 78: 611–16.

HERI (Higher Education Research Institute). 2014. *Your First College Year Survey 2014*. Los Angeles, CA: Cooperative Institutional Research Program, University of California-los Angeles.

Kachgal, M. M., L. S. Hansen and K. T. Nutter. 2001. "Academic Procrastination Prevention/Intervention: Strategies and Recommendations." *Journal of Developmental Education* 25(1): 2–12.

Lakein, A. 1973. *How to Get Control of Your Time and Your Life*. New York: New American Library.

Light, R. J. 2001. *Making the Most of College: Students Speak Their Minds*. Cambridge, MA: Harvard University Press.

McCance, N., and T. A. Pychyl. August, 2003. *From Task Avoidance to Action: An Experience Sampling Study of Undergraduate Students' Thoughts, Feelings and Coping Strategies in Relation to Academic Procrastination.* Paper presented at the Third Annual Conference for Counseling Procrastinators in the Academic Context, University of Ohio, Columbus.

Morgenstern, J. 2004. *Time Management from the Inside Out: The Foolproof System for Taking Control of Your Schedule and Your Life*. 2nd ed. New York: Henry Holt & Co.

Onwuegbuzie, A. J. 2000. "Academic Procrastinators and Perfectionistic Tendencies among Graduate Students." *Journal of Social Behavior and Personality* 15: 103–9.

Rhodewalt, F., and K. D. Vohs. 2005. Defensive Strategies, Motivation, and the Self. In *Handbook of Competence and Motivation,* edited by A. Elliot and C. Dweck, 548–65. New York: Guilford Press.

Solomon, L. J., and E. D. Rothblum. 1984. "Academic Procrastination: Frequency and Cognitive-behavioral Correlates." *Journal of Counseling Psychology* 31(4): 503–9.

Steel, P. 2007. "The Nature of Procrastination: A Meta-analytic and Theoretical Review of Quintessential Self-regulatory Failure." *Psychological Bulletin,* 133(1): 65–94.

Szalavitz, M. July/August, 2003. "Tapping Potential: Stand and Deliver." *Psychology Today* 50–4.

Chapter 8 Exercises

8.1 Quote Reflections

Review the sidebar quotes contained in this chapter and select two that were especially meaningful or inspirational to you.

For each quote, provide a three- to five-sentence explanation why you chose it.

8.2 Term at a Glance

Review the syllabus (course outline) for each course you're enrolled in this term, and complete the following information for each:

Term _____ Year _____

Course ↓	Professor ↓	Exams ↓	Projects & Papers ↓	Other Assignments ↓	Attendance Policy ↓	Late & Makeup Assignment Policy ↓

1. Is the overall workload what you expected? Are you surprised by the amount of work required in any particular course or courses?

2. At this point in the term, what do you see as your most challenging or demanding course or courses? Why?

3. Do you think you can handle the total workload required for the full set of courses you're enrolled in this term?

4. What adjustments or changes could you make to your personal schedule that would make it easier to accommodate your academic workload this term?

8.3 Developing a Task Management Plan for Your First Term in College

1. Review the *course syllabus (course outline)* for each class you are enrolled in this term and highlight all major exams, tests, quizzes, assignments, and papers and the dates on which they are due.

2. Obtain a *large calendar* for the academic term (available at your campus bookstore or learning center) and record all the highlighted information for your exams and assignments for all your courses in the calendar boxes that represent their due dates. To fit this information within the calendar boxes, use creative abbreviations to represent different tasks, such as RA for reading assignment, E for exam, and TP for term paper. When you're done, you'll have a detailed chart or map of deadline dates and a master schedule for the entire term. There are several online calendars that can assist in managing your schedule (e.g., http://www.cozi.com/family-calendar.htm and http://pomodorotechnique.com/).

3. Activate the calendar and task lists functions on your smartphone. Enter your schedule, important dates, deadlines, and set alert reminders. By carrying your cell phone with your regularly, you will always have this information at your fingertips.

Reflections

1. Is your overall workload what you expected? Are your surprised by the amount of work time you will need to devote to your courses?

2. At this point in the term, what course is demanding the greatest amount of out-of-class work time? Have you been able to put in this time?

3. What adjustments or changes (if any) could you make to your personal schedule this term to create more time to handle your academic workload?

8.4 Time Analysis Inventory

1. Go to the following website: *pennstatelearning.psu.edu/resources/study-tips/time-mgt* Click on the link for the "time-management exercise."

2. Complete the time management exercise at this site. The exercise asks you to estimate the hours per day or week that you engage in various activities (e.g., sleeping, employment, and commuting). When you enter the amount of time devoted to each activity, this website will automatically compute the total number of remaining hours you have available in the week for academic work.

3. After completing your entries, answer the following questions (or provide your best estimate).

   a. How many hours per week do you have available for academic work?

   b. Do you have two hours available for academic work outside of class for each hour you spend in class? If you don't, what activities could be eliminated or reduced to create more time for academic work outside of class?

8.5 Developing a Time Management Plan for Your First Term in College

Keep in mind the task management plan you developed in Exercise 8.2, use the following Week-at-a-Glance Grid to map out your typical or average week for this term. Start by recording what you usually do on these days, including the times you're in class, when you work, and when you relax or recreate. You can use abbreviations (e.g., CT for class time, HW for homework, J for job, and R&R for rest and relaxation). List the abbreviations you created at the bottom of the page so that your instructor can follow them.

If you're a *full-time* student, plan for 25 *hours* in your week for homework (HW). (If you're a *part-time* student, find 2 *hours* you could devote to homework *for every hour* you're in class—i.e., if you're in class 9 hours per week, find 18 hours of homework time).

> The amount of free time you have in college is much more than in high school. Always have a weekly study schedule to go by. Otherwise, time slips away and you will not be able to account for it."
>
> —*Advice to new college students from a first-year student (Rhoads 2005)*

These homework hours could take place at any time during the week, including weekends. If you combine 25 hours per week of out-of-class school work with the amount of time you spend in class each week, you'll end up with a 40-hour academic workweek—comparable to a full-time job—which is how college should be viewed.

Week-at-a-Glance Grid

	Sunday	Monday	Tuesday	Wednesday	Thursday	Friday	Saturday
7:00 am							
8:00 am							
9:00 am							
10:00 am							
11:00 am							
12:00 pm							
1:00 pm							
2:00 pm							
3:00 pm							
4:00 pm							
5:00 pm							
6:00 pm							
7:00 pm							
8:00 pm							
9:00 pm							
10:00 pm							
11:00 pm							

Reflections:

1. How likely are you to put this time management plan into practice? Circle one: Definitely Probably Unlikely

2. What would *promote or encourage* you to put this plan into practice?

3. What would *prevent or discourage* you from putting this plan into practice?

4. How do you think other students would answer the above three questions?

8.6 Ranking Priorities

Look at the tasks below and decide if they are A, B, or C priorities:

_____ Going for a run

_____ Writing a paper that is due tomorrow

_____ Paying your electric bill that is due next week

_____ Checking out what your friends are doing on Facebook

_____ Getting your haircut

_____ Making an appointment with your academic advisor to register for classes

_____ Playing your favorite video game

_____ Making it to your doctor's appointment

_____ Helping your sister plan her wedding

_____ Picking up your child's prescription from the pharmacy

_____ Studying for your final exams

_____ Calling your cousin to catch up on family gossip

_____ Making reservations for your vacation

_____ Going to see the hot new movie that has come out

_____ Getting your oil changed in your car

_____ Getting your car washed

8.7 Reality Bite

Procrastination: The Vicious Cycle

Delayla has a major paper due at the end of the term. It's now past midterm and she still hasn't started to work on it. She keeps telling herself, "I should have started sooner," but she continues to postpone her work and is becoming increasingly anxious and guilty. To relieve her growing anxiety and guilt, Delayla starts doing other tasks instead, such as cleaning her room and returning e-mails. This makes her feel a little better because these tasks keep her busy, take her mind off the term paper, and give her the feeling that at least she's getting something accomplished. Time continues to pass; the deadline for the paper grows dangerously close. Delayla now finds herself in the position of having lots of work to do and little time in which to do it.

Adapted from *Procrastination: Why You Do It, and What to do about It* (Burka and Yuen 2008).

Reflection and Discussion Questions

1. What do you expect Delayla will do at this point? Why?

2. What grade do you think she'll end up receiving on her paper?

3. Other than simply starting sooner, what else could Delayla (and other procrastinators like her) do to break the cycle of procrastination?

4. Can you relate to this student's predicament, or do you know other students who often find themselves in this predicament?

8.8 Time Management PEPS Reflection

Look back at your PEPS Learning Style Inventory Report and answer the following questions.

1. Is your time of day preference late day, early day, or did you have no preference? Knowing this, when is the best time of day for you to take classes? To study?

2. How can you make your time of day preference part of your time management plan?

Chapter 8 Reflection

Looking back on suggestions from this chapter, what are three things you can do start managing your time better?

1.

2.

3.

Explain how you are going to make this happen.

CHAPTER 9

STUDY AND TEST WISE IN HIGHER EDUCATION ENVIRONMENTS

STRATEGIC STUDYING AND TEST-TAKING SKILLS AND STRATEGIES

CHAPTER PREVIEW

This chapter supplies you with a systematic set of strategies for improving your performance on different types of tests that can be used before, during, and after exams, helping you to become more "test wise" and less "test anxious."

PERFORMANCE OBJECTIVE

Acquire effective strategies to improve your performance on multiple-choice, true-false and essay tests.

PRE-REFLECTION

Do I tend to feel prepared when I am about to take a test?

PURPOSE FOR READING THIS CHAPTER

Doing well on tests is a process and each type of test requires some different strategies to be successful. After marking the text by circling key terms and bracketing specific strategies describe, choose three strategies you believe will help you, two strategies you're already doing, and present one specific case where using the skill since you've been in college has helped you in test taking.

Learning in college courses typically takes place in a three-stage process: (1) acquiring information from lectures and readings; (2) studying that information and storing it in your brain as knowledge; and (3) demonstrating that knowledge on exams.

STRATEGIC STUDYING: LEARNING DEEPLY AND REMEMBERING LONGER

Studying isn't a short sprint that takes place just before test time. Instead, it's more like a long-distance run that takes place over time. Studying the night before an exam should be the last step in a sequence of test-preparation steps that take place well before test time, which include: (a) taking accurate and complete notes in class, (b) doing the assigned reading, and (c) seeking help from professors or peers along the way for any concepts that are unclear or confusing. After these steps have been taken, you are then well-positioned to study the material you've acquired and learn it deeply.

Described below is a series of study strategies you can use to promote deep and durable (long-lasting) learning.

Writing in the Margins: Six Strategies at a Glance

The following table provides six annotation strategies that help readers analyze and understand texts. While making connections, clarifying information, or doing other work defined below, the student can record thoughts in the margins of the text.

Visualize	Summarize
Visualize what the author is saying and draw an illustration in the margin. Visualizing what authors say will help clarify complex concepts and ideas. When visualizing ask:	Briefly summarize paragraphs or sections of a text. Summarizing is a good way to keep track of essential information while gaining control of lengthier passages. Summaries will:
• What does this look like?	• State what the paragraph is about.
• How can I draw this concept/idea?	• Describe what the author is doing.
• What visual and/or symbol best represents this idea?	• Account for key terms and/or ideas.
Clarify	Connect
Clarify complex ideas presented in a text. Readers clarify ideas through a process of analysis, synthesis, and evaluation. Pausing to clarify ideas will increase understanding of ideas in the text. In order to clarify information:	Make connections within the reading to personal experiences and to the world. Making connections will improve comprehension of the text. While reading, ask:
• Define key terms.	• How does this relate to me?
• Reread sections of the text.	• How does this idea relate to other ideas in the text?
	• How does this relate to the world?
Respond	Question
Respond to ideas in the text as you read. Responses can be personal or analytical in nature. Thoughtful responses will increase engagement and comprehension. Readers will often respond to:	Question both the ideas in the text and personal understanding of the text. Asking good questions while reading will increase critical reading skills. While reading, ask:
• Interesting ideas.	• What is the author saying here?
• Emotional arguments.	• What is the author doing?
• Provocative statements.	• What do I understand so far?
• Authors' claims.	• What is the purpose of this section?
• Facts, data, and other support.	• What do I agree/disagree with?

MARKING THE TEXT: *SOCIAL SCIENCE*

This strategy has three distinct marks:

1. **Number the paragraphs.** ①	① Before you read, take a moment and number the paragraphs in the section that you are planning to read. Start with the number one and continue numbering sequentially until you reach the end of the text or reading assignment. Write the number near the paragraph indention and circle the number; write it small enough so that you have room to write in the margin. ② As with page numbers, paragraph numbers will act as a reference, so you can easily refer to specific sections of the text.
2. Ⓒⓘⓡⓒⓛⓔ **key terms, cited authors, and other essential words or numbers.**	You might circle: • Key concepts • Lesson-based content vocabulary • Concept-based vocabulary _____ • Words that signal relationships (i.e., *This led to…* or *As a result…*) _____ • Names of people • Names of historical events _____ • Dates • Numbers
3. <u>Underline</u> **the author's claims and other information relevant to the reading purpose.**	While reading informational texts (i.e., textbooks, reference books, articles, or journals), read carefully to identify information that is relevant to the reading task. Relevant information might include the following: • Central claims • Evidence • Details relating to a theology, philosophy, or ideology _____ • Facts about a person, place, thing, or idea _____ • Descriptions of a person, place, thing, or idea _____ • Cause-and-effect relationships

Some strategies to help students identify essential information in the reading are as follows:

• Read the introduction to the primary or secondary source.

• Scan the text for visuals, vocabulary, comprehension questions, or other reading aids.

• Review your notes for key concepts.

• Preview chapter or unit reviews.

Note: If you are not working with consumables, consider photocopying sections of a text that are essential to writing assignments, course content, exams, or other class activities.

MARKING THE TEXT: *SCIENCE*

This strategy has three distinct marks:

1. **Number the paragraphs.**	① Before you read, take a moment and number the paragraphs in the section that you are planning to read. Start with the number one and continue numbering sequentially until you reach the end of the text or reading assignment. Write the number near the paragraph indention and circle the number; write it small enough so that you have room to write in the margin.
	② As with page numbers, paragraph numbers will act as a reference, so you can easily refer to specific sections of the text.

3. (Circle) **key terms, cited authors, and other essential words or numbers.**	You might circle: • Key concepts • Lesson-based vocabulary • Content-based vocabulary • Names of people, theories, and/or experiments • Properties • Elements • Formulas • Units of measure • Variables • Values • Percentages • _____ • _____ • _____

4. <u>Underline</u> **the author's claims and other information relevant to the reading purpose.**	While reading informational texts (i.e., textbooks, reference books, articles, or journals), read carefully to identify information that is relevant to the reading task. Relevant information might include the following:

• Concerns	• Guiding language		
• Claims			
• Data	• Hypotheses	• _____	
• Definitions	• "If/Then"		
• Descriptions	statements	• _____	
• Evidence	• Main ideas		
• Examples	• Methods	• _____	
• Explanations	• Processes		

Some strategies to help students identify essential information in the reading are as follows:

• Read the introduction to the chapter, lab, or article.

• Scan the text for visuals, vocabulary, comprehension questions, or other reading aids.

• Review your notes for key concepts.

• Preview chapter or unit reviews.

Note: If you are not working with consumables, consider photocopying sections of a text that are essential to labs, courses, content, exams, or other class activities.

MARKING THE TEXT: *MATHEMATICS* (*WORD PROBLEMS*)

This strategy has four distinct marks:

1. **Number the paragraphs.**	① When reading a word problem that is only one paragraph, number each sentence. ② For longer word problems, start with the number one and number sentences by fives (1, 5, 10).	
2. **Circle key terms, cited authors, and other essential words or numbers.**	You might circle: • Action words • Sum, Add, More Than • Multiply • Simplify • Divide • Difference, Subtract • Units • Amounts • Values • Percentages • Variables • Formulas • Solve	• _____ • _____ • _____
3. **Underline verbal models.**[1]	You might also underline: • A process • Definitions • Descriptions • Explanations	
4. **Box the question.**	In a word problem or multiple choice question, draw a box around the question.	

MARKING THE TEXT: *FICTION*

This strategy has three distinct marks:

1. **Number the paragraphs.**	① Before you read, take a moment and number the paragraphs in the section that you are planning to read. Start with the number one and continue numbering sequentially until you reach the end of the text or reading assignment. Write the number near the paragraph indention and circle the number; write it small enough so that you have room to write in the margin. ② As with page numbers, paragraph numbers will act as a reference, so you can easily refer to specific sections of the text.

(continued)

---

[1] A verbal model is an expression or equation that uses words to represent a real-life situation.

2. (Circle) descriptive words and names of people, places, and things.	You might circle: • Vivid language • Concrete nouns • _____ • Names of characters • Names of places • _____ • Vocabulary • Word choice • _____ • Diction
3. Underline descriptions, figurative language, or other information relevant to the reading purpose.	While reading fictional texts (i.e., novels, short stories, or poems), read carefully to identify information that is relevant to the reading task. Relevant information might include the following: • Analogies • Literary devices • _____ • Characterization • Dialogue • _____ • Imagery • Context clues • _____ • Descriptions

Note: If you are not working with consumables, consider photocopying passages of texts that are essential to class discussions or closing activities. For example, if you want students to write an essay where they examine the monologues of a certain character, you might consider photocopying those places in the text where the monologues take place. What other passages would you like to have available for students to mark?

MARKING THE TEXT: NON- FICTION (ARGUMENT)

This strategy has three distinct marks:

1. **Number the paragraphs.**	(1.) Before you read, take a moment and number the paragraphs in the section that you are planning to read. Start with the number one and continue numbering sequentially until you reach the end of the text or reading assignment. Write the number near the paragraph indention and circle the number; write it small enough so that you have room to write in the margin. (2.) As with page numbers, paragraph numbers will act as a reference, so you can easily refer to specific sections of the text.
2. (Circle) key terms, cited authors, and other essential words or numbers.	In order to identify a key term, consider if the word or phrase is: • Repeated • Defined by the author • Used to explain or represent an idea • Used in an original or unique way • A central concept or idea • Relevant to one's reading purpose

3. <u>Underline</u> the author's claims and other information relevant to the reading purpose.	A claim is an arguable statement or assertion made by the author. Data, facts, or other backing should support an author's assertion. Consider the following statements: • A claim <u>may appear anywhere</u> in the text (beginning, middle, or end). • A claim <u>may not appear explicitly</u> in the argument, so the reader must infer it from the evidence presented in the text. • Often, an <u>author will make several claims</u> throughout his or her argument. • An <u>author may signal his or her claim,</u> letting you know that this is his or her position.

Ultimately, what you underline and circle will depend on your reading purpose. In addition to marking key terms and claims, you might be asked to mark other essential information, such as the author's evidence, descriptions, stylistic elements, or language in the text that provide some insight into the author's values and beliefs.

ANALYZING A WRITING PROMPT[2]

Students should develop the habit of asking critical questions that will help them understand and prepare for a formal writing assignment. Even though prompts provide language that helps direct a student's thinking, students must analyze the prompt, in order to respond accurately and effectively. The following questions will help students work through and respond to complex writing prompts.

1. **What am I supposed to *do* as a writer when I respond to this prompt?**
   Does the prompt ask me to make an argument, inform my readers about a particular issue, or describe an event? Do I have to explain the significance of a particular topic? If you don't understand what you're being asked to do, seek clarification.
2. **What am I expected to cover in this essay?**
   What content should I include?
3. **From which perspective or persona am I being asked to write this essay?**
   Does the prompt ask me to speak from a particular perspective? Should I write this essay as an ordinary student or someone else? Some prompts will ask inexperienced writers to take on the persona of celebrities, leaders, government officials, and so on.
4. **Who is my audience?**
   To whom am I writing this essay (an organization, the mayor, a city council member, or some other individual or group)? What language is most appropriate for my audience? What does my audience know and/or believe?

---
[2] Johns, A. (2008). *AVID college readiness: Working with sources, grades 11-12.* San Diego, CA: AVID Press.

5. **What type of text am I being asked to write? What do I know about this genre?**

   Am I being asked to write a business letter or a personal statement? How about a book review? You might want to ask your instructor about the writing type expected and specifically how to organize the content.

6. **Does the prompt ask me to use sources? If so, what sources should I use?**

   Does the prompt specify whether the sources should be primary (e.g., speeches, interviews, autobiographies, etc.) or secondary (e.g., biographies, analyses, or commentaries on events, ideas, people, etc.)? What types of sources are appropriate? Sources might include magazine or journal articles, films, or other source material. How many different types of sources should I use?

7. **Does the prompt tell me to focus on a specific text?**

   What does the prompt ask me to consider? How should I focus my analysis? How many elements and/or strategies am I being asked to analyze?

8. **Are there clues in the prompt that will help me organize my paper?**

   Does the prompt use transition words? Is there a series of questions to consider? Does it make sense to discuss a specific portion of the prompt first, second, and third?

> "You can do several things at once, but only if they are easy and undemanding. You are probably safe carrying on a conversation with a passenger while driving on an empty highway [but] you could not compute the product of 17 x 24 while making a left turn into dense traffic, and you certainly should not try."
>
> —*Daniel Kahneman, professor emeritus of Psychology, and author of Thinking Fast and Slow*

Give Studying Your Undivided Attention

The human attention span has limited capacity—we have only so much of it available to us at any point in time and we can give all or part of it to whatever task(s) we're working on. As the phrase "paying attention" suggests, it's like paying money, we only have so much of it to spend. Thus, if attention while studying is spent on other activities at the same time (e.g., listening to music, watching TV, or text messaging friends), there's a deduction in the amount of attention paid to studying. In other words, studying doesn't receive our undivided attention.

Studies show that when people multitask they don't pay equal attention to all tasks at the same time; instead, they divide their attention by shifting it back and forth between tasks (Howard 2014). Their performance on the task that demands the most concentration or deepest thinking is the one that suffers the most (Crawford and Strapp 1994). When performing complex mental tasks that cannot be done automatically or mindlessly, the brain needs quiet, internal reflection time for permanent connections to form between brain cells—which is what must happen if deep, long-lasting learning is to take place (Jensen 2008). If the brain must simultaneously engage in other tasks or process other sources of external stimulation, this connection-making process is interfered with and learning is impaired.

So, give study time your undivided attention by unplugging all your electronic accessories. You can even use apps to help you do so (e.g., to silence your phone). Another strategy would be to set aside a short block of time to check electronic messages after you've completed a longer block of study time (e.g., as a study break); this allows you to use social media as a reward *after* putting in a stretch of focused study time. Just don't do both at the *same* time.

Multitasking while studying interferes with learning by dividing up attention and driving down comprehension and retention.

AUTHOR'S JOURNEY

When I was in college there were so many distractions for me. I had a job that I could work as many hours as I wanted to work. I had organizations where I was offered leadership positions. In addition, there were so many attractive girls. Then there were all these demanding classes that required me to study. To be honest, I enjoyed some of these distractions more than others. Well, that's another story for another day and another book. What I did know was that my education was the most important thing to me so I had to prioritize it. Thus, I had to study, learn, and do well in order to graduate. To do this I had to **REDUCE MY DISTRACTIONS!!** So, I developed Thompson's plan of action. They were: 1. Find a friend or two who also wanted to learn who could be study partners. What I realized was that my primary learning style is auditory (this worked well when I needed to study for a test). 2. If I was studying alone, find a place that was quiet where I could not listen to music or turn on the TV (the library was my favorite place to do this). BTW, in today's terms, that means no internet, text, phone, etc. 3. Never study when I am hungry and tired. 4. Give myself enough time to complete the assigned study task where I did not feel I had to rush through the material.

—*Aaron Thompson*

MAKE MEANINGFUL ASSOCIATIONS

Deep learning doesn't take place by simply absorbing information like a sponge—in exactly the same, prepackaged form as you received it from a textbook or lecture. Instead, deep learning involves actively translating the information you receive into a form that makes sense to you (Biggs and Tang 2007; Mayer 2002).

AUTHOR'S JOURNEY

When my son was about three years old, we were riding in the car together and listening to a song by the Beatles titled, *Sergeant Pepper's Lonely Hearts Club Band*. You may be familiar with this tune, but in case you're not, there's a part in it where the following lyrics are sung repeatedly: "Sergeant Pepper's Lonely, Sergeant Pepper's Lonely, Sergeant Pepper's Lonely . . . ."

When this part of the song was being played, I noticed that my three-year-old son was singing along. I thought it was pretty amazing for a boy his age to be able to understand and repeat those lyrics. However, when that part of the song came on again, I listened to him more closely and noticed he wasn't singing "Sergeant Pepper's Lonely, Sergeant Pepper's Lonely . . ." Instead, he was singing: "Sausage Pepperoni, Sausage Pepperoni . . ." (which were his two favorite pizza toppings).

My son's brain was doing what all human brains tend to naturally do. It took unfamiliar information—song lyrics that didn't make any sense to him—and transformed it into a form that was meaningful to him.

—Joe Cuseo

NOTE

Deep learning is not about teachers transmitting information to students; it's about students transforming that information into knowledge that's meaningful to them.

The brain's natural learning tendency is to translate unfamiliar information into a familiar form that makes sense and has personal meaning. This is illustrated in the experience.

❝

Learning these WICOR strategies is helpful for all my classes, but I realized it will help me with whatever career I choose—how to manage my time, creative thinking, and critical reading so I can identify client needs or a program's desired outcomes, and working with diverse groups of people.

—AHE Third-year student

You can experience the brain's natural inclination for meaning-making by reading the following passage, which once appeared anonymously on the Internet.

Aoccdrnig to rscheearch at Cmabridge Uinverstisy, it deos't mattaer in what order the ltteers in a word are, the only iprmoetnt thing is that the frist and lsat ltteer be at the rghit pclae. The rset can be a total mses and you can still raed it wouthit a porbelm. This is bcusae the human mind deos not raed ervey lteter by istlef, but the word as a wlohe. Amzanig huh?

Notice how easily you made meaning out of unfamiliar, misspelled words by naturally transforming them into familiar, meaningful words—which were already stored in your brain. Whenever you're learning something new, capitalize on the brain's natural tendency to find meaning by trying to connect what you're trying to understand to what you already know.

Learning the specialized terminology associated with different academic disciplines may seem like learning a foreign language for a student with little or no experience with these terms. However, before you start brutally beating these terms into your brain through sheer repetition, try to find meaning in them. One way to do so is by looking up the term's word root in the dictionary or by identifying its prefix or suffix, which may give away the term's meaning. For instance, suppose you're taking a biology course and studying the autonomic nervous system—the part of the nervous system that operates without conscious awareness or voluntary control (e.g., your heart and lungs). The meaning of this biological term is found in its prefix "auto," meaning self-controlling or "automatic" (e.g., automatic transmission). Once you find meaning in a term, you can learn it faster and retain it longer than by memorizing it through sheer repetition.

If looking up an academic term's root, prefix, or suffix doesn't reveal its meaning, see if you can make it meaningful to you in some other way. Suppose you looked up the root of the term "artery" and nothing about the origins of this term helped you understand its meaning or purpose.

You could create your own meaning for this term by taking its first letter (a), and have it stand for "away"—to help you remember that arteries carry blood away from the heart. By so doing, you take a meaningless term and make it personally meaningful and memorable.

Journal Reflection 9.1

Think of a technical academic term or concept you're learning in a course this term, and create a meaningful association you could use to remember it.

_____

_____

_____

_____

_____

Another way you can make learning meaningful is by *comparing and contrasting* what you're learning with what you already know. When you're studying, get in the habit of asking yourself the following questions:

1. How is this idea similar or comparable to something that I've already learned? (Compare)
2. How is this idea different from what I've already learned? (Contrast)

Research indicates that this simple strategy is one of the most powerful ways to promote learning of academic information (Marzano, Pickering, and Pollock 2001). When you ask yourself the question, "How is this similar to and different from concepts I already know?" you make the learning process more meaningful and relevant because you're relating what you're trying to learn to what you already know or have already experienced.

Integrate Information from Lectures and Readings

Connect ideas from your lecture notes and reading assignments that relate to the same concept. Get them in the same place by recording them on the same index card under the same category heading. Index cards can be used like a portable file cabinet, whereby each card functions like the hub of a wheel, around which individual pieces of related information can be attached like spokes. In contrast, when ideas pertaining to the same point or concept are spread all over the place, they're more likely to take that form in your mind—leaving them mentally disconnected and leaving you more confused or overwhelmed (and stressed out).

NOTE

When learning, go for meaning first, memorization last. If you can connect what you're trying to learn to what you already know, the deeper you'll learn it and the longer you'll remember it.

" The extent to which we remember a new experience has more to do with how it relates to existing memories than with how many times or how recently we have experienced it."

—*Morton Hunt,* The Universe Within: A New Science Explores the Human Mind

NOTE

Deep learners ask questions like: How can this specific piece of information be categorized or classified into a larger concept? How does this particular idea relate to or "fit into" something bigger?

" Hurriedly jam-packing a brain is akin to speed-packing a cheap suitcase—it holds its new load for a while, then most everything falls out."

—*Benedict Carey, author,* How We Learn: Throw Out the Rule Book and Unlock Your Brain's Potential

Distribute Study Time across Separate Study Sessions

Learning deeply depends not only on how you learn (your method), but when you learn (your timing). Equally important as how much time you spend studying is how you distribute or spread out your study time. Research consistently shows that for students of all abilities and ages, distributing study time across several shorter sessions results in deeper learning and longer retention than channeling all study time into one long session (Brown, Roediger, and McDaniel 2014; Carey 2014; Dunlosky et al. 2013). Distributed practice improves your learning and memory in two major ways:

* It minimizes loss of attention due to fatigue or boredom.
* It reduces mental interference by giving the brain some downtime to cool down and lock in information it has received before being interrupted by the need to deal with additional information (Malmberg and Murnane 2002; Murname and Shiffrin 1991). Memory works like a muscle: after it's been exercised, if given some "cool down" time before it's exerted again, it builds greater strength—that is, stronger memory for what it previously learned (Carey 2014). On the other hand, if the brain's downtime is interfered with by the arrival of additional information, it gets overloaded and its capacity for handling information becomes impaired. That's what cramming does—it overloads the brain with lots of information in a limited period of time. In contrast, distributed study does just the opposite—it uses shorter sessions with downtime between sessions—giving the brain time to slow down and retain the information it's previously processed (studied) and more time to move that information from short-term to long-term memory (Willis 2006).

Distributed study is also less stressful and more motivating than cramming. You're more likely to start studying when you know you won't be doing it for a long stretch of time (or lose any sleep doing it). It's also easier to sustain attention for tasks that are done for a shorter period of time.

Although cramming just before exams is better than not studying at all, it's far less effective than studying that's spread out across time. Instead of frantically cramming total study time into one long session ("massed practice"), use *distributed practice*—"distribute" or space out your study time over several shorter sessions.

 Journal Reflection 9.2

Are you more likely to study in advance of exams or cram just before exams? Explain.

_____

_____

_____

_____

How do you think most students would answer this question?

_____

_____

_____

_____

_____

Use the "Part-to-Whole" Study Method

A natural extension of distributed practice is the part-to-whole method. This method involves breaking up the material you need to learn into smaller parts and studying those parts in separate sessions in advance of the exam; then you use your last study session just before the exam to review (restudy) the parts you previously studied in separate sessions. Thus, your last session isn't a cram session or even a study session, it's a review session.

Research shows that students of all ability levels learn material in college courses more effectively when it's studied in small units and when progression to the next unit takes place only after the previous unit has been mastered or understood (Pascarella and Terenzini 1991, 2005).

Don't buy into the myth that studying in advance is a waste of time because you'll forget it all by test time. (Procrastinators often use this argument to rationalize their habit of putting off studying until the very last moment, which forces them to cram frantically the night before exams.) Even if you aren't able to recall what you previously studied when you look at it again closer to test time, research shows that once you start reviewing it, you can relearn it in a fraction of the time it took the first time. Since it takes much less time to relearn the material because the brain still has a memory trace for information studied in the earlier sessions (Kintsch 1994), it proves you didn't completely forget it and that studying it in advance wasn't a waste of time. Another key advantage of breaking material you're learning into smaller parts and studying those parts in advance of major exams is that it allows you to check your understanding of the part you studied before moving on to learning the next part. This is a particularly important advantage in courses where learning the next unit of material builds on your understanding the previous unit (e.g., math and science).

Capitalize on the Power of Visual Learning

The human brain consists of two hemispheres (half spheres)—left and right (see **Figure 9.1**). Each of these hemispheres specializes in a different type of learning. The left hemisphere specializes in verbal learning; it deals primarily with words. In contrast, the right hemisphere specializes in visual–spatial learning; it deals primarily with perceiving images, patterns, and objects that occupy physical place or space. If you involve both hemispheres

FIGURE 9.1

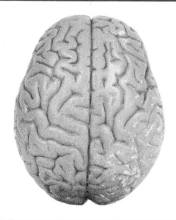

The human brain is comprised of two half spheres (hemispheres): the left hemisphere specializes in verbal learning, and the right hemisphere specializes in visual learning.

©JupiterImages Corporation.

of the brain while studying, two different memory traces are recorded—one in each major hemisphere (half) of the brain. This process of laying down dual memory traces (verbal and visual) is referred to as *dual coding* (Paivio 1990). Since two memory traces are better than one, dual coding results in deeper learning and longer retention.

To capitalize on the advantage of dual coding, be sure to use all the visual aids available to you, including those found in your textbook and those provided by your instructor in class. You can also create your own visual aids by representing what you're learning in the form of pictures, symbols, or concept maps—such as flowcharts, timelines, spider webs, wheels with hubs and spokes, or branching tree diagrams. (See **Figure 9.2** for an example of a concept map.) Visit https://coggle.it/ for help in creating your own concept/mind maps. When you transform material you're learning into a visual pattern, you're putting it into a form that's compatible with the

FIGURE 9.2: Concept Map for the Human Nervous System

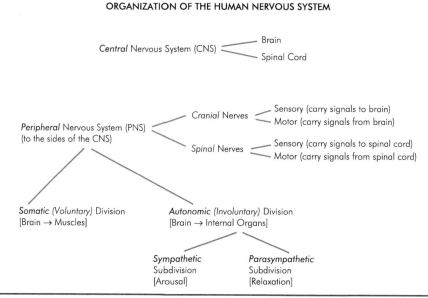

ORGANIZATION OF THE HUMAN NERVOUS SYSTEM

Central Nervous System (CNS)
— Brain
— Spinal Cord

Peripheral Nervous System (PNS)
(to the sides of the CNS)

Cranial Nerves
— Sensory (carry signals to brain)
— Motor (carry signals from brain)

Spinal Nerves
— Sensory (carry signals to spinal cord)
— Motor (carry signals from spinal cord)

Somatic (Voluntary) Division
[Brain → Muscles]

Autonomic (Involuntary) Division
[Brain → Internal Organs]

Sympathetic Subdivision
[Arousal]

Parasympathetic Subdivision
[Relaxation]

brain's tendency to store information in neurological networks (Willis 2006). Drawing also keeps you actively engaged in the process of learning, and by representing verbal information in visual form, you double the number of memory traces recorded in your brain. As the old saying goes, "A picture is worth a thousand words."

NOTE

Don't forget that drawings and visual illustrations can be more than just forms of artistic expression; they can also be powerful learning tools—you can draw to learn!

💡 Journal Reflection 9.3

Think of a course you're taking this term in which related pieces of information could be joined together to form a concept map. Make a rough sketch of this map that includes the information you need to remember.

_____

_____

_____

_____

Build Variety into the Study Process

Infusing variety and change of pace into your study routine can increase your motivation to study and your concentration while studying. Here are some practical strategies for doing so.

Mix it up: periodically shift the type of academic tasks you perform during a study session. Changing the nature of the academic work you do while studying increases your alertness and concentration by reducing *habituation*—attention loss that occurs after repeatedly engaging in the same type of mental task (Thompson 2009). You can combat attention loss due to habituation by varying the type of tasks you perform during a study session. For instance, you can shift periodically among tasks that involve reading, writing by hand, typing on a keyboard, reviewing, reciting, and solving problems. Similar to how athletes benefit from mixing different types of drills into their workouts (e.g., separate drills for building strength, speed, and endurance), studies of human learning show that "interleaving" (mixing) different academic subjects or academic skills while studying results in deeper learning and stronger memory (Brown, Roediger, and McDaniel 2014; Carey 2014).

Study in different places. In addition to spreading out your studying at different times, it's also a good idea to spread it out in different places. Studying in different locations provides different environmental contexts for learning; this reduces the amount of mental interference that normally builds up when all information is studied in the same place. The great public speakers in ancient Greece and Rome used this method of changing places to remember long speeches by walking through different rooms while rehearsing their speech, learning each major part of their speech in a different room (Higbee 2001).

Although it's useful to have set times for studying so that you get into a regular work routine, this doesn't mean you learn best by always studying in the same place. Periodically changing the academic tasks you perform while studying, as well as the environment in which you perform them, has been found to improve attention to (and retention of) what you're studying (Carey 2014; Druckman and Bjork 1994).

Break up long study sessions with short study breaks that involve physical activity (e.g., a short jog or brisk walk). Study breaks that include physical activity refresh the mind by giving it a rest from studying. Physical activity also stimulates the mind by increasing blood flow to your brain—helping you retain what you've studied and regain concentration for what you'll study next.

The following sections of this chapter contain strategies relating primarily to the third stage of this learning process and they are divided into three categories:

- Strategies to use *in advance* of a test,
- Strategies to use *during* a test, and
- Strategies to use *after* test results are returned.

PRE-TEST STRATEGIES: WHAT TO DO *IN ADVANCE* OF TESTS

NOTE

Notice how many of the strategies have these same three categories—pre-, during, and after a particular activity. In most cases, such as the pre-reading activities, these early activities are designed to build your comfort level before you actually start your work—reading or, in this case, test-taking.

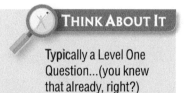

THINK ABOUT IT

Typically a Level One Question...(you knew that already, right?)

Your ability to remember material on a test that you studied prior to the test depends not only on how long and how well you studied, but also on the type of test questions used to test your memory. You may be able to remember what you've studied if you're tested in one format (e.g., multiple-choice) but not if tested in a different format (e.g., essay). Thus, the type of questions that will appear on an upcoming test should influence the type of study strategies you use to prepare for the test. Test questions can be classified into the following two major categories, depending on the type of memory required to answer them.

1. *Recognition test questions* ask you to select or choose the correct answer from choices that are provided for you. Falling into this category are multiple-choice, true–false, and matching questions. These test questions don't require you to supply or produce the correct answer on your own; instead, you're asked to recognize or pick out the correct answer—similar to picking out the "correct" criminal from a lineup of potential suspects.

2. *Recall test questions* require you to retrieve information you've studied and reproduce it on your own. As the word "recall" implies, you have to re-call ("call back") information and supply it yourself—as opposed to picking it out from information supplied for you. Recall test questions include essay and short-answer questions that require you to provide your own answer—in writing.

Since recognition test questions (e.g., multiple-choice or true–false) ask you to recognize or pick out the correct answer from answers provided for you, reading your class notes and textbook highlights and identifying key information may be an effective study strategy—because it matches the type of mental activity you'll be performing on the exam—reading test questions and identifying correct answers provided to you.

On the other hand, recall test questions, such as essay questions, require you to retrieve information and generate your own answers. They don't involve answer recognition; they require answer *production*—you produce the answer in writing. If you study for essay tests by just looking over your class notes and reviewing your reading highlights, you're using a study strategy that doesn't align with or match what you'll be expected to do on the test itself, which is to supply the correct information yourself. To prepare for essay test questions, you need to practice *retrieval*—recalling the information on your own—without looking at it.

Two essay-test preparation strategies that ensure you engage in memory retrieval are: (a) recitation and (b) creation of retrieval cues. Each of these strategies is described below.

Recitation

Stating aloud the information we want to remember—without looking at that information—is a memory-improvement strategy known as *recitation*. Memory is strengthened substantially when we reproduce on our own what we're trying to remember, instead of simply looking it over or rereading it (Roediger and Karpicke 2006). Recitation strengthens memory and better prepares you for essay tests because it:

- Requires *more mental effort* to dig out (retrieve) the answer on its own, which strengthens memory for the answer and allows the brain to practice exactly what it's expected to do on essay tests.
- Gives you clear *feedback* about whether or not you know the material. If you can't retrieve and recite it without looking at it, you know for sure that you won't be able to recall it at test time and need to study it further. You can provide yourself with this feedback by putting the question on one side of an index card and the answer on the flip side. If you find yourself flipping over the index card to look at the answer in order to remember it, this shows you can't retrieve the information on your own and you need to study it further. (To create electronic flash cards, see: www.studystack.com or studyblue.com)
- Encourages you to use your own words. If you can paraphrase it—rephrase what you're studying in your own words—it's a good indication you really understand it; and if you really understand it, you're more likely to recall it at test time.

Recitation can be done silently, by speaking aloud, or by writing out what you're trying to recall. Speaking aloud or writing out what you're reciting are particularly effective essay-test preparation strategies because they involve physical activity, which ensures that you're actively involved and engaged in the learning process.

Creating Retrieval Cues

A *retrieval cue* is a type of memory reminder (like a string tied around your finger) that brings back to mind what you've temporarily forgotten.

THINK ABOUT IT

Here is where you will see your professors focusing on Level Two and Level Three Questions.

NOTE

If you've been using Cornell Notes, you can check the questions on the left side of the pages of your notes—the answer should be on the right side of the page.

Research shows that students who can't remember previously studied information are better able to recall that information if they're given a retrieval cue. By taking pieces of information you need to recall on an essay test and organizing it into categories, you can then use the category names as retrieval cues at test time. Retrieval cues work because memories are stored in the brain as part of an interconnected network. So, if you're able to recall one piece or segment of the network (the retrieval cue), it can trigger recall of other pieces of information linked to it in the same network (Willingham 2009).

Another strategy for creating retrieval cues is to come up with your own catchword or catchphrase to "catch" or batch together all related ideas you're trying to remember. Acronyms can serve as catchwords, with each letter acting as a retrieval cue for a batch of related ideas. For instance, suppose you're studying for an essay test in abnormal psychology that will include questions testing your knowledge of different forms of mental illness. You could create the acronym SCOT as a retrieval cue to help you remember to include the following key elements of mental illness in your essay answers: Symptoms (S), Causes (C), Outcomes (O), and Therapies (T).

"Avoid flipping through notes (cramming) immediately before a test. Instead, do some breathing exercises and think about something other than the test."
—*Advice to first-year students from a college sophomore*

Strategies to Use *Immediately before* a Test

1. **Before the exam, take a brisk walk or light jog.** Physical activity increases mental alertness by increasing oxygen flow to the brain; it also decreases tension by increasing the brain's production of emotionally "mellowing" brain chemicals (e.g., serotonin and endorphins).
2. **Come fully armed with all the test-taking tools you need.** In addition to the basic supplies (e.g., no. 2 pencil, pen, blue book, Scantron, calculator, etc.), bring backup equipment in case you experience equipment failure (e.g., an extra pen in case your first one runs out of ink or extra pencils in case your original one breaks).
3. **Get to the classroom as early as possible.** Arriving early allows you to take a few minutes to get into a relaxed pretest state of mind by thinking positive thoughts, taking slow, deep breaths, and stretching your muscles.
4. **Sit in the same seat you normally occupy in class.** Research indicates that memory is improved when information is recalled in the same place where it was originally received or reviewed (Sprenger 1999). Thus, taking a test in the same place where you heard the information delivered will likely improve your test performance.

THINK ABOUT IT

It may surprise you to know that there also are some nutritional strategies you can use to strengthen your test performance. It's not so much what you eat but how much you eat. For example, it helps to eat a light breakfast on the day of a test. Bring an energy bar or piece of fruit to the exam if it's a long one where your energy might begin to lag. And, surprisingly, avoid caffeine! It could make you "antsy" or worse, make you wish you could take a bathroom break during the test!

"No man can be wise on an empty stomach."
—*George Eliot, 19th-century English novelist*

STRATEGIES TO USE *DURING* TESTS

1. **Before you receive a copy of the test, write down any hard-to-remember terms, formulas, and equations and any memory-retrieval cues you may have created as soon as you start the exam.** This will help ensure you don't forget this important information when you start focusing your attention on the test itself.

2. **First answer questions you know well and carry the most points.** Before automatically attacking the first question that appears on test, take a moment to

Consuming large doses of caffeine or other stimulants before exams is likely to increase your alertness, but it's also likely to increase your level of stress and test anxiety.

check out the overall layout of the test and note the questions that are worth the most points and the questions you're best prepared to answer. Tackle these questions first. Put a checkmark next to questions whose answers you're unsure of and come back to them later—after you've answered the questions you're sure of—to ensure you get these points added to your total test score before you run out of test time.

3. **If you experience "memory block" for information you know, use the following strategies to unlock it.**
   * Mentally put yourself back in the environment in which you studied. Recreate the situation by mentally picturing the place where you first heard or saw the information and where you studied it—including sights, sounds, smells, and time of day. This memory-improvement strategy is referred to as *guided retrieval*, and research supports its effectiveness for recalling information of any kind, including information recalled by eyewitnesses to a crime (Glenberg 1997; Glenberg et al. 1983).
   * Think of any idea or piece of information that relates to the information you can't remember. Studies show that when students forget information they studied, they're more likely to suddenly remember that information if they first recall a piece related to it in some way (Reed 2013). This strategy works because related pieces of information are typically stored in the same area of the brain—as part of an interconnected neural network.
   * Take your mind off the question by turning to another question. This frees your subconscious to focus on the forgotten information, which can suddenly trigger your conscious memory of it. Moving on to other test questions also allows you to find information included in later test questions that may enable you to recall information related to the earlier question that you previously forgot.
   * Before turning in your test, carefully review and double-check your answers. This is the critical last step in the test-taking process. Sometimes the performance pressure and anxiety associated

with test taking can cause students to overlook details, misread instructions, unintentionally skip questions, or make absent-minded mistakes. So take time to look over your answers and check for any mindless mistakes you may have made. Avoid the temptation to immediately cut out of class after answering the last test question because you're pooped out or stressed out. When you think about the amount of time and effort you put into preparing for the exam, it's foolish not to take a little more time to detect and correct any silly mistakes you made that could cost you points and lower your test score.

Notes on Pythagorean Theorem

Questions:	Notes:
What is the formula for Pythagorean theorem?	Pythagorean theorem: $a^2 + b^2 = c^2$.
What is a right triangle?	This theory involves right triangles of any size. A right triangle is a triangle with a right (90 degree) angle in it. Legs a, b, and hypotenuse c can be of any value as long as c is the longest of all three values.
When would this formula be used?	
How do I label the legs of a right triangle?	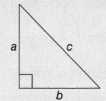 Hypotenuse: A hypotenuse is the longest leg of a right triangle and is always the side opposite of the right angle.
Which leg is the hypotenuse and what makes it significant?	
What are we looking to solve for in this problem?	It does not matter which leg a or b is as long as neither of them is representing the hypotenuse. That is to say leg a and leg b will never be labeled as the hypotenuse when using the Pythagorean theorem.
When plugging the values into the formula, how do I determine which leg is a, which is b, and which is c?	In order to solve for any leg or hypotenuse of a right triangle, take the given values and plug them into this formula: $$a^2 + b^2 = c^2.$$ Now solve for the missing value. When solving for the length of a leg or the hypotenuse in a right triangle always remember to plug your given values into the Pythagorean theorem:
How do I solve for c?	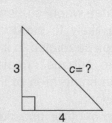 $3^2 + 4^2 = c^2.$ $9 + 16 = c^2.$ $25 = c^2.$ $\sqrt{25} = \sqrt{c^2}.$ $5 = c.$
How can I confirm my answer?	
What else is significant about this triangle?	

> The sum of the squares of the lengths of the legs of a right triangle is equal to the square of the length of the hypotenuse or
> $$a^2 + b^2 = c^2.$$
> where a and b are the legs of the right triangle and c is the hypotenuse.

Summary:
When working with right triangles and the length of the legs or the hypotenuse, it is important to always remember the Pythagorean theorem: $a^2 + b^2 = c^2$. This simple formula helps us determine the length of a missing side of a right triangle while providing an opportunity to check and confirm the discovered answer by plugging it back in and checking the answer. Similar questions can be posed to check the three different lengths.

American Government (Mock #2)
Notes on American Government: Political Socialization

Question/ Main Ideas:	Essential Questions:
What are the four factors that help shape a person's political socialization?	**Essential Questions:** How were your political attitudes formed and how were they influenced? How is the citizen plugged into the political system? **NOTES:** People peak out in terms of political socialization by 18–22 years of age and determine basic political attitudes and values for life. This socialization is similar to other countries. There are four basic "agents" of the political socialization process in American society. They are: 1. Family—most important as families impart values to their children. This included political party preference, ideology, and participation. • Includes voting or not voting habits, running for office. • If you get mixed views, some studies say in father dominate families, children follow mother. Another study says this is true because of the maternal nurturing. • Dewhirst anecdotal evidence says children follow the more outspoken parent. • If parents are politically super active, then children will be (Bushes, Kennedys, etc.). • Voter suppression backfired in 2012. 2. Schools—studies focus on public schools as there is less data on private. Impact is from civic education (proper role of a good citizen) and culture of school (cues to behave based on surroundings, neighborhood). Schools tend not to teach partisanship. • Children taught importance of compliance with law, rules are fair and punishment is an inevitable consequence of breaking law. • With age, they question fairness of the rules and are more aware of alternative roles and protesting. For example, Maryville High fired football coach and children left school protesting. 3. Peer groups tend to reinforce notions. Peer groups tend to be homogenous (same socio-economic background, religion, race, etc.). • College is also a factor as child ages; they listen to roommates, and find those disagreeing to be "ignorant" and those agreeing to be "smart." 4. Mass media—the real question is how and to what extent, not if, it effects political socialization. • Selective use of media: Narrowcasting—we tend to follow viewpoints that we know ahead of time agree with us • Selective perception—when two people see the same thing, hear the same thing, and come to different conclusions. For example, Kennedy vs. Nixon debates (Democrats said Kennedy won and Republicans said Nixon won). • Mental gymnastics—we will do any kind of rationalization other than say we were wrong. • Because of mass media, public more accepting of violence, and a growth in acceptance of violence as a solution (death penalty, violent intervention in other countries). Males more likely to grasp onto this than females. Video games increased if more violent which has created crime that has created political consequences.
Which of the four agents is most influential, or is one more influential than the others?	

(continued)

(continued)

	There is resocialization of political attitudes after childhood particularly when people reach college age. These changes are caused by the following.
	1. College: Females attending East coast colleges. Usually females come in very conservative and leave super liberal. They begin to accept people different from them, different background. The better educated, the more tolerant people tend to be of differences.
	2. Changes in socio-economic standings: As factory worker fathers send sons to college, they return making more money and go from more liberal to super conservative.
	3. Dramatic contemporary events: American Civil War resocialized generations and effected subsequent generations. The Great Depression is another example.
	4. Some resocialization occurs over slower periods of time. Civil Rights movement, women's rights, and immigration issues with Hispanics.
Why are females and males so different in how socio-economic standings and events affect them?	There are different ways that we are socialized by race, ethnicity, and subculture. People in the majority are socialized differently than those socialized in minority groups.
	• Efficacy: The feeling that what you do can will make a difference.
	• Socio-economic class differences: Lower political efficacy and less likely to vote Gender differences: boys taught politics as impersonal and instrumental and girls' views are in terms of benevolence and personal.
	Gender Gaps: Women tend to vote Democrat and Men republican.

Summary:
Our political views are shaped as children by family, school, media, and peers; however, they can be adjusted in early adulthood by college and social events. Other factors that can affect political views are race, ethnicity, gender, and subculture.

| Cornell Notes
AVID
Decades of College Dreams | Topic/Objective: Identify significant literary devices that define a writer's style and use to interpret work | Name: _____ |
| | | Comp. Lit. Class |

Essential Question:
How does Langston Hughes' poem, "Mother to Son", advice the reader to overcome difficulty and keep from giving up in life?

Questions:	Notes:
① What is the significance of the speaker in the poem?	① Speaker - ✱ voice that communicates a poem's ideas, actions, descriptions, & feelings - similar to narrator - can be unknown or specific (like character)
② How does a poet's choice of speaker affect the mood/meaning of a poem?	② Impt. - Poet's choice of speaker - contributes to the poems mood/meaning - who speaks is as impt. as what is said - different points of view regarding same event (ie. parent, child, elderly person) - ✱ the person telling the story gives point of view and affects the message told ← P.O.V ✱ writer's/poets style
③ How does Hughes use vocabulary to contribute to and convey his message?	③ Vocab - helps to understand meaning "crystal stair" = luxuries (metaphor) compares 2 things ie. "Life for me ain't been no crystal stair" "reachin'" - replace letter at end of word (dialect) "'cause" = because → Slang var. lang used by group speech patt.

Summary:
The speaker/voice in the poem is important because it communicates the ideas/feelings of the poem. Who the poet chooses as the speaker identifies the point of view and affects the message/meaning. Hughes uses vocabulary and style to convey the message that life is hard when Mother says "Life for me aint been no crystal staircase."

Questions:	Notes:	
④ How are literary elements used in "Mother to Son" to convey the author's message?	④ Literary Elements: Speaker: – voice of poem – creates tone (attitude) – attitude based on P.O.V. Character: – person	Ⓐ Mother (Hughes – author) Ⓑ mother – hardworking, determ. son – wants to give up because life is diff.
⑤ How does the poets choice of speaker contribute to the mood / meaning of the poem?	⑤ Mood: – emotional quality – atmosphere ← feeling get from poem Meaning: message in poem lesson (use on essay test as ex.)	Ⓒ Mother – uses her victory & survival of diff. exp. to motivate son Ⓓ Hard life – filled with many difficulties * – "tacks","splinters","torn-up boards" – "climbin', reachin', turnin'= struggle – "goin' in the dark" w/o light to guide the way not giving up is like climbing stairs... if she could do it so can he (Mother's message)

Theme of a fable equals its moral or teaching. The theme of a fiction work is its view about life and how people behave. You determine the theme by what the characters say, do and by the setting of the story or poem. It is the main communication by the author to the reader. It is an underlying truth that tries to connect with the reader.

Summary: The mother's words in Hughes' poem "Mother to Son" shows life as a climb up a staircase full of tacks, splinters, torn up boards and sometimes without light; but even though it is a hard climb, she says don't sit down on the steps and give up, keep climbing until you achieve

ANSWERING MULTIPLE-CHOICE TEST QUESTIONS

You're likely to encounter multiple-choice questions on college tests (particularly in large classes), on certification or licensing exams for particular professions (e.g., nursing and teaching), as well as on admissions tests for graduate school (e.g., master's and doctoral degree programs) and professional school (e.g., law school and medical school). Since you're likely to take multiple-choice tests frequently in college and beyond, this section of the text is devoted to a detailed discussion of strategies for taking such tests. These strategies are also applicable to *true–false* questions, which are really essentially multiple-choice questions with two choices: true or false.

1. **Read the question and think of the answer in your head before looking at the possible answers.** If the answer you thought of is in the list of possible answers, it is likely that is the correct answer. However, if you see an answer that is similar but you feel is more correct, select that answer. Thinking of the answer in your head allows you to recall what you studied before recognizing it.

2. **Read all choices listed and use a *process-of-elimination* approach.** Search for the correct answer by first eliminating choices that are clearly wrong; continue to do so until you're left with one choice that represents the best option. Keep in mind that the correct answer is often the one that has the highest probability or likelihood of being true; it doesn't have to be absolutely true—just truer than all the other choices listed.

To be or not to be?
(a) Orange Julius
(b) Julius Erving ("Dr. J.")
(c) Julius Caesar
(d) Caesar Salad
(e) Casarean Section

A process-of-elimination approach is an effective test-taking strategy to use when answering difficult multiple-choice questions.

3. **For a choice to be correct, the *entire statement* must be true.** If any part of the statement is inaccurate or false, eliminate it because it's an incorrect answer.

4. **Use *test-wise* strategies when you cannot narrow down your choice to one answer.** Your first strategy on any multiple-choice question should be to choose an answer based on your knowledge of the material, not by guessing the correct answer based on how the question is worded. However, if you've relied on your knowledge, used the process-of-elimination strategy to eliminate clearly wrong choices, and you're still left with two or more answers that appear to be correct, then you should turn to being *test wise*—use the wording or placement of the test question itself to increase your chances of selecting the correct answer (Flippo and Caverly 2009). Here are three test-wise strategies you can use for multiple-choice questions when more than one choice appears to be correct:
   - **Pick the answer that contains qualifying words.** Correct answers are more likely to contain modifying words such as "usually," "probably," "often," "likely," "sometimes," "perhaps," or "may." Knowledge often doesn't come neatly packaged as absolute or unqualified truths, so choices are more likely to be false if they make broad generalizations or contain words such as "always," "every," "never," "only," "must," and "completely."
   - **Pick the longest answer.** True statements often require more words to make them true.
   - **Pick a middle answer rather than the first or last answer.** If you've narrowed down the correct answer to either "a" or "c," go with "c." Similarly, if you've narrowed your choices to "b" or "d," your best bet may be to go with "b." Studies show that instructors have a tendency to place the correct answer in the middle, rather than as the first or last choice (Miller, Linn, and Gronlund 2012)—perhaps because they think the correct answer will be too obvious or stand out if it's placed at the top or bottom of the list.

5. **Check to be sure that your answers are aligned with the right questions.** When looking over your test before turning it in, search carefully for questions you may have skipped and intended to go back to later. Sometimes you may skip a test question on a multiple-choice test and forget to skip the number of that question on the answer form. This will throw off all your other answers by one space or line and result in a disastrous "domino effect" of wrong answers that can do major damage to your total test score.

6. **Don't feel that you must remain locked into your first answer.** When reviewing your answers on multiple-choice and true–false tests, don't be afraid to change an answer after you've given it more thought. Don't buy into the common belief that your first answer is always your best answer. There have been numerous studies on the topic of changing answers on multiple-choice and true–false tests, dating all the way back to 1928 (Kuhn 1988). These studies consistently show that most changed test answers go from being incorrect to correct,

resulting in improved test scores (Bauer, Kopp, and Fischer 2007; Prinsell, Ramsey, and Ramsey 1994).

If you have good reason to think an answer change should be made, don't be afraid to make it. The only exception to this general rule is when you find yourself changing many of your original answers; this may indicate that you were not well prepared for the exam and are just doing a lot of guessing and second-guessing.

Be sure you don't overthink the question and talk yourself into changing a correct answer. Sometimes "go with your gut" is the best decision if you are not sure. Don't change an answer if you are not sure the new answer is correct.

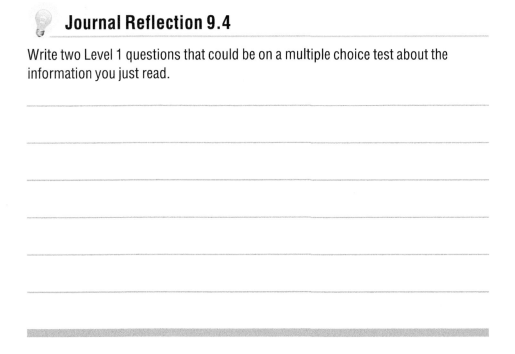

Journal Reflection 9.4

Write two Level 1 questions that could be on a multiple choice test about the information you just read.

ANSWERING ESSAY QUESTIONS

Along with multiple-choice questions, essay questions are among the most common types of test questions on college exams. The following strategies are recommended for strengthening your performance on essay questions.

1. **Look for "mental action" verbs in the question that point to the type of thinking your instructor expects you to demonstrate in your answer.** Box 9.2 contains a list of thinking verbs you're likely to see in essay questions and the type of mental action typically called for by each of these verbs. As you read this list, place a check mark next to the verbs that represent a type of thinking you've rarely or never been asked to do in the past.

Box 9.2

Mental Action Verbs Commonly Found in Essay-Test Questions

Analyze. Break the topic down into its key parts and evaluate the parts in terms of their accuracy, strengths and weaknesses.

Compare. Identify the similarities and differences between major concepts.

Contrast. Identify the differences between ideas, particularly sharp differences and clashing viewpoints.

Describe. Provide details (e.g., who, what, where, and when).

Discuss. Analyze (break apart) and evaluate the parts (e.g., strengths and weaknesses).

Document. Support your judgment and conclusions with scholarly references or research evidence.

Explain. Provide reasons that answer the questions "why?" and "how?"

> I keep six honest serving men. They taught me all I knew. Their names are what and why and how and when and where and who."
>
> —Rudyard Kipling, "The Elephant's Child," The Just-So Stories

Illustrate. Supply concrete examples or specific instances.

Interpret. Draw your own conclusion and explain why you came to that conclusion.

Support. Back up your ideas with logical reasoning, persuasive arguments, or statistical evidence.

Note

The operative word here is "quick"! You do not want to spend so much time on this that you do not have enough time to finish the exam.

2. **Make an outline of your key ideas before you start writing sentences.** First, do a quick "information dump" by jotting down the main points you plan to make in your essay answer in outline form. Outlines are effective for several reasons:

    *   **An outline ensures you don't forget to include your most powerful points.** The points listed in your outline serve as memory-retrieval cues that help you remember the "big picture" before getting lost in all the details.
    *   **An outline earns you points by improving your answer's organizational quality.** In addition to reminding you of the points you need to make, an outline gives you a plan for ordering your ideas in a sequence that flows smoothly from beginning to middle to end. One factor instructors consider when awarding points for an essay answers is how well that answer is organized. An outline will make your answer's organization clearer and more coherent to the reader, which will increase the amount of points you're awarded.
    *   **An outline helps reduce test anxiety.** By organizing your points ahead of time, you can focus on expressing (writing) those points without the added stress of figuring out *what* you're going to say at the same time you're trying to figure out *how* to say it.
    *   **An outline can add points to answers you don't have time to complete.** If you run out of test time before writing out your full answer to an essay question, an outline shows your instructor what you planned to include in your written answer. The outline itself is likely to earn you some points because it demonstrates your knowledge of the major points called for by the question.

Exhibit 1

Identical twins
Adoption
Parents/family tree

6/6

1. There are several different studies that scientists conduct, but one study that they conduct is to find out how genetics can influence human behavior in <u>identical twins</u>. Since they are identical, they will most likely end up very similar in behavior because of their identical genetic makeup. Although environment has some impact, genetics are still a huge factor and they will, more likely than not, behave similarly. Another type of study is with <u>parents and their family trees</u>. Looking at a subject's family tree will explain why a certain person is bipolar or depressed. It is most likely caused by a gene in the family tree, even if it was last seen decades ago. Lastly, another study is with adopted children. If an <u>adopted child</u> acts a certain way that is unique to that child, and researchers find the parents' family tree, they will most likely see similar behavior in the parents and siblings as well.

No freewill
No afterlife

2. The monistic view of the mind-brain relationship is so strongly opposed and criticized because there is a belief or assumption that <u>free will</u> is taken away from people. For example, if a person commits a horrendous crime, it can be argued "monistically" that the chemicals in the brain were the reason, and that a person cannot think for themselves to act otherwise. This view limits responsibility.

6/6

   Another reason that this view is opposed is because it has been said that <u>there is no</u> <u>afterlife</u>. If the mind and brain are one and the same, and there is <u>NO</u> difference, then once the brain is dead and is no longer functioning, so is the mind. Thus, it cannot continue to live beyond what we know today as life. <u>And</u> this goes against many religions, which is why this reason, in particular, is heavily opposed.

A college sophomore's answers to short essay questions that demonstrate effective use of bulleted lists or short outlines (in the side margin) to ensure recall of key points.

3. **Get directly to the point on each question.** Avoid elaborate introductions that take up your test time (and your instructor's grading time) but don't earn you any points. An answer that begins with the statement "This is an interesting question that we had a great discussion on in class . . ." is pointless because it doesn't add points to your test score. Timed essay tests often leave you pressed for time; don't waste that time on flowery introductions that contribute nothing to your test grade.

   One effective way to get directly to the point on essay questions is to include part of the question in the first sentence of your answer. For example, suppose the test question asks you to, "Argue for or against capital punishment by explaining how it will or will not reduce the nation's homicide rate." Your first sentence could be, "Capital punishment will not reduce the homicide rate for the following reasons . . ." Thus, your first sentence becomes your thesis statement—it points you directly to the major points you're going to make in your answer and earns immediate points for your answer.

4. **Answer essay questions with as much detail as possible.** Don't assume that your instructor already knows what you're talking about or will be bored by details. Instead, take the approach that you're

NOTE

As a general rule, it's better to over-explain than under-explain your answers to essay questions.

writing to someone who knows little or nothing about the subject—as if you're an expert teacher who is explaining it from scratch.

5. **Support your points with evidence—facts, statistics, quotes, or examples.** When you're answering essay questions, take on the mindset of a lawyer: make your case by presenting concrete evidence (exhibit A, exhibit B, etc.).

6. **Leave space between your answers to each essay question.** This strategy will enable you to easily add information to your original answer if you recall something later in the test that you would like to include.

7. **Proofread your answers for spelling and grammar.** Before turning in your test, proofread what you've written and correct any spelling or grammatical errors you find. Catching and correcting clerical errors will improve your test score. Even if your instructor doesn't explicitly state that grammar and spelling count toward your grade, these mechanical mistakes are still likely to influence your professor's overall evaluation of your written work.

8. **Neatness counts.** Many years of research indicate that neatly written essays are scored higher than sloppy ones, even if the answers are essentially the same (Huck and Bounds 1972; Hughes, Keeling, and Tuck 1983; Pai et al. 2010). These findings aren't surprising when you consider that grading essay answers is a time-consuming, labor-intensive task that requires your instructor to plod through multiple answers written by students with multiple styles of handwriting—ranging from crystal clear to quasi-cryptic. If you make your instructor's job a little easier by writing as clearly as possible and cleaning up any sloppy markings before turning in your test, you're likely to earn more points for your answers.

STRATEGIES FOR ONLINE TESTS

More instructors are using technology to enhance their courses. It is very possible that you could have to take an online test even when you are not taking an online course. When taking a test online, you should always read the instructions carefully. Below are some things you should consider when taking online tests.

1. **Online tests are often timed.** Because you are taking these tests outside of class, you are able to use your notes and books. For this reason, many instructors will place a time limit on the test. If you do not complete the test in time, it will shut off when your time is up and you won't be able to do the rest of the test. Be sure to study for online timed tests. You will not have enough time to look up all of the answers, and if you don't study, you won't do well.

2. **Backtracking might be prohibited.** Sometimes you have to answer a question before you can move on to the next question, and once you move on, you cannot go back and change an answer. If this is a timed test, be sure to use your time wisely and don't spend too much time on any one question.

If you have not taken an online test before, be sure to ask your instructor what to expect. Online tests can be created just like an in-class test. Don't assume that online tests will be made up of only multiple-choice and true–false questions.

Be sure you do not wait until the last minute to take your online test. Because you are dealing with technology something can (and often will) go wrong. Be prepared for something to go wrong (e.g., you lose your internet connection in the middle of the test) by giving yourself enough time to deal with any problems that might arise during the test.

When taking online tests, be sure you are using a reliable computer and you are free from anything that could take your focus away from the test (e.g., cell phone, children, etc.). If something does go wrong during the test, be sure to contact your instructor immediately.

POST-TEST STRATEGIES: WHAT TO DO *AFTER* RECEIVING YOUR TEST RESULTS

Successful test performance involves both forethought (preparation before the test) and afterthought (reflection after the test). Often, when students get a test back, they check to see what grade they got, then stuff it in a binder or toss it into the nearest wastebasket. Don't fall prey to this unproductive habit; instead, use your test results as feedback to improve your future performance. Reflect on your results and ask yourself: How can I learn from this? How can I put it to use to correct my mistakes and repeat my successes? Remember: A test score isn't an end result; it may tell you where you are now, but it doesn't tell you where you'll end up. Use your results as a means to another end—a higher score on the next test.

Journal Reflection 9.5

What do you usually do with tests and assignments after they're returned to you? Why?

_____

_____

_____

_____

_____

Listed below are strategies you can use to transform your test results into performance-enhancing feedback.

1. **When you get a test back, determine where you gained points and lost points.** Pinpoint what went right so you do it again, and troubleshoot what went wrong so you don't make the same mistake again. On test questions where you lost points, use the strategies summarized in **Box 9.3** to pinpoint the source of the problem.

NOTE

If you do poorly on an exam, don't get bitter—get better. View your mistakes in terms of what they can do for you, not to you. A poor test performance can be turned into a productive learning experience, particularly if it occurs early in the course when you're still learning the rules of the game. You can use your test results as a valuable source of feedback for improving your future performance and final course grade.

NOTE

Do not skip reviewing your test! This is the most important part of the learning process.

Box 9.3

Strategies for Pinpointing the Source of Lost Points on Tests

On test questions where you lost points, identify the stage in the learning process where the breakdown occurred by asking yourself the following questions.

- **Did I have the information I needed to answer the question correctly?** If you didn't have the information needed to answer the question, where should you have acquired it in the first place? Was it information presented in class that didn't get into your notes? If yes, consider adopting strategies for improving your classroom listening and note-taking (such as those found on **p. 358**). If the missing information was contained in your assigned reading, check whether you're using effective reading strategies (such as those listed on **pp. 348–349**).

- **Did I have the information but didn't study it because I didn't think it was important?** If you didn't expect the information to appear on the test, review the strategies for detecting the most important information delivered during class lectures and in reading assignments (see strategies on **p. 362**).

- **Did I study it, but didn't retain it?** Not remembering information you studied may mean one of three things:

  (a) You didn't learn it deeply and didn't lay down a strong enough memory trace in your brain for you to recall it at test time. This suggests you need to put in more study time or use a different study strategy to learn it more deeply (see **p. 272 for specific strategies**).

  (b) You may have tried to cram in too much study time just before the exam and may have not given your brain time enough to "digest" (consolidate) the information and store it in long-term memory. The solution may be to distribute your study time more evenly in advance of the next exam and take advantage of the "part-to-whole" study method (see **pp. 38–39**).

  (c) You studied hard and didn't cram, but you may need to study smarter or more strategically (see strategies on **p. 75**).

- **Did I study the material but didn't really understand it or learn it deeply?** This suggests you may need to self-monitor your comprehension more carefully while studying to track whether you're truly understanding the material and moving beyond **"shallow" or "surface" learning (see p. 45)**.

- **Did I know the material but lost points due to careless test-taking mistakes?** If this happened, the solution may simply be to take more time to review your test after completing it and check for absent-minded errors before turning it in. **Or,** your careless errors may have resulted from test anxiety that interfered with your concentration and memory. If you think this was the factor, consider using strategies for reducing test anxiety.

2. **Get feedback from your instructor.** Start by noting any written comments your instructor made on your exam; keep these comments in mind when you prepare for the next exam. You can seek additional feedback by making an appointment to speak with your instructor during office hours. Come to the appointment with a positive mindset about improving your next test performance, not complaining about your last test grade.

3. **Seek feedback from professionals in your Learning Center or Academic Support Center.** Tutors and other learning support professionals can also be excellent sources of feedback about adjustments you can make in your test preparation and test-taking strategies. Ask these professionals to take a look at your tests and seek their advice about how to improve your test performance.

4. **Seek feedback from your classmates.** Your peers can also be a valuable source of information on how to improve your performance. You can review your test with other students in class, particularly with

students who did well. Their test answers can provide you with models of what type of work your instructor expects on exams.

Teaming up after tests and assignments *early in the term* is especially effective because it enables you to get a better idea of what the instructor will expect from students throughout the remainder of the course. You can use this information as early feedback to diagnose your initial mistakes, improve your next performance, and raise your overall course grade—while there's still plenty of time in the term to do so. (See **Box 9.4** for a summary of the type of feedback you should seek from others to best strengthen your academic performance.)

BOX 9.4

Key Features of Performance-Enhancing Feedback

When asking for feedback from others on your academic performance, seek feedback that has the following performance-improvement features:

- Effective feedback is *specific.* Seek feedback that identifies precisely what you should do to improve your performance and how you should go about doing it. After a test, seek feedback that provides you with more than information about what your grade is, or why you lost points. Seek specific information about what particular adjustments you can make to improve your next performance.

- Effective feedback is *prompt.* After receiving your grade on a test or assignment, *immediately* review your performance and seek feedback as soon as possible. This is the time when you're likely most motivated to find out what you got right and wrong, and it's also the time when you're most likely to retain the feedback you receive.

- Performance-enhancing feedback is *proactive.* Seek feedback *early* in the learning process. Be sure to ask for feedback at the start of the term. This will leave you with plenty of time and opportunity to use the feedback throughout the term to accumulate points and earn a higher final grade.

STRATEGIES FOR REDUCING TEST ANXIETY

High levels of anxiety can interfere with the ability to recall information that's been studied and increases the risk of making careless concentration-related errors on tests—such as, overlooking key words in test questions (Fernández-Castillo and Caurcel 2014; Tobias 1993). Studies also show that students who experience high levels of test anxiety are more likely to use ineffective "surface"-level study practices that rely on memorization, rather than more effective "deep-learning" strategies that involve seeking meaning and understanding (Biggs and Tang 2007; Ramsden 2003). The strategies listed below can help you recognize and minimize test anxiety.

1. **Understand what test anxiety is and what it's not.** Don't confuse anxiety with stress. Stress is a physical reaction that prepares your body for action by arousing and energizing it; this heightened level of arousal and energy can actually strengthen your performance. In fact, to be totally stress-free during an exam may mean that you're too laid back and could care less about how well you're doing. Peak levels of performance—whether academic or athletic—are not achieved by

completely eliminating stress. Research shows that experiencing a *moderate* level of stress (neither too high nor too low) during exams and other performance-testing situations serves to maximize alertness, concentration, and memory (Sapolsky 2004).

If you often experience the following physical and psychological symptoms during tests, it probably means your stress level is too high and may be accurately called *test anxiety*.

- You feel bodily symptoms of tension during the test, such as pounding heartbeat, rapid pulse, muscle tension, sweating, or a queasy stomach.
- You have difficulty concentrating or maintaining your focus of attention while answering test questions.
- Negative thoughts and feelings rush through your head, such as fear of failure or self-putdowns (e.g., "I always mess up on exams.")
- You rush through the test just to get it over with and get rid of the uncomfortable feeling you're experiencing.
- Even though you studied and know the material, you go blank during the test and forget much of what you studied. However, after turning in the test and leaving the test situation, you're often able to remember the information you were unable to recall during the exam.

2. **Use effective test preparation strategies prior to the test.** Test-anxiety research indicates that college students who prepare well for tests and use effective study strategies prior to tests—such as those discussed in Chapter 6—experience less test anxiety during tests (Zeidner 1995; Zohar 1998). Studies also show that there is a strong relationship between test anxiety and procrastination—that is, students who put off studying to the very last minute are more likely to report higher levels of test anxiety (Carden, Bryant, and Moss 2004). The high level of pretest tension caused by last minute rushing to prepare for an exam often carries over to the test itself, resulting in higher levels of tension during the exam. Furthermore, late night cramming deprives the brain of stress-relieving dream (REM) sleep (Voelker 2004), causing the sleep-deprived student to experience higher levels of anxiety the following day—the day of the test.

3. **Stay focused on the test in front of you, not the students around you.** Don't spend valuable test time looking at what others are doing and wondering whether they're doing better than you are. If you came to the test well prepared and still find the test difficult, it's very likely that other students are finding it difficult too. If you happen to notice that other students are finishing before you do, don't assume they breezed through the test or that they're smarter than you. Their faster finish may simply reflect the fact that they didn't know many of the answers and decided to give up and get out, rather than prolong the agony.

4. **During the test, concentrate on the here and now.** Devote your attention fully to answering the test question that you're currently working on; don't spend time thinking (and worrying) about the test's outcome or what your grade will be.

5. **Focus on the answers you're getting right and the points you're earning, rather than worrying about what you're getting wrong and how many points you're losing.** Our thoughts can influence our

emotions (Ellis 2004), and positive emotions—such as those associated with optimism and a sense of accomplishment—can improve mental performance by enhancing the brain's ability to process, store, and retrieve information (Fredrickson and Branigan 2005). One way to maintain a positive mindset is to keep in mind that college tests are often designed to be more difficult than high school tests, so it's less likely that students will get 90% to 100% of the total points. You can still achieve a good grade on a college test without having to achieve a near-perfect test score.

6. **Don't forget that it's just a test, not a measure of your intelligence, academic ability, or self-worth.** No single test can measure your true intellectual capacity or academic talent. In fact, the test grade you earn may not be a true indicator of how much you've actually learned. A low test grade also doesn't mean you're not capable of doing better work or destined to end up with a poor grade in the course—particularly if you adopt a "growth mindset" that views mistakes as learning opportunities and uses test results as feedback for improving future performance.

7. **If you continue to experience test anxiety after trying to overcome it on your own, seek assistance from a professional in your Learning (Academic Support) Center or Personal Counseling Office.** You can try to overcome test anxiety (or any other personal issue) through the use of self-help strategies. However, if the problem persists after you've done your best to overcome it, there's no need to keep struggling on your own; instead, it's probably time to seek help from others. This doesn't mean you're weak or incompetent; it means you have the emotional intelligence and resourcefulness to realize your limitations and capitalize on the support networks available to you.

> If you focus on growth . . . on making progress instead of proving yourself, you are less likely to get depressed because you won't see setbacks and failures as reflecting your own self worth." And you are less likely to stay depressed, because feeling bad makes you want to work harder and keep striving."
>
> —Heidi Grant Halvorson, psychologist and author of *Succeed: How We Can Reach Our Goals*

CHAPTER SUMMARY AND HIGHLIGHTS

Effective performance on college tests involves strategies used in advance of the test, during the test, and after test results are returned. Good test performance starts with good test preparation and awareness of the type of test questions you will be expected to answer (e.g., multiple-choice or essay). Test questions can be classified into two major categories, depending on the type of memory required to answer them: (1) *recognition* questions and (2) *recall* questions. Each of these types of questions tests your knowledge and memory in a different way.

Recognition test questions ask you to select or choose the correct answer from choices provided for you. Falling into this category are multiple-choice, true–false, and matching questions. These test questions don't require you to supply or produce the correct answer on your own; instead, you recognize or pick out the correct answer. Since recognition test questions ask you to recognize or select the correct answer from among answers provided for you, reviewing your class notes and textbook highlights may be an effective study strategy for multiple-choice and true–false test questions because it matches the type of mental activity you'll be asked to perform on the exam—which is to read test questions and look for the correct answer.

Recall test questions, on the other hand, require you to retrieve information you've studied and reproduce it on your own. This means you have to recall (re-call or "call back") the information you studied and supply it yourself. Recall test questions include essay and short answer questions; these questions don't involve answer recognition, but answer *production*— you produce the answer in writing. Studying for these types of test questions require *retrieval*—such as reciting the information without looking at it.

Effective test performance not only involves effective test-preparation strategies, but also effective test-taking strategies. For multiple-choice tests, effective test-taking strategies include using a *process-of-elimination* approach to weed out incorrect answers before identifying the best option, and *test-wise* strategies that use the wording of test questions to increase the likelihood of choosing the correct answer (e.g., choosing the longest answer and eliminating answers that contain absolute truths or broad generalizations).

Lastly, effective test performance involves carefully reviewing test results and using them as feedback to improve your future performance and final course grade. When test results are returned, determine where you earned and lost points. Pinpoint what went right so you continue doing it, and troubleshoot what went wrong so you prevent it from happening again.

LEARNING MORE THROUGH THE WORLD WIDE WEB: INTERNET-BASED RESOURCES

For additional information on strategic test-taking and managing test anxiety, see the following websites:

Test-Taking Strategies:
https://miamioh.edu/student-life/rinella-learning-center/academic-counseling/self-help/test-taking/index.html
https://www.stmarys-ca.edu/academics/academic-resources-support/student-academic-support-services/tutorial-academic-skills-8

Overcoming Test Anxiety:
http://www.studygs.net/tstprp8.htm
http://www.sic.edu/files/uploads/group/34/PDF/TestAnxiety.pdf

REFERENCES

Bauer, D., V. Kopp, and M. R. Fischer. 2007. "Answer Changing in Multiple Choice Assessment: Change that Answer When in Doubt and Spread the Word!" *BMC Medical Education* 7: 28–32.

Biggs, J., and C. Tang. 2007. *Teaching for Quality Learning at University.* 3rd ed. Buckingham: SRHE and Open University Press.

Brown, P. C., H. L. Roediger III, and M. A. McDaniel. 2014. *Make it Stick: The Science of Successful Learning.* Cambridge, MA: The Belknap Press of Harvard University Press.

Carden, R., C. Bryant, and R. Moss. 2004. "Locus of Control, Test Anxiety, Academic Procrastination, and Achievement among College Students." *Psychological Reports* 95(2): 581–82.

Carey, B. 2014. *How We Learn.* London: Random House.

Crawford, H. J., and C. H. Strapp. 1994. "Effects of Vocal and Instrumental Music on Visuospatial and Verbal Performance as Moderated by Studying Preference and Personality." *Personality and Individual Differences* 16(2): 237–45.

Druckman, D., and R. A. Bjork, eds. 1994. *Learning, Remembering, Believing: Enhancing Human Performance.* Washington, DC: National Academies Press.

Dunlosky, J., K. A. Rawson, E. J. Marsh, M. J. Nathan, and D. T. Willingham. 2013. "Improving Students' Learning with Effective Learning Techniques: Promising Directions from Cognitive and Educational Psychology." *Psychological Science in the Public Interest* 14(1): 4–58.

Ellis, A. 2004. *Rational Emotive Behavior Therapy: It Works for Me It Can Work for You*. Amherst, NY: Prometheus Books.

Fernández-Castillo, A., and M. J. Caurcel. 2014. "State Test-anxiety, Selective Attention and Concentration in University Students." *International Journal of Psychology* 50(4): 265–71.

Flippo, R. F., and D. C. Caverly. 2009. *Handbook of College Reading and Study Strategy Research*. 2nd ed. New York: Lawrence Erlbaum Associates.

Fredrickson, B. L., and C. Branigan. 2005. "Positive Emotions Broaden the Scope of Attention and Thought-action Repertoires." *Cognition & Emotion* 19: 313–32.

Glenberg, A, M. 1997. "What Memory Is for." *Behavioral and Brain Sciences* 20: 1–55.

Higbee, K. L. 2001. *Your Memory: How It Works and How to Improve It*. New York: Marlowe.

Howard, P. J. 2014. *The Owner's Manual for the Brain: Everyday Applications of Mind-brain Research*. 4th ed. New York: HarperCollins.

Huck, S., and W. Bounds. 1972. "Essay Grades: An Interaction between Graders' Handwriting Clarity and the Neatness of Examination Papers." *American Educational Research Journal* 9(2): 279–83.

Hughes, D. C., B. Keeling, and B. F. Tuck. 1983. "Effects of Achievement Expectations and Handwriting Quality on Scoring Essays." *Journal of Educational Measurement* 20(1): 65–70.

Jensen, E. 2008. *Brain-based Learning*. Thousand Oaks, CA: Corwin Press.

Kintsch, W. 1994. "Text Comprehension, Memory, and Learning." *American Psychologist* 49: 294–303.

Kuhn, L. 1988. "What Should We Tell Students about Answer Changing?" *Research Serving Teaching* 1(8).

Malmberg, K. J., and K. Murnane. 2002. "List Composition and the Word-frequency Effect for Recognition Memory." *Journal of Experimental Psychology: Learning, Memory, and Cognition* 28: 616–30.

Marzano, R. J., D. J. Pickering, and J. Pollock. 2001. *Classroom Instruction That Works: Research-based Strategies for Increasing Student Achievement*. Alexandria, VA: Association for Supervision and Curriculum Development.

Mayer, R. E. 2002. "Rote Versus Meaningful Learning." *Theory into Practice* 41(4): 226–32.

Miller, M. D., R. L. Linn, and N. E. Gronlund. 2012. *Measurement and Assessment in Teaching*. 7th ed. Englewood Cliffs, NJ: Pearson.

Murname, K., and R. M. Shiffrin. 1991. "Interference and the Representation of Events in Memory." *Journal of Experimental Psychology: Learning, Memory, & Cognition* 17: 855–74.

National Resource Center for the First-year Experience and Students in Transition. 2004. *The 2003 Your First College Year (YFCY) Survey*. Columbia, SC: Author.

Pai, M. R., N. Sanji, P. G. Pai, and S. Kotian. 2010. "Comparative Assessment in Pharmacology Multiple Choice Questions versus Essay with Focus on Gender Differences." *Journal of Clinical and Diagnostic Research* [serial online] 4(3): 2515–20.

Paivio, A. 1990. *Mental Representations: A Dual Coding Approach*. New York: Oxford University Press.

Pascarella, E., and P. Terenzini. 1991. *How College Affects Students: Findings and Insights from Twenty Years of Research*. San Francisco: Jossey-bass.

Pascarella, E., and P. Terenzini. 2005. *How College Affects Students: A Third Decade of Research*. vol. 2. San Francisco: Jossey-bass.

Prinsell, C. P, P. H. Ramsey, and P. P. Ramsey. 1994. "Score Gains, Attitudes, and Behaviour Changes due to Answer-changing Instruction." *Journal of Educational Measurement* 31: 327–37.

Ramsden, P. 2003. *Learning to Teach in Higher Education*. 2nd ed. London: RoutledgeFalmer.

Reed, S. K. 2013. *Cognition: Theory and Applications*. 3rd ed. Belmont, CA: Wadsworth/Cengage.

Roediger, H., and J. Karpicke. 2006. "The Power of Testing Memory: Basic Research and Implications for Educational Practice." *Perspectives on Psychological Science* 1(3): 181–210.

Sapolsky, R. 2004. *Why Zebras Don't Get Ulcers*. New York: W. H. Freeman.

Sprenger, M. 1999. *Learning and Memory: The Brain in Action*. Alexandria, VA: Association for Supervision and Curriculum Development.

Thompson, R. F. 2009. "Habituation: A hHistory." *Neurobiology of Learning and Memory* 92(2): 127–34.

Tobias, S. 1993. *Overcoming Math Anxiety*. New York: W.W. Norton.

Voelker, R. 2004. "Stress, Sleep Loss, and Substance Abuse Create Potent Recipe for College Depression." *Journal of the American Medical Association* 291: 2177–79.

Willingham, D. B. 2009. *Cognition: The Thinking Animal*. Upper Saddle River, NJ: Pearson.

Willis, J. 2006. *Research-based Strategies to Ignite Student Learning: Insights from a Neurologist and Classroom Teacher*. Alexandria, VA: ASCD.

Zeidner, M. 1995. "Adaptive Coping with Test Situations: A Review of the Literature." *Educational Psychologist* 30(3), 123–33.

Zohar, D. 1998. "An Additive Model of Test Anxiety: Role of Exam-specific Expectations." *Journal of Educational Psychology* 90: 330–40.

Chapter 9 Exercises

9.1 Quote Reflections

Review the sidebar quotes contained in this chapter and select two that were especially meaningful or inspirational to you.

For each quote, provide a three- to five-sentence explanation why you chose it.

9.2 Reality Bite

Bad Feedback: Shocking Midterm Grades

Fred has enjoyed his first weeks on campus. He has met lots of people and really likes being in college. He's also very pleased to discover that, unlike high school, his college schedule doesn't require him to be in class for five to six hours per day. That's the good news. The bad news is that unlike high school, where his grades were all As and Bs, Fred's first midterm grades in college are three Cs, one D, and one F. He's stunned and a bit depressed by his midterm grades because he thought he was doing well. Since he never received grades this low in high school, he's beginning to think that he's not college material and may flunk out.

Reflection Questions

1. What factors may have caused or contributed to Fred's bad start?

2. What are Fred's options at this point?

3. What do you recommend Fred do right now to get his grades up and avoid being placed on academic probation?

4. What might Fred do in the future to prevent this midterm setback from happening again?

9.3 Self-Assessment of Test-Taking Habits and Strategies

Rate yourself in terms of how frequently you use these test-taking strategies according to the following scale: 4 = always, 3 = sometimes, 2 = rarely, 1 = never

1. I take tests in the same seat I usually sit in to take class notes.	4	3	2	1
2. I answer easier test questions first.	4	3	2	1
3. I use a process-of-elimination approach on multiple-choice questions to eliminate choices until I find one that is correct or appears to be the most accurate option.	4	3	2	1
4. Before answering essay questions, I look for key action words indicating what type of thinking I should display in my answer (e.g., "analyze," "compare").	4	3	2	1
5. On essay questions, I outline or map out the major ideas I'll include in my answer before I start writing sentences.	4	3	2	1
6. I look for information included on the test that may help me answer difficult questions or that may help me remember information I've forgotten.	4	3	2	1

7. I leave extra space between my answers to essay questions in case I want to come back and add more information later.   4   3   2   1

8. I carefully review my work, double-checking for errors and skipped questions before turning in my tests.   4   3   2   1

Self-Assessment Reflections

Which of the above strategies do you already use?

Of the ones you don't use, which one are you *most* likely to implement and *least* likely to implement? Why?

9.4 Midterm Self-Evaluation

At this point in the term, you may be experiencing the "midterm crunch"—a wave of midterm exams and due dates for assignments. This is a good time to step back and assess your academic progress.

Using the form below, list the courses you're taking this term and the grades you are currently receiving in each of these courses. If you don't know what your grade is, take a few minutes to check your syllabus for your instructor's grading policy and add up your scores on completed tests and assignments; this should give you at least a rough idea of where you stand in your courses. If you're having difficulty determining your grade in a course, even after checking your course syllabus and returned tests or assignments, ask your instructor how you could estimate your current grade.

	Course No.	Course Title	Grade
1.			
2.			
3.			
4.			
5.			

Reflection Questions

1. Were these the grades you *expected*? If not, were they better or worse than you anticipated?

2. Were these the grades you were *hoping* for? Are you pleased or disappointed?

3. Do you see any patterns in your performance that suggest what you're doing well and what you need to improve?

4. If you had to pinpoint one action you could immediately take to improve your lowest course grades, what would it be?

9.5 Calculating Your Midterm Grade Point Average

Use the information below to calculate what your grade point average (GPA) would be if your current course grades turn out to be your final grades for the term.

How to Compute Your Grade Point Average (GPA)

Most colleges and universities use a grading scale ranging from 0 to 4 to calculate a student's grade point average (GPA) or QPA (quality point average). Some schools use a grading system that involves only letters (A, B, etc.), while other institutions use letters as well as pluses and minuses (A–, B+, etc.). Check you college catalog or student handbook to determine what grading system is used at your campus.

The typical point value (points earned) by different letter grades are listed below.

Grade = Point Value

A = **4.0**
A– = 3.7
B+ = 3.3
B = **3.0**
B– = 2.7
C+ = 2.3
C = **2.0**
C– = 1.7
D+ = 1.3
D = **1.0**
D– = .7
F = 0

1. **Calculate the grade points you're earning in each of your courses this term by multiplying the course's number of units (credits) by the point value of the grade you're now earning in the course.** For instance, if you have a grade of B in a three-unit course, that course is earning you 9 grade points; if you have a grade of A in a two-unit course, that course is earning you 8 grade points.

2. **Calculate your grade point average by using the following formula:**

$$\text{GRADE POINT AVERAGE (GPA)} = \frac{\text{Total Number of Grade Points for all Courses}}{\text{Divided by Total Number of Course Units}}$$

For instance, see the fictitious example below:

Course	Units	×	Grade	=	Grade Points
Roots of Rock 'n' Roll	3	×	C (2)	=	6
Daydreaming Analysis	3	×	A (4)	=	12
Surfing Strategies	1	×	A (4)	=	4
Wilderness Survival	4	×	B (3)	=	12
Sitcom Analysis	2	×	D (1)	=	2
Love and Romance	3	×	A (4)	=	12
	16				**48**

$$\text{GPA} = \frac{48}{16} = 3.0$$

Reflection Questions

1. What is your GPA at this point in the term?

2. At the start of this term, was this the GPA you expected to attain? If there is a gap between the GPA you expected to achieve and the GPA you now have, what do you think accounts for this discrepancy?

3. Do you think your actual GPA at the end of the term will be higher or lower than it is now? Why?

Note: It's very typical for GPAs to be lower in college than they were in high school, particularly during the first year of college. Here are the results of one study that compared students' high school GPAs with their GPAs after their first year of college:

- A total of 29% of beginning college students had GPAs of 3.75 or higher in high school, but only 17% had GPAs that high at the end of their first year of college.

- A total of 46% had high school GPAs between 3.25 and 3.74, but only 32% had GPAs that high after the first year of college (National Resource Center for the First-Year Experience and Students in Transition 2004).

Chapter 9 Reflection

What are some ways that you currently prepare for tests that do not seem to be working? Why do you think these methods of preparing for tests do not work?

List and explain three ways you can change your current methods of preparing for tests that you believe will help you perform better on tests.

1.

2.

3.

What are two things you can do during the test that will help you perform better?

1.

2.

What are two things you can do after you get your test back that can help you perform better on future tests?

1.

2.

CHAPTER 10

ACADEMIC PLANNING AND DECISION-MAKING

This chapter will help you develop a plan for making educational decisions that will best enable you to reach your long-term goals.

Students will learn the effective strategies to pursue the educational path that meets their personal interests, talents, and goals.

Equip you with effective strategies for pursuing an educational path that's compatible with your personal interests, talents, and goals.

 Journal Reflection 10.1

At this point in your college experience, are you decided or undecided about a major?

1. What resources or mentors have you consulted in relationship to selection of a major and/or minor? If you're undecided, what subjects are you considering as possible majors?

2. If you're decided:

   a) What's your choice?

b)   What led you to this choice?

_____

_____

_____

_____

c)   How sure are you about this choice? (Circle one.)

absolutely sure   fairly sure   not too sure   likely to change

TO BE OR NOT TO BE DECIDED: WHAT RESEARCH SHOWS ABOUT STUDENTS' CHOICE OF A COLLEGE MAJOR

At age five, Joe told his parents he wanted to be a fireman. They laughed and wondered how many times he would change his mind before he started on a career. As a teen, he dutifully went to a four-year college and graduated. And then he went to Firefighting Academy. At age 30, Joe had been a fireman for seven years and loved the work. "It's just what I wanted." Some people do know what they want to major in from the time their children. However, most aren't so lucky.

Studies of student decisions about a college major show that:

- Fewer than 10% of new college students feel they know a great deal about the field they intend to major in;
- As students proceed through the first year of college, they grow more uncertain about the major they chose when they entered college;
- More than one-third of new students change their mind about their major during their first year of college;
- Only one in three college seniors eventually major in the same field they had in mind when they began college (Cuseo 2005; HERI 2014).

These findings demonstrate that the vast majority of first-year students are uncertain about their academic specialization. Typically, they don't make a final decision about their major *before* starting college; instead, they reach that decision *during* their college experience.

Some are undecided because they have multiple interests; this is a healthy form of indecision indicating they have a wide range of interests and a high level of intellectual curiosity. Students may also be undecided because they are reflective and deliberate decision-makers who prefer to explore their options carefully before making a firm and final commitment. In a national study of students who were undecided about a major at the start of college, 43% of them had some majors in mind but weren't quite ready to make a final commitment to one of them (Gordon and Steele 2003).

NOTE

Thus, being initially undecided about a major isn't something you should be worried or embarrassed about; it doesn't mean you're clueless. It may just mean you're open-minded. In fact, studies show that new students are often undecided for very good reasons.

For new students to be at least somewhat uncertain about their educational goals at the start of their college experience is only natural because they haven't yet experienced the variety of subjects included in the college curriculum. One goal of general education courses is to help new students develop the critical thinking skills needed to make wise choices and well-informed decisions, including their decision about a college major.

The college curriculum will introduce you to new fields of study, some of which you never experienced before and all of which represent possible choices for a college major. A key benefit of experiencing the variety of courses in the general education curriculum is that they help you become more aware of the range of academic disciplines and subject areas available to you as potential majors, while at the same time, helping you become more aware of yourself. As you gain experience with the college curriculum, you will gain greater self-insight into your academic interests, strengths, and weaknesses. Take this self-knowledge into consideration when choosing a major because you want to pursue a field that capitalizes on your intellectual curiosity, abilities, and talents.

THE IMPORTANCE OF LONG-RANGE EDUCATIONAL PLANNING

Being undecided doesn't mean you have no plan; your plan is to find out what your major will be. Now is the time to start the major selection process by testing your interests and narrowing down your choices. If you're at a community college and planning to transfer, it's better to reach a sound decision about a major sooner rather than later because you will probably have to declare a major at the time you apply to a four-year campus and begin major-specific coursework almost immediately after you're accepted (Miller and Nadler 2004). Thus, it's important to develop an educational plan during your first term in college so that you can immediately begin to select and enroll in transferable courses.

On the other hand, if you've already chosen a major, this doesn't mean that you'll never have to give any more thought to that decision. Instead, you should continue the exploration process by carefully testing your first choice, making sure it's a choice that is compatible with your abilities and interests. Take the approach that this is your *current* choice; whether it becomes your firm and *final* choice will depend on how well you perform (and how interested you are) in the first courses you take in the field.

Developing a long-range educational plan enables you to take a *proactive* approach to your education—you take charge of it by taking early and preemptive action that anticipates your future. Rather than waiting and passively letting your educational future happen *to* you, advanced planning makes it happen *for* you.

EDUCATIONAL PATHWAYS FOR COMMUNITY COLLEGE STUDENTS

As a beginning community college student, you have two primary educational paths to choose from: Career Technical Education or Transfer Preparation.

NOTE

Developing a long-range educational plan takes time so make an appointment to meet with an advisor at a time other than during the mad rush of course registration. This will give you both the opportunity to focus on your transfer plans and long-range goals, rather than focusing on short-term scheduling of next term classes.

NOTE

Keep in mind that a long-range educational plan isn't something set in stone. As you gain more educational experience, your specific academic and career interests may change and so may the specifics of your long-range plan. The purpose of a plan is not to tie you up or pin you down, but provide you with a roadmap to keep you on track and moving along the right pathway.

1. **Career Technical Education Pathway.** This pathway prepares you for a specific particular occupation or trade and immediate employment after completing either (a) a short-term (e.g., one year or less) credential or certificate program, or (b) a two-year associate degree—such as an *Associate of Applied Science (AAS) or an Associate of Applied Technology (AAT)* degree. Some community colleges offer "stackable credentials" that allow you to earn a short-term credential that you can build on later by taking additional courses to earn longer-term credentials that allow you to move up a career ladder and advance to higher-paying positions. For example, you can continue to earn educational credits along the pathway to an associate degree by completing a series of shorter credentials that focus on mastering skills for specific technologies, which prepare them to gain entry level work in the field of information technology and eventually advance to higher positions in that field.

2. **Transfer Preparation Pathway.** This pathway prepares you for transfer to a four-year college or university and a four-year (bachelor's) degree. These programs typically lead to degrees such as an *Associate of Arts (AA)* or an *Associate of Science (AS)*. Some community colleges offer *Inverted Degree* programs, whereby students can complete a degree in a career technical education program (e.g., an AAS degree) and then transfer to a four-year college to complete general education to earn a bachelor's degree. Many community colleges also have *Reverse Transfer* programs whereby students who transfer to a four-year college before completing an associate degree are allowed to transfer credits completed at the four-year campus back to their previous two-year campus to receive the Associate Degree.

Journal Reflection 10.2

Are you currently planning to pursue a career technical education pathway or a transfer preparation pathway? How sure are you about this choice?

_____

_____

_____

_____

_____

_____

BOX 10.1

A Checklist of Course-Recognition Registration Reminders for Community College Students

Achieving your educational goals requires both long- and short-range planning. Your long-range plan involves completing your degree, and your short-range plan involves continuing your enrollment in college from term to term. When planning to register for the next academic term, keep the following list of reminders handy to ensure that your term-to-term transition proceeds smoothly.

- Check the registration dates and be prepared to register at the earliest date that's available to you.
- Check with an academic adviser to be sure that you're planning to take the right classes for your program, major, and any four-year school you plan to transfer to.

- Let your advisor know what your educational goals are and if you've changed your goals since the last time you registered.
- Let your advisor know the total number of hours per week you plan to work so that you create a schedule that will allow you to successfully balance school-work and for-pay work.
- If you're receiving financial aid, meet with a financial aid counselor or advisor to be sure that you have adequate funds to cover next term's tuition, book costs, and parking fees.
- Once you've registered periodically check the status of your courses, because last-minute changes can occur in the time and day when courses meet and it's possible that one of your courses might be canceled (e.g., due to insufficient enrollment).

FACTORS TO CONSIDER WHEN CHOOSING A MAJOR OR FIELD OF STUDY

Self-awareness is the critical first step in the process of making any effective personal decision or choice. You need to know yourself well before knowing what major is best for you. When choosing a major, self-awareness should include awareness of your:

- Mental abilities and talents
- Personal interests and curiosities

Research indicates that students who choose majors that are compatible with their personal characteristics are more likely to be academically successful in college and complete their degree (Leuwerke et al. 2004; Pascarella and Terenzini 2005).

Multiple Intelligences: Becoming Aware of Your Mental Abilities and Talents

Based on studies of gifted and talented individuals, experts in different lines of work, and research on the human brain, psychologist Howard Gardner (1993, 1999, 2006) has identified the multiple forms of intelligence listed in **Box 10.2.** Keep these forms of intelligence in mind when you're choosing a college major because different majors emphasize different intellectual skills (Brooks 2009). Ideally, you want to pursue an academic field that allows you to utilize your strongest mental attributes and talents. If you do, you're likely to master the concepts and skills required by your major more efficiently and more deeply, excel in courses required by your major, and experience a higher level of academic self-confidence and motivation to continue your education.

> "Exceptional individuals have a special talent for identifying their own strengths and weaknesses."
>
> —*Howard Gardner,*
> Extraordinary Minds

BOX 10.2

Multiple Forms of Intelligence

As you read through the following forms of intelligence, place a checkmark next to the type that you think represents your strongest ability or talent. (You can possess more than one type.)

1. *Linguistic* Intelligence: ability to comprehend the meaning of words and communicate through language (e.g., verbal skills relating to speaking, writing, listening, and learning foreign languages).
2. *Logical-Mathematical* Intelligence: aptitude for understanding logical patterns (e.g., making and following logical arguments) and solving mathematical problems (e.g., working well with numbers and quantitative calculations).
3. *Spatial* Intelligence: aptitude for visualizing relationships among objects arranged in different spatial positions and ability to perceive or create visual images (e.g., forming mental images of three-dimensional objects; detecting detail in objects or drawings; drawing, painting, sculpting, and graphic design; strong sense of direction and capacity to navigate unfamiliar places).
4. *Musical* Intelligence: ability to appreciate or create rhythmical and melodic sounds (e.g., playing, writing, or arranging music).
5. *Interpersonal (Social)* Intelligence: ability to relate to others and accurately identify their needs, motivations, or emotional states; effective at expressing emotions and feelings to others (e.g., interpersonal communication skills, ability to accurately "read" the feelings of others and meet their emotional needs).

6. *Intrapersonal (Self)* Intelligence: ability to introspect and understand your own thoughts, feelings, and behaviors (e.g., capacity for personal reflection; emotional self-awareness; self-insight into personal strengths and weaknesses).
7. *Bodily–Kinesthetic (Psychomotor)* Intelligence: ability to control one's own body skillfully and learn through bodily sensations or movements; skilled at tasks involving physical coordination, working well with hands, operating machinery, building models, assembling things, and using technology.

 I used to operate a printing press. In about two weeks I knew how to run it and soon after I could take the machine apart in my head and analyze what each part does, how it functioned, and why it was shaped that way.

—*Response of college sophomore to the questions: "What are you really good at? What comes easily or naturally to you?"*

8. *Naturalist* Intelligence: ability to carefully observe and appreciate features of the natural environment; keen awareness of nature or natural surroundings; ability to understand causes and consequences of events occurring in the natural world.
9. *Existential* Intelligence: ability to conceptualize phenomena and ponder experiences that go beyond sensory or physical evidence, such as questions involving the origin of human life and the meaning of human existence.

Sources: Gardner (1993, 1999, 2006).

💡 Journal Reflection 10.3

Look back at the nine forms of intelligence listed in **Box 10.2.**

Which of these types of intelligence do you think represents your strongest talent(s)?

_____

_____

_____

_____

Which college major(s) do you think may best match your natural talents?

_____

_____

_____

_____

Discovering a Major that's Compatible with Your Personal Interests and Talents

In addition to knowing your intellectual strengths and learning styles, another key to factor into your decisions about a college major are your _interests_. Here are some specific strategies for exploring and confirming whether a major is compatible with your educational interests.

Reflect on past learning experiences you found stimulating and were productive. Think about previous classes that piqued your curiosity and in which you produced your best work. The subjects of these courses may be major fields of study that match up well with your interests, talents, and learning style.

At the website _www.mymajors.com_, you can enter information about your academic performance in high school courses. Your inputted information will be analyzed and you'll receive a report on what college majors appear to be a good match for you. You can do the same analysis for the first courses you complete in college.

NOTE

When considering college majors, first think about general fields rather than specific jobs. For example, focusing on the health professions offers you greater flexibility than deciding immediately to be a lab technician.

Take a look at introductory textbooks in the field you're considering as a major. Review the table of contents and read a few pages of the text to get some sense of the writing style used in the field and whether the topics are compatible with your educational interests. You should be able to conveniently find introductory textbooks for different fields of study in your college media center.

Seek out students majoring in the subject you're considering and ask them about their experiences. Talk to several students to get a different and balanced perspective on what the field is like. You can find these students by visiting student clubs on campus related to the major (e.g., psychology club or history club). The following questions may be good ones to ask students in a major you're considering:

- What attracted you to this major?
- What would you say are the advantages and disadvantages of majoring in this field?
- Knowing what you know now, would you choose the same major again?

Also, ask students about the quality of teaching and advising in the department offering the major. Studies show that different departments within the same college or university can vary greatly in terms of the quality of teaching as well as their educational philosophy and attitude toward students (Pascarella and Terenzini 1991, 2005).

Sit in on some classes in the field you're considering as a major. If the class you'd like to visit is large, you may be able to just slip into the back row and listen. If the class is small, ask the instructor for permission. When visiting a class, focus on the content or ideas being covered rather than the instructor's personality or teaching style. Remember: you're trying to decide whether to major in the subject, not the teacher.

Discuss the major you're considering with an academic advisor or career counselor. To get unbiased feedback about the pros and cons of majoring in a particular field, it's probably best to speak with an academic advisor who works with students from a variety of majors. If you're still interested, you can follow up by getting more detailed information by consulting with an advisor who works primarily with students in that particular major.

Speak with faculty members in the department. Consider asking them the following questions:

* What academic skills or qualities are needed for a student to be successful in your field?
* What are the greatest challenges faced by students majoring in your field?
* What can students do with a major in your field after graduation?
* What types of graduate programs or professional schools would a student in your major be well prepared to enter?

Surf the website of the professional organization associated with the field you're considering as a major. These websites often contain useful information for students interested in pursuing a major in the field. To locate the professional website for a field you would like to explore as a major, ask a faculty member in that field or complete a search on the web by simply entering the name of the field followed by the word "association." For example, if you're thinking about becoming an anthropology major, check out the website of the American Anthropological Association. If you're considering history as a major, take a look at the website of the American Historical Association. The website of the American Philosophical Association contains information about nonacademic careers for philosophy majors, and the American Sociological Association's website identifies various careers that sociology majors are qualified to pursue.

Use your elective courses to test your interest in subjects that you might major in. As its name implies, "elective" courses are those you elect or choose to take. They come in two forms: free electives and restricted electives. *Free electives* are any courses you take that count toward your college degree but aren't required for general education or a major. *Restricted electives* are courses you must take, but you get to choose them from a restricted list (menu) of possible courses that have been specified by your college to fulfill a requirement in general education or a major. For example, your campus may have a general education requirement in the social or behavioral sciences that stipulates you must take two courses in this field, but you choose what those two courses are from a list of options (e.g., anthropology, economics, political science, psychology, or sociology). If you're considering one of these fields as a possible major, you can take an introductory course in that subject to test your interest in the subject while simultaneously fulfilling a general education requirement needed for graduation. This strategy allows you to use general education as the main highway for travel toward your final destination (a college degree) while using your restricted electives to explore side roads (potential majors) along the way. You can use the same strategy with your free electives.

> "I took it (Biology) to satisfy the distribution requirement and I ended up majoring in it."
> —*Pediatrician (quoted in Brooks 2009)*

Be sure you're aware of all courses required for the major you've chosen or are considering. You can find this information in your college catalog, university bulletin, or campus website. If you're in doubt, seek assistance from an academic advisor.

Sometimes college majors require courses you would never expect to be required. Students interested in majoring in the field of forensics are often surprised by the number of science courses for this major. Keep in mind that college majors often require courses in fields outside of the major that are designed to support the major. For instance, psychology majors are often required to take at least one course in biology, and business majors are often required to take calculus.

If you're interested in majoring in a particular field, be sure you are fully aware of such outside requirements and are comfortable with them. Once you've accurately identified all courses required for the major you're considering, ask yourself the following two questions:

1. Do the course titles and descriptions appeal to my interests and values?
2. Do I have the abilities or skills needed to do well in these courses?

AUTHOR'S JOURNEY

As an academic advisor, I often see students who are confused about what they want to major in, especially traditional (18 to 24 year old) students. I can relate to these students because I changed my major multiple times before I reached a final decision. The first piece of advice I give students about choosing majors is to use their resources (e.g., academic advisement) and to do some research on the courses required for the majors they're considering. Over the last few years, I've seen many students who want to major in forensic science—largely due to the popularity of the CSI shows. I then ask them how they feel about science and math, and many of these students tell me they hate those subjects. When I inform them that becoming forensic scientist involves a minimum of a master's in chemistry, they decide to look at other majors. Fewer surprises like this would occur if students did at least some research on what courses are required for the majors and careers they're considering.

—*Julie McLaughlin*

When completing your bachelor degree, consider the possibility of completing a college minor in a field that complements your major. A college minor usually requires about half the number of credits (units) required for a major. Most campuses allow you the option of completing a minor along with your major. Check your course catalog or consult with an academic advisor for college minors that may interest you.

If you have a strong interest in two different fields, a minor will allow you to major in one of these fields while minoring in the other. Thus, you're able to pursue two fields of interest without having to sacrifice one for the other. Another advantage of a minor is that it can usually be completed with a major without delaying your time to graduation. In contrast, a double major is likely to lengthen your time to graduation because it requires completing all requirements for both majors.

Another way to complete a second field of study without increasing your time to graduation is by completing a "concentration" or "cognate area"—an academic specialization that requires fewer courses to complete than a minor (e.g., four to five courses vs. seven to eight courses). A concentration area may have even fewer requirements (only three to four courses).

Taking a cluster of courses in a field outside your major can be an effective way to strengthen your resume and your employment prospects; it demonstrates your versatility and ability to acquire knowledge and skills in areas that may be missing or underemphasized in your major. For example, by taking a cluster of courses in fields such as mathematics (e.g., statistics), technology (e.g., computer science), and business (e.g., economics), students majoring in the fine arts (e.g., music or theater) or humanities (e.g., English or history) can acquire knowledge and skills in areas not strongly emphasized by their major, thereby increasing their prospects for employment after graduation.

 Journal Reflection 10.4

Consider the following statement: "Choosing a major is a life-changing decision because it will determine what you will do for the rest of your life."

Would you agree or disagree?

Why?

MYTHS ABOUT THE RELATIONSHIP BETWEEN MAJORS AND CAREERS

Numerous misconceptions exist about the relationship between college majors and careers, some of which can lead students to make uninformed or unrealistic decisions about a major. Here are four common myths about the major–career relationship you should be aware of and factor into your decision about a college major.

Myth 1. When you choose your major, you're choosing your career.

While some majors lead directly to a specific career, most do not. Majors leading directly to specialized careers are often called preprofessional or pre-vocational majors; they include such fields as accounting, engineering, and nursing. However, the relationship between most college majors and future careers is often not direct or linear; you don't travel on a monorail straight from your major to a single career that's directly connected to your major. For instance, all physics majors don't become physicists, all philosophy majors don't become philosophers, all history majors don't become historians, and all English majors don't become Englishmen (or Englishwomen). Instead, the same major typically leads you to a variety of career options.

The truth is that for most college students the journey from college major to future career(s) is less like scaling a vertical pole and more like climbing a tree. As illustrated in **Figure 10.1**, you begin with the tree's trunk, the foundation provided by general education (the liberal arts); this leads to separate limbs (choices for college majors), which, in turn, lead to different branches (different career paths or options). Note that different sets of branches (careers) grow from the same limb (major).

> " Linear thinking can keep you from thinking broadly about youroptionsandbeingopen-minded to new opportunities."
>
> *—Katharine Brooks, author,* You Majored in What?

FIGURE 10.1: The Relationship between General Education (Liberal Arts), College Majors, and Careers

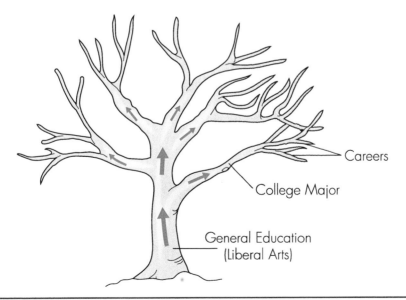

Careers

College Major

General Education
(Liberal Arts)

Similarly, different career clusters or "career families" grow from the same major. An English major can lead to a variety of careers that involve writing (e.g., editing, journalism, or publishing), and a major in Art can lead to different careers that involve visual media (e.g., illustration, graphic design, or art therapy).

Furthermore, different majors can lead to the same career. For instance, a variety of majors can lead a student to law school and a career as a lawyer; in fact, there's really no such thing as a "law major" or "pre-law major." Students with a variety of majors (or minors) can also enter medical school as long as they have a solid set of foundational courses in biology and chemistry and score well on the medical college admissions test.

Studies show that today's workers change jobs 10 times in the two decades following college and the job-changing rate is highest for younger workers (AAC&U 2007). Research also indicates that only half of new college graduates expect to be working in the same field in which they're currently employed (Hart Research Associates 2006); they frequently change positions during their first two decades of employment following college completion, and the further along they proceed in their career path, the more likely they are to be working in a field that's unrelated to their college major (Millard 2004).

So, don't assume that your major *is* your career, or that your major automatically turns into your lifelong career. It's this belief that can result in some students procrastinating about choosing a major; they think they're making a lifelong decision and fear that if they make the "wrong" choice, they'll be stuck doing something they hate for the rest of their life. Although it's important to think about how your choice of a college major will affect your career path, for most college students—particularly those not majoring in preprofessional fields—choice of a major and choice of a career are not identical decisions made at the same time. Choosing a specific major is a decision that should be made by your sophomore year; choosing a career is a decision that can be made later.

NOTE

Don't assume that choosing your college major means you're choosing what you'll be doing for the remainder of your working life. Deciding on a major and deciding on a career are not identical decisions that must be made simultaneously.

Myth 2. If you want to continue your education after college graduation, you must continue in the same field as your college major.

After graduating with a four-year (baccalaureate) degree, you have two primary paths available to you: (a) enter the workforce immediately, and/or (b) continue your education in graduate school or professional school. (See **Figure 10.2** for a visual map of the stages and milestones in the college experience and the paths available to you after college.)

FIGURE 10.2: A Snapshot of the College Experience and Beyond

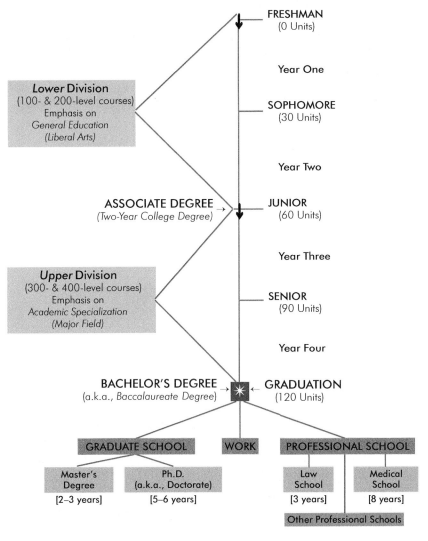

Notes

1. On average, about one-third of the courses required for a college degree are general education courses selected from the liberal arts curriculum. However, the number of required general education courses varies from campus to campus and can vary at the same campus depending on the student's major.

2. The word "freshman" originated in England in 1596, when every college student was a "fresh" (new) "man." Today, the term "freshman" is frequently being replaced by "first-year student" because this is a more gender-neutral term.

3. The term "baccalaureate" derives from "Bacchus"—the Greek god of wine and festive celebration, and "laurel"—a wreath made from the laurel plant that ancient Greeks draped around the neck of Olympic champions.

4. It often takes college students longer than four years to graduate due to a variety of reasons, such as working part-time and taking fewer courses per term, needing to repeat courses that were failed or dropped, or making a late change to a different major and needing to fulfill additional requirements for the new major.

5. Graduate and professional schools are options for continuing to higher levels of education after completion of an undergraduate (college) education.

6. Students going to graduate school on a full-time basis can sometimes support themselves financially by working part-time as a teaching assistant (TA) or research assistant (RA). It's also possible to enroll in some graduate or professional school programs on a part-time basis while holding a full-time job.

7. The term "Ph.D." refers to "Doctor of Philosophy," respecting the fact that the first scholars were the ancient Greek philosophers (e.g., Socrates, Plato, and Aristotle). However, a Ph.D. can be earned in many different academic fields (Mathematics, Music, Economic, etc.).

8. Compared to graduate school, professional school involves advanced education in more "applied" professions (e.g., pharmacy or public administration).

"The first week of law school, one of my professors stressed the importance of 'researching, analyzing and writing.' I thought this was an interesting thing to say, because English majors learn and practice these skills in every class."

—*English major attending law school*

Journal Reflection 10.5

Reflect back on the timeline depicted in Figure 10.2, which suggests that an associate degree is designed to be completed in two years and a bachelor's degree in four years.

Do you see yourself completing an associate degree in two years or a bachelor's degree in four years? Why or why not?

_____

_____

_____

_____

_____

_____

Once you earn a college diploma, you can continue your education in a field that's not directly related to your college major. This is particularly true for students majoring in liberal arts fields that don't lead directly to a specific career after graduation (Pascarella and Terenzini 1991, 2005). For example, an English major can go to graduate school in a subject other than English, or go to law school, or get a master's degree in business administration. In fact, most students who attend graduate school in the field of business (e.g., MBA programs) were not business majors when they were in college (Zlomek 2012).

Myth 3. Since most college graduates are employed in business organizations or corporations, you should major in business.

NOTE

Many colleges offer business courses for specific professions—dentists, lawyers, engineers, IT professionals—that typically are taken by people who want to go into business for themselves. These may be taken as course for a major or even after graduation.

Most college graduates are employed in business settings, so students (and their parents) often conclude that if students are going to work for a business, they better major in business. This belief likely explains why business is the most popular major among college students (National Center for Education Statistics 2014). However, college graduates now working in business settings have majored in variety of fields besides business, and many CEOs of today's most profitable companies did not major in business (Elliot 2015). Certainly, if you have an interest in and passion for majoring in business, by all means major in business; however, don't choose a business major because you think it's the only major that will qualify you to work for and succeed in a business organization after graduation.

AUTHOR'S JOURNEY

My undergraduate degree was in political science and sociology. When I graduated from college, I spent the first eight years of my professional life becoming a corporate manager. I did not major in business, but found that my liberal arts background gave me the problem-solving and communication skills that were crucial in working with a variety of people in my profession. You do not need to major in business to be a successful business person. Indeed, employers are telling us that they are looking for those who can solve, critically think, write and speak well, and work with a diversity of people and thoughts.

—*Aaron Thompson*

Myth 4. If you major in a liberal arts field, the only career available to you is teaching.

A commonly held myth is that all you can do with a major in a liberal arts subject is to teach the subject you majored in (e.g., math majors become math teachers; history majors become history teachers). The truth is that students majoring in different liberal arts fields go on to enter, advance, and prosper in a wide variety of careers. College graduates with degrees in the liberal arts who went on to achieve professional success in careers other than teaching include:

- Jill Barad (English major), CEO, Mattel Toys
- Willie Brown (liberal studies major), Mayor of San Francisco
- Ken Chenault (History major), CEO, American Express
- Christopher Connor (Sociology major), CEO, Sherwin Williams
- Robert Iger (Communications major), CEO, Walt Disney Company

Research also reveals that the career mobility and career advancement of liberal arts majors working in the corporate world are comparable to business majors. For example, liberal arts majors are just as likely to advance to the highest levels of corporate leadership as majors in such preprofessional fields as business and engineering (Pascarella and Terenzini 2005). The point we're making here is that if you have a passion for and talent in a liberal arts field, don't dismiss it as being "impractical," and don't be dismayed or discouraged by those who challenge your choice by asking: "What are you going to do with a degree in that major?" (Brooks 2009).

> They asked me during my interview why I was right for the job and I told them because I can read well, write well and I can think. They really liked that because those were the skills they were looking for."
>
> —*English major hired by a public relations firm*

AUTHOR'S JOURNEY

My brother, Vinny, was a philosophy major in college. He came home one Christmas wearing a tee-shirt on which was printed the message: "Philosophy major. Will think for food." With his major in philosophy, my brother went to graduate school, completed a Master's degree in higher education, and is now making a six-figure salary working as a college administrator. Looking back, his old tee-shirt should have read: "Philosophy major. Will think for money."

—*Joe Cuseo*

Journal Reflection 10.6

Look back at the four myths about the relationships between majors and careers. Which of these four myths did you know were false? Which myths did you previously think were true? Explain.

STRATEGIES FOR SUCCESSFUL TRANSFER TO A FOUR-YEAR COLLEGE OR UNIVERSITY

Almost one-half of all people in this country with a bachelor's degree started their college education at a two-year college before transferring to and graduating from a four-year college or university (National Student Clearing House Research Center 2015). Listed below are strategies you can use to prepare for successful transfer and join the ranks of Americans who began their college education at a two-year college and went on to complete a four-year degree. More information is provided on them online. Be sure to review them carefully if transferring is your objective.

Connect early and often with an academic advisor. National surveys show that community college students rank academic advising higher than any other student support service: Almost two-thirds of community college students rate it as a "very important" service. However, only about one-third of community college students report using advising "often" and over one-third report using advising "rarely or never" (Center for Community College Engagement 2008, 2010).

If you are a community college student planning to transfer, it's important to determine what courses at the community college will transfer for credit to the four-year college you hope to attend.

To maximize your number of transferable course credits, ask an advisor about whether your community college has any of the following programs that ensure transfer credit:

- **Transfer Articulation Agreements or Transfer Agreement Pacts.** Agreement between two and four-year colleges that allow for "Block Transfer"—transfer of a whole group (block) of courses at the same time (e.g., all general education courses taken at a community college are accepted for credit at a four-year college).

- **Guaranteed Admission Agreement (aka, Joint Admissions or "2+2 Agreement").** Agreement between a two and four-year college that allows students who complete the general education program at their community college with a satisfactory GPA to be automatically admitted to the four-year college campus as upper-division students (junior status) without having to complete a formal application for admission and acceptance.
- **Concurrent Enrollment Program:** An agreement between two- and four-year colleges that allows potential transfer students at the two-year college to cross-register for courses offered by the four-year college. For instance, a four-year university may offer courses to community college students that allows them to obtain "advanced transfer credit."

If you are an adult student who has received credit at your community college for experiential learning that took place in noncollege settings (e.g., previous work or military experiences), ask an advisor if your community college has any agreements that allow you to transfer these experiential credits to four-year colleges.

Lastly, keep in mind that community college courses may transfer to fulfill a general education requirement, a requirement in your major, or as elective credit. If possible, you want your transferable courses to fulfill general education requirements or requirements in your intended major. Check with your advisor to see if your community college has *Major-Specific (aka, Program-Major-to-Program-Major) Agreements*, which ensure that community college courses taken in your intended major are automatically accepted as fulfilling graduation requirements in your major at the four-year college to which you intend to transfer.

Save your course syllabi and course assignments. You may be able to use materials to answer any questions a four-year college may have about the nature and transferability of your courses.

Capitalize on available resources to help you prepare for successful transfer. Transfer resources may be available to you online, in print, and in person. Some campuses even have transfer student clubs where you can meet others planning on transferring. Also, check to see if there are Transfer Fairs at which you can visit with advisors and students from the prospective university campus. They include the following resources.

- *Common Course Numbering System:* a computer-based system offered in some states that places the same number and prefix on courses that count for credit at both the community college and the four-year college to which you intend to transfer.
- Checklists or worksheets developed by advisors at your community college that make it easy for you to identify general education requirements and required courses in specific majors at different four-year colleges.
- Transfer workshops and transfer events on campus, especially "Transfer Days" or "Transfer Fairs" at which transfer advisors and college admissions representatives from four-year institutions help community college students plan for successful transfer.

- Campus visits and tours of four-year colleges provided by your community college.
- Transfer student clubs, committees, councils, and honor associations (e.g., Phi Theta Kappa).

Complete your associate degree before transferring. Transfer students who complete an associate degree before transferring to a four-year college perform better after transferring and are more likely to complete a four-year degree (Community College Research Center 2014; Thurmond 2007). Listed below are key advantages of an associate degree that probably account for why transfer students who complete this degree are more successful.

Advantages of Completing an Associate Degree Prior to Four-Year College Transfer

1. **Many four-year campuses give priority admission to transfer students who have completed an associate degree.** (CSU Student Transfer 2015; Washington State Board for Community and Technical Colleges 2015). Thus, earning an associate degree will increase your transfer chances and options. It also allows you to capitalize on articulation agreements between two- and four-year campuses that grant "block transfer" of all general education credits earned for an associate degree. Research shows that students with more transfer credits at the time they enter a four-year college are more likely to complete a bachelor's degree (CCRC 2014).

2. **By completing an associate degree, you buy extra time and advising support to reach a final decision about your college major and what four-year college you'll transfer to.** If you're unsure about what major you want to declare, or what four-year college you want to attend, returning to your community college for your sophomore year provides an additional year of time and advising support to reach both of these important decisions.

   What field of study you major in and what four-year college you attend are often interrelated decisions. Some majors may only be offered at certain colleges, and the nature and quality of the same major may vary from one campus to the next. A second year at your community college can provide the time and support you need to reach a well-informed decision about what four-year campus is the best choice for your major.

3. **Research shows that students who complete an associate degree make a smoother academic transition to four-year campuses.** Students who transfer before completing an associate degree tend to experience more "transfer shock"—a sharper drop in GPA after transferring to a four-year institution—than do students who transfer after completing an associate degree (Laanan 2001). The superior post-transfer performance of students who complete an associate degree may be due to the fact that they (a) develop a stronger set of transferable skills by completing more academic skill-building courses (writing, math, oral communication) prior to transfer and (b) acquire a broader base of knowledge by completing the wide range of general education courses required for the associate degree. In addition, completing an associate degree allows you to complete all these academic skill-building courses

and general education requirements at a community college—where classes are smaller and courses are taught by experienced instructors whose primary responsibility is teaching, not research. (At larger universities, first- and second-year courses are often taught by the least experienced professors or graduate students.)

4. **Earning an associate degree opens up more opportunities for you to obtain internships, part-time employment during the academic year, or full-time employment during the summers in between your junior and senior years of college.** Having an associate degree increases your chances of being hired and also increases the amount you're paid for the work you're hired to do (Gagliardi and Heimstra 2013; Mullin and Phillippe 2013). Employees possessing an associate degree earn substantially more money than individuals with a high school diploma (Ganzglass 2014; Tinto 2012). This may be particularly advantageous if, for some reason, you're unable to complete a four-year degree or have to postpone its completion.

5. **Completing an associate degree supplies you with more time and opportunity to accumulate academic awards and honors prior to transfer (e.g., graduating with honors and participating in Phi Theta Kappa—national honor society for two-year college student).** Such awards increase your chances of receiving scholarships and grants from four-year colleges. Furthermore, since these accomplishments remain on your permanent college record after completing a bachelor's degree, they strengthen your job prospects after college graduation, as well as your chances of acceptance to graduate or professional school.

6. **Completing an associate degree provides you with more opportunity for leadership development and recognition during your sophomore year.** As a community college student, you become eligible for a variety of resume-building and character-building leadership opportunities during your second year (e.g., orientation week leader, peer tutor, or peer mentor). At four-year colleges and universities, sophomores are often unable to assume these leadership positions because they may be reserved for more experienced juniors and seniors. At two-year colleges, sophomores are the "seniors" and you can engage in leadership experiences during your sophomore year that will: (a) increase your chances of acceptance at four-year colleges, (b) qualify you for similar leadership positions at the four-year college to which you transfer, and (c) enhance your job prospects during your last two years of college and after completing your four-year degree.

7. **Completing an associate degree gives you the opportunity to participate in your community college's graduation ceremony.** Even if you plan to transfer and graduate from a four-year college with a bachelor's degree, don't underestimate the importance of celebrating your attainment of an associate degree. This is a significant achievement because:
   • It indicates you have survived and thrived during the two most critical years of the college experience. (Research shows that almost 75% of those students who withdraw from college will do so during the freshman and sophomore years [American College Testing 2015].)

- It signifies that you've successfully completed the general education component of the college experience. In many ways, this is the most important component of your college career because it represents the acquisition of breadth of knowledge and the development of essential, transferable skills (e.g., writing, speaking, critical thinking, and quantitative reasoning) that spell success in all majors and all careers.

- It's an opportunity for you to be recognized publicly—in front of family, friends, faculty, and fellow students. Research indicates that student involvement in college rituals or ceremonial events (such as graduation) reinforces their commitment to continue their education and reach their educational goal (Kuh et al. 2005). Proof of the power of the graduation experience is illustrated in the following excerpt of a letter written by a student who graduated with an associate degree from a two-year college and transferred to a four-year campus to complete her bachelor's degree.

> *"I just wanted to get in touch and let you know how I am doing. I successfully graduated from USF [a four-year college]. Looking back, the two-year college experience helped me achieve successful habits that brought me to where I am today. Also, during the graduation ceremony for my associate degree, I saw some fellow students wearing the yellow shawl that represented walking with honors. I thought to myself, 'I am going to walk with honors when I get my B.A.' And that I did! Who would have ever thought? [Now] I have decided that I want to go to graduate school."*

—Letter from a two-year college graduate received by Joe Cuseo

Factors to Consider when Choosing a Four-Year College for Transfer

Keep in mind that not all four-year colleges and universities are created equal. Some are more "transfer student friendly" than others; they welcome and value transfer students by reaching out to recruit them and supporting them once they've been recruited. Listed below are key things to look for, ask about, and factor into your decision about what four-year campuses to apply to and attend.

Outreach to Community College Students:
- Does the four-year college show interest in transfer students by supplying community college students with transfer information in the form of transfer websites, brochures, newsletters, guides, or handbooks?
- Has a representative from the four-year college visited your community college campus to recruit transfer students?
- Does the four-year college hold transfer fairs and campus visits for transfer students?

Financial Aid:
- Does the four-year college set aside financial aid, scholarships, grants, and campus employment opportunities for transfer students?

- Does the four-year college provide transfer students with early notification about how much financial aid they will receive?
- Does the four-year college offer specialized financial counseling for transfer students?

Transfer Audit (aka Transfer Credit Evaluation): Does the four-year campus provide early evaluation of transfer students' transcripts so they know exactly how many courses will be accepted for transfer credit and where the credit will be applied (e.g., toward general education, the major, or electives).

Registration: Are transfer students allowed to register at the same time as other students, or must they wait until all other students at the college (freshman through seniors) have already registered?

Housing:
- Does the college reserve on-campus housing spaces for transfer students?
- Does the college help transfer students find off-campus housing?

Transfer Student Orientation: Does the college offer an orientation program designed specifically for new transfer students? (Or, must transfer students participate in the same orientation program designed for freshmen?)

Transfer Advisors: Does the college offer specialized academic advising for transfer students?

Transfer Center: Does the college have a transfer resource center that provides a place for transfer students to gather and receive support?

Peer Support: Does the college have peer mentors for transfer students to help them navigate their new environment and develop social networks?

Transfer Orientation Course (aka, Transfer Student Seminar): Does the college offer a first-term course specifically for new transfer students that's designed to promote their success?

Transfer Honors Program: Does the college have an honors program specifically designed for transfer students (e.g., Tau Sigma Honor Society—a national honors and scholarship program for transfer students who earn a 3.5 GPA after their first term on campus or rank among the top 20% of their entering transfer class in academic performance).

HOW FOUR-YEAR COLLEGES AND UNIVERSITIES EVALUATE TRANSFER STUDENTS

The following criteria are those that four-year colleges will most likely use to evaluate your application and decide on your acceptance.

Academic Record. Four-year colleges will look at your overall GPA, as well as your grades for courses in your major. (Be sure to have the registrar's office send your academic record in the form of an *official transcript*—a verified record of your completed course work that's signed and date-stamped by the registrar's office to verify that the information contained in it is up-to-date, accurate, and hasn't been altered.)

Out-of-class Experiences. Your involvement in leadership activities and volunteer experience in the community or on campus can play a role in your acceptance at a four-year college.

Personal Statement. In your letter of application for college admission, demonstrate your knowledge of:

- *Yourself* (e.g., your personal interests, abilities, and values),
- Your intended *major* (e.g., why you're interested in it and what you might do with it after graduation), and
- The *college* to which you're applying to show that you know something specific about the school—such as its mission, philosophy, and specific programs—especially the particular program to which you're applying.

Course Transcript

At the same time that grades are important, so are the types of courses you take. Employers want to see that you challenged yourself and took challenging courses outside your major field.

Your course transcript is a listing of all courses you enrolled in and the grades you received in those courses. Two pieces of information included on your college transcript can strongly influence employers' hiring decisions or admissions committee decisions about your acceptance to a graduate or professional school: (a) the grades you earned in your courses and (b) the types of courses you completed.

Simply stated, the better the grades you earn in college, the better are your employment prospects after college. Research on college graduates indicates that the higher their grades, the higher:

- The prestige of their first job
- Their total earnings (salary and fringe benefits)
- Their job mobility (ability to change jobs or positions).

This relationship between higher college grades and career advantages holds true for students at all types of colleges and universities, regardless of the perceived reputation or prestige of the school they attended (Pascarella and Terenzini 1991, 2005).

Co-curricular Experiences

Participation in student clubs, campus organizations, and other types of co-curricular activities represent a valuable source of experiential learning that complements classroom-based learning and contributes to career preparation and development. A sizable body of research supports the power of these experiences for career success (Astin 1993; Hart Research Associates 2006, 2014; Kuh 1993; Pascarella and Terenzini 1991, 2005). Co-curricular experiences that are especially relevant to career development and career success are those that:

- Allow you to develop leadership and mentoring skills—such as, participating in leadership retreats, student government, college committees, peer counseling, or peer tutoring.
- Enable you to interact with others from diverse ethnic and racial groups—such as, multicultural or international clubs and organizations.

NOTE

As a first-year student, it could be said that you're in the early stages in the process of developing your product. Begin the process now by identifying and packaging your skills and attributes so by the time you graduate you'll have a well-developed product that potential employers will be interested in purchasing.

- Relate to your academic major or career interests—such as, involvement in student clubs in your college major or intended career field.

Don't forget that co-curricular experiences are also resume-building experiences; they serve as evidence of social responsibility to your communities on and off campus. Be sure to showcase these experiences to prospective employers. Also, don't forget that campus professionals with whom you may interact while participating in co-curricular activities (e.g., the director of student activities or dean of students) can serve as valuable references and provide you with letters of recommendation to future employers, graduate schools, or professional schools.

Personal Resume

A resume may be described as a listed or bulleted summary of your most important accomplishments, skills, and credentials. If you haven't yet accumulated enough experiences to construct a fully developed resume, you can start building a "skeletal resume" that contains major categories or headings (the skeleton) which you'll eventually flesh out with your specific experiences and accomplishments. (See **Box 10.3** for a sample skeleton resume.)

Portfolio

Unlike a resume, which simply lists your experiences, a portfolio contains actual products or samples of your work. You may have heard the word "portfolio" referred to as a collection of artwork that professional artists put together to showcase or advertise their artistic ability. However, the term *portfolio* has a broader meaning; it can be a collection of any material that depicts a person's skills and talents, or demonstrates educational and personal development. For example, a portfolio could include items such as:

- Outstanding papers, exam performances, research projects, and lab reports
- Work samples and photos from study abroad experiences, service learning, and internships
- Video footage of oral presentations and public performances
- Performance evaluations received from professors, student development professionals, and employers
- Letters of recognition or commendation from professors, student development professionals, and employers.

As a first-year student, you can begin the process of portfolio development right now by saving your best work and performances, including those done in classes, co-curricular experiences on campus, or service and work experiences off campus. Store them in a traditional portfolio folder, or save them on a flash drive to create an electronic portfolio. You could also create a website and upload your materials there. Eventually, you should be able to build a well-stocked portfolio that showcases your skills and demonstrates your achievements to future employers or future schools.

NOTE

Look for co-curricular activities enable you to actively practice and discuss the concepts and skills you are learning in your curricular courses.

Box 10.3

Constructing a Skeletal Resume

Use this skeletal resume as an outline or template or blueprint to begin constructing your personal resume and setting future goals. (If you have already created a resume, use this template to identify and add categories that may be missing from your current one.)

NAME
(First, Middle, Last)

Current Addresses:
Postal address
E-mail address
Phone no.

Permanent Addresses:
Postal address
E-mail address
Phone no.

EDUCATION: Name of College or University, City, State
Degree Name (e.g., Bachelor of Science)
College Major (e.g., Accounting)
Graduation Date
GPA (if 3.0 or higher)

RELATED WORK   Position Title, City, State   Start and stop dates
EXPERIENCES: (Begin the list with your most recent experiences.)
(List skills you used or developed.)

VOLUNTEER (COMMUNITY SERVICE) EXPERIENCES
(List skills you used or developed.)

NOTABLE COURSEWORK
(e.g., leadership, interdisciplinary, or intercultural courses; study abroad experiences)

CO-CURRICULAR EXPERIENCES
(e.g., student government or peer leadership)
(List skills used or developed.)

PERSONAL SKILLS AND POSITIVE QUALITIES
(List as bullets; be sure to include those that are especially relevant to the position for which you're applying.)

HONORS AND AWARDS
(Include those received prior to college and outside of college.)

REFERENCES
(Names and contact information for those who can speak to your work experience.)

 Journal Reflection 10.7

What do you predict will be your best work products in college—those that you would most likely showcase in a portfolio?

Why?

_____

_____

_____

Letters of Recommendation (Letters of Reference)

Letters of recommendation can come from course instructors, academic advisors, or other student support professionals. Provide the following courtesies for those you ask to write letters for you:

- Give the person advanced notice (at least two weeks).
- Provide a *fact sheet* about yourself that will enable them to cite concrete examples or specific evidence of your achievements and contributions—(this will make the letter much more powerful).
- If your letter is to be mailed, supply a *stamped, addressed* envelope (a personal courtesy that makes the job a little easier for your reference).
- Send a *thank you note* close to the date the letter is due. This isn't only the polite thing to do, it also serves as a gentle reminder for the person to write your letter.

The quality of your letters of recommendation will be strengthened if you give careful thought to (a) who will serve as your references, (b) how to approach them, and (c) what to provide them. Specific strategies for doing so are summarized in **Box 10.4**.

 ## Journal Reflection 10.8

Have you met anyone on campus who you could be in a position to write a letter of recommendation for you?

_____

If you have, who is this person, and what position does he or she hold on campus?

_____

_____

_____

If you haven't, who might be a good future candidate?

_____

_____

_____

Box 10.4

The Art and Science of Requesting Letters of Recommendation: Effective Strategies and Common Courtesies

1. **Select recommendations from people who know you well.** Think about individuals with whom you've had an ongoing relationship, who know you by name, and who have observed your strongest performances and skills. Good candidates are instructors who you've had for more than one course, an academic advisor whom you see often, or an employer who has witnessed your work habits for an extended period of time.

2. **Seek a balanced blend of letters from people who have observed your performance in different settings or situations.** The following are performance-based settings where people may have observed how well you performed:
   - The classroom—a professor who can speak on your academic performance
   - On campus—a student life professional who can comment on your contributions to a club or organization
   - Off campus—a professional for whom you've performed volunteer service, part-time work, or an internship

3. **Pick the right time and place to make your request.** Be sure to request letters of recommendation well in advance of the letter's deadline date (at least two weeks). First, ask the person if he or she is willing to write you a letter of recommendation. Don't approach the person with the form in your hand because it may send the message that you have assumed the person will say yes or are pressuring the person to say yes. This isn't the most socially sensitive message to send someone whom you're about to ask a favor.

   Also, pick a place and time where the person can give full attention to your request. Make a personal visit to the person's office, rather than making the request in a busy hallway or in front of a classroom full of students.

4. **Provide your references with a fact sheet about yourself.** Include your experiences and achievements—both inside and outside the classroom. This will help make your references' job a little easier by providing points for them to focus on. It's also likely to make your letter stronger because it will contain specific examples that draw directly from your personal experiences and accomplishments. On your fact sheet, be sure to include high grades you may have earned in certain courses, as well as volunteer services, leadership experiences, awards or forms of recognition, and special interests or talents relevant to your academic major and career choice. Your fact sheet is the place to "toot your own horn," so don't fear coming across as a braggart. You're not being boastful or showboating; you're just highlighting your strengths.

5. **If the letter is to be mailed, provide your references with a stamped, addressed envelope.** This is a simple courtesy that makes their job easier and demonstrates your social sensitivity.

6. **Waive your right to see the letter.** If you have the option to waive (give up) your right to see the letter of recommendation, waive your right—as long as you feel reasonably certain that you will receive a good letter of recommendation. By waiving your right to see the letter, you show confidence that the letter will be positive and assures the person reading the letter that you didn't inspect or screen it to ensure it was good before sending it.

7. **Follow up with a thank you note.** Send this note at about the time your letter of recommendation should be sent. This is the right thing to do because it shows your appreciation; it's also the smart thing to do because if the letter hasn't been sent, the thank you note serves as a gentle reminder to your reference that the letter should be sent soon.

8. **Let your references know the outcome of your application.** If you've been offered the position or been admitted to the school to which you applied, let your references know. This is the socially sensitive thing to do, and your references are likely to notice and remember your social sensitivity—which should strengthen the quality of any future letters of recommendation you may request from them.

CHAPTER SUMMARY AND HIGHLIGHTS

Studies show that the vast majority of students entering college are uncertain about their academic specialization. Most students do not reach a final decision about their major *before* starting college; typically, they make that decision *during* their college experience. As you gain experience with the college curriculum, you will gain greater self-insight into your academic interests, strengths, and weaknesses. Take this self-knowledge into consideration when choosing a major to help you select a field that capitalizes on your personal interests, abilities, and talents.

To make a well-informed choice of a college major, there are several myths you should be aware of:

- When you choose your major, you're choosing your career.
- After you graduate with a college degree, any further education you pursue must be in the same field as your college major.
- Since most college graduates work in business settings, you should major business.
- If you major in a liberal arts subject, the only career available to you is teaching.

LEARNING MORE THROUGH THE WORLD WIDE WEB: INTERNET-BASED RESOURCES

For additional information related to educational planning and choosing a major, see the following websites.

Identifying and Choosing College Majors:
www.mymajors.com

www.princetonreview.com/majors.aspx

Relationships between Majors and Careers:
http://uncw.edu/career/WhatCanIDoWithaMajorIn.html

Developing a Personalized Career Plan: www.mapping-your-future.org

Navigating the Job Market: www.mymajors.com

Career Descriptions and Future Employment Outlook: www.bls.gov/

Position Openings & Opportunities:
www.rileyguide.com

www.monster.com

Resume Writing & Job Interviewing: www.quintcareers.com

REFERENCES

AAC&U (Association of American Colleges and Universities). 2007, 2013. *It Takes More Than a Major: Employer Priorities for College Learning and Success*. Washington, DC: Author.

American College Testing. 2015. *College Student Retention and Graduation Rates from 2000 Through 2015*.

Astin, A. W. 1993. *What Matters in College?* San Francisco: Jossey-bass.

Baumeister, R., and M. R. Leary. 1995. "The Need to Belong: Desire for Interpersonal Attachments as a Fundamental Human Motivation." *Psychological Bulletin* 117, 497–529.

Bolles, R. N. 1998. *The New Quick Job-hunting Map*. Toronto, Ontario, Canada: Ten Speed Press.

Brooks, K. 2009. *You Majored in What? Mapping Your Path from Chaos to Career*. New York: Penguin.

Brown, S. D., and N. E. R. Krane. 2000. Four (or Five) Sessions and a Cloud of Dust: Old Assumptions and New Observations About Career Counseling. In *Handbook of Counseling Psychology*. 3rd ed., edited by S. D. Brown and R. W. Lent, pp. 740–66. New York: Wiley.

Casserly, M. 2012. "10 Jobs That Didn't Exist 10 Years Ago." *Forbes*. http://www.forbes.com/sites/meghancasserly/2012/05/11/10-jobs-that-didnt-exist-10-years-ago/.

Center for Community College Student Engagement. 2008. *High Expectations and High Support* (2008 CCSSE findings). Austin, Texas: The University of Texas at Austin, Community College Leadership Program.

Center for Community College Student Engagement. 2010. *The Heart of Student Success: Teaching, Learning, and College Completion (2010 CCSSE Findings)*. Austin, TX: The University of Texas at Austin, Community College Leadership Program.

Chua, S. N., and R. Koestner. 2008. "A Self-determination Theory Perspective on the Role of Autonomy in Solitary Behavior." *The Journal of Social Psychology* 148(5), 645–7.

Community College Research Center (CCRC). 2014. "Earning an Associate Degree Increases Likelihood of Completing Bachelor's Degree." http://ccrc.tc.columbia.edu/press-releases/earning-associate-before-transfer-press-release.html.

Crosby, O. 2002. "Informational Interviewing: Get the Scoop on Careers." *Occupational Outlook Quarterly* (Summer), 32–7.

CSU Student Transfer. 2015. The Student Transfer Achievement Reform Act. http://www.calstate.edu/transfer/degrees/.

Cuseo, J. B. 2005. ""Decided," "Undecided," and "in Transition": Implications for Academic Advisement, Career Counseling, and Student Retention." In *Improving the First Year of College: Research and Practice*, edited by R. S. Feldman, 27–50. Mahwah, NJ: Lawrence Erlbaum.

Deci, E., and R. Ryan, eds. 2002. *Handbook of Self-determination Research*. Rochester, NY: University of Rochester Press.

Education Commission of the States. 1995. *Making Quality Count in Undergraduate Education*. Denver, CO: ECS Distribution Center.

Elliott, M. 2015. *CEOs Who Didn't Pursue Undergrad Business Degrees*. http://www.usatoday.com/story/money/business/2015/03/29/cheat-sheet-ceos-college-business/70442270/.

Figler, H., and R. N. Bolles. 2007. *The Career Counselor's Handbook*. Berkeley, CA: Ten Speed Press.

Gagliardi, J., and H. Hiemstra. 2013. *College Still Pays*. Kentucky Postsecondary Education Policy Brief. http://cpe.ky.gov/NR/rdonlyres/8DE2CF1E-51A2-4C27-8C2B-41FB126252FE/0/CollegeStillPayspolicybrief.pdf.

Ganzglass, E. 2014. *Scaling "Stackable Credentials": Implications for Implementation and Policy. Center for Postsecondary and Economic Success*. http://www.clasp.org/resources-and-publications/files/2014-03-21-Stackable-Credentials-Paper-FINAL.pdf.

Gardner, P. D. March, 1991. *Learning the Ropes: Socialization and Assimilation into the Workplace*. Paper presented at the Second National Conference on the Senior Year Experience, San Antonio, TX.

Gardner, H. 1993. *Frames of Mind: The Theory of Multiple Intelligences*. 2nd ed. New York: Basic Books.

Gardner, H. 1999. *Intelligence Reframed: Multiple Intelligences for the 21st Century*. New York: Basic Books.

Gardner, H. 2006. *Changing Minds. The Art and Science of Changing Our Own and Other People's Minds*. Boston, MA: Harvard Business School Press.

Gordon, V. N., and G. E. Steele. 2003. "Undecided First-year Students: A 25-year Longitudinal Study." *Journal of the First-year Experience and Students in Transition* 15(1): 19–38.

Hagedorn, L. S., H. S. Moon, S. Cypers, W. E. Maxwell, and J. Lester. 2006. "Transfer Between Community Colleges and Four-year Colleges: The All-American Game." *Community College Journal of Research and Practice* 30(3): 223–42.

Hart Research Associates. 2006. *How Should Colleges Prepare Students to Succeed in Today's Global Economy?* Based on surveys among employers and recent college graduates. Conducted on behalf of the Association of American Colleges and Universities. Washington, DC: Author.

Hart Research Associates. July, 2014. *How Should Colleges Prepare Students to Succeed in Today's Global Economy?* http://dpdproject.info/details/how-should-colleges-prepare-students-to-succeed-in-todays-global-economy-peter-d-hart-research-associates/.

HERI (Higher Education Research Institute). 2014. *Your First College Year Survey 2014.* Los Angeles, CA: Cooperative Institutional Research Program, University of California-los Angeles.

Hildenbrand, M., and P. A. Gore, Jr. 2005. "Career Development in the First-year Seminar: Best Practice versus Actual Practice." In *Facilitating the Career Development of Students in Transition*, edited by P. A. Gore, monograph no. 43, 45–60. Columbia: National Resource Center for the First-year Experience and Students in Transition, University of South Carolina.

Knouse, S., J. Tanner, and E. Harris. 1999. "The Relation of College Internships, College Performance, and Subsequent Job Opportunity." *Journal of Employment Counseling* 36: 35–43.

Kuh, G. D. 1993. "In Their Own Words: What Students Learn Outside the Classroom." *American Educational Research Journal* 30: 277–304.

Kuh, G. D., J. Kinzie, J. H. Schuh, E. J. Whitt. 2005. *Student Success in College: Creating Conditions that Matter.* San Francisco, CA: Jossey-bass.

Laanan, F. S. 2001. "Transfer Student Adjustment." In *Transfer Students: Trends and Issues*, edited by F. S. Laanan, 5–13. New Directions for Community Colleges, no. 114. San Francisco: Jossey-bass.

Leuwerke, W. C., S. B. Robbins, R. Sawyer, and M. Hovland. 2004. "Predicting Engineering Major Status from Mathematics Achievement and Interest Congruence." *Journal of Career Assessment* 12: 135–49.

Lock, R. D. 2004. *Taking Charge of Your Career Direction.* 5th ed. Belmont, CA: Brooks Cole.

Millard, B. November 7, 2004. *A Purpose-based Approach to Navigating College Transitions.* Preconference workshop presented at the Eleventh National Conference on Students in Transition, Nashville, Tennessee.

Miller, M. T., and D. P. Nadler. 2004. "Transfer Trends in the Future of Higher Education." In *The "College Transfer Student in America: The Forgotten Student*, edited by B. C. Jacobs, 188–201. Washington, DC: American Association of Collegiate Registrars and Admissions Officers.

Mullin, C., and K. Phillippe. 2013. *Community College Contributions* (No. AACC Policy Brief 2013-01PB). American Association of Community Colleges. http://www.aacc.nche.edu/Publications/Briefs/Documents/2013PB_01.pdf.

National Association of Colleges and Employers. 2012. *Internship and Co-op Survey.* Bethlehem, PA: Author.

National Association of Colleges and Employers. 2013. *Job Outlook: The Candidate Skills/Qualities Employers Want.* http://www.naceweb.org/s10022013/job-outlook-skills-quality.aspx.

National Association of Colleges and Employers. 2014. *2014 Internship and Co-op Survey,* executive summary. https://www.naceweb.org/uploadedFiles/Content/static-assets/downloads/executive-summary/2014-internship-co-op-survey-executive-summary.pdf.

National Center for Education Statistics. 2014. *Fast Facts: Most Popular Majors.* Washington, DC: U.S. Department of Education. http://nces.ed.gov/fastfacts/display.asp?id=37.

National Student Clearing House Research Center. 2015. *Contribution of Two-year Institutions to Four-year Completions.* https://nscresearchcenter.org/snapshotreport-twoyearcontributionfouryearcompletions17/.

Pascarella, E., and P. Terenzini. 1991. *How College Affects Students: Findings and Insights from Twenty Years of Research.* San Francisco: Jossey-bass.

Pascarella, E., and P. Terenzini. 2005. *How College Affects Students: A Third Decade of Research.* Vol. 2. San Francisco: Jossey-bass.

Pope, L. 1990. *Looking Beyond the Ivy League.* New York: Penguin Press.

Ryan, R. 1995. "Psychological Needs and the Facilitation of Integrative Processes." *Journal of Personality* 63: 397–427.

Ryan, R. M., and Deci, E. L. 2000. "Self-determination Theory and the Facilitation of Intrinsic Motivation, Social Development, and Well-being." *American Psychologist* 55: 68–78.

Smith, D. D. 2005. "Experiential Learning, Service Learning, and Career Development." In *Facilitating the Career Development of Students in Transition*, edited by P. A. Gore, monograph no. 43, 205–22. Columbia: National Resource Center for the First-year Experience and Students in Transition, University of South Carolina.

Thurmond, K. C. 2007. Transfer Shock: Why Is a Term Forty Years Old Still Relevant? *NACADA Clearinghouse of Academic Advising Resources* website: http://www.nacada.ksu.edu/Resources/Clearninghouse/View-Articles/Dealing-with-transfer-shock.aspx.

Tinto, V. 2012. *Completing College: Rethinking Institutional Action*. Chicago: The University of Chicago Press.

Washington State Board for Community and Technical Colleges. 2015. *Transfer Associate Degrees*. http://www.sbctc.ctc.edu/college/_e-transferdegrees.aspx

Zlomek, E. March 26, 2012. As MBA Applicants, Business Majors Face an Uphill Battle. *Bloomburg Business.* http://www.bloomberg.com/bw/articles/2012-03-26/as-mba-applicants-business-majors-face-an-uphill-battle.

Chapter 10 Exercises

10.1 Quote Reflections

Review the sidebar quotes contained in this chapter and select two that were especially meaningful or inspirational to you.

For each quote, provide a three- to five-sentence explanation why you chose it.

10.2 Gaining Self-Awareness of Personal Interests, Talents, and Values

No one is in a better position to discover who you are, and who you want to be, than *you*. One effective way to gain deeper self-insight is through self-questioning. You can become more self-aware by asking yourself questions that cause you to think carefully about your inner qualities and characteristics. Responding honestly to the following questions can sharpen awareness of your true interests, abilities and values, and help you determine what major or career is a good "fit" for you. As you read each question, briefly note what thought(s) come to mind about yourself.

Personal Interests

1. What tends to grab your attention and hold it for long periods of time?
2. What sorts of things are you naturally curious about or frequently intrigue you?
3. What do you really enjoy doing and do as often as you possibly can?
4. What do you look forward to, or get excited about?
5. What are your favorite hobbies or pastimes?
6. When you're with your friends, what do you like to talk about or spend time doing?
7. What has been your most stimulating or enjoyable learning experience?
8. If you've had previous work or volunteer experience, what jobs or tasks did you find most interesting or stimulating?
9. When time seems to "fly by" for you, what are you usually doing?
10. What do you like to read about?
11. When you open a newspaper or log onto the Internet, where do you tend to go first?
12. When you find yourself daydreaming or fantasizing about your future, what is it usually about?

From your responses to the above questions, identify a career that appears to be most compatible with your personal *interests*? In the space below, note the career and your interests that are compatible with it.

Personal Talents and Abilities

1. What seems to come naturally to you?
2. What would you say is your greatest talent or personal gift?
3. What are your most advanced or well-developed skills?

4. What seems to come easily to you that others have to work harder to do?

5. What would you say has been your greatest personal accomplishment or achievement in life thus far?

6. What about yourself are you most proud of, or that you take most pride in doing?

7. When others come to you for advice or assistance, what is it usually for?

8. What would your best friend(s) say is your best quality, trait, or characteristic?

9. When you've done something that left you feeling like you really were successful, what was it that you did?

10. If you have received awards or other forms of recognition, what have they been for?

11. On what types of learning tasks or activities have you experienced the most success?

12. In what types of courses do you tend to earn the highest grades?

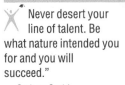

Never desert your line of talent. Be what nature intended you for and you will succeed."

—Sydney Smith, 18th-century English writer and defender of the oppressed

From your responses to the above questions, identify a career that appears to be most compatible with your personal *talents and abilities*? In the space below, note the career and your talents and abilities that are compatible with it.

Personal Values

1. What matters most to you?

2. If you were to single out one thing you really stand for or believe in, what would it be?

3. What would you say are your highest priorities in life?

4. Whenever you get the feeling you've done what was good or right, what was it that you did?

5. If there were one thing in the world you could change, improve, or make a difference in, what would it be?

6. When you have extra spending money, what do you usually spend it on?

7. When you have free time, what do you usually find yourself doing?

8. What does living a "good life" mean to you?

9. How would you define success? (What would it take for you to feel that you achieved success?)

10. How do you define happiness? (What would it take for you to be happy?)

To love what you do and feel that it matters—how could anything be more fun?"

—Katharine Graham, former CEO of the Washington Post and Pulitzer Prize–winning author

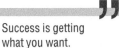

Success is getting what you want. Happiness is wanting what you get."

—Dale Carnegie, author of the best-selling book, How to Win Friends and Influence People *and founder of The Dale Carnegie Course—a worldwide program for business based on his teachings*

11. Do you have a hero or anyone you admire, look up to, or feel has set an example worth following? (If yes, who and why?)

12. Would you rather be thought of as:

   a. smart,
   b. wealthy,
   c. creative, or
   d. caring?

(Rank from 1 to 4, with 1 being the highest)

From your responses to the above questions, identify a career that appears to be most compatible with your personal *values*? In the space below, note the career and your values that are compatible with it.

10.3 Developing a Long-Range Academic Plan for Your Coursework

This exercise is designed to help you design a detailed yet flexible, two-year academic plan. While it may seem a bit overwhelming to develop a long-range plan at this stage of your college experience, you will receive guidance from your course instructor. This is an opportunity to begin customizing your college experience and mapping your educational future. Remember: an educational plan isn't something set in stone, it can change depending on changes in your academic and career interests. As you create, shape, and follow your plan, consult frequently with an academic advisor. If you're planning to transfer to a particular four-year college or university, be aware of its requirements as you develop this academic plan.

Overview of Courses Comprising Your Plan

Your trip through the college curriculum will involve taking courses in the following three key categories:

1. *General education* courses required of all college graduates regardless of their major

2. *Required courses in your chosen major*

3. *Elective* courses you choose to take from any listed in your college catalog.

What follows are planning directions for each of these types of courses. By building these three sets of courses into your educational plan, you can create a roadmap that guides your future coursework. Once you've reserved slots for these three key categories of courses you will have a blueprint to guide (not dictate) your educational future. If you later change your mind about a particular course you originally planned to take, you can do so without interfering with your educational progress by substituting another course from the same category. For instance, if your original plan was to take psychology to fulfill a general education requirement in the Social and Behavioral Sciences, but you decide later to take anthropology instead, you have a space reserved in your plan to make the switch.

As you gain more educational experience, your specific academic and career interests are likely to change and so may the specifics of your long-range plan. The purpose of this plan is not to tie you up or pin you down, but to supply you with a map that keeps you on course and moving in the right direction. Since this is a flexible plan, it's probably best to complete it in pencil or electronically so you can make future changes as needed.

Once you've developed your plan, hold onto it, and keep an up-to-date copy of it throughout your time in college. Bring it with you when you meet with advisors and career development specialists, and come prepared to discuss your progress on the plan as well as any changes you'd like to make to your plan.

Part A. Planning for General Education

Step 1. Use your course catalog (bulletin) to identify the general education requirements for graduation. You're likely to find these requirements organized into general divisions of knowledge (Humanities, Natural Sciences, etc.). Within each of these divisions, courses will be listed that you can take to fulfill the general education requirement(s) for that particular division. (Course catalogs can sometimes be tricky to navigate or interpret; if you run into any difficulty, seek help from your course instructor or an academic advisor.) You'll probably be able to choose courses from a list of different options. Use your freedom of choice to choose general education courses whose descriptions capture your curiosity and contribute to your personal development and career plans. You can use general education courses not only to fulfill general education requirements, but also to test your interest and talent in different fields—one of which may end up becoming your major (or minor).

Step 2. Identify courses in the catalog you plan to take to fulfill your general education requirements and list them on the following form. Some courses you're taking this term may be fulfilling general education requirements, so be sure to list them as well.

Planning Grid for *General Education* Courses

Course Title	Units	Course Title	Units

Total Number of Units Required for *General Education* = _____

Part B. Planning for a College Major

The point of this portion of your educational plan is not to force you to commit to a major right now, but to develop a flexible plan that will allow you to reach a well-informed decision about your major. If you have already chosen a major, this exercise will help you lay out exactly what's ahead of you and confirm whether the coursework required by your major is what you expected and "fits" well with your interests and talents.

Step 1. Go to your college catalog and locate the major you've chosen or are considering. If you're completely undecided, select a field that you might consider as a possibility. To help you identify possible majors, peruse your catalog or go online and answer the questions at *www.mymajors.com.*

Another way to identify a major for this exercise is to first identify a career you might be interested in and work backward to find a major that leads to this career. If you would like to use this strategy, the following website will guide you through the process: *http://uncw.edu/career/WhatCanIDoWithaMajorIn.html.*

Step 2. After you've selected a major, consult with an academic advisor about what courses are required for that major. The advising center on campus may have "major planning sheets" that list the specific course requirements for different majors.

A college major will require all students majoring in that field to complete specific set of courses. For instance, all business majors are required to take microeconomics and macroeconomics. Other courses required for a major may be chosen from a menu or list of options (e.g., "choose any three courses from the following list of six courses"). Such courses are often called "major electives." For these major electives, read their course descriptions carefully and use your freedom of choice wisely to select courses that interest you and are most relevant to your future plans.

Note: You can "double dip" by taking courses that fulfill a major requirement and a general education requirement at the same time. For instance, if your major is psychology, you may be able to take a course in General or Introductory Psychology that counts simultaneously as a required major course and a required general education course in the area of Social and Behavioral Sciences.

Step 3. Identify courses you plan to take to fulfill your major requirements and major electives and list them on the following form. Courses you're taking this term may be fulfilling requirements in the major you've selected, so be sure to list them as well.

Planning Grid for Courses in Your *Major*

Course Title	Units	Course Title	Units

Total Number of Units Required for Your *Major* = _____

Plan C. Planning Your Free Electives

Now that you've built general education courses and major courses into your educational map, you're well positioned to plan your *free electives*—courses not required for general education or your major but that are needed to reach the minimum number of units required for your degree or program. These are courses you are free to choose from any listed in the college catalog.

To determine how many free elective units you have, add up the number of course units you're taking to fulfill general education and major requirements, then subtract this number from the total number of units you need to graduate. The number of course units remaining represents your total number of free electives.

Planning Grid for Your *Free Electives*

Course Title	Units	Course Title	Units

Total Number of *Free Elective* Units = _____

Part D. Putting It Altogether: Developing a Comprehensive Graduation Plan

In the previous three sections, you built three key sets of college courses into your plan: general education courses, major courses, and free elective courses. Now you're positioned to tie these three sets of courses together and create a comprehensive graduation plan.

Using the "Long-Range Graduation Planning Form" on **p. 330,** enter the courses you selected to fulfill general education requirements, major requirements, and free electives. In the space provided next to each course, use the following shorthand notations to designate its category:

GE = *general education* course

M = *major* course

E = *elective* course

Notes:

1. If there are courses in your plan that fulfill two or more categories at the same time (e.g., a general education requirement and a major requirement), note both categories.

2. To complete an associate degree (approximately 60 units) in two years, you should plan to complete about 30 course credits each academic year. Keep in mind that you can take college courses in the summer as well as the fall and spring.

3. Keep in mind that the number associated with a course indicates the year in the college experience when the course is usually taken. Courses numbered in the 100s (or below) are typically taken in the first year of college and 200-numbered courses in the sophomore year.

NOTE ✗

Unlike high school, taking summer courses in college doesn't mean you've fallen behind or need to retake a course you failed during the "normal" school year (fall and spring terms). Instead, summer term can be used to get ahead and reduce your time to graduation. Adopt the mindset that summer term is a regular part of the college academic year; use it strategically to stay on track to complete your degree in a timely fashion.

4. If you haven't decided on a major, a good strategy is to focus on completing general education requirements during your first year of college. This first-year strategy will open more slots in your course schedule during your sophomore year—by that time, you may have a better idea of what you'll major in and what four-year college you want to attend, so you can fill these open slots with courses required for the major you've chosen. (This first-year strategy will also allow you to use general education courses in different subjects to test your interest in majoring in one of these subjects.)

5. Be sure to check whether the course you're planning to take has any *prerequisites*—courses that need to be completed *before* you can enroll in the course you're planning to take. For example, before you can enroll in literature course, you may need to complete at least one prerequisite course in writing or English composition.

6. Your campus may have a *degree audit program* that allows you to electronically track the courses you've completed and the courses you still need to complete a degree in your chosen major. If such a program is available, take advantage of it.

7. You're not locked into taking all your courses in the exact terms you originally placed them in your plan. You can trade terms if it turns out that the course isn't offered during the term you were planning to take it, or if it's offered at a time that conflicts with another course in your schedule.

8. Keep in mind that not all college courses are offered every term, every year. Typically, college catalogs do not contain information about when courses will be scheduled. If you're unsure when a course will be offered, check with an academic advisor. Some colleges develop *a projected plan of scheduled courses* that shows what academic term(s) courses will be offered for the next few years. If such a projected schedule of courses is available, take advantage of it. It will enable you to develop an educational plan that not only includes *what* courses you will take, but also *when* you will take them.

9. Don't forget to include out-of-class learning experiences as part of your educational plan, such as co-curricular experiences on campus and volunteer work or internships.

Long-Range Graduation Planning Form

FRESHMAN YEAR
Fall Term

Course Title	Course Type General Ed. (GE), Major (M), Elective (E)	Course Units

Total Units = _____

Spring Term

Course Title	Course Type General Ed. (GE), Major (M), Elective (E)	Course Units

Total Units = _____

Summer Term

Course Title	Course Type General Ed. (GE), Major (M), Elective (E)	Course Units

Total Units = _____

SOPHOMORE YEAR
Fall Term

Course Title	Course Type General Ed. (GE), Major (M), Elective (E)	Course Units

Total Units = _____

Spring Term

Course Title	Course Type General Ed. (GE), Major (M), Elective (E)	Course Units

Total Units = _____

Summer Term

Course Title	Course Type General Ed. (GE), Major (M), Elective (E)	Course Units

Total Units = _____

Reflection Questions

1. What is the total number of credits in your graduation plan? Does it equal or exceed the total number of credits needed to graduate with an associate degree?

2. How many credits will you be taking in the following areas?

   a. General Education =
   b. Major =
   c. Free Electives =

3. Look over the course required for the major you selected:

   a. Are there required courses you were surprised to see or didn't expect would be required?
   b. Are you still interested in majoring in this field?
   c. How likely is it that you will change the major you selected?
   d. If you were to change your major, what would "Plan B" likely be?

4. Did completing this long-range graduation plan help you clarify your educational goals?

Why or why not?

CHAPTER 11

HIGHER-LEVEL THINKING

MOVING BEYOND BASIC KNOWLEDGE TO CRITICAL AND CREATIVE THINKING

National surveys consistently show that the primary goal of college faculty is teaching students how to think critically. This chapter will help you understand what critical thinking is and empower you to think in this way. You will be provided with thinking strategies that move you beyond memorization to higher levels of thinking and learn how to demonstrate higher-level thinking on college exams and assignments.

CHAPTER PREVIEW

This chapter provides an overview of what higher level thinking is and will demonstrate how to use higher level thinking on college exams and assignments.

LEARNING OBJECTIVE

You will recognize various levels of thinking and demonstrate your knowledge by developing study questions at three levels of sophistication.

PERFORMANCE OBJECTIVE

Do I spend my time in a way on studying critical elements of my courses or am I focusing on less important details.

PRE-REFLECTION

 Journal Reflection 11.1

THOUGHT STARTER

To me, critical thinking is . . .

_____

_____

_____

_____

_____

(At a later point in this chapter, we'll ask you to flashback to the response you made here.)

©Rafael Ramirez/Shutterstock.com

WHAT IS HIGHER-LEVEL THINKING?

Contestants on TV quiz shows like *Jeopardy* are asked questions that call for knowledge of facts: Who? What? When? or Where? If game show contestants were asked higher-level thinking questions, they'd be responding to questions such as: "Why?" "How?" "What if?" Higher-level thinking (a.k.a. higher-order thinking) refers to a more advanced level of thought than that used to acquire factual knowledge. It involves reflecting on knowledge and taking it to a higher level—evaluating its validity, integrating it with something else you've learned, or creating new ideas. As its name implies, higher-level thinking involves raising the bar and jacking up your thinking to a level that goes beyond merely remembering, reproducing, or regurgitating factual information.

In national surveys of college professors teaching freshman-level through senior-level courses in various academic fields, more than 95% of faculty report that the most important goal of a college education is to develop students' ability to think critically (Gardiner 2005; Milton 1982). Similarly, college professors teaching introductory courses for freshmen and sophomores report that the primary educational purpose of their courses is to develop students' critical thinking skills (Higher Education Research Institute 2009; Stark et al. 1990). Simply stated, professors are more concerned with teaching you *how* to think than teaching you *what* to think (i.e., what facts to remember).

Compared to high school, college courses focus less on memorizing information and more on thinking about issues, concepts, and principles (Conley 2005). Remembering information in college may get you a grade of "C," demonstrating comprehension of that information may get you a "B," and going beyond comprehension to demonstrate higher-level thinking will earn you an "A." This is not to say that acquiring knowledge and basic comprehension are unimportant; they provide the stepping stones needed to climb to higher levels of thinking—as illustrated in **Figure 11.1**.

" To me, thinking at a higher level means to think and analyze something beyond the obvious and find the deeper meaning."

—*AHE First-year student*

NOTE

The focus of higher-level thinking is not just to answer questions but also to question answers.

" What is the hardest task in the world? To think."

—*Ralph Waldo Emerson, celebrated 19th-century American essayist and lecturer*

FIGURE 11.1: The Relationship between Knowledge, Comprehension, and Higher-Level Thinking

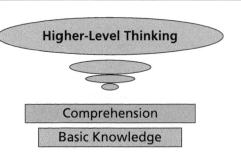

©Kendall Hunt Publishing Company

Studies show that memory for factual information acquired in college fades quickly with the passage of time. However, higher-level thinking is a *skill* (like learning to ride a bike) that's retained on a long-term basis and used for an entire lifetime (Pascarella and Terenzini 1991, 2005).

DEFINING AND DESCRIBING THE MAJOR FORMS OF HIGHER-LEVEL THINKING

When your college professors ask you to "think critically," they're usually asking you to use one or more of the eight forms of thinking listed in **Box 11.1**. As you read the descriptions of each form of thinking, note whether you've heard of it before.

BOX 11.1

Seven Major Forms of Higher-Level Thinking

1. Analysis (Analytical Thinking). Breaking down information to identify its essential parts and underlying elements.
2. Synthesis (Integrative Thinking). Building up ideas by connecting them to form a larger whole or more comprehensive system.

> " In college . . . you will be expected to get inside what you are learning to apply it, make comparisons and connections, draw implications, and use ideas."
>
> —*Robert Shoenberg, author,* Why Do I Have to Take This Course?

3. Application (Applied Thinking). Putting thinking into practice to solve problems and resolve issues.
4. Multidimensional Thinking. Viewing issues from a variety of vantage points to gain a more complete or comprehensive perspective.
5. Balanced Thinking. Carefully considering arguments for and against a particular position or viewpoint.
6. Critical Thinking (Evaluation). Judging the quality of arguments, conclusions, and thought processes— including all forms of thinking on this list.
7. Creative Thinking. Generating ideas that are unique, original, or distinctively different.

💡 Journal Reflection 11.2

Look back at the seven forms of thinking described in **Box 11.1**. Which of these forms of thinking have you used on high school exams or assignments?

_____

_____

_____

_____

_____

NOTE

You might want to add these words to your vocabulary list. They can be tricky but they're important to your understanding of what you may be asked to do in your college classes.

Analysis (Analytical Thinking)

The mental process of analysis is similar to the physical process of peeling an onion. When you analyze something, you take it apart and pick out its key parts, main points, or underlying elements. For example, if you were to analyze a chapter in this book, you would do more than cover its content; you would try to uncover or discover its main ideas by detecting its essential points and distinguishing them from background information or incidental details.

Synthesis (Integrative Thinking)

When you engage in *synthesis*, you're using a thought process that's basically the opposite of analysis. Instead of breaking down or taking apart ideas, you piece them together to form an integrated whole—like piecing together parts of a puzzle. Connecting ideas learned in different courses is a form of synthesis, such as integrating ethical concepts learned in a philosophy course with marketing concepts learned in a business course to develop a comprehensive set of ethical guidelines for marketing and advertising products.

NOTE

Synthesis is not just a summary of ideas produced by someone else, it's a thought process that integrates isolated pieces of information to generate a comprehensive product of your own.

Application (Applied Thinking)

When you learn something deeply, you transform information into knowledge; when you translate knowledge into practice, you engage in a higher-level thinking process known as *application*. It's a powerful form of higher-level thinking that allows you to transfer your knowledge to real-life situations and put it to use for practical purposes. For instance, you're engaging in application if you use the knowledge you've acquired about human relations in Chapter 10 to become more assertive, or when you take knowledge acquired in an accounting course to help manage your personal finances.

Multidimensional Thinking

Important issues don't exist in isolation but as parts of a complex, interconnected system that involves interplay of multiple factors and perspectives. When you view yourself and the world around you from different perspectives or vantage points to gain a comprehensive perspective, you're engaging in *multidimensional thinking*. For instance, multidimensional thinkers are able to think from the following four key perspectives and see how each of them influences, and is influenced by, the issue they're examining:

> *To me, thinking at a higher level is when you approach a question or topic thoughtfully, when you fully explore every aspect of that topic from all angles."*
> —*AHE First-year student*

1. Perspective of **Person (Self):** How does this issue affect individuals on a personal basis?
2. Perspective of **Place:** What impact does this issue have on people living in different parts of the country or world?
3. Perspective of **Time:** How will future generations of people be affected by this issue?
4. Perspective of **Culture:** How is this issue likely to be interpreted or experienced by groups of people who share different social customs and traditions? (the perspective of culture)

Journal Reflection 11.3

Group activity: Many colleges and universities have been grappling with issues revolving around free speech. Let's look at it from various perspectives. What do you think the view would be if you were the president of an institution where students had protested? How about the view of a student protester, a parent, and a student who didn't participate in the protest. Don't forget to provide the rationale for your view.

Balanced Thinking

When we seek out and carefully consider arguments *for* and *against* a particular position, we're engaging in balanced thinking. The process of finding supporting evidence or reasons for a position is referred to as *adduction*—when you adduce, you identify reasons *for* a position; the process of finding evidence or reasons that contradicts a position is called *refutation*—when you refute, you provide a rebuttal *against* a particular position.

Balanced thinking involves both adduction and refutation. Each position's stronger arguments are acknowledged, and its weaker ones are refuted (Fairbairn and Winch 1996). The goal of a balanced thinker is not to stack up evidence for one position or the other but to be an impartial judge looking at supporting and opposing evidence for both sides of an issue, and striving to draw a conclusion that's neither biased nor one-sided. When you consider the strengths and weaknesses of opposing arguments at the same time, it reduces the likelihood that you'll fall prey to an overly simplistic form of thinking typical of many first-year students—known as *dualistic* thinking—seeking the "truth" in the form of clear-cut, black-or-white answers or solutions to complex issues—where one position or theory is "right" and the others "wrong" (Perry 1970, 1999).

Don't be surprised and frustrated if you find scholars disagreeing about what particular positions or theories are more accurate or account for most of the "truth" in their field. This is a healthy thought process known as *dialectic* or *dialogic* thinking (deriving from the root "dialogue" or "conversation"). It's a productive form of intellectual dialogue (Paul and Elder 2014) that acknowledges different sides of a complex issue and results in a more balanced, integrated understanding of it.

NOTE

Select one of the seven modes of higher level thinking and explain it using a Freyer Model.

Lastly, balanced thinking involves more than just totaling the number of arguments for and against a position; it also involves *weighing* the strength of each argument. Arguments can vary in terms of their degree of importance or level of support. When weighing arguments, ask yourself, "What is the quality and quantity of evidence supporting it?" Consider whether the evidence is:

1. **Definitive**—so strong or compelling that a definite conclusion should be reached;
2. **Suggestive**—strong enough to suggest that a tentative or possible conclusion may be reached; or
3. **Inconclusive**—too weak to reach any conclusion.

When making class presentations and writing papers or reports, be mindful of how much weight should be assigned to different arguments and explain how their weight has been factored into your conclusion.

If you find that the more you learn, the more complicated things seem to become, this is good news. It means you're moving from simplistic to complex thinking that's more multidimensional and balanced.

Critical Thinking (Evaluation)

When we *evaluate* or *judge* the quality of an argument or work product, we're engaging in a form of higher-level thinking known as *critical thinking*. It's a skill highly valued by professors teaching students at all stages in the college experience and all subjects in the college curriculum (Higher Education Research Institute 2009; Stark et al. 1990). By working on developing your critical thinking skills as a first-year student, you will significantly improve you academic performance throughout your college experience.

Many students misinterpret critical thinking to mean "being critical"—criticizing something or somebody. Although critical thinking does involving making an evaluation or judgment, the evaluation can be either positive or negative. For instance, a movie critic can give a good (thumbs up) or bad (thumbs down) review of a film.

Critical thinking is a skill that enables you to "read between the lines" and cut through the fog or smog of ideas and arguments—including your own. Whether the evaluation is positive or negative (or some combination thereof), critical thinking involves backing up your evaluation with specific, well-informed reasons or evidence that support the critique. Failure to do so makes the criticism unfounded—that is, lacking any foundation or basis of support.

You can start developing the mental habit of critical thinking by using the following criteria as standards for evaluating ideas or arguments:

1. **Validity (Truthfulness).** Is it true or accurate?
2. **Morality (Ethics).** Is it fair or just?
3. **Beauty (Aesthetics).** Does it have artistic merit or value?
4. **Practicality (Usefulness).** Can it be put to use for practical or beneficial purposes?
5. **Priority (Order of Importance or Effectiveness).** Is it better than other ideas and alternative courses of action?

NOTE

Balanced thinking enables you to become a more complex and comprehensive thinker capable of viewing issues from opposing sides and multiple perspectives.

" Critical thinking is an evaluative thought process that requires deep thinking."

—*AHE first-year student*

Journal Reflection 11.4

How do they differ?

_____

_____

_____

_____

Logical Fallacies: Inferential Reasoning Errors

Unfortunately, errors can be made in the inferential reasoning process, which are commonly referred to as *logical fallacies*. Listed below is a summary of the major types of logical fallacies. Be mindful of them in your thinking and when evaluating the thinking of others. Several examples of logical fallacies are given below.

- **Non sequitur.** Drawing a conclusion that doesn't follow from or connect with the premise—the initial statement or observation. (*Non sequitur* derives from Latin, which literally means, "it does not follow.") Example: There was a bloody glove found at the murder scene and it doesn't fit the defendant, therefore the defendant must be innocent.
- **Dogmatism.** Stubbornly clinging to a personal point of view unsupported by evidence while remaining closed-minded (nonreceptive) to other viewpoints better supported by evidence. Example: Arguing that adopting a national health system is a form of socialism that cannot work in a capitalistic economy, while ignoring the fact that there are many other nations in the world that have both a national health care system and a capitalistic economy.
- **Double Standard.** Having two sets of judgment standards—a higher standard for judging others and a lower standard for judging oneself. Example: Critically evaluating and challenging the opinions of others, but not our own.
- **Wishful Thinking.** Thinking something is true not because of logic or evidence, but because the person *wants* it to be true. Example: A teenage girl who believes she will not become pregnant, even though she and her boyfriend are having sex without any form of contraception.
- **Jumping to a Conclusion.** Making a leap of logic to a conclusion that's based on a single reason or factor while ignoring other possible reasons or contributing factors. Example: A shy person immediately concludes that a person who doesn't make eye contact with her doesn't like her, without considering the possibility that the lack of eye contact may be due to the fact that the other person was distracted or shy himself.
- **False Cause and Effect (a.k.a. Correlational Error).** Concluding that if two things co-occur at about the same time or in close sequence,

> " Facts do not cease to exist because they are ignored."
> —*Aldous Huxley, English writer and author of* Brave New World.

one must *cause* the other. Example: The old belief that sexual activity causes acne because when children become teenagers, they are more sexually active and also are more likely to develop acne.

- **Ad Hominem Argument.** Attacking the person, not the person's argument. (Literally translated, *ad hominem* means "to the man.") Example: discounting a young person's argument by saying: "you're too young and inexperienced to know what you're talking about," or discounting an older person's argument by stating: "you're too old-school to understand this issue."

- **Smoke Screen.** Intentionally disguising or camouflaging the truth by providing confusing or misleading explanations. Example: A politician who opposes gun control legislation by arguing that it's a violation of the constitutional right to bear arms, when in reality, the reason for his position is that he's receiving financial support from gun manufacturing companies.

- **Rhetorical Deception.** Using deceptive language to conclude that something is true without actually providing reasons or evidence. Example: Using glib words such as: "*Clearly* this is . . ." "It's *obvious* that . . ." or "Any *reasonable* person can see . . .", without explaining why it's so "clear," "obvious," or "reasonable."

- **Circular Reasoning (a.k.a. "Begging the Question").** Drawing a conclusion by merely rewording or restating one's position without providing any supporting reasons or evidence, thus leaving the original question unanswered. This logical fallacy basically offers a conclusion that's simply a circular restatement of the premise—it's true because it's true. Example: Concluding that "stem cell research isn't ethical because it's morally wrong."

> "Political talk shows have become shouting matches designed to push emotional hot buttons and drive us further apart. We desperately need to exchange ideas with one another rationally and courteously."
>
> —*David Boren, president, University of Oklahoma and longest-serving chairman of the U.S. Senate Intelligence Committee*

Creative Thinking

Creative thinking leads you to ask the question: "Why not?" (e.g., "Why not do it a different way?"). When you generate something new or different— an original idea, strategy, or work product—you're thinking creatively.

The process of creative thinking may be viewed as an extension or higher form of synthesis. Like synthesis, separate ideas are integrated, but they're combined in a way that results in something distinctively different (Anderson and Krathwohl 2001). For instance, the musical genre of hard rock was created by combining elements of blues and rock and roll, and folk rock was born when Bob Dylan combined musical elements of acoustic blues and amplified rock (Shelton et al. 2003). Robert Kearns (subject of the film, "Flash of Genius") combined preexisting mechanical parts to create the intermittent windshield wiper (Seabrook 2008).

Keep in mind that creative thinking is not restricted to the arts, it can occur in all subject areas—even in fields that seek precision and definite answers. In math, creative thinking involves using new approaches or strategies for arriving at a correct solution to a problem. In science, creativity takes place when a scientist first uses imaginative thinking to create a hypothesis or logical hunch ("What might happen if . . . ?") and then conducts an experiment to test out whether the hypothesis turns out to be true.

Box 11.2

The Process of Brainstorming

1. Generate as many ideas as you can, jotting them down rapidly without stopping to evaluate their validity or practicality. Studies show that worrying about whether an idea is correct often blocks creativity (Basadur, Runco, and Vega 2000). So, at this stage of the process, just let your imagination run wild; don't be concerned about whether the idea you generate is impractical, unrealistic, or outrageous.

2. Review the ideas you generated and use them as a springboard to trigger additional ideas, or combine them into larger ideas.

3. After you run out of ideas, critically evaluate the list of ideas you've generated and eliminate those that you think are least effective.

4. From the remaining list of ideas, choose the best idea or best combination of ideas.

Note that the first two steps in the brainstorming process involve *divergent thinking*—a form of creative thinking that allows you to go off in different directions and generate diverse ideas. In contrast, the last two steps in the process involve *convergent thinking*—a form of critical thinking in which you converge (focus in) and narrow down the ideas, evaluating each of them for their effectiveness.

As this multistage process suggests, creativity doesn't just happen suddenly or effortlessly (the so-called "stroke of genius"); instead, it takes sustained mental effort (De Bono 2007; Paul and Elder 2004). Although creative thinking may occasionally involve spontaneous or intuitive leaps, it typically involves careful reflection and evaluation of whether any of those leaps actually land you on a good idea.

AUTHOR'S JOURNEY

I was once working with a friend to come up with ideas for a grant proposal. We started out by sitting at his kitchen table, exchanging ideas while sipping coffee; then we both got up and began to pace back and forth, walking all around the room while bouncing different ideas off each other. Whenever a new idea was thrown out, one of us would jot it down (whoever was pacing closer to the kitchen table at the moment).

After we ran out of ideas, we shifted gears, slowed down, and sat down at the table together to critique the ideas we generated during our "binge-thinking" episode. After some debate, we finally settled on an idea that we judged to be the best of all the ideas we produced, and we used this idea for the grant proposal—which, ultimately, was awarded to us.

Although I wasn't fully aware of it at the time, the stimulating thought process my friend and I were engaging in was called brainstorming: first we engaged in creative thinking—our fast-paced, idea-production stage—followed by critical thinking—our slower-paced, idea-evaluation stage.

—*Joe Cuseo*

Creativity is allowing oneself to make mistakes; art is knowing which ones to keep."

—*Scott Adams, creator of the Dilbert comic strip and author of* The Dilbert Principle

USING HIGHER-LEVEL THINKING SKILLS TO IMPROVE ACADEMIC PERFORMANCE

Thus far, this chapter has focused primarily on helping you get a clear idea of what higher-level thinking is and what its major forms are. The remainder of the chapter focuses on helping you develop habits of higher-level thinking that can be applied to improve your performance in college and beyond.

NOTE

Creative thinking is about generating new answers and solutions. Critical thinking is about evaluating the quality of answers and solutions we generate.

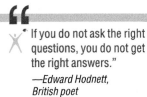

This first semester has changed my views on college. I hadn't realized skills I would gain in addition (what I) needed to earn my degree. In the past, I would read articles and have passionate opinions on topics, but in an argument or discussion, I couldn't articulate my thoughts. It was frustrating. I realize now, I just lacked the skills.

—Allison Scott

Note

When reading, be sure to engage with what you're reading by writing in the margins. Similar to talking back to a movie while playing or reflecting/writing ideas from your thought bubble (e.g., cartoons), make notes of what the author appears to be doing, how things resonate with your understanding/ experience, comments that might contradict one another, etc.

If you do not ask the right questions, you do not get the right answers."

—Edward Hodnett, British poet

Connect ideas you acquire in class with related ideas found in your assigned reading. When you discover information in your reading that relates to something you've learned about in class (or vice versa), make a note of it in the margin of your textbook or your class notebook. By integrating knowledge you've obtained from these two major sources, you're engaging in the higher-level thinking skill of synthesis, which you can then demonstrate on exams and assignments to improve your course grades.

When listening to lectures and completing reading assignments, pay attention not only to the content being covered but also the thought process used to cover the content. Periodically ask yourself what form of higher-level thinking your instructors are using during class presentations and authors are using when you're reading their writing. The more conscious you are of the type of higher-level thinking skills you're being exposed to, the more likely you are to develop those thinking skills yourself and demonstrate them on exams and assignments.

Periodically pause to reflect on your own thinking process. When working on different academic tasks, ask yourself what type of thinking you're doing (e.g., analysis, synthesis, or evaluation). Thinking about and becoming aware of how you're thinking while you're thinking is a mental process called *metacognition* (Flavell 1979; Hartman 2001). It's a mental habit that's associated with higher-level thinking and improved problem-solving skills (Halpern 2013; Resnick 1986).

Asking yourself higher-level thinking questions during lectures should prevent you from asking questions like this one.

Develop habits of higher-level thinking by asking yourself higher-level thinking questions. One simple yet powerful way to help you reflect on your thinking is through self-questioning. Since thinking often involves

© Kendall Hunt Publishing Company

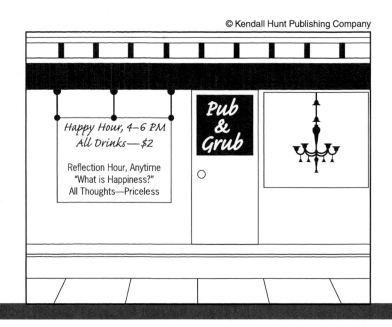

talking to ourselves silently (or aloud), if we ask ourselves high-quality, thought-provoking questions, you can train your mind to think at a higher level. A good question can launch you on a quest or voyage to answer it by using higher-level thinking skills. Getting in the habit of asking yourself higher-level thinking questions while learning will increase the likelihood you'll display higher levels of thinking during class discussions, as well as on course exams and assignments.

Journal Reflection 11.5

1. Why do bars and restaurants selling drinks have a happy hour?
   After analyzing some possible reasons, discuss some of the most common ones with a study group or online with your classmates.

2. What are arguments for and against this practice?
   Review all of the responses of your group and provide evidence for why this is or is not a good practice.

Box 11.3 contains key questions you can use to trigger different forms of higher-level thinking. The questions are constructed as incomplete sentences so you can fill in the blank with any topic or concept you're studying in any course you may be taking. Research indicates that when students get in the habit of using question stems such as these, they develop and demonstrate higher levels of thinking in college courses (King 1990, 1995, 2002). As you read the questions under each of the seven forms of higher-level thinking in the following box, think about how they may be applied to material you're learning in courses this term.

When engaged in Socratic Seminars and/or Philosophical Chairs the following information will guide your active involvement.

BOX 11.3

Self-Questioning Strategies to Trigger Different Forms of Higher-Level Thinking

1. Analysis (Analytical Thinking)—breaking down information into its essential elements or parts.

   Trigger Questions:
   - What are the main ideas contained in _____?
   - What are the important aspects of _____?
   - What are the key issues raised by _____?
   - What are the major purposes of _____?
   - What hidden assumptions are embedded in _____?
   - What are the reasons behind _____?

2. Synthesis (Integrative Thinking)—integrating separate pieces of information to form a more complete and coherent product or pattern.

   Trigger Questions:
   - How can this idea be joined or connected with _____ to create a more complete or comprehensive answer?
   - How could these different _____ be grouped together into a more general class or category?
   - How could these separate _____ be reorganized or rearranged to produce a comprehensive understanding of the big picture?

3. Application (Applied Thinking)—using knowledge for practical purposes to solve problems and resolve issues.

   Trigger Questions:
   - How can this idea be used to _____?
   - How can this theory be put into practice to _____?
   - What could be done to improve or strengthen _____?
   - What could be done to prevent or reduce _____?

4. Balanced Thinking—carefully considering reasons for and against a particular position or viewpoint.

   Trigger Questions:
   - Have I considered both sides of _____?
   - What are the strengths (advantages) and weaknesses (disadvantages) of _____?
   - What evidence supports and contradicts _____?
   - What are arguments for and counterarguments against _____?

5. Multidimensional Thinking—thinking that involves viewing yourself and the world around you from different angles or vantage points.

   Trigger Questions:
   - Have I taken into consideration all factors that could influence _____ or be influenced by _____?
   - How would _____ affect different dimensions of myself (emotional, physical, etc.)?
   - What broader impact would _____ have on the social and physical world around me?
   - How might people living in different times (e.g., past and future) experience _____?
   - How would people from different cultural backgrounds interpret or react to _____?

6. Critical Thinking (Evaluation)—making critical judgments or assessments.

   Trigger Questions for Evaluating *Empirical Evidence:*
   - What examples support the argument that _____?
   - What research evidence is there for _____?
   - What statistical data document or back up this _____?

   Trigger Questions for Evaluating *Logical Consistency:*
   - If ____ is true, does it follow that ____ is also true?
   - If I believe in _____, should I practice _____?
   - To draw this conclusion means I'm assuming that ____?

   Trigger Questions for Evaluating *Morality (Ethics):*
   - Is _____ fair?
   - Is _____ just?
   - Is this action consistent with the professed or stated values of _____?

   Trigger Questions for Evaluating Beauty (Aesthetics):
   - Does _____ meet established criteria for judging artistic beauty?
   - What is the aesthetic merit or value of _____?
   - Does _____ contribute to or detract from the beauty of the environment?

Trigger Questions for Evaluating *Practicality (Usefulness):*
- Will _____ work?
- What practical value does this _____ have?
- What potential benefits and drawbacks would result if this ____ were put into practice?

Trigger Questions for Evaluating *Priority (Order of Importance or Effectiveness):*
- Which one of these _____ is the most important?
- Is this _____ the best option or choice available?
- How do these _____ rank from first to last (best to worst) in terms of their effectiveness?

7. Creative Thinking—generating ideas that are unique, original, or distinctively different.
   Trigger Questions:
   - What could be invented to _____?
   - Imagine what would happen if _____?
   - What might be a different way to _____?

- How would this change if _____?
- What would be an innovative approach to _____?

Note: Save these higher-level thinking questions and use them when completing different academic tasks required in your courses (e.g., preparing for exams, writing papers or reports, and participating in class discussions or study group sessions). Get in the habit of periodically stepping back to reflect on your thinking and ask yourself what form of thinking you're engaging in (analysis, synthesis, application, etc.). You could even keep a "thinking log" or "thinking journal" to increase self-awareness of the thinking strategies you're using and developing. This strategy will not only help you acquire higher-level thinking skills, it will also help you communicate these skills in job interviews and letters of application for career positions.

INQUIRY

Although inquiry is critical to the entire Socratic tutorial process, it is the focus of Step 4. Tutors facilitate learning when they check for understanding and have the student articulate the processes or steps that clarified the student's point of confusion. This inquiry process helps students accept responsibility for their own learning. Any advanced preparation for the tutorial session on a TIF is reinforced when the student can clearly identify the point of confusion—the point where the student gets muddled. Students process their notes by reading and adding additional information identified in the tutoring session, capture summarizing thoughts to fill in the gaps, and mark and annotate written information. Finally, students capture questions that are explained in the notes.

> "Effective problem solvers know how to ask questions to fill in the gaps between what they know and what they don't know. Effective questioners are inclined to ask a range of questions."
> —*Costa and Kallick 2000*

Using the art of inquiry, a tutor provides a scaffold to help students:

- identify foundational knowledge (Level 1) such as facts, definitions, and steps;
- make comparisons (Level 2), distinguishing the differences between parts or steps; and
- analyze and apply the information (Level 3).

In other words, students make sense out of information, process the information that has been gathered, and make connections to create or identify new relationships using that information. This increased level of thinking and understanding prepares students to evaluate and/or create new ideas, products, or points of view. Innovation and speculation moves students to the highest level of thinking.

Tutors may need to establish the foundational knowledge to identify any gaps in student understanding. Using Level 1 questions to make students reflect on class notes, readings of assigned texts, and other assigned resources empowers students to know that they have collected the right information. This Level 1 reflection supports the Level 2 thinking, wherein students look for similarities or differences and assimilate the new information. Learning is best when students can relate new information to what they already know. The memory part of the brain builds new synapses and is able to relate to and retain the information better.

Inquiry Learning Process: Aligned with the 6-Step AHE Socratic Tutorial Process

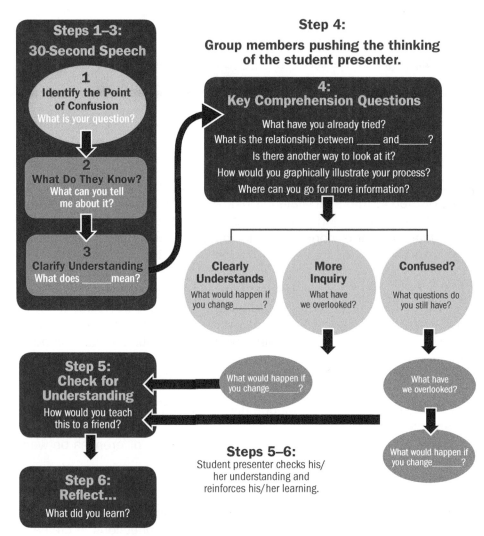

Adapted from Comparison by Andrew Churches at http://edorigami.wikispaces.com/Bloom%27s+Digital+Taxonomy and http://ww2.odu.edu/educ/roverbau/Bloom/blooms_taxonomy.htm

Bloom's & Costa's Levels of Thinking Comparison

Level	Costa's	Bloom's	Vocabulary Levels of Thinking		
Higher Order Thinking Skills HOTS	**OUTPUT (Level 3)** **Applying Information:** Applying and evaluating actions, solutions, and connections made in order to predict	**Creating:** *Can the students:* • Create/generate new ideas, products or points of view • Combine ideas/thoughts to develop an innovative idea, solution, or way of thinking	Assemble Build Construct Create Design	Develop Devise Formulate Imagine Invent	Make Plan Produce Write
		Evaluating: *Can the students:* • Justify a stand or decision • Judge the value of an idea, item, or technique by creating and applying standards/criteria	Appraise Argue Check Critique Defend Detect	Forecast Generalize Hypothesize If/Then Judge Predict	Select Speculate Support Test Valuate Value
	PROCESSING (Level 2) **Processing Information:** Making sense out of information; processing the information gathered by making connections and creating relationships	**Analyzing:** *Can the students:* • Distinguish between the different parts • Explore and understand relationships between the components/parts	Attribute Classify Compare Contrast Criticize Deconstruct Differentiate	Discriminate Distinguish Examine Experiment Infer	Integrate Organize Outline Question Sort Structure
		Applying: *Can the students:* • Use the information in a similar situation • Apply learned concepts, strategies, principles and theories in a new way	Carry out Choose Demonstrate Do Dramatize	Employ Execute Illustrate Implement Interpret	Operate Schedule Sketch Solve Using
Lower Order Thinking Skills LOTS	**INPUT (Level 1)** **Gathering Information:** Identifying and recalling information	**Understanding:** *Can the students:* • Explain ideas or concepts • Understand information provided	Classify Complete Describe Discuss	Explain Identify Locate Paraphrase	Recognize Report Select Translate
		Remembering: *Can the students:* • Recall or remember the information • Recognize specific information	Define Duplicate List	Memorize Recall Repeat	Reproduce State

Daws, T. and P. Schiro, 2012. AVID Tutorial Guide: Creating Rigorous Tutorials to Increase Student Achievement in Academic Classes. San Diego, CA: AVID Press.

English Content—Specific Questions

Level 1	Level 2	Level 3
• What information is provided? • Locate in the story where . . . • When did the event take place? • Point to the . . . • List the . . . • Name the . . . • What is . . .? • Who was/were . . .? • Illustrate the part of the story that . . . • Make a map of . . . • What is the origin of the word ____? • What events led to . . .?	• What would happen to you if . . .? • Would you have done the same thing as . . .? • What occurs when . . . ? • Compare and contrast ____ to ____. • What is the main idea of the story (event)? • What information supports your explanation? • What was the message in this piece (event)? • Give me an example of . . . • Describe in your own words what ___ means. • What does ____ suggest about _____'s charter? • What lines of the poem express the poet's feelings about _____? • What is the author trying to prove? • What evidence does he/she present?	• Design a ____ to show . . . • Predict what will happen to ____ as ____ is changed. • Write a new ending to the story (event). • Describe the events that might occur if . . . • Add something new on your own that was not in the story. • Pretend you are . . . • What would the world be like if . . . ? • Pretend you are a character in the story. Rewrite the episode from your point of view. • What do you think will happen to ____? Why? • What is most compelling to you in this _____? Why? • Could this story have really happened? Why or why not? • If you were there, would you . . . ? • How would you solve this problem in your life?

Math Content—Specific Questions

Level 1	Level 2	Level 3
• What information is provided? • What are you being asked to find? • What formula would you use in this problem? • What does ____ mean? • What is the formula for . . .? • List the . . . • Name the . . . • Where did . . .? • What is . . .? • When did . . .? • Explain the concept of . . . • Give me an example of . . . • Describe in your own words what ____ means. • What mathematical concepts does this problem connect to? • Draw a diagram of . . . • Illustrate how ____ works.	• What additional information is needed to solve this problem? • Can you see other relationships that will help you find this information? • How can you put your data in graphic form? • What occurs when . . .? • Does it make sense to . . .? • Compare and contrast ____ to ____. • What was important about . . .? • What prior research/formulas support your conclusions? • How else could you account for . . .? • Explain how you calculate . . . • What equation can you write to solve the word problem?	• Predict what will happen to ____ as ____ is changed. • Using a math principle, how can we find . . .? • Describe the events that might occur if . . . • Design a scenario for . . . • Pretend you are . . . • What would the world be like if . . .? • How can you tell if your answer is reasonable? • What would happen to ____ if ____ (variable) were increased/decreased? • How would repeated trials affect your data? • What significance is this formula to the subject you are learning? • What type of evidence is most compelling to you?

Science Content—Specific Questions

Level 1	Level 2	Level 3
• What information is provided? • What are you being asked to find? • What formula would you use in this problem? • What does ____ mean? • What is the formula for . . .? • List the . . . • Name the . . . • Where did . . .? • What is . . .? • When did . . .? • Describe in your own words what ____ means. • What science concepts does this problem connect to? • Draw a diagram of . . . • Illustrate how ____ works.	• What additional information is needed to solve this problem? • Can you see other relationships that will help you find this information? • How can you put your data in graphic form? • How would you change your procedures to get better results? • What method would you use to . . .? • Compare and contrast ____ to ____. • Which errors most affected your results? • What were some sources of variability? • How do your conclusions support your hypothesis? • What prior research/formulas support yourconclusions? • How else could you account for . . .? • Explain the concept of . . . • Give me an example of . . .	• Design a lab to show . . . • Predict what will happen to ____ as ____ is changed. • Using a science principle, how can we find . . .? • Describe the events that might occur if . . . • Design a scenario for . . . • Pretend you are . . . • What would the world be like if . . .? • What would happen to ____ if ____ (variable) were increased/decreased? • How would repeated trials affect your data? • What significance is this experiment to the subject you are learning? • What type of evidence is most compelling to you? • Do you feel ____ experiment is ethical? • Are your results biased?

Social Science Content—Specific Questions

Level 1	Level 2	Level 3
• What information is provided?	• What would happen to you if . . .?	• Design a _____ to show . . .
• What are you being asked to find?	• Can you see other relationships that will help you find this information?	• Predict what will happen to _____ as _____ is changed?
• When did the event take place?	• Would you have done the same thing as . . .?	• What would it be like to live . . .?
• Point to the . . .	• What occurs when . . .?	• Write a new ending to the event.
• List the . . .	• If you were there, would you . . .?	• Describe the events that might occur if . . .
• Name the . . .	• How would you solve this problem in your life?	• Pretend you are _____ and explain how events would have changed. Why?
• Where did . . .?	• Compare and contrast _____ to _____.	• What would the world be like if . . .?
• What is . . .?	• What other ways could _____ be interpreted?	• How can you tell if your analysis is reasonable?
• Who was/were . . .?	• What things would you have used to . . .?	• What do you think will happen to _____? Why?
• Make a map of . . .	• What is the main idea in this piece (event)?	• What is the significance of this event in the global perspective?
	• What information supports your explanation?	• What is most compelling to you in this _____? Why?
	• What was the message in this event?	• Do you feel _____ is ethical? Why or why not?
	• Explain the concept of . . .	
	• Give me an example of . . .	

FOR INCREASING HIGHER LEVEL THINKING

In addition to self-questioning strategies, the following attitudes and practices can be used to stimulate creative thinking:

• **Be flexible.** Think about ideas and objects in alternative and unconventional ways. The power of flexible and unconventional thinking was well illustrated in the movie "Apollo 13," based on the true story of an astronaut who saved his life by creatively using duct tape as an air filter. The inventor of the printing press (Johannes Gutenberg) made his groundbreaking discovery while watching a machine being used to crush grapes at a wine harvest. He thought that the same type of machine could be used for a different purpose—to press letters onto paper (Dorfman, Shames, and Kihlstrom 1996).

• **Be experimental.** Play with ideas; try them out to see whether they'll work or work better than the status quo. Studies show that creative people tend to be mental risk-takers who are willing to experiment with different ideas and techniques (Sternberg 2001). Consciously resist the temptation to settle for the security of familiarity. When people cling rigidly to what's conventional or traditional, they're clinging to the comfort or security of what's most familiar and predictable; this often blocks originality, ingenuity, and openness to change. Tom Kelley, co-founder of the famous IDEO design firm in Palo Alto, California, has found that innovative thinking emerges from an exploratory mindset that's "open to new insights every day" (Kelley and Littman 2005).

- **Get mobile.** Stand up and move around while you're thinking. Research shows that taking a walk—either inside or outside—stimulates the production of creative ideas (Oppezzo and Schwartz 2014). Even by standing up, our brain gets approximately 10% more oxygen than it does when sitting down (Sousa 2011). Since oxygen provides fuel for the brain, our ability to think creatively is energized when we're up on our feet and moving around.

- **Get it down.** Ideas can often pop into our mind at the most unexpected times. Scholars refer to the sudden birth of creative ideas as *incubation*—just like incubated eggs can hatch at any time, so too can original ideas suddenly hatch and pop into our consciousness. However, just as great ideas can suddenly come to mind, they can also slip out of mind as soon as we start thinking about something else. You can prevent this slippage from happening by having the right equipment on hand to record your creative ideas before they slip away. Carry a pen and a small notepad, a packet of sticky notes, or a portable electronic recording device at all times to immediately record original ideas the instant you have them.

- **Get diverse.** Seek ideas from diverse social and informational sources. Bouncing your ideas off of different people and getting their feedback about your ideas is a good way to generate mental energy, synergy (multiplication of ideas), and serendipity (accidental discoveries). Studies show that creative people venture well beyond the boundaries of their particular area of training or specialization (Baer 1993; Kaufman and Baer 2002). They have wide-ranging interests and knowledge, which they draw upon and combine to generate new ideas (Riquelme 2002). So, be on the lookout to combine the knowledge and skills you acquire from different subjects and different people, and use them to create bridges to new ideas.

- **Take breaks.** If you're having trouble discovering a solution to a problem, stop working on it for a while and come back to it later. Creative solutions often come to mind after you stop thinking about the problem you're trying to solve. What often happens when you work intensely on a problem or challenging task for a sustained period of time, your attention can get rigidly riveted on just one approach to its solution (German and Barrett 2005; Maier 1970). By taking your mind off of it and returning to it later, your focus of attention is likely to shift to a different feature or aspect of the problem. This new focus may enable you to view the problem from a different angle or vantage point, which can lead to a breakthrough idea that was blocked by your previous perspective (Anderson 2010). Furthermore, taking a break allows the problem to incubate in your mind at a lower level of consciousness and stress, which can sometimes give birth to a sudden solution.

- **Reorganize the problem.** When you're stuck on a problem, try rearranging its parts or pieces. Reorganization can transform the problem into a different pattern that may enable you to suddenly see a solution you previously overlooked—similar to how changing the order of letters in a word jumble can help you find the hidden word. You can use the same strategy to change the wording of any problem you're working on, or by recording ideas on index cards (or sticky notes) and laying them out in different sequences and patterns.

If you're having trouble solving a problem that involves a sequence of steps (e.g., a math problem), try reversing the sequence and start by working from the end or middle. The new sequence makes you to take a different approach to the problem; this forces you to come at it from a different direction, which can lead you to an alternative path to its solution.

* **Be persistent.** Studies show that creativity takes time, dedication, and hard work (Ericsson 2006; Ericsson and Charness 1994). Creative insights typically don't occur effortlessly, but emerge after repeated reflection and sustained commitment.

CHAPTER SUMMARY AND HIGHLIGHTS

Higher-level thinking (also known as higher-order thinking) refers to a more advanced level of thought than that used to acquire factual knowledge. It involves reflecting on knowledge acquired and taking it to a higher level—by performing additional mental action on it—such as evaluating its validity, integrating it with other ideas, or applying it to solve problems.

In this chapter, seven major forms of higher-level thinking skills were identified along with strategies for developing each of them:

1. *Analysis (Analytical Thinking)*—breaking down information to identify its key parts and underlying elements;
2. *Synthesis (Integrative Thinking)*—building up ideas by connecting them to form a larger whole or more comprehensive system;
3. *Application (Applied Thinking)*—putting knowledge into practice to solve problems and resolve issues;
4. *Multidimensional Thinking*—taking multiple perspectives (i.e., viewing issues from different vantage points);
5. *Balanced Thinking*—carefully considering arguments for and against a particular argument or position;
6. *Critical Thinking*—evaluating (judging the quality of) arguments, conclusions, and ideas;
7. *Creative Thinking*—generating ideas that are unique, original, or distinctively different.

Besides achieving academic excellence in college, there are other key benefits of developing higher-level thinking skills.

1. **Higher-level thinking is essential for success in today's "information age"—a time when new information is being generated at faster rates than at any other time in human history.** The majority of new workers in the information age no longer work with their hands, they will work with their heads (Miller 2003). Employers now value college graduates who have inquiring minds and possess higher-level thinking skills (Harvey et al. 1997; Peter D. Hart Research Associates 2006).

2. **Higher-level thinking skills are vital for citizens in a democratic nation.** Authoritarian political systems, such as dictatorships and fascist regimes, suppress critical thought and demand submissive obedience to authority. In contrast, citizens of a democracy are able to control their political destiny by making wise choices about the political leaders they elect. Thus, effective use of higher-level thinking skills, such as critical thinking, is an essential civic responsibility for people living in a democratic nation.

3. **Higher-level thinking is an important safeguard against prejudice, discrimination, and hostility.** Racial, ethnic, and national prejudices are often rooted in narrow, self-centered or group-centered thinking (Paul and Elder 2014). Oversimplified, dualistic thinking can lead individuals to categorizing others into either "in" groups (us) or "out" groups (them). Such dualistic thinking can lead, in turn, to ethnocentrism—the tendency to view one's own racial or ethnic group as the superior "in" group and see other groups as inferior "out" groups. Development of higher-level thinking skills, such as taking multiple perspectives and using balanced thinking, counteracts the type of dualistic, ethnocentric thinking that leads to prejudice, discrimination, and hate crimes.

4. **Higher-level thinking helps preserve mental and physical health.** Simply put: Those who use their mind don't lose their mind. As they age, mentally active people are less likely to suffer memory loss or experience dementia (Wilson, Mendes, and Barnes 2002). Thinking is not only a mental activity, it's also a physical activity that exercises the brain, much like physical activity exercises muscles in other parts of the body. Thinking requires higher levels of energy, which stimulates biological activity among brain cells, invigorates them, and reduces the likelihood they will deteriorate with age.

©Kendall Hunt Publishing Company

Contrary to common belief, problem solving and other forms of higher-level thinking will not "fry" your brain but will stimulate and exercise it, reducing the likelihood that you'll experience Alzheimer's disease and other causes of memory loss in later life.

LEARNING MORE THROUGH THE WORLD WIDE WEB: INTERNET-BASED RESOURCES

For additional information on thinking skills, see the following websites:

Higher-Level Thinking Skills: http://edorigami.wikispaces.com/Bloom%27s+Digital+Taxonomy

Critical Thinking:
www.criticalthinking.org

Creative Thinking:
www.amcreativityassoc.org

Thinking Errors:
www.psychologytoday.com/blog/what-mentally-strong-people-dont-do/201501/10-thinking-errors-will-crush-your-mental-strength

www.factcheck.org (site for evaluating the factual accuracy of statements made by politicians in TV ads, debates, speeches, interviews, and news releases)

REFERENCES

Anderson, J. R. 2010. *Cognitive Psychology and its Implications*. New York: Worth Publishers.

Anderson, L. W., and D. R. Krathwohl, eds. 2001. *A Taxonomy for Learning, Teaching, and Assessing: A Revision of Bloom's Taxonomy of Educational Objectives*. New York: Addison Wesley Longman.

Baer, J. M. 1993. *Creativity and Divergent Thinking*. Hillsdale, NJ: Erlbaum.

Basadur, M., M. A. Runco, and L. A. Vega. 2000. "Understanding How Creative Thinking Skills, Attitudes and Behaviors Work Together: A Causal Process Model." *Journal of Creative Behavior* 34 (2): 77–100.

Conley, D. T. 2005. *College Knowledge: What It Really Takes for Students to Succeed and What We Can Do to Get Them Ready*. San Francisco: Jossey-bass.

De Bono, E. 2007. *How to Have Creative Ideas*. London, UK: Vermillion.

Donald, J. G. 2002. *Learning to Think: Disciplinary Perspectives*. San Francisco: Jossey-bass.

Dorfman, J., J. Shames, and J. F. Kihlstrom. 1996. "Intuition, Incubation, and Insight." In *Implicit Cognition, edited by* G. Underwood, 257–296. New York: Oxford University Press.

Ericsson, K. A. 2006. "The Influence of Experience and Deliberate Practice on the Development of Superior Expert Performance. In *Cambridge Handbook of Expertise and Expert Performance*, edited by K. A. Ericsson, N. Charness, P. Feltovich, and R. R. Hoffman, 685–706. Cambridge, UK: Cambridge University Press.

Ericsson, K. A., and N. Charness. 1994. "Expert Performance: Its Structure and Acquisition." *American Psychologist* 49 (8): 725–47.

Fairbairn, G. J., and C. Winch 1996. *Reading, Writing and Reasoning: A Guide for Students*. 2nd ed. Buckingham: OU Press.

Flavell, J. H. 1979. "Metacognition and Cognitive Monitoring: A New Area of Cognitive developmental Inquiry." *American Psychologist* 34 (10): 906–11.

Gardiner, L. F. 2005. "Transforming the Environment for Learning: A Crisis of Quality." *To Improve the Academy* 23: 3–23.

German, T. P., and H. C. Barrett. 2005. "Functional Fixedness in a Technologically Sparse Culture." *Psychological Science* 16: 1–5.

Halpern, D. F. 2013. *Thought & Knowledge: An Introduction to Critical Thinking*. 5th ed. New York: Psychology Press.

Hartman, H. J., ed. 2001. *Metacognition in Learning and Instruction: Theory, Research and Practice*. Dordrecht: Kluwer Academic Publishers.

Harvey, L., S. Moon, V. Geall, and R. Bower. 1997. *Graduates Work: Organizational Change and Students' Attributes*, Birmingham, Centre for Research into Quality, University of Central England.

Higher Education Research Institute (HERI). 2009. *The American College Teacher: National Norms for 2007–2008*. Los Angeles: HERI, University of California, Los Angeles.

Kaufman, J. C., and J. Baer. 2002. "Could Steven Spielberg Manage the Yankees? Creative Thinking in Different Domains." *Korean Journal of Thinking & Problem Solving* 12 (2): 5–14.

Kelley, T., and J. Littman. 2005. *The Ten Faces of Innovation: IDEO's Strategies for Beating the Devil's Advocate & Driving Creativity Throughout Your Organization*. New York: Currency/Doubleday.

King, A. 1990. "Enhancing Peer Interaction and Learning in the Classroom through Reciprocal Questioning. "*American Educational Research Journal* 27 (4): 664–87.

King, A. 1995. Guided Peer Questioning: A Cooperative Learning Approach to Critical Thinking." *Cooperative Learning and College Teaching* 5 (2): 15–9.

King, A. 2002. "Structuring Peer Interaction to Promote High-level Cognitive Processing." *Theory into Practice* 41 (1): 33–9.

Maier, N. R. F. 1970. *Problem Solving and Creativity in Individuals and Groups*. Belmont, CA: Brooks/Cole.

Miller, M. A. September/October, 2003. "The Meaning of the Baccalaureate." *About Campus* 8 (4): 2–8.

Milton, O. 1982. *Will That Be on the Final?* Springfield, IL: Charles C. Thomas.

National Resources Defense Council. 2005. *Global Warming: A Summary of Recent Findings on the Changing Global Climate*. http://www.nrdc.org/globalwarming/science/2005.asp.

Oppezzo, M., and D. L. Schwartz. 2014. "Give Your Ideas Some Legs: The Positive Effect of Walking on Creative Thinking." *Journal of Experimental Psychology: Learning, Memory, and Cognition* 40 (4): 1142–52.

Pascarella, E., and P. Terenzini. 1991. *How College Affects Students: Findings and Insights from Twenty Years of Research*. San Francisco: Jossey-bass.

Pascarella, E., and P. Terenzini. 2005. *How College Affects Students: A Third Decade of Research*. Vol. 2. San Francisco: Jossey-bass.

Paul, R., and L. Elder. 2004. *The Nature and Functions of Critical and Creative Thinking*. Dillon Beach, CA: Foundation for Critical Thinking.

Paul, R., and L. Elder. 2014. *Critical Thinking: Tools for Taking Charge of Your Professional and Personal Life*. Upper Saddle River, NJ: Pearson Education.

Perry, W. G. 1970, 1999. *Forms of Intellectual and Ethical Development During the College Years: A Scheme*. New York: Holt, Rinehart and Winston.

Peter D. Hart Research Associates. 2006. *How Should Colleges Prepare Students to Succeed in Today's Global Economy?* The Association of American Colleges and Universities by Peter D. Hart Research Associates, Inc.

Resnick, L. B. 1986. *Education and Learning to Think*. Washington, DC: National Academy Press.

Riquelme, H. 2002. "Can People Creative in Imagery Interpret Ambiguous Figures Faster than People less Creative in Imagery?" *Journal of Creative Behavior* 36 (2): 105–16.

Seabrook, J. 2008. *Flash of Genius and Other True Stories of Invention*. New York: St. Martin's Press.

Shelton, D. R., J. A. Van Kessel, M. R. Wachtel, K. T. Belt, J. S. Karns. December, 2003. "Evaluation of Parameters Affecting Quantitative Detection of Escherichia coli O157 in Enriched Water Samples Using Immunomagnetic Electrochemiluminescence." *J. Microbiology Methods* 55 (3): 717–25.

Sousa, D. A. 2011. *How the Brain Learns*. Thousand Oaks, CA: Sage.

Stark, J. S., M. A. Lowther, R. J. Bentley, M. P. Ryan, G. G. Martens, M. L. Genthon, P. A. Wren, K. M. Shaw. 1990. *Planning Introductory College Courses: Influences on Faculty*. Ann Arbor: National Center for Research to Improve Postsecondary Teaching and Learning, University of Michigan. (ERIC Document Reproduction Services No. 330 277 370.)

Staudinger, U. M. 2008. "A Psychology of Wisdom: History and Recent Developments. "*Research in Human Development* 5: 107–20.

Sternberg, R. J. 2001. "What Is the Common Thread of Creativity?" *American Psychologist* 56 (4): 360–2.

Wilson, R. S., C. F. Mendes, L. L. Barnes, J. A. Schneider, J. L. Bienias, D. A. Evans, D. A. Bennett. 2002. "Participation in Cognitively Stimulating Activities and Risk of Incident Alzheimer's Disease." *Journal of the American Medical Association* 287 (6): 742–8.

Chapter 11 Exercises

11.1 Quote Reflections

Review the sidebar quotes contained in this chapter and select two that were especially meaningful or inspirational to you.

For each quote, provide a three- to five-sentence explanation why you chose it.

11.2 Reality Bite

Trick or Treat: Confusing Test or Challenging Test?

Students in Professor Plato's philosophy course just got their first exam back and they're going over the test together in class. Some students are angry because they feel the professor deliberately included "trick questions" to confuse them. Professor Plato responds by saying that his test questions were not designed to trick the class but to "challenge them to think."

Reflection and Discussion Questions

1. What do you think may have led some students to conclude that the professor was trying to trick or confuse them?
2. What type of test questions do you suspect the professor created to "challenge students to think"?
3. On future tests, what might the students do to reduce the likelihood that they'll feel tricked again?
4. On future tests, what might Professor Plato do to reduce the likelihood that students will complain about being asked "trick questions"?

11.3 Faculty Interview

Make an appointment to visit a faculty member on campus, either in a course you're taking this term, or in a field of study you're likely to pursue as your major. During your visit, ask the following questions:

1. In your field of study, what key questions do scholars ask?
2. How are answers to these questions investigated and discovered?
3. How do scholars in your field demonstrate critical and creative thinking?
4. What types of thinking skills does it take for students to succeed or excel in your field?

11.4 Self-Assessment of Higher-Level Thinking Characteristics

Thinking at a higher level is not just an intellectual process, it's also a personal attribute. Listed below are attributes of higher-level thinkers, accompanied by specific behaviors associated with each attribute. As you read the behaviors under each of the general attributes, place a checkmark (✓) next to any behavior that's true of you now and an asterisk (*) next to any behavior you think you need to work on.

1. *Tolerant and Accepting*

   _____ Don't tune out ideas that conflict with your own

   _____ Keep your emotions under control when someone criticizes your personal viewpoint

   _____ Feel comfortable discussing controversial issues

   _____ Try to find common ground with others holding opposing viewpoints

2. *Inquisitive and Open Minded*

    _____ Eager to continue learning new things from different people and different experiences

    _____ Willing to seek out others who hold viewpoints different than your own

    _____ Find differences of opinion and opposing viewpoints to be interesting and stimulating

    _____ Attempt to understand why people have opposing viewpoints

3. *Reflective and Tentative*

    _____ Take time to consider all perspectives or sides of an issue before drawing conclusions, making choices, or reaching decisions

    _____ Give fair consideration to ideas that others may instantly disapprove of or find distasteful

    _____ Acknowledge the complexity, ambiguity, and uncertainty of certain issues, and am willing to say: "I need to give this more thought" or "I need more evidence before I can draw a conclusion"

    _____ Periodically reexamine your own viewpoints to determine whether they should be maintained or changed

4. *Honest and Courageous*

    _____ Willing to examine your views to see if they're biased or prejudiced

    _____ Willing to challenge others' ideas that are based on personal bias or prejudice

    _____ Willing to express viewpoints that may not conform to those of the majority

    _____ Willing to change previously held opinions and personal beliefs when they're contradicted by sound arguments or new evidence

Look back at the list and count the number of checkmarks and asterisks you placed in each of the four general areas:

	Checkmarks	**Asterisks**
Tolerant and Accepting:	_____	_____
Inquisitive and Open Minded:	_____	_____
Reflective and Tentative:	_____	_____
Honest and Courageous:	_____	_____

Reflection questions:

*   Under which of the four attributes did you place (a) the most *checkmarks*, (b) the most *asterisks*? What do you think accounts for the difference?

*   What could you do in college to strengthen your weakest area (the attribute below which you had the most asterisks)?

Chapter 11 Reflection

How can you use critical thinking to be a more successful student? Explain. List three action steps you can do to make this happen.

How can you use critical thinking to improve your personal life? Explain.

How can you use creative thinking to be a more successful student? Explain. List three action steps you can do to make this happen.

How can you use creative thinking to improve your personal life? Explain.

CHAPTER 12

FINANCIAL LITERACY

MANAGING MONEY AND MINIMIZING DEBT

This chapter provides you with specific strategies for tracking cash flow, minimizing and avoiding debt, balancing time spent on schoolwork and working for pay, and making wise spending and saving decisions while you're in college.

Become more aware, knowledgeable, and strategic about managing money, financing your college education and handling your future finances. To provide students with strategies that promote good money management

You will develop a SMART goal that enables them to reduce debt or keep them from going into debt.

Describe your current financial plan for college.

What strategies would improve my financial foundation during college?

Purpose for Reading this Chapter: There are an increasing number of options to help you spend—and helo you save money. As you read, circle phrases that support good money management in blue and undesirable financial practices in red. Create a SMART goal (with subgoals if necessary) to assist you in developing and practicing sound money management.

For many students, starting college marks the start of greater personal independence and greater responsibilities for financial self-management and decision-making. The issue of money management for college students is growing in importance for a number of reasons. The higher cost of a college education requires more difficult fiscal decisions about what options (or combination of options) to use to meet college expenses. Unfortunately, research indicates that many students today are making decisions about financing their college education in ways that do not effectively promote their academic success and progress to graduation (King 2005).

Another reason why money management is growing in importance for college students is the availability and convenience of credit cards. It's never been easier for college students to access, use, and abuse credit cards. Credit agencies and bureaus now closely monitor college students' credit card payments and routinely report their "credit score" to credit card companies and banks. Since research shows that there is a statistical relationship between using credit cards responsibly and being a responsible employee (Ring 1997; Susswein 1995), employers check these credit scores and use them as indicators or predictors of how responsible a student will be as an employee. Thus, being irresponsible with credit while in college can affect a student's ability to land a job after (or during) college. Students' credit scores also affect their likelihood of qualifying for car loans and home loans as well as their ability to rent an apartment (Pratt 2011). College graduates today can do everything right while they are in college, such as get good grades, get involved on campus, and get work experience before graduating, but a poor credit history as college students can harm them after college—reducing their chance of obtaining credit and their job prospects (Nellie Mae 2005; Sallie Mae 2009).

Furthermore, accumulating high levels of debt while in college is associated with higher levels of student stress (Nelson et al. 2008), lower academic performance (Susswein 1995), and greater risk of withdrawing from college (Ring 1997). On the positive side of the ledger, studies show that when college students learn to use effective money management strategies (such as those discussed below), they can reduce unnecessary spending, minimize accumulation of debt, and lower their overall level of stress (Health and Soll 1996; Kidwell and Turrisi 2004; Walker 1996).

SOURCES OF INCOME FOR FINANCING A COLLEGE EDUCATION

College students' income typically comes from three sources:

- Scholarships or grants that are not repaid, and
- Loans that must be repaid, and
- Salary earned from part- or full-time work.

The *Free Application for Federal Student Aid (FAFSA)* is the application used by the U.S. Department of Education to determine financial aid eligibility for students. It asks for personal and family financial information to determine a student's eligibility for federal, state, and college-sponsored financial aid, including grants, loans, and work-study employment. A formula is used to determine the student's *estimated family contribution (EFC)*—the amount of money estimated by the government that a family can contribute to the educational costs incurred by a family member attending college.

Grants

When exploring options to pay for college, start by considering what grants might be available. Because grants are "gift aid," and typically do not require

NOTE

You need to complete the FAFSA every year! It is free to fill out and submit and the earlier you submit the better. Mark your calendar and review the form to make sure you have all the information you need prior to filling it out.

NOTE

Get ready to write! Many nonacademic scholarships require essays. Access the writing center or professors to assist you with crafting your winning essay.

repayment, they enable students to fund their college education without burdensome debt repayments during college or after graduation.

About two-thirds of all college students receive grant aid, which, on average, reduces their tuition bills by more than half. The Federal Pell Grant is the largest grant program; it provides need-based aid to low-income undergraduate students. The amount of the grant depends on criteria such as: (1) the anticipated contribution of the family to the student's education (EFC), (2) the cost of the postsecondary institution that the student is attending, and (3) the enrollment status of the student (part-time or full-time). Pell Grants are the largest individual grant program, there are others that should be explored. First, check to see if your state offers any grants funding. The Cal Grant A or the Texas Grants program are two examples of general state grants that are available. Because funding is limited, however, states often set an income cut off for eligibility. There also are targeted grants that are for subsets of students, such as foster children, children of military dependents or of policemen or firemen who died in the line of duty. Be sure to check all possibilities.

NOTE

Even though grants do not need to be paid back, students must maintain certain academic standards to remain eligible to receive grant funds. Most require a certain grade point average and, sometimes, that a student be full-time.

Scholarships

Scholarships are available from many sources, including the institution you choose to attend. They are awarded based on various criteria that may include a written essay, ACT or SAT scores, and high school grade point average (GPA). In addition to academic scholarships, scholarships are awarded based on organizations you may have been a part of, race or ethnicity, the region of the country you live in, athletics, artistic talents, and so on. It is important to remember that all scholarships are competitive and deadlines are observed by the awarding agencies or institutions. Be aware of the application material deadlines and submit your materials well in advance of these deadlines.

You should contact the Financial Aid Office of the institution you are attending to find available scholarships. You can also conduct an Internet search to find many sites that offer scholarship information (like www.fastweb.com), but it is important to remember that you should not enter credit card or bank account information on any site.

THINK ABOUT IT

Don't miss out on scholarship opportunities! Explore, Explore, Explore!

Student Loans

Keep in mind that not all loans are created equal. Compared to private loans, federally guaranteed student loans are relatively low-cost and may be paid off slowly after graduation. On the other hand, private lenders of student loans are like credit card companies; they charge extremely high interest rates (that can go even higher at any time) and the loans must be paid off quickly. Private loans should not be used as a primary loan to help pay for college and they should only be used as a last resort—when no other options are available for covering college expenses.

Despite the much higher interest rate of private loans, they're the fastest-growing type of loans taken out by college students—largely because of aggressive, and sometimes misleading, irresponsible, or unethical advertising on loan-shopping websites. Students sometimes think they're getting a federal loan only to find out later they've taken on a more expensive private loan (Hamilton 2012; Kristof 2008).

Apply for as much grant aid as possible before borrowing, and then seek lower-interest federal student loans before tapping private ones. There is a lot of student aid that can help make the expense [of college] more manageable."

—Sandy Baum, senior policy analyst, College Board (quoted in Gordon 2009)

Also, keep in mind that federal and state regulations require that if you're receiving financial aid, you must maintain "satisfactory academic progress." In most cases this means you must do the following:

1. Maintain a satisfactory GPA—such as, 2.0 or above. Your entire academic record will be reviewed, even if you have paid for some of the classes with your own resources.
2. Make satisfactory academic progress—such as, 12 to 15 units per semester for full-time students and 6 to 9 hours for part-time students. You must successfully complete approximately 70% of the classes you attempt. Your academic progress will be evaluated at least once per year, usually at the end of each spring semester.
3. Complete a degree or certificate program with a reasonable number of units. There is a maximum number of course hours you can attempt per degree. (Check with your institution's Financial Aid Office for details.)

Loans need to be repaid after a student graduates from college. Listed below are some of the more well-known, federally funded student loan programs.

NOTE

Don't forget! Federal programs and opportunities change often. When determining what you wish to apply for, frequently check the FAFSA Web page.

NOTE

Some loans may require a co-signer with good credit. Review your state's Higher Education Agency for reputable lenders. Texans— Your state has loan programs from the state!

- *The Federal Perkins Loan*: A low-interest loan awarded to exceptionally needy students. Repayment of the loan begins nine months after a student is no longer enrolled at least half-time.
- *The Federal Subsidized Stafford Loan*: Available to students enrolled at least half-time, has a fixed interest rate established each year on July 1. The federal government pays the interest on the loan while the student is enrolled. Repayment for this loan begins six months after a student is no longer enrolled at least half-time.
- *The Federal Unsubsidized Stafford Loan*: A loan not based on need that has the same interest rate as the Federal Subsidized Stafford Loan. Students are responsible for paying the interest on this loan while they're enrolled in college. Repayment for this loan begins 6 months after a student is no longer enrolled at least half-time.

Keep in mind that federal and private loans differ in the following ways:

- *Federal* loans have fixed interest rates that are comparatively low (currently less than 7%) and cannot go higher.
- *Private* loans have variable interest rates that are very high (currently more than 15%) and can go higher at any time.

Student Loans and Credit Scores

Be aware that students loans are a type of loan and can affect your credit score. For many community college students, credit is now a reality and will be for the rest of you when you graduate from college. College loans can hurt or enhance your credit score depending on how you treat the loan.

Your credit score is a number that tells lenders and creditors how financially responsible you are. It assists them in judging the level of risk you present to them as a borrower.

This score will dictate how easily you can obtain credit cards, loans, houses, renting an apartment, etc. The score is based on the following percentages:

- 35% based on payment history: how consistently you pay bills on time
- 30% based on how much you currently owe

- 15% based on credit history: have you had credit before and handled it responsibly?
- 10% based on new credit: how many new applications and acceptances of other credit you've had
- 10% based on types of credit: credit card, student loan, auto loan, etc.

Thus, having loans (including student loans) can be good or bad and sometimes both, depending on how you use them and how you repay them. Making your student loan payments in full and on time each month will assist your credit score and help you to establish a good credit history. However, missing payments or not paying at all can be devastating to your credit and credit score.

Lastly, if you find yourself temporarily short of funds and need just a small loan to recover, many colleges have an *emergency student loan program*, whereby they provide students with an immediate, interest-free loan to help them cover short-term expenses (e.g., cost of textbooks) or deal with financial emergencies (e.g., accidents and illnesses). Emergency student loans are typically granted within 24 to 48 hours, sometimes even the same day, and usually need to be repaid within two months.

Veterans Benefits

If you are currently a veteran, you may be eligible for the GI Bill benefits.

Fact #1.

You have 10–15 years to use your GI Bill benefits. Once you have separated from the service you have 10 years to use all of your benefits under the Montgomery GI Bill and 15 years to use your Post-9/11 GI Bill benefits. Although separating from service "starts the clock" on your time limit, you should know that if you rejoin active-duty service for more than 90 days before your time limit expires the clock resets. In other words, you get 10–15 years from your last discharge.

For resources to explore the GI Bill, visit www.military.com. Example: Seaman Smith left active duty and joined the Navy Reserve. Three years later she returned to active duty with twelve years remaining on her GI Bill clock. At that point, the clock is reset at the 15-year mark when she leaves the active duty service again, at which point the 15 year clock will start ticking again. She now has a fresh 15 years left to use ALL of her benefits or she will lose her remaining balance, which then returns to Uncle Sam.

Fact #2.

The GI Bill is not Federal Financial Aid. The GI Bill is not considered Financial Aid in the traditional sense. College and University financial aid departments do not consider the GI Bill financial aid because it is normally paid directly to you, not the school. Most schools will require you to sign a promissory note or apply for student loans to pay them upfront. You will then be required to pay these loans–hopefully with your GI Bill payments.

This also means that you are eligible for student loans, scholarships, and Pell Grants along with the GI Bill.

Note: Although un-taxable, GI Bill benefit payments reduce the amount of student financial aid you are eligible to receive.

Fact #3.

You can stop and start using the GI Bill as needed. Unfortunately, many people believe that once you apply for benefits you have to remain enrolled in school to get the full benefit. Thankfully that's not true; you can use the GI Bill for any period of time. Take time off and re-apply to use it again at a later date (keeping in mind fact number one).

You can also use it as you progress towards your education goal. If you use your benefits wisely, your GI Bill benefits can help you finish your associates, work on your bachelor's, and later, complete your master's degree.

Fact #4.

A "month" of benefits doesn't always mean a month. The GI Bill benefit provides 36 months of education benefits. The term "months" can often be confusing. The "36 months" of benefits does not mean you have only 36 months to use it, nor does it mean you must use it all in one 36 month period.

There are two ways the term month is used. One way is for active duty, and the other is used for veterans. The following should help you to better understand this aspect of the GI Bill.

For the Post-9/11 GI Bill: If you go to classes full time for either 1 month or 30 days you use 1 month worth of benefits. For example, if your classes go from February 1 to March 15 you use 1.5 months of benefits (1 month for February—since it is a calendar month, and 1/2 month for March—since you were in classes for 15 days.)

For the Montgomery GI Bill: If you are a veteran you are basically charged one month of entitlement for each month of full-time training you take.

If you are on active duty and you go to school full-time for four months, but your tuition is only $1,000, you will still be charged for four months of your 36 month entitlement. In this example a "month" actually does mean a month.

If you are using your GI Bill for training other than college or vocational training, there are different rules. See our Flight Training, Apprenticeship/On-the-Job Training, or National Testing Programs pages for specific information.

Fact #5.

The GI Bill pays according to the number of credits you take and how much active duty service you have.

The Post-9/11 GI Bill pays according to several factors, the main factors being number of months served on active duty and the number of credit pursued. If you are attending a public school, the Post-9/11 GI Bill can pay your full tuition directly to the school. You will receive a monthly housing allowance and up to $1000 a year for books and supplies. The housing allowance is paid at a percentage based on your active duty service, and your credit load. See our Post-9/11 Overview page for detailed information.

The Montgomery GI Bill payment rates are based on several factors, the biggest being your credit load. For example a full-time student using the Montgomery GI Bill will get up to $1,857, while a half-time student will only get half that amount. Learn more about how GI Bill Payment Rates work.

You can apply for the GI Bill online by going to the VA's vets.gov website and completing an online application. For more details, see the Post-9/11 GI Bill Application Process and get started using your benefits today! www.military.com GI Bill Top 5 things to know.

The Post 9/11 GI Bill is the largest and most extensive veterans' program available for postsecondary education. It can help veterans, and in some cases, their dependents, pay for their college education as well as other necessities. Benefits can include housing cost allotments as well as funds for books and supplies. There are numerous other VA programs and funding sources that might be tapped, but the first step is to find out where your colleges houses its Veterans Affairs office.

Salary Earnings

Tips for Working While in College

- If you're relying on salary from off-campus work to pay for college tuition, check with your employer to see if the company you're working for offers tuition reimbursement.

- Check with the Billing Office (sometimes referred to as the Cashier's Office) on your campus to determine whether payment plans are available that allow you to pay tuition costs on an installment schedule that aligns with the timing of your paychecks. These tuition-payment plans may provide you with some flexibility in terms of amount due per payment, deadlines for payments, and how remaining debt owed to the institution is dealt with at the end of the term. (Keep in mind that your college may not allow you to register for the following term until tuition for the previous term has been completely paid.)

- If possible, try to find work *on campus* rather than off campus. Research shows that when students work on campus they're more likely to succeed in college (Astin 1993; Pascarella and Terenzini 1991, 2005). This is probably due to the fact that they become more connected to the college (Cermak and Filkins 2004; Tinto 1993) and because on-campus employers are more flexible than off-campus employers in allowing students to meet their academic commitments (Leonard 2008). For instance, on-campus employers are more willing to schedule students' work hours around their class schedule and allow students to modify their work schedule when their academic workload increases (e.g., at midterm and finals). Thus, if at all possible, rather than seeking work off campus, try to find work on campus and capitalize on its proven capacity to promote college success.

 Journal Reflection 12.1

If you're using any of the following financial resources to help pay for your college education, circle it: loans, grants, scholarships, salary earnings, savings, monetary support from parents or other family members, other resources.

Which of the above resources is the primary or main source of funding for your college education? Which of the resources above might you be able to use?

DEVELOPING A MONEY MANAGEMENT PLAN

Gain Financial Self-Awareness

Development of any good habit begins with the critical first step of self-awareness. Developing effective money-management habits begins with awareness of your *cash flow*—the amount of money you have coming in and going out. As illustrated here, cash flow is tracked by monitoring:

Income ⟷ Expenses

Savings ⟷ Debt

- Income—the amount of money you have coming in versus the amount going out (expenses or expenditures), and
- Savings—the amount of money you've earned and not spent versus the amount you've borrowed and haven't paid back (debt).

Once you're aware of the amount of money you have coming in (and from what sources) plus the amount of money you're spending (and for what reasons), your next step is to develop a plan for managing your cash flow. The bottom line is to ensure that the sum of money you have coming in (income) is equal to or greater than the sum of money you have going out (expenses). If the amount of money going out exceeds the amount coming in, you're "in the red" or have "negative cash flow."

Track Your Cash Flow

You can track cash flow by using any of the following tools:

- Checking accounts
- Credit cards
- Charge cards
- Debit cards

Checking Accounts

A checking account may be obtained from a bank or credit union; its typical costs include a deposit ($20–$25) to open the account, a monthly service fee (e.g., $10), and small fees for checks.

Along with your checking account, banks usually provide you with an automatic teller machine (ATM) card that you can use to get cash. Look for a checking account that offers a free service along with your checking account, rather than one that charges a separate fee for ATM transactions.

Strategies for Wisely Using Checking Accounts.

- Know what you're getting. Different institutions set different requirements for checking accounts. Some charge a monthly fee, others may charge you by the check. Some will do both. Others may require a

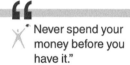

"Never spend your money before you have it."
—*Thomas Jefferson, third president of the United States and founder of the University of Virginia*

minimum balance, others waive fees if a greater balance is maintained. It's up to you to explore different options before signing up for a checking account.

- Keep track of your ATM withdrawals and expenditures. Remember that an ATM is just like a check without the paper. When you use your ATM, it might save you from having to carry checks, but funds are still being withdrawn from your account. If you don't keep track, you're in danger of overdrawing your checking account.
- Check your monthly bank statements carefully. If you get your statement online, don't just file it, review it first. If you see a discrepancy between what you thought checks and/or service charges should be, contact your bank immediately.

Credit Cards

A credit card is basically money loaned to you by the credit card company issuing the card, which you pay back to the company on a monthly basis. You can pay the whole bill or a portion of the bill each month—as long as some minimum payment is made. However, for any remaining (unpaid) portion of your bill, you're charged a high interest rate—which can be as much as 30%. Consequently, if you decide to use.

Strategies for Wisely Using Credit Cards

- Start with one. When you started college, you probably got several offers for credit cards. Remember that those offers are advertisements that show the good and discuss the bad—interest rates, grace periods, lines of credit—in very small print. Start with one card that will be useful in most places you shop and that has a reasonable interest rate. If you already have more than one card, take all of them out of your wallet and leave them at home. Or cut them up!
- Read the contract carefully. A credit card contract is not interesting reading but it is important. Be sure to check on interest rates, what the grace period is, and what to do if the card is lost or stolen. And if you don't understand something, be sure you get it explained by a representative from the company.
- View your use of the card as a short-term loan. You are using the card for convenience, not to buy a lot of things you really can't afford. Each month, decide how much you can spend and pay off. And stick to it.
- Pay off credit cards each month. THIS IS THE MOST IMPORTANT RULE! Credit card companies vary in terms of what they will charge you if you don't pay the entire amount on time. Fees can be as high as 30% on some cards. While your bill will tell you the minimum amount you can pay, that figure is for the card's benefit, not yours! The less you pay the more money the company gets in interest fees that will keep mounting. If you can't pay it all off, pay as much as you can and not just the minimum amount.
- Don't ever miss a payment entirely. Remember that you are now building a credit history. As you buy and pay off credit cards, you are creating a history that follows you for a lifetime. Getting a good start on this journey is critical, especially as you look at large scale expenditures like computer systems or cars. If you can not make a monthly payment, call the company and see if you can't work out some kind of

> "What I don't do that I know I should do is pay my bills on time, like my cell phone and credit cards."
>
> —First-year student

> "I need to pay attention to my balance more closely and actually allot certain amounts for certain things."
>
> —First-year student

arrangement. This probably will be expensive, however. If you get overwhelmed by credit card debt, you may want to consider a personal loan. While you will still have to make payments, they will be for a set amount each month, which will let you plan on it in your budget. Also, the interest rate will be much lower.

Credit card companies make their profit by the interest they collect from cardholders who don't pay back their credit on time. Just as procrastinating about completing schoolwork is a poor time-management habit that hurts your grades, procrastinating about paying your credit card bills is a poor money-management habit that hurts your pocketbook by forcing you to pay high interest rates.

Don't allow credit card companies to make profit at your expense. Pay your total balance on time and avoid paying exorbitantly high interest rates. If you can't pay the total amount owed at the end of the month, instead of making the minimum monthly payment, pay as much as you possibly can. If you keep making only the minimum payment each month, you'll begin piling up huge amounts of debt.

Box 12.1

Credit Cardholders' Bill of Rights Act of 2009

Congress passed legislation in 2009 that enacted certain protections for consumers who use credit cards. Here are the specific reforms that affect college students:

- Creditors are forbidden from offering credit to consumers under the age of 18 (unless they are emancipated under state law, or the consumer's parent or legal guardian is the primary account holder).

- College students without a cosigner will have their credit line limited to the greater amount of 20 percent of their annual gross income or $500. The collective amount of credit available on all credit cards will be limited to 30 percent of the student's annual gross income.

- Creditors are not allowed to open a credit-card account for a college student who does not have a verifiable annual gross income or already has a credit-card account with that creditor or any of its affiliates (Chan 2009).

NOTE

If you keep making charges on your credit card while you have an unpaid balance (debt), you no longer have a grace period to pay back your charges; instead, interest is charged immediately on all your purchases.

Charge Cards (a.k.a Smart Cards)

A charge card works similar to a credit card in that you're given a short-term loan for one month; the only difference is that you must pay your bill in full at the end of each month and you cannot carry over any debt from one month to the next. Its major disadvantage relative to a credit card is that it has less flexibility—no matter what your expenses may be for a particular month, you must still pay up or lose your ability to obtain credit for the following month. However, if you're someone who consistently has trouble paying your monthly credit card bill on time, this is an advantage of a charge card because it will prevent you from accumulating debt.

Debit Cards

A debit card looks almost identical to a credit card (e.g., it has a *Master-Card* or *Visa* logo), but it works differently. When you use a debit card, money is immediately taken out or subtracted from your checking account. Like a check or ATM withdrawal, any purchase you make with a debit card is immediately subtracted from your balance. Thus, you can only use money that's already in your account (rather than borrowing money). At the end of the month, you don't receive a bill; instead, you get a statement with information about checks you deposited and cashed, as well as your debit card transactions. If you attempt to purchase something with a debit card that costs more than the amount of money you have in your account, your card will not allow you to do so. Similar to a bounced check, a debit card will not permit you to pay out any money that's not in your account.

Like a credit card, a major advantage of the debit card is that it provides you with the convenience of plastic; however, unlike a credit card, it prevents you from spending beyond your means and accumulating debt. For this reason, many financial advisors recommend using a debit card rather than a credit card (Knox 2004; Tyson 2012).

NOTE

SSN numbers are needed for payroll. Do your best to memorize your SSN. Keep it secure and hidden.

BOX 12.2

Minimize Your Risk of Identity Theft

Identity thieves steal your personal information to make transactions or purchases in your name. This can damage your credit status and cost you time and money to restore your financial credibility. Listed below are key strategies for reducing your risk of identity theft.

If you have a passport, keep it secure and hidden.

- Don't share personal identity information over the phone with anyone you don't know and trust, especially your social security or credit card number.
- Don't share identity information over the phone with anyone who claims to be an Internal Revenue Service (IRS) agent and threatens you with arrest or deportation, or who requests personal information the purpose of sending you a refund. The IRS will contact you in writing if it needs anything.
- Don't respond to e-mails from anyone claiming to be from the IRS. This is always a scam because the IRS doesn't initiate contact with taxpayers by e-mail or social media to request personal or financial information. (The only legitimate communication you will receive from the IRS is through postal mail.)
- Don't click on links or open e-mail attachments from anyone unfamiliar to you. Scam artists create fake websites and send "phishing" e-mails—which are attempts to acquire personal information such as usernames, passwords, and credit card details, often using the names of trustworthy electronic sources (e.g., an Internet service provider).
- Don't enter your credit card or bank account information on any websites.
- Install firewalls and virus detection software on your computer, to protect yourself against "cyber crime."

- When using your laptop in public, shield your screen from "shoulder surfers."
- Don't carry your Social Security (SSN) card in your wallet or write it on your checks. Only give out your SSN to people you know and trust.
- Conceal your personal identification number (PIN). Don't supply it to anyone and don't keep it in your wallet.
- Shred documents containing personal information you no longer need. (Some identity thieves are "dumpster divers" who go through the garbage to get your personal information.)
- Compare your receipts with your account statements and credit card statements to be sure there are no transactions you didn't authorize. If you have an online account, you can check your account at any time. It's a good idea to get in the habit of checking it at least once a week (e.g., every Sunday evening).
- If you believe you've been victimized by identity theft, contact your local police department and any of the following credit reporting companies to place a fraud alert:

Experian: https://www.experian.com/freeze/center.html

TransUnion: https://freeze.transunion.com/sf/security-Freeze/landingPage.jsp

Equifax: https://www.freeze.equifax.com/Freeze/jsp/SFF_PersonalIDInfo.jsp

Sources:
Prevent and Report Identity Theft: https://www.irs.gov/Individuals/Identity-Protection

Identity Protection Tips–Internal Revenue Service: www.irs.gov/Individuals/Identity-Protection-Tips

Tips to Avoid Identity Theft: http://www.bbb.org/sacramento/news-events/consumer-tips/2015/03/how-to-avoid-identity-theft/

NOTE

Remaining aware of the distinction between essentials that must be purchased and incidentals that may or may not be purchased is an important first step toward budgeting effectively and minimizing debt.

> " I need to save money and not shop so much and impulse buy."
>
> —*First-year student*

> " My money management skills are poor. If I have money, I will spend it unless somebody takes it away from me. I am the kind of person who lives from paycheck to paycheck."
>
> —*First-year student*

NOTE

What you're willing to sacrifice and save for, and what you're willing to spend money on and go into debt for, says a lot about who you are and what you value.

Similar to managing your time, the first step in planning and managing money is to prioritize. Identify your most important expenses—the indispensable necessities you can't live without—and separate them from incidentals—dispensable luxuries you can live without and can be reduced or eliminated if necessary. People easily confuse *essentials* (things they really *need*) with *desirables* (stuff they just *want*). For instance, if a piece of merchandise happens to be on sale, it may be a desirable purchase at that time because of its reduced price; however, it's not an essential purchase if you don't need that piece of merchandise at that particular time.

DEVELOPING A PLAN FOR MANAGING MONEY AND MINIMIZING DEBT

The ultimate goal of money management is to save money and dodge debt. Here are some strategies for accomplishing both of these goals.

Prepare a personal budget. A budget is simply a plan for coordinating income and expenses in a way that ensures you're left with sufficient money to cover your expenses. It enables you to be your own accountant who keeps an accurate account of your own income and expenses.

Postponing short-term satisfaction of material desires is a key element of long-term financial success. Unfortunately, humans are often more motivated by short-range thinking because it produces quicker results and more immediate gratification (Goldstein and Hogarth 1997; Lowenstein, Read, and Baumeister 2003). This is why so many people pile up credit card debt; they choose to experience the short-term pleasure of the immediate purchase instead of postponing gratification to save money in the long run.

We need to remain mindful of whether we're spending money *impulsively* on what we want rather than *reflectively* on what we need. The truth is that humans spend money for a host of psychological reasons (conscious or subconscious), many of which are unrelated to actual need. Some people spend money to build their self-esteem or self-image, to combat personal boredom, or because of an emotional "high" they experience when they buy things for themselves (Dittmar 2004; Furnham and Argyle 1998). Other people can become obsessed with spending money, shop compulsively, and develop an addiction to purchasing products. Just as Alcoholics Anonymous (AA) functions as a support group for alcoholics, Debtors Anonymous serves as a support group for shopaholics and includes a similar 12-step recovery program.

AUTHOR'S JOURNEY

I was a student who had to manage my own college expenses, so I soon became an expert in managing small budgets. The first thing I always took care of was my tuition. I was going to go to school even if I starved. The next thing I budgeted for was food, housing, clothing, and transportation needs. If I ran out of money, I would then work additional hours if it didn't interfere with my school work.

Rather than making and spending money while I was in college, I was working to make a better future life for myself. To be successful, I had to be a great money manager because there was so little of it to manage. This took a lot of focus and strong will, but did it pay off? Absolutely.

—*Aaron Thompson*

Financial Self-Awareness Worksheet

	Estimate	Actual
Income Sources		
Parents/Family		
Work/Job		
Grants/Scholarships		
Loans		
Savings		
Other:		
TOTAL INCOME		
Essentials (Fixed Expenses)		
Living Expenses: Food/Groceries		
Rent/Room & Board		
Utilities (gas/electric)		
Essentials (Fixed Expenses) *(continued)*		
Living Expenses (continued): Clothing		
Laundry/Dry Cleaning		
Phone		
Computer		
Household Items (dishes, etc.)		
Medical Insurance Expenses		
Debt Payments (loans/credit cards)		
Other:		
School Expenses: Tuition		
Books		
Supplies (print cartridges, etc.)		
Special Fees (lab fees, etc.)		
Other:		
Transportation: Public Transportation (bus fees, etc.)		
Car Insurance		
Car Maintenance		
Fuel (gas)		
Car Payments		
Other:		
Incidentals (*Variable* Expenses)		
Entertainment: Movies/Concerts		
DVDs/CDs		
Restaurants (eating out)		
Other:		

Financial Self-Awareness Worksheet *(continued)*

	Estimate	Actual
Personal Appearance/Accessories: Hairstyling/Coloring		
Cosmetics/Manicures		
Fashionable Clothes		
Jewelry		
Other:		
Hobbies: Travel (trips home, vacations)		
Gifts		
Other:		
TOTAL EXPENSES		

Fill in either the exact amount or an estimate of your income and essential expenses you have each month.

How much extra money do you have left?

Now complete the chart for incidental expenses. Does your money after essential expenses cover your incidentials.

In a helping trio, discuss with two other classmates what your budget reveals and see if they can help you focus and prioritize your incidental items.

Who's In Charge?

Financial Priorities

It is the first week of the term and you still don't have your books. You are getting irritated because your instructors are telling you that you are already falling behind and if you don't get your books soon, you will fail the class! You explain that you don't have the money right now and next week you need to get your nails done and buy an iPod® because your daughter broke yours. You think your instructors are plain mean and don't want to help you. Who is really at fault here? What could have been done differently in this situation?

_____

_____

_____

_____

Make all your bills visible and, if possible, pay them as soon as you see them. When bills are in your sight, they're on your mind and you're less likely to forget to pay them, or forget to pay them on time. Try to get in the habit of paying a bill as soon as you open it and have it in your hands, rather than setting it aside and running the risk of forgetting to pay it (or losing it altogether).

Also, consider setting up an online banking program that will enable you to visually track your transactions and make credit card payments automatically. The advantage of an online account is that it's paperless and you don't have to deal with bills sent to you through postal mail. However, its disadvantage is that it doesn't appear in tangible form in your mailbox—which provides you with clear, visual reminder to pay it. So, if you set up an online account, get into an ongoing habit of checking it. Otherwise, what's out of sight stays out of mind and your bills may not get paid on time.

Live within your means. Simply stated: Don't purchase what you can't afford. If you're spending more money than you're taking in, it means you're living *beyond* your means. To begin living *within* your means, you have two options:

1. Decrease your expenses (reduce your spending), or
2. Increase your income (earn more money).

NOTE

Add required payment due dates to your calendar (paper or electronic). Set a reminder to be sure and pay it early! Fines are often added to late payments.

THINK ABOUT IT

Research (Kingkade 2014) shows that working too many hours hurts student performance and progress. It is much better to reduce spending than it is to increase work hours.

AUTHOR'S JOURNEY

When I was young, my mom was always cutting out coupons and looking for what was on sale. If it was not on sale or she did not have a coupon, she usually did not buy it. As a child, it drove me nuts and I thought she was crazy! Now that I am older, I find I am a lot like her when it comes to money. I am always looking for coupons and I rarely buy anything if it is not on sale. Even when I do buy something I stop and think, "Do I really need this?" or "How much use will I get out of this?" It is because of this that I am able to save up some of my money and do things I really enjoy (season tickets for football games, traveling, etc.), and I am thankful my mom taught me how to save.

—*Julie McLaughlin*

Strategies To Help Manage Your Money. Intelligent consumers use critical thinking skills when purchasing products. When preparing to buy something, check online to see if there are sales, discounts, or coupons you can take advantage of now or in the near future. Before pressing the "Buy" button though, check how much postage and handling might add to the cost. Consider whether a name brand is worth it—drug store brands often have the same ingredients for much less money. Finally, consider cooperative buying with some friends. Often you can get items cheaper if you buy in bulk.

Downsize. Cut down or cut out spending for products you don't need. Avoid conspicuous consumption or exhibitionistic (look-at-me) spending just to keep up with or show off to your friends. Don't allow peer pressure to determine your spending habits; your consumer decisions should reflect your ability to think critically, not your desire to conform socially.

"We choose to spend more money than we have today. Choose debt, or choose freedom, it's your choice."

—*Bill Pratt, Extra Credit: The 7 Things Every College Student Needs to Know About Credit, Debt & Cash*

NOTE

Advertising creates product familiarity, not product quality. The more money manufacturers pay for advertising and creating well-known brands, the more money we pay for their product.

Save money by living with others rather than living alone. You lose some privacy when you share living quarters, but you save a substantial amount of money. Living with others may also bring with it the fringe social benefit of spending time with people (roommates or housemates) with whom you're compatible and whose company you enjoy.

Give gifts of time instead of money. Spending money on gifts for family, friends, and romantic partners isn't the only way to show you care. The point of gift giving isn't to show others you aren't cheap, it's to show you care. You can demonstrate caring by making something special or doing something meaningful for those you care about. Gifts of time and kindness are often more personal and special than store-bought gifts.

Develop your own money-saving strategies and habits. You can save money by doing little things that eventually add up to big savings over time. The following tips for saving money were suggested by students in a first-year seminar class. Some of these strategies may work for you as well.

- Don't carry a lot of extra money in your wallet. (It's just like food; if it's easy to get to, you'll be more likely to eat it up.)
- Shop with a list—get in, get what you need, and get out.
- Put all your extra change in a jar.
- Put extra cash in a piggy bank that requires you to smash the piggy to get at it.
- Seal your savings in an envelope.
- When you get extra money get it immediately into the bank (and out of your hands).
- Bring (don't buy) your lunch.
- Hide your credit card or put it in the freezer so that you don't use it on impulse.
- Use cash (instead of credit cards) because you can set aside a certain amount of it for yourself and you can clearly see how much of it you have at the start of a week (as well as how much is left at any point during the week).

AUTHOR'S JOURNEY

When my wife (Mary) and I were first dating, I was trying to gain weight because I was on the thin side. One day when I came home from school, I found this hand-delivered package in front of my apartment door. I opened it up and there was a homemade loaf of whole wheat bread made from scratch by Mary. That gift didn't cost her much money, but she took the time to do it and she remembered to do something that was important to me (gaining weight). That gift really touched me; it's a gift I've never forgotten. Since I eventually married Mary and we're still happily married, I guess you could say that inexpensive loaf of bread was a "gift that kept on giving."

—Joe Cuseo

When making purchases, always factor in their total, long-term cost. Short-term thinking leads to poor long-term money management and financial planning. Those small (monthly) installment plans that businesses offer to entice you to buy expensive products may make the cost of those products appear attractive and affordable in the short run. However, when you factor in the interest rates you pay on monthly installment plans, plus the length of time (number of months) you're making installment payments, you get a more accurate picture of the product's total cost in the long run. Taking this long-range perspective can quickly alert you to the reality that a product's sticker price represents its partial and seemingly affordable short-term cost—not its total long-term cost—which is much less affordable and more likely to exceed your budget.

> People don't realize how much work it is to stay in college. It's its own job in itself, plus if you've got another job you go to, too. I mean, it's just a lot."
> —*College student (quoted in Engle, Bermeo, and O'Brien 2006)*

LONG-RANGE FISCAL PLANNING: FINANCING YOUR COLLEGE EDUCATION

Thus far, our discussion has focused primarily on short- and mid-range financial planning strategies that will keep you out of debt on a monthly or yearly basis. We turn now to issues involving long-term financial planning for your entire college experience. While there's no one "correct" strategy for financing a college education, certain strategies are more effective than others. Studies show that financing a college education by obtaining a student loan and working no more than 15 hours per week is an effective long-range strategy for students at all income levels. Students who use this strategy are more likely to graduate from college, graduate in less time, and graduate with higher grades than full-time college students who work part-time for more than 15 hours per week or students who work full-time and attend college part-time (King 2002; Perna and DuBois 2010).

Unfortunately, almost 50% of first-year students choose a strategy that research indicates is the least likely to be associated with college success: borrowing nothing and trying to work more than 15 hours per week. Students who use this strategy increase their risk of lowering their grades significantly and withdrawing from college altogether (King 2005), probably because they can't handle the academic work load required of a full-time student on top of all the hours they're working each week. Working longer hours also increases the likelihood that students switch from full-time and part-time enrollment, which delays their time to graduation and increases their risk of not graduating at all (Tinto 2012). Thus, a good strategy for balancing learning and earning is to try to limit work for pay to 15 or fewer hours per week.

Students who work more than 15 hours per week not only take longer to graduate from college, but they also end up losing money in the long run. The hourly pay most part-time jobs students earn while they're in college is less than half than what they'll earn from working in full-time positions as college graduates (King 2005). Thus, the longer they take to graduate, the longer they must wait to enter higher-paying, full-time positions that a college diploma qualifies them for; this delays their opportunity to "cash in" on the monetary benefits of a college degree.

Journal Reflection 12.2

Do you need to work part-time to meet your college expenses?

_____

If you answered "yes" to the above question, are you working more than 15 hours per week?

_____

If you answered "yes" to the above question, can you reduce your work time to 15 or fewer hours per week and still make ends meet?

_____

_____

_____

_____

_____

NOTE

Student loans are provided by the American government with the intent of helping its citizens become better educated. In contrast, for-profit businesses (such as credit card companies) lend students money with no intent of helping them become better educated, but with the clear intent of helping themselves make money—from the high rates of interest they collect from students who fail to pay off their debt in full at the end of each month.

Furthermore, studies show that two out of three college students have at least one credit card and nearly one-half of students with credit cards carries an average balance of more than $2,000 per month (Nellie Mae 2005; Sallie Mae 2009). A debt level this high is likely to force many students into working more than 15 hours a week to pay it off. ("I owe, I owe, so off to work I go.") These students often end up taking fewer courses per term so they can work more hours to pay off their credit card debt, which results in their taking longer to graduate and to start earning a college graduate's salary.

Instead of paying almost 20% interest to credit card companies for their monthly debt, these students would be better off obtaining a student loan at a much lower interest rate, which they will start paying back six months after graduation—when they'll be making more money in full-time positions as college graduates. Despite this clear advantage of student loans compared to credit-card loans, only about 25% of college students with credit cards take out student loans (King 2002).

Keep in mind that not all debt is bad. Debt can be good if it represents an investment in something that will appreciate with time—that is, something that will gain in value and eventually turn into profit for the investor. Purchasing a college education on credit is a good investment because you're investing in yourself and your future, which, over time, will *appreciate*—that is, increase its monetary return in the form of higher salaries and benefits accumulated over the remainder of your life. In contrast, purchasing a new car is a bad long-term investment because it begins to *depreciate* or lose monetary value immediately after it's purchased. The instant you drive that new car off the dealer's lot, you become the proud owner of a used car that's worth much less than what you just paid for it.

You may have heard the expression: "Time is money." One way to interpret this expression is that the more money you spend, the more time you must spend making money. College students who spend more time earning money to cover the costs of material things they want, but don't need, typically spend less time studying, complete fewer classes, and earn lower grades. You can avoid this negative cycle by viewing academic work as work that "pays" you back in terms of completed courses and higher grades. If you put in more academic time to earn more course credits in less time, you're paid back sooner by graduating sooner and beginning to earn the full-time salary of a college graduate—which will pay you about twice as much per hour than you'll earn doing part-time work without a college degree (plus additional "fringe benefits" like health insurance and paid vacation time). Furthermore, the time you put into earning higher grades in college will earn you more pay in your first full-time position after college because research shows that for students graduating in the same field, those with higher grades earn higher starting salaries (Pascarella and Terenzini 2005).

> Unlike a car that depreciates in value each year that you drive it, an investment in education yields monetary, social, and intellectual profit. A car is more tangible in the short term, but an investment in education (even if it means borrowing money) gives you more bang for the buck in the long run."
>
> —Eric Tyson, financial counselor and national best-selling author of Personal Finance for Dummies

Journal Reflection 12.3

In addition to college, what might be other good, long-term investments you could make now or in the near future?

_____

_____

_____

_____

_____

> If a man empties his purse into his head, no one can take it away from him. An investment in knowledge always pays the best interest."
>
> —Benjamin Franklin, 18th-century scientist, inventor, and a founding father of the United States

BOX 12.3

Financial Literacy: Understanding the Language of Money Management

As you can tell from the number of financial terms used in this chapter, there's an entire language we must master to be _financially literate_. As you read the financial terms listed below, place a checkmark next to any term you didn't know.

Account. A formal business arrangement in which a bank provides financial services to a customer (e.g., checking account or savings account).

Annual Fee. Yearly fee paid to a credit card company to cover the cost of maintaining the cardholder's account.

Annual Percentage Rate (APR). Interest rate that must be paid when monthly credit card balances aren't paid in full.

(continued)

Box 12.3 *(continued)*

Balance. Amount of money in a person's account or amount of unpaid debt.

Bounced Check. A check written for a greater amount of money than the amount contained in a personal checking account; it typically requires the person paying a charge to the bank and possibly to the business that attempted to cash the bounced check.

Budget. A plan for balancing income and expenses to ensure that sufficient money is available to cover personal expenses.

Cash Flow. Amount of money flowing in (income) and flowing out (expenses); "negative cash flow" occurs when the amount of money going out exceeds the amount coming in.

Credit. Money obtained with the understanding that it will be paid back.

Credit History. Past record of how timely and completely a credit card holder has paid off credit.

Credit Line (a.k.a. Credit Limit). The maximum amount of money (credit) made available to a borrower.

Credit Score. Measure used by credit card companies to determine if someone applying for a credit card is "credit worthy," that is, likely to repay. (An applicant with a low credit score may be denied credit.)

Debt. Amount of money owed.

Default. Failure to meet a financial obligation (e.g., a student who fails to repay a college loan "defaults" on that loan).

Emergency Student Loan. Immediate, interest-free loan provided by a college or university to help financially strapped students cover short-term expenses (e.g., cost of textbooks) or deal with financial emergencies (e.g., accidents and illnesses). Emergency student loans are typically granted within 24 to 48 hours, sometimes even the same day, and usually need to be repaid within two months.

Deferred Student Payment Plan. A plan allowing student borrowers to temporarily defer or postpone loan payments for some acceptable reason (e.g., to pursue an internship or do volunteer work after college).

Estimated Family Contribution (EFC). Amount of money the government has determined a family can contribute to the educational costs of a family member attending college.

Fixed Interest Rate. A loan with an interest rate that stays the same for the entire term of the loan.

Free Application for Federal Student Aid (FAFSA). Free application that asks for personal and family financial information to determine a student's eligibility for federal, state, and college-sponsored financial aid, including grants, loans, and work-study employment.

Grace Period. Amount of time a credit card holder has—after a monthly credit card statement has been issued—to pay back the company without paying added interest fees.

Grant. Money received that doesn't have to be repaid.

Gross Income. Income generated before taxes and other expenses are deducted.

Identity Theft. A crime committed by obtaining someone's personal identity information and assumes that person's identity to make financial transactions or purchases.

Insurance Premium. Amount of money paid in regular installments to an insurance company to remain insured.

Interest. Amount of money paid to a customer for deposited money (as in a bank account) or paid by a customer for borrowed money (e.g., interest on a loan). Interest is usually calculated as a percentage of the total amount of money deposited or borrowed.

Interest-Bearing Account. A bank account that earns interest if the customer keeps a minimum amount of money in the bank.

Loan Consolidation. Consolidating (combining) separate student loans into one larger loan to make the process of tracking, budgeting, and repayment easier. Loan consolidation typically requires the borrower to pay slightly more interest.

Loan Premium. The amount of money loaned without interest.

Merit-Based Scholarship. Money awarded to a student on the basis of performance or achievement that doesn't have to be repaid.

Need-Based Scholarship. Money awarded to a student on the basis of financial need that doesn't have to be repaid.

Net Income. Money earned after all expenses and taxes have been paid.

Principal. Total amount of money borrowed or deposited, not counting interest.

Variable Interest Rate. An interest rate on a loan that can vary (up or down) over the term of the loan.

Work Study. Financial assistance that college students earned by working on campus (funded by the federal government).

Yield. Revenue gained beyond amount invested or paid. (For example, revenue gained by college graduates through higher lifetime salaries beyond the amount they paid for a college education.)

Now that you've had a quick review of the financial literacy, develop a monthly SMART goal that enables you to:

- go to school full-time
- work no more than 15 hours
- covers all essential expenses AND
- enables you to save $5 a week.

If you can achieve the goal, at the end of the month, take 10% of your savings and reward yourself.

CHAPTER SUMMARY AND HIGHLIGHTS

Similar to time management, if you manage your money effectively and gain control of how you spend it, you gain greater control over the quality of your life. Research shows that accumulating high levels of debt while in college is associated with higher levels of stress, lower academic performance, and greater risk of withdrawing from college. The good news is that research demonstrates that students who learn to use effective money-management strategies are able to reduce unnecessary spending, decrease their risk of debt and stress, and increase the quality of their academic performance.

In this chapter, effective strategies for money management were identified and discussed, such as the following:

- **Financing your college education wisely.** Explore all sources of income for financing your college education, including FAFSA, scholarships, grants, loans, salary earnings, and personal savings.
- **Utilizing your Financial Aid Office.** Check periodically to see if you qualify for additional sources of income, such as part-time employment on campus, low-interest loans, grants, or scholarships.
- **Gaining financial self-awareness.** Become aware of your cash flow—amount of money coming in versus going out.
- **Managing money effectively.** Use available financial tools and instruments to track and maximize cash flow, such as checking accounts, credit cards, or debit cards.
- **Preparing a personal budget.** Keep an accurate account of your money to ensure you have sufficient amount to cover your expenses.
- **Paying your bills when they arrive.** Take care of bills when you first get them to reduce the risk of forgetting to pay them or paying them late.

- **Living within your means.** Don't purchase what you can't afford.
- **Economizing.** Be an intelligent consumer who uses critical thinking skills to evaluate and prioritize purchases.
- **Downsizing.** Don't buy products you don't need and don't allow peer pressure to dictate your spending habits.
- **Working for better grades now and better pay later.** Taking out a student loan and working part-time for 15 or fewer hours per week is the most effective long-range financial and educational strategy for students at all income levels. It improves grades, enables students to earn their degree sooner, and allows them to gain earlier entry to higher-paying jobs that require a college degree.

LEARNING MORE THROUGH THE WORLD WIDE WEB: INTERNET-BASED RESOURCES

For additional information on fiscal literacy, money management, and financial planning, see the following websites.

Fiscal Literacy & Money Management:
www.360financialliteracy.org
www.cashcourse.org

Financial Aid & Federal Funding Sources for a College Education:
www.students.gov
https://studentloans.gov/myDirectLoan/index.action

Student Loan Management Strategies:
https://firsttechfed.studentchoice.org/.../managing.../student-loan-repayment strategies

Spending Habits & Consumer Self-Awareness:
beyondthepurchase.org

REFERENCES

Astin, A. W. 1993. *What Matters in College?* San Francisco: Jossey-bass.

Cermak, K., and J. Filkins. 2004. *On-campus Employment as a Factor of Student Retention and Graduation*. DePaul University. http://oipr.depaul.edu/open/gradereten/oce.asp.

Cude, B. J., F. C. Lawrence, A. C. Lyons, K. Metzger, E. LeJeune, L. Marks, and K. Machtmes. 2006. "College Students and Financial Literacy: What They Know and What We Need to Learn. *Proceedings of the Eastern Family Economics and Resource Management Association Conference* 102–9.

Dittmar, H. 2004. "Understanding and Diagnosing Compulsive Buying." In *Handbook of Addictive Disorders: A Practical Guide to Diagnosis and Treatment*, edited by R. Coombs, 411–50. New York, NY: Wiley.

Engle, J. A. Bermeo, and C. O'Brien. 2006. *Straight from the Source: What Works for First-generation College Students*. Washington, DC: The Pell Institute for the Study of Opportunity in Higher Education.

Furnham, A., and M. Argyle. 1998. *The Psychology of Money*. New York: Routledge.

Goldstein, W. M., and R. M. Hogarth, eds. 1997. *Research on Judgment and Decision Making*. Cambridge, UK: Cambridge University Press.

Gordon, L. October 21, 2009. "College Costs up in Hard Times." *Los Angeles Times* A13.

Hamilton, H. 2012. "Student Loan Blues." *Los Angeles Times*, B1, B8.

Health, C., and J. Soll. 1996. "Mental Budgeting and Consumer Decisions." *Journal of Consumer Research* 23: 40–52.

Kidwell, B., and R. Turrisi. 2004. "An Examination of College Student Money Management Tendencies." *Journal of Economic Psychology* 25 (5): 601–16.

King, J. E. 2002. *Crucial Choices: How Students' Financial Decisions Affect Their Academic Success.* Washington, DC: American Council on Education.

King, J. E. 2005. "Academic Success and Financial Decisions: Helping Students Make Crucial Choices." In *Improving the First Year of College: Research and Practice*, edited by R. S. Feldman, 3–26. Mahwah, NJ: Lawrence Erlbaum.

Kingkade, T. August 27, 2014. "Sleepy College Students Are Worried about Their Stress Levels." *The Huffington Post.* http://www.huffingtonpost.com/2014/08/27/college-students-sleep-stress_n_5723438.html.

Knox, S. 2004. *Financial Basics: A Money Management Guide for Students.* Columbus: Ohio State University Press.

Kristof, K. M. 2008. "Hooked on Debt: Students Learn too Late the Costs of Private Loans." *Los Angeles Times*, A1: A18–19.

Leonard, G. 2008. *A Study on the Effects of Student Employment on Retention.* uc.iupui.edu/Portals/155/uploadedFiles/.../StudEmpRetentionRprt.pdf.

Lowenstein, G., D. Read, and R. G. Baumeister, eds. 2003. *Time and Decision: Economic and Psychological Perspectives on Intertemporal Choice.* New York: Russell Sage Foundation.

Nellie Mae. 2005. *Undergraduate Students and Credit Cards in 2004: An Analysis of Usage Rates and Trend.* Wilkes-barre, PA: Nellie Mae.

Nelson, M. C., K. Lust, M. Story, and E. Ehlinger. 2008. "Credit Card Debt, Stress and Key Health Risk Behaviors among College Students." *American Journal of Health Promotion* 22 (6): 400–7.

Niederjohn, M. S. 2008. "First-year Experience Course Improves Students' Financial Literacy." *ESource for College Transitions* [Electronic newsletter published by the National Resource Center for the First-year Experience and Students in Transition] 6 (1): 9–11.

Pascarella, E., and P. Terenzini. 1991. *How College Affects Students: Findings and Insights from Twenty Years of Research.* San Francisco: Jossey-bass.

Pascarella, E., and P. Terenzini. 2005. *How College Affects Students: A Third Decade of Research.* Vol. 2. San Francisco: Jossey-bass.

Perna, L. W., and G. DuBois, eds. 2010. *Understanding the Working College Student: New Research and its Implications for Policy and Practice.* Sterling, VA: Stylus.

Pratt, B. 2008. *Extra Credit: The 7 Things Every College Student Needs to Know about Credit, Debt, & Cash.* Keedysville, MD: ExtraCreditBook.com.

Pratt, B. 2011. *Extra Credit: The 7 Things Every College Student Needs to Know About Credit, Debt & Cash.* 2nd ed. Winterville, NC: Financial Relevancy.

Ring, T. October, 1997. "Issuers Face a Visit to the Dean's Office." *Credit Card Management* 10: 34–9.

Sallie Mae April, 2009. *How Undergraduate Students Use Credit Cards: Sallie Mae's National Study of Usage Rates and Trends 2009.* http://static.mgnetwork.com/rtd/pdfs/20090830_iris.pdf.

Susswein, R. 1995. "College Students and Credit Cards: A Privilege Earned?" *Credit World* 83: 21–3.

Tinto, V. 1993. *Leaving College: Rethinking the Causes and Cures of Student Attrition.* 2nd ed. Chicago: University of Chicago Press.

Tinto, V. 2012. *Completing College: Rethinking Institutional Action.* University of Chicago Press, Chicago, IL.

Tyson, E. 2012. *Personal Finance for Dummies.* 7th ed. Hoboken, NJ: John Wiley and Sons.

Walker, C. M. 1996. "Financial Management, Coping, and Debt in Households under Financial Strain." *Journal of Economic Psychology* 17: 789–807.

Chapter 12 Exercises

12.1 Quote Reflections

Review the sidebar quotes contained in this chapter and select two that were especially meaningful or inspirational to you.

For each quote, provide a three- to five-sentence explanation why you chose it.

12.2 Reality Bite

Problems Paying for College

A college student posted the following message on the Internet:

"I went to college for one semester, failed some of my classes, and ended with $900 in student loans. Now I can't even get financial aid or a loan because of some stupid thing that says if you fail a certain amount of classes you can't get aid or a loan. And now since I couldn't go to college this semester they want me to pay for my loans already, and I don't even have a job."

Any suggestions?

Reflection and Discussion Questions

1. What suggestions do you have for this student? What should the student do immediately? Eventually?

2. What should the student have done to prevent this from happening in the first place?

3. Do you know of any students who are in a similar predicament or soon could be?

12.3 Self-Assessment of Financial Attitudes and Habits

Answer the following questions about yourself as accurately and honestly as possible.

	Agree	Disagree
1. I pay my rent or mortgage on time each month.	_____	_____
2. I avoid maxing out or going over the limit on my credit cards.	_____	_____
3. I balance my checkbook each month.	_____	_____
4. I set aside money each month for savings.	_____	_____
5. I pay my phone and utility bills on time each month.	_____	_____
6. I pay my credit card bills in full each month to avoid interest charges.	_____	_____
7. I believe it's important to buy the things I want when I want them.	_____	_____
8. Borrowing money to pay for college is a smart thing to do.	_____	_____
9. I have a monthly or weekly budget that I follow faithfully.	_____	_____
10. The thing I enjoy most about making money is spending money.	_____	_____
11. I limit myself to one credit card.	_____	_____
12. Getting a degree will get me a good job and a good income.	_____	_____

Sources: Cude et al. (2006), Niederjohn (2008).

Give yourself one point for each item that you marked "agree"—except for items 7, 9, and 10. For these items, give yourself a point if you marked "disagree."

A perfect score on this short survey would be 12.

Reflection Questions:

1. What was your total score?

2. Which items lowered your score?

3. Do you detect any pattern across the items that lowered your score?

4. Do you see any realistic way(s) to improve your score on this test?

12.4 Financial Self-Awareness: Monitoring Money & Tracking Cash Flow

Step 1. Use the "Financial Self-Awareness" worksheet on the next page to *estimate* your income and expenses per month, and enter them in column 2.

Step 2. *Track* your actual income and expenses for a month and enter them in column 3. (To help you do this accurately, keep a file of your cash receipts, bills paid, and credit card or checking account records for the month.)

Step 3. After one month of tracking your cash flow, answer the following questions.

a. Were your estimates generally accurate?

b. On what items were there the largest discrepancies between your estimated cost and their actual cost?

c. Comparing your bottom-line total for income and expenses, are you satisfied with how your monthly cash flow is going?

d. What changes could you make to create more positive cash flow—that is, to increase your income or savings and reduce your expenses or debt?

e. How likely is it that you'll make the changes you mentioned in the previous question?

Chapter 12 Reflection

How are you financing your college education? Do you feel this is the best way for you to pay for college? Why or why not?

Do you feel you have good or poor money management skills? Explain.

List and describe at leave five principles discussed in this chapter that you can use to better manage your money.

1.

2.

3.

4.

5.

Now explain HOW you can put these principles into practice.

CAREER PLANNING AND DECISION-MAKING

This chapter will help you develop a plan for making career decisions that will best enable you to reach your long-term goals.

Equip you with effective strategies for pursuing a career path that's compatible with your personal interests, talents, and goals.

 Journal Reflection 13.1

At this point in your college experience, are you decided or undecided about a career?

What resources or mentors have you consulted in relationship to selection of a career or career field?

1. If you're undecided, what career pathways or career field?

2. If you're decided:

   a) What's your choice?

   b) What led you to this choice?

_____

_____

_____

c) How sure are you about this choice? (Circle one.)

absolutely sure   fairly sure   not too sure   likely to change

Do What You Are (DWYA)

1. According to your DWYA report, what are your career satisfiers? Do you agree or disagree with these? Explain.

_____

_____

_____

_____

2. Look at your DWYA report and your "pretty interested" or "somewhat interested" career suggestions. Of these careers, which are your top three choices? Why are these your top three choices?

_____

_____

_____

_____

3. How do your career satisfiers tie in with the three careers you chose in question two?

_____

_____

_____

_____

The Importance of Career Planning

Most of the remaining hours of your life will be spent working; the only other single activity you'll spend more time doing is sleeping. Since such a sizable portion of your life is spent on your vocation, it's easy to see why your career can have such a strong influence on your identity and personal happiness. Choosing a career path is one of the most important decisions you'll make in your life, so the process of career exploration and choice should begin right now—during your first year in college. The need to do so is highlighted by a national survey of first-year college student: almost 60% of them strongly agreed that it's important to be thinking about their career path; however, only 25% reported they had a clear idea on how to achieve their career goals (HERI 2014).

Even if you have decided on a career that you've been dreaming about since you were a preschooler, you still need to confirm this choice and will likely need to decide on a specialization within your chosen field. For instance, if you're interested in pursuing a career in law, you'll need to decide what branch of law you will practice (criminal law, corporate law, family law, etc.). You will also need to decide what employment sector or type of industry you'd like to work in (e.g., nonprofit, for-profit, education, or government). Thus, no matter how certain or uncertain you are about your career path, you still need to explore specific career options and begin to devise a career development plan.

STRATEGIES FOR CAREER EXPLORATION AND PREPARATION

Reaching an effective decision about a career path involves four key steps:

1.

Awareness of *yourself*—insight into your personal, interests, talents, needs, and values

↓

2.

Awareness of your *career options*—knowing the different career choices available to you

↓

3.

Awareness of what career options provide the *best "fit"* for you—knowing what career(s) best match your personal interests, talents, needs, and values

↓

4.

Awareness of the key *steps and strategies* needed to reach your career goal—knowing how to prepare for and gain entry to the career of your choice

In short, effective career decision-making begins with a clear under-standing of who you are, where you can go, where you will go, and how you will get there.

Step 1. Awareness of Self

The career you decide to pursue says a lot about who you are, what you want from life, and how you want to impact the lives of others. Thus, self-awareness is the critical first step in the process of career planning. A wise career choice begins with a clear understanding of who you are; from there you can determine where you want to go and how to get there. You must know yourself before you know what career is best for you. While this may seem obvious, self-awareness and self-discovery are often overlooked aspects of the career decision-making process. By deepening your self-awareness, you put yourself in a better position to choose a career path that's true to the person you are and the person you want to be.

Self-awareness is the first and most important step in the career planning process. Meaningful career goals and effective career choices are built on a deep understanding of self.

You can increase your self-awareness by asking yourself questions that stimulate introspection—reflection on your inner qualities and personal priorities. Introspective questions launch you on an inner quest for self-insight and self-discovery that leads you to a career that's consistent with who you are and who you want to be. You can begin this introspective process by asking yourself questions relating to your personal:

- **Interests:** what you *like* doing;
- **Talents:** what you're *good* at doing;
- **Needs:** what you find personally *satisfying* or *fulfilling;* and
- **Values:** what you believe is *important* to do or is *worth* doing.

💡 Journal Reflection 13.2

Complete the following sentences:

- My primary interests are . . .

  _____

  _____

  _____

  _____

- My strongest abilities or talents are . . .

  _____

  _____

  _____

  _____

- What brings me the greatest sense of personal satisfaction and fulfillment is ...

- What I value the most is ...

How do your above answers compare with results from the "Your Career Satisfiers" section of your *Do What You Are* report?

One way to gain greater self-awareness is by taking psychological tests or assessments. These assessments allow you to see how your interests and values compare with other students and with working professionals who are satisfied and successful with their careers. This comparative perspective provides you with an important reference point for assessing whether your level of interest in a career is high, average, or low relative to other students and to professionals working in that field. To take a career interest test, as well as other career exploration assessments, consult the Career Development Office on your campus.

In addition to your personal interests, another factor you should consider when choosing a career is your personal needs. A *need* may be described as something stronger than an interest. When you do something that satisfies a personal need, you're doing something that you find highly motivating and personally fulfilling (Melton 1995). Psychologists have identified several important human needs that vary in strength or intensity from person to person (Ryan 1995; Ryan and Deci 2000). Listed in **Box 13.1** are personal needs that are especially important to consider when making a career choice.

> I believe following my passion is more crucial than earning money. I think that would come itself eventually."
>
> —*College sophomore responding to the question, "What are you looking for in a career?"*

BOX 13.1

Personal Needs to Consider when Making Career Choices

After reading about each need in this box, make a note indicating how strong that need is for you (high, moderate, or low).

1. **Autonomy.** Need for working independently without close supervision or control. Individuals with a high need for autonomy experience greater fulfillment working in careers that allow them to be their own boss, make their own choices or decisions, and control their own work schedule. Individuals low in this need may experience greater satisfaction working in careers that are more structured and allow them to work with a supervisor who provides direction, assistance, and frequent feedback.

> *Our research [on happiness] indicates prosperity is not the most important factor. Personal freedom is more important, and it's freedom in all kinds of ways. . . political freedom and freedom of choice."*
> —*Ronald Inglehart, happiness researcher, University of Michigan*

AUTHOR'S JOURNEY

As a college junior with half of my degree completed, I had an eye-opening experience. I wish this experience had happened in my first year, but better late than never. When I chose a career during my first year of college, my decision-making process was not systematic and didn't involve critical thinking. I chose a major based on what sounded prestigious and would pay me the most money. Although these are not necessarily bad factors, my failure to use a systematic and reflective process to evaluate my career choice. In my junior year, I asked one of my professors why he decided to get his PhD and become a professor. He simply answered, "I wanted autonomy." This was an epiphany for me. He explained that when he reflected on what mattered most to him, he realized that he needed a career that offered independence. So, he began looking at career options that would allow him to work independently. After hearing his explanation, "autonomy" became my favorite word, and this story became a guiding force in my life. After going through a critical introspective process, I determined that autonomy was exactly what I desired and a professor is what I became.

—*Aaron Thompson*

2. **Affiliation (Belongingness).** Need for social interaction, a sense of belonging, and the opportunity to collaborate with others. Individuals with a high need for affiliation experience greater fulfillment working in careers that involve teamwork and frequent interpersonal interaction with coworkers. Individuals low in this need are more likely to be satisfied working alone or in competition with others.

> *To me, an important characteristic of a career is being able to meet new, smart, interesting people."*
> —*First-year student*

3. **Achievement (Competence).** Need to experience challenge and a sense of personal accomplishment. Individuals with high achievement needs feel more

> *I want to be able to enjoy my job and be challenged by it at the same time. I hope that my job will not be monotonous and that I will have the opportunity to learn new things often."*
> —*First-year student*

fulfilled working in careers that push them to solve problems, generate creative ideas, and continually learn new information or master new skills. Individuals with a low need for achievement are likely to be more satisfied with careers that don't continually test their abilities and don't repeatedly challenge them to stretch their skills with new tasks and different responsibilities.

4. **Recognition.** Need for prestige, status, and respect from others. Individuals with high recognition needs

are likely to feel satisfied working in high-status careers that society perceives as prestigious. Individuals with a low need for recognition would feel comfortable working in a career that they find self-satisfying, regardless of how impressive or enviable their career appears to others.

5. **Sensory Stimulation.** Need for experiencing variety, change, and risk. Individuals with high sensory stimulation needs are more likely to be satisfied working in careers that involve frequent changes of pace and place (e.g., travel), unpredictable events (e.g., work tasks that require them to think on their feet), and some stress (e.g., working under pressure of competition or deadlines). Individuals with a low need for sensory stimulation may feel more comfortable working in careers that involve regular routines, predictable situations, and minimal risk or stress.

> For me, a good career is very unpredictable and interest-fulfilling. I would love to do something that allows me to be spontaneous."
>
> —First-year student

Sources: Baumeister and Leary (1995); Chua and Koestner (2008); Deci and Ryan (2002); Ryan (1995)

Journal Reflection 13.3

Looking back at the five needs listed in **Box 13.1,** which one(s) did you identify as being strong needs for you?

What career or careers do you think would best match your strongest needs?

_____

_____

_____

_____

_____

_____

> Don't expect a recluse to be motivated to sell, a creative thinker to be motivated to be a good proofreader day in and day out, or a sow's ear to be happy in the role of a silk purse."
>
> —Pierce Howard, author of The Owner's Manual for the Brain

In sum, four key personal characteristics should be considered when exploring and choosing a career: abilities, interests, values, and needs. As illustrated in **Figure 13.1**, these core characteristics are the pillars that provide the foundational support for making effective career choices and decisions. Ideally, you want to be in a career that you're good at, interested in, passionate about, and brings you a sense of personal satisfaction and fulfillment.

The opportunity to make a reasonable amount of money is certainly one factor to consider when choosing a career, but a good career choice

FIGURE 13.1: Personal Characteristics providing the Foundation for Effective Career Choice

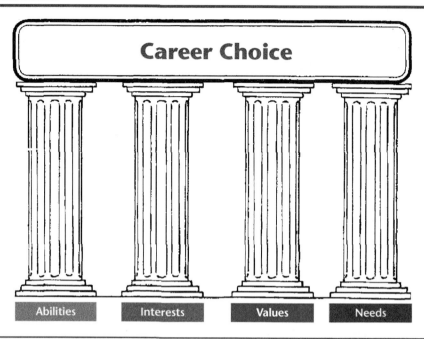

©Kendall Hunt

involves more factors than just starting salary. It's a decision that should also involve deep awareness and strong consideration of your special abilities, what you're passionate about, and what is meaningful to you. It's noteworthy that the word *vocation* derives from the Latin "vocatio" meaning "a calling." This suggests that a career is more than a money-making venture; it should call out to you and call forth your true talents and interests.

Step 2. Awareness of Career Options

In addition to self-awareness and knowledge about yourself, effective career decision-making requires knowledge about your range of career options and the realities of the work world. When you look at the list of occupations in **Box 13.2**—none of which existed ten years ago—you can see how the nature of today's work world is changing more rapidly than at any other time in history.

Collaboration Opportunity

Take a piece of paper and divide it in half vertically and horizontally so you have four boxes on the page. Label the first box "abilities," the second, "interests," the third, "values," and the fourth "needs." Visually represent what you believe are your attributes related to each of the labeled boxes. In a group of four, discuss each others' chart, and discuss the pros and cons of various career choices.

BOX 13.2

Occupations That Didn't Exist Ten Years Ago

1. **App developer:** When you hear "there's an app for that," it's because a career track emerged for program developers who have professional knowledge and skills in the world of mobile devices.
2. **Market research data miner:** Ever wonder how retailers know how to create customized advertisements especially for you? Market researcher data miners collect data on consumer behaviors and predict trends for advertisers to use to develop marketing strategies.
3. **Educational or admissions consultant:** Some parents take extra steps to ensure their children are accepted at the "right" school (from preschool to college). Educational or admissions consultants are hired to guide families through the application and interview process.
4. **Millennial generation expert:** It's now very common to find people from different generations working together in the same organization. Millennial generation experts help employers maximize the potential of their staff by providing advice on working with their youngest employees and mentoring them for future success.
5. **Social media manager:** The business world now makes greater use of social media to market and advertise their products and services. Social media managers target their marketing to users of different social media sites.
6. **Chief listening officer:** Similar to a social media manager, a chief listening officer uses social media to monitor consumer discussions and shares this information with marketing agents so they can design strategies that appeal to various segments of the population.
7. **Cloud computing services:** Most websites used every day by consumers store incredibly large amounts of data. Computer engineers with expertise in data management, store and index tremendous volumes of bytes for companies—about a quadrillion!
8. **Elder care:** Life expectancy is increasing and along with it the need for individuals who possess the knowledge, skills, and compassion to serve the elderly, their families, and the agencies and companies that assist them.
9. **Sustainability expert:** For environmental and economic reasons, companies are now seeking ways to minimize their carbon emissions. This has created a demand for professionals with expertise in the science of sustainability and the ability to develop "green" business practices that are also cost-effective.
10. **User experience design:** User experience designers do exactly what their titles suggest: they create experiences for consumers through technology. These designers use current technology to create color, sound, and images by using tools like HTML, Photoshop, and CSS.

Source: Casserly (2012)

Career Information Resources

There are numerous resources you can use to find out about careers that provide information on required schooling, wages and compensation, and possible transfer opportunities. Here is a list to get you started:

Dictionary of Occupational Titles **(DOT) (www.occupationalinfo.org).** This is the largest printed resource on careers; it contains concise definitions of more than 17,000 jobs. It also includes information on:

- Work tasks typically performed in different careers.
- Background experiences of people working in different careers that qualified them for their positions.

- Types of knowledge, skills, and abilities required for different careers.
- Personal interests, values, and needs of individuals in different occupations who are satisfied and successful in their line of work.

Occupational Outlook Handbook (OOH) (www.bls.gov/oco). This is one of the most widely available and used resource on careers. It contains descriptions of approximately 250 positions, including information on: the nature of the work; work conditions; places of employment; training or education required for career entry and advancement; salaries and benefits; and additional sources of information about particular careers (e.g., professional organizations and governmental agencies associated with a career). A distinctive feature of this resource is that it also contains information about the *future employment outlook* for different careers.

Encyclopedia of Careers and Vocational Guidance (Chicago: Ferguson Press). As the name suggests, this is an encyclopedia of information on entry qualifications, salaries, and advancement opportunities for a wide variety of careers.

Occupational Information Network (O*NET) Online (www.online. onetcenter.org). This is America's most comprehensive online source of online information about careers. It contains up-to-date descriptions of almost 1,000 careers, plus lots of other career-related information similar to what you would find in the *Dictionary of Occupational Titles*.

In addition to these general sources of information, your Career Development Center and College Library should have resources relating to specific careers or occupations (e.g., careers for English majors). You can also learn a great deal about specific careers by simply reading advertisements for position openings in your local newspaper or online (e.g., www.careerbuilder.com and college.monster.com). When reading position descriptions, make special note of the tasks, duties, or responsibilities they involve and ask yourself whether these positions are compatible with your personal talents, interests, needs, and values.

Career Planning and Development Workshops

Periodically during the academic year, your campus is likely to offer programs devoted to career exploration and career preparation. For example, the Career Center may sponsor career exploration or career planning workshops that you can attend for free. Research indicates that career development workshops are effective in helping students plan for and choose careers (Brown and Krane 2000; Hildenbrand and Gore 2005). Your Career Center may also organize career fairs, at which professionals working in different career fields have booths where you can visit with them and ask questions about their careers.

Career Development Courses

Your college may offer career development courses for elective credit. These courses typically include self-assessments of your career interests, information about different careers, and strategies for career preparation. Since you need to do career planning while you're enrolled in college, why not do it by enrolling in a career planning course that gives you college credit for doing it? Studies show that students benefit from participating in these courses (Pascarella and Terenzini 2005).

You may also be able to explore career interests in a writing or speech course that allows you to choose the topic that you write or speak about. If you're given the freedom to choose any topic to research, consider researching a career you're exploring and make that the topic of your paper or presentation.

Information Interviews

One of the best and most overlooked ways to get accurate information about a career is to interview professionals working in that career. Career development specialists refer to this strategy as information interviewing. Don't assume that working professionals aren't interested in taking time to speak with a student; most are open to being interviewed and many report they like doing it (Crosby 2002).

Information interviews provide you with "inside information" about what the career is really like because you're getting it directly from the horse's mouth—the person actually working in the career on a day-to-day basis. Information interviewing also helps you gain experience and confidence in interview situations, which may help you prepare for future job interviews. Furthermore, if you make a good impression during information interviews, the people you interview may suggest that you contact them again after graduation to see if there's a position opening. If there is an opening, you might find yourself being the interviewee instead of the interviewer, and find yourself being hired.

Because interviews can supply you with valuable information about careers and provide possible contacts for future employment, we strongly encourage you to complete the information interview assignment at the end of this chapter.

Career Observation (Shadowing)

In addition to reading about careers and interviewing professionals, you can also learn about careers by observing professionals performing their daily duties in their place of work. Two college-sponsored programs may be available on your campus that will allow you to observe working professionals:

Job Shadowing Program. Following (shadowing) and observing a professional during a typical workday.

Externship Program. An extended version of job shadowing that lasts for a longer time period (e.g., two to three days).

Visit your Career Development Center to learn about what job shadowing or externship programs may be available on your campus. If you're unable to find a campus program for the career field you're exploring, consider finding one on your own by using strategies similar to the recommendations for information interviews at the end of this chapter. It's basically the same process; the only difference is that instead of asking the person for an interview, you're asking if you could observe that person at work. In fact, you could ask the person who granted you an information interview if you could observe (shadow) that person at work. Just a day or two of job shadowing can give you valuable information about a career.

AUTHOR'S JOURNEY

When my sister was in the last year of her nursing degree, she decided she wanted to be a pediatric nurse and work at one of the top 10 pediatric hospitals in the country. At the time, I lived in a city with an excellent pediatric hospital. My sister decided to come visit me for an extended weekend and made appointments to shadow different units in that hospital on her visit. She fell in love with the place and decided she definitely wanted to work there! A few months later, when she was in her last semester of school, that hospital called her and asked if she wanted to come and interview for jobs on all four units. They'd been just as impressed with her when she shadowed as she was with them, and they made a note on her resume to call her when she was close to graduating. She interviewed and was offered all four jobs! It turned out her shadowing experience actually ended up being a "pre-interview," and she had a job before she even graduated!

—*Julie McLaughlin*

 Journal Reflection 13.4

If you were to interview or observe a working professional in a career that interests you, what type of work would that person be doing?

_____

_____

_____

_____

_____

_____

Information interviewing, job shadowing, and externships supply you with great information about a career. However, information is not experience. In order to avoid the "no experience" syndrome after graduation, consider one of the following options:

- Internships
- Cooperative education programs
- Volunteer work or service learning
- Part-time work

In contrast to job shadowing and externships—which involve observing someone at work—an internship actively involves you in the work itself and gives you the opportunity to perform career-related work duties. The key advantage of internships is that they give you hands-on experience in a real work environment. Many colleges recognize the need its students have when they graduate and offer internships in a variety of fields. These may provide academic credit and enable a recent graduate to include work experience on future resumes. Surveys show that more than 75% of employers prefer candidates with internships (National Associate of Colleges & Employers 2010).

Cooperative Education (Co-op) Programs

Co-op programs are similar to internships but involve work experiences that last longer than one academic term and often require students to stop their coursework temporarily to participate in the program. Some co-op programs, however, allow you to continue to take classes while working part time at a co-op position; these are sometimes referred to as "parallel co-ops." Students are paid for participating in co-op programs and their co-op experience is officially noted on their college transcript (Smith 2005).

The value of co-ops and internships is strongly supported by research, which indicates that students who have these experiences during college:

- Are more likely to report that their college education was relevant to their career;
- Receive higher evaluations from employers who recruit them on campus;
- Have less difficulty finding an initial position after graduation;
- Are more satisfied with their first career position following graduation; and
- Earn higher starting salaries (Gardner 1991; Knouse, Tanner, and Harris 1999; Pascarella and Terenzini 1991, 2005).

When employers are asked to rank various factors they consider important when hiring new college graduates, internships or cooperative education programs receive the highest ranking (National Association of Colleges & Employers 2012, 2014). Employers also report that when full-time positions open up in their organization or company, they usually turn first to their own interns and co-op students (National Association of Colleges & Employers 2013). While both co-ops and internships are typically available for juniors and seniors, community college students seeking certification in a variety of fields also have opportunities to explore options.

Volunteer Work or Service Learning

Volunteer service not only gives you the opportunity to serve your community, it also gives you the opportunity to explore different work environments and gain work experience in career fields relating to your area of service. For example, volunteer work performed for different age groups (children, adolescents, or the elderly) and in different work environments (hospital, school, or laboratory) provides you with firsthand, resume-building experience and the opportunity to test your interest in careers related to these age groups and work environments. Volunteer experience also enables you to network with professionals who can serve as personal references for you and provide you with letters of recommendation. Furthermore, if these professionals are impressed with your service they may hire you on a part-time basis while you're still in college, or full-time after you graduate.

Another course-integrated option for gaining work experience is by enrolling in courses that include a *practicum* or *field work*. For instance, if you're interested in working with children, courses in child psychology or early childhood education may offer experiential learning opportunities in a preschool or daycare center on campus.

Lastly, it may be possible to do volunteer work on campus in different college offices, or by assisting a faculty member. Volunteering as a research or teaching assistant can be a very valuable experience if you intend to go to graduate school. If you have a good relationship with faculty members in an academic field that interests you, consider asking them whether they would like some assistance with their teaching or research responsibilities. You might also check out your professors' web pages to find out what type of research projects they're working on; if any of these projects interest you or relate to a career path you're considering, contact the professor and offer your help. Volunteer work done for a college professor could lead to your making a presentation with your professor at a professional conference or may even result in your name being included as a coauthor on an article published by the professor.

Part-Time Work

Jobs you hold during the academic year or summer break shouldn't be overlooked as career development experiences. Part-time work can supply you with opportunities to develop skills and personal qualities that may be relevant to any future career you decide to pursue, such as organizational skills, communication skills, and ability to work effectively with coworkers from diverse backgrounds and cultures. It's also possible that work in a part-time position may eventually turn into a full-time career—as illustrated in the following story.

 ## Journal Reflection 13.5

If you have participated in internships, volunteer, or part-time work experiences, what did you learn about yourself from these experiences that might influence your career plans, or acquire skills that could be applied to a future career?

AUTHOR'S JOURNEY

While he was enrolled in college, a former student of mine (Matt), an English major, worked part time for an organization that provides special assistance to students with disabilities. After he completed his English degree, the organization offered him a full-time position that he accepted. While working full-time at this position with students with disabilities, Matt decided to go to graduate school part-time and eventually completed a master's degree in special education. This degree qualified him for a promotion to a more advanced position in the organization, which he also accepted. Moral of the story: Part-time work in college can play an important role in opening up a future career path.

—*Joe Cuseo*

It might also be possible for you to obtain part-time work experience on campus through your school's work-study program. Work-study jobs can be done in a variety of campus settings (e.g., Financial Aid Office, Library, Public Relations Office, or Computer Services Center), and they can be built around your course schedule. Just like off-campus work, on-campus work can provide you with valuable career exploration and resume-building experiences, and the professionals for whom you work can also serve as excellent references for letters of recommendation to future employers. To see whether you are eligible for your school's work-study program, visit the Financial Aid Office on your campus. If you don't qualify for work-study jobs, ask about other forms of campus employment that are not funded through the work-study program.

There's simply no substitute for gaining knowledge about careers than direct, hands-on learning experience in actual work settings—such as shadowing, internships, volunteer services, and part-time work. These firsthand experiences represent the ultimate career "reality test." They allow you direct access to what careers are really like—as opposed to the glamorized and unrealistic picture of them portrayed in the media.

Tying it altogether, experiencing work in real-life work settings has five powerful career advantages:

- You get a realistic picture of what work is like in a particular field
- You get to test your interests and skills for certain types of work
- You strengthen your resume by adding experiential learning to academic (classroom) learning
- You acquire contacts who can serve as personal references and sources for letters of recommendation
- You network with employers who may hire you or refer you for a position after graduation.

In addition, getting work experience *early* in college makes you a more competitive candidate for internships and part-time positions you may apply for later in your college experience.

To locate and participate in work experiences that relate to your career interests, use all resources available to you, including campus resources (e.g., the Career Development Center and Financial Aid Office), local resources (e.g., Chamber of Commerce), and personal contacts (e.g., family and friends). Take these experiences seriously, learn as much as

NOTE

A key characteristic of effective goal setting is to set goals that are realistic. In the case of career goals, getting firsthand experience in actual work settings allows you to get a much more realistic view of what work in a field is really like—before committing to that field as your career goal.

you can from them, and build relationships with the people you work with—these are the people who can provide you with future contacts, references, and referrals. Don't forget that almost three of every four jobs are obtained through personal relationships, aka "networking" (Brooks 2009).

Step 3. Awareness of Career Options that Provide the Best "Fit" for You

As we've emphasized throughout this chapter, the factor that should carry the greatest weight in career decision-making is the match between your career choice and your personal talents, interests, needs, and values. Since a career choice is a long-range decision that affects your life well beyond college, the process of self-awareness should not only involve reflection on who you are now, but also on how your career choice relates to where you see yourself in the future.

 Journal Reflection 13.6

> I think that a good career has to be meaningful for a person. It should give a person a sense of fulfillment."
>
> —First-year student

Answer the following questions about a career you're considering or have chosen:

1. Why are you attracted to this career? (What led or caused you to become interested in it?)

_____

_____

_____

_____

_____

2. Would you say that your interest in this career is characterized primarily by *intrinsic* motivation—something "inside" of you, such as your personal abilities, interests, needs, and values? Or, would you say that your interest in the career is driven by *extrinsic* motivation—something "outside" of you, such as starting salary, pleasing your family, or meeting expectations of your gender (i.e., an expected career role for a male or female)? Explain.

_____

_____

_____

_____

3. If money weren't an issue and you could earn a comfortable living working in another career, would you still continue to pursue the same career you're currently considering? Why or why not?

_____

_____

_____

_____

> It's easy to make a buck. It's a lot tougher to make a difference."
>
> —Tom Brokaw, award-winning television journalist and author

Step 4. Awareness of the Major Steps Needed to Reach Your Career Goal

Whether you're keeping your career options open or you think you've already decided on a particular career, you can start now by taking early steps for successful entry into any career by using the following strategies.

Self-Monitoring: Watching and Tracking Your Skills and Attributes

Keep in mind that the *academic* skills you're developing in college are also *professional* skills you'll use beyond college. Said in another way, learning skills become earning skills. When you're engaged in the process of completing academic tasks—such as note-taking, reading, writing papers, and taking tests—you're also developing career-relevant skills—such as listening, interpreting, analyzing, and problem-solving.

What matters more to employers of college graduates than their degree credentials or the courses on their transcript are the skills and personal qualities they've developed and can bring to the position (Education Commission of the States 1995; Figler and Boles 2007) You can start building these skills and qualities through effective *self-monitoring*—that is, monitoring (watching) yourself and tracking the skills you're using and developing during your college experience. Skills are habits, and like other habits that are repeatedly practiced, their development can be so gradual and subtle that you may not even notice how much growth has taken place (like watching grass grow). Thus, career development specialists recommend that you consciously and carefully reflect on the skills you're using so you remain aware of their development and are able to articulate them to potential employers (Lock 2004).

One way to track your developing skills is by keeping a *learning journal* in which you reflect on the academic tasks and assignments you've completed, along with the skills you developed while completing them. Your journal should also include skills developed outside the classroom—such as those acquired through co-curricular experiences, leadership development programs, volunteer experiences, and part-time jobs.

Since skills are actions, it's best to track and record them in your journal as *verbs*. You're likely to find that many of these action verbs reflect the type of work-related skills that employers seek in today's job candidates. **Box 13.3** contains a sample of action-oriented career skills you're likely to develop in college that are relevant to successful performance in a variety of careers.

Box 13.3

Transferable Skills Relevant to Successful Career Performance

The following behaviors represent a sample of flexible skills that are relevant to success in virtually all careers (Bolles 1998; Figler and Bolles 2007). As you track your learning experiences in college, remain mindful of whether you're developing these (and other) skills, both inside and outside the classroom.

advise	create	initiate	produce	supervise
assemble	delegate	measure	research	synthesize
calculate	design	motivate	resolve	
coach	evaluate	negotiate	sequence	
coordinate	explain	present	summarize	

In addition to tracking your skills, also keep track of the positive traits and attributes you're developing. While skills are best recorded as *verbs* because they represent actions you can perform for anyone who hires you, personal attributes are best recorded as *adjectives* because they describe who you are and what positive qualities you can bring to any position. **Box 13.4** below identifies examples of personal traits and attributes that are relevant to successful performance in any career.

Box 13.4

Personal Traits and Attributes Relevant to Successful Career Performance

As you proceed through college, keep track of these and other personal attributes or character traits you are developing.

collaborative	conscientious	considerate	curious	dependable
determined	energetic	enthusiastic	ethical	flexible
imaginative	industrious	loyal	observant	open-minded
outgoing	patient	persuasive	positive	precise
prepared	productive	prudent	punctual	reflective
sincere	tactful	team player	thorough	thoughtful

Self-Marketing: Packaging and Presenting Your Personal Strengths and Achievements

Studies show that students who convert their college degree into a successful career have two common characteristics: personal initiative and a positive attitude (Pope 1990). They don't take a passive approach and assume a good position will just fall into their lap; nor do they believe they are owed a position simply because they have a college degree or credential. Instead, they take an active role involved in defining their strengths and showcasing them in the job-search process (Brown and Krane 2000).

One way you can convert your college degree into gainful employment is to view yourself (a college graduate) as a product and view employers as customers who may be interested in purchasing your product (your skills and attributes). As a first-year student, it could be said that you're in the early stages in the process of developing your product. Begin the process now by identifying and packaging your skills and attributes so by the time you graduate you'll have a well-developed product that potential employers will be interested in purchasing.

By developing an effective self-marketing plan, you give employers a clear idea of what you can bring to the table and do *for them*. You can market your personal skills, qualities, and achievements to future employers through the following formats.

Networking

Would it surprise you to learn that 80% of jobs are never advertised? This means that jobs you see listed in a classified section of the newspaper and posted in a Career Development Center or employment center represent only 20% of available openings at any given time. Almost one-half of all job hunters find employment through people they know or have met, such as friends, family members, and casual acquaintances. When it comes to locating positions, *who* you know can be as important as *what* you know or how good your resume looks. Consequently, it's important to continually expand the circle of people who are aware of your career interests and abilities, because they can be a valuable source of information about employment opportunities.

Also, be sure to share copies of your resume with friends and family members, just in case they come in contact with employers who are looking for somebody with your career interests and qualifications.

Personal Interview

A personal interview is your opportunity to make a positive in-person impression. You can make a strong first impression during any interview by showing that you've done your homework and have come prepared. In particular, you should come to the interview with knowledge about yourself and your audience.

You can demonstrate knowledge about yourself by bringing a mental list of your strongest selling points to the interview and being ready to speak about them when the opportunity arises. You can demonstrate knowledge of your audience by doing some homework on the organization you are applying to, the people who are likely to be interviewing you,

NOTE

Embedded in your work and class experiences are transferable skills and personal qualities that are applicable to a variety of careers. Tracking these skills and qualities and articulating them to potential employers is as important to successful entry into a future career as the courses listed on your transcript and the major listed on your resume.

"

The bottom line for most employers is 'Will this person fit in our environment?' One of the keys to marketing yourself is to make a connection, to get out of your mindset and into your audience's.

—*Katharine Brooks, author, You Majored in What? Mapping Your Path from Chaos to Career*

NOTE

Explore organization's mission statements. Consider how you might support the organization in addressing their mission. Incorporate your contribution into your interview responses.

NOTE

Be prepared with quality questions. This is not the time to ask "How much vacation time do I get?" Rather, ask, "What attributes are you looking for in a candidate?" or "Is there opportunity for growth within the company?"

and the questions they are likely to ask you. Try to acquire as much information about the organization and its key employees as is available to you online and in print. When you know your audience (who your interviewers are likely to be and what they're likely to ask), and when you know yourself well (what about yourself you're going to say), you should then be ready to answer what probably is the most important interview question of all: "What can *you* do for *us*?"

To prepare for interviews, visit your Career Development Center and inquire about questions that are commonly asked during personal interviews. You might also try to speak with seniors who have interviewed with recruiters and ask them whether certain questions tended to be frequently asked. Once you begin to participate in actual interviews, make note of the questions you are asked. Although you may be able to anticipate some of the more general questions that are asked in almost any interview, there likely will be unique questions asked of you that relate specifically to your personal qualifications and experiences. If these questions are asked in one of your interviews, there's a good chance they'll be asked in a future interview. As soon as you complete an interview, mentally review it and attempt to recall the major questions you were asked before they slip your mind. Consider developing an index card catalog of questions that you've been asked during interviews, with the question on one side and your prepared response on the reverse side. By being better prepared for personal interviews, you'll increase the quality of your answers and decrease your level of anxiety. You should also have a list of questions to ask at the interview. This shows that you are interested and did your homework. Finally, remember to dress appropriately for an interview. If you are unsure how to dress, consult a professional you trust on campus.

Lastly, remember to send a thank-you note to the person who interviewed you. This is not only the courteous thing to do, but also the smart thing to do because it demonstrates your interpersonal sensitivity and reinforces the person's memory of you.

Technology and Career Placement

Once you start looking for a job, internship, or co-op, it is very important to consider how you use technology:

1. **Your email address.** Make sure it is professional and would not offend anyone.
2. **Your cell phone.** Consider your "ring-back tone." If it is music that has offensive language, remove it. Also, make sure your voicemail message is short and professional. Time is precious and people don't want to listen to a two-minute voicemail message, no matter what it is about.
3. **Facebook, Twitter, and so on.** Make sure anything you post would not turn off any potential employers. Even if your page is marked "private," employers are hiring people to get all the dirt on you!

It is important when you are looking for a job to put your best self out there—this includes your digital self.

CHAPTER SUMMARY AND HIGHLIGHTS

Reaching an effective decision about a career path involves four forms of awareness: involved in setting

1. Awareness of *self*—insight into your personal interests, talents, needs, and values
2. Awareness of your *career options*—knowledge of different career fields available to you
3. Awareness of what options provide the *best "fit" for you*—knowing what careers most closely match your personal interests, talents, needs, and values
4. Awareness of the major *steps needed to reach your career goal*—knowing how to prepare for and gain entry into the career of your choice

   You can gain valuable information about careers by:

- Accessing printed and online career resources (e.g., *Dictionary of Occupational Titles*; *Occupational Outlook Handbook*)
- Taking career development courses
- Attending career fairs on campus
- Conducting information interviews with professionals in careers that interest you
- Shadowing (observing) professionals at work
- Engaging in service learning, internships, or cooperative education programs

LEARNING MORE THROUGH THE WORLD WIDE WEB: INTERNET-BASED RESOURCES

For additional information related to educational planning and choosing a major, see the following websites.

Identifying and Choosing College Majors:
www.mymajors.com

www.princetonreview.com/majors.aspx

Relationships between Majors and Careers:
http://uncw.edu/career/WhatCanIDoWithaMajorIn.html

Developing a Personalized Career Plan: www.mapping-your-future.org

Navigating the Job Market: www.mymajors.com

Career Descriptions and Future Employment Outlook: www.bls.gov/

Position Openings & Opportunities:
www.rileyguide.com

www.monster.com

Resume Writing & Job Interviewing: www.quintcareers.com

REFERENCES

AAC&U (Association of American Colleges and Universities). 2007. *It Takes More than a Major: Employer Priorities for College Learning and Success*. Washington, DC: Author.

Astin, A. W. 1993. *What Matters in College?* San Francisco: Jossey-bass.

Baumeister, R., and M. R. Leary. 1995. "The Need to Belong: Desire for Interpersonal Attachments as a Fundamental Human Motivation." *Psychological Bulletin* 117: 497–529.

Bok, D. 2006. *Our Underachieving Colleges*. Princeton, NJ: Princeton University Press.

Bolles, R. N. 1998. *The New Quick Job-hunting Map*. Toronto, ON, Canada: Ten Speed Press.

Brooks, K. 2009. *You Majored in What? Mapping Your Path from Chaos to Career*. NY: Penguin.

Brown, S. D., and N. E. R. Krane. 2000. "Four (or Five) Sessions and a Cloud of Dust: Old Assumptions and New Observations about Career Counseling." In *Handbook of Counseling Psychology*, edited by S.D. Brown and R. W. Lent, 3rd ed., 740–66. New York: Wiley.

Casserly, M. 2012. "10 Jobs That Didn't Exist 10 Years Ago." *Forbes.* http://www.forbes.com/sites/meghancasserly/2012/05/11/10-jobs-that-didnt-exist-10-years-ago/.

Center for Community College Student Engagement. 2008. *High Expectations and High Support* (2008 CCSSE findings). Austin, TX: The University of Texas at Austin, Community College Leadership Program.

Center for Community College Student Engagement. 2010. *The Heart of Student Success: Teaching, Learning, and College Completion* (2010 CCSSE findings). Austin, TX: The University of Texas at Austin, Community College Leadership Program.

Chua, S. N., and R. Koestner. 2008. "A Self-determination Theory Perspective on the Role of Autonomy in Solitary Behavior." *The Journal of Social Psychology* 148(5): 645–7.

Community College Research Center (CCRC). 2014. "Earning an Associate Degree Increases Likelihood of Completing Bachelor's Degree." http://ccrc.tc.columbia.edu/press-releases/earning-associate-before-transfer-press-release.html.

Crosby, O. 2002. "Informational Interviewing: Get the Scoop on Careers." *Occupational Outlook Quarterly* (Summer): 32–7.

Cuseo, J. B. 2005. " "Decided," "Undecided," and "in Transition": Implications for Academic Advisement, Career Counseling, and Student Retention." In *Improving the First Year of College: Research and Practice*, edited by R. S. Feldman, 27–50. Mahwah, NJ: Lawrence Erlbaum.

Deci, E., and R. Ryan, eds. 2002. *Handbook of Self-determination Research*. Rochester, NY: University of Rochester Press.

Education Commission of the States. 1995. *Making Quality Count in Undergraduate Education*. Denver, CO: ECS Distribution Center.

Elliott, M. 2015. *CEOs Who Didn't Pursue Undergrad Business Degrees*. http://www.usatoday.com/story/money/business/2015/03/29/cheat-sheet-ceos-college-business/70442270/.

Figler, H., and R. N. Bolles. 2007. *The Career Counselor's Handbook*. Berkeley, CA: Ten Speed Press.

Gardner, P. D. March, 1991. *Learning the Ropes: Socialization and Assimilation into the Workplace*. Paper presented at the Second National Conference on the Senior Year Experience, San Antonio, TX.

Gardner, H. 1993. *Frames of Mind: The Theory of Multiple Intelligences*. 2nd ed. New York: Basic Books.

Gardner, H. 1999. *Intelligence Reframed: Multiple Intelligences for the 21st Century*. New York: Basic Books.

Gardner, H. 2006. *Changing Minds. The Art and Science of Changing Our Own and Other People's Minds*. Boston, MA: Harvard Business School Press.

Gordon, V. N., and G. E. Steele. 2003. "Undecided First-year Students: A 25-year Longitudinal Study." *Journal of the First-year Experience and Students in Transition* 15(1): 19–38.

Hagedorn, L. S., H. S. Moon, S. Cypers, W. E. Maxwell, and J. Lester. 2006. "Transfer between Community Colleges and Four-year Colleges: The All-American Game." *Community College Journal of Research and Practice* 30(3): 223–42.

Hart Research Associates. 2006. *How Should Colleges Prepare Students to Succeed in Today's Global Economy?* Based on surveys among employers and recent college graduates. Conducted on behalf of the Association of American Colleges and Universities. Washington, DC: Author.

Hart Research Associates. July, 2014. *How Should Colleges Prepare Students to Succeed in Today's Global Economy?* http://dpdproject.info/details/how-should-colleges-prepare-students-to-succeed-in-todays-global-economy-peter-d-hart-research-associates/.

HERI (Higher Education Research Institute). 2014. *Your First College Year Survey 2014*. Los Angeles,

CA: Cooperative Institutional Research Program, University of California-los Angeles.

Hildenbrand, M., and P. A. Gore, Jr. 2005. "Career Development in the First-year Seminar: Best Practice versus Actual Practice." In *Facilitating the Career Development of Students in Transition*, edited by P. A. Gore, Monograph No. 43, 45–60. Columbia: National Resource Center for the First-year Experience and Students in Transition, University of South Carolina.

Knouse, S., J. Tanner, and E. Harris. 1999. "The Relation of College Internships, College Performance, and Subsequent Job Opportunity." *Journal of Employment Counseling* 36: 35–43.

Kuh, G. D. 1993. "In Their Own Words: What Students Learn Outside the Classroom." *American Educational Research Journal* 30: 277–304.

Leuwerke, W. C., S. B. Robbins, R. Sawyer, and M. Hovland. 2004. "Predicting Engineering Major Status from Mathematics Achievement and Interest Congruence." *Journal of Career Assessment* 12: 135–49.

Lock, R. D. 2004. *Taking Charge of Your Career Direction.* 5th ed. Belmont, CA: Brooks Cole.

Melton. 1995.

Millard, B. November 7, 2004. *A Purpose-based Approach to Navigating College Transitions*. Preconference workshop presented at the Eleventh National Conference on Students in Transition, Nashville, Tennessee.

National Association of Colleges & Employers. 2012. *Internship and Co-op Survey.* Bethlehem, PA: Author.

National Association of Colleges & Employers. 2013. *Job Outlook: The Candidate Skills/Qualities Employers Want.* http://www.naceweb.org/s10022013/job-outlook-skills-quality.aspx.

National Association of Colleges & Employers. 2014. *2014 Internship and Co-op Survey,* executive summary. https://www.naceweb.org/uploadedFiles/Content/static-assets/downloads/executive-summary/2014-internship-co-op-survey-executive-summary.pdf.

National Center for Education Statistics. 2014. *Fast Facts: Most Popular Majors.* Washington, DC: U. S. Department of Education. http://nces.ed.gov/fastfacts/display.asp?id=37.

National Student Clearing House Research Center. 2015. *Contribution of Two-year Institutions to Four-year Completions*. https://nscresearchcenter.org/snapshotreport-twoyearcontributionfouryearcompletions17/.

Pascarella, E., and P. Terenzini. 1991. *How College Affects Students: Findings and Insights from Twenty Years of Research.* San Francisco: Jossey-bass.

Pascarella, E., and P. Terenzini. 2005. *How College Affects Students: A Third Decade of Research.* Vol. 2. San Francisco: Jossey-bass.

Pope, L. 1990. *Looking beyond the Ivy League.* New York: Penguin Press.

Ryan, R. 1995. "Psychological Needs and the Facilitation of Integrative Processes." *Journal of Personality* 63: 397–427.

Ryan, R. M., and E. L. Deci. 2000. "Self-determination Theory and the Facilitation of Intrinsic Motivation, Social Development, and Well-being." *American Psychologist* 55: 68–78.

Smith, D. D. 2005. "Experiential Learning, Service Learning, and Career Development." In *Facilitating the Career Development of Students in Transition*, Monograph No. 43, edited by P. A. Gore, 205–22. Columbia: National Resource Center for the First-year Experience and Students in Transition, University of South Carolina.

Thurmond, K. C. 2007. Transfer Shock: Why Is a Term Forty Years Old Still Relevant? *NACADA Clearinghouse of Academic Advising Resources* website: http://www.nacada.ksu.edu/Resources/Clearninghouse/View-Articles/Dealing-with-transfer-shock.aspx.

Useem, M. 1989. *Liberal Education and the Corporation: The Hiring and Advancement of College Graduates.* Piscataway, NJ: Aldine Transaction.

Zamani, E. 2001. "Institutional Responses to Barriers to the Transfer Process." In *Transfer Students: Trends and Issues*, edited by F. Laanan, 15–24. New Directions for Community Colleges, No. 114. San Francisco: Jossey-bass.

Zlomek, E. March 26, 2012. "As MBA Applicants, Business Majors Face an Uphill Battle." *Bloomburg Business.* http://www.bloomberg.com/bw/articles/2012-03-26/as-mba-applicants-business-majors-face-an-uphill-battle.

Chapter 13 Exercises

13.1 Quote Reflections

Review the sidebar quotes contained in this chapter and select two that were especially meaningful or inspirational to you.

For each quote, provide a three- to five-sentence explanation why you chose it.

13.2 Reality Bite

Career Choice: Conflict and Confusion

Josh is a first-year student whose family has made a great financial sacrifice to support his college education. He deeply appreciates the sacrifice his family members has made and wants to pay them back as soon as possible. Consequently, he's been looking into careers that offer the highest starting salaries immediately after graduation. Unfortunately, none of these careers seem to match Josh's natural abilities and personal interests. He's now conflicted, confused, and worried. He knows he'll have to make a decision soon because the careers with high starting salaries involve majors that have many course requirements. If he expects to graduate in four years, he'll have to start taking some of these courses next semester.

Reflection and Discussion Questions

1. If you were Josh, what would you do?

2. Do you see any way that Josh might balance his desire to pay back his family as soon as possible with his desire to pursue a career that's compatible with his interests and talents?

3. What questions or factors do you think Josh should consider before making his decision about a career?

4. Can you relate to Josh's story, or do you know of students in a similar predicament?

13.3 Gaining Self-Awareness of Personal Interests, Talents, and Values

No one is in a better position to discover who you are, and who you want to be, than *you*. One effective way to gain deeper self-insight is through self-questioning. You can become more self-aware by asking yourself questions that cause you to think carefully about your inner qualities and characteristics. Responding honestly to the following questions can sharpen awareness of your true interests, abilities, and values, and help you determine what major or career is a good "fit" for you. As you read each question, briefly note what thought(s) come to mind about yourself.

Personal Interests

1. What tends to grab your attention and hold it for long periods of time?

2. What sorts of things are you naturally curious about or frequently intrigue you?

3. What do you really enjoy doing and do as often as you possibly can?

4. What do you look forward to, or get excited about?

5. What are your favorite hobbies or pastimes?

6. When you're with your friends, what do you like to talk about or spend time doing?

7. What has been your most stimulating or enjoyable learning experience?

8. If you've had previous work or volunteer experience, what jobs or tasks did you find most interesting or stimulating?

9. When time seems to "fly by" for you, what are you usually doing?

10. What do you like to read about?

11. When you open a newspaper or log onto the Internet, where do you tend to go first?

12. When you find yourself daydreaming or fantasizing about your future, what is it usually about?

From your responses to the above questions, identify a career that appears to be most compatible with your personal *interests.* In the space below, note the career and your interests that are compatible with it.

Personal Talents and Abilities

1. What seems to come naturally to you?

2. What would you say is your greatest talent or personal gift?

3. What are your most advanced or well-developed skills?

4. What seems to come easily to you that others have to work harder to do?

5. What would you say has been your greatest personal accomplishment or achievement in life thus far?

6. What about yourself are you most proud of, or that you take most pride in doing?

7. When others come to you for advice or assistance, what is it usually for?

8. What would your best friend(s) say is your best quality, trait, or characteristic?

9. When you've done something that left you feeling like you really were successful, what was it that you did?

10. If you have received awards or other forms of recognition, what have they been for?

11. On what types of learning tasks or activities have you experienced the most success?

12. In what types of courses do you tend to earn the highest grades?

> "Never desert your line of talent. Be what nature intended you for and you will succeed."
>
> —*Sydney Smith, 18th-century English writer and defender of the oppressed*

From your responses to the above questions, identify a career that appears to be most compatible with your personal *talents and abilities.* In the space below, note the career and your talents and abilities that are compatible with it.

Personal Values

1. What matters most to you?

2. If you were to single out one thing you really stand for or believe in, what would it be?

3. What would you say are your highest priorities in life?

4. Whenever you get the feeling you've done what was good or right, what was it that you did?

> "To love what you do and feel that it matters—how could anything be more fun?"
>
> —*Katharine Graham, former CEO of the Washington Post and Pulitzer Prize–winning author*

5. If there were one thing in the world you could change, improve, or make a difference in, what would it be?

6. When you have extra spending money, what do you usually spend it on?

7. When you have free time, what do you usually find yourself doing?

8. What does living a "good life" mean to you?

9. How would you define success? (What would it take for you to feel that you achieved success?)

10. How do you define happiness? (What would it take for you to be happy?)

11. Do you have a hero or anyone you admire, look up to, or feel has set an example worth following? (If yes, who and why?)

12. Would you rather be thought of as:

   a. smart,

   b. wealthy,

   c. creative, or

   d. caring?

(Rank from 1 to 4, with 1 being the highest)

From your responses to the above questions, identify a career that appears to be most compatible with your personal *values*. In the space below, note the career and your values that are compatible with it.

13.5 Conducting an Information Interview

One of the best ways to acquire accurate information about a career is to interview a working professional in that career. This career exploration strategy is known as an *information interview*. An information interview enables you to (a) get an insider's view of what the career is really like, (b) network with a professional in the field, and (c) gain confidence in interview situations that prepares you for future job interviews.

Steps in the Information Interview Process

1. Select a career you may be interested in pursuing. Even if you're currently keeping your career options open, pick a career that might be a possibility.

2. Find someone in the career you've selected and set up an information interview with that person. To locate possible interview candidates, consider members of your family, friends of family members, and family members of your friends. Any of these people may be working in the career you are considering and may be good interview candidates, or they may know others who could be good candidates. The Career Development Center on your campus, as well as the Alumni Association may also be able to provide you with contacts who are willing to talk about their careers with students—such as alumni or professionals working in the local community near your campus. The Internet may be another source for locating interview candidates.

3. Once you've identified someone you would like to interview, send that person a short letter or email, or give them a call, asking about the possibility of scheduling a short interview and mention that you would be willing to conduct the interview in person or by phone—whichever would be more convenient. If you don't hear back within a reasonable period (7–10 days), send a follow-up message. If you don't receive a response to the follow-up message, try contacting someone else.

4. After you have found someone to interview, here are some strategies for conducting the interview:

   • Thank the person for taking the time to speak with you. This should be the first thing you do after meeting the person—before you officially begin the interview.
   • Prepare your interview questions in advance. Here are some questions that you might consider asking:
     1. During a typical day's work, what tasks occupy most of your time?
     2. What do you like most about your career?
     3. What are the most difficult or frustrating aspects of your career?
     4. What personal skills or qualities do you see as being critical for success in your career?
     5. How did you decide on your career?
     6. What personal qualifications or prior experiences enabled you to enter your career?
     7. How does someone find out about openings in your field?
     8. What steps did you take to locate your current position?
     9. What advice would you give first-year students about what they might do at this stage of their college experience to begin preparing for a career in your field?
     10. How does someone advance in your career?
     11. Are there any moral issues or ethical challenges that tend to arise in your career?
     12. Are members of diverse groups likely to be found in your career? (This is an especially important question to ask if you're a member of an ethnic, racial, or gender group that is underrepresented in the career field.)
     13. What impact does your career have on your home life or personal life outside of work?
     14. If you had to do it all over again, would you choose the same career?

15. Would you recommend that I speak with anyone else to obtain additional information or a different perspective on your career field? (If the answer is "yes," you may follow up by asking: "May I mention that you referred me?") It's always a good idea to obtain more than one person's perspective before making any important choice, such as your career choice.

- **Take notes during the interview.** This not only helps you remember what was said, it also sends a positive message to the persons you interview because it shows them that their ideas are important and noteworthy (worth taking notes on).
- **If the interview goes well, consider asking if it might be possible to observe or shadow that person at work.**

Self-Assessment Questions

After completing your interview, take a moment to reflect on it and answer the following questions:

1. What information did you receive that impressed you about the career?

2. What information did you receive that distressed (or depressed) you about the career?

3. What was the most useful piece of information you took away from the interview?

4. Based on the information you acquired during the interview, would you still be interested in pursuing a career in this field? Why?

Chapter 13 Reflection

What is your ideal career?

What would your work day be like?

Make a detailed plan for how you can get this career.

What are some things you can utilize from this chapter to make it happen?

LEARNING THE LANGUAGE OF HIGHER EDUCATION

A GLOSSARY AND DICTIONARY OF COLLEGE VOCABULARY

Academic Advisors: faculty or professional staff who advise college students on course selection, help them understand college procedures, and guide their academic progress toward completion of a college degree.

Academic Calendar: the scheduling system used by a college or university to divide the academic year into shorter terms (e.g., semesters, trimesters, or quarters).

Academic Credits (Units): how students receive credit for courses counting toward completing a college degree. Academic credit is typically counted in terms of how many hours the class meets each week (e.g., a course that meets for three hours per week counts for three credits).

Academic Discipline: a field of study (biology, psychology, philosophy, etc.).

Academic Probation: a period of time (usually one term) during which students with a grade point average that does not meet the college's minimum requirement for graduation (e.g., less than 2.0) are given a chance to improve their grades. If grades improve to the point that they meet or exceed the college's minimum requirement, probation is lifted; if not, the student may be academically dismissed from the college.

Academic Support Center: place on campus where students can obtain individual assistance from professionals and trained peers to support and strengthen their academic performance.

Active Involvement (aka Engagement): the amount of *time* a student devotes to learning in college and the degree of personal *effort* or *energy* (mental and physical) the student puts into the learning process.

Analysis (Analytical Thinking): a form of higher-level thinking, which involves breaking down information and identifying its key parts or underlying elements, and detecting what's most important or relevant.

Aptitude: ability to do something well or to the potential to do it well.

Associate of Applied Science Degree (AAS Degree): community college degree in science-related fields that lead directly to a job rather than transfer to a 4-year college or university.

Associate of Applied Technology Degree (AAT Degree): community college degree in technology-related fields that lead directly to a job rather than transfer to a four-year college or university.

Associate of Arts Degree: community college degree that represents completion of general education and premajor requirements needed for transfer to a four-year college or university with a major in a nonscience field(arts).

Associate of Science Degree: community college degree that represents completion of general education and pre-major requirements needed for transfer to a four-year college or university in a science-related field.

Bachelor's (Baccalaureate) Degree: degree awarded by four-year colleges and universities that represents completion of general education requirements and requirements for a major.

Career: the sum total of vocational experiences throughout an individual's work life.

Career Advancement: working up the career ladder to higher levels of authority and socioeconomic status.

Career Development Center: key campus resource where students learn about the nature of different careers and acquire strategies for locating career-related work experiences.

Career Development Courses: college courses that typically include self-assessment of career interests, information about different careers, and strategies for career preparation.

Certificate: credential received by students at a community or technical college to signify completion of a vocational or occupational training program, which qualifies them for a specific job or occupation.

Citation: an acknowledgment of the source of any piece of information included in a written paper or oral report that is not the writer's original work.

Co-curricular Experiences: student learning and development that results from experiences taking place outside the classroom.

College Catalog (Bulletin): an official publication of a college or university that identifies its mission, curriculum, academic policies and procedures, as well as the names and educational background of its faculty.

Commuter Student: college students who do not live on campus.

Concept: a system or network of related ideas.

Concept Map: a diagram that represents or maps out main categories of ideas and depicts their relationships in a visual–spatial format.

Cooperative Education (Co-op) Program: program in which students gain work experience relating to their college major, either by stopping their course work temporarily to work full-time at the co-op position, or by continuing to take classes while working part-time at the co-op position.

Counseling Services: personal counseling provided by professionals with expertise in promoting self-awareness and self-development, particularly with respect to social and emotional aspects of life.

Cramming: packing study time into one study session immediately before an exam.

Creative Thinking: a form of higher-level thinking that generates unique ideas, strategies, or products.

Critical Thinking: a form of higher-level thinking that involves making well-informed evaluations or judgments.

Culture: a distinctive pattern of beliefs and values learned by a group of people who share the same social heritage and traditions.

Dean: a college or university administrator who is responsible for running a particular unit of the college (e.g., Dean of Fine Arts).

Diversity Appreciation: valuing the experiences of different groups of people and interest in learning from their experience.

Diversity Courses: courses designed to promote diversity awareness and appreciation of multiple cultures.

Doctoral Degree: an advanced degree obtained after completion of the bachelor's (baccalaureate) degree, which typically requires five to six years of full-time study in graduate school, including completion of a thesis or doctoral dissertation.

Double Major: a bachelor's degree in two majors that is attained by meeting the course requirements in both fields of study.

Electives: courses that students are not required to take, but which they elect (choose) to take.

Ethnic Group (Ethnicity): a group of people who share the same culture.

Experiential Credit: college credit granted for prior learning experiences that took place in noncollege settings (e.g., previous work or military experiences).

Experiential Learning: out-of-class experiences that promote learning and development.

Faculty: the collection of instructors on campus whose primary role is to teach courses offered in the college curriculum.

FAFSA (Free Application for Federal Student Aid): a form prepared annually by current and prospective college students (undergraduate and graduate) in the United States to determine their eligibility for student financial aid.

Fine Arts: a division of the liberal arts curriculum that focuses largely on artistic performance and appreciation of artistic expression by pursuing such questions as: What is beautiful? How do humans express and appreciate aesthetic (sensory) experiences, imagination, creativity, style, grace, and elegance?

Free Electives: courses that students may elect to enroll in, which count toward a college degree, but are not required for general education or an academic major.

Freshman 15: a phrase commonly used to describe the 15-pound weight gain that some students experience during their first year of college.

Full-time Student: a student enrolled in at least 12 units of coursework during the academic term.

General Education Curriculum: collection of courses designed to provide breadth of knowledge and transferable skills needed for success in any major or career.

Grade Points: number of points earned for a course, which is calculated by multiplying the course grade by the number of credits carried by the course.

Grade Point Average (GPA): translation of students' letter grades into a numeric system, whereby the total number of grade points earned in all courses is divided by the total number of course units.

Graduate School: education pursued after completing a bachelor's degree.

Graduate Student: student who has completed a four-year (bachelor's) degree and is enrolled in graduate school to obtain an advanced degree (e.g., Master's or Ph.D.).

Grant: money received that does not have to be repaid.

Guaranteed Admission Agreement (aka, Joint Admissions or "2+2 Agreements"): Agreement between a two-year and four-year college that stipulates if students complete the general education program at their community college with a satisfactory GPA, they are automatically admitted to the four-year college campus as upper division students (junior status) without having to complete a formal application for admission and acceptance.

Higher Education: formal education beyond high school.

Higher-Level Thinking: thinking at a higher or more complex level than merely acquiring factual knowledge or memorizing information.

Holistic (Whole Person) Development: development of the total self, which includes intellectual, social, emotional, physical, spiritual, ethical, and vocational aspects of personal development.

Honors Program: a special program of courses and related learning experiences designed for students who have demonstrated exceptionally high levels of academic achievement.

Humanities: division of the liberal arts curriculum that focuses on the human experience, human culture, and questions relating to the human condition, such as: Why are we here? What is the meaning or purpose of our existence? How should we live? What is the good life? Is there life after death?

Humanity: common elements of the human experience shared by all human beings.

Hypothesis: an informed guess that might be true, but still needs to be tested to confirm or verify its truth.

Intellectual Development: acquiring knowledge, learning how to learn, and learning to think deeply.

Intercultural Competence: ability to appreciate and capitalize on human differences, and to interact effectively with people from diverse cultural backgrounds.

Interdisciplinary: courses or programs that are designed to help students integrate knowledge from two or more academic disciplines (fields of study).

International Student: a student attending college in one nation, but who is a citizen of another nation.

Internship: work experience related to a college major for which students receive academic credit and, in some cases, financial compensation.

Interpret: to draw a conclusion about something and support that conclusion with evidence.

Job Shadowing: a program that allows a student to follow (shadow) and observe a professional during a typical workday.

Leadership: ability to influence people in a positive way (e.g., motivating peers to do their best), or the ability to produce positive change in an organization or institution (e.g., improving the quality of a school, business, or political organization).

Learning Habits: the usual approaches, methods, or techniques a student uses while learning.

Learning Style: the way in which an individual prefers to perceive information (receive or take it in) and process information (deal with it once it has been taken in).

Letters of Reference: a letter of reference typically written for students who are applying for entry into positions or schools after college, and for students applying for special academic programs, student leadership positions on campus, or part-time employment.

Liberal Arts: the component of a college education that represents the essential foundation or backbone for the college curriculum, which is designed to equip students with a versatile set of skills that promotes their success in any academic major or career.

Lifelong Learning: learning how to learn and how to continue learning throughout life.

Major: the academic field students choose to specialize in while in college.

Major-Specific (aka, Program-Major-to-Program-Major) Agreements: courses taken by students at community college in a field they intend to major in after transferring to a four-year college are automatically accepted by the four-year college as fulfilling graduation requirements in that major.

Master's Degree: degree obtained after completion of the bachelor's (baccalaureate) degree that typically requires two to three years of full-time study in graduate school.

Mentor: someone who serves as a role model and personal guide to help students reach their educational or occupational goals.

Merit-Based Scholarship: money awarded on the basis of performance or achievement that does not have to be repaid.

Metacognition: thinking about how you are thinking while you are thinking.

Midterm: the midpoint of an academic term.

Minor: a field of study designed to complement and strengthen a major, which usually consists of about half the number of courses required for a college major (e.g., six to seven courses for a minor).

Mnemonic Device: a memory improvement method for retaining and recalling information (e.g., an acronym or rhyming pattern).

Multicultural Center: place on campus designed for interaction among and between members of diverse cultural groups.

Multidimensional Thinking: a form of higher-level thinking that involves taking multiple perspectives and vantage points.

Multiple Intelligences: the theory that humans display intelligence and mental ability in a variety of ways (e.g., social intelligence and emotional intelligence).

Natural Sciences: a division of the liberal arts curriculum that focuses on the systematic observation of the physical world and underlying explanations of natural phenomena, asking such questions as: "What causes the physical events that take place in the natural world?" "How can we predict and control natural events?"

Need-Based Scholarship: money awarded to students on the basis of financial need that does not have to be repaid.

Netiquette: applying principles of social etiquette and interpersonal sensitivity when communicating online.

Official Transcript: college transcript signed and date-stamped by the registrar's office to verify that the information contained in it is up-to-date, accurate, and not altered by the student. For students intending to transfer, an official transcript must be sent by the registrar's office to the colleges to which the student intends to transfer.

Paraphrase: restating or rephrasing information in your own words.

Part-Time Student: a college student who enrolls in fewer than 12 units during an academic term.

Part-to-Whole Study Method: a study strategy in which material to be learned is divided into smaller parts and studied in a series of short sessions in advance of an exam; on the day before the exam, the previously studied parts are reviewed as a whole.

Phi Theta Kappa: a national honor society that recognizes outstanding academic achievement of students at two-year colleges.

Plagiarism: intentional or unintentional use of someone else's work without acknowledging it, giving the impression that it is one's own work.

Portfolio: a collection of work materials or products that illustrates an individual's skills and talents, or demonstrates educational and personal development.

Postsecondary Education: formal education beyond secondary (high school) education.

Prerequisite Course: a course that must be completed before a more advanced course can be taken.

Prewriting: an early stage in the writing process where the focus is on generating and organizing one's own ideas, rather than expressing or communicating ideas to someone else.

Process-of-Elimination Approach: test-taking strategy for multiple-choice exams whereby choices that are clearly wrong are "weeded out" or eliminated until the best possible answer is identified.

Professional School: formal education pursued after a bachelor's degree in a school that prepares students for an "applied" profession (e.g., Pharmacy, Medicine, or Law).

Proofreading: final stage of editing that focuses on detecting mechanical errors relating to referencing, grammar, punctuation, and spelling.

Recall Test Question: a type of test question that requires students to generate or produce the correct answer on their own (e.g., essay question).

Recitation (Reciting): a study strategy that involves recalling and speaking aloud information to be remembered without looking at it.

Recognition Test Question: a type of test question that requires students to select or choose a correct answer from answers that are provided to them (e.g., multiple-choice, true–false, and matching questions).

Reflection: a thoughtful review of what one has already done, is in the process of doing, or is planning to do.

Registrar's Office: campus office that maintains college transcripts and other official records associated with student coursework and academic performance.

Research Skills: ability to locate, access, retrieve, organize, and evaluate information from a variety of sources, including library and technology-based (computer) systems.

Residential Students: students who live on campus or in a housing unit owned and operated by the college.

Restricted Electives: courses that students choose to take from a restricted set or list of possible courses that have been specified by the college.

Resume: a list of an individual's credentials, accomplishments, skills, and awards.

Reverse Transfer Agreement: community college students who transfer to a four-year college before completing an associate degree are allowed to transfer credits completed at the four-year campus back to their previous two-year campus to receive the associate degree.

Rough Draft: an early stage in the writing process whereby the writer's major ideas are expressed without close attention to the mechanics of writing (e.g., punctuation, grammar, or spelling).

Self-Assessment: the process of reflecting on and evaluating personal characteristics, such as personality traits, personal interests, or learning habits.

Self-Monitoring: maintaining self-awareness of what you're doing and how well you're doing it.

Service Learning: a form of experiential learning in which students serve or help others while also acquiring skills through hands-on experience that can be used to strengthen their resumes and explore potential careers.

Sexually Transmitted Infections (STIs): a group of contagious infections spread through sexual contact.

"shallow" or "surface" learning: an approach to learning in which the student's study time is spent repeating and memorizing information in the exact form in which it's presented, rather than transforming it into words that are meaningful to the student.

Social and Behavioral Sciences: a division of the liberal arts curriculum that focuses on the observation of human behavior, individually and in groups, asking such questions as: What causes humans to behave the way they do? How can we predict, control, or improve human behavior?

Socially Constructed: knowledge that is built up through interaction and dialogue with others.

Stackable Credentials: short-term credentials that students can earn at a community colleges that can eventually be built on by taking additional courses to longer-term credentials that allow students to advance up a career ladder or across career pathways to higher-paying jobs. (For example, students can continue to earn educational credits along the pathway to an associate degree by completing a series of shorter credentials that focus on mastering skills for specific technologies, which prepare them to gain entry-level work in the field of information technology and eventually advance to higher positions.)

Student Activities: co-curricular experiences offered outside the classroom designed to promote student involvement in campus life.

Study Abroad Program: taking courses at a college or university in a foreign country.

Student Handbook: an official college publication that identifies student roles and responsibilities, violations of campus rules and policies, and opportunities for student involvement in co-curricular programs, such as student clubs, campus organizations, and student leadership positions.

Syllabus: an academic document that outlines course requirements, attendance policies, grading scale, course topics by date, test dates and dates for completing reading and other assignments, as well as information about the instructor (e.g., office location and office hours).

Synthesis: a form of higher-level thinking that involves integrating (connecting) smaller, separate pieces of information into a more comprehensive and coherent product.

Tau Sigma Honor Society: a national honors and scholarship program offered at some four-year colleges that is specifically designed for transfer students. To be eligible, transfer students must earn at least a 3.5 GPA after their first term on campus or rank among the top 20% of their entering transfer class in academic performance.

Test Anxiety: a state of emotional tension that can weaken test performance by interfering with concentration, memory, and ability to think at a higher level.

Test-Wise: using characteristics of the test question itself (e.g., its wording or format) to increase the probability of choosing the correct answer.

Theory: a body of conceptually related concepts and general principles that help organize, understand, and apply knowledge that has been acquired in a particular field of study.

Thesis Statement: a one- to three-sentence statement contained in the introduction to a paper, which serves as a summary of the key point or main argument the writer intends to make and support with evidence.

Transfer Advisors: professionals working at either two-year or four-year colleges who specialize in advising transfer students.

Transfer Articulation Agreements (aka, Transfer Agreement Pacts): agreements between two-year and four-year colleges about how course credit will be transferred from one college to the other.

Transfer Audit (aka Transfer Credit Evaluation): process whereby a four-year college evaluates a transferring student's transcript to determine how many courses will be accepted for transfer credit and where the credit will be applied (e.g., as credit toward general education, a college major, or an elective).

Transfer Fair: an event held at a two-year or four-year campus whereby transfer advisors and college admissions representatives from four-year institutions help community college students plan for successful transfer.

Transfer Orientation Course: an educational program experienced before the first academic term in college that's designed to help new students make a smooth transition to higher education.

Transfer Shock: cultural adjustment and dip in GPA typically experienced by transfer students during their first term on the four-year campus; however, after surviving this initial adjustment and dip, transfer students' grades improve and their graduation rates

are similar to students who begin their college education at four-year colleges.

Transfer-Student Orientation: program offered at a four-year college designed specifically for new transfer students to facilitate their transition to the college.

Transfer Orientation Course (aka, Transfer Student Seminar: course offered at a four-year college specifically for new transfer students during their first term on campus to facilitate their transition to the college.

Transferable Skills: skills that can be transferred or applied across different subjects, careers, and life situations.

Undergraduate: student enrolled in a two-year or four-year college.

Visual Aids: charts, graphs, diagrams, or concept maps that improve learning and memory by enabling the learner to organize information into a picture or image.

Visual Memory: memory that relies on the sense of vision.

Visualization: a memory improvement strategy that involves creating a mental image or picture of what is to be remembered, or by imagining it in a familiar site or location.

Vocational Development: exploring career options, making career choices wisely, and developing skills needed for career success.

Waive: to give up one's right to access information (e.g., waiving the right to see a letter of recommendation).

Wellness: a state of optimal health, peak performance, and positive well-being that results from balancing and integrating different dimensions of the "self" (body, mind, and spirit).

Withdrawal: dropping a class after the drop/add deadline, which results in a student receiving a "W" for the course and no academic credit.

Work-Study Program: a federal program that supplies colleges and universities with funds to provide on-campus employment for students who are in financial need.

Writing Center: a campus support service where students receive assistance at any stage of the writing process, whether it be collecting and organizing ideas, composing a first draft, or proofreading a final draft.

REFERENCES

AAC&U (Association of American Colleges and Universities). 2007, 2013. *It Takes More Than a Major: Employer Priorities for College Learning and Success*. Washington, DC: Author.

Abbey, A. 2002. "Alcohol-related Sexual Assault: A Common Problem Among College Students." *Journal of Studies on Alcohol* 14: 118–28.

Acredolo, C., and J. O'Connor. 1991. "On the Difficulty of Detecting Cognitive Uncertainty." *Human Development* 34: 204–23.

Advisory Committee on Student Financial Assistance. September, 2008. *Apply to Succeed: Ensuring Community College Students Benefit from Need-based Financial Aid*. Washington DC: Author. https://www2.ed.gov/about/bdscomm/list/acsfa/applytosucceed.pdf.

Agus M. S., J. F. Swain, C. L. Larson, E. A. Eckert, and D. S. Ludwig. 2000. "Dietary Composition and Physiologic Adaptations to Energy Restriction." *American Journal of Clinical Nutrition* 74(4): 901–07.

AhYun, K. 2002. "Similarity and Attraction." In *Interpersonal Communication Research*, edited by M. Allen, R. W. Preiss, B. M. Gayle, and N. A. Burrell, 145–67. Mahwah, NJ: Erlbaum.

Allport, G. W. 1954. *The Nature of Prejudice.* Cambridge, MA: Addison-Wesley.

Allport, G. W. 1979. *The Nature of Prejudice*. 3rd ed. Reading, MA: Addison-Wesley.

American Association of Community Colleges 2009 Fact Sheet. 2009. http://www.aacc.nche.edu/About/Documents/factsheet2009.pdf.

American Association of Community Colleges. 2009. 2009 Fact Sheet. http://www.aacc.nche.edu/About/Documents/factsheet2009.pdf.

American College Testing. 2015. *College Student Retention and Graduation Rates from 2000 through 2015*. http://www.act.org/research/policymakers/pdf/retain_2015.pdf.

American Psychiatric Association. 2015. *Diagnostic and Statistical Manual of Mental disorders, DSM-IV-TR*. 5th ed. Washington, DC: Author.

Amir, Y. 1969. "Contact Hypothesis in Ethnic Relations." *Psychological Bulletin* 71: 319–42.

Amir, Y. 1976. "The Role of Intergroup Contact in Change of Prejudice and Ethnic Relations." In *Towards the Elimination of Racism*, edited by P. A. Katz, 245–308. New York: Pergamon Press.

Anderson, C. J. 2003. "The Psychology of Doing Nothing: Forms of Decision Avoidance Result from Reason and Emotion." *Psychological Bulletin* 129: 139–67.

Anderson, J. R. 2010. *Cognitive Psychology and its Implications*. New York: Worth Publishers.

Anderson, L. W., and D. R. Krathwohl, eds. 2001. *A Taxonomy for Learning, Teaching, and Assessing: A Revision of Bloom's Taxonomy of Educational Objectives*. New York: Addison Wesley Longman.

Anderson, M., and S. Fienberg. 2000. *"Race and Ethnicity and the Controversy Over the US Census." Current Sociology* 48(3): 87–110.

Andres, L., and J. Wyn. 2010. *The Making of a Generation: The Children of the 1970s in Adulthood*. Buffalo, NY: University of Toronto Press.

Appleby, D. C. June, 2008. *Diagnosing and Treating the Deadly 13th Grade Syndrome*. Paper presented at the Association of Psychological Science Convention, Chicago, IL.

Arnedt, J. T., G. J. S. Wilde, P. W. Munt, and A. W. MacLean. 2001. "How Do Prolonged Wakefulness and Alcohol Compare in the Decrements they Produce on a Simulated Driving Task?" *Accident Analysis and Prevention* 33: 337–44.

Aronson, E., T. D. Wilson, and R. M. Akert. 2013. *Social Psychology*. 8th ed. Upper Saddle River, NJ: Pearson/Prentice Hall.

Arum, R., and J. Roska. 2011. *Academically Adrift: Limited Learning on College Campuses*. Chicago: The University of Chicago Press.

Association of American Colleges & Universities (AAC&U). 2002. *Greater Expectations: A New Vision for Learning as a Nation Goes to College*. Washington, DC: Author.

Association of American Colleges & Universities (AAC&U). 2004. *Our Students' Best Work*. Washington, DC: Author.

Astin, A. W. 1993. *What Matters in College?* San Francisco: Jossey-bass.

Ausubel, D., J. Novak, and H. Hanesian. 1978. *Educational Psychology: A Cognitive View*. 2nd ed. New York: Holt, Rinehart & Winston.

Averell, L., and A. Heathcote. 2011. "The Form of the Forgetting Curve and the Fate of Memories." *Journal of Mathematical Psychology* 55(1): 25–35.

Avolio, B. and F. Luthans. 2006. *The High Impact Leader*. New York: McGraw Hill.

Avolio, B. J., F. O. Walumbwa, and T. J. Weber. 2009. "Leadership: Current Theories, Research, and Future Directions." *Annual Review of Psychology* 60: 421–49.

Baca, J. S. March 3, 2014. *Coming into Language*. https: //pen.org/coming-into-language.

Baddeley, A. D. 1999. *Essentials of Human Memory*. Hove: Psychology.

Baer, J. M. 1993. *Creativity and Divergent Thinking*. Hillsdale, NJ: Erlbaum.

Bailey, G. 2009. *University of North Carolina, Greensboro Application for NADE Certification, Tutoring Program*. NADE Certification Council Archives. Searcy, AR: Harding University.

Bandura, A. 1994. Self-efficacy. In *Encyclopedia of Human Behavior*, edited by V. S. Ramachaudran. Vol. 4, 71–81. New York: Academic Press.

Bandura, A., and D. Cervone. 1983. "Self-evaluative and Self-efficacy Mechanisms Governing the Motivational Effects of Goal Systems." *Journal of Personality and Social Psychology* 45(5): 1017–28.

Barefoot, B. O., C. L. Warnock, M. P. Dickinson, S. E. Richardson, and M. R. Roberts, eds. 1998. *Exploring the Evidence: Vol. 2. Reporting Outcomes of First-year Seminars*. Monograph No. 29. Columbia: National Resource Center for the First-year Experience and Students in Transition, University of South Carolina.

Barker, L. and K. W. Watson. 2000. *Listen Up: How to Improve Relationships, Reduce Stress, and Be More Productive by Using the Power of Listening*. New York: St. Martin's Press.

Baron, R. A., R. N. Branscombe, and D. R. Byrnne. 2008. *Social Psychology*. 12th ed. Boston, MA: Allyn and Bacon.

Bartels, A. and S. Zeki. 2000. "The Neural Basis of Romantic Love." *European Journal of Neuroscience* 12: 172–93.

Bartlett, T. 2002. "Freshman Pay, Mentally and Physically, as they Adjust to College Life." *Chronicle of Higher Education* 48: 35–37.

Basadur, M., M. A. Runco, and L. A. Vega. 2000. "Understanding How Creative Thinking Skills, Attitudes and Behaviors Work Together: A Causal Process Model." *Journal of Creative Behavior* 34(2): 77–100.

Bassham, G., W. Irwin, H. Nardone, and J. M. Wallace. 2013. *Critical Thinking: A Student's Introduction*. 5th ed. New York: McGraw-Hill.

Bauer, D., V. Kopp, and M. R. Fischer. 2007. "Answer Changing in Multiple Choice Assessment: Change that Answer When in Doubt and Spread the Word!" *BMC Medical Education* 7: 28–32.

Baum, S., J. Ma, and K. Payea. 2013. *Education Pays 2013: The Benefits of Higher Education for Individuals and Society*. Washington DC: The College Board. http://trends.collegeboard.org/sites/default/files/education-pays-2013-full-report-022714.pdf.

Baumeister, R., and M. R. Leary. 1995. "The Need to Belong: Desire for Interpersonal Attachments as a Fundamental Human Motivation." *Psychological Bulletin* 117, 497–529.

Beck, B. L., S. R. Koons, and D. L. Milgram. 2000. "Correlates and Consequences of Behavioural Procrastination: The Effects of Academic Procrastination, Self-consciousness, Self-esteem and Self-handicapping [Special issue]. *Journal of Social Behaviour & Personality* 15(5): 3–13.

Belenky, M. F., B. Clinchy, N. R. Goldberger, and J. M. Tarule. 1986. *Women's Ways of Knowing: The Development of Self, Voice, and Mind*. New York: Basic Books.

Bellet, P. S. and M. J. Maloney. 1991. "The importance of empathy as an interviewing skill in medicine." *JAMA* 266(13): 1831–2. doi:10.1001/jama.1991.03470130111039.

Benedict, M. E., and J. Hoag. 2004. "Seating Location in Large Lectures: Are Seating Preferences or Location Related to Course Performance?" *Journal of Economics Education* 35: 215–31.

Bennett, W., and J. Gurin. 1983. *The Dieter's Dilemma*. New York: Basic Books.

Benson, H. and W. Proctor. 2011. *The Relaxation Revolution: The Science and Genetics of Mind Body Healing*. New York: Scribner.

Bergen-Cico, D. 2000. "Patterns of Substance Abuse and Attrition Among First-year Students." *Journal of the First-year Experience and Students in Transition* 12(1): 61–75.

Berndt, T. J. 1992. "Friendship and Friends' Influence in Adolescence." *Current Directions in Psychological Science* 1(5): 156–59.

Biggs, J. and C. Tang. 2011. *Teaching for Quality Learning at University*. New York: Open Education Press.

Biggs, J., and C. Tang. 2007. *Teaching for Quality Learning at University*. 3rd ed. Buckingham: SRHE and Open University Press.

Bippus, A. M. and S. L. Young. 2005. "Owning Your Emotions: Reactions to Expressions of Self-versus Other-attributed Positive and Negative Emotions." *Journal of Applied Communication Research* 33(1): 26–45.

Blair, I. V. 2002. "The Malleability of Automatic Stereotypes and Prejudice." *Personality and Social Psychology Review* 6(3): 242–61.

Bligh, D. A. 2000. *What's the Use of Lectures?* San Francisco: Jossey Bass.

Bok, D. 2006. *Our Underachieving Colleges: A Candid Look at How Much Students Learn and Why They Should Be Learning More.* Princeton, New Jersey: Princeton University Press.

Bok, D. 2006. *Our Underachieving Colleges.* Princeton, NJ: Princeton University Press.

Bolles, R. N. 1998. *The New Quick Job-hunting Map.* Toronto, Ontario, Canada: Ten Speed Press.

Booth, F. W., and D. R. Vyas. 2001. "Genes, Environment, and Exercise." *Advances in Experimental Medicine and Biology* 502: 13–20.

Boudreau, C., and J. Kromrey. 1994. "A Longitudinal Study of the Retention and Academic Performance of Participants in a Freshman Orientation Course." *Journal of College Student Development* 35: 444–49.

Bowen, H. R. 1977. *Investment in Learning: The Individual and Social Value of American Higher Education.* San Francisco: Jossey-bass.

Bowen, H. R. 1997. *Investment in Learning: The Individual and Social Value of American Higher Education.* 2nd ed. Baltimore: Johns Hopkins Press.

Bowlby, J. 1980. *Attachment and Loss: Loss, Sadness, and Depression.* Vol. 3. New York: Basic Books.

Bradburn, E. M. 2002. *Short-term Enrollment in Postsecondary Education: Student Background and Institutional Differences in Reasons for Early Departure, 1996–1998.* Washington, DC: National Center for Education Statistics, U.S. Department of Education.

Bridgeman, B. 2003. *Psychology and Evolution: The Origins of Mind.* Thousand Oaks, CA: Sage Publications.

Brissette, I., S. Cohen, and T. E. Seeman. 2000. "Measuring Social Integration and Social Networks." In *Social Support Measurement and Intervention,* edited by S. Cohen, L. G. Underwood, and B. H. Gottlieb, 53–85. New York: Oxford University Press.

Bronfenbrenner, U., ed. 2005. *Making Human Beings Human: Bioecological Perspectives on Human Development.* Thousand Oaks, CA: Sage.

Brookfield, S. D. 1987. *Developing Critical Thinkers.* San Francisco: Jossey-bass.

Brooks, I. 2009. Organisational Behaviour. 4th ed. Englewood Cliffs, NJ: Prentice Hall.

Brooks, K. 2009. *You Majored in What? Mapping Your Path from Chaos to Career.* New York: Penguin.

Brown, K. T., T. N. Brown, J. S. Jackson, R. M. Sellers, and W. J. Manuel. 2003. "Teammates On and Off the Field? Contact with Black Teammates and the Racial Attitudes of White Student Athletes." *Journal of Applied Social Psychology* 33: 1379–403.

Brown, P. C., H. L. Roediger III, and M. A. McDaniel. 2014. *Make it Stick: The Science of Successful Learning.* Cambridge, MA: The Belknap Press of Harvard University Press.

Brown, R. D. 1988. "Self-quiz on Testing and Grading Issues." *Teaching at UNL (University of Nebraska–Lincoln)* 10(2): 1–3.

Brown, S. A., S. F. Tapert, E. Granholm, and D. C. Delis. 2000. "Neurocognitive Functioning of Adolescents: Effects of Protracted Alcohol Use." *Alcoholism: Clinical & Experimental Research* 24(2): 164–71.

Brown, S. D., and N. E. R. Krane. 2000. "Four (or Five) Sessions and a Cloud of Dust: Old Assumptions and New Observations About Career Counseling." In *Handbook of Counseling Psychology.* 3rd ed., edited by S. D. Brown and R. W. Lent, pp. 740–66. New York: Wiley.

Brown, T. D., F. C. Dane, and M. D. Durham. 1998. "Perception of Race and Ethnicity." *Journal of Social Behavior and Personality* 13(2): 295–306.

Bruffee, K. A. 1993. *Collaborative Learning: Higher Education, Interdependence, and the Authority of Knowledge.* Baltimore: Johns Hopkins University Press.

Bruner, J. 1990. *Acts of Meaning.* Cambridge, MA: Harvard University Press.

Burka, J. B., and L. M. Yuen. 2008. *Procrastination: Why You Do It, What to Do About It Now.* Cambridge, MA: De Capo Press.

Bushman, B. J., and H. M. Cooper. 1990. "Effects of Alcohol on Human Aggression: An Integrative Research Review." *Psychological Bulletin* 107(3): 341–54.

Cabrera, A., A. Nora, P. Terenzini, E. Pascarella, and L. S. Hagedorn. 1999. "Campus Racial Climate and the Adjustment of Students to College: A Comparison Between White Students and African American Students." *The Journal of Higher Education* 70(2): 134–60.

Caine, R. and G. Caine. 1994. *Making Connections: Teaching and the Human Brain.* Menlo Park, CA: Addison-Wesley.

Caine, R., and G. Caine. 2011. *Natural Learning for a Connected World: Education, Technology and the Human Brain.* New York, NY: Teachers College Press.

Caplan, P. J., and J. B. Caplan. 2008. *Thinking Critically About Research on Sex and Gender.* 3rd ed. New York: HarperCollins College Publishers.

Carden, R., C. Bryant, and R. Moss. 2004. "Locus of Control, Test Anxiety, Academic Procrastination, and Achievement among College Students." *Psychological Reports* 95(2): 581–82.

Carey, B. 2014. *How We Learn*. London: Random House.

Carlson, J. N., Keller, R. W., Glick, S. D. 1990. "Individual Differences in the Behavioral Effects of Stressors Attributable to Lateralized Differences in Mesocortical Dopamine Systems." *Society for Neuroscience Abstracts 16.233.*

Carlson, N. R., H. Miller, C. D. Heth, J. W. Donahoe, and G. N. Martin. 2009. *Psychology: The Science of Behaviour*. 7th ed. Toronto, ON: Pearson Education Canada.

Carneiro, P., C. Crawford, and A. Goodman. 2006. *Which Skills Matter?* Centre for the Economics of Education, London School of Economics, Discussion Paper 59. http://cee.lse.ac.uk/ceedps/ceedp59.pdf.

Carnevale, A. P., J. Strohl, and M. Melton. 2011. *What's in Worth? The Economic Value of College Majors*. Washington DC: Center on Education and the Workforce, Georgetown University. http:cew.georgetown.edu/whatsitworth/

Casserly, M. 2012. "10 Jobs That Didn't Exist 10 Years Ago." *Forbes.* http://www.forbes.com/sites/meghancasserly/2012/05/11/10-jobs-that-didnt-exist-10-years-ago/.

Cates, J. R., N. L. Herndon, S. L. Schulz, and J. E. Darroch. 2004. *Our Voices, Our Lives, Our Futures: Youth and Sexually Transmitted Diseases*. Chapel Hill, NC: University of North Carolina at Chapel Hill School of Journalism and Mass Communication.

Center for Community College Student Engagement. 2008. *High Expectations and High Support* (2008 CCSSE findings). Austin, Texas: The University of Texas at Austin, Community College Leadership Program.

Center for Community College Student Engagement. 2010. *The Heart of Student Success: Teaching, Learning, and College Completion (2010 CCSSE Findings)*. Austin, TX: The University of Texas at Austin, Community College Leadership Program.

Centers for Disease Control and Prevention. 2010. *Teen Drivers Fact Sheet*. http://www.cdc.gov/motorvehiclesafety/teen_drivers/teendrivers_factsheet.html.

Cermak, K., and J. Filkins. 2004. *On-campus Employment as a Factor of Student Retention and Graduation*. DePaul University. http://oipr.depaul.edu/open/gradereten/oce.asp.

Chen, B., and A. Hirumi. 2009. "Effects of Advance Organizers on Learning for Differentiated Learners in a Fully Web-based Course." *International Journal of Instructional Technology & Distance Learning.* http://itdl.org/Journal/Jun_09/article01.htm

Chickering, A. W., and N. K. Schlossberg. 1998. "Moving on: Seniors as People in Transition." In *The Senior Year Experience* edited by J. N. Gardner, G. Van der Veer, et al., 37–50. San Francisco: Jossey-bass.

Chu, A. H. C., and J. N. Cho. 2005. "Rethinking Procrastination: Positive Effects of "Active" Procrastination Behavior on Attitudes and Performance." *The Journal of Social Psychology* 145(3): 245–64.

Chua, S. N., and R. Koestner. 2008. "A Self-determination Theory Perspective on the Role of Autonomy in Solitary Behavior." *The Journal of Social Psychology* 148(5): 645–7.

Ciancotto, J. 2005. *Hispanic and Latino Same-sex Couple Households in the United States: A Report from the 2000 Census*. New York: The National Gay and Lesbian Task Force Policy Institute and the National Latino/a Coalition for Justice.

Colcombe, S. J., K. Erickson, P. E. Scalf, J. S. Kim, R. Prakash, and E. McAuley. 2006. "Aerobic Exercise Training Increases Brain Volume in Aging Humans." *Journal of Gerontology: Medical Sciences* 61A(11): 1166–70.

Colombo, G., R. Cullen, and B. Lisle. 2013. *Rereading America: Cultural Contexts for Critical Thinking and Writing*. 9th ed. Boston: Bedford Books of St. Martin's Press.

Community College Research Center (CCRC). 2014. "Earning an Associate Degree Increases Likelihood of Completing Bachelor's Degree." http://ccrc.tc.columbia.edu/press-releases/earning-associate-before-transfer-press-release.html.

Conaway, M. S. 1982. "Listening: Learning Tool and Retention Agent." In *Improving Reading and Study Skills*. 51–63. San Francisco: Jossey-bass.

Conley, D. T. 2005. *College Knowledge: What It Really Takes for Students to Succeed and What We Can Do to Get Them Ready*. San Francisco: Jossey-bass.

Cook, S. W. 1984. "Cooperative Interaction in Multiethnic Contexts." In *Groups in Contact: The Psychology of Desegregation*, edited by N. Miller and M. B. Brewer, 291–302. New York: Academic Press.

Corbin, C. B., R. P. Pangrazi, and B. D. Franks. 2000. "Definitions: Health, Fitness, and Physical Activity." *President's Council on Physical Fitness and Sports Research Digest* 3(9): 1–8.

Covey, S. R. 1990. Seven Habits of Highly Effective People. 2nd ed. New York: Fireside.

Covey, S. R. 2004. *Seven Habits of Highly Effective People.* 3rd ed. New York: Fireside.

Crawford, H. J., and C. H. Strapp. 1994. "Effects of Vocal and Instrumental Music on Visuospatial and Verbal Performance as Moderated by Studying Preference and Personality." *Personality and Individual Differences* 16(2): 237–45.

Credé, M., S. G. Roch, and U. M. Kieszczynka. 2010. "Class Attendance in College: A Meta-analytic Review of the Relationship of Class Attendance with Grades and Student Characteristics." *Review of Educational Research*, 80(2): 272–95.

Crosby, O. 2002. "Informational Interviewing: Get the Scoop on Careers." *Occupational Outlook Quarterly* (Summer): 32–7.

Cross, K. P., E. F. Barkley, and C. H. Major. 2005. *Collaborative Learning Techniques: A Handbook for College Faculty.* San Francisco: Jossey-bass.

CSU Student Transfer. 2015. The Student Transfer Achievement Reform Act. http://www.calstate.edu/transfer/degrees/.

Cude, B. J., F. C. Lawrence, A. C. Lyons, K. Metzger, E. LeJeune, L. Marks, and K. Machtmes. 2006. "College Students and Financial Literacy: What They Know and What We Need to Learn. *Proceedings of the Eastern Family Economics and Resource Management Association Conference* 102–9.

Cuseo, J. B. 1996. *Cooperative Learning: A Pedagogy for Addressing Contemporary Challenges and Critical Issues in Higher Education.* Stillwater, OK: New Forums Press.

Cuseo, J. B. 2003. Comprehensive Academic Support for Students During the First Year of College. In *Student Academic Services: An Integrated Approach,* edited by G. L. Kramer et al., 271–310. San Francisco: Jossey-bass.

Cuseo, J. B. 2005. " "Decided," "Undecided," and "in Transition": Implications for Academic Advisement, Career Counseling, and Student Retention." In *Improving the First Year of College: Research and Practice*, edited by R. S. Feldman, 27–50. Mahwah, NJ: Lawrence Erlbaum.

Cuseo, J. B., A. Thompson, J. McLaughlin. 2013. *Thriving in Community College & Beyond: Strategies for Academic Success and Personal Development.* Dubuque, IA: Kendall Hunt Publishing Company.

Cuseo, J. B., A. Thompson, M. Campagna, and V. S. Fecas. 2013. *Thriving in College & Beyond: Research-based Strategies for Academic Success and Personal Development.* 3rd ed. Dubuque, IA: Kendall Hunt.

Cuseo, J. B., A. Thompson, M. Campagna, and V. S. Fecas. 2013. *Thriving in College & Beyond: Research-based Strategies for Academic Success and Personal Development.* 3rd ed. Dubuque, IA: Kendall Hunt.

Cuseo, J. B., and B. O. Barefoot. 1996. "A Natural Marriage: The Extended Orientation Seminar and the Community College." In *The Community College: Opportunity and Access for America's First-year Students* edited by J. Henkin, 59–68. Columbia: National Resource Center for the First-year Experience and Students in Transition, University of South Carolina.

Daniels, D. and L. J. Horowitz. 1997. *Being and Caring: A Psychology for Living.* Prospect Heights, IL: Waveland Press.

De Bono, E. 2007. *How to Have Creative Ideas.* London, UK: Vermillion.

Deci, E., and R. Ryan, eds. 2002. *Handbook of Self-determination Research.* Rochester, NY: University of Rochester Press.

Dee, T. 2004. "Are There Civic Returns to Education?" *Journal of Public Economics* 88: 1697–720.

Dement, W. C., and C. Vaughan. 2000. *The Promise of Sleep: A Pioneer in Sleep Medicine Explores the Vital Connection between Health, Happiness, and a Good Night's Sleep.* New York: Dell.

Demmert, W. G., Jr., and J. C. Towner. 2003. *A Review of the Research Literature on the Influences of Culturally Based Education on the Academic Performance of Native American Students.* The Northwest Regional Educational Laboratory, Portland, Oregon. http://educationnorthwest.org/sites/default/files/cbe.pdf.

DeNavas-Walt, C., B. D. Proctor, and J. C. Smith. 2013. *Income, Poverty, and Health Insurance Coverage in the United States, 2012.* U.S. Census Bureau, Current Population Reports, P60-245, Washington, DC: U.S. Government Printing Office.

Dessel, A. 2012. "Effects of Intergroup Dialogue: Public School Teachers and Sexual Orientation Prejudice." *Small Group Research* 41(5): 556–92.

Dittmar, H. 2004. "Understanding and Diagnosing Compulsive Buying." In *Handbook of Addictive Disorders: A Practical Guide to Diagnosis and Treatment*, edited by R. Coombs, 411–50. New York, NY: Wiley.

Dolan, M., and L. Romney. June 27, 2015. "Law in California Is Now a Right for All." *Los Angeles Times*: A1 and A8.

Donald, J. G. 2002. *Learning to Think: Disciplinary Perspectives.* San Francisco: Jossey-bass.

Doran, G. T. 1981. "There's a S.M.A.R.T. Way to Write Management's Goals and Objectives." *Management Review* 70(11): 35–6.

Dorfman, J., J. Shames, and J. F. Kihlstrom. 1996. "Intuition, Incubation, and Insight." In *Implicit Cognition, edited by* G. Underwood, 257–296. New York: Oxford University Press.

Dovidio, J. F., A. Eller, and M. Hewstone. 2011. "Improving Intergroup Relations Through Direct, Extended and Other Forms of Indirect Contact." *Group Processes & Intergroup Relations* 14: 147–60.

Driver, J. 2010. *You Say More than You Think: A 7-day Plan for Using the New Body Language to Get What You Want*. New York: Crown Publishers.

Druckman, D., and R. A. Bjork, eds. 1994. *Learning, Remembering, Believing: Enhancing Human Performance*. Washington, DC: National Academies Press.

Drum, D., C. Brownson, A. B. Denmark, S. E. Smith. 2009. "New Data on the Nature of Suicidal Crises in College Students: Shifting the Paradigm." *Professional Psychology: Research and Practice* 40(3): 213–22.

Dryden, G., and J. Vos. 1999. *The Learning Revolution: To Change the Way the World Learns*. Torrance, CA and Auckland, New Zealand: The Learning Web.

Duckworth, A. L., C. Peterson, M. D. Matthews, and D. R. Kelly. 2007. "Grit: Perseverance and Passion for Long-term Goals." *Journal of Personality and Social Psychology* 92(6): 1087–101.

Dunlosky, J., K. A. Rawson, E. J. Marsh, M. J. Nathan, and D. T. Willingham. 2013. "Improving Students' Learning with Effective Learning Techniques: Promising Directions from Cognitive and Educational Psychology." *Psychological Science in the Public Interest* 14(1): 4–58.

Dweck, C. S. 2006. *Mindset: The New Psychology of Success*. New York: Random House.

Education Commission of the States. 1995. *Making Quality Count in Undergraduate Education*. Denver, CO: ECS Distribution Center.

Education Commission of the States. 1995. *Making Quality Count in Undergraduate Education*. Denver, CO: ECS Distribution Center.

Eimers, M. T., and G. R. Pike. 1997. "Minority and Nonminority Adjustment to College: Differences or Similarities." *Research in Higher Education* 38(1): 77–97.

Einstein, G. O., J. Morris, and S. Smith. 1985. "Note-taking, Individual Differences, and Memory for Lecture Information." *Journal of Educational Psychology* 77(5): 522–32.

Ekman, P. 2009. *Telling Lies: Clues to Deceit in the Marketplace, Politics, and Marriage*. Revised ed. New York: W. W. Norton.

Elliott, M. 2015. *CEOs Who Didn't Pursue Undergrad Business Degrees*. http://www.usatoday.com/story/money/business/2015/03/29/cheat-sheet-ceos-college-business/70442270/.

Ellis, A. 2004. *Rational Emotive Behavior Therapy: It Works for Me It Can Work for You*. Amherst, NY: Prometheus Books.

Ellis, A., and W. J. Knausm. 2002. *Overcoming Procrastination*. Rev. ed. New York: New American Library.

Engle, J. A. Bermeo, and C. O'Brien. 2006. *Straight from the Source: What Works for First-generation College Students*. Washington, DC: The Pell Institute for the Study of Opportunity in Higher Education.

Epstein, L., and S. Mardon. 2007. *The Harvard Medical School Guide to a Good Night's Sleep*. New York: The McGraw-Hill Companies.

Erickson, B. L., C. B. Peters, and D. W. Strommer. 2006. *Teaching First-year College Students*. San Francisco: Jossey-bass.

Ericsson, K. A. 2006. "The Influence of Experience and Deliberate Practice on the Development of Superior Expert Performance. In *Cambridge Handbook of Expertise and Expert Performance*, edited by K. A. Ericsson, N. Charness, P. Feltovich, and R. R. Hoffman, 685–706. Cambridge, UK: Cambridge University Press.

Ericsson, K. A., and N. Charness. 1994. "Expert Performance: Its Structure and Acquisition." *American Psychologist* 49(8): 725–47.

Ewell, P. T. 1997. "Organizing for Learning." *AAHE Bulletin* 50(4), 3–6.

Fairbairn, G. J., and C. Winch 1996. *Reading, Writing and Reasoning: A Guide for Students*. 2nd ed. Buckingham: OU Press.

Family Care Foundation. 1997–2012. *If the World Were a Village of 100 People*. http://www.familycare.org/special-interest/if-the-world-were-a-village-of-100-people/.

Feagin, J. R., and C. B. Feagin. 2007. Racial and Ethnic Relations. 8th ed. Englewood Cliffs, NJ: Prentice Hall.

Feldman, K. A., and T. M. Newcomb. 1994. *The Impact of College on Students*. New Brunswick, NJ: Transaction Publishers (original work published 1969).

Fernández-Castillo, A., and M. J. Caurcel. 2014. "State Test-anxiety, Selective Attention and Concentration in University Students." *International Journal of Psychology* 50(4): 265–71.

Festinger, L. 1954. "A Theory of Social Comparison Processes." *Human Relations* 7: 117–40.

Fezler, W. 1989. *Creative Imagery: How to Visualize in All Senses*. New York: Simon & Schuster.

Fidler, P., and M. Godwin. 1994. "Retaining African-American Students through the Freshman Seminar." *Journal of Developmental Education* 17: 34–41.

Figler, H., and R. N. Bolles. 2007. *The Career Counselor's Handbook*. Berkeley, CA: Ten Speed Press.

Fixman, C. S. 1990. "The Foreign Language Needs of U.S. Based Corporations." *Annals of the American Academy of Political and Social Science* 511: 25–46.

Flavell, J. H. 1979. "Metacognition and Cognitive Monitoring: A New Area of Cognitive developmental Inquiry." *American Psychologist* 34(10): 906–11.

Fletcher, A., N. Lamond, C. J. van den Heuvel, and D. Dawson. 2003. "Prediction of Performance During Sleep Deprivation and Alcohol Intoxication using a Quantitative Model of Work-Related Fatigue." *Sleep Research Online* 5: 67–75.

Flippo, R. F., and D. C. Caverly. 2009. *Handbook of College Reading and Study Strategy Research*. 2nd ed. New York: Lawrence Erlbaum Associates.

Flowers, L., S. Osterlind, E. Pascarella, and C. Pierson. 2001. "How Much Do Students Learn in College? Cross-sectional Estimates Using the College Basic Academic Subjects Examination." *Journal of Higher Education* 72: 565–83.

Foreman, J. June 22, 2009. "Dear, I Love You with All My Brain." *Los Angeles Times*. http://www.latimes.com/features/health/la-he-love22-2009jun22,0,6897401.column.

Fredrickson, B. L., and C. Branigan. 2005. "Positive Emotions Broaden the Scope of Attention and Thought-action Repertoires." *Cognition & Emotion* 19: 313–32.

Freedner, N., L. H. Freed, Y. W. Yang, and S. B. Austin. 2002. "Dating Violence among Gay, Lesbian, and Bisexual Adolescents: Results from a Community Survey." *Journal of Adolescent Health* 31: 469–74.

Friedman, T. L. 2005. *The World Is Flat: A Brief History of the Twenty-first Century: Revitalizing the Civic Mission of Schools*. Alexandria, VA.

Furnham, A., and M. Argyle. 1998. *The Psychology of Money*. New York: Routledge.

Gagliardi, J., and H. Hiemstra. 2013. *College Still Pays*. Kentucky Postsecondary Education Policy Brief. http://cpe.ky.gov/NR/rdonlyres/8DE2CF1E-51A2-4C27-8C2B-41FB126252FE/0/CollegeStillPayspolicybrief.pdf.

Ganzglass, E. 2014. *Scaling "Stackable Credentials": Implications for Implementation and Policy. Center for Postsecondary and Economic Success*. http://www.clasp.org/resources-and-publications/files/2014-03-21-Stackable-Credentials-Paper-FINAL.pdf.

Gardiner, L. F. 2005. "Transforming the Environment for Learning: A Crisis of Quality." *To Improve the Academy* 23: 3–23.

Gardner, H. 1993. *Frames of Mind: The Theory of Multiple Intelligences*. 2nd ed. New York: Basic Books.

Gardner, H. 1999. Intelligence Reframed: Multiple Intelligences for the 21st Century. New York: Basic Books.

Gardner, H. 2006. *Changing Minds. The Art and Science of Changing Our Own and Other People's Minds*. Boston, MA: Harvard Business School Press.

Gardner, P. D. March, 1991. *Learning the Ropes: Socialization and Assimilation into the Workplace*. Paper presented at the Second National Conference on the Senior Year Experience, San Antonio, TX.

German, T. P., and H. C. Barrett. 2005. "Functional Fixedness in a Technologically Sparse Culture." *Psychological Science* 16: 1–5.

Giles, L. C., F. V. Glonek, M. A. Luszcz, and G. R. Andrews. 2005. "Effect of Social Networks on 10-year Survival in Very Old Australians: The Australia Longitudinal Study of Aging." *Journal of Epidemiology and Community Health* 59: 574–79.

Gilles, R. M., and F. Adrian. 2003. *Cooperative Learning: The Social and Intellectual Outcomes of Learning in Groups*. London: Farmer Press.

Glass, J., and M. Garrett. 1995. "Student Participation in a College Orientation Course: Retention, and Grade Point Average." *Community College Journal of Research and Practice* 19: 117–32.

Glenberg, A, M. 1997. "What Memory Is for." *Behavioral and Brain Sciences* 20: 1–55.

Goldsmith, E. B. 2010. *Resource Management for Individuals and Families*. 4th ed. Upper Saddle River, NJ: Prentice Hall.

Goldstein, W. M., and R. M. Hogarth, eds. 1997. *Research on Judgment and Decision Making*. Cambridge, UK: Cambridge University Press.

Goleman, D. 1995. *Emotional Intelligence: Why It Can Matter More than IQ*. New York: Random House.

Goleman, D. 2000. *Working with Emotional Intelligence*. New York: Bantam Dell.

Goleman, D. 2006. *Social Intelligence: The New Science of Human Relationships*. New York: Dell.

Goleman, D., Boyatzis, R., and McKee, A. 2013. *Primal Leadership: Realizing the Potential of Emotional Intelligence*. Boston, MA: Harvard Business School Press.

Gordon, L. October 21, 2009. "College Costs up in Hard Times." *Los Angeles Times* A13.

Gordon, V. N., and G. E. Steele. 2003. "Undecided First-year Students: A 25-year Longitudinal Study." *Journal of the First-year Experience and Students in Transition* 15(1): 19–38.

Gordon, V. N., and G. E. Steele. 2003. "Undecided First-year Students: A 25-year Longitudinal Study." *Journal of the First-year Experience and Students in Transition* 15(1): 19–38.

Gorski, P. C. 2009. *Key Characteristics of a Multicultural Curriculum*. Critical Multicultural Pavilion: Multicultural Curriculum Reform (An EdChange Project). www.edchange.org/multicultural/curriculum/characteristics.html.

Gottman, J. 1994. *Why Marriages Succeed and Fail*. New York: Fireside.

Gottman, J. 1999. *The Seven Principles for Making Marriage Work*. New York: Three Rivers Press.

Gould, E., and H. Wething. 2013. "Health Care, the Market and Consumer Choice." *Inquiry* 50(1): 85–6.

Grunder, P., and D. Hellmich. 1996. "Academic Persistence and Achievement of Remedial Students in a Community College's Success Program." *Community College Review* 24: 21–33.

Gurin, P. 1999. "New Research on the Benefits of Diversity in College and Beyond: An Empirical Analysis." *Diversity Digest* 3(3), 5–15. http://www.diversityweb.org/Digest/Sp99/benefits.html.

Guttmacher Institute. 2009. *A Real-Time Look at the Impact of the Recession on Women's Family Planning and Pregnancy Decisions*. New York: Guttmacher Institute.

Hagedorn, L. S., H. S. Moon, S. Cypers, W. E. Maxwell, and J. Lester. 2006. "Transfer Between Community Colleges and Four-year Colleges: The All-American Game." *Community College Journal of Research and Practice* 30(3): 223–42.

Halpern, D. F. 2013. *Thought & Knowledge: An Introduction to Critical Thinking*. 5th ed. New York: Psychology Press.

Halvorson, H. G. 2010. *Succeed: How We Can Reach Our Goals*. New York: Plume.

Hamilton, H. 2012. "Student Loan Blues." *Los Angeles Times*, B1, B8.

Hamilton, W. December 29, 2011. "College Still Worth it, Study Says." *Los Angeles Times*, p. B2.

Hamilton, W. June 25, 2014. "College Still Good Bet, Study Says." *Los Angeles Times*, p. B4.

Harriot, J. and J. R. Ferrari. 1996. "Prevalence of Procrastination among Samples of Adults." *Psychological Reports* 78: 611–16.

Harris, A. 2010. "Leading System Transformation." *School Leadership and Management* 30(3): 197–207.

Harris, M. B. 2006. "Correlates and Characteristics of Boredom and Proneness to Boredom." *Journal of Applied Social Psychology* 30(3): 576–98.

Hart Research Associates. 2006. *How Should Colleges Prepare Students to Succeed in Today's Global Economy?* Based on surveys among employers and recent college graduates. Conducted on behalf of the Association of American Colleges and Universities. Washington, DC: Author.

Hart Research Associates. 2006. *How Should Colleges Prepare Students to Succeed in Today's Global Economy?* Based on surveys among employers and recent college graduates. Conducted on behalf of the Association of American Colleges and Universities. Washington, DC: Author.

Hart Research Associates. 2013. *It Takes more than a Major: Employer Priorities for College Learning and Student Success*. Washington, DC: Author.

Hart Research Associates. July, 2014. *How Should Colleges Prepare Students to Succeed in Today's Global Economy?* http://dpdproject.info/details/how-should-colleges-prepare-students-to-succeed-in-todays-global-economy-peter-d-hart-research-associates/.

Hart Research Associates. July, 2014. *How Should Colleges Prepare Students to Succeed in Today's Global Economy?* http://dpdproject.info/details/how-should-colleges-prepare-students-to-succeed-in-todays-global-economy-peter-d-hart-research-associates/.

Hartley, J. 1998. *Learning and Studying: A Research Perspective*. London: Routledge.

Hartley, J., and S. Marshall. 1974. "On Notes and Note Taking." *Universities Quarterly* 28: 225–35.

Hartman, H. J., ed. 2001. *Metacognition in Learning and Instruction: Theory, Research and Practice*. Dordrecht: Kluwer Academic Publishers.

Harvey, L., S. Moon, V. Geall, and R. Bower. 1997. *Graduates Work: Organizational Change and Students' Attributes*, Birmingham, Centre for Research into Quality, University of Central England.

Hashaw, R. M., C. J. Hammond, and P. H. Rogers. 1990. "Academic Locus of Control and the Collegiate Experience." *Research & Teaching in Developmental Education* 7(1): 45–54.

Hatfield, E., and Rapson, R. L. 1993. *Love, Sex, and Intimacy: Their Psychology, Biology, and History*. New York: HarperCollins.

Hatfield, E., and Rapson, R. L. 2000. "Love." In *The Concise Corsini Encyclopedia of Psychology and Behavioral Science*, edited by W. E. Craighead and C. B. Nemeroff, 898–901. New York: John Wiley & Sons.

Health, C., and J. Soll. 1996. "Mental Budgeting and Consumer Decisions." *Journal of Consumer Research* 23: 40–52.

Heath, H. 1977. *Maturity and Competence: A Transcultural View*. New York: Halsted Press.

Herbert, W. 2014. "Ink on Paper: Some Notes on Note Taking." Association for Psychological Science (APS). http://www.psychologicalscience.org/index.php/news/were-only-human/ink-on-paper-some-notes-on-note-taking.html

HERI (Higher Education Research Institute). 2013. *Your First College Year Survey 2012*. Los Angeles, CA: Cooperative Institutional Research Program, University of California-Los Angeles.

HERI (Higher Education Research Institute). 2014. *Your First College Year Survey 2014*. Los Angeles, CA: Cooperative Institutional Research Program, University of California-Los Angeles.

Hertel, P. T., and Brozovich, F. 2010. "Cognitive Habits and Memory Distortions in Anxiety and Depression." *Current Directions in Psychological Science* 19: 155–60.

Higbee, K. L. 2001. *Your Memory: How It Works and How to Improve It*. New York: Marlowe.

Higher Education Research Institute (HERI). 2009. *The American College Teacher: National Norms for 2007–2008*. Los Angeles: HERI, University of California, Los Angeles.

Hildenbrand, M., and P. A. Gore, Jr. 2005. "Career Development in the First-year Seminar: Best Practice versus Actual Practice." In *Facilitating the Career Development of Students in Transition*, edited by P. A. Gore, monograph no. 43, 45–60. Columbia: National Resource Center for the First-year Experience and Students in Transition, University of South Carolina.

Hollenbeck, J. R., C. R. Williams, and H. J. Klein. 1989. "An Empirical Examination of the Antecedents of Commitment to Difficult Goals." *Journal of Applied Psychology* 74(1): 18–23.

Holmes, K. K., R. Levine, and M. Weaver. 2004. "Effectiveness of Condoms in Preventing Sexually Transmitted Infections." *Bulletin of the World Health Organization* 82: 254–464.

Howard, P. J. 2014. *The Owner's Manual for the Brain: Everyday Applications of Mind-brain Research*. 4th ed. New York: HarperCollins.

Howe, M. J. 1970. "Note-Taking Strategy, Review, and Long-Term Retention of Verbal Information." *Journal of Educational Psychology* 63: 285.

Huck, S., and W. Bounds. 1972. "Essay Grades: An Interaction between Graders' Handwriting Clarity and the Neatness of Examination Papers." *American Educational Research Journal* 9(2): 279–83.

Hugenberg, K., and G. V. Bodenhausen. 2003. "Facing Prejudice: Implicit Prejudice and the Perception of Facial Threat." *Psychological Science* 14: 640–43.

Hughes, D. C., B. Keeling, and B. F. Tuck. 1983. "Effects of Achievement Expectations and Handwriting Quality on Scoring Essays." *Journal of Educational Measurement* 20(1): 65–70.

Hunter, M. A., and C. W. Linder. 2005. "First-year Seminars." In *Challenging and Supporting the First-year Student: A Handbook for Improving the First Year of College*, edited by M. L. Upcraft, J. N. Gardner, B. O. Barefoot, et al., 275–91. San Francisco: Jossey-bass.

IES Abroad News. 2002. Study Abroad: A Lifetime of Benefits. www.iesabroad.org/study-abroad/news/study-abroad-lifetime-benefits.

Jablonski, N. G., and G. Chaplin. 2002. "Skin Deep." *Scientific American* (October): 75–81.

Jairam, D., and K. A. Kiewra. 2009. "An Investigation of the SOAR Study Method." *Journal of Advanced Academics* August: 602–29.

Jenkins, J. G., and K. M. Dallenbach. 1924. Oblivescence during Sleep and Waking. *American Journal of Psychology* 35: 605–12.

Jensen, E. 2008. *Brain-based Learning.* Thousand Oaks, CA: Corwin Press.

Jernigan, C. G. 2004. "What Do Students Expect to Learn? The Role of Learner Expectancies, Beliefs, and Attributions for Success and Failure in Student Motivation." *Current Issues in Education* [On-line], 7(4). Retrieved January 16, 2012, from cie.asu.edu/ojs/index.php/cieatasu/article/download/824/250

Johnson, D. W., R. T. Johnson, and K. A. Smith. 1998. *Active Learning: Cooperation in the College Classroom*. Edina, MN: Interaction Book Company.

Johnson, D., R. Johnson, and K. Smith. 1998. "Cooperative Learning Returns to College: What Evidence Is There that It Works?" *Change* 30: 26–35.

Johnson, M. P., and Ferraro, K. J. 2000. "Research on domestic violence in the 1990s: Making distinctions." *Journal of Marriage and the Family* 62: 948–63.

Johnston, L. D., P. M. O'Malley, J. G. Bachman, and J. E. Schulenberg. 2005. *Monitoring the Future National Survey Results on Drug Use, 1975–2004:Vol 2. College Students and Adults Ages 19–45*. National Institute on Drug Abuse: Bethesda, MD: 2005. NIH Publication No. 05-5728.

Johnstone, A. H., and W. Y. Su. 1994. "Lectures: A Learning Experience?" *Education in Chemistry* 31(1): 65–76, 79.

Judd, C. M., C. S. Ryan, and B. Parke. 1991. "Accuracy in the Judgment of In-Group and Out-Group Variability." *Journal of Personality and Social Psychology* 61: 366–79.

Julien, R. M., C. D. Advokat, and J. E. Comaty. 2011. *A Primer of Drug Action*. New York: Worth.

Kachgal, M. M., L. S. Hansen and K. T. Nutter. 2001. "Academic Procrastination Prevention/Intervention: Strategies and Recommendations." *Journal of Developmental Education* 25(1): 2–12.

Karjane, Fisher, and Cullen. 2002/2005. *Campus Sexual Assault: How America's Institutions of Higher Education Respond*, final report to the National Institute of Justice, October 2002, NCJ 196676.

Kaufman, J. C., and J. Baer. 2002. "Could Steven Spielberg Manage the Yankees? Creative Thinking in Different Domains." *Korean Journal of Thinking & Problem Solving* 12(2): 5–14.

Kaufmann, N. L., J. M. Martin, and H. D. Weaver. 1992. *Students Abroad: Strangers at Home: Education for a Global Society.* Yarmouth, ME: Intercultural Press.

Kelley, T., and J. Littman. 2005. *The Ten Faces of Innovation: IDEO's Strategies for Beating the Devil's Advocate & Driving Creativity Throughout Your Organization*. New York: Currency/Doubleday.

Kelly, K. 1994. *Out of Control: The New Biology of Machines, Social Systems, and the Economic World*. Reading, MA: Addison-Wesley.

Khoshaba, D., and S. R. Maddi. 2005. *HardiTraining: Managing Stressful Change*. 4th ed. Newport Beach, CA: Hardiness Institute.

Kidwell, B., and R. Turrisi. 2004. "An Examination of College Student Money Management Tendencies." *Journal of Economic Psychology* 25(5): 601–16.

Kiewra, K. A. 1985. "Students' Note-Taking Behaviors and the Efficacy of Providing the Instructor's Notes for Review." *Contemporary Educational Psychology* 10: 378–86.

Kiewra, K. A. 2000. "Fish Giver or Fishing Teacher? The Lure of Strategy Instruction." *Teaching at UNL (University of Nebraska Lincoln)* 22(3): 1–3.

Kiewra, K. A. 2005. *Learn How to Study and SOAR to Success*. Upper Saddle River, NJ: Pearson Prentice Hall.

Kiewra, K. A., and N. F. DuBois. 1998. *Learning to Learn: Making the Transition from Student to Lifelong Learner*. Needham Heights, MA: Allyn and Bacon.

Kiewra, K. A., K. Hart, J. Scoular, M. Stephen, G. Sterup, and B. Tyler. 2000. "Fish Giver or Fishing Teacher? The lure of strategy instruction." *Teaching at UNL (University of Nebraska Lincoln)* 22(3).

King, A. 1990. "Enhancing Peer Interaction and Learning in the Classroom through Reciprocal Questioning. "*American Educational Research Journal* 27(4): 664–87.

King, A. 1995. Guided Peer Questioning: A Cooperative Learning Approach to Critical Thinking." *Cooperative Learning and College Teaching* 5(2): 15–9.

King, A. 2002. "Structuring Peer Interaction to Promote High-level Cognitive Processing." *Theory into Practice* 41(1): 33–9.

King, J. E. 2002. *Crucial Choices: How Students' Financial Decisions Affect Their Academic Success*. Washington, DC: American Council on Education.

King, J. E. 2005. "Academic Success and Financial Decisions: Helping Students Make Crucial Choices." In *Improving the First Year of College: Research and Practice*, edited by R. S. Feldman, 3–26. Mahwah, NJ: Lawrence Erlbaum.

Kingkade, T. August 27, 2014. "Sleepy College Students Are Worried about Their Stress Levels." *The Huffington Post*. http://www.huffingtonpost.com/2014/08/27/college-students-sleep-stress_n_5723438.html.

Kintsch, W. 1994. "Text Comprehension, Memory, and Learning." *American Psychologist* 49: 294–303.

Kitchener, K., P. Wood, and L. Jensen. August, 2000. *Curricular, Co-Curricular, and Institutional Influence on Real-World Problem-Solving.* Paper Presented at the Annual Meeting of the American Psychological *Associa*tion, Boston.

Knouse, S., J. Tanner, and E. Harris. 1999. "The Relation of College Internships, College Performance, and Subsequent Job Opportunity." *Journal of Employment Counseling* 36: 35–43.

Knox, S. 2004. *Financial Basics: A Money Management Guide for Students*. Columbus: Ohio State University Press.

Knox, W. E., P. Lindsay, and M. N. Kolb. 1993. *Does College Make a Difference? Long-term Changes in Activities and Attitudes*. Westport, CT: Greenwood.

Kochlar, R., R. Fry, and P. Taylor. 2011. "Wealth Gaps Rise to Record Highs Between Whites, Blacks, Hispanics, Twenty-to-One." *Pew Research Social and Demographics Trends* (July). http://www.pewsocialtrends.org/2011/07/26/wealth-gaps-rise-to-record-highs-between-whites-blacks-hispanics/.

Kramer, A. F., and K. I. Erickson. 2007. "Capitalizing on Cortical Plasticity: Influence of Physical Activity on Cognition and Brain Function." *Trends in Cognitive Sciences* 11(8): 342–48.

Kristof, K. M. 2008. "Hooked on Debt: Students Learn too Late the Costs of Private Loans." *Los Angeles Times*, A1: A18–19.

Kuh, G. D. 1993. "In Their Own Words: What Students Learn Outside the Classroom." *American Educational Research Journal* 30: 277–304.

Kuh, G. D. 1995. "The Other Curriculum: Out-of-class Experiences Associated with Student Learning and Personal Development." *Journal of Higher Education* 66(2): 123–53.

Kuh, G. D. 2005. "Student Engagement in the First Year of College." In *Challenging and Supporting the First-year Student: A Handbook for Improving the First Year of College,* edited by M. L. Upcraft, J. N. Gardner, B. O. Barefoot, & Associates, 86–107. San Francisco: Jossey-bass.

Kuh, G. D. et al. 2005. Student Engagement in the First Year of College. In *Challenging and Supporting the First-year Student: A Handbook for Improving the First Year of College,* edited by M. L. Upcraft, J. N. Gardner, B. O. Barefoot, et al., 86–107. San Francisco: Jossey-bass.

Kuh, G. D., J. Kinzie, J. H. Schuh, E. J. Whitt. 2005. *Student Success in College: Creating Conditions that Matter.* San Francisco, CA: Jossey-bass.

Kuh, G. D., K. B. Douglas, J. P. Lund and J. Ramin-Gyurnek. 1994. *Student Learning Outside the Classroom: Transcending Artificial Boundaries.* ASHE-ERIC Higher Education Report No. 8. Washington, DC: George Washington University, School of Education and Human Development.

Kuhn, L. 1988. "What Should We Tell Students About Answer Changing?" *Research Serving Teaching* 1(8).

Kuriyama, K., K. Mishima, H. Suzuki, S. Aritake, and M. Uchiyama. 2008. "Sleep Accelerates Improvement in Working Memory Performance." *The Journal of Neuroscience* 28(4): 10145–50.

Laanan, F. S. 2001. "Transfer Student Adjustment." In *Transfer Students: Trends and Issues*, edited by F. S. Laanan, 5–13. New Directions for Community Colleges, no. 114. San Francisco: Jossey-bass.

Lack, L. C., M. Gradisar, E. J. W. Van Someren, H. R. Wright, and K. Lushington. 2008. The Relationship between Insomnia and Body Temperatures. *Sleep Medicine Reviews* 12(4): 307–17.

Lakein, A. 1973. *How to Get Control of Your Time and Your Life.* New York: New American Library.

Lancaster, L., and D. Stilman. 2002. *When Generations Collide: Who They Are. Why They Clash.* New York: HarperCollins.

Latané, B., J. H. Liu, A. Nowak, N. Bonevento, and L. Zheng, 1995. "Distance Matters: Physical Space and Social Impact." *Personality and Social Psychology Bulletin* 21: 795–805.

Latham, G. and E. Locke. 2007. "New Developments in and Directions for Goal-setting Research." *European Psychologists* 12: 290–300.

Launius, M. H. 1997. "College Student Attendance: Attitudes and Academic Performance." *College Student Journal* 31(1): 86–93.

Leavy, P., A. Gnong, and L. S. Ross. 2009. "Femininity, Masculinity, and Body Image Issues among College-Age Women: An In-depth and Written Interview Study of the Mind-body Dichotomy." *The Qualitative Report* 14(2): 261–92.

LeDoux, J. 2002. *Synaptic Self: How Our Brains Become Who We Are.* New York: Penguin Books.

Lehrer, P., D. H. Barlow, R. L. Woolfolk, and W. E. Sime, eds. 2007. *Principles and Practice of Stress Management.* 3rd ed. New York: The Guilford Press.

Leibel, R. L., M. Rosenbaum, and J. Hirsch. 1995. "Changes in Energy Expenditure Resulting from Altered Body Weight." *New England Journal of Medicine* 332: 621–28.

Leonard, G. 2008. *A Study on the Effects of Student Employment on Retention.* uc.iupui.edu/Portals/155/uploadedFiles/.../StudEmpRetentionRprt.pdf.

Leung, A. K., W. W. Maddux, A. D. Galinsky, and C.-Y. Chiu. 2008. "Multicultural Experience Enhances Creativity: The When and How." *American Psychologist* 63(3): 169–81.

Leuwerke, W. C., S. B. Robbins, R. Sawyer, and M. Hovland. 2004. "Predicting Engineering Major Status from Mathematics Achievement and Interest Congruence." *Journal of Career Assessment* 12: 135–49.

Lewis, M., G. W. Paul, and C. D. Fenning, eds. 2014. Ethnologue: Languages of the World. 17th ed. Dallas, Texas: SIL International. Online Version: http://www.ethnologue.com.

Liebertz, C. 2005a. "A Healthy Laugh." *Scientific American Mind* 16(3): 90–91.

Liebertz, C. 2005b. "Want Clear Thinking? Relax." *Scientific American Mind* 16(3): 88–89.

Light, R. J. 2001. *Making the Most of College: Students Speak their Minds.* Cambridge, MA: Harvard University Press.

Light, R. L. 1990. *The Harvard Assessment Seminars.* Cambridge, MA: Harvard University Press.

Light, R. L. 1992. *The Harvard Assessment Seminars, Second Report.* Cambridge, MA: Harvard University Press.

Lock, R. D. 2004. *Taking Charge of Your Career Direction.* 5th ed. Belmont, CA: Brooks Cole.

Locke, E. 1977. An Empirical Study of Lecture Note-Taking Among College Students." *Journal of Educational Research* 77: 93–99.

Locke, E. A. 2000. Motivation, Cognition, and Action: "An Analysis of Studies of Task Goals and Knowledge." *Applied Psychology: An International Review* 49: 408–29.

Locke, E. A., and G. P. Latham. 1990. *A Theory of Goal Setting and Task Performance*. Englewood Cliffs, NJ: Prentice Hall.

Locke, E. A., and G. P. Latham. 2002. "Building a Practically Useful Theory of Goal Setting and Task Motivation." *American Psychologist*, 57, 705–17.

Lotkowski, V. A., S. B. Robbins, and R. J. Noeth. 2004. *The Role of Academic and Non-academic Factors in Improving student retention*. ACT Policy Report. https://www.act.org/research/policymakers/pdf/college_retention.pdf.

Lowenstein, G., D. Read, and R. G. Baumeister, eds. 2003. *Time and Decision: Economic and Psychological Perspectives on Intertemporal Choice*. New York: Russell Sage Foundation.

Lucler, K. L. 2015. "15 Ways to Stay Safe while in College." http://collegelife.about.com/od/healthwellness/qt/SafetyTips.htm

Luhman, R. 2007. *The Sociological Outlook*. Lanham, MD: Rowman & Littlefield.

Lumina Foundation. 2013. *A Stronger Nation Through Higher Education*. Indianapolis IN: Author. http://www.pesc.org/library/docs/about_us/whitepapers/a-stronger-nation-2013lumina.pdf.

Lumina Foundation. 2015. *A Stronger Nation Through Higher Education*. Indianapolis IN: Author. http://www.luminafoundation.org/files/publications/A_stronger_nation_through_higher_education-2015.pdf.

Luthra, R., and C. A. Gidycz. 2006. "Dating Violence among College Men and Women: Evaluation of a Theoretical Model." *Journal of Interpersonal Violence*. 21: 717–31.

Maddux, W. W., and A. D. Galinsky. 2009. "Cultural Borders and Mental Barriers: the Relationship Between Living Abroad and Creativity." *Journal of Personality and Social Psychology* 96(5): 1047–61.

Magolda, M. B. B. 1992. *Knowing and Reasoning in College*. San Francisco: Jossey-bass.

Maier, N. R. F. 1970. *Problem Solving and Creativity in Individuals and Groups*. Belmont, CA: Brooks/Cole.

Malik, S., S. B. Sorenson, and C. S. Aneshensel. 1997. "Community and Dating Violence among Adolescents: Perpetration and Victimization." *Journal of Adolescent Health* 1997(5): 291–302.

Malinauskas, B. M., V. G. Aeby, R. F. Overton, T. Carpenter-Aeby, and K. Barber-Heidal. 2007. "A Survey of Energy Drink Consumption Patterns among College Students." *Nutrition Journal* 6(1): 35.

Malmberg, K. J., and K. Murnane. 2002. "List Composition and the Word-Frequency Effect for Recognition Memory." *Journal of Experimental Psychology: Learning, Memory, and Cognition* 28: 616–30.

Malvasi, M., C. Rudowsky, and J. M. Valencia. 2009. *Library Rx: Measuring and Treating Library Anxiety, a Research Study*. Chicago: Association of College and Research Libraries.

Marczinski, C., G. Estee, and V. Grant. 2009. *Binge Drinking in Adolescent and College Students*. New York: Nova Science Publishers.

Marzano, R. J., D. J. Pickering, and J. Pollock. 2001. *Classroom Instruction That Works: Research-based Strategies for Increasing Student Achievement*. Alexandria, VA: Association for Supervision and Curriculum Development.

Matthews, G., M. Zeidner, and R. D. Roberts. 2007. *The Science of Emotional Intelligence: Knowns and Unknowns*. New York: Oxford University Press.

Mayer, R. E. 2002. "Rote Versus Meaningful Learning." *Theory into Practice* 41(4): 226–32.

Mayo Clinic. 2015. "Rev Up Your Workout with Interval Training: Interval Training Can Help You Get the most Out of Your Workout." http://www.mayoclinic.org/healthy-living/fitness/in-depth/interval-training/art-20044588?pg=1

Mayo Clinic. 2015a. *Anxiety: Definition*. http://www.mayoclinic.org/diseases-conditions/anxiety/basics/definition/con-20026282.

Mayo Clinic. 2015b. *Depression: Definition*. http://www.mayoclinic.org/diseases-conditions/depression/basics/definition/con-20032977.

Mazurek K., K. Karwczyk, P. Zemijeeski, H. Norkoski, and M. Czajkowska. 2014. "Effects of Aerobic Interval Training versus Continuous Moderate Exercise Programme on Aerobic and Anaerobic Capacity, Somatic Features and Blood Lipid Profile in Collegiate Females." *Annals of Agricultural and Environmental Medicine* 21(4): 844–49.

McCance, N., and T. A. Pychyl. August, 2003. *From Task Avoidance to Action: An Experience Sampling Study of Undergraduate Students' Thoughts, Feelings and Coping Strategies in Relation to Academic Procrastination*. Paper presented at the Third Annual Conference for Counseling Procrastinators in the Academic Context, University of Ohio, Columbus.

McDrury, J. and M. G.Alterio 2002. *Learning through Storytelling: using reflection and experience in higher education contexts*. Palmerston North: Dunmore Press.

McKay, M., M. Davis, and P. Fanning. 2009. *Messages: The Communication Skills Book*. 2nd ed. Oakland, CA: New Harbinbger.

Meilman, P. W., and C. A. Presley. 2005. "The First-year Experience and Alcohol Use." In *Challenging and Supporting the First-year Student: A Handbook for Improving the First Year of College*, edited by M. L. Upcraft, J. N. Gardner, B. O. Barefoot, et al. 445–68. San Francisco: Jossey-bass.

Melton. 1995.

Mendez, F., T. Krahn, B. Schrack, A. M. Krahn, K. Veeramah, A. Woerner, F. L. Fomine, M. Bradman, N., M. Thomas, T. Karafet, and M. Hammer. 2013. "An African American Paternal Lineage Adds an Extremely Ancient Root to the Human Y Chromosome Phylogenetic Tree." *The American Journal of Human Genetics* 92: 454–59.

Meredith, M. 2011. *Born in Africa: The Quest for the Origins of Human Life*. New York: Public Affairs.

Meyer, P. J. 2003. "What Would You Do if You Knew You Couldn't Fail? Creating S.M.A.R.T. Goals." *In Attitude Is Everything: If You Want to Succeed Above and Beyond*. Meyer Resource Group, Incorporated.

Millard, B. November 7, 2004. *A Purpose-based Approach to Navigating College Transitions*. Preconference workshop presented at the Eleventh National Conference on Students in Transition, Nashville, Tennessee.

Miller, L. M. 2011. "Physical Abuse in a College Setting: A Study of Perception and Participation in Abusive Dating Relationships." *Journal of Family Violence* 26(1): 71–80.

Miller, M. A. September/October, 2003. "The Meaning of the Baccalaureate." *About Campus* 8(4): 2–8.

Miller, M. D., R. L. Linn, and N. E. Gronlund. 2012. *Measurement and Assessment in Teaching*. 7th ed. Englewood Cliffs, NJ: Pearson.

Miller, M. T., and D. P. Nadler. 2004. "Transfer Trends in the Future of Higher Education." In *The College Transfer Student in America: The Forgotten Student*, edited by B. C. Jacobs, 188–201. Washington, DC: American Association of Collegiate Registrars and Admissions Officers.

Milton, O. 1982. *Will That Be on the Final*? Springfield, IL: Charles C. Thomas.

Morgenstern, J. 2004. *Time Management from the Inside Out: The Foolproof System for Taking Control of Your Schedule and Your Life*. 2nd ed. New York: Henry Holt & Co.

Mueller, P. A., and D. M. Oppenheimer. 2014. "The Pen is Mightier Than the Keyboard: Advantages of Longhand over Laptop Note Taking." *Psychological Science* 25(6): 1159–68.

Mullin, C., and K. Phillippe. 2013. *Community College Contributions* (No. AACC Policy Brief 2013-01PB). American Association of Community Colleges. http://www.aacc.nche.edu/Publications/Briefs/Documents/2013PB_01.pdf.

Multon, S. D., K. D., Brown, and R. W. Lent. 1991. "Relation of Self-efficacy Beliefs to Academic Outcomes: A Meta-Analytic Investigation." *Journal of Counseling Psychology* 38(1): 30–8.

Murname, K., and R. M. Shiffrin. 1991. "Interference and the Representation of Events in Memory." *Journal of Experimental Psychology: Learning, Memory, & Cognition* 17: 855–74.

Murray, C. E. and K. N. Kardatzke. 2007. "Dating Violence among College Students: Key Issues for College Counselors." *Journal of College Counseling* 10(1): 79.

Myers, D. G. 1993. *The Pursuit of Happiness: Who Is Happy and Why?* New York: Morrow.

Myers, D. G. 2000. *The American Paradox: Spiritual Hunger in an Age of Plenty*. New Haven, CT: Yale University Press.

Nagda, B. R., P. Gurin, and S. M. Johnson. 2005. "Living, Doing and Thinking Diversity: How Does Pre-College Diversity Experience Affect First-year Students' Engagement with College Diversity?" In *Improving the First Year of College: Research and Practice*, edited by R. S. Feldman, 73–110. Mahwah, NJ: Lawrence Erlbaum.

Nathan, R. 2005. *My Freshman Year: What a Professor Learned by Becoming a Student*. Ithaca, NY: Cornell University Press.

Nathan, R. 2005. *My Freshman Year: What a Professor Learned by Becoming a Student*. London: Penguin.

National Association of Colleges & Employers. 2012. *Internship and Co-op Survey*. Bethlehem, PA: Author.

National Association of Colleges & Employers. 2013. *Job Outlook: The Candidate Skills/Qualities Employers Want*. http://www.naceweb.org/s10022013/job-outlook-skills-quality.aspx.

National Association of Colleges & Employers. 2014. *2014 Internship and Co-op Survey,* executive summary. https://www.naceweb.org/uploadedFiles/Content/static-assets/downloads/executive-summary/2014-internship-co-op-survey-executive-summary.pdf.

National Association of Colleges and Employers (NACE). 2003. Job Outlook 2003 Survey. Bethlehem, PA: Author.

National Association of Colleges and Employers (NACE). 2007. Job Outlook 2007 Survey. Bethlehem, PA: Author.

National Association of Colleges and Employers. 2012. *Internship and Co-Op Survey*. Bethlehem, PA: Author.

National Association of Colleges and Employers. 2013. *Job Outlook: The Candidate Skills/Qualities Employers Want*. http://www.naceweb.org/s10022013/job-outlook-skills-quality.aspx.

National Association of Colleges and Employers. 2014. *2014 Internship and Co-Op Survey,* executive summary. https://www.naceweb.org/uploadedFiles/Content/static-assets/downloads/executive-summary/2014-internship-co-op-survey-executive-summary.pdf.

National Center for Education Statistics. 2011. *Digest of Education Statistics, Table 237. Total Fall Enrollment in Degree-Granting Institutions, by Level of Student, Sex, Attendance Status, and Race/Ethnicity: Selected Years, 1976 Through 2010.* Alexandria, VA: U.S. Department of Education. http://neces.ed/gov/programs/digest/d11/tables/dt11_237.asp

National Center for Education Statistics. 2014. *Fast Facts: Most Popular Majors.* Washington, DC: U. S. Department of Education. http://nces.ed.gov/fastfacts/display.asp?id=37.

National Center for Victims of Crime. 2012.

National Institute of Mental Health. 2014. *What Are Eating Disorders?* Washington, DC: U.S. Department of Health and Human Services. http://www.nimh.nih.gov/health/publications/eating-disorders-new-trifold/index.shtml.

National Resource Center for the First-year Experience and Students in Transition. 2004. *The 2003 Your First College Year (YFCY) Survey.* Columbia, SC: Author.

National Resources Defense Council. 2005. *Global Warming: A Summary of Recent Findings on the Changing Global Climate.* http://www.nrdc.org/globalwarming/science/2005.asp.

National Student Clearing House Research Center. 2015. *Contribution of Two-year Institutions to Four-year Completions.* https://nscresearchcenter.org/snapshotreport-twoyearcontributionfouryearcompletions17/.

National Survey of Student Engagement. 2009. *NSSE Annual Results 2009. Assessment for Improvement: Tracking Student Engagement over Time.* Bloomington, IN: Author.

National Survey of Women Voters. 1998. *Autumn Overview Report Conducted by DYG Inc.* http://www.diversityweb.org/research_and_trends/research_evaluation_impact_/campus_community_connections/national_poll.cfm

Navarro, J. 2008. *What Every BODY Is Saying.* New York: Harper Collins.

Nellie Mae. 2005. *Undergraduate Students and Credit Cards in 2004: An Analysis of Usage Rates and Trend.* Wilkes-Barre, PA: Nellie Mae.

Nelson, M. C., K. Lust, M. Story, and E. Ehlinger. 2008. "Credit Card Debt, Stress and Key Health Risk Behaviors among College Students." *American Journal of Health Promotion* 22(6): 400–7.

Newell, A., and H. A. Simon. 1959. *The Simulation of Human Thought.* Santa Monica, CA: Rand Corporation.

Ng, M., T. Fleming, M. Robinson, B. Thomson, N. Graetz, C. Margono, E. C. Mullany, et al. 2014. "Global, Regional, and National Prevalence of Overweight and Obesity in Children and Adults during 1980–2013: A Systematic Analysis for the Global Burden of Disease Study 2013. *The Lancet* 384 (9945): 766–81.

Nhan, D. 2012. "Census: Minorities Constitute 37 Percent of U.S. Population." *National Journal: The Next America-Demographics 2012.* http://www.nationaljournal.com/thenextamerica/demographics/census-minorities-constitute-37-percent-of-u-s-population-20120517

NHTSA/FARS and U.S. Census Bureau. 2012. *Underage Drunk Driving Fatalities.* www.centurycouncil.org/drunk-driving/underage-drunk-driving-fatalities.

Nichols, M. P. 2009. *The Lost Art of Listening.* New York: Guilford Press.

NIDDK (National Institute of Diabetes and Digestive Kidney Diseases). 2010. *Overweight and Obesity Statistics.* Washington, DC: U.S. Department of Health and Human Services.

Niederjohn, M. S. 2008. "First-year Experience Course Improves Students' Financial Literacy." *ESource for College Transitions* [Electronic newsletter published by the National Resource Center for the First-year Experience and Students in Transition] 6(1): 9–11.

Nora, A., and A. Cabrera, 1996. "The Role of Perceptions of Prejudice and Discrimination on the Adjustment of Minority College Students." *The Journal of Higher Education* 67(2): 119–48.

Oettingen, G. 2000. "Expectancy Effects on Behavior Depend on Self-Regulatory Thought." *Social Cognition* 14: 101–29.

Oettingen, G., and E. Stephens. 2009. "Mental Contrasting Future and Reality: A Motivationally Intelligent Self-Regulatory Strategy." In *The Psychology of Goals*, edited by G. Moskowitz and H. Grant. New York: Guilford.

Office of Research. 1994. *What Employers Expect of College Graduates: International Knowledge and Second Language Skills.* Washington, DC: Office of Educational Research and Improvement, U.S. Department of Education.

Ohayon, M. M., M. A. Carskadon, C. Guilleminault, and M. V. Vitiello. 2004. "Meta-Analysis of Quantitative Sleep Parameters from Childhood to Old Age in Healthy Individuals: Developing Normative Sleep Values Across the Human Lifespan." *Sleep* 27: 1255–73.

Olson, L. 2007. "What Does "Ready" Mean?" *Education Week* 40: 7–12.

Onwuegbuzie, A. J. 2000. "Academic Procrastinators and Perfectionistic Tendencies among Graduate Students." *Journal of Social Behavior and Personality* 15: 103–9.

Oppezzo, M., and D. L. Schwartz. 2014. "Give Your Ideas Some Legs: The Positive Effect of Walking on Creative Thinking." *Journal of Experimental Psychology: Learning, Memory, and Cognition* 40(4): 1142–52.

Ottens, A. J., and K. Hotelling. 2001. *Sexual Violence on Campus: Politics, Programs, and Perspectives.* New York: Springer Publishing Company, Inc.

Pace, C. 1990. *The Undergraduates: A Report of Their Activities.* Los Angeles: University of California, Center for the Study of Evaluation.

Pace, C. May, 1995 *From Good Processes to good Products: Relating Good Practices in Undergraduate Education to Student Achievement.* Paper presented at the meeting of the Association for Institutional Research, Boston.

Pai, M. R., N. Sanji, P. G. Pai, and S. Kotian. 2010. "Comparative Assessment in Pharmacology Multiple Choice Questions versus Essay with Focus on Gender Differences." *Journal of Clinical and Diagnostic Research* [serial online] 4(3): 2515–20.

Paivio, A. 1990. *Mental Representations: A Dual Coding Approach.* New York: Oxford University Press.

Palank, J. July 17, 2006. *Face It: "Book" no Secret to Employers.* http://www.washtimes.com/business/20060717-12942-1800r.htm.

Parker-Pope, T. 2010. "Vigorous exercise linked with better grades." http://query.nytimes.com/gst/fullpage.html?res=9A03EEDE103EF93BA35755C0A9669D8B63.

Pascarella, E. T. 2005. *How College Affects Students: Ten Directions for Future Research.* San Francisco: Jossey-bass.

Pascarella, E. T. November/December, 2001. "Cognitive Growth in College: Surprising and Reassuring Findings from the National Study of Student Learning." *Change*, 21–27.

Pascarella, E. T., and P. T. Terenzini. 2005. *How College Affects Students, Volume 2, A Third Decade of Research.* San Francisco, CA: Jossey-bass.

Pascarella, E., and P. Terenzini. 1991. *How College Affects Students: Findings and Insights from Twenty Years of Research.* San Francisco: Jossey-bass.

Pascarella, E., and P. Terenzini. 2005. *How College Affects Students: A Third Decade of Research.* Vol. 2. San Francisco: Jossey-bass.

Pascarella, E., B. Palmer, M. Moye, and C. Pierson. 2001. "Do Diversity Experiences Influence the Development of Critical Thinking?" *Journal of College Student Development* 42(3): 257–91.

Paul, R., and L. Elder. 2004. *The Nature and Functions of Critical and Creative Thinking.* Dillon Beach, CA: Foundation for Critical Thinking.

Paul, R., and L. Elder. 2014. *Critical Thinking: Tools for Taking Charge of Your Professional and Personal Life.* Upper Saddle River, NJ: Pearson Education.

Penfold, R. B. 2006. *Dragonslippers: This Is What an Abusive Relationship Looks Like.* New York: Grove/Atlantic.

Peoples, J., and G. Bailey. 2011. *Humanity: An Introduction to Cultural Anthropology.* Belmont, CA: Wadsworth, Cengage Learning.

Perna, L. W., and G. DuBois, eds. 2010. *Understanding the Working College Student: New Research and its Implications for Policy and Practice.* Sterling, VA: Stylus.

Perry, W. G. 1970, 1999. *Forms of Intellectual and Ethical Development During the College Years: A Scheme.* New York: Holt, Rinehart and Winston.

Peter D. Hart Research Associates. 2006. *How Should Colleges Prepare Students to Succeed in Today's Global Economy?* The Association of American Colleges and Universities by Peter D. Hart Research Associates, Inc.

Pettigrew, T. F. 1997. "Generalized Intergroup Contact Effects on Prejudice." *Personality and Social Psychology Bulletin* 23: 173–85.

Pettigrew, T. F. 1998. "Intergroup Contact Theory." *Annual Review of Psychology* 49: 65–85.

Pettigrew, T. F., and L. R. Tropp. 2000. "Does Intergroup Contact Reduce Prejudice? Recent Meta-analytic Findings." In *Reducing Prejudice and Discrimination*, edited by S. Oskamp, 93–114. Mahwah, NJ: Lawrence Erlbaum Associates.

Pew Research Center. February, 2014. *The Rising Cost of not Going to College.* http://www.pewsocialtrends.org/2014/02/11/the-rising-cost-of-not-going-to-college/.

Piaget, J. 1978. *Success and Understanding.* Cambridge, MA: Harvard University Press.

Pinker, S. 2000. *The Language Instinct: The New Science of Language and Mind.* New York: Perennial.

Pintrich, P. R., and D. H. Schunk. 2002. *Motivation in Education: Theory, Research, and Applications.* Upper Saddle River, NJ: Merrill-Prentice Hall.

Pope, L. 1990. *Looking Beyond the Ivy League.* New York: Penguin Press.

Porter, S. R., and R. L. Swing. 2006. "Understanding How First-year Seminars Affect Persistence." *Research in Higher Education* 47(1): 89–109.

Pratt, B. 2008. *Extra Credit: The 7 Things Every College Student Needs to Know about Credit, Debt, & Cash.* Keedysville, MD: ExtraCreditBook.com.

Pratt, B. 2011. *Extra Credit: The 7 Things Every College Student Needs to Know About Credit, Debt & Cash.* 2nd ed. Winterville, NC: Financial Relevancy.

Pratto, F., J. H. Liu, S. Levin, J. Sidanius, M. Shih, H. Bachrach, and P. Hegarty. 2000. "Social Dominance Orientation and the Legitimization of Inequality Across Cultures." *Journal of Cross-Cultural Psychology* 31: 369–409.

Prentice. M., C. Storin, and G. Robinson. 2012. *Make It Personal: How Pregnancy Planning and Prevention Help Students Complete College*. Washington, DC: American Association of Community Colleges.

Price, R. H., J. N. Choi, and A. D. Vinokur. 2002. "Links in the Chain of Adversity Following Job Loss: How Financial Strain and Loss of Personal Control Lead to Depression, Impaired Functioning, and Poor Health." *Journal of Occupational Health Psychology* 7(4): 302–12.

Prinsell, C. P, P. H. Ramsey, and P. P. Ramsey. 1994. "Score Gains, Attitudes, and Behaviour Changes due to Answer-Changing Instruction." *Journal of Educational Measurement* 31: 327–37.

Pryor, J. H., L. De Angelo, B. Palucki-Blake, S. Hurtado, and S. Tran. 2012. *The American Freshman: National Norms Fall 2011*. Los Angeles: Higher Education Research Institute, UCLA.

Public Service Enterprise Group (PSEG). 2009. *Diversity*. www.pseg.com/info/environment/sustainability/2009/.../diversity.jsp

Purdy, M., and D. Borisoff, eds. 1996. *Listening in Everyday Life: A Personal and Professional Approach*. Lanham, MD: University Press of America.

Putman, R. D. 2000. *Bowling Alone: The Collapse and Revival of American Community*. New York: Simon & Schuster.

Ramsden, P. 2003. *Learning to Teach in Higher Education*. 2nd ed. London: RoutledgeFalmer.

Ravizza, S. M., D. Z. Hambrick, and K. M. Fenn. 2014. "Non-Academic Internet Use in the Classroom is Negatively Related to Classroom Learning Regardless of Intellectual Ability." *Computers & Education* 78: 109–14.

Reed, S. K. 2013. *Cognition: Theory and Applications*. 3rd ed. Belmont, CA: Wadsworth/Cengage.

Reid, G. B. R., and R. Hetherington. 2010. *The Climate Connection: Climate Change and Modern Evolution*. Cambridge, UK: Cambridge University Press.

Rennels, M. R., and R. B. Chaudhair. 1988. "Eye-Contact and Grade Distribution." *Perceptual and Motor Skills*, 67 (October): 627–32.

Resnick, L. B. 1986. *Education and Learning to Think*. Washington, DC: National Academy Press.

Rhodewalt, F., and K. D. Vohs. 2005. Defensive Strategies, Motivation, and the Self. In *Handbook of Competence and Motivation,* edited by A. Elliot and C. Dweck, 548–65. New York: Guilford Press.

Ring, T. October, 1997. "Issuers Face a Visit to the Dean's Office." *Credit Card Management* 10: 34–9.

Riquelme, H. 2002. "Can People Creative in Imagery Interpret Ambiguous Figures Faster than People less Creative in Imagery?" *Journal of Creative Behavior* 36(2): 105–16.

Rivera, C. July 1, 2015. "College Safety Gets a Tech Boost." *Los Angeles Times*, B2.

Roediger, H. L., Y. Dudai, and S. M. Fitzpatrick. 2007. *Science of Memory: Concepts*. New York, NY: Oxford University Press.

Roediger, H., and J. Karpicke. 2006. "The Power of Testing Memory: Basic Research and Implications for Educational Practice." *Perspectives on Psychological Science* 1(3): 181–210.

Rohrbaugh, J. B. 2006. "Domestic Violence in Same-Gender Relationships." *Family Court Review* 44(2): 287–99.

Rotter, J. 1966. "Generalized Expectancies for Internal versus External Controls of Reinforcement." *Psychological Monographs: General and Applied* 80(609): 1–28.

Roxburgh, B. H., P. B. Nolan, R. M. Weatherwax, L. C. Dalleck, 2014. "Is Moderate Intensity Exercise Training Combined with High Intensity Interval Training more Effective at Improving Cardiorespiratory Fitness than Moderate Intensity Exercise Training Alone?" *Journal of Sports Science and Medicine* 13(3):702–07.

Ruggiero, V. R. 2011. *Beyond Feelings: A Guide to Critical Thinking*. New York: McGraw-Hill Education.

Ryan, R. 1995. "Psychological Needs and the Facilitation of Integrative Processes." *Journal of Personality* 63: 397–427.

Ryan, R. M., and E. L. Deci. 2000. "Self-determination Theory and the Facilitation of Intrinsic Motivation, Social Development, and Well-being." *American Psychologist* 55: 68–78.

Sallie Mae April, 2009. *How Undergraduate Students Use Credit Cards: Sallie Mae's National Study of Usage Rates and Trends 2009*. http://static.mgnetwork.com/rtd/pdfs/20090830_iris.pdf.

Salovey, P. and J. D. Mayer. 1990. "Emotional Intelligence." *Imagination, Cognition, and Personality* 9: 185–211.

Sapolsky, R. 2004. *Why Zebras Don't Get Ulcers*. New York: W. H. Freeman.

Sax, L. J. 2003. "Our Incoming Students: What Are They Like? *About Campus* July–August: 15–20.

Sax, L. J., A. N. Bryant, and S. K. Gilmartin, 2004. "A Longitudinal Investigation of Emotional Health among Male and Female First-year College Students." *Journal of the First-year Experience and Students in Transition* 16(2): 29–65.

Sax, L. J., A. N. Bryant, and S. K. Gilmartin. 2004. "A Longitudinal Investigation of Emotional Health Among Male and Female First-year College Students." *Journal of the First-year Experience,* 16: 39–65.

Schacter, D. L. 2001. *The Seven Sins of Memory: How the Mind Forgets and Remembers.* Boston: Houghton Mifflin.

Schilling, K. August, 2001. *Plenary Address.* Presented at The Summer Institute on First-year Assessment, Asheville, North Carolina.

Schlosser, E. 2005. *Fast Food Nation: The Dark Side of the All-American Meal.* New York: Harper Perennial.

Schunk, D. H. 1995. "Self-Efficacy and Education and Instruction." In *Self-Efficacy, Adaptation, and Adjustment: Theory, Research, and Application,* edited by J. E. Maddux, 281–303. New York: Plenum Press.

Seabrook, J. 2008. *Flash of Genius and Other True Stories of Invention.* New York: St. Martin's Press.

Seaward, B. L. 2011. *Managing stress: Principles and Strategies for Health and Well-being.* Burlington, MA: Jones & Bartlett Learning.

SECFHE. 2006. *A National Dialogue: The Secretary of Education's Commission on the Future of Higher Education.* U.S. Department of Education Boards and Commissions: A Draft Panel Report. http://www.ed.gov/about/bdscomm/list/hiedfuture/reports/0809-draft.pdf

Segall, M. H., D. T. Campbell, and M. J. Herskovits. 1966. *The Influence of Culture on Visual Perception.* Indianapolis: Bobbs-Merrill.

Seifert, T. A., K. M. Goodman, N. Lindsay, J. D. Jorgensen, G. C. Wolniak, E. T. Pascarella, and C. Blaich. 2008. "The Effects of Liberal Arts Experiences on Liberal Arts Outcomes." *Research in Higher Education* 49: 107–25.

Senn, C. Y., M. Eliasziw, P. C. Barata, W. E. Thurston, I. R. Newby-Clark, H. L. Radtke, and K. L. Hobden. 2015. "Efficacy of a Sexual Assault Resistance Program for University Women." *New England Journal of Medicine* 372: 2326–35.

Shah, A. 2009. *Global Issues: Poverty Facts and Stats.* http://www.globalissues.org/article/26/poverty-facts-and-stats.

Shanley, M., and C. Witten. 1990. "University 101 Freshman Seminar Course: A Longitudinal Study of Persistence, Retention, and Graduation Rates." *NASPA Journal* 27: 344–52.

SHEEO (State Higher Education Executive Officers). 2012. *State Higher Education Finance, FY 2011.* http://www.sheeo.org/sites/default/files/publications/SHEF_FY11.pdf.

Shelton, D. R., J. A. Van Kessel, M. R. Wachtel, K. T. Belt, J. S. Karns. December, 2003. "Evaluation of Parameters Affecting Quantitative Detection of Escherichia coli O157 in Enriched Water Samples Using Immunomagnetic Electrochemiluminescence." *J. Microbiology Methods* 55(3): 717–25.

Shelton, J. T., E. M. Elliot, S. D. Eaves, and A. L. Exner. 2009. "The Distracting Effects of a Ringing Cell Phone: An Investigation of the Laboratory and the Classroom Setting." *Journal of Environmental Psychology* (March). http://news-info.wustl.edu/news/page/normal/14225.html.

Sherif, M., D. J. Harvey, B. J. White, W. R. Hood, and C. W. Sherif. 1961. *The Robbers' Cave Experiment.* Norman, OK: Institute of Group Relations.

Shimoff, E., and C. A. Catania. 2001. "Effects of recording attendance on grades in Introductory Psychology." *Teaching of Psychology* 23(3): 192–5.

Shiraev, E. D., and D. Levy. 2013. *Cross-Cultural Psychology: Critical Thinking and Contemporary Applications.* 5th ed. Upper Saddle River, NJ: Pearson Education.

Sidanius, J., S. Levin, H. Liu, and F. Pratto. 2000. "Social Dominance Orientation, Anti-egalitarianism, and the Political Psychology of Gender: An Extension and Cross-Cultural Replication." *European Journal of Social Psychology* 30: 41–67.

Sidle, M., and J. McReynolds. 1999. "The Freshman Year Experience: Student Retention and Student Success." *NASPA Journal* 36: 288–300.

Singh, N. A., K. M. Clements, and M. A. Fiatarone. 1997. "A Randomized Controlled Trial of the Effect of Exercise on Sleep." *Sleep* 20: 95–101.

Sinsky, R. 2011. "Reppler has a New Way to Rate Your Social Network Image." http://venturebeat.com/2011/09/27 /reppler/.

Slavin, R. E. 1995. *Cooperative Learning.* 2nd ed. Boston: Allyn & Bacon.

Smith, D. D. 2005. "Experiential Learning, Service Learning, and Career Development." In *Facilitating the Career Development of Students in Transition,* edited by P. A. Gore, monograph no. 43, 205–22. Columbia: National Resource Center for the First-year Experience and Students in Transition, University of South Carolina.

Smith, D. D. 2005. "Experiential Learning, Service Learning, and Career Development." In *Facilitating the Career Development of Students in Transition,* Monograph No. 43, edited by P. A. Gore, 205–22. Columbia: National Resource Center for the First-year Experience and Students in Transition, University of South Carolina.

Smith, D. G., L. Guy, G. L. Gerbrick, M. A. Figueroa, G. H. Watkins, T. Levitan, L. C. Moore, P. A. Merchant, H. D. Beliak, and B. Figueroa. 1997. *Diversity Works: The Emerging Picture of How Students Benefit.* Washington, DC: Association of American Colleges and Universities.

Smith, J. B., T. L. Walter, and G. Hoey. 1992. "Support Programs and Student Self-efficacy: Do First-year Students Know When They Need Help?" *Journal of the Freshman Year Experience* 4(2): 41–67.

Snyder, C. R. 1995. Conceptualizing, Measuring, and Nurturing Hope." *Journal of Counseling and Development* 73 (January/February): 355–60.

Snyder, C. R., C. Harris, J. R. Anderson, S. A. Holleran, L. M. Irving, S. T. Sigmon, L. Yoshinobu, J. Gibb, C. Langelle, and P. Harney. 1991. "The Will and the Ways: Development and Validation of an Individual-Differences Measure of Hope." *Journal of Personality and Social Psychology* 60: 570–85.

Solomon, L. J., and E. D. Rothblum. 1984. "Academic Procrastination: Frequency and Cognitive-behavioral Correlates." *Journal of Counseling Psychology* 31(4): 503–9.

Sousa, D. A. 2011. *How the Brain Learns.* Thousand Oaks, CA: Sage.

Sprenger, M. 1999. *Learning and Memory: The Brain in Action.* Alexandria, VA: Association for Supervision and Curriculum Development.

Stangor, C., G. B. Sechrist, and J. T. Jost. 2001. "Changing Racial Beliefs by Providing Consensus Information." *Personality and Social Psychology Bulletin* 27: 484–94.

Stark, J. S., M. A. Lowther, R. J. Bentley, M. P. Ryan, G. G. Martens, M. L. Genthon, P. A. Wren, K. M. Shaw. 1990. *Planning Introductory College Courses: Influences on Faculty.* Ann Arbor: National Center for Research to Improve Postsecondary Teaching and Learning, University of Michigan. (ERIC Document Reproduction Services No. 330 277 370.)

Starke, M. C., M. Harth, and F. Sirianni. 2001. "Retention, Bonding, and Academic Achievement: Success of a First-year Seminar." *Journal of the First-year Experience and Students in Transition* 13(2): 7–35.

Staudinger, U. M. 2008. "A Psychology of Wisdom: History and Recent Developments. "*Research in Human Development* 5: 107–20.

Staudinger, U. M. 2008. A psychology of wisdom: History and recent developments. *Research in Human Development* 5: 107–20.

Staying Safe on Campus. July 20, 2012. http://www. nytimes.com/2012/07/20/education/edlife/students-fear-venturing-out-alone-at-night-on-campus. html?pagewanted=all.

Steel, P. 2007. "The Nature of Procrastination: A Meta-analytic and Theoretical Review of Quintessential Self-regulatory Failure." *Psychological Bulletin,* 133(1): 65–94.

Sternberg, R. J. 2001. "What Is the Common Thread of Creativity?" *American Psychologist* 56(4): 360–2.

Stoltz, P. G. 2014. *Grit: The New Science of What It Takes to Persevere, Flourish, Succeed.* San Luis Obispo: Climb Strong Press.

Suls, J., R. Martin, and L. Wheeler. 2002. Social Comparison: Why, with Whom, and with What Effect? *Current Directions in Psychological Science* 11(5): 159–63.

Susswein, R. 1995. "College Students and Credit Cards: A Privilege Earned?" *Credit World* 83: 21–3.

Szalavitz, M. July/August, 2003. "Tapping Potential: Stand and Deliver." *Psychology Today* 50–4.

Tagliacollo, V. A., G. L. Volpato, and A. Pereira Jr. 2010. "Association of Student Position in Classroom and School Performance." *Educational Research* 1(6): 198–201.

Taylor, S. E., L. A. Peplau, and D. O. Sears. 2006. *Social Psychology.* 12th ed. Upper Saddle River, NJ: Pearson/Prentice-Hall.

The Hamilton Project. 2014. *Major Decisions: What Graduates Earn over Their Lifetimes.* Washington, DC: Brookings Institution. http://www. hamiltonproject.org/papers/major_decisions_what_ graduates_earn_over_their_lifetimes/

Thompson, A., and J. Cuseo. 2014. *Diversity and the College Experience.* Dubuque, IA: Kendall Hunt.

Thompson, R. F. 2009. "Habituation: A hHistory." *Neurobiology of Learning and Memory* 92(2): 127–34.

Thomson, R. 1998. "University of Vermont." In *Exploring the Evidence: Vol. 2. Reporting Outcomes of First-year Seminars*, edited by B. O. Barefoot, C. L. Warnock, M. P. Dickinson, S. E. Richardson, and M. R. Roberts, Monograph No. 29, 77–78. Columbia: National Resource Center for the First-year Experience and Students in Transition, University of South Carolina.

Thurmond, K. C. 2007. Transfer Shock: Why Is a Term Forty Years Old Still Relevant? *NACADA Clearinghouse of Academic Advising Resources* website: http://www.nacada.ksu.edu/Resources/ Clearninghouse/View-Articles/Dealing-with-transfer-shock.aspx.

Tinto, V. 1993. *Leaving College: Rethinking the Causes and Cures of Student Attrition.* 2nd ed. Chicago: University of Chicago Press.

Tinto, V. 2012. *Completing College: Rethinking Institutional Action.* University of Chicago Press, Chicago, IL.

Titsworth, S., and K. A. Kiewra. 2004. "Organizational Lecture Cues and Student Note Taking." *Contemporary Educational Psychology* 29: 447–61.

Tobias, S. 1993. *Overcoming Math Anxiety*. New York: W.W. Norton.

Tobolowsky, B. F. 2005. *The 2003 National Survey on First-year Seminars: Continuing Innovations in the College Curriculum,* Monograph No. 41. Columbia, SC: University of South Carolina, National Resource Center for the First-year Experience and Students in Transition.

Tomsho, R. April 22, 2009. "Study Tallies Education's Gap on GDP." *Wall Street Journal*. http://www.wsj.com/articles/SB124040633530943487

Topping, K. 1998. "Peer Assessment between Students in Colleges and Universities." *Review of Educational Research* 68(3): 249–76.

Tyson, E. 2012. *Personal Finance for Dummies*. 7th ed. Hoboken, NJ: John Wiley and Sons.

U.S. Bureau of Labor Statistics. 2015. *Employment Projections*. United States of Department of Labor. http://www.bls.gov/emp/ep_chart_001.htm.

U.S. Census Bureau. 2008. *Bureau of Labor Statistics*. Washington, DC: Author.

U.S. Census Bureau. 2013. *Poverty*. Washington, DC: Author. https://www.census.gov/hhes/www/poverty/data/threshld/.

Useem, M. 1989. *Liberal Education and the Corporation: The Hiring and Advancement of College Graduates*. Piscataway, NJ: Aldine Transaction.

Van Dongen, H. P., G. Maislin, J. M. Mullington, and D. F. Dinges. 2003. "The Cumulative Cost of Additional Wakefulness: Dose Response Effects on Neurobehavioral Functions and Sleep Physiology from Chronic Sleep Restriction and Total Sleep Deprivation." *Sleep* 26: 117–26.

Van Overwalle, F. I., I. Mervielde, and J. De Schuyer. 1995. "Structural Modeling of the Relationships Between Attributional Dimensions, Emotions, and Performance of College Freshmen." *Cognition and Emotion* 9(1): 59–85.

Viorst, J. 1998. *Imperfect Control: Our Lifelong Struggles with Power and Surrender*. New York: Simon Schuster.

Voelker, R. 2004. "Stress, Sleep Loss, and Substance Abuse Create Potent Recipe for College Depression." *Journal of the American Medical Association* 291: 2177–79.

Vygotsky, L. S. 1978. "Internalization of Higher Cognitive Functions." In *Mind in Society: The Development of Higher Psychological Processes*, edited and translated by M. Cole, V. John-Steiner, S. Scribner, and E. Souberman. 52–57. Cambridge, MA: Harvard University Press.

Wabash National Study of Liberal Arts Education. 2007. *Liberal Arts Outcomes*. http:www.liberalarts.wabash.edu/ study-overview/.

Walker, C. M. 1996. "Financial Management, Coping, and Debt in Households under Financial Strain." *Journal of Economic Psychology* 17: 789–807.

Walsh, K. 2005. *Suggestions from More Experienced Classmates*. http://www.uni.edu/walsh/introtips.html.

Walsh, N. P., M. Gleeson, R. J. Shephard, J. A. Woods, N. C. Bishop, M. Fleshner, C. Green, B. K. Pedersen, L. Hoffman-Goetz, C. J. Rogers, H. Northoff, A. Abbasi, and P. Simon. 2011. "Position Statement. Part One: Immune Function and Exercise." *Exercise Immunology Review* 17: 6–63.

Walter, T. L., and J. Smith. April, 1990. *Self-assessment and Academic Support: Do Students Know They Need Help?* Paper presented at the annual Freshman Year Experience Conference, Austin, Texas.

Walter, T. W., G. M. Knudsvig, and D. E. P. Smith. 2003. *Critical Thinking: Building the Basics*. 2nd ed. Belmont, CA: Wadsworth.

Washington State Board for Community and Technical Colleges. 2015. *Transfer Associate Degrees*. http://www.sbctc.ctc.edu/college/_e-transferdegrees.aspx

Weinstock, H., S. Berman, and W. Cates, Jr. 2004. "Sexually Transmitted Diseases among American youth: Incidence and Prevalence Estimates, 2000." *Perspectives on Sexual and Reproductive Health* 36(10): 6–10.

Weschsler, H., and B. Wuethrich. 2002. *Dying to Drink: Confronting Binge Drinking on College Campuses*. Emmaus, PA: Rodale.

Wheelright, J. March, 2005. "Human, Study Thyself." *Discover*: 39–45.

White, J. W. and M. P. Koss. 1991. "Courtship Violence: Incidence in a National Sample of Higher Education Students." *Violence and Victims* 6: 247–56.

Wiederman, M. W. 2007. "Gender Differences in Sexuality." *Family Journal Counseling and Therapy* 9(4): 468–71.

Wilhite, S. 1990. "Self-efficacy, Locus of Control, Self-Assessment of Memory Ability, and Student Activities as Predictors of College Course Achievement." *Journal of Educational Psychology* 82(4): 696–700.

Willingham, D. B. 2009. *Cognition: The Thinking Animal*. Upper Saddle River, NJ: Pearson.

Willis, J. 2006. *Research-based Strategies to Ignite Student Learning: Insights from a Neurologist and Classroom Teacher*. Alexandria, VA: ASCD.

Willis, J. 2007. *Brain-friendly strategies for the inclusion classroom*. Alexandria, VA: Association for Supervision and Curriculum Development.

Wilson, R. S., C. F. Mendes, L. L. Barnes, J. A. Schneider, J. L. Bienias, D. A. Evans, D. A. Bennett. 2002. "Participation in Cognitively Stimulating Activities and Risk of Incident Alzheimer's Disease." *Journal of the American Medical Association* 287(6): 742–8.

Youngstedt, S. D. 2005. "Effects of exercise on sleep." *Clinical Sports Medicine* 24(2): 355–65.

Zajonc, R. B. 1968. "Attitudinal Effects of Mere Exposure." *Journal of Personality and Social Psychology* 9 (monograph supplement no. 2, part 2): 1–27.

Zajonc, R. B. 1970. "Brainwash: Familiarity Breeds Comfort." *Psychology Today* (February): 32–5, 60–2.

Zajonc, R. B. 2001. "Mere Exposure: A Gateway to the Subliminal." *Current Directions in Psychological Science* 10: 224–28.

Zamani, E. 2001. "Institutional Responses to Barriers to the Transfer Process." In *Transfer Students: Trends and Issues*, edited by F. Laanan, 15–24. New Directions for Community Colleges, No. 114. San Francisco: Jossey-bass.

Zeidner, M. 1995. "Adaptive Coping with Test Situations: A Review of the Literature." *Educational Psychologist* 30(3), 123–33.

Zimbardo, P. G., R. L. Johnson, and V. McCann. 2012. *Psychology: Core Concepts.* 7th ed. Boston: Pearson.

Zlomek, E. March 26, 2012. "As MBA Applicants, Business Majors Face an Uphill Battle." *Bloomburg Business.* http://www.bloomberg.com/bw/articles/2012-03-26/as-mba-applicants-business-majors-face-an-uphill-battle.

Zohar, D. 1998. "An Additive Model of Test Anxiety: Role of Exam-Specific Expectations." *Journal of Educational Psychology* 90: 330–40.

Zull, J. E. 2002. *The Art of Changing the Brain: Enriching Teaching by Exploring the Biology of Learning.* Sterling, VA: Stylus.

INDEX